Virtualization and Private Cloud with VMware Cloud Suite

Virtualization and Private Cloud with VMware Cloud Suite

Lee Chao

CRC Press
Taylor & Francis Group
Boca Raton London New York

CRC Press is an imprint of the
Taylor & Francis Group, an **informa** business

AN AUERBACH BOOK

CRC Press
Taylor & Francis Group
6000 Broken Sound Parkway NW, Suite 300
Boca Raton, FL 33487-2742

First issued in hardback 2018

Version Date: 20161025

ISBN 13: 978-1-138-37379-2 (hbk)
ISBN 13: 978-1-4987-8432-0 (pbk)

Library of Congress Cataloging-in-Publication Data

Names: Chao, Lee, 1951- author.
Title: Virtualization and private cloud with VMware Cloud suite / Lee Chao.
Description: Boca Raton : Taylor & Francis, 2017.
Identifiers: LCCN 2016041874 | ISBN 9781498784320 (pb : alk. paper)
Subjects: LCSH: VMware. | Virtual computer systems. | Cloud computing.
Classification: LCC QA76.9.V5 C425 2017 | DDC 005.4/3--dc23
LC record available at https://lccn.loc.gov/2016041874

**Visit the Taylor & Francis Web site at
http://www.taylorandfrancis.com**

**and the CRC Press Web site at
http://www.crcpress.com**

Contents

Preface

Cloud Computing with VMware vCloud Suite

Cloud computing is a new platform for the current enterprise information technology (IT) infrastructure. The cloud computing platform has the flexibility in delivering the IT infrastructure based on demands. Cloud computing can maximize the efficiency of IT infrastructure development. For a forward-thinking enterprise, cloud computing is the next big thing that can revolutionize the way the enterprise runs its business.

E-commerce and education institutions can particularly benefit from the cloud-based IT infrastructure. A company or an education institution often requires some specifically designed IT infrastructure to meet the computing requirements. It may not be easy for a company to rebuild its own IT infrastructure to meet these requirements. Cloud computing is particularly helpful for meeting this type of requirements. Without constructing its own IT infrastructure, a company or an education institution can subscribe the software, application development platform, or ready-built IT infrastructure from cloud providers. A cloud subscriber only needs to pay for the usage of the software and hardware. In such a way, the cloud subscriber can significantly reduce the time and cost of the IT infrastructure development and management.

Another benefit of cloud computing is its scalability. In a cloud computing environment, a company or an education institution can easily upscale or downscale its IT requirements as needed. A cloud provider provides adequate computing resources to handle planned or unplanned spikes. As an organization grows, the organization can subscribe more computing resources from the cloud provider to accommodate the growing needs for computing.

Cloud providers also provide backup and recovery mechanisms for better reliability. In a cloud computing environment, multiple copies of data are stored in different storage devices and at different locations. In case of an error, the IT infrastructure can be migrated from one datacenter to another datacenter. The fault tolerance mechanism can be used for zero downtime operation. With fault tolerance, two servers can be configured to run simultaneously. In case that one of the servers goes down, the other one will continue to operate.

Motivation

As enterprises are moving from the traditional client–server platform to the cloud computing platform, the IT industry supports the transition by providing the cloud development software and hardware. To support cloud-based e-commerce or online teaching, VMware provides VMware vCloud Suite, including vSphere used as a virtualization operating system, vSphere Client used as a client application for vSphere management, vCenter used as a centralized management tool for a vSphere cluster, vCloud Director used for cloud computing management, VMware Workstation used as a desktop development and management tool of virtual machines, and many other tools. VMware offers the VMware Academic Program package, which includes all the above-mentioned software and more. It also provides similar packages for small businesses. VMware vCloud Suite is designed to run on x86-compatible computers. Therefore, it is relatively easy for education institutions and small businesses to create their private clouds.

More and more companies and educational institutions are planning to adopt the cloud-based IT infrastructure. The market trend generates a huge demand for IT professionals with skills in the cloud technology. For many students majoring in IT-related fields and entry-level IT professionals, there are a handful of challenges on implementing the cloud computing environment at the enterprise level. The best way for them to master the cloud technology is to develop a fully functioning cloud-based IT infrastructure with their own hands. By understanding the needs, the author is motivated to write this book, which includes systematic coverage of the implementation of cloud-based IT infrastructure on x86-platform personal computers (PCs) with VMware vCloud Suite.

Objectives of the Book

With the above-mentioned motivation, this book is designed with the following objectives. Firstly, it will provide the knowledge of cloud computing. Through examples, it will demonstrate how small businesses and education institutions can benefit from the cloud-based IT infrastructure. Secondly, the book will provide the necessary knowledge about the components included in VMware vCloud Suite. It will explain the functionalities provided by these components and how each of these components works in a cloud environment. Thirdly, this book will help IT professionals to get a quick start on developing a cloud-based IT infrastructure. The book is designed to enhance readers' hands-on skills by providing hands-on lab activities. The book will lead the readers to create a lab environment on x86-based PCs. In the VMware vCloud Suite lab, a cloud-based IT infrastructure will be developed to provide cloud services. These cloud services will be accessible from external networks.

Features of the Book

This book covers the implementation of a cloud-based IT infrastructure with VMware vCloud Suite. The following are the features that make the book valuable for readers who are interested in learning about the cloud-based IT infrastructure:

- *Lab-based learning environment:* This book's readers will learn about the cloud technology and IT infrastructure through developing a cloud-based IT infrastructure that is built with VMware vCloud Suite.
- *Real-world approach:* The cloud-based IT infrastructure built in this book can be used for a real-world business. It is built with the hardware and software commonly available in the current IT industry.
- *Step-by-step approach:* The step-by-step instruction and the screenshots are used to guide the lab activities. The comprehensive lab activities help readers make the connection between theory and practice.
- *Self-contained content:* For readers' convenience, the book is self-contained. It includes some necessary cloud computing, operating system, database, directory service, network shared storage device, and networking concepts. It also includes IT infrastructure design strategies.
- *Suitable for self-study:* This book provides detailed instructions that are suitable for self-study. It explains the theory and concepts through examples, illustrations, and hands-on activities.
- *Designed for VMware:* The book is specially designed for VMware, which is one of the popular packages for developing cloud-based IT infrastructure on x86-platform PCs. All the hands-on activities can be carried out with VMware vCloud Suite.
- *Instructional materials:* To help with teaching and learning, this book includes instructional materials such as an instructor's manual, PowerPoint presentations, and solutions.

With these features, readers can get a quick start on implementing the cloud-based IT infrastructure. This book focuses on its goal to make sure that readers can start quickly with less difficulty.

Intended Audience

This book is suitable for undergraduate and beginning graduate students who major in computing-related fields. The content of the book is designed for teaching cloud computing–related courses. This book is also suitable for IT professionals who do self-study on cloud computing and those who are interested in learning about VMware vCloud Suite.

Organization of the Book

This book has 11 chapters. Each chapter contains an introduction of the content to be covered by that chapter, the main body of the chapter, the Summary section to summarize the discussion in the chapter, and the Review Questions section to help readers review the knowledge learned from the chapter. The chapters also include hands-on activities to help readers better understand the content covered in the chapters.

Chapter 1. Introduction to Cloud Computing: This chapter introduces cloud computing concepts and architecture. It describes the process of setting up a cloud-based IT infrastructure. In the lab activity in this chapter, an IT infrastructure is built for hosting the VMware lab environment.

Chapter 2. Domain Controller Installation and Configuration: This chapter discusses the domain controller, which is the server with the directory service software installed. The directory service will be used for the centralized authentication for the VMware lab environment. In the lab activity, Windows Server 2012 will be installed and configured to provide the directory service. In this chapter, Windows Server 2012 is also configured to be a server for the network-based installation of the Elastic Sky X Integrated (ESXi) host and the time server.

Chapter 3. ESXi Installation and Configuration: This chapter covers the hypervisor ESXi. It explains the installation of ESXi, which will be used to create a virtualized environment. In the lab activity, the readers will follow the step-by-step instruction to install and configure ESXi.

Chapter 4. vCenter Installation and Configuration: This chapter introduces the vCenter software, which will be used to manage the VMware lab environment. In the lab activity, vCenter will be installed and configured so that it is ready for the centralized management of the virtualized lab environment.

Chapter 5. Virtual Networks: This chapter introduces virtual networks. In the VMware computing environment, the domain controllers, ESXi host servers, vCenter Servers, network shared storage devices, and virtual machines communicate with each other through virtual networks. This chapter explains how a virtual network works. It also shows how to create a virtual network through the hands-on activity.

Chapter 6. Network Shared Storage: In this chapter, a network will be established to connect the ESXi hosts to the network storage so that the ESXi hosts can share the network storage device. In the lab activity, the ESXi hosts will be connected to the Internet Small Computer System Interface–based network shared storage device through a specially designed network.

Chapter 7. Virtual Machines, Templates, and vApps: In this chapter, virtual machines, templates, and vApps will be created for various applications. In the lab activity, vApps will be created with multiple virtual machines and vApp internal networks.

Chapter 8. High Availability and Resource Balancing: This chapter introduces the features related to high availability and fault tolerance. These features are for the enterprise computing environment that requires high business continuity. vMotion is also introduced in this chapter. In the lab activity, readers will get hands-on practice on the VMware tools for high availability, fault tolerance, and distributed resource scheduler. In the lab activity, a specially designed network is established for migrating running virtual machines from one ESXi host to another ESXi host.

Chapter 9. Managing vSphere Security: This chapter introduces some security measures, such as the firewall, user authentication, and server certificate, included in VMware vCloud Suite. This chapter focuses on the subjects related to user authentication and authorization. This chapter's hands-on activity practices the configuration of some measures to enhance the security of ESXi and vCenter. It also covers the management of certificates for the ESXi and vCenter Servers.

Chapter 10. vCloud Networking and Security: VMware vCloud Networking and Security is the software used to manage the networking and security of a vCloud environment. It includes components such as the virtual firewall, virtual private network, load balancing, network address translation, Dynamic Host Configuration Protocol, and virtual extensible local area network–extended networks. In the lab activity, the software will be installed and configured to link and secure the networks created for vCloud Director.

Chapter 11. vCloud Director: This chapter prepares the installation of vCloud Director for providing the cloud services for customers. It describes the features of vCloud Director and shows what can be done with vCloud Director. In the lab activity, vCloud Director will be installed and configured. The lab activity demonstrates how to control computing resources, how to set up organizations and catalogs, and how to create templates and use the templates to develop vApps to implement cloud-based services.

Appendix A. IT Infrastructure Preparation for Supporting Business: In this section, a physical IT infrastructure is prepared for installing VMware vCloud Suite. The physical IT infrastructure consists of physical server computers and network devices specified in Chapter 1. As an example, a basic implementation that costs about $10,000 is demonstrated in this section.

Appendix B. SQL Server Database Installation and Configuration: This section establishes a database system that is used to store user and machine information for the management of the VMware lab environment. In the lab activity, Microsoft SQL Server is installed and configured for managing vCenter data.

Appendix C. Installing and Configuring vCenter Server with SQL Server Database: In a production environment, vCenter is often installed on a physical server for better reliability and performance. This section illustrates how to install and configure vCenter on a physical server.

As the cloud-based IT infrastructure will be built cumulatively through these hands-on activities, it is recommended that readers complete the activity in each chapter before starting the hands-on activity in the next chapter.

Acknowledgments

I thank my family for their love and support, their patience, and their understanding of my work.

My special gratitude goes to my students and Dr. Jenny Huang for their participation in the book-proofreading process. They carefully reviewed the manuscript. Their suggestions and corrections significantly improved the quality of the book.

I also thank the wonderful editorial staff and other personnel at Auerbach Publications of Taylor & Francis Group for their support of this project. I sincerely appreciate the collaboration of Mr. John Wyzalek, senior acquisitions editor, and all the other people who have been involved in this book project. The book would not be possible without their encouragement and great effort.

Lee Chao

Author

Dr. Lee Chao is currently a professor of the science, technology, engineering, and mathematics division at the University of Houston–Victoria, Texas. He received his PhD from the University of Wyoming, Laramie, Wyoming. Dr. Chao has been teaching information technology (IT) courses for over 20 years. His current research interests are IT infrastructure development and cloud computing. Dr. Chao is also the author of numerous research articles and books in various areas of IT.

Chapter 1

Introduction to Cloud Computing

Objectives

- Comprehend cloud computing
- Get familiar with VMware vCloud Suite
- Analyze hardware and software requirements
- Understand virtualized information technology infrastructure

1.1 Introduction

The goal of this chapter is to provide an overview of the cloud-based information technology (IT) infrastructure. Cloud computing is an Internet-based computing platform. In the cloud computing environment, instead of developing its own IT infrastructure and application development platform, and supporting the software, an organization can subscribe these services from a cloud provider. The cloud provider provides computing resources such as software, application development platform, and virtualized IT infrastructure to cloud service subscribers. The cloud subscribers only pay for the services and computing resources they use to reduce cost. Without constructing an IT infrastructure to support e-commerce or online teaching activities, there will be no upfront expenditure on the IT infrastructure for the company or the education institution. Right after the computing resources have been subscribed from the cloud provider, the company or the education institution can get a quick start to meet their computation needs. The physical IT infrastructure supporting the cloud services will be managed by the cloud provider. This means that the subscriber can further reduce cost on the maintenance of the IT infrastructure.

In addition, cloud computing is more efficient on the usage of computing resources. As the business grows, the company or the education institution can subscribe more services and computing resources. Cloud computing is a more flexible computing platform; it is relatively easy for a subscriber to alter an application development platform or the virtualized IT infrastructure to meet its needs. A public cloud is especially useful for handling peak demands by scaling up the computing resources without delay. Another advantage of cloud computing is the cloud services such as the software, the application development platform, or the virtualized IT infrastructure, which can be accessed through the Internet anywhere and anytime. Subscribing cloud services from cloud providers can be a great solution for small businesses that lack computing resources and skills to support their own IT infrastructure.

Cloud services can be subscribed from a public cloud provider, from a private cloud provider, or from a cloud provider combining both public and private clouds. For a public cloud, cloud subscribers can get computing resources and services from a third-party cloud provider such as Amazon Elastic Compute Cloud, IBM Blue Cloud, and Microsoft Windows Azure. The cloud services can be categorized into three major types: (1) software as a service (SaaS), (2) infrastructure as a service (IaaS), and (3) platform as a service (PaaS).

Software as a service: SaaS provides application software to subscribers. The application software provided by SaaS is accessible through personal computing devices such as notebook computers or mobile devices anywhere and anytime. Some of the well-known public SaaS services are available for subscribers. Google provides cloud-based application software such as Google Mail, Google Docs, Google Cloud Print, and Google Calendar. Similarly, Microsoft also provides cloud-based applications such as Microsoft Office 365. In addition to Web-based Office software such as Word, Excel, PowerPoint, and OneNote, Microsoft Office 365 includes software for cloud-based email, shared calendars, personal computer (PC)–to-PC calling, videoconferencing, and antivirus and antispam filters.

Platform as a service: PaaS provides a Web-based application development platform for cloud subscribers. The application development platform includes software such as server operating systems (OSs), databases, middleware,

Web servers, and project management tools. By subscribing to a PaaS service, subscribers do not have to construct and maintain the application development platform and the IT infrastructure that supports the application development platform. They can then focus on designing, developing, testing, deploying, and upgrading their application projects. The PaaS service allows application developers to work collaboratively on a project through the Internet.

One of the publicly available PaaS services is Microsoft Azure, which provides a platform that consists of data storage, network infrastructure, and application development software. Microsoft Azure also provides tools for testing and deploying application projects. With Microsoft Azure, application developers are able to create various Web-based applications, as well as mobile applications.

Infrastructure as a service: IaaS provides the virtualized IT infrastructure that consists of networks, servers, data storage, and client computers. With IaaS, subscribers can create their own IT infrastructure such as their own networks and their own client–server infrastructure. They can run their own database servers, Web servers, domain controllers, Dynamic Host Configuration Protocol (DHCP) service, and domain name service.

Amazon is such a public cloud provider that provides IaaS through Amazon Web Services (AWS). AWS IaaS provides cloud subscribers with virtual network servers, virtual desktop computers, data storage, and Internet Protocol (IP) addresses. The IaaS service provided by AWS allows the subscribers to choose prebuilt virtual machines installed with various OSs and application software. The cloud subscribers can also install their own software on the virtual machines provided by AWS. This means that a cloud subscriber is able to install free or open-source software such as the open-source database MySQL, which runs on a Linux OS. AWS IaaS also provides the virtual private cloud technology, which allows cloud subscribers to create their own private networks on the Amazon cloud. Once the virtual machines provided by AWS IaaS service are properly assigned IP addresses, these virtual machines will be accessible through the Internet. The AWS IaaS service also allows cloud subscribers to integrate a company's own IT infrastructure with the virtualized IT infrastructure provided by Amazon.

Subscribing computing resources from a public cloud provider can greatly improve the flexibility and availability on IT infrastructure development and management. On the other hand, by subscribing cloud services from a public cloud provider, a cloud subscriber has to pay monthly for the cloud services. The subscription fee can be too costly for many small businesses and education institutions. Also, cloud subscribers have no control over where their data are stored. Many subscribers may share the same data storage. Sometimes, the data may even be stored in a datacenter located in a foreign country. This may cause some concerns about the public cloud. For instance, as required by the federal government, an educational institution is responsible for keeping its students' privacy. It may violate state or federal government regulations if the student data are stored in a foreign country.

To take advantage of the cloud computing platform meanwhile to meet the data safety requirements, a company or an education institution can provide cloud services for private use. A private cloud can be constructed on the existing IT infrastructure owned by an organization. Cloud services and computing resources can be provided by the organization's IT department. The private cloud allows the organization to have total control of its own data, and the cloud subscribers are authenticated by the organization. The private cloud allows the subscribers to take advantage of the security, flexibility, and availability provided by cloud computing without paying subscription fees. The disadvantage of a private cloud is that the company or the education institution has to develop and manage the IT infrastructure, which requires capital expenditure, time, and a group of skilled technical personnel.

Software packages for developing a private cloud are widely available. There are some well-known private cloud development software, such as VMware vCloud Suite, Microsoft Hyper-V and System Center Virtual Machine Manager, and Xen Cloud Platform, to name a few. Among them, Microsoft Hyper-V depends on the Windows OS to interact with the hardware; Xen depends on the Linux OS to interact with the hardware; and VMware is able to directly interact with the hardware. However, VMware can only work with certified hardware such as server computers, storage devices, and network devices.

To take advantage of the public cloud and the private cloud, a company or an education institution can integrate them to form a hybrid cloud. The sensitive data will be saved to the private datacenter; meanwhile, the users will enjoy the scalability and availability of the public cloud. As many organizations already have their own IT infrastructure in place, it is relatively easy to construct a private cloud on top of the existing IT infrastructure. The private cloud can be used to support the security-sensitive departments such as their financial and human resources departments. In the meantime, they can use the public cloud to support the less sensitive business processes such as the company's Web applications. On the other hand, the hybrid cloud has some disadvantages. It has to deal with both the private cloud and public cloud. A company or an education institution needs to maintain the existing IT infrastructure on its private cloud and pay the subscription fee for the third-party public cloud provider. It takes more effort to manage both the public cloud and the private cloud at the same time. If the hybrid cloud is too much for a small business or an education institution to handle, a private cloud can be considered as an alternative.

In addition to the public, private, and hybrid clouds, the personal cloud has become available. A brief introduction of this type of cloud services is given as follows.

Personal cloud: The personal cloud is designed for storing and managing personal data that are accessible through the Internet. A personal cloud provider allows subscribers to share their personal data such as photos, movies, contacts, email, and documents with their friends, family, and coworkers online. By using the services provided by the personal cloud provider, the subscribers are able to store, retrieve, and organize their own data anywhere and anytime. They are also able to update, back up, and replicate all the personal data with their mobile devices.

iCloud is one of the well-known personal cloud providers. More than an online storage service, iCloud does everything for the subscriber to manage his or her personal data. iCloud keeps a person's email, contacts, and calendars up to date across his or her devices. With iCloud, a person's data content will be available on all of his or her computing devices, including iPhone, iPad, iPod touch, Mac, or PC.

Windows Live SkyDrive is the Microsoft version of the personal cloud. It is also used to store, organize, and share personal data anywhere and anytime through the Internet. Subscribers can create a contact list and grant permissions to access specific folders so that friends and family members can share photos, videos, music, and other data content. SkyDrive allows the subscribers to link the stored data to

their blogs or Web pages. In addition to the above two personal clouds, many other companies provide personal cloud services for their customers.

As described above, cloud computing works well in e-commerce and online education environments. The goal of this book is to provide the knowledge and skills to develop cloud services. The book provides an overview of cloud architecture and helps readers understand the software and hardware requirements of developing a cloud. Let us start with the description of cloud architecture in the next section.

1.2 Cloud Architecture

In a client–server environment, the server hosts some of the network-capable applications such as a database or email. Multiple users can access these applications through client computers from remote locations, as shown in Figure 1.1.

The advantage of a client–server solution is that the computing workload is distributed to both the server and the client computers. For a large computing task, the workload may be distributed to a group of servers and a group of client computers. The distributed structure can significantly reduce the workload of each individual computer. By placing the security-sensitive

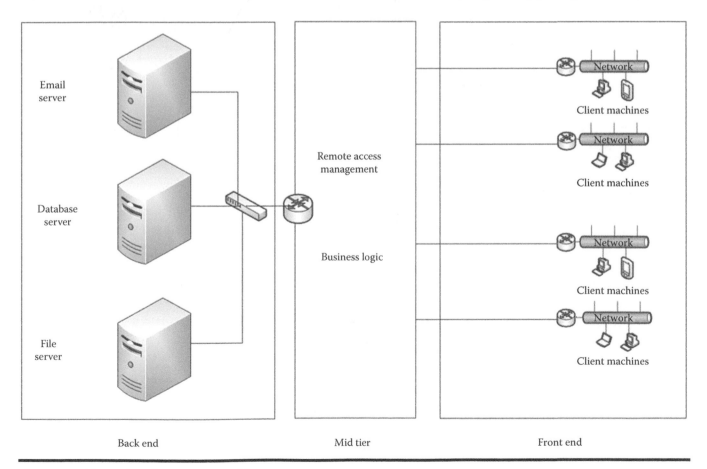

Email server

Database server

File server

Remote access management

Business logic

Network
Client machines

Network
Client machines

Network
Client machines

Network
Client machines

Back end   Mid tier   Front end

Figure 1.1   Three-tier client–server architecture.

content to the server machine, the client–server solution is more secure as the server is better protected. The client–server architecture is more reliable when the data are replicated to two or more servers. The client–server solution provides a flexible architecture. When a new version of application software is available, it can be installed on a new server and make it available to those client computers that need to access the new-version software. Meanwhile, keep the old-version software on another server for those clients who still need the old-version software. Also, the client–server architecture is suitable for centralized authentication and user management. With these advantages, the client–server architecture is adopted by most of the e-commerce and education institutions.

In many ways, the client–server architecture resembles SaaS in cloud computing. The clients at the front end work like cloud subscribers, and the servers at the back end serve the role of a cloud provider. The difference is that SaaS is no longer enterprise centric in the case of the public cloud. The back-end tier in the client–server architecture evolves to a more scalable, reliable, and flexible datacenter that consists of a cluster of servers and storage devices. In the case of the public cloud, the datacenter can be managed by a third-party cloud provider. The application software provided by the cloud provider largely becomes Web enabled. The cloud subscribers connect to the application software mainly through a Web browser. Unlike the client in the client–server architecture, the cloud subscribers only pay for the software and computing resources they use. In addition to the SaaS services, the cloud provider can provide the PaaS and IaaS services by applying the virtualization technology.

A cloud provider constructs its server side on a set of nodes, each of which includes data storage devices and a number of server computers installed in a blade enclosure. For reliability, each node has two or more backup nodes. The data in each node are replicated to backup nodes. These nodes are interconnected with high-speed wires and switches and are controlled by a unit called fabric controller (FC). The FC works with the load balancer to make sure that none of the nodes is overworked. The cloud architecture is illustrated in Figure 1.2.

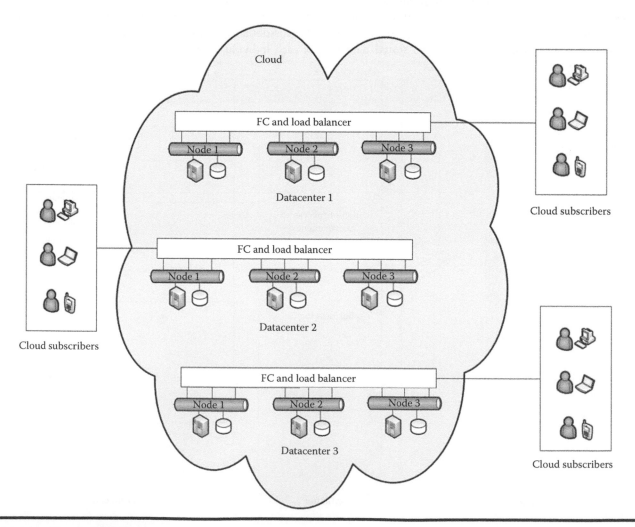

Figure 1.2 Cloud architecture.

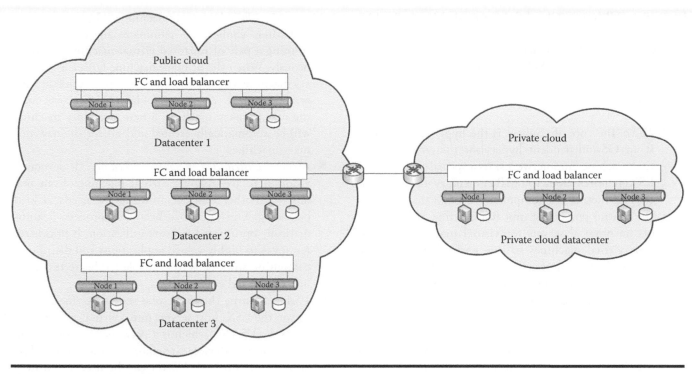

Figure 1.3 Hybrid cloud.

The private cloud has a similar architecture to the one shown in Figure 1.2, except that the datacenter is built on an organization's private network, and the cloud subscribers are the employees who are authenticated by the organization.

In a hybrid cloud, the cloud subscribers can access the cloud services from the public cloud provider, as well as from the private cloud provider. The applications created on the public cloud can access the datacenter constructed on the private cloud or vice versa. Due to limited resources, the private cloud may not be able to handle a large increase of demand on computing resources. In such a case, the private cloud can offload some of its workload to the integrated public cloud. The private cloud is connected to the public cloud through two routers with the firewall built in. One router is used to connect the private network to the Internet, and the other one is used to connect the Internet to the public cloud provider's network. Figure 1.3 illustrates the architecture of a hybrid cloud.

1.3 Cloud Development: Software and Hardware Overview

This section provides an overview about the hardware and software for cloud development. It also takes a look at virtualization and its application in providing cloud services. Let us start with the overview of the software.

1.3.1 Software Overview

Many small businesses and education institutions have their IT infrastructure built on computers with the x86 platform. VMware vCloud Suite is a widely deployed software suite for virtualization and cloud computing on x86-compatible computers. VMware vCloud Suite bundles a group of VMware products, including ESXi, vCenter, vRealize, and so on, to make it easier for creating a cloud computing environment. With VMware, an enterprise can provide virtual machines and virtual networks to form an IT infrastructure to replace many disparate, disorganized, and unproductive physical hardware devices. As an enterprise-level software suite, VMware vCloud Suite can be expensive for many small businesses and education institutions. To help those small businesses and education institutions, VMware provides low-cost packages such as VMware vSphere Essentials Kit, VMware vSphere Essentials Plus Kit, and the VMware Academic Program (VMAP). VMware vSphere Essentials Kit is a starter kit for small businesses to virtualize and centralize their physical hardware devices. The VMAP provides students and faculty members with low-cost VMware software to implement cloud computing into their curriculum.

Low-cost packages, such as the VMAP, will be used to support all the lab activities covered in this book. With a systematic approach, readers will be able to build a cloud computing environment for a small business or an education institution. VMware vCloud Suite provided by the VMAP includes components such as Elastic Sky X Integrated (ESXi) Server, VMware vCenter Server, vSphere Client, VMware vSphere Web Client, vSphere vMotion, vSphere High Availability (HA), vSphere Distributed Resource Scheduler (DRS), and so on.

- *ESXi:* The core of vSphere is the hypervisor ESXi. It is an OS-independent hypervisor that manages virtual machines and networks. As a special-purpose OS, ESXi requires about 130 MB of memory to work properly. VMkernel is a component in ESXi that allocates the central processing unit (CPU) time and memory of the physical servers for virtual machines. It controls virtual machines so that each virtual machine gets its computing resources in turn so that the virtual machines would not interrupt each other. Two or more identical copies of ESXi are usually installed on two or more physical servers called hosts, which form a server cluster. In case that one of the physical servers fails, the computing tasks run by the failed server will be taken over by the other servers in the same cluster. By doing so, the virtualized IT infrastructure can significantly reduce the system downtime.
- *VMware vCenter Server:* It is the software that provides centralized management of data storage, virtual machines, and hosts. It controls services such as remote access, performance monitoring, and alarm management. vCenter Server is used for the implementation of enterprise features such as vMotion, VMware HA, and VMware DRS. vCenter Server also provides directory services and data storage for managing and storing the information about ESXi hosts and virtual machines. VMware offers a prebuilt vCenter appliance, which is the vCenter Server installed on a virtual machine with SUSE Linux as the guest OS.
- *vSphere Client:* It is the software used to remotely access to the ESXi host or vCenter Server from any Windows PC.
- *VMware vSphere Web Client:* It is the software used to remotely access vCenter Server from a Web browser.
- *vSphere vMotion:* It is used to manually migrate running virtual machines from one ESXi host to another ESXi host.
- *vSphere High Availability:* It is the software used to detect hardware and guest OS failures. During a power outage or if a failure is detected, the HA utility can automatically restart a virtual machine from a different ESXi host. In a virtualized IT environment, HA provides uniform, cost-effective failover protection against a hardware or OS breakdown.
- *vSphere Fault Tolerance (FT):* Like vSphere HA, FT is also used against system failures. However, by restarting failed virtual machines, HA has a short downtime. vSphere FT eliminates any downtime by running a pair of mirrored virtual machines simultaneously. When the primary machine fails, the secondary machine will step in to take over the workload with zero downtime. As the secondary machine becomes the new primary machine, a new secondary machine will be automatically created and mirror the new primary machine.
- *vSphere Distributed Resource Scheduler:* It leverages vMotion to live-migrate virtual machines from one host to another host according to the needs of load balancing. During a load-balancing process, it automatically optimizes hardware utilization. It prioritizes resources to highly valued applications and distributes computing workloads to available hardware resources in a virtualized environment.
- *VSAN:* It turns the local solid-state drive (SSD) storage on the ESXi host servers into a virtual storage area network (VSAN), which is a network interconnecting shared storage devices. It requires at least three ESXi hosts to be involved. VSAN can be used to create a datastore across multiple ESXi hosts. It can improve input/output (I/O) performance.

To support cloud computing, VMware vCloud Suite provided by the VMAP includes VMware vCloud Director (vCD) used to create and manage cloud services and vCloud Networking and Security (vCNS), which provides security service such as VPN and firewall. vCNS can also be used to isolate one cloud subscriber's virtual IT infrastructure from another cloud subscriber's virtual IT infrastructure. Currently, VMware has replaced vDC and vCNS with vRealize and NSX in the commercial VMware vCloud Suite package. However, at the time of writing, VMware still keeps vCD and vCNS in the VMAP. VMware also provides vCD for cloud service providers. Figure 1.4 shows the design diagram of the VMware setup for a small business or for a cloud-based teaching environment.

In Figure 1.4, vCD can be built to provide multitenant cloud services. In vCD, a VMware administrator can create multiple organizations, each of which can be used to support a small business (the cloud service subscriber). For online teaching, an organization can represent the IT infrastructure to support a class taught online. The organizations are separated from each other and are completely secure. Through vCD, the VMware administrator can allocate computing resources for each organization and configure virtual organization networks. An organization network can be configured to connect to a private network, such as a private classroom network, so that it can communicate with other computing devices on the private network. Through vCNS, the organization network can be

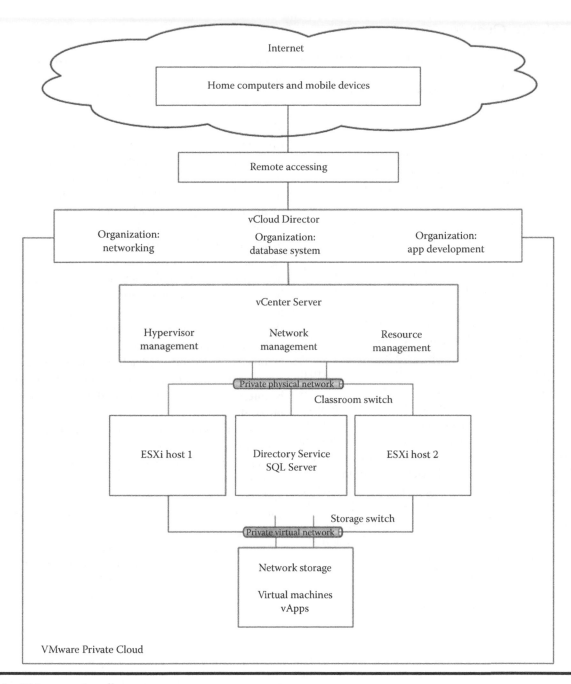

Figure 1.4   VMware setup diagram.

configured to communicate with the Internet. By doing so, a client in a remote location can access the cloud services provided by vCD through the Internet.

A vApp consists of virtual machines, virtual networks, and applications for the users. Through the vApp, one can deliver IaaS, which provides the IT infrastructure, PaaS, which provides an application development platform, or SaaS, which provides application software for the cloud subscribers. The vApp is portable so that it can be transferred from one VMware computing environment to another VMware computing environment. For an online class, the

vApp can be cloned so that each group of students can work on a similar IT infrastructure for their hands-on practice.

On the other end, vCD is connected to vCenter, which is a server installed with the vCenter software. Through vCenter, the VMware administrator can manage vCD, ESXi hosts, the Directory Services server, the database server, network storage, and the virtual and physical networks such as the classroom network and storage network. vCenter can also be used to create and manage virtual machines created on ESXi hosts. However, vCenter does not directly create cloud services as vCD does.

1.3.2 Hardware Overview

Hardware devices include server computers, storage devices, power supplies, and network devices. First, we need to select the hardware on the VMware compatibility list from the following Web site:

http://www.vmware.com/resources/compatibility/search .php

For example, suppose that we are interested to purchase rack or tower computers from Dell to install VMware ESXi 6.0 or a later version. The server computer selection is based on the functionality and affordability. The selection depends on many factors such as CPU, random access memory (RAM), NIC, storage, and compatibility with other hardware devices.

ESXi hosts are connected to vCenter, as well as network storage. An ESXi host is an x86 server with the ESXi software installed. Usually, two or more ESXi hosts are installed for redundancy. Multiple ESXi hosts share one or more network storage devices so that virtual machines can be easily moved between two ESXi hosts. ESXi works with hardware such as CPU and memory directly for resource allocation to virtual machines. It works with network interface cards (NICs) and the device connection bus. It manages drivers that are used for the communication between hardware and software. ESXi also includes drivers to work with network storage devices. Virtual NICs and virtual switches can be created within ESXi to connect the virtual machines running inside the ESXi hosts. There are two versions of virtual switches: (1) the standard vSwitch and (2) the distributed vSwitch. Through the standard vSwitch, several virtual machines on a single ESXi host can share a physical NIC. Through the distributed vSwitch, the vSwitches on each ESXi host can form a single logical network switch.

The amount of memory required for the ESXi server is based on the number of virtual machines running simultaneously. VMware with the OverCommit feature allows virtual machines to run when the total required memory size exceeds the memory available on the ESXi server. If virtual machines consume all the ESXi server's memory, then the ESXi server will reclaim memory from virtual machines and redistribute the ESXi memory, in an efficient and fair manner, to all virtual machines so that the memory resource is best utilized.

1.3.3 Virtualized IT Infrastructure

Cloud computing can greatly benefit from a virtualized IT infrastructure. For better flexibility and scalability, cloud services can be provided through the virtualized IT infrastructure. The following describes how the virtualized IT infrastructure works and how it can be used to provide cloud services.

When dealing with an urgent request for the IT infrastructure to support a new project, instead of purchasing, installing, and networking the IT infrastructure, we can create virtualized servers and networks in a short time to meet the needs. We can make a virtualized IT infrastructure as a template and clone it when needed. We can take a snapshot of the virtualized IT infrastructure. When the IT infrastructure crashes due to power failure or other reasons, the IT infrastructure can be quickly recovered by using the snapshots. The virtualized IT infrastructure can be easily moved from one server to another server or from one storage device to another storage device without any downtime.

In VMware vCloud Suite, the software ESXi can be used to simulate an IT infrastructure. The virtualization technology can be used to generate virtual machines and virtual networks. These virtual machines and virtual networks will be stored on the network storage and will run on an ESXi host. Depending on the computing resources available on the ESXi host, a number of virtual machines can run on the ESXi host simultaneously. ESXi keeps each virtual machine completely independent. Each virtual machine is capable of running its own OS and application software and will not be interrupted by the other virtual machines running on the physical machine.

ESXi supports network virtualization. It provides vNetwork Standard Switch (vSS) and vNetwork Distributed Switch (vDS) for constructing networks. vSS can be used to connect the virtual machines managed by the ESXi host and the physical network so that the virtual machines can communicate with each other on a virtual network, as well as with physical machines on a company's network. For better resource management of large, complicated physical networks, both vSS and vDS can be used to connect and manage multiple virtual local area networks (VLANs). A VLAN can be used to divide a large physical network into a few smaller logical networks. Each logical network can be configured so that it is isolated from other logical networks. For example, a network built for a finance department is often isolated from other networks in a company. It is much easier to reconfigure a VLAN without physically relocating the connected computers. The VLAN technology also provides better network security and manageability. vSS and vDS also support NIC teaming, which is a technology that integrates multiple network adapters on a host to form a team for bandwidth aggregation and preventing the loss of connection.

In addition, vDS provides centralized management of virtual networks. That is, it connects and monitors the virtual machines managed by multiple ESXi hosts. vDS supports private virtual local area networks (PVLANs), which can achieve port isolation. That is, a VLAN contains switch ports that can only communicate with a given uplink port. vDS is able to handle load balancing and is therefore able to support vMotion, which migrates the running virtual

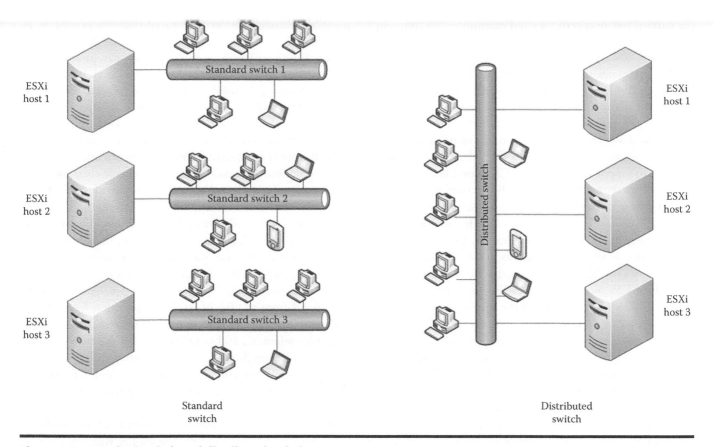

Figure 1.5   Standard switch and distributed switch.

machines from one ESXi host to another with zero down-time. vDS also supports the collecting, monitoring, and analyzing of IP traffic information. Figure 1.5 illustrates the architecture of vSS and vDS.

Even though the standard switch lacks some features, it is adequate for developing the virtualized IT infrastructure for many medium and small businesses. The distributed switch offers some features for task automation and for large network management.

1.4   Process of Cloud-Based IT Infrastructure Development

The development of a cloud-based IT infrastructure can be complicated. It requires careful planning. The development process starts with the phase of requirement analysis that investigates the requirements for the to-be-built IT infrastructure in order to meet the project's goal. The next phase is to draft a blueprint to lay out the details of about the future IT infrastructure on paper. Based on the requirements, specify the hardware and software that will be used to build the IT infrastructure. Make sure that the hardware and software specified in the blueprint can achieve the design goal. Once confirmed, the implementation phase begins. In this phase,

according to the blueprint, the hardware and software will be purchased, and the construction of the IT infrastructure can take off. Once the proposed IT infrastructure is implemented, the next phase is to deploy the IT infrastructure to the customers. The last phase of the development process is collecting users' feedback and summarizing the experience gained from the project development. The last phase will help the development team to further improve the underlying project. Let us take a brief look at each IT infrastructure development phase.

1.4.1   Requirement Analysis

The first task is to investigate the requirements for the IT infrastructure to be developed. A well-designed IT infrastructure stems from a thorough requirement analysis. The designers need to find out what business processes will be supported by the IT infrastructure, the number of users to work on the IT infrastructure, the number of computers to be installed, the requirements for the network capacity, the security measure to be enforced, and the rules and limitations to be imposed on the future IT infrastructure. To collect the needed information, the design team should conduct interviews with the key players of the business process. The team can also collect the needed information by observing the current business activities and examining the company's mission and long-term planning. As an example, let us consider the following scenario.

The computer information systems (CIS) department is looking at developing an IT infrastructure for the hands-on practice in many CIS courses. It is desired if the IT infrastructure can be used to support courses such as programming, database, networking, Web development, security, system administration, and so on. Often, the IT infrastructure designed to support one type of the CIS course may not be suitable for other types of CIS courses. For example, the IT infrastructure designed for a networking course is not suitable for teaching Web development. Students in the networking class often change the network configuration. Once the network configuration is altered, the students in the Web development class may not be able to connect to the Web server. Therefore, some of the CIS courses require their own IT infrastructure.

As the CIS students may get the administrator's privilege so that they can perform the system management tasks on the server side, these students must be prevented from accessing the university's private network. It is required that the IT infrastructure created for the teaching of CIS courses be isolated from the university's network.

The IT infrastructure should provide an application development platform to allow collaboration by groups of students. In some CIS courses, students are grouped and are working on a software engineering project. For example, a group member may be responsible for developing the billing system; another member may be responsible for developing a database system and other server side applications; yet another member is to develop client applications; and so on. Ideally, the students should be aware of the activities performed by their peers. Therefore, the application development platform should be constructed to support all the collaboration activities.

The IT infrastructure should be designed to help the CIS department to catch up with the fast-moving trend of the IT industry. Frequently upgrading the IT infrastructure can be a financial burden on an education institution. It also requires well-trained technicians to carry out the reconstruction work. Therefore, the proposed cloud-based IT infrastructure should be easily upgraded and able to keep the reconstruction cost affordable.

1.4.2 System Design

Once the design team figures out the requirements, it is time to design the logical IT infrastructure that serves as a blueprint for the future IT infrastructure. Without designing and planning, one may encounter problems with compatibility, availability, meeting the deadline, budgeting, and achieving the project goal. Based on the requirements, the IT infrastructure should be flexible enough for different courses. It should be isolated from a university's network, should be

suitable for collaboration, and should be less expensive. A cloud-based IT infrastructure can meet all these requirements. The cloud-based IT infrastructure can provide SaaS, PaaS, or IaaS specially designed to support each type of CIS courses. SaaS can be used to support the courses that require network-based software. PaaS can be used to support collaboration. IaaS can be used to support courses that require their own IT infrastructure. The virtual networks can be easily isolated from the university's private network and allow students to remotely access, create, and manage their own virtual machines and virtual networks. To provide SaaS, PaaS, and IaaS, a private cloud can be built to accomplish the tasks.

At this phase, hardware and software should be specified to run the private cloud. In this case study, the selected software is VMware vCloud Suite for implementing virtualization and cloud services, and Active Directory for the user and computer management. To host the software, hardware must be selected from the list of hardware provided by VMware Compatibility Guide. The hardware may include servers, network equipment, and storage devices. The hardware must be powerful enough to support the software. For example, to support multiple courses in a CIS program, the system should be designed to meet the following requirements:

■ The future cloud-based IT infrastructure needs to support at least 60 virtual machines with lightweight workloads.
■ It requires a multitenant environment so that each CIS class can have a workplace for its own use.
■ It requires the IT infrastructure to provide the IaaS service, which allows students to design and construct their own vApps.

Some of the CIS classes may need just a few virtual machines. However, in some cases, a CIS class may require 40–60 virtual machines running the Linux OS. Each student has two virtual machines; one is the server, and the other one is the client. The virtual machines have the following configuration (Table 1.1).

For hands-on practice, these virtual machines have fairly light resource requirements and will be shut down soon after the lab assignment is completed. The VMAP entitles ESXi to use four physical CPUs. Suppose that each CPU has four cores. Each core can support 8–10 virtual machines if the requirement on the computing resources is light. Assume that each ESXi host server has two CPUs; then each ESXi

Table 1.1 Virtual Machine Requirements

Operating System	Hard Disk	Memory	NIC
Ubuntu Server	20 GB	1 GB	2
Ubuntu Desktop	20 GB	1 GB	2

server has eight cores that can support up to 64–80 virtual machines if the requirement on the computing resource is light. If two such ESXi servers are installed, we should be able to handle up to 160 virtual machines. As each virtual machine requires 1-GB memory, to run 80 virtual machines on an ESXi server, it will be enough to have 84-GB RAM installed on the ESXi server. In fact, the 80 virtual machines can run simultaneously with much less RAM on the ESXi server with the OverCommit feature.

As each virtual machine requires 20-GB hard disk storage space, 80 virtual machines will require at least 1.6-TB hard disk storage space. ESXi itself needs 4-GB hard disk storage space. Later, as the demand for memory and storage increases, more memory and storage space can be added. Table 1.2 summarizes the specifications of an ESXi server.

The two-port NIC is used for redundancy to prevent NIC failure. The specified requirements are more than what we need to meet the requirements for our case study. On the other hand, more computing resources will be needed if we consider supporting multiple CIS courses concurrently. For the servers to host Domain Controller, Database, vCenter, vCNS, and vCD, we have the following specifications shown in Table 1.3.

The specified requirements in Table 1.3 are more than the minimum requirements. Lightweight tasks can be carried out with much less computing resources than what is listed in Table 1.3. VMware also provides the ready-made vCenter Appliance, vCD Appliance, or vCNS Appliance built on a virtual machine. With the appliances, servers can be directly installed on an ESXi host server. In that case, the memory and storage requirements in Table 1.2 should be modified accordingly.

The use of appliances is more proper for small projects. The deployment of appliances is straightforward. Many useful tools such as Auto Deploy Server are already installed on the appliances. An appliance can be directly uploaded to the ESXi server. After a few configurations, the appliance is ready to run. As the IT infrastructure is designed for hands-on practice, students can get a quick start with these appliances.

Often, the bottleneck of a system is the I/O of the storage device. The I/O bottleneck can be resolved by using SSD

Table 1.2 ESXi Server Requirements

Item	Description	Quantity
CPU	Intel Xeon E52643, 6 Core, 3.4 GHz	2
RAM	16-GB registered dual in-line memory module (RDIMM), 2,133 MT/s, Dual Rank	12
Hard drive	300-GB 15K-rpm Serial-Attached SCS (SAS) 6 Gbps 2.5 in, redundant array of independent disks (RAID) 1	2
NIC	Intel I350 QP—Gigabit Ethernet × 2 Ports	4

Table 1.3 Other Server Requirements

Server	Processor	Memory	Disk Storage	NIC
DC	Intel x64, 2 Core, 2 GHz	2 GB	60 GB	2 × 1 Gb
SQL Server	Intel x64, 2 Core, 2 GHz	4 GB	60 GB	2 × 1 Gb
vCenter	Intel x64, 4 Core, 2 GHz	8 GB	140 GB	2 × 1 Gb
vCNS	Intel x64, 2 Core, 2 GHz	8 GB	60 GB	2 × 1 Gb
vCD	Intel x64, 2 Core, 2 GHz	2 GB	8 GB	2 × 1 Gb

hard disks that may get 10 times faster in I/O performance than that of a traditional SAS hard drive. For better reliability, we may consider using RAID 1, which requires twice as many SSD hard disks as no RAID 1. For better reliability, as well as better performance, we may consider using RAID 5 or RAID 10, which requires three or four times as many SSD hard disks. The summary of network storage devices is given in Table 1.4.

Again, the configuration is more than what we need for our case study. The extra storage space will be reserved for more CIS courses.

Assume that the ESXi servers are rack mounted. Each of the servers has four built-in 1-Gb network adapters. The network should be designed to support a management network, a vMotion network, a remote access network, and a network for storage devices and virtual machines. The management network will be used to monitor and manage the host servers and virtual machines. The storage network connects the network storage devices that store the virtual machines. The vMotion network is for moving virtual machines and other failover activities. The remote access network allows

Table 1.4 Network Storage Requirements

Item	Description	Quantity
Network-attached storage (NAS)	12 Bay 2U Rackmount NAS	1
SSD	1-TB 2.5-in. SATA III Internal SSD	12
Switch	16-Port Gigabit Ethernet Switch	2

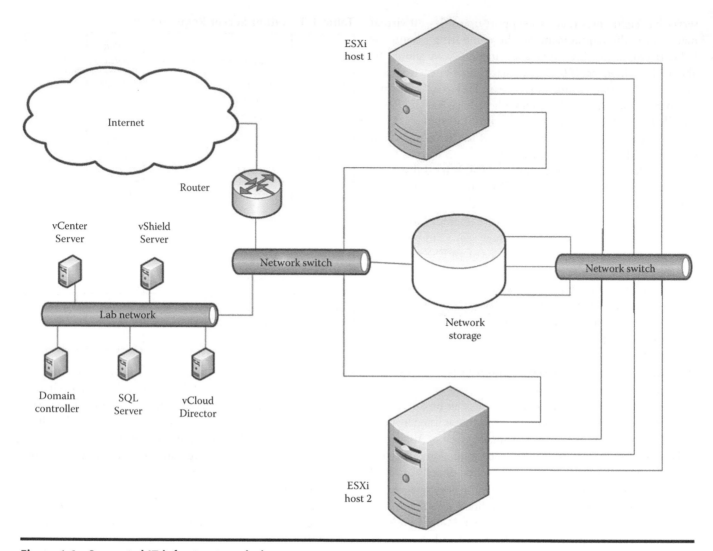

Figure 1.6 Suggested IT infrastructure design.

communication between users and virtual machines. It also allows the communication between two virtual machines running on two different host servers. When four 1-Gb NICs, each with two ports, are installed on each ESXi server, we may assign two NICs for the shared storage: one NIC for vMotion and one for management; virtual machine activities can be distributed to all four NICs, and one of them is connected to the public network for remote access.

The IT infrastructure should be designed so that it is adequate to meet the requirements on the number of users and computers. It should be designed to comply with the security requirements and the organization's rules and limitations. For example, the cost of hardware and software should be within the budget limit. The blueprint will be verified by the design team and the customers to make sure that the design goal has been achieved. It may take several rounds of modifications before the blueprint can be finalized. In summary, the suggested logical IT infrastructure may look like the one in Figure 1.6.

1.4.3 System Implementation

Once the blueprint is finalized, the implementation phase begins. During this phase, hardware and software will be purchased, installed, and configured according to the blueprint. As an example, the following describes how the software and hardware are purchased and installed.

Hardware specification and installation: Server computers will be selected so that they can meet the requirements listed in Tables 1.2 and 1.3. Among many choices, we may choose the rack mount PowerEdge R730 Intel Xeon E5-2600-v3 Series server or the older mini tower PowerEdge T710 Intel Xeon 55xx Series server. For example, the PowerEdge R730 can be configured, as shown in Table 1.5.

At the time of writing, each server costs about $10,000. If the price is too high for some small businesses, one may also consider the older PowerEdge T710 server with the specifications shown in Table 1.6.

Table 1.5   Quotation of Two PowerEdge R730 Servers

Quantity	Description
2	PowerEdge R730 Server (210-ACXU)
4	Intel Xeon E5-2637 v3 3.5 GHz,15M Cache, 9.60 GT/s
8	Intel i350AM2 Dual-Port 1-Gb NIC
2	RAID 1 for H330/H730/H730P (2 HDDs or SSDs)
32	16-GB RDIMM, 2,133 MT/s, Dual Rank, x4 Data Width
4	300-GB 10K rpm SAS 6-Gbps 2.5-in Hot-plug Hard Drive
2	DVD-ROM, SATA, INTERNAL
2	Dual, Hot-plug, Redundant Power Supply (1 + 1), 750 W

Table 1.6   Quotation of Two PowerEdge T710 Servers

Quantity	Description
2	PowerEdge T710
4	Intel Xeon E5-2640 2.50 GHz, 15M Cache, 7.2 GT/s QuickPath Interconnect
8	Broadcom 5720 DP 1-Gb NIC
24	8-GB RDIMM, 1333 MHz, Low Volt, Single Rank, x4
4	300-GB 7.2K-rpm SATA 3.5-in Hot-plug Hard Drive
2	DVD-ROM, SATA, INTERNAL
2	Dual, Hot-plug, Redundant Power Supply (1 + 1), 750 W

The price of this type of server is about $3,000 each. Used servers may cost significantly lower.

The selection of storage is also a critical decision. ESXi supports three types of storage devices: (1) Fibre Channel–based storage or Fibre Channel over Ethernet (FCoE) storage, (2) Internet Small Computer System Interface (iSCSI)–based storage, and (3) Network File System (NFS)–based storage. The selection may be based on the following factors:

■ The storage should be compatible with the existing ESXi servers and network devices.
■ The IT staff members should be knowledgeable about the selected storage technology.
■ The performance of the storage device should meet the requirements of the proposed IT infrastructure.

To match the servers specified in Table 1.5, one may consider the storage device Dell PowerVault MD3220i iSCSI SAN Storage Array. It is a cost-effective Ethernet-based storage array with the following features:

■ It supports up to 24 2.5-in. SAS, Near-Line SAS, and SSD drives. With an optional Premium Feature Key, it can be expanded to support 120 hard drives.
■ With a single controller, 4 servers can be directly connected to the device. With a double controller, 8 servers can be directly connected to the device. Through an Ethernet switch, 32 servers can be connected to the device.
■ The device supports RAID levels 0, 1, 10, 5, and 6.
■ It provides failover management of redundant data paths between the server and storage array.
■ For each controller, it provides four RJ-45 1-Gb Ethernet network cards.

If the PowerVault MD3220i is too big for a small business, one may consider Synology Disk Station DS1815+, which has the following specifications:

■ The device has eight SATA II hard disk drive (HDD)/ SSD drive bays and supports up to 48-TB data storage capacity.
■ It supports RAID levels 0, 1, 10, 5, and 6 and just a bunch of disks (JBOD).
■ The device includes a 2.4-GHz Intel Atom Quad-Core CPU, 2-GB DDR3 Memory, and 4 x USB 3.0/2 x eSATA Ports.
■ It provides 4 x Gigabit LAN/Wake on LAN/WAN.

The selection of NICs and physical switches should meet the requirements by the ESXi servers and storage devices. For example, for tasks such as ESXi management, vMotion, FT, communication between ESXi servers and storage devices, and communication among virtual machines, the gigabit NICs or even the 10-Gb NICs should be considered. For instance, an NIC may be assigned to ESXi management, and another NIC should be assigned to vMotion. The NIC assigned to vMotion can be used as a standby NIC for ESXi management, or vice versa. For redundancy, a pair of NICs will be assigned for FT. If available, a pair of 10-Gb NICs should be considered. Another pair of NICs should be used for the communication between ESXi servers and storage devices. Also, a pair of NICs should be used for the communication among virtual machines. If there is a busy traffic among virtual machines, 10-Gb NICs should be considered.

To connect the servers and storage devices, we need some network devices such as network switches and routers. To be compatible with VMware, we may select PowerConnect 6224 Managed Switch (Table 1.7).

Table 1.7 Specifications of Dell PowerConnect 6224 Managed Switch

Name	Description
Ports	24 10/100/1000BASE-T auto-sensing Gigabit Ethernet switching ports; 4 SFP combo ports for fiber media support
Authentication	RADIUS, Secure Shell v.2 (SSH2), TACACS+
Encryption	SSL, SSL 2.0, SSL 3.0
Cabling type	Ethernet 1000Base-T, Ethernet 100Base-TX, Ethernet 10Base-T
Management protocol	HTTP, HTTPS, RMON, SNMP 1, SNMP 2c, SNMP 3, Telnet
Switching protocol	Ethernet
Routing protocol	DVMRP, OSPF, OSPFv2, OSPFv3, RIP-1, RIP-2, VRRP, static IP routing
Support	ARP, BOOTP, Broadcast Storm Control, DHCP, DoS attack prevention, IGMP snooping, IPv6, Syslog, VLAN, auto-negotiation, auto-uplink, flow control, port mirroring

In addition, we may need three lower-cost eight-port gigabit desktop switches and a digital subscriber line router for accessing the Internet. Although the Category 5 (Cat 5) cable works with the gigabit switches, it is better to use Cat 5e or Cat 6 cables to minimize the electromagnetic interference.

For the software specification and installation, one needs to install the software provided by VMware vCloud Suite including ESXi, vCenter, vSphere Client, vCNS, and vCD. The software can be installed on separate physical server computers for better performance and FT, or installed on a cluster of virtual machines hosted by the ESXi host server for convenience. Windows Server 2012 should also be installed on a server computer to provide services such as DHCP for automatic IP address assignment, domain name system for computer name resolution, and Active Directory for user authentication. If a separate database server is required, a server computer installed with Microsoft SQL Server 2012 can be considered. In later chapters, there will be some hands-on activities to illustrate software installation and configuration.

Once the hardware and software are installed, before the newly developed IT infrastructure can be used in the business process, it needs to be tested to see if the IT infrastructure is able to meet all the requirements. Based on the testing

results, the IT infrastructure will be modified and tested again until it meets all the requirements.

In the above, you have gone through the main steps in the development of IT infrastructure to support a private cloud.

Once the IT infrastructure is implemented, the next phase is to provide technical support, prepare documentation, and collect feedback from the users. As the IT infrastructure is deployed, maintenance and troubleshooting are the main tasks to be accomplished by the IT department. When the IT infrastructure is ready to use, the users are encouraged to verify if they can log on to the IT infrastructure and are able to use it. In our case, the instructors are encouraged to develop teaching materials such as lab instructions for their classes. Successful deployment of the IT infrastructure requires training and technical support. The users should be trained on how to use the IT infrastructure. There should be some operation instructions written for the users. The technical support team should be organized to help the users with troubleshooting.

For the improvement of the IT infrastructure, we need to collect the users' experience. Data can be collected from the troubleshooting reports, system failure reports, users' feedback, and the expenditure report on the system maintenance. In our case, the teaching and learning practice on the IT infrastructure will be closely observed and modified to achieve better impact on learning and teaching. The instructors' and students' opinions and suggestions will be collected. The data about the engagement of the instructors and students with the IT infrastructure will be documented for future improvement.

1.5 Activity 1: Preparing Hands-On Practice

In this lab activity, you will create an environment for hands-on practice. The physical PC used to implement the project can be either a gaming computer or a workstation. As an example, the physical PC can be configured, as shown in Table 1.8.

Although one can run the virtual machines on a PC with less than 16-GB RAM, a PC with 32-GB RAM has much better performance. It is not too difficult to find a PC with 32-GB RAM. For example, most of the gaming computers can meet the requirements. Some of the workstation computers can also meet the requirements. For instance, the Dell Precision M6500 or later laptop computer can have 32-GB RAM installed. The Dell Precision T1700 Minitower or later can also have 32-GB RAM installed.

This activity illustrates how to install the software VMware Workstation on a PC specified in Table 1.8. In later

Table 1.8 Configuration of PC Hosting VMware vCloud Suite

Name	Description
CPU	Intel core_i7 Processor 2.3 GHz. The virtualized Intel VT-x/EPT or AMD-v/RVI feature needs to be enabled on the CPU.
RAM	Minimum 16-GB DDR3
Hard disk	750 GB 7200 rpm with 8-GB ExpressCache SSD
NIC	Integrated 10/100/1000 Network Card and 802.11 abg/n Wireless LAN
Screen	17.3″ Full HD 1080P LED
DVD	SuperMulti Double Layer DVD with Blu-ray
OS	Windows 8.1 64 Bit Professional or later
Hypervisor	VMware Workstation 9 or later

chapters, VMware Workstation will be used to create virtual machines used as server computers to install ESXi, vCenter, vCNS, vCD, storage, and Windows Server 2012.

For the hands-on practice, the network storage is not necessary. The SSD hard disk specified in Table 1.8 is good enough. In fact, it is even OK to use a 500-GB SATA 7200-rpm hard drive, which has slower performance. Assume that the PC is installed with the OS Windows Server 2012. The first task is to install VMware Workstation with the following steps:

1. Download VMware Workstation from the following Web site. On the Web site, search for the latest version of VMware Workstation:
   https://my.vmware.com/web/vmware/downloads
2. Once the installation exe file is downloaded, double-click the download file to start the installation wizard.
3. On the Setup Type page, select the option **Typical** and click **Next**.
4. On the Ready to Perform the Requested Operations page, click **Continue**.
5. On the Enter a license key page, enter the license key or skip the license key for 30-day evaluation. (Students may ask the instructor for the license key.)
6. Click **Finish** to complete the installation. The installed VMware Workstation is shown in Figure 1.7.
7. Click the **Edit** menu and select **Preferences** to open the Preferences dialog shown in Figure 1.8. You may change the preferences setting to meet your needs.
8. One needs to reserve the memory for the virtual machines. Windows 10 OS needs about 2.5-GB memory. Subtracting 2.5 GB from the total available memory, we have the amount of memory reserved for the virtual machines. For example, for a computer with 16-GB memory, about 13.8 GB is reserved for the virtual machines, as shown in Figure 1.9. When the memory is running out, the option **Allow some virtual machine**

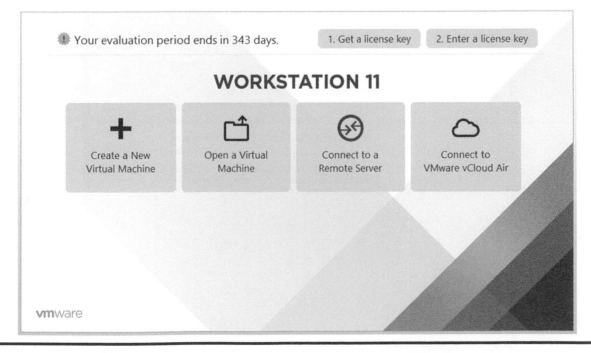

Figure 1.7 VMware Workstation.

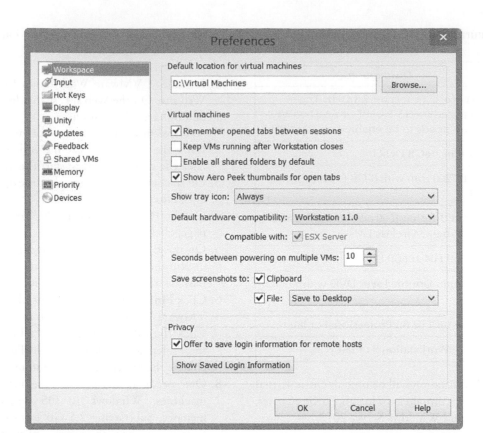

Figure 1.8   Location of virtual machines.

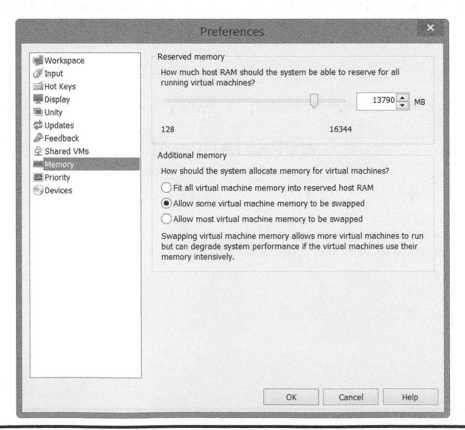

Figure 1.9   Reserved memory.

memory to be swapped allows the virtual machines to use part of SSD or HDD as the virtual memory.

9. Click **OK** to complete the configuration of performance.

Network preparation: After VMware Workstation is installed, one needs to create a private network to connect virtual machines used as server machines for the hands-on practice. VMware Workstation offers three types of virtual networks:

1. *Bridged virtual network:* This type of virtual network allows virtual machines to access the physical network. The virtual machines can communicate directly with the computers and network devices on the physical network.
2. *NAT virtual network:* This type of virtual network allows virtual machines on the same host to communicate with each other. The virtual machines can also directly communicate with the host machine. When communicating with other computers on the physical network where the host computer is connected, this virtual network translates the IP address of a virtual machine to the host's IP address and vice versa.
3. *Host-only virtual network:* This type of network is isolated from the host and physical network. It only allows the virtual machines on the same host to communicate with each other. When an isolated network is required, this kind of network is created for keeping the virtual machines disconnected from the external network.

The following steps illustrate how to get started:

1. Start VMware Workstation and click the **Home** tab.
2. Click the **Edit** menu and select **Virtual Network Editor**. Then, click the **Change Settings** button.
3. Click the **Add Network** button and select **VMnet2** on the dropdown list. Then, click **OK**.

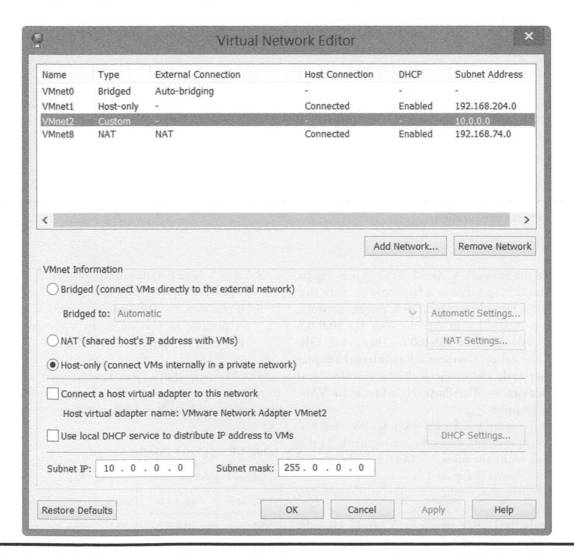

Figure 1.10   VMnet2 configuration.

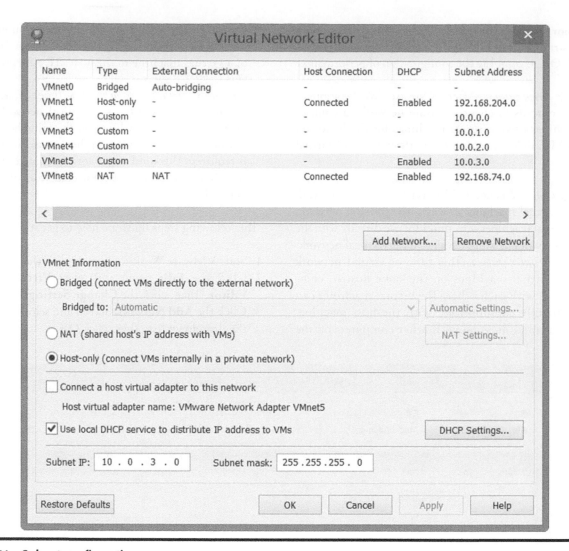

Figure 1.11 Subnet configuration.

4. Configure the network VMnet2, as shown in Figure 1.10. VMnet2 is specified as a host-only network that connects the virtual machines on a private network. VMnet2 is assigned a private network ID **10.0.0.0** with the network mask **255.0.0.0**. Then, click **OK**. Uncheck the option **Connect a host virtual adapter to this network** and uncheck the option **Use local DHCP service to distribute IP address to VMs**. Then, click **Apply**.

5. As shown in Figure 1.6, for vMotion, failover, and network storage, multiple networks are required. At this stage, let us create the subnets VMnet3, VMnet4, and VMnet5, as shown in Figure 1.11.

6. Table 1.9 lists the configurations for the subnets VMnet3, VMnet4, and VMnet5.

7. To configure the DHCP service for VMnet5, click the DHCP button. The DHCP service is configured, as shown in Figure 1.12. Then, click **OK**.

8. Later, a more detailed description of these subnets will be given when we use these subnets in lab development.

9. At this step, the infrastructure is ready for the hands-on practice in this book. In VMware Workstation, click the **File** menu and select **Exit**.

In the steps above, you have created a lab environment for the hands-on practice. For supporting a business or supporting cloud-based IT education, one may want to

Table 1.9 Subnet Configurations

Network	Network ID	Subnet Mask	DHCP Service
VMnet3	10.0.1.0	255.255.255.0	Not required
VMnet4	10.0.2.0	255.255.255.0	Not required
VMnet5	10.0.3.0	255.255.255.0	Required

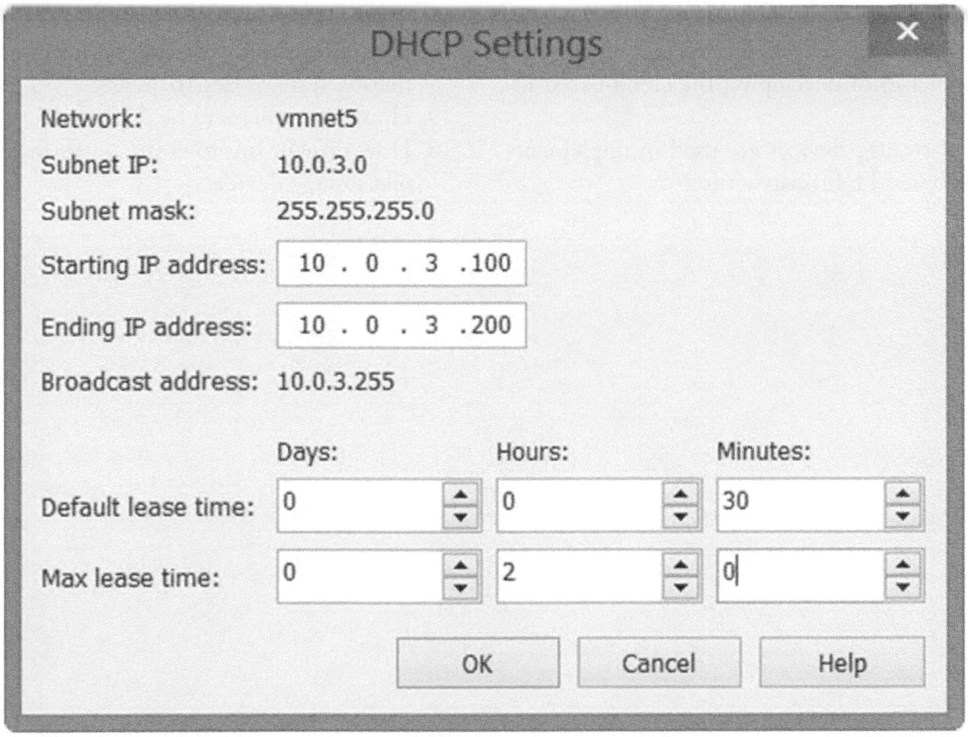

Figure 1.12   DHCP service configuration.

implement the IT infrastructure on a set of physical servers. Details about the implementation on a set of physical servers are included in Appendix A.

1.6 Summary

This chapter provides an overview of cloud-based IT infrastructure. It introduces cloud computing concepts such as public cloud, private cloud, and hybrid cloud. Also, it explains cloud services such as IaaS, PaaS, and SaaS. This chapter describes the cloud architecture, which illustrates how the cloud is constructed and how the hardware and software are used in supporting cloud computing. For better flexibility and scalability, cloud services are provided through the virtualized IT infrastructure. This chapter also describes how the virtualized IT infrastructure works and how it can be used to provide cloud services. As an overview, this chapter goes through the development process to create a cloud infrastructure. It explains how to conduct the requirement analysis, how to select the hardware and software, and how to specify the hardware and software to support the IT infrastructure to implement cloud services. The software used in this book is VMware vCloud Suite, which is used for developing an enterprise-level private cloud. The hardware includes servers and network equipment used for supporting VMware vCloud Suite. The hands-on activity in

this chapter gives instruction on creating an environment for the hands-on practice for the rest of the book. With the environment established, the next task is to develop a domain controller, which will be used for user authentication and for managing the components of VMware vCloud Suite. The topics of domain controller will be covered in Chapter 2.

REVIEW QUESTIONS

1. What is the software often provided by SaaS?
2. What components are included in the PaaS provided by Microsoft Windows Azure?
3. What do you do with IaaS?
4. What are the advantages and disadvantages of a public cloud?
5. What are the advantages and disadvantages of a private cloud?
6. Describe how a hybrid cloud works.
7. What is ESXi, and how does it work?
8. What is VMware vCenter Server, and what do you do with it?
9. What do you do with vSphere vMotion?
10. Describe how vSphere HA works.
11. Describe how vSphere FT works.
12. Describe how vSphere DRS works.
13. What do you do with VSAN?

14. What is a vApp, and how do you use it?
15. How does the virtualized IT infrastructure work?
16. Describe the phases of developing the cloud-based IT infrastructure.
17. What types of storage devices are used in implementing the cloud-based IT infrastructure?
18. What are the challenges for the IT infrastructure used to support the hands-on practice required by an information systems department?
19. How can appliances be deployed?
20. How do you improve the performance and reliability of a storage device?

Chapter 2

Domain Controller Installation and Configuration

Objectives

- Understand the role played by domain controller
- Install and configure Active Directory
- Manage domain name service

2.1 Introduction

As described in Chapter 1, there are multiple Elastic Sky X Integrated (ESXi) host servers installed in an information technology (IT) infrastructure to support cloud computing. In such a case, for each ESXi host server, you need to create a group of local users. As a local user, the user account created for one ESXi server does not work on another ESXi server. In addition to the ESXi servers, you may need to create user accounts for other servers such as the vCenter server, database server, vCloud Networking and Security (vCNS) server, and vCloud Director server. Therefore, it is necessary to have a directory service that is used for centralized user authentication. In addition to centralized user authentication, the directory service can be used for the management of computers and network devices in the IT infrastructure.

VMware supports the widely deployed directory service, Active Directory, included in the Windows Server 2012 operating system or later. Active Directory Domain Services (AD DS) is used for user authentication. It stores information about users, computers, and other network resources. The server that hosts the directory service is called the *domain controller*. The domain controller can also be configured to provide name service. This chapter discusses the AD DS concepts and demonstrates how to install and configure the domain controller for VMware vCloud Suite.

2.2 AD DS

In an enterprise, the management of hardware, software, and users can be a tedious task. AD DS is the software for centralized administration. With centralized management, a user does not have to have an account for each individual computer in an IT infrastructure. AD DS, included in the Windows Server operating system, can be used to perform the following tasks:

- It provides the directory service to store information about the IT infrastructure components such as users, computers, network devices, and application-specific data.
- With the directory service, one can configure the authentication or authorization mechanisms for sharing computing resources.
- It can be used to implement remote access control for a cloud-based computing environment.

The tasks are described in Sections 2.2.1 through 2.2.3.

2.2.1 Storing Information of an IT Infrastructure

AD DS can be used to store information about the objects in an IT infrastructure. In a distributed database, the objects stored in AD DS are represented as entities such as users and groups. Each entity is characterized by its attributes, such as the username and password, that specify the object user. In AD DS, a schema is used to define an object and its attributes. There are two types of objects: (1) leaf object and (2) container object. When an object has no child object, it is the leaf object. When an object contains other objects, it is the container object. Table 2.1 lists some commonly used leaf objects. Table 2.2 lists come commonly used container objects.

A group object is a generic AD DS container. In Active Directory, a group policy cannot be applied to a generic AD DS container. It can be used to define user and computer objects. That is, the group policy can decide what a user can do or cannot do. For example, it gives permission for a user to access an application. Although the group policy cannot be directly applied to a group object, the group object can receive the group policy inherited from a higher-level container object such as OU.

The OU object is the lowest-level container object that can be assigned a group policy. It can be used to support business activities at the department level. For example, according to the group policy, the user objects in the OU can be assigned a specially designed desktop. Through the OU, a group of users can be granted permission to access certain application software. Also, the OU object can be used to set the password expiration period. Figure 2.1 illustrates an OU object.

In AD DS, a domain object is used for managing the computing environment of a company or organization. Each domain is an administrative boundary. That is, the leaf objects and OU objects are authenticated by the same domain controller. A domain controller is a server installed with AD DS to provide the directory service. For a company to have the centralized administrative control of the IT infrastructure, a domain controller should be installed, and a domain object should be created. A domain object can designate its administrative duty to lower-level objects such as the OU. In such a way, the OU administrator can perform some of the administrative tasks at the domain level. Figure 2.2 illustrates a domain object.

A tree object is a collection of one or more domains that are related in a tree structure. The first domain in a tree is the root domain. A domain attached to the root domain is a child domain. The child domain can have its own child domains. A domain with a child domain is called a parent domain. Figure 2.3 shows a domain tree with three domains:

Table 2.1 Commonly Used Leaf Objects

Object	Description
User	This object contains information about users. The attributes of the user object are the username, password, and so on. Each instance of the user object is an individual user account.
Computer	This object contains information about computers. Each instance of the computer object is an individual computer account.
Contact	This object contains contact information about an organization's contractors and suppliers and other people who have connection with the organization.

Table 2.2 Commonly Used Container Objects

Object	Description
Group	This object contains information about a group, which contains user accounts, computer accounts, and other groups.
Organizational unit (OU)	This is a container object that contains group objects, user objects, and other leaf objects. It may also contain information about other OU objects.
Domain	This object contains information about OU objects and leaf objects. It also contains objects that are used to help with communication among domains such as trusted domain objects (TDOs) and site link objects.
Domain tree	The object contains a collection of domains. In a domain tree object, domains are grouped in a hierarchical structure.
Forest	This object contains one or more domains or domain trees. A forest object is the top-level container object.

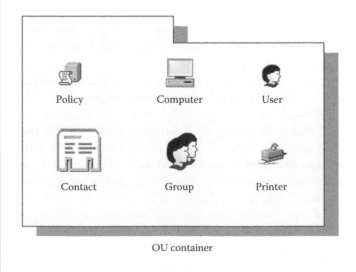

Figure 2.1   OU object.

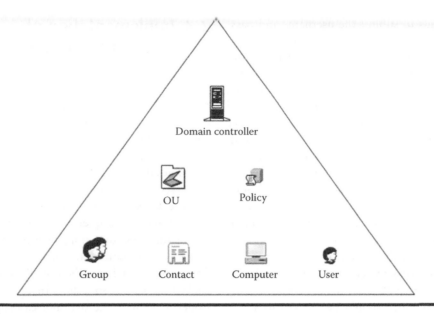

Figure 2.2   Domain object.

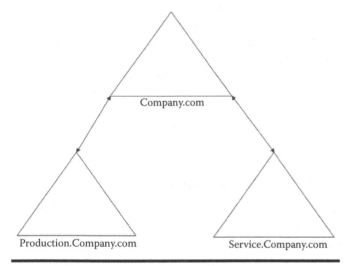

Figure 2.3   Domain tree.

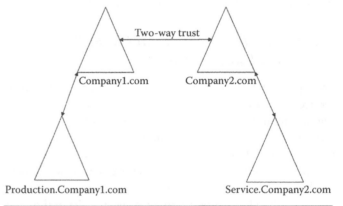

Figure 2.4   Forest object.

Company.com and its two child domains, Production .Company.com and Service.Company.com.

As a top-level container object, a forest object contains one or more domains or domain trees. The forest is also known as a collection of domains. The forest can be considered the boundary of Active Directory. In the forest, objects are saved in a distributed data repository called a global catalog. Two domains in a forest may be related with a two-way transitive trust relationship. When a domain is trusted by another domain, the trusting domain allows the administrator of the trusted domain to alter its objects. If two domains have a two-way transitive trust relationship, each domain allows the administrator of another domain to alter its objects. For

example, there are two companies; each has its own domain. After they merge, the merged company creates a new forest to include the two domains and create a two-way trust relationship between these two domains. Figure 2.4 illustrates the forest object for the merged company.

The logical structure in Figure 2.4 reveals the relationships between two companies. The forest object allows the two companies to keep their domain names so that their customers and contractors can still access the same Web page; meanwhile, the IT staff members from both companies are able to manage both domains.

2.2.2 Authentication and Authorization

With Active Directory, a company can keep all of its users' information stored on a domain controller for centralized management. For a user to log on to a computer in a company, the user needs to submit the username and password to that computer for authentication. It can be a tedious job to create a user account on each computer that the user is allowed to log on to. When AD DS is implemented, it is not necessary for a user to have an account on an individual computer in the company. Instead, the user's username and password will be sent to the domain controller. The directory service is able to verify the user's username and password. Once approved, the domain controller will inform that computer to allow the user to log on even though the user has no local account on that computer. As VMware vCloud Suite is designed for constructing the enterprise-level computing environment, AD DS is critical for implementing and managing the authentication service for a private cloud.

In a company, for users with different job assignments, permissions assigned to the users to access computing resources should be different. For example, only some people working in the human resources office should be allowed to access the employees' information. Authorization is the process that grants or denies specific permissions to an authenticated user. Authorization can be carried out through AD DS. Permission-related information will be stored in AD DS.

2.2.3 Directory Services in Cloud-Based IT Infrastructure

To support VMware vCloud Suite, it requires a directory service that can provide the authentication service for both the on-premises and cloud applications. With the directory service, users can access the cloud services remotely through the Internet. Before logging on to a cloud portal, a user must be authenticated by the directory service. Cloud subscribers need to be authenticated before they can access those cloud services. The cloud subscribers also need to be authorized so that they can get permission to access certain computing resources.

For the management of the IT infrastructure that is used to host VMware vCloud Suite, the directory service is also necessary. The authentication information about the ESXi servers, vCenter servers, vCNS servers, vCloud Director servers, and virtual machines hosted by ESXi will be stored in the directory service. The users of these servers and virtual machines will also be managed by the directory service. A domain controller provides the name resolution service and the time synchronization service for the servers and virtual machines. The domain controller can also be used to support network-based software installation.

In addition to performing the authentication and authorization tasks, the directory service stores information about applications that are used to support the cloud services. It contains the application configuration information, network configuration information, and so on.

2.3 Implementation of Domain Controller

In order to implement a domain controller, you need to install Windows Server 2012 R2 or a later version of the operating system on a physical machine or virtual machine. Once the operating system is installed, you can install and configure the AD DS role to provide the directory service. Implementing the domain controller on a virtual machine has some advantages. It eliminates the installation of a physical server and a network linking the server to other computers. The domain controller receives queries for authentication and responds to the queries. Normally, it has a relatively light workload. Therefore, implementing the domain controller on a virtual machine can still have acceptable performance. As a virtual machine, the domain controller can be easily backed up with a snapshot. In case that the domain controller is crashed, the snapshot can speed up the process of data recovery. For the hands-on practice in this book, you will implement the domain controller on a virtual machine. Figure 2.5 shows that the domain controller is implemented on a virtual machine in VMware Workstation.

In a production environment, if the workload is heavy, the domain controller can be implemented on a physical machine with more computing resources.

Being a server, the virtual machine should be configured with a fixed Internet Protocol (IP) address so that the client computers know where to find this server. Figure 2.6 illustrates the configuration of an NIC for the domain controller.

2.3.1 AD DS Installation

Once the Windows Server operating system is installed, you may want to change the computer name to DC so that the server can be recognized as a domain controller. To install AD DS, select **Active Directory Domain Services** in the Add Role and Features Wizard, as shown in Figure 2.7.

Once the AD DS role is installed on a virtual machine, it is the time to promote the virtual machine to a domain controller, as shown in Figure 2.8.

The promotion process can be done with the Active Directory Domain Services Configuration Wizard. By using the wizard, you will be able to create a default forest object to host the new domain, or you can attach the new domain to an existing domain. You can specify a name for the domain and a location to store the AD DS files. Once the promotion process is completed, you will see that the AD DS–related services are added to the Tools menu shown in Figure 2.9.

For example, under the Active Directory Users and Computers service, you should be able to see a set of user objects created for VMware vCloud Suite management shown in Figure 2.10.

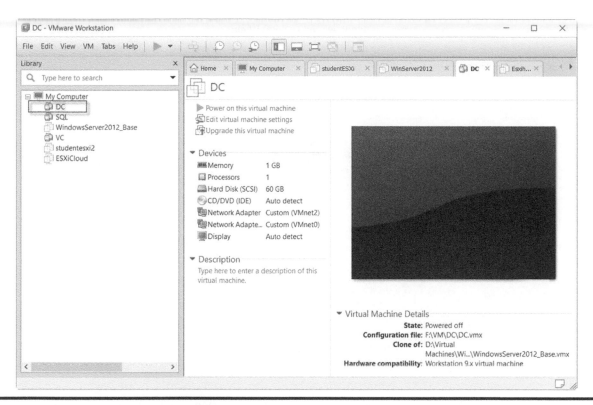

Figure 2.5 Domain controller on virtual machine.

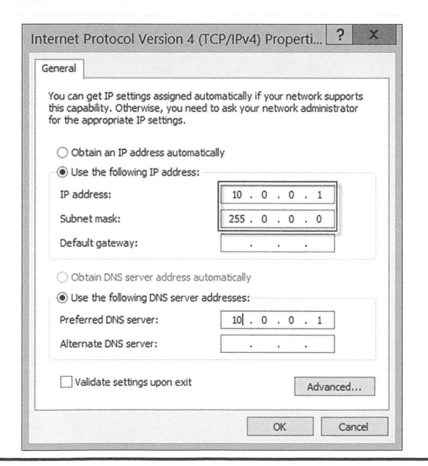

Figure 2.6 Fixed IP address.

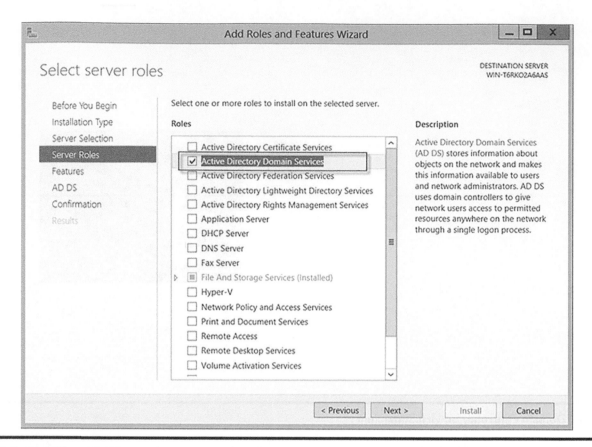

Figure 2.7 Installing AD DS.

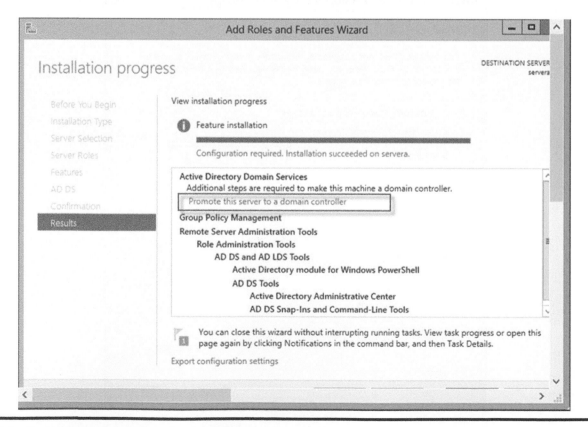

Figure 2.8 Promoting server to domain controller.

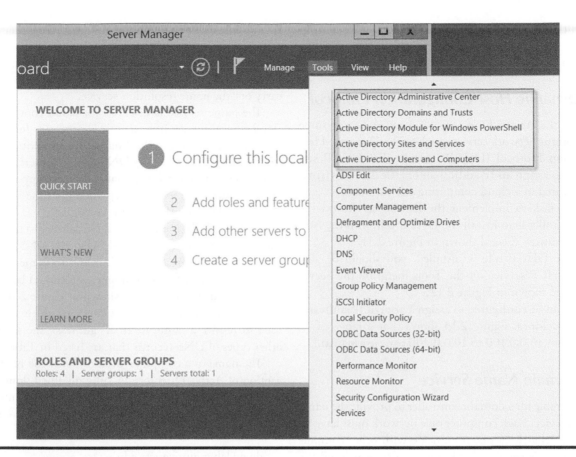

Figure 2.9 AD DS services.

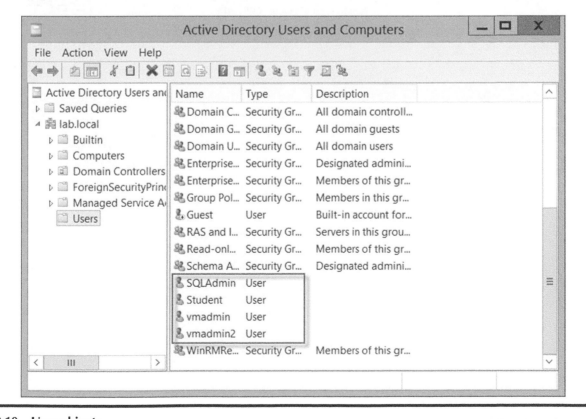

Figure 2.10 User objects.

In addition to the directory service, the domain controller can be used to provide the other services, which will be described in the next section.

2.3.2 *Dynamic Host Configuration Protocol*

Aside from the Active Directory services, there are some other important network services such as the Dynamic Host Configuration Protocol (DHCP) service. The DHCP service is used to assign an IP address automatically to a virtual machine created in a cloud computing environment.

The first task to implement the DHCP service on the domain controller is to install the DHCP role with the Add Roles and Features Wizard shown in Figure 2.11.

Once the DHCP role is installed, you should be able to see the DHCP service on the Tools menu on the Server Manager page shown in Figure 2.12.

DHCP can be configured to assign a pool of IP addresses to virtual machines. Figure 2.13 shows that a range of IP addresses from 10.0.0.100 to 10.0.0.200 can be assigned.

2.3.3 *Domain Name Service*

It is also desirable for a domain controller to provide the name resolution service. Each computer on a network must have an IP address so that it can communicate with other computers. However, it is impossible for a user to remember all the IP addresses. Users prefer a meaningful name that reveals a computer's function. The name service resolves meaningful computer names to IP addresses and vice versa. Windows Server 2012 provides the domain name system (DNS) to carry out the name resolution service.

The name service is essential for cloud computing. In a cloud computing environment, it is necessary for cloud providers to provide meaningful names for subscribers to access the cloud logon portal. The DNS can help users to remotely access the IT infrastructure that is used to support VMware vCloud Suite. This section briefly describes the implementation of the DNS on the domain controller.

As shown in Figure 2.14, the DNS can be installed with the Add Roles and Features Wizard. After the DNS is installed, you will have the service available in the Tools menu shown in Figure 2.15. Open **DNS Manager**; you should be able to see the name and IP address pairs shown in Figure 2.16.

In Figure 2.16, the type of DNS record is A, which is used to resolve a name to an IP address. There are several other types of DNS records that are listed in Table 2.3.

The name of a computer should follow the naming convention of Active Directory. A fully qualified domain name (FQDN) has two parts: (1) the name for a computer and (2) the domain name. For example, to name the domain controller created for a computer lab, you have

dc.mylab.myuniversity.edu

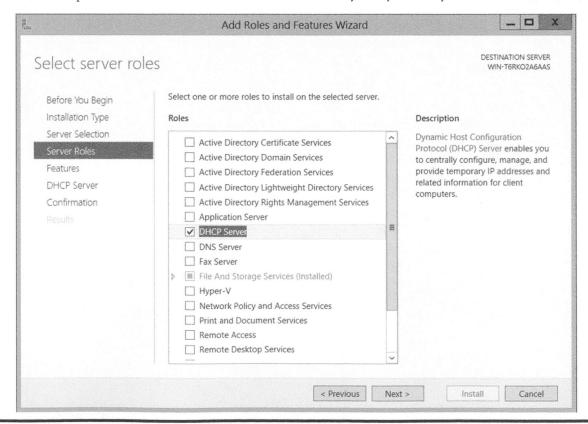

Figure 2.11   Installing DHCP role.

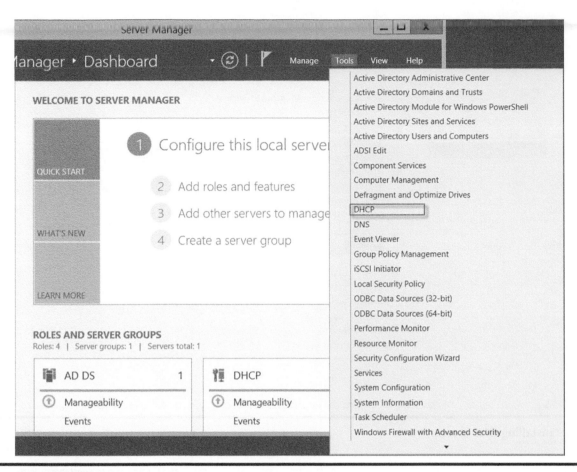

Figure 2.12   DHCP service.

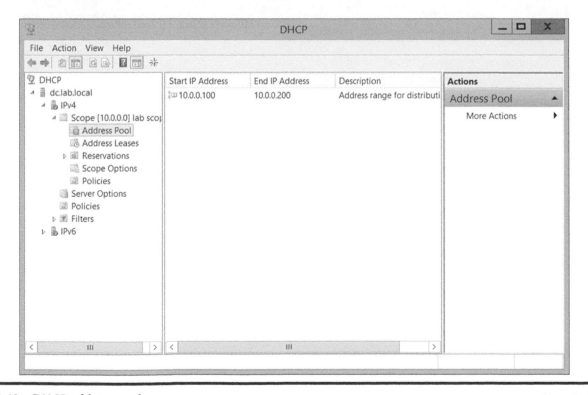

Figure 2.13   DHCP address pool.

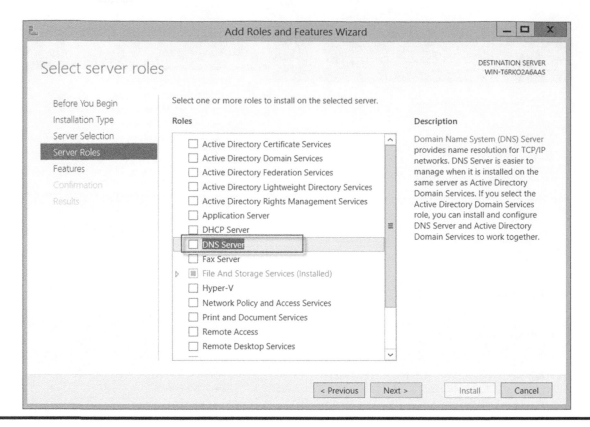

Figure 2.14 Installing DNS server.

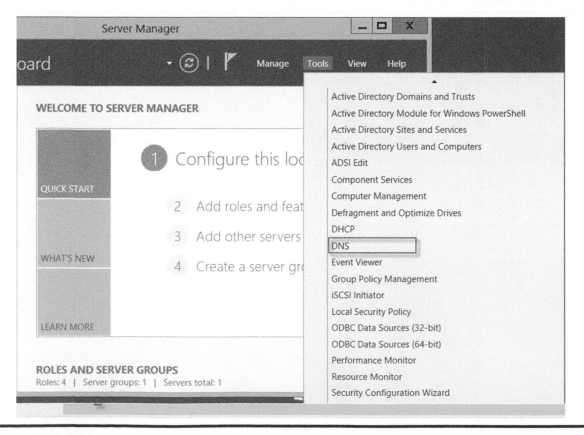

Figure 2.15 DNS service.

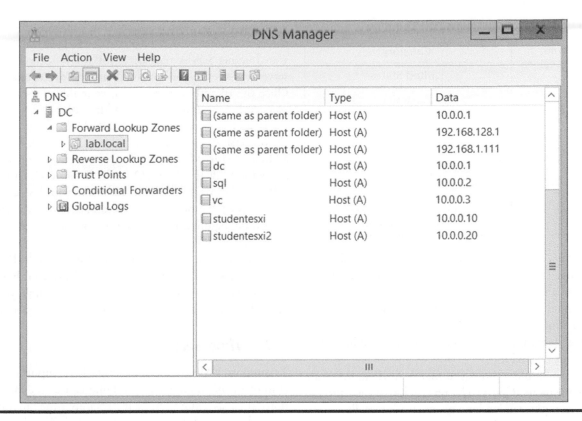

Figure 2.16 DNS Manager.

where dc is the computer name, and mylab.myuniversity.edu is the domain name set for Active Directory. The name represents the hierarchical structure of a university where the domain controller is located. The leftmost name is the least general name, and the rightmost name is the most general name. The name edu is the top-level domain. The commonly used top-level domains are listed in Table 2.4.

Table 2.3 Types of DNS Records

Type	Usage
A	It is used to resolve a host name to an IPv4 IP address.
AAAA	It is used to resolve a host name to an IPv6 IP address.
CNAME	It is used to assign an alias to a host name.
MX	It is used to bind an IP address to a specified mail server.
NS	It is used to bind an IP address to a specified DNS server.
PTR	It is the pointer type of record, which is used to resolve an IP address to a host name.
SOA	It is the start-of-authority type of record, which contains the configuration information about the domain that this DNS server is responsible for.
SRV	It is the service type of record, which is used to store the locations of domain controllers.

Table 2.4 Commonly Used Top-Level Domains

Domain Name	Category
.biz	Business
.com	Commercial
.edu	Education
.gov	Government
.info	Information
.int	International use
.mil	Military
.museum	Museums
.net	Network organization
.org	Nonprofit organization

Table 2.5 Country-Code Top-Level Domains

Domain Name	Category
.us	United States
.au	Australia
.ca	Canada
.cn	China
.de	Germany
.ru	Russia
.uk	United Kingdom

Sometimes, top-level domains can also be named as the country code. Table 2.5 illustrates some country code–based top-level domains.

For a cloud to be accessible from the Internet, a company or an education institution needs to register to one of the top-level domains. Otherwise, a computer can be named locally such as dc.lab.local.

Forward lookup is a process to match an IP address for a given domain name. Conversely, reverse lookup is a process to match a computer name for a given IP address. For example, to communicate with the domain controller from your home computer through the Internet, it is necessary to have the domain controller's IP address. Suppose that the FQDN

dc.lab.university.edu

is entered in your Web browser. After you press the Enter key, the forward look search begins. Your request will be sent to your Internet Service provider's (ISP's) DNS server. The DNS server will ask the root for the IP address of the top-level edu. Once the IP address is returned, your ISP's DNS server will contact the edu server for the IP address of the university. Once the IP address is returned, your ISP's DNS server will contact the university server for the IP address of the lab. Once the IP address is returned, your ISP's DNS server will contact the lab server for the dc IP address. Once the IP address is returned, the ISP's DNS server sends the IP address to your home computer so that your computer can communicate with the computer named dc. Figure 2.17 illustrates the name resolution process in the hierarchical system.

After your computer gets the dc IP, it caches the IP address. Next time, to search for the same IP address, your home computer will check the cache first. If there is a match, your computer does not need to conduct a full search all over again.

2.3.4 Time Service

To support VMware vCloud Suite, it is important to synchronize time among servers. Time can affect many functions such as expiration date, backup time, maintenance schedule, and valid authorization period. The domain controller can be configured to provide the time service, which synchronizes time among internal servers.

Windows Server 2012 provides the time synchronization service through the Network Time Protocol (NTP). In the

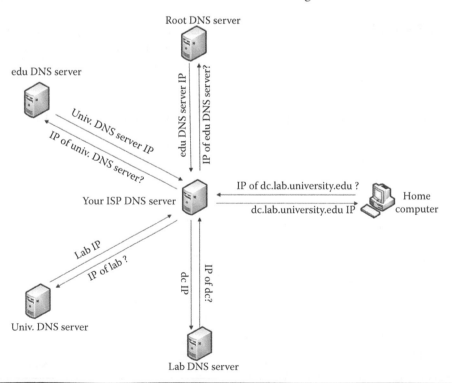

Figure 2.17 Name resolution process.

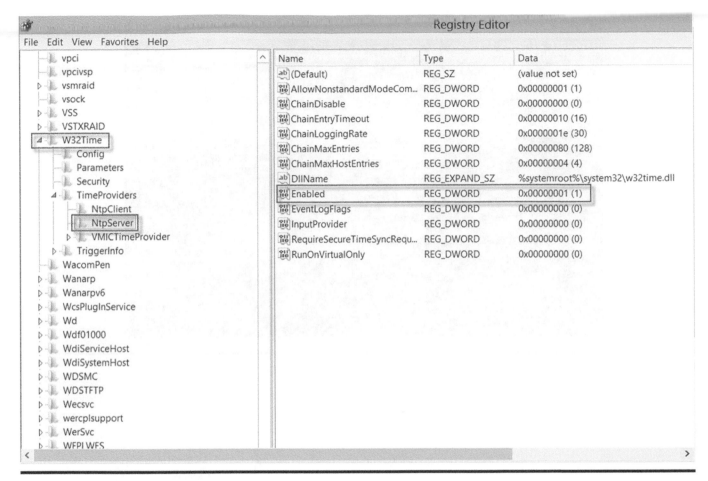

Figure 2.18   Enable NTP server.

domain controller, the NTP server can be enabled in the registry editor. Figure 2.18 illustrates that the NTP is enabled by setting the Enabled item to 1. Once the NTP server is enabled, run the following command to update the current configuration, as shown in Figure 2.19:

```
w32tm/config/update
```

In addition to the time service, the domain controller can be used for network-based operating system installation, which will be covered in the next section.

2.3.5 Network-Based Operating System Installation

The installation of ESXi can be done through the Preboot Execution Environment (PXE), which installs software over a network. The PXE-based installation does not require the boot image attached to a virtual machine. This technology can used to install ESXi in a cluster environment that includes a large number of servers. It can be used to implement an unattended installation. For hands-on practice, one can take advantage of the PXE boot to create a vApp for practicing the installation of the ESXi server in a cloud

environment. The PXE boot requires a client–server environment. For example, the domain controller can be used as the PXE server, and the client is the virtual or physical machine where ESXi is to be installed. The network protocols used in the PXE boot are DHCP and Trivial File Transfer Protocol (TFTP). Figure 2.20 illustrates the PXE boot process.

To implement the PXE service on the domain controller, you need to accomplish the following tasks:

- Download and configure the PXE tool for ESXi installation
- Extract the ESXi ISO file to the folder that the PXE tool can reach
- Configure the firewall and network to allow DHCP communication

There is some free and open-source software that can be used to set up the PXE server on the Windows Server 2012 operating system. For example, from the following Web site, you can find the freeware ESXiPXE to set up the PXE service on Windows Server 2012 R2:

http://wp.secretnest.info/archives/812

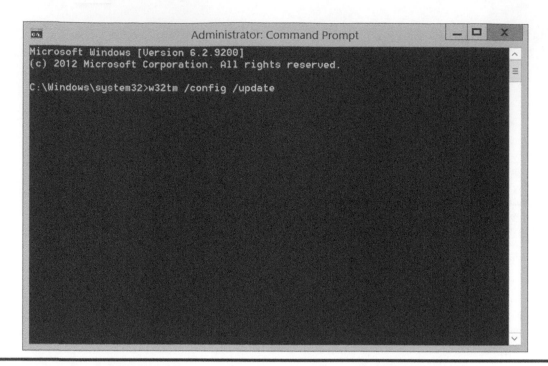

Figure 2.19 Update NTP server configuration.

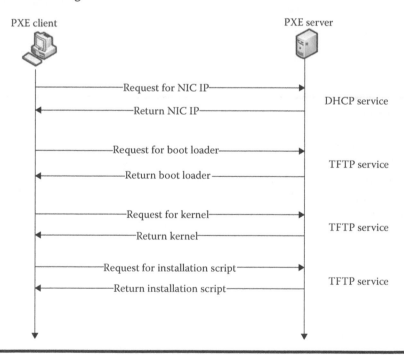

Figure 2.20 PXE boot process.

The freeware provides the DHCP and TFTP services for the installation of ESXi. After the software is downloaded, the freeware can be extracted into the folder ESXiPXE where the configuration and execution files are stored, as shown in Figure 2.21.

To be able to install ESXi over the network, you need to extract the content of the ESXi ISO file into the folder ESXi, as shown in Figure 2.21. To implement the DHCP service,

the firewall should be configured to allow the inbound and outbound DHCP traffic to go through the User Datagram Protocol (UDP) port 67 and UDP port 69, as shown in Figure 2.22.

To configure the NIC for DHCP communication, you need to assign the IP address 192.168.128.1 to one of the NICs reachable by the virtual machine to be used to install ESXi. Figure 2.23 illustrates the network configuration.

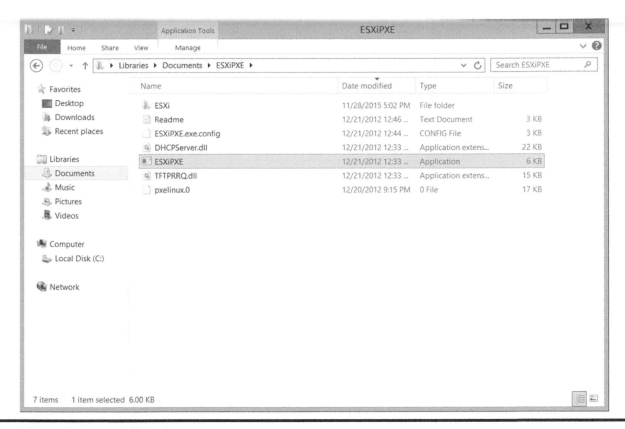

Figure 2.21   ESXiPXE installation files.

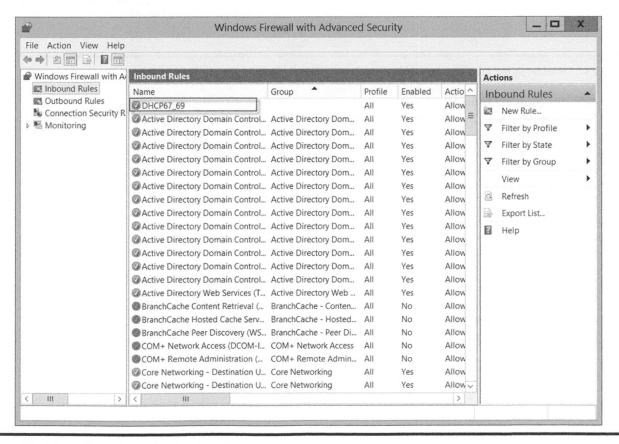

Figure 2.22   Firewall configuration for DHCP.

Figure 2.23 IP address for DHCP communication.

As shown in Figure 2.23, the IP address 192.168.128.1 has been added to the NIC for DHCP communication. Once the virtual machine is booted up, it will search for the DHCP server. After the domain controller receives the request, it will offer an IP address to the virtual machine to establish communication. Then, by using the TFTP service, the boot loader, the kernel, and the installation script can be loaded to the targeted virtual machine.

In the above, you have a few services needed for the VMware vCloud Suite installation. Details for the implementation of these services are given in the following activity.

2.4 Activity 1: Implementing Domain Controller

In this activity, you are going to install AD DS on a virtual machine used as a domain controller. The following tasks will be performed:

- *Task 1:* Preparing domain controller virtual machine
- *Task 2:* Configuring domain controller
- *Task 3:* Configuring DNS
- *Task 4:* Configuring DHCP
- *Task 5:* Configuring NTP service
- *Task 6:* Configuring PXE service

In this activity, the tasks are performed on a virtual machine. In a production environment, if the workload is heavy, it is advised that the domain controller should be implemented on a physical machine.

2.4.1 Task 1: Preparing Domain Controller Virtual Machine

In this section, you will create a virtual machine that has Windows Server 2012 as the guest operating system. To begin with, you need to download and install Windows Server 2012.

1. Students can download the Windows Server 2012 installation file from the following Web site:

   https://www.dreamspark.com/Student/Default.aspx

2. From the Web site, download the Windows Server 2012 R2 installation image file. If you prefer to install the operating system by using the DVD drive, burn the image file to a DVD disk.
3. Start VMware Workstation. Click the **Home** tag and click **Create a New Virtual Machine**.
4. On the Welcome to the New Virtual Machine Wizard page, select the option **Custom (advanced),** as shown in Figure 2.24, and click **Next**.
5. On the Choose the Virtual Machine Hardware Compatibility page, you can specify the hardware compatibility. To be backward compatible with the older version of VMware Workstation, for example, you may specify the hardware compatibility to **Workstation 11.0,** as shown in Figure 2.25. If you want to take full advantage of the latest VMware Workstation, you can specify the latest version of VMware Workstation for hardware compatibility. After the hardware compatibility is specified, click **Next**.
6. On the Guest Operating System Installation page, there are different ways to install the guest operating system. If an installation DVD is available, you can select the option **Installer disc**. If there is an installation image file available, you can specify the option **Installer disc image file**. If you have not yet decided which guest operating system to install, you can choose the option **I will install the operating system later**. In our case, select the option **Installer disc image file,** as shown in Figure 2.26. Then, click **Next**.
7. On the Easy Install Information page, enter the product key, the user name, and the password (Figure 2.27). Then, click **Next**.
8. On the Name the Virtual Machine page, name the virtual machine **DC,** as shown in Figure 2.28, and click **Next**. For better performance, a physical solid-state drive disk should be used for the DC virtual machine.
9. On the Firmware Type page, select **BIOS** and click **Next**.
10. VMware Workstation allows you to select the number of processors, which cannot exceed the limit of processors on the host computer. On the Processor Configuration page, specify the virtual machine to have 1 processor with 1 core, as shown in Figure 2.29. Then, click **Next**.
11. A virtual machine uses the memory of the host computer. It needs to have adequate memory to run. The minimum memory requirement to run Windows Server 2012 is 1 GB. Additional memory can improve the virtual machine's performance if used properly. Since we are dealing with a small lab, on the Memory for the Virtual Machine page, take the minimum memory size, which is 1 GB (Figure 2.30). Then, click **Next**.

Figure 2.24   New Virtual Machine Wizard.

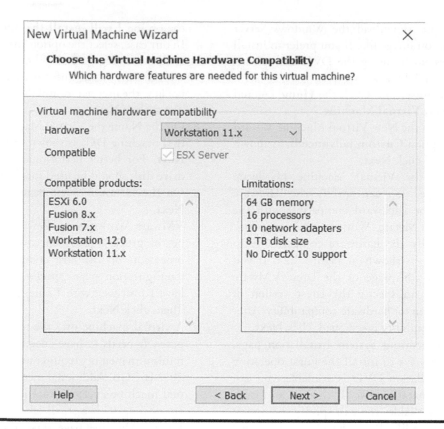

Figure 2.25 Hardware compatibility.

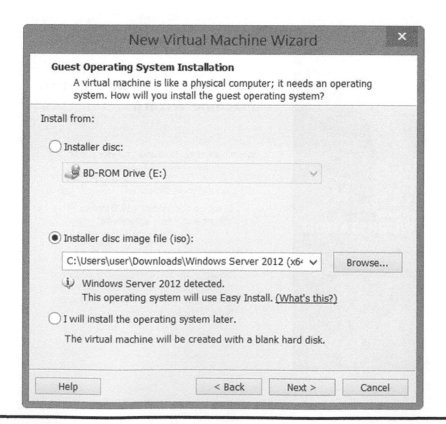

Figure 2.26 Installation method.

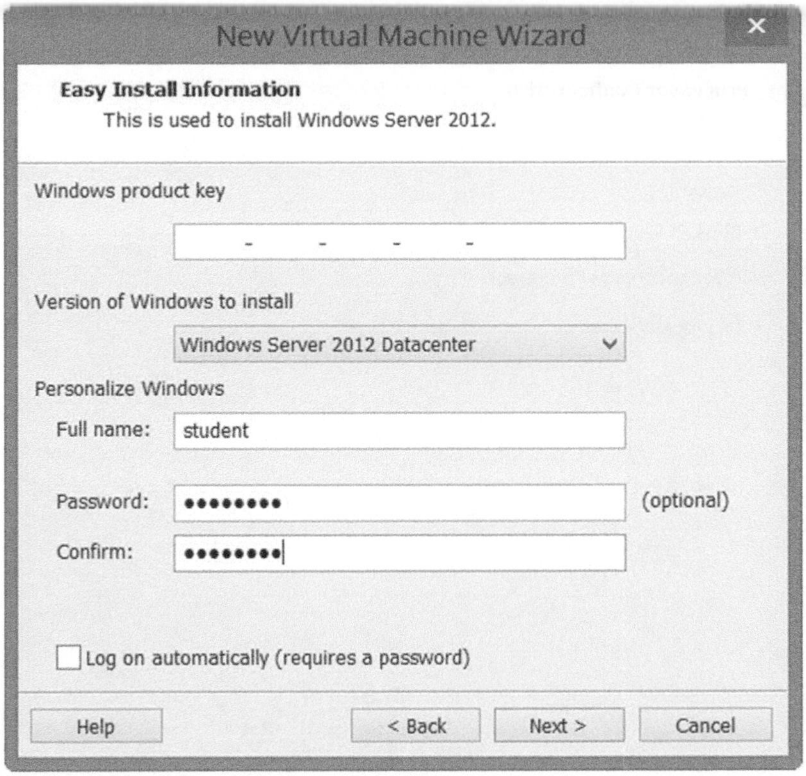

Figure 2.27   Guest operating system.

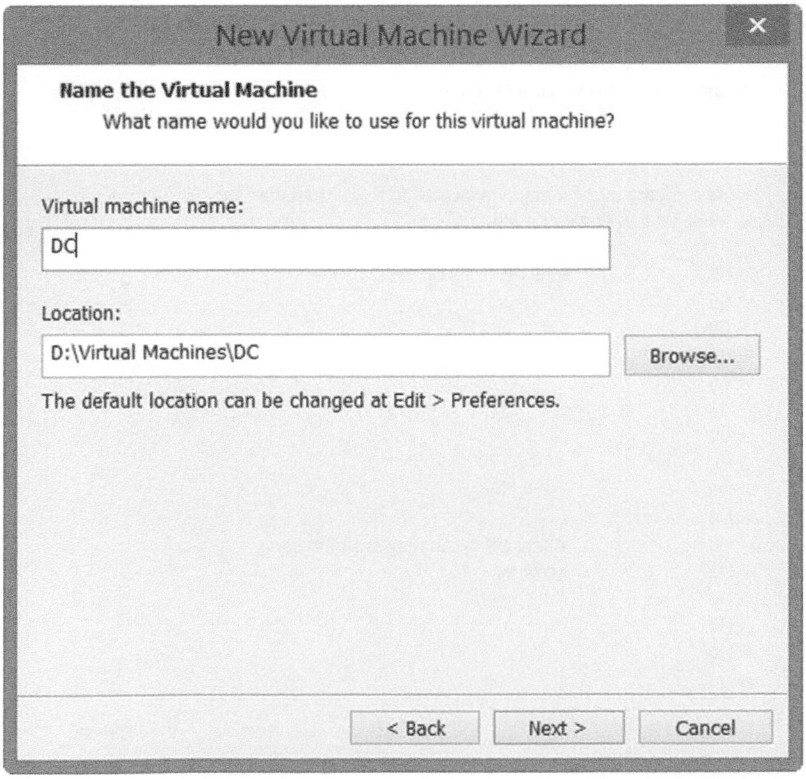

Figure 2.28   Virtual machine name.

Figure 2.29 Processor configuration.

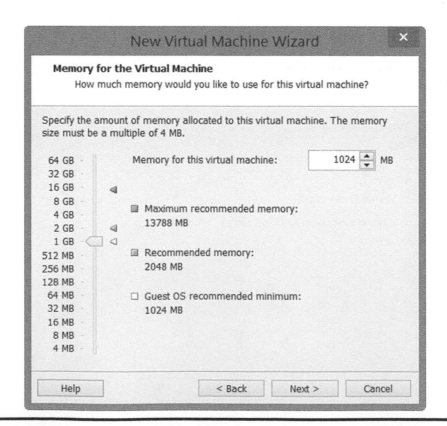

Figure 2.30 Amount of memory.

12. A network will be used to connect servers such as the domain controller, SQL Server, and vCenter. At this moment, the network has not been created. Therefore, on the Network Type page, select the option **Do not use a network connection,** as shown in Figure 2.31, and click **Next.**

13. On the Select I/O Controller Type page, keep the recommended controller **LSI Logic SAS,** which is required by Windows Server 2012 for failover and load balancing. Then, click **Next.**

14. On the Select a Disk Type page, select the recommended disk type **SCSI,** which stands for Small Computer System Interface. SCSI has faster input/output data transfer. Therefore, SCSI is commonly used as a data drive that has no operating system installed. Then, click **Next.**

15. On the Select a Disk page, you can choose to create a new virtual disk, use an existing virtual hard disk or use a physical hard disk. Select the option **Create a new virtual disk,** as shown in Figure 2.32, and click **Next.**

16. On the Specify Disk Capacity page, take the recommended disk size **60GB** and select the option **Store virtual disk as a single file,** as shown in Figure 2.33. Then, click **Next.**

17. On the Specify Disk File page, take the default and click **Next.**

18. On the Ready to Create Virtual Machine page, uncheck the option **Power on this virtual machine after creation,** as shown in Figure 2.34. Then, click **Finish** to start the installation.

2.4.2 Task 2: Configuring Domain Controller

In this section, we will configure the DC virtual machine so that it can provide the directory service for the lab. The following are the steps for creating Windows Server 2012 Active Directory service:

1. Start VMware Workstation. Right-click the **DC** virtual machine and select **Settings**.
2. In the Virtual Machine Settings dialog, click the **Add** button.
3. On the Hardware Type page, click **Network Adapter,** as shown in Figure 2.35, and then click **Next.**
4. On Network Adaptor Type page, select **Custom** and then select **VMnet2,** as shown in Figure 2.36. Then, click **Finish**.
5. Similarly, you can add the second network adapter VMnet0 (Figure 2.37), which can be used to connect to the Internet. Click **Finish,** and then click **OK.**

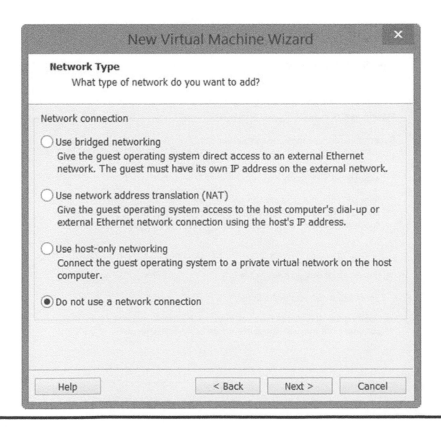

Figure 2.31　Network type.

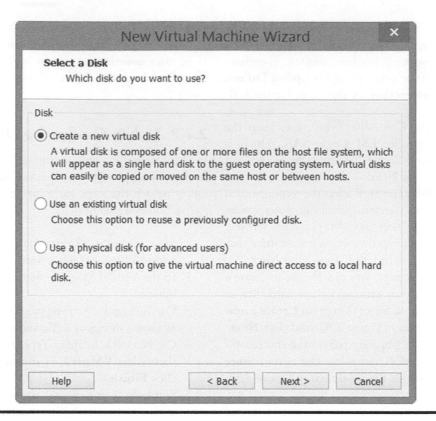

Figure 2.32 Disk selection.

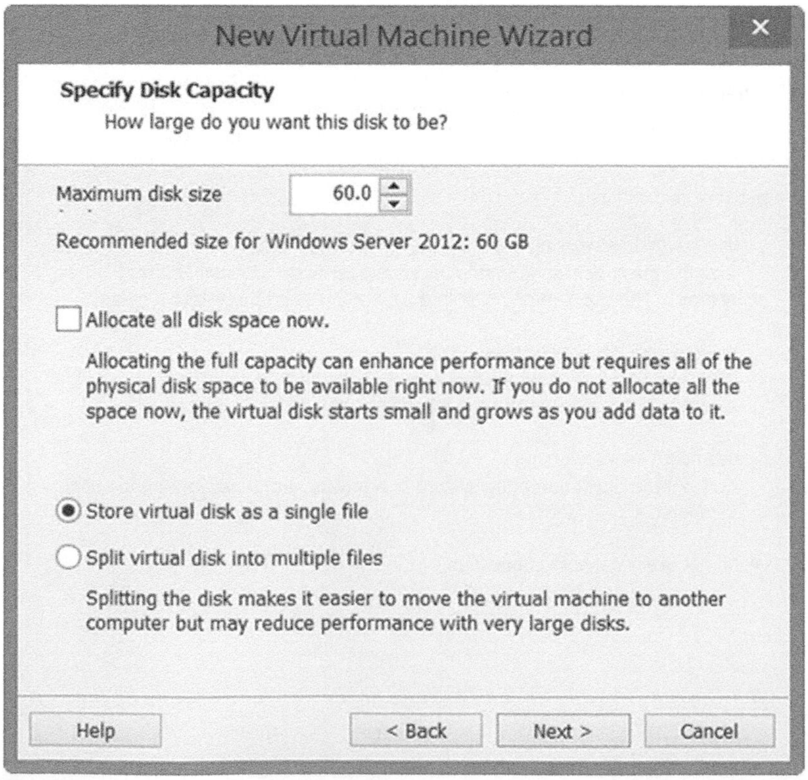

Figure 2.33 Disk capacity.

Figure 2.34   Summary of settings.

Figure 2.35   Adding network adapter.

Figure 2.36   VMnet2 network adapter.

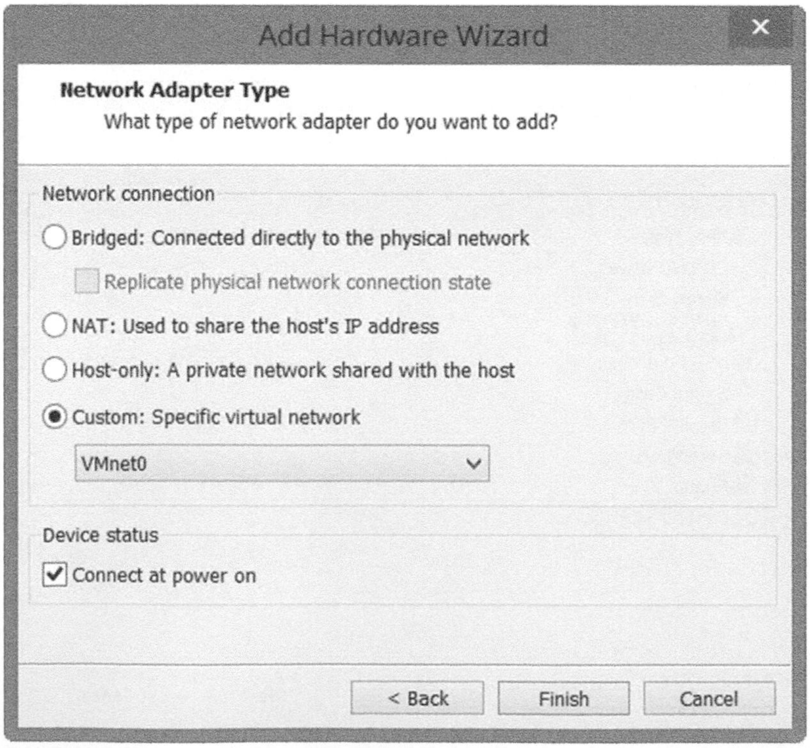

Figure 2.37   VMnet0 network adapter.

6. Now, you can power on the virtual machine DC. Right-click the **DC** tab and select **Ctrl+Alt+Delete**.
7. Log on to the virtual machine with your password.
8. A server needs a fixed IP address. To assign the network interface card (NIC) that is connected to the network VMnet2 a fixed IP address, at the lower-right corner of the screen, right-click the network icon and select **Open Network and Sharing Center,** as shown in Figure 2.38.
9. On the Network and Sharing Center page, click the link **Change adapter settings**.
10. Right-click the Ethernet icon for the NIC, which is connected to the network VMnet2, and select **Properties**.
11. After the Ethernet Properties dialog is opened, click **Internet Protocol Version 4**. Then, click the **Properties** button.
12. In the Internet Protocol Version 4 Properties dialog, select the option **Use the following IP address** and specify the IP address as **10.0.0.1**, network mask as **255.0.0.0,** and the preferred DNS server as **10.0.0.1** (Figure 2.39). Then, click **OK**.
13. Next, you need to rename the virtual machine as DC.lab.local. To do so, on the Dashboard of Server Manager, click **Local Server** on the left-hand side of the screen. Then, click the computer name **DC**.
14. In the System Properties dialog, click the **Change** button.
15. Click the **More** button and enter the domain name **lab.local,** as shown in Figure 2.40. Then, click **OK** several times. Then, restart the virtual machine.
16. To open the Add Roles and Features Wizard in Server Manager, on the Dashboard of Server Manager, select **Add Roles and Features**.
17. Click **Next** a few times to go to the **Select server roles** page. Click **Active Directory Domain Services,** as shown in Figure 2.41.
18. In the Add features that are required for Active Directory Domain Services dialog, click **Add Features,** as shown in Figure 2.42. Then, click **Next**.
19. On the Select features page, click **Next** several times to go to the **Confirm installation selections** page. Check the check box **Restart the destination server automatically if required** and click **Install**. The Installation progress page displays the status during the installation process, as shown in Figure 2.43.
20. When the process completes, in the message details, click **Promote this server to a domain controller,** and the Active Directory Domain Services Configuration Wizard will open.
21. On the Deployment Configuration page, select **Add a new forest,** as shown in Figure 2.44. For the Root domain

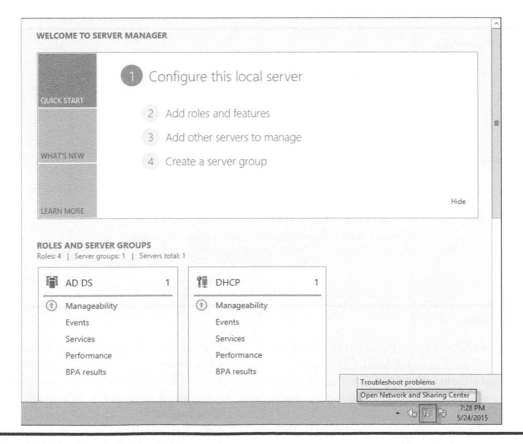

Figure 2.38   Open Network and Sharing Center.

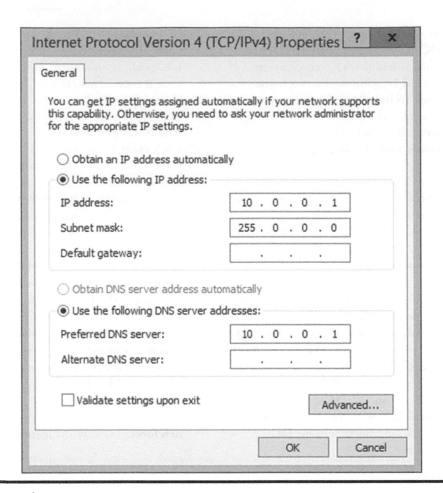

Figure 2.39   IPv4 Properties.

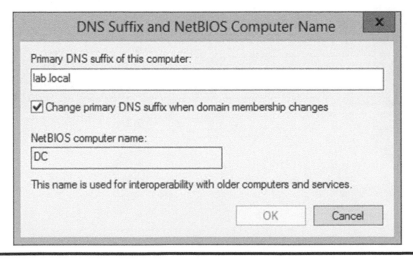

Figure 2.40   DNS suffix.

name, type the FQDN for your domain. For example, if your FQDN is lab.local, type **lab.local**. Click **Next**.

22. On the **Domain Controller Options** page, type the password of your choice and confirm it (Figure 2.45); click **Next**.

23. On the DNS Options page, click **Next** several times until you get to the **Review Options** page.

24. On the Review Options page, review your selections. Click **Next**.

25. On the Prerequisites Check page, your selections are validated (Figure 2.46). When the check completes, click **Install**.

26. Once the installation is complete, you will see that AD DS is added to the Dashboard list (Figure 2.47).

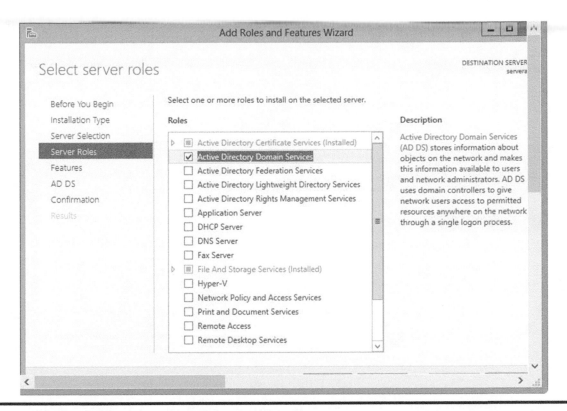

Figure 2.41   Server role selection.

Figure 2.42   Adding features.

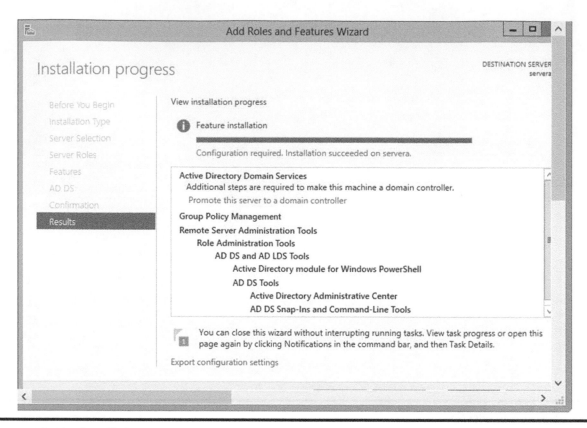

Figure 2.43   Viewing installation progress.

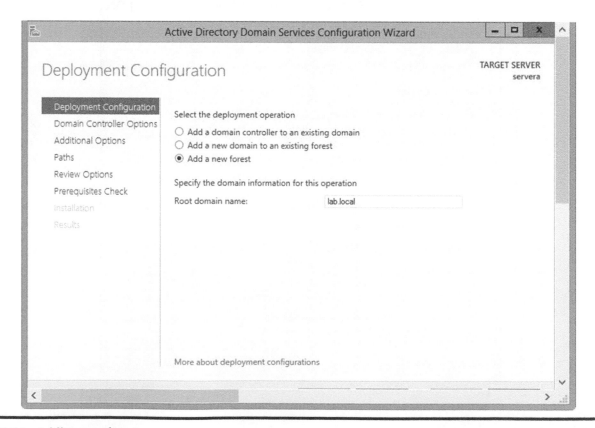

Figure 2.44   Adding new forest.

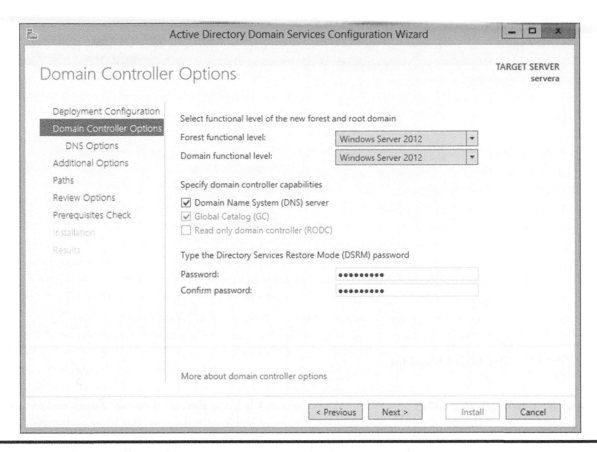

Figure 2.45 **Domain controller options.**

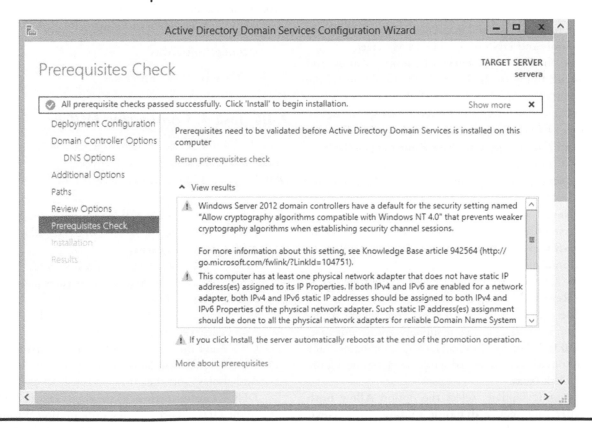

Figure 2.46 **Prerequisites check.**

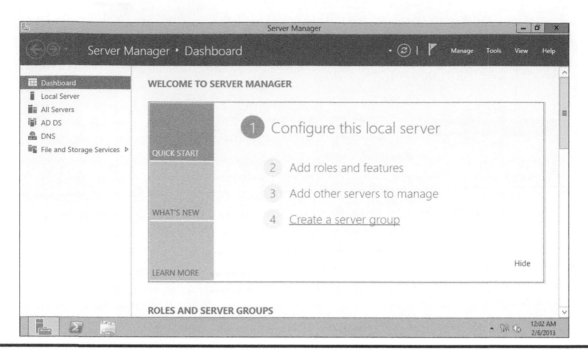

Figure 2.47 AD DS added to dashboard list.

2.4.3 Task 3: Configuring DNS

After Active Directory is installed, the DNS is installed with it. The first configuration task is to create a reverse lookup zone for the DNS service.

1. Log on to the DC virtual machine. In System Manager, click **Tools** and **DNS** to open DNS Manager.
2. Expand the **DC** node, **Forward Lookup Zones**, and **lab.local**. In Figure 2.48, you should be able to see the dc records registered under the DNS node.
3. The next task is to create a reverse lookup. To do so, in the DNS Manager dialog, right- click **Reverse Lookup Zones**, and select **New Zone** to open the New Zone Wizard.
4. Click **Next** in the Welcome to the New Zone Wizard. Then, select **Primary zone** for the zone type. Then, click **Next**.
5. In Active Directory Zone Replication Scope, select **To all DNS servers running on domain controllers in this domain: lab.local**. Then, click **Next**.
6. On the first Reverse Lookup Zone Name page, select **IPv4 Reverse Lookup Zone**. Click **Next**.
7. On the second Reverse Lookup Zone Name page, type the network ID of your subnetwork. In our case, type **10.0.0**. For the Reverse lookup zone name, take the automatically generated name, as shown in Figure 2.49. Click **Next**.
8. In Dynamic Update, select the option **Allow both insecure and secure dynamic update**. Click **Next**. Then, click **Finish**.

9. Click the **Reverse Lookup Zones** node to expand it. Double-click the node **0.0.10.in-addr.arpa**. You should be able to see the reverse lookup records shown in Figure 2.50.
10. In the Command Prompt window, run the following command, as shown in Figure 2.51:

    ipconfig/registerdns

    Then, press the **Enter** key.

2.4.4 Task 4: Configuring DHCP

With the DHCP service, when a virtual machine is created, it is automatically assigned an IP address. In this section, the DHCP service is implemented with Windows Server 2012.

1. Assume that you are still logged on to the DC virtual machine. On the Dashboard of Server Manager, click **Add Roles and Features**.
2. In the Add Roles and Features Wizard, click **Next** three times. On the **Select server roles** page, click the **DHCP Server** checkbox.
3. When you are prompted to add required features, click **Add Features,** as shown in Figure 2.52.
4. Click **Next** three times, and then click **Install**.
5. Wait for the installation process to complete. In the Add Roles and Features Wizard, click **Complete DHCP configuration,** as shown in Figure 2.53.
6. In the DHCP Post-Install Configuration Wizard, click **Next** and then click **Commit**. Then, click **Close**.

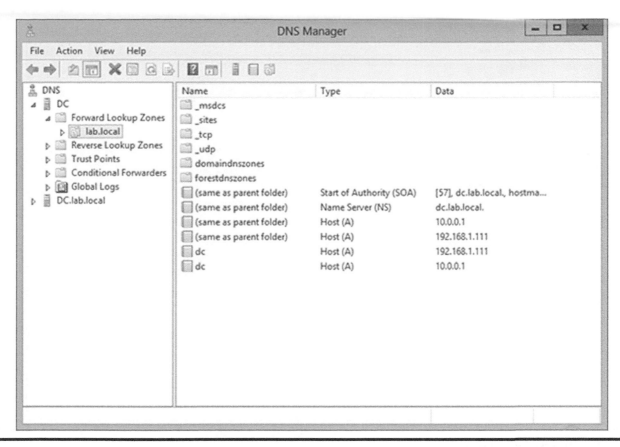

Figure 2.48   DNS records.

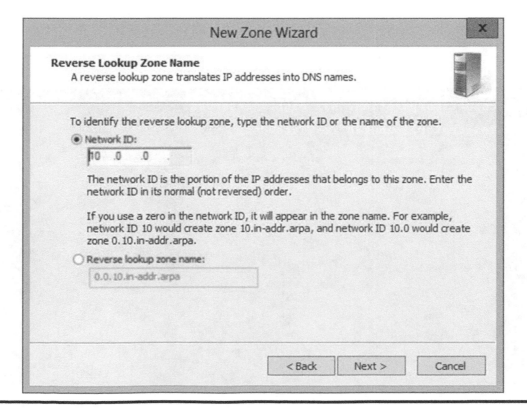

Figure 2.49   Reverse lookup zone.

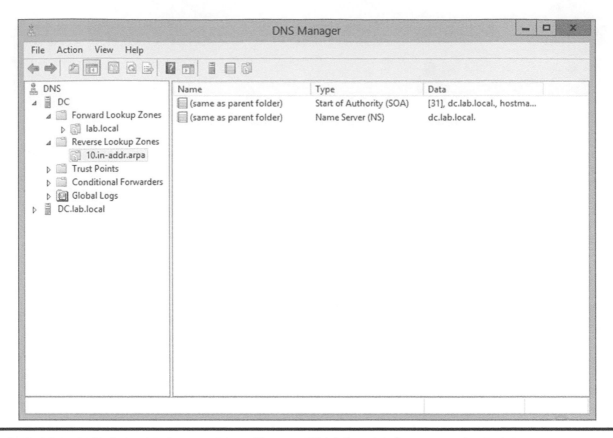

Figure 2.50 Reverse lookup records.

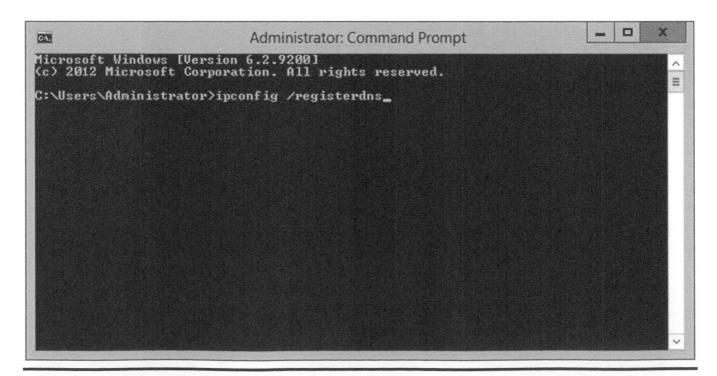

Figure 2.51 Registering DNS.

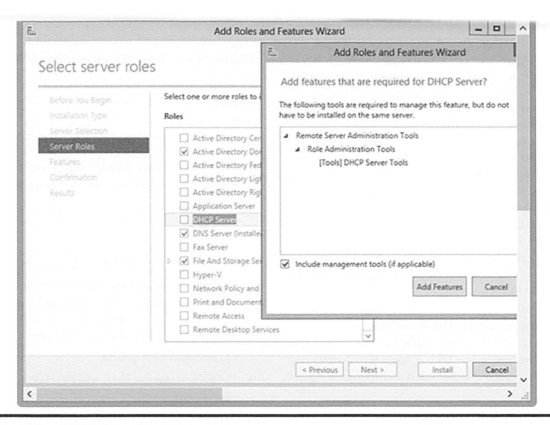

Figure 2.52   Adding DHCP server features.

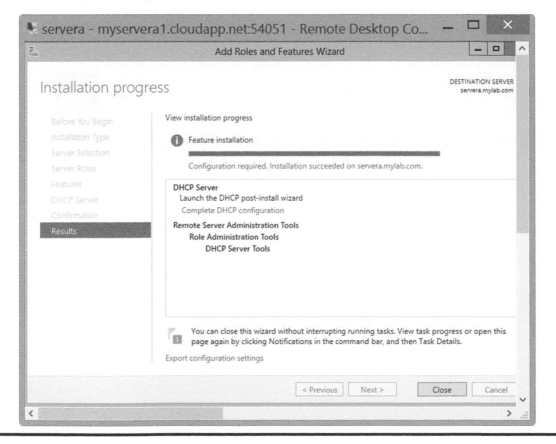

Figure 2.53   Completing DHCP configuration.

7. On the Server Manager menu bar, click **Tools** and then select **DHCP**. The DHCP console will open.

8. On the DHCP console tree, navigate to **IPv4**. Right-click **IPv4** and then click **New Scope**. The **New Scope Wizard** will open.

9. Click **Next** and then type a name for the new scope next to **Name** (e.g., **lab-scope** in Figure 2.54).

10. Click **Next**. Then, for the IP address range, type **10.0.0.100** next to **Start IP address**, type **10.0.0.200** next to **End IP address**, and type **8** next to **Length**. The value of the subnet mask will change automatically to **255.0.0.0** (Figure 2.55).

11. Click **Next** three times to go to the **Domain Name and DNS Servers** page. Verify that the Parent domain is **lab.local**, the server name is **dc.lab.local**, and **10.0.0.1** is listed as the only DNS server IP address (Figure 2.56).

12. Click **Next** twice, and then in Activate Scope, select **Yes, I want to activate this scope now**.

13. Click **Next**, and then click **Finish**.

14. Refresh the view in the DHCP console and verify that IPv4 is checked and lab-scope is active (Figure 2.57).

2.4.5 Task 5: Configuring NTP Service

In this task, you will configure the NTP service to make the domain controller a time server. Later, other servers will synchronize time with this domain controller. For this task, the time server is implemented with Windows Server 2012. The following are the implementation steps:

1. Assume that you are still logged on to the DC virtual machine. Press the Windows's icon on your keyboard to open the Start menu. Type the word **regedit**, and click the regedit icon to open the Registry Editor, as shown in Figure 2.58.

2. Once the Registry Editor is open, click the following sequence of folders to get to the NtpServer folder:

```
HKEY_LOCAL_MACHINE\SYSTEM\CurrentControl
Set\Services\W32Time\NtpServer
```

3. In the NtpServer folder, set the Enabled value to **1,** as shown in Figure 2.59. Then, close the Registry Editor.

4. To update time, on the Start menu, type **cmd**. Click the cmd icon to start the Command Prompt window. Then, enter the command below (Figure 2.60). Then, press the **Enter** key to execute the command.

```
w32tm/config/update
```

5. To check if the time server is enabled, run the following command:

```
w32tm/query/configuration
```

6. You will see that the value for Enabled is set to 1, as shown in Figure 2.61.

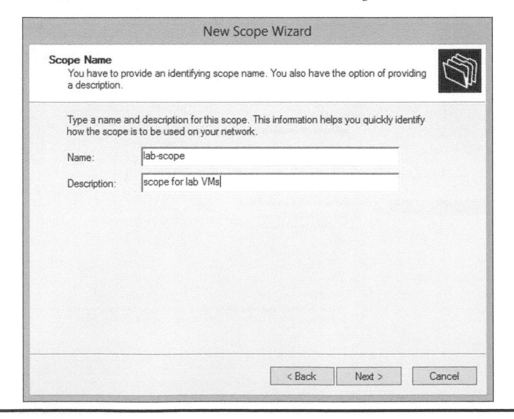

Figure 2.54   Scope name.

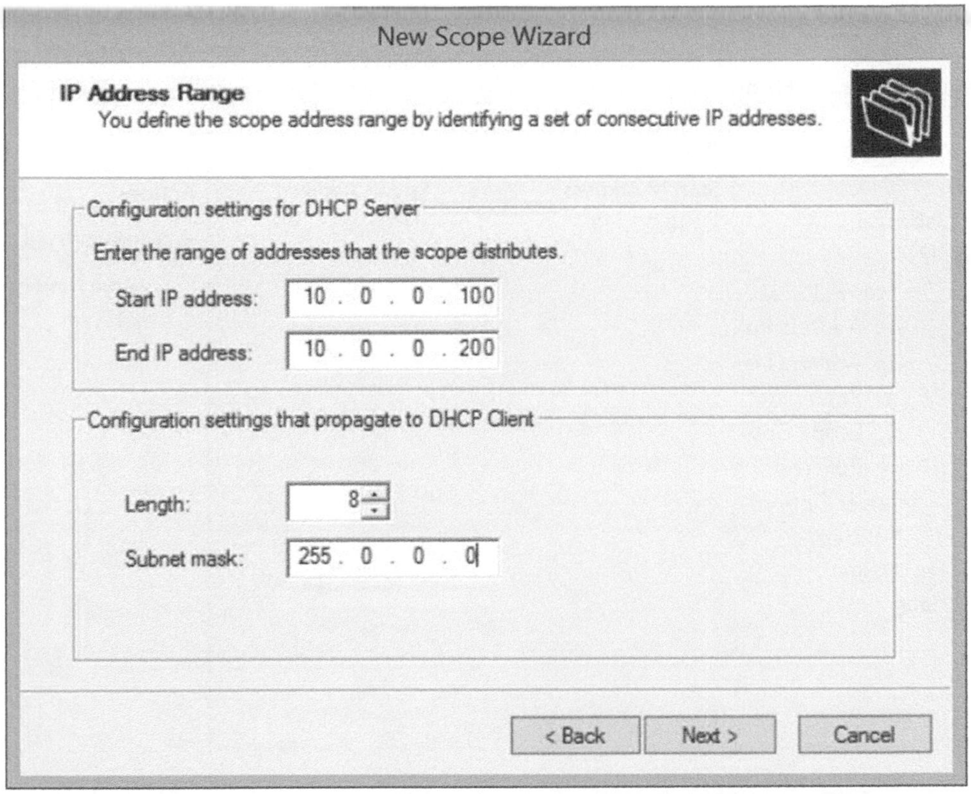

Figure 2.55   Specifying scope range.

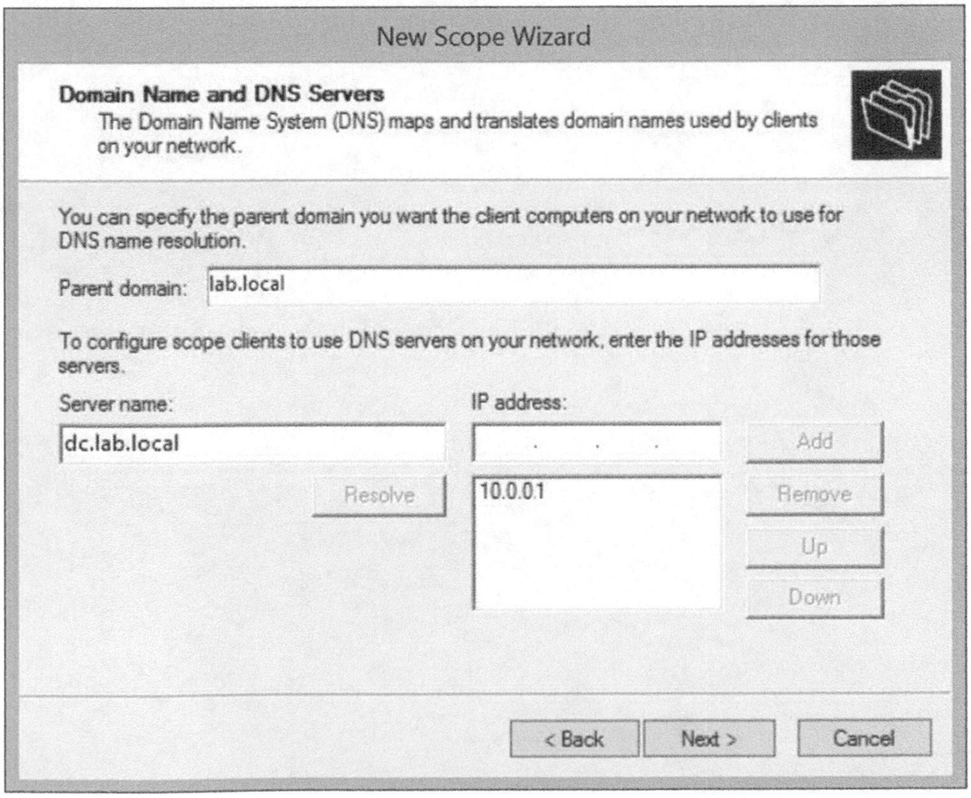

Figure 2.56   Verifying parent domain, server name, and IP address.

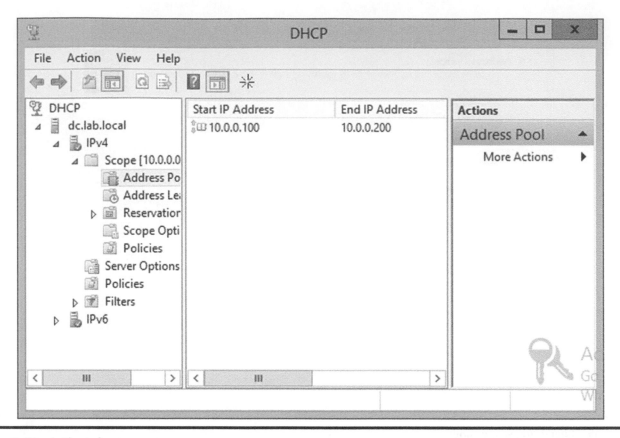

Figure 2.57 Activated scope.

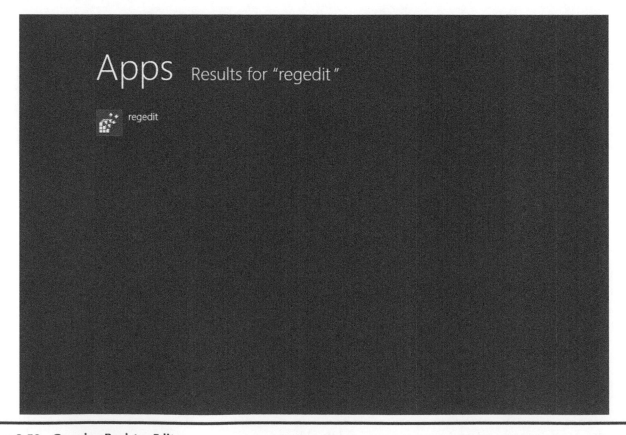

Figure 2.58 Opening Registry Editor.

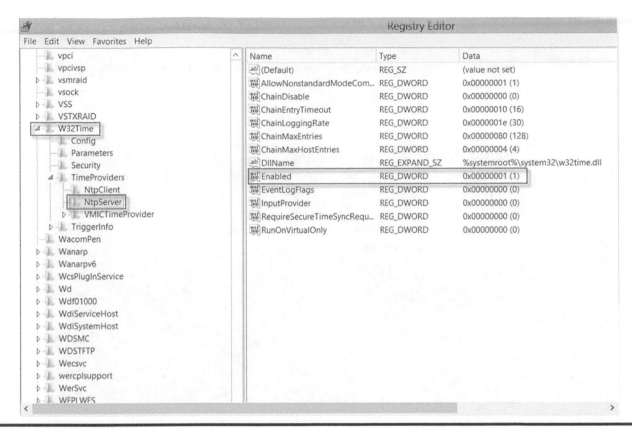

Figure 2.59   Start NtpServer.

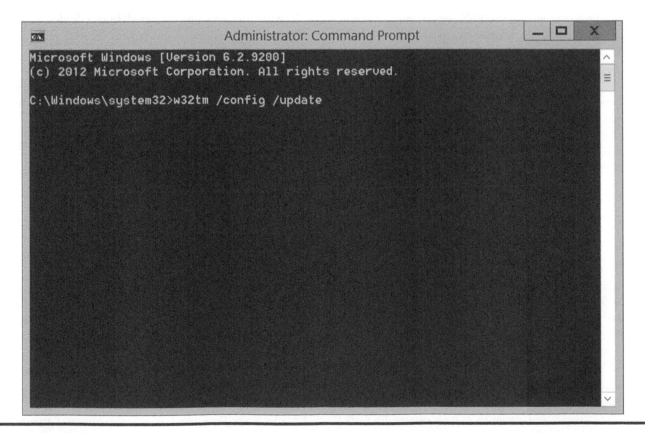

Figure 2.60   Update time server.

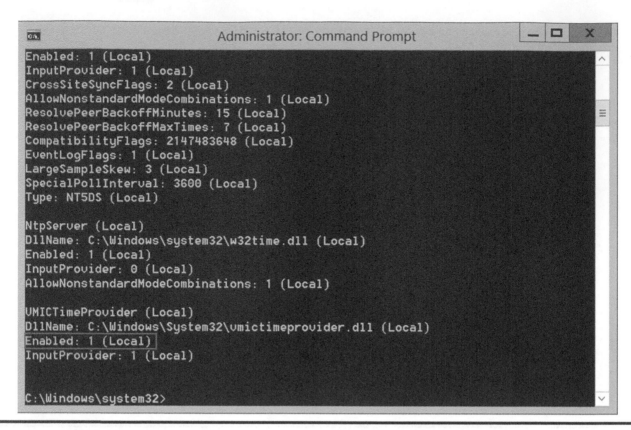

Figure 2.61 Enabled time server.

Later, when configuring the ESXi server, you can configure the ESXi server to synchronize time with this time server.

2.4.6 Task 6: Configuring PXE Service

For this task, you will configure the PXE service for network-based operating system installation. In this part of the activity, the PXE server will be installed and configured on the domain controller DC. The following are the steps to accomplish this task:

1. Download ESXiPXE from the following Web site, as shown in Figure 2.62:

   http://wp.secretnest.info/archives/812

2. ESXiPXE is a RAR file. It can be extracted by using the tool called 7-Zip. You can download 7-Zip from the following Web site. As shown in Figure 2.63, you need to download the 64-bit.exe file for Windows Server 2012 R2.

   http://www.7-zip.org/download.html

3. Double-click the .exe file to install 7-Zip.
4. After 7-Zip is installed, right-click the downloaded ESXiPXE.rar and select 7-Zip to extract ESXiPXE into a folder, as shown in Figure 2.64.

5. After the files are extracted into a folder, copy and paste the folder to a convenient location such as your Document folder.
6. Inside the ESXiPXE folder, create the ESXi folder (Figure 2.65) to host the VMware installation files.
7. You can download VMware ESXi 6.0 from the following Web site:

   https://my.vmware.com/web/vmware/details?productId=491&downloadGroup=ESXI600U1

8. To extract the content of the VMware ESXi 6.0 installer file, double-click it (Figure 2.66).
9. The content of the installer file will be extracted to the virtual compact disc (CD) drive, as shown in Figure 2.67. Copy all the files in the CD drive and paste them to the ESXi folder created earlier.
10. To configure the firewall to allow network traffic go through the ports 67 and 69, click the **Tools** menu on the Server Manager desktop. Click **Windows Firewall with Advanced Security,** as shown in Figure 2.68.
11. To create an inbound rule for the ports 67 and 69, click **Inbound Rules**, **Action**, and **New Rule** to open the New Inbound Rule Wizard.
12. On Rule Type page, check the option **Custom** and click **Next** twice.

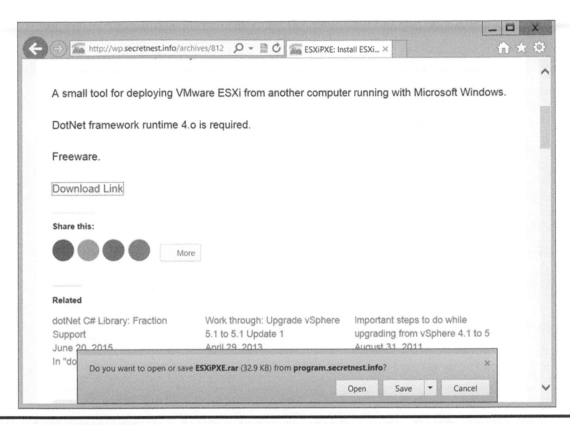

Figure 2.62   Downloading ESXiPXE.

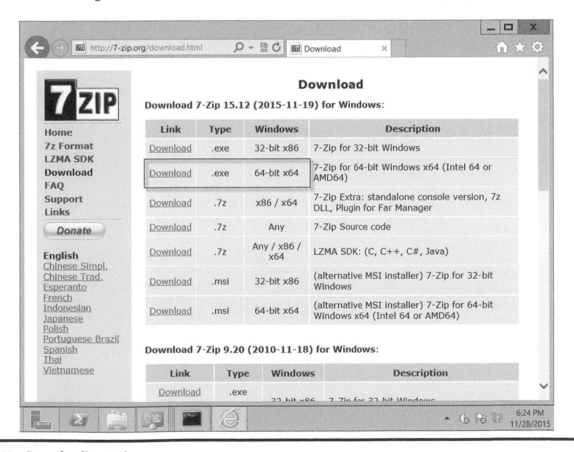

Figure 2.63   Downloading 7-Zip.

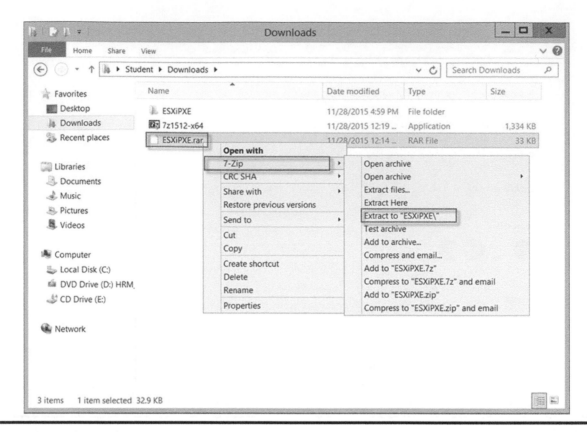

Figure 2.64   Extracting ESXiPXE.

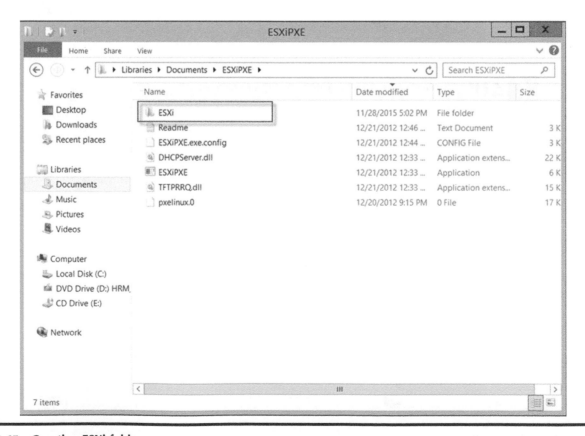

Figure 2.65   Creating ESXi folder.

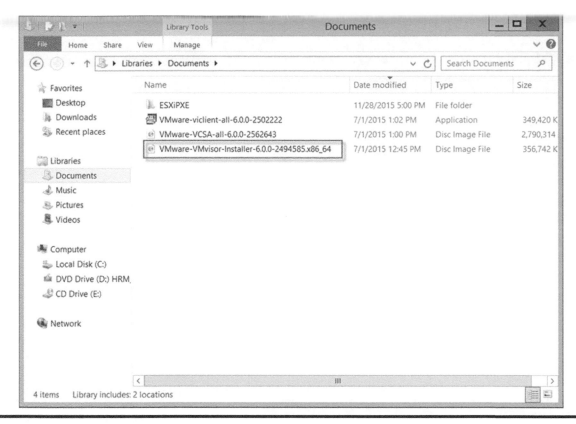

Figure 2.66 Extracting ESXi installer.

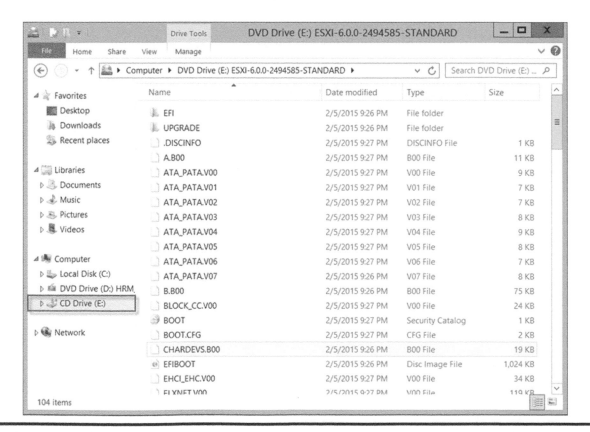

Figure 2.67 Content of installer file.

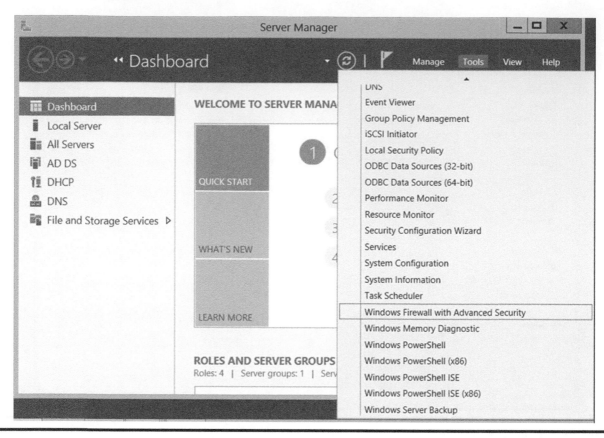

Figure 2.68   Opening Windows Firewall with Advanced Security.

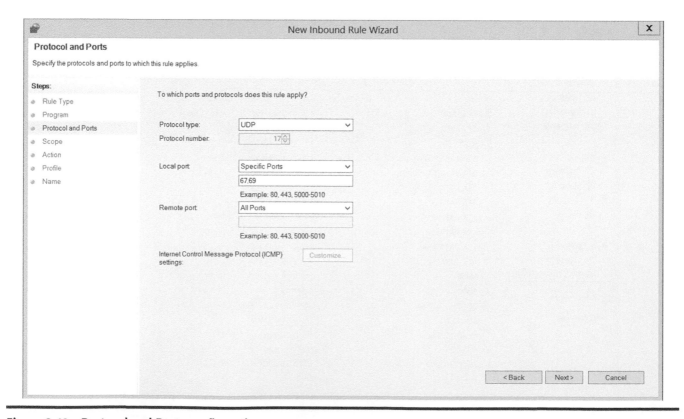

Figure 2.69   Protocol and Ports configuration.

13. On the Protocol and Ports page, configure the ports 67 and 69, as shown in Figure 2.69. Then, click **Next** twice.
14. On the Action page, make sure the option **Allow the connection** is checked. Then, click **Next** twice.
15. On the Name page, enter the name such as DHCP67_69. Then, click **Finish**.
16. Similarly, create an outbound rule and name it DHCPOutBound67_69, as shown in Figure 2.70. You can now close the Windows Firewall and Advance Security Wizard.
17. Once the firewall is configured, the next job is to configure the NIC. To do so, right-click the network icon and select **Open Network and Sharing Center,** as shown in Figure 2.70.
18. On the Network and Sharing Center page, click **Change adapter setting**.
19. On the Network Connection page, right-click the Ethernet NIC, which will be connected to the target VM for installation. Then, select **Properties,** as shown in Figure 2.71.
20. In the Ethernet Properties dialog, click **Internet Protocol Version 4** and click **Properties**.

21. In the Properties dialog, click the **Advanced** button.
22. In the Advanced TCP/IP Settings dialog, click the **Add** button.
23. Enter the IP address shown in Figure 2.72. Then, click the **Add** button. Then, click **OK** twice.
24. In the Command Prompt window, enter the **ipconfig** command to make sure that the IP address is added (Figure 2.73).

Now, your PXE server is ready for the network-based installation. On the same network, when the target virtual machine is booted up, it will contact the DHCP service provided by ESXiPXE for the IP address. After the target server gets its IP address, the installation process begins.

Similarly, by following the steps here, you can create a domain controller on a virtual machine hosted by the IT infrastructure whose implementation is demonstrated in Appendix A, or on a physical server. If you need to install SQL Server as a separate database for a production environment, refer to Appendix B for the installation of SQL Server.

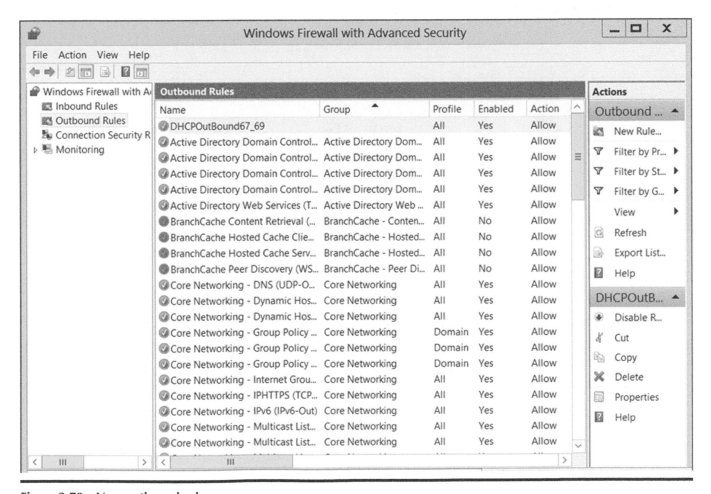

Figure 2.70   New outbound rule.

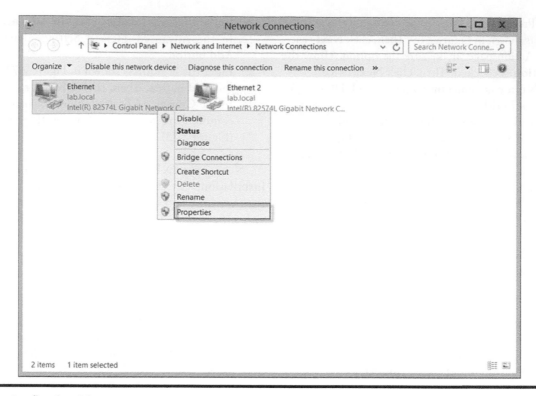

Figure 2.71   Configuring Ethernet.

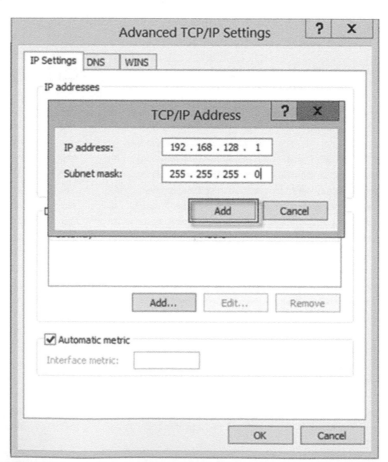

Figure 2.72   Assigning IP address for ESXiPXE.

```
                          Command Prompt                    _ □ X

C:\Users\student>ipconfig

Windows IP Configuration


Ethernet adapter Ethernet 2:

   Connection-specific DNS Suffix  . :
   Link-local IPv6 Address . . . . . : fe80::28b2:e97c:7453:2bac%15
   IPv4 Address. . . . . . . . . . . : 192.168.1.111
   Subnet Mask . . . . . . . . . . . : 255.255.255.0
   Default Gateway . . . . . . . . . : 192.168.1.1

Ethernet adapter Ethernet:

   Connection-specific DNS Suffix  . :
   Link-local IPv6 Address . . . . . : fe80::c4c1:9dcf:bcd2:2213%13
   IPv4 Address. . . . . . . . . . . : 10.0.0.1
   Subnet Mask . . . . . . . . . . . : 255.0.0.0
   IPv4 Address. . . . . . . . . . . : 192.168.128.1
   Subnet Mask . . . . . . . . . . . : 255.255.255.0
   Default Gateway . . . . . . . . . :

Tunnel adapter isatap.(C89B8AE3-D2E4-4634-A6E3-42765ADFE1CE):
```

Figure 2.73　Checking IP address.

2.5　Summary

This chapter has examined the domain controller, which is used to support the IT infrastructure used for VMware vCloud Suite. The domain controller services such as AD DS, DHCP, DNS, Ntp, and PXE are discussed in this chapter. With the AD DS service, the domain controller can provide the directory service that performs authentication and authorization for remote access. The directory service can also be used to store information of the objects in the IT infrastructure. DHCP automatically assigns IP addresses to network hosts. In the hands-on activity, the DHCP service is implemented with Windows Server 2012. The DNS service is essential for the cloud computing environment. It associates an IP address with a human-friendly name, or vice versa. The hands-on activity in this chapter implements the DNS service in Windows Server 2012 R2. The time service is used to synchronize time among servers used in the cloud computing environment. The time service is also implemented with Windows Server 2012 R2. The last service implemented in this chapter is the PXE service with the freeware tool ESXiPXE. The PXE service is used to provide network-based operating system installation.

REVIEW QUESTIONS

1. What is directory service?
2. What is a domain controller?
3. What is AD DS, and what do you do with it?
4. Describe the commonly used leaf objects in AD DS.
5. Describe the commonly used container objects in AD DS.
6. How is the directory service used to support VMware cloud services?
7. What are the advantages of implementing the domain controller on a virtual machine?
8. What is DHCP, and what do you do with it?
9. What is DNS, and what do you do with it?
10. What is the usage of the A type of DNS record?
11. What is the usage of the CNAME type of DNS record?
12. What is the usage of the PTR type of DNS record?
13. What is the usage of the SOA type of DNS record?
14. By using an example, describe an FQDN.
15. What is a forward lookup, and what is a reverse lookup?
16. By using an example, describe the forward lookup process.
17. Why does one need to synchronize time among servers?
18. What is NTP, and how is the NTP server enabled?
19. Describe the PXE-based installation.
20. What are the protocols required by the PXE-based installation?

2.5 Summary

Chapter 3

ESXi Installation and Configuration

Objectives

■ Explain how ESXi works
■ Understand the role played by ESXi
■ Install and configure ESXi

3.1 Introduction

The key component in VMware vCloud Suite is ESXi, which stands for Elastic Sky X Integrated. ESXi is a hypervisor used for virtualization. The virtualization technology can efficiently use physical hardware. This technology can significantly reduce information technology (IT) cost and improve availability and security. ESXi is also the primary product in vSphere, which is a suite of products for virtualization.

Like an operating system, ESXi has a kernel that manages the drivers for communication between hardware and software. Unlike the general-purpose operating system, ESXi has a compact architecture that requires small disk space. ESXi is designed for quick deployment, rapid performance, high scalability, and optimized virtualization. For these purposes, ESXi provides a remote command-line interface for management and configuration.

As a compact hypervisor, the code size of ESXi is less than 100 MB. With such a compact size, ESXi has a few advantages. Less code means less vulnerability. Hackers have less chance to find security holes. Less code also means less configuration and less management. This advantage makes the management of ESXi more efficient. The compactness also means that there will be less service running on ESXi. Therefore, the service process (daemon) is actually running on the machine that remotely accesses the ESXi server. In this way, the performance of ESXi can be improved. Even though ESXi is ultracompact, it supports all the virtualization products such as vMotion, vCenter, Virtual Symmetric Multiprocessing, VMware

High Availability, Virtual Machine File System (VMFS), VMware Consolidated Backup, VMware Distributed Resource Scheduler, and VMware Update Manager.

3.2 ESXi Components

This section describes some of the key elements in the ESXi architecture. It explains how the architecture meets the requirements of virtualization. Figure 3.1 illustrates the overview of the ESXi architecture.

In the following, you will get a closer look at the detailed descriptions of each of the components shown in Figure 3.1.

VMkernel: The key component included in ESXi is VMkernel. VMkernel is used to manage the communication between hardware and software. For example, when software issues an input/output (I/O) request, VMkernel translates the request into code that can be used to instruct the central processing unit (CPU) to act accordingly. ESXi also includes some processes running in VMkernel. VMkernel uses these processes to monitor hardware, control hardware devices, and manage virtual machines and computing resources. The following are some of the commonly used processes run in VMkernel:

■ *Virtual Machine Executable (VMX):* This process deals with communication among user interface, remote console, and snapshot managers. It also handles I/O requests to devices.
■ *Virtual Machine Monitor (VMM):* The process is used to construct an execution environment for a virtual machine. It deals with the virtual CPU in a virtual machine. Running in VMkernel, this process passes requests for network I/O or for storage to VMkernel. It also delivers all other requests to the VMX process.
■ *Mouse Keyboard Screen:* This process handles user inputs for a guest operating system. It is also responsible for rendering the guest video.

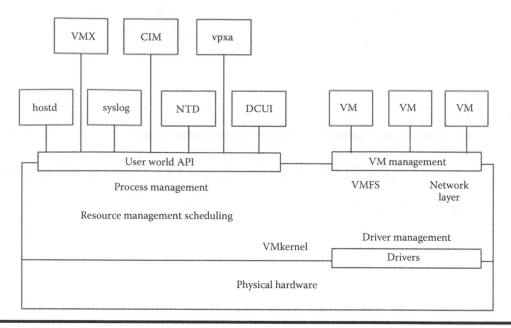

Figure 3.1 ESXi architecture.

- *vpxa:* This process is used to connect ESXi to vCenter. vpxa is installed on the ESXi server and is managed by vCenter. Therefore, it serves as a vCenter agent.
- *Common Information Model (CIM) system:* This process is responsible for hardware monitoring and health status. From a remote application, this process provides an interface for querying the health status of hardware.
- Various ESXi agents are used to enable high-level VMware infrastructure management from remote applications. For example, when connecting vCenter to ESXi, hostd is the daemon used for handling the connection. The syslog agent is a daemon used for logging messages of VMkernel and other system components to log files. It is able to place log files to a remote syslog server.
- *Direct Console User Interface (DCUI):* This process provides a console for ESXi management. Through this console, the administrator can perform some basic configuration. Figure 3.2 illustrates the DCUI.

File system: The main file system used by VMkernel is the VMware VMFS. This file system is designed to store virtual machines. It is optimized to handle large files such as virtual disks and swap files, which may either be stored on the ESXi server's hard disk or on a shared network storage device. The files can be remotely accessed through a browser with https. VMkernel also provides an in-memory file system that can be used to store config files, log files, and staged patches.

User world: "user world" in the ESXi architecture means the executable binary code compiled and scheduled by VMkernel. Being managed by VMkernel, "user world" can directly access the CPU, which reduces the memory requirement. A swap file is used to store operation data for "user world." The swap file can be automatically created as a Virtual File Allocation Table partition or specified in a datastore by the administrator. For each ESXi server, a swap file is about 1 GB in size. "user world" is specially designed for running processes such as hostd, vpxa, syslog, VMX, and VMM. These processes are considered native VMkernel applications. Therefore, the "user world" management is equivalent to the process management.

Resource scheduling and management: ESXi has a scheduler that controls how the guest operating systems on virtual machines fairly access the underlying computing resources. On an ESXi server, physical CPUs are shared by the virtual machines. The virtual machines are scheduled to wait in line for a free physical CPU/core to be available. If each virtual machine is configured to run on a single virtual CPU, the scheduler will assign a physical CPU/core to that virtual machine once the physical CPU/core is available. In the case that a virtual machine is configured to run on multiple virtual CPUs, the virtual machine has to wait for multiple physical CPUs/cores to be available. The wait time will be much longer if the number of required virtual CPUs/cores is much larger than the number of physical CPUs/cores. For example, if the number of virtual CPUs/cores is four times the available physical CPUs/cores, the virtual machines will only run at one-fourth native speed of the ESXi server. VMkernel provides several tools to make the memory usage more efficient:

- *Ballooning:* When an ESXi host server needs to reclaim some of the memory from virtual machines, it uses a balloon driver to request the unneeded memory pages

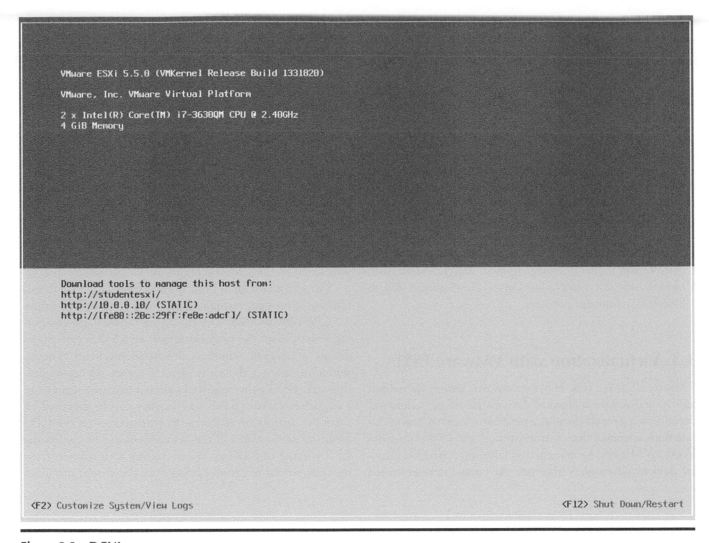

```
VMware ESXi 5.5.0 (VMKernel Release Build 1331820)

VMware, Inc. VMware Virtual Platform

2 x Intel(R) Core(TM) i7-3630QM CPU @ 2.40GHz
4 GiB Memory




Download tools to manage this host from:
http://studentesxi/
http://10.0.0.10/ (STATIC)
http://[fe80::20c:29ff:fe8e:adcf]/ (STATIC)
```

```
<F2> Customize System/View Logs                              <F12> Shut Down/Restart
```

Figure 3.2   DCUI.

from the guest operating system running on a virtual machine. Once the virtual machine allocates the unneeded memory, it *inflates* the balloon driver. The balloon driver informs the ESXi host server about the unneeded physical memory pages. Then, the ESXi host server reclaims the physical memory pages back using the balloon driver.

■ *Memory sharing:* When multiple virtual machines use the same operating system running on an ESXi host server, VMkernel scans the memory for duplicated memory pages. If it finds some, it will make these virtual machines share the duplicated memory. By doing so, VMkernel can save a lot of memory. For management, multiple regions of the physical memory can be mapped to a single region of virtual memory or vice versa. VMkernel can also leave a specific region of the physical memory and virtual memory unmapped.

■ *Swapping:* When the size of the memory allocated to the virtual machines is larger than the actual physical memory, swapping is the technology used by the ESXi host server to make more memory available to the virtual machines. Swapping uses a swap file on the hard drive as the memory for the virtual machines. Although the virtual machines can use the swap file as memory, it will significantly slow the virtual machines' performance. Another use of swapping is to reclaim the memory used by the virtual machines. When the ESXi host server needs to reclaim some of the memory for its own use, but the balloon driver cannot find any unneeded memory page from the virtual machines, the ESXi host server forces or swaps the memory used by a virtual machine to a swap file. Then, the ESXi host server can reclaim the physical memory originally allocated to that virtual machine.

Network layer: In the network layer, a VMkernel adapter can be configured with an IP address on a vSphere standard switch. The VMkernel adapter provides connectivity to ESXi hosts for the management of ESXi. It also handles network traffic generated by ESXi components such as vMotion and fault tolerance.

Driver management: ESXi has a Native Device Driver model interface built in VMkernel for managing device drivers. This interface allows a hardware device driver to communicate directly with VMkernel. In addition, for those legacy device drivers, VMkernel includes a management layer called vmklinux to deal with the drivers supported by Linux. The Native Device Driver model interface has many advantages. First, it can improve performance by allowing the drivers to directly access VMkernel. It supports new features such as Peripheral Component Interconnect Express (PCIe) hot-plug for the hot-swapping of PCIe devices. It is more efficient and flexible. Therefore, VMware encourages hardware vendors to develop drivers to meet the requirements of the Native Device Driver model interface. To assist driver development, VMware provides the Native Driver Development Kit to VMware development partners.

3.3 Virtualization with VMware ESXi

VMware ESXi is a type of hypervisor that creates virtualized hardware directly on physical devices. Therefore, it does not depend on a general-purpose operating system to communicate with a storage device or network device. ESXi provides its own VMkernel to manage and communicate with physical devices. Through VMkernel, the virtual devices hosted by an ESXi server can communicate with physical CPUs, memory, hard drives, and network devices. Figure 3.3 illustrates the use of VMkernel.

When a virtual machine gets started, VMkernel allocates memory and schedule CPU operation for the virtual machine. In such a way, VMkernel can allocate physical hardware resources to several running virtual machines. Therefore, a VMware ESXi server can host multiple virtual machines, each installed with different operating systems.

To allow communication between a guest operating system with a physical machine, VMkernel provides drivers of the physical hardware for carrying out the information exchange. As an ultralight kernel, VMkernel does not provide a wide range of drivers like a general-purpose operating system does. This is why an ESXi server only supports the hardware listed on the VMware Hardware Compatibility List.

Virtualization can be done in three ways: (1) CPU virtualization, (2) memory virtualization, and (3) I/O virtualization.

CPU virtualization: Depending on the available computing resources on the physical server, an ESXi server allows dozens of or even hundreds of virtual machines running simultaneously on the same physical server. To accomplish this task, ESXi either translates virtual machine requests to a sequence of instructions so that they can be executed on the CPU or directly executes the instructions on the CPU for better performance if the instructions can be run on the CPU without translation. When dealing with requests from multiple virtual machines, ESXi runs the virtual machines

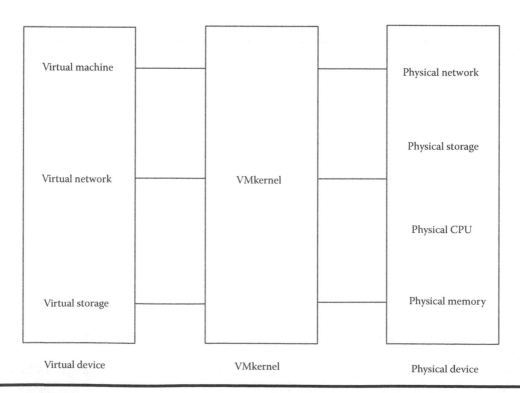

Figure 3.3 Use of VMkernel.

in turns. During a time share interval, ESXi allocates a share of the physical resources (including the specified number of CPUs) to a virtual machine.

Memory virtualization: Memory virtualization allows virtual machines to share the physical memory on ESXi servers. Each virtual machine needs to have its own memory for running its own operating system and its applications. ESXi allocates memory for each virtual machine. When running an application on the virtual machine, the address of the virtual memory used by the virtual machine needs to be translated to the address of the physical memory. The virtual memory is divided into blocks called pages, which have corresponding physical memory pages. When the physical memory is used up, the data will be stored to the hard disk.

I/O virtualization: The I/O virtualization technology allows multiple virtualized network interface cards (NICs) to share a single physical network adapter card. After an I/O request is issued by the guest operating system on a virtual machine, the guest operating system selects the corresponding driver and forwards the request to the driver. The driver processes the request and forwards the request to the selected communication port. ESXi then calls the corresponding driver loaded on the physical server to handle the request and send the request to the destination physical device.

3.4 Use of ESXi

As a hypervisor, ESXi can carry out the following tasks:

■ Hosting and consolidating a cluster of servers
■ Cloning virtual machines and other virtual devices
■ Recovering from system failure
■ Desktop virtualization
■ Simplifying the management of virtualization

Server cluster: By hosting multiple virtual machines on the same physical server, the ESXi server can be used to host a cluster formed by the multiple virtual machines. The size of the cluster can be changeable by adding or removing virtual machines. The servers in a cluster can be configured to start and shut down in a predefined order. The computing task of one server can be replicated to another server. In the case that one of the servers in the cluster fails, another server can replace the failed server without shutting down the operation. In a cluster, computing resources can be configured to meet different requirements. For example, among three servers, if one of them requires a large amount of CPU processing power and memory, the administrator can allocate more computing resources to that particular server.

Virtual machine cloning: ESXi makes the duplication of a virtual machine easier. To create a large number of virtual machines with similar configuration, ESXi allows the administrator to clone an entire virtual machine or just clone the virtual hard drive. The cloned virtual hard drive can be used to create a number of new virtual machines. With the cloning tool, new virtual machines can be created in minutes or even in seconds. Cloning makes the upgrade of virtual machines relatively easy. The administrator can upgrade one virtual machine and use it as the template. Then, the template is used to generate new virtual machines that are upgraded.

Disaster recovery: By virtualizing the hardware, ESXi makes disaster recovery affordable and flexible. Virtual machines, virtual networks, and virtual storage are just files. It is relatively easier to migrate, back up, and recover the files. Backing up a virtual machine can be done by simply making a copy of the virtual machine file. With the ESXi server, one can make a snapshot of a running virtual machine. The snapshot can be used as the backup of the virtual machine. In the case that the virtual machine is crashed, one can reload the snapshot to get the virtual machine back to the running state. In such a way, one can minimize the complexity of a recovery process. To help with recovery planning, the administrator can test the recovery mechanism on a set of virtual machines without stopping the physical hardware operation. Also, in case one of the ESXi servers fails, the virtual machine managed by the failed ESXi server can be booted up by another ESXi server. This can significantly simplify the data transfer from a storage device to a recovery site.

Desktop virtualization: Sometimes, students or employees may need to work on multiple PCs installed with different operating systems. They may also need to remotely access these PCs while on a trip. ESXi can virtualize the desktop of a PC. The virtualized desktop can be used as an interface to a virtual machine. ESXi allows remote access to the virtual desktop through a Web browser or through thin client software.

Virtualization management: ESXi provides tools and a user interface for the management of physical servers, physical networks, physical storage, virtual machines, virtual networks, and virtual storage. The tools can be used to add more memory, configure network parameters, upload/download virtual machines, view alert and warning messages, log operational information, and connect to storage devices. As time passes, ESXi allows the administrator to update computing resource allocations accordingly.

3.5 Activity 1: Installation and Configuration of ESXi

ESXi can be installed on a physical machine or on a virtual machine. In a production environment, it is advisable to install ESXi on a physical machine. The IT infrastructure in Appendix A provides an environment where ESXi is installed on physical machines. For the hands-on practice, you can install ESXi on a virtual machine. To install ESXi on a virtual machine, you need to create a virtual machine. Make sure that VMware Workstation has been installed and properly configured. The installation and configuration of ESXi can be accomplished with the following tasks:

- *Task 1:* ESXi installation preparation
- *Task 2:* ESXi installation
- *Task 3:* ESXi server configuration

Let us start with Task 1.

3.5.1 Task 1: ESXi Installation Preparation

There are three ways to install ESXi:

1. Install ESXi interactively with an ESXi installation media DVD or with an installation image Iso file. The installation can also be done through a PXE server.
2. Install ESXi automatically with a script.
3. Install ESXi automatically by remotely connecting to the Auto Deploy server.

In this lab activity, you will need to prepare two virtual machines for two ESXi servers. To accomplish this, follow the steps below:

1. Start VMware Workstation. Click the **File** menu and select **New Virtual Machine**.
2. On the Welcome to the New Virtual Machine Wizard page, select the **Custom** option, as shown in Figure 3.4. Then, click **Next**.
3. On the Choose the Virtual Machine Hardware Compatibility page, choose **Workstation 11.x** for Hardware, as shown in Figure 3.5. Then, click **Next**.
4. On the Guest Operating System Configuration page, select the option **I will install the operating system later,** as shown in Figure 3.6. Then, click **Next**.
5. On the Select a Guest Operating System page, check the **VMware ESX** option and select the version **VMware ESXi 6,** as shown in Figure 3.7. Then, click **Next**.
6. On the Name the Virtual Machine page, enter the virtual machine name such as **LabESXi1** and the location where you will save the virtual machine. For

Figure 3.4 New Virtual Machine Wizard.

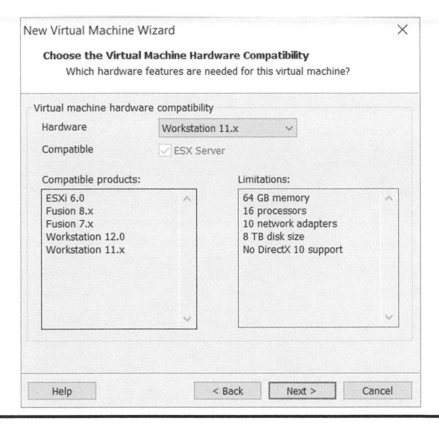

Figure 3.5   Hardware compatibility.

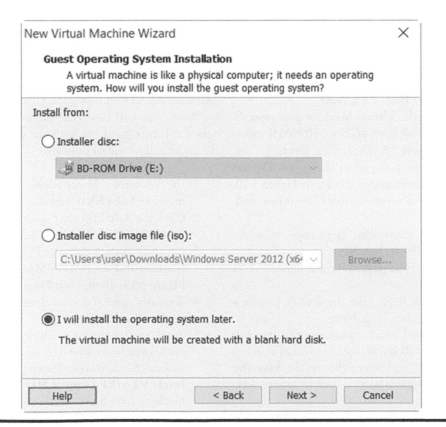

Figure 3.6   Installation of ESXi.

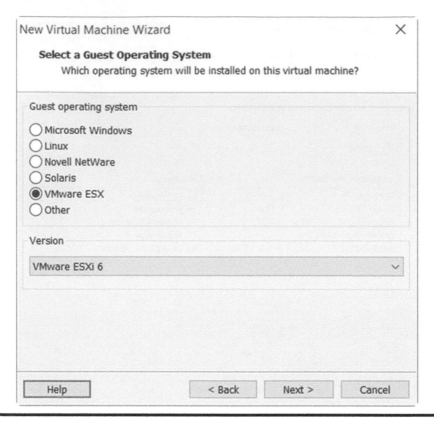

Figure 3.7 Selecting guest operating system.

better performance, it is better to save LabESXi1 to Solid-state drive.

7. On the Processor Configuration page, set the virtual machine to have **2** processors, each with **2** cores, as shown in Figure 3.8. Then, click **Next**.

8. On the Memory for the Virtual Machine page, specify the virtual machine to have **4GB** or **4096MB** memory, as shown in Figure 3.9. Then, click **Next**.

9. On the Network Type page, select the option **Do not use a network connection,** as shown in Figure 3.10. You will configure the network after ESXi is installed. Then, click **Next**.

10. On the Select I/O Controller Type page, take the default **LSI Logic**. Then, click **Next**.

11. On the Select Disk Type page, take the default **SCSI** and click **Next**.

12. On the Select a Disk page, take the default **Create a New Virtual Disk**. Then click **Next**.

13. On the Specify Disk Capacity page, specify the disk size as **40GB** or **140GB** if you intend to install vCenter on this ESXi server, and select the option **Save the virtual disk as a single file,** as shown in Figure 3.11. Then, click **Next**.

14. On the Specify Disk File page, take the default file name and click **Next**.

15. On the Ready to Create Virtual Machine page, examine the configuration and click **Finish**.

If the virtual machine starts automatically, cancel the installation and shut down the virtual machine.

Next, you will configure the network so that the ESXi server can communicate with the domain controller (DC). To do so, follow the steps below:

1. In VMware Workstation, right-click the virtual machine **LabESXi1** and select **Settings**.

2. Click the **Add** button (Figure 3.12). On the Hardware Type page, click **Network Adapter** and click **Next**.

3. On the Network Adapter Type page, select the option **Custom** and select the **VMnet2** network, as shown in Figure 3.13. Then, click **Finish**.

4. Similarly, add the second network adapter, which is also specified in Figure 3.13.

5. To allow the virtual machine LabESXi1 to host other virtual machines (that is, to let LabESXi1 be a nested virtual machine), you need to enable the feature **Virtualize Intel VT-x/EPT or AMD-V/RVI** for the virtual machine LabESXi1. To do so, in the Virtual Machine Settings dialog, click **Processors** and check the option **Virtualize Intel VT-x/EPT or AMD-V/RVI**.

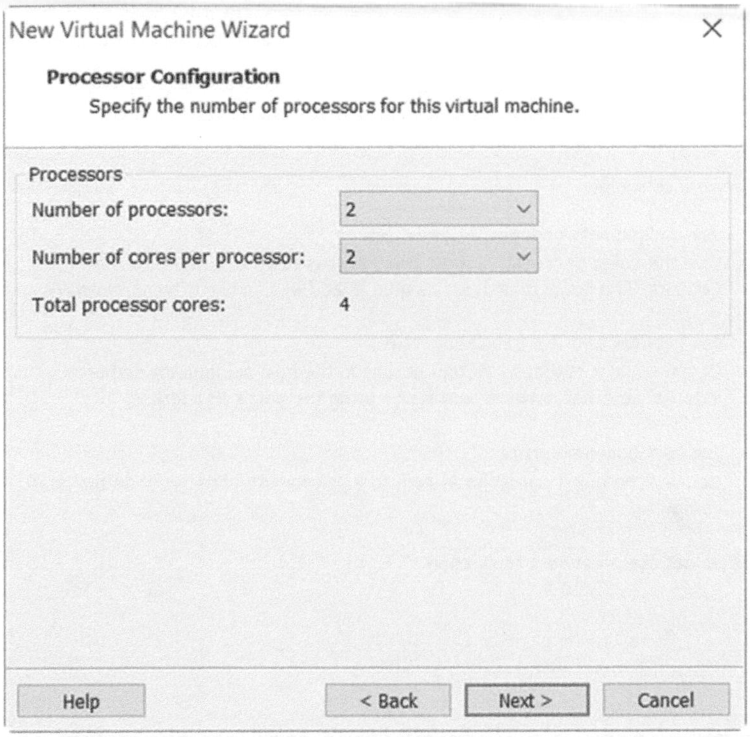

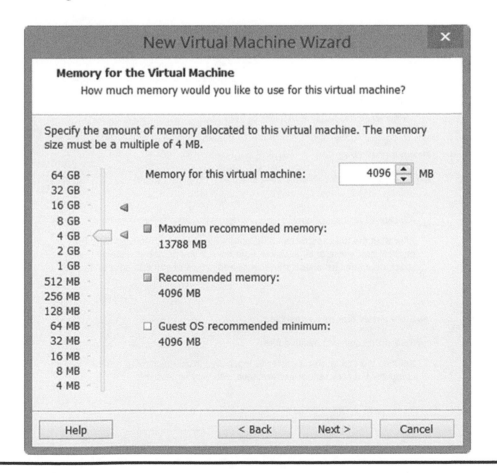

Figure 3.8   Processor configuration.

Figure 3.9   Memory configuration.

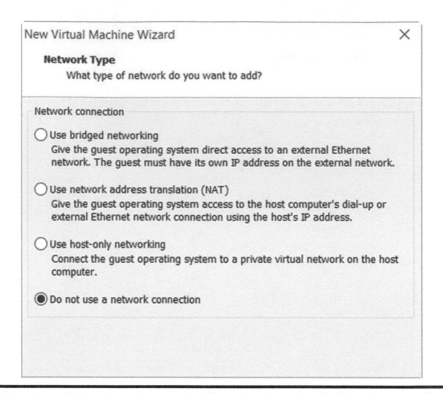

Figure 3.10   Network connection.

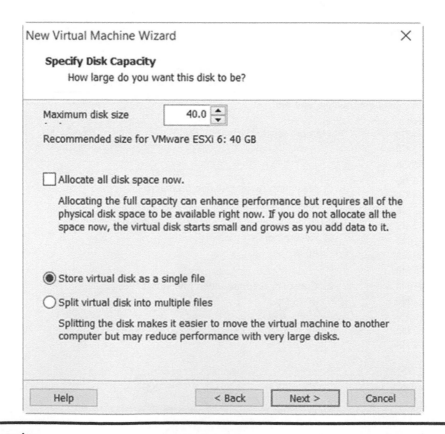

Figure 3.11   Disk capacity.

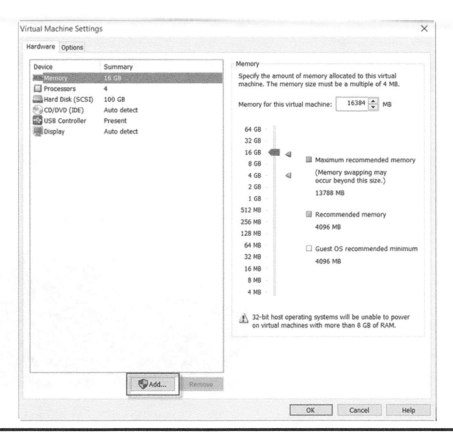

Figure 3.12   Adding network adapter.

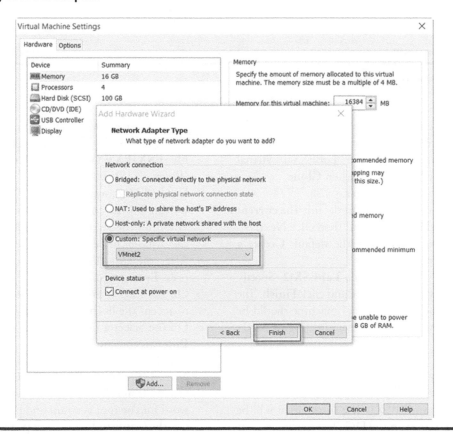

Figure 3.13   Network adapter configuration.

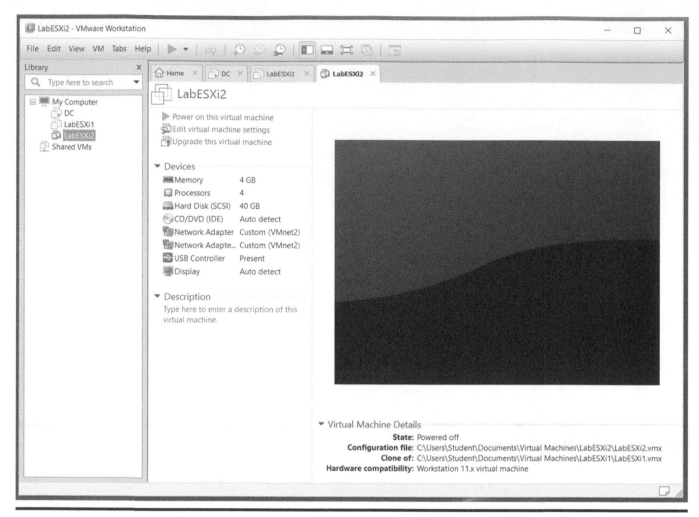

Figure 3.14 Configuration of second virtual machine.

6. You can clone the LabESXi1 virtual machine to get the second ESXi server. To do so, in the Virtual Machine Settings dialog, right-click the LabESXi1 virtual machine and select **Manage** and then **Clone**.
7. On the Welcome page, click **Next**.
8. On the Clone Source page, take the default **The current state in the virtual machine,** and then click **Next**.
9. On the Clone Type page, take the default **Create a linked clone** and click **Next**.
10. Name the second virtual machine **LabESXi2**. Specify the location of the virtual machine and click **Finish**. The configuration of the second virtual machine should be similar to that of the first virtual machine (Figure 3.14).

3.5.2 Task 2: ESXi Installation

For this task, you will install ESXi. The installation will be done through the PXE server on the DC. The following steps illustrate how to install ESXi:

1. In VMware Workstation, power on the DC. Navigate to the folder ESXiPXE. Right-click the file **ESXiPXE** and select **Run as administrator** (Figure 3.15).
2. Figure 3.16 shows the started PXE server. The server is waiting for the contact from a virtual machine.
3. Power on the virtual machine **LabESXi1** and wait for the installer to be loaded, as shown in Figure 3.17.
4. After the installer is loaded, on the Welcome page, press **Enter** to continue.
5. On the End User License Agreement page, Press **F11** to accept the license and **Enter** to continue.
6. On the Select a Disk to Install or Upgrade page, press **Enter** to continue.
7. On the Select a Keyboard Layout page, specify the keyboard layout and press the **Enter** key to continue.
8. On the Enter the Root Password page, enter your password for the root account and press **Enter** to continue.
9. On the Confirm Installation page, press the **F11** key to install ESXi.

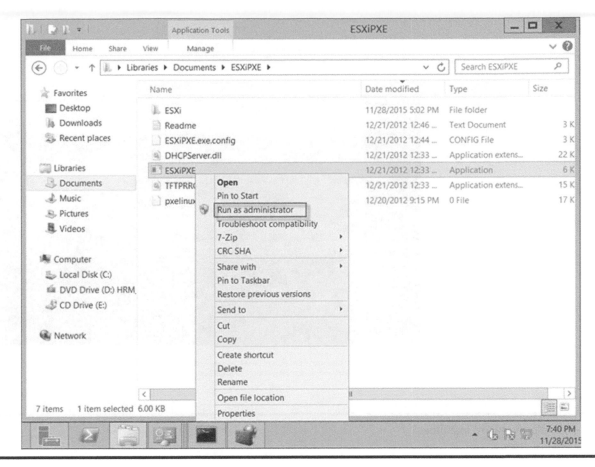

Figure 3.15 Starting PXE server.

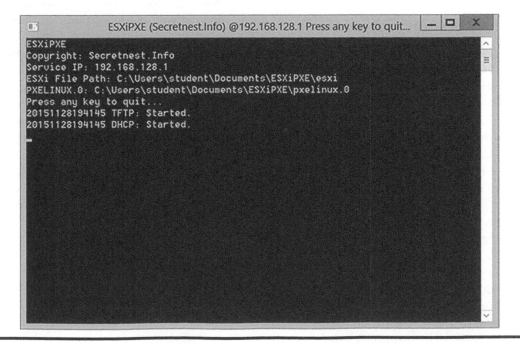

Figure 3.16 PXE server started.

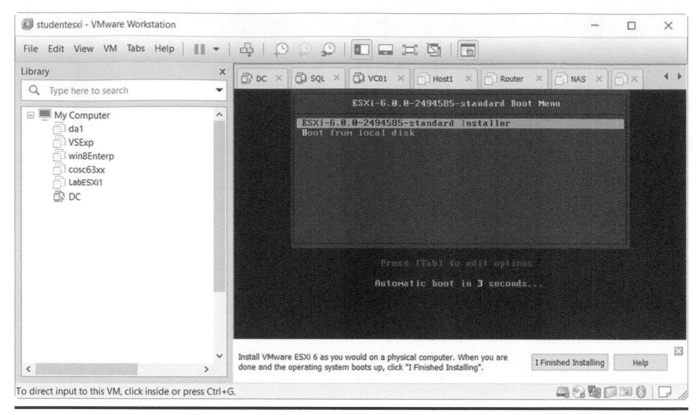

Figure 3.17 Loading VMware installer.

10. After the installation is complete, press **Enter** to reboot the system. After the system is rebooted, you will get the screen shown in Figure 3.18.

3.5.3 Task 3: ESXi Server Configuration

The warning message in Figure 3.18 indicates that the network has not been configured. In this section, you will configure the ESXi server so that it can communicate with other servers in the VMware computing environment.

1. To log on to the ESXi server **LabESXi1**, press **F2** to bring up the Authentication page.
2. Enter the login name **root**. Press the **Tab** key on your keyboard and enter your password, as shown in Figure 3.19.
3. On the System Customization page, use the keyboard to select **Configure Management Network,** as shown in Figure 3.20. Then, press **Enter**.
4. On the Configure Management Network page, select **Network Adapters** and press the **Enter** key.
5. On the Network Adapter page, select **vmnic1** and press the **Space** bar to add the NIC vmnic1 to the virtual machine (Figure 3.21). Then, press **Enter** to accept the configuration.

6. On the Configure Management Network page, select **IPv4 Configuration** (Figure 3.22). Then, press **Enter**.
7. On the IPv4 Configuration page, use the **Arrow** key to move the cursor to the option **Set static IPv4 address and network configuration**. Then, use the **Space** bar to select the option shown in Figure 3.23.
8. Also, on the IPv4 Configuration page, set the IP Address as 10.0.0.10, Subnet Mask as 255.0.0.0, and Default Gateway as 10.0.0.1 (Figure 3.24). 10.0.0.1 is the IP address of the DC server. Then, press **Enter**.
9. On the Configure Management Network page, select **DNS Configuration,** as shown in Figure 3.25. Then, press **Enter**.
10. On the DNS Configuration page, enter **10.0.0.1** as the IP address of Primary DNS Server and **dc.lab.local** as the complete Hostname. Then, press the **Enter** key (Figure 3.26).
11. On the Configure Management Network page, press the **Esc** key to exit.
12. On the Confirm page, press the **Y** key to apply the changes and restart the management, as shown in Figure 3.27.
13. Press the **Esc** key again to log out. Then, press **F12** to shut down the virtual machine. You will be asked to enter the password and then press **F2** to shut down the virtual machine.

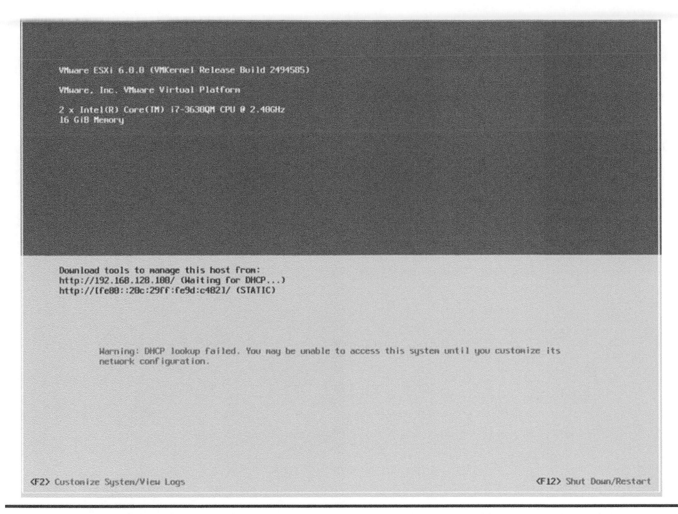

Figure 3.18 ESXi installed.

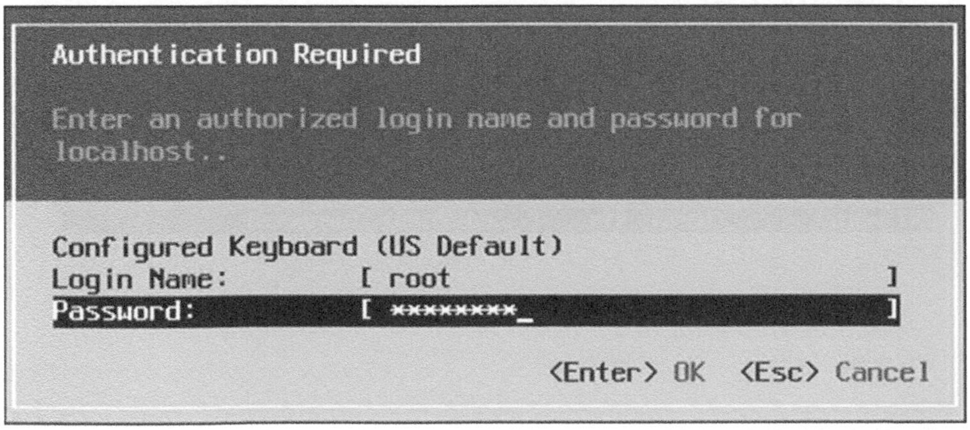

Authentication Required

Enter an authorized login name and password for localhost..

Configured Keyboard (US Default)
Login Name: [root   ]
Password: [********_   ]

                              <Enter> OK   <Esc> Cancel

Figure 3.19 Logging in as root.

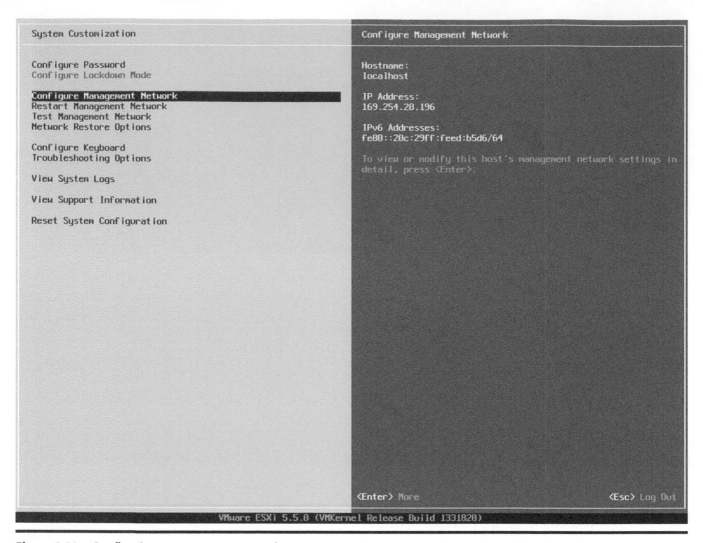

Figure 3.20   Configuring management network.

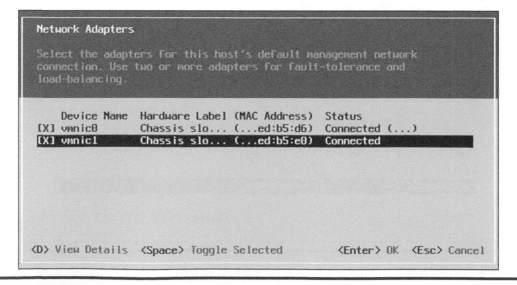

Figure 3.21   Adding vmnic1.

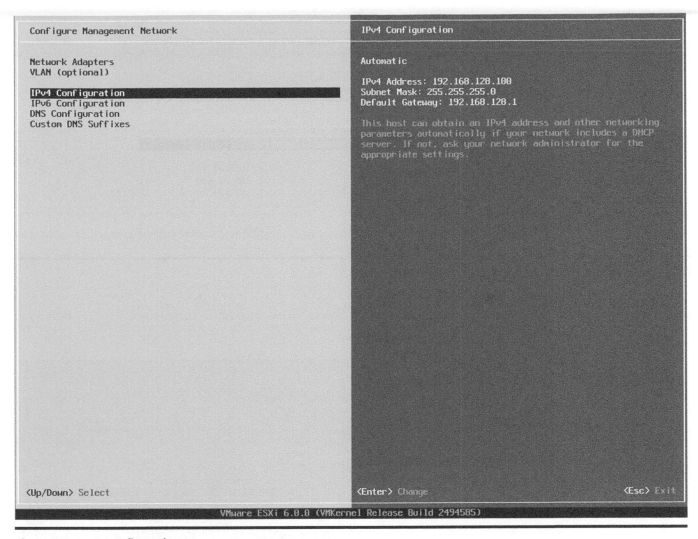

Figure 3.22   IP configuration.

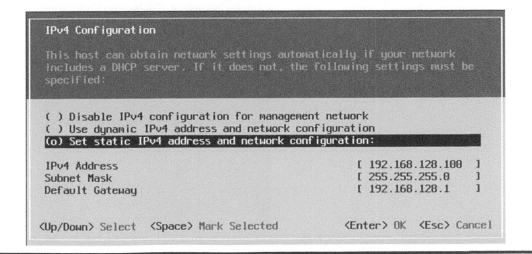

Figure 3.23   Static IP configuration.

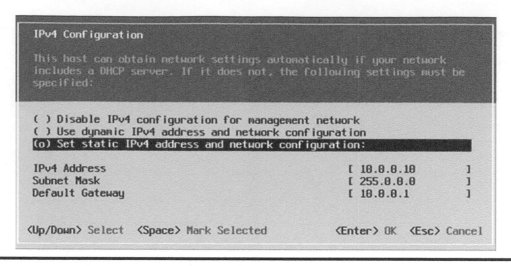

Figure 3.24 Configuration of NIC.

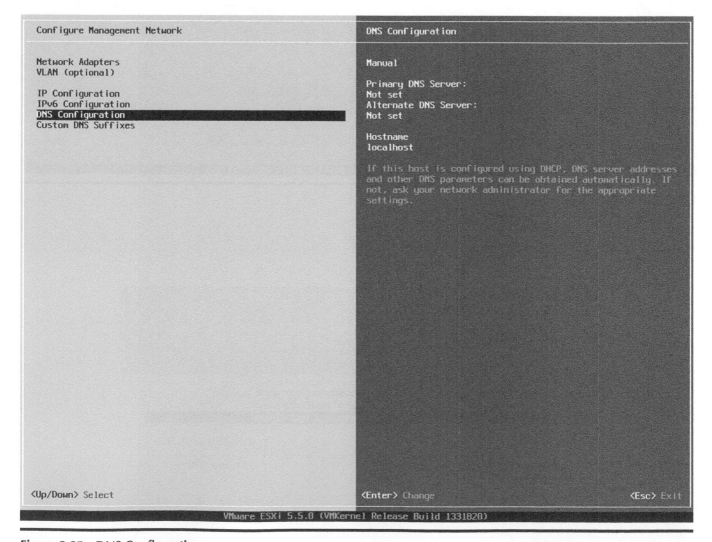

Figure 3.25 DNS Configuration.

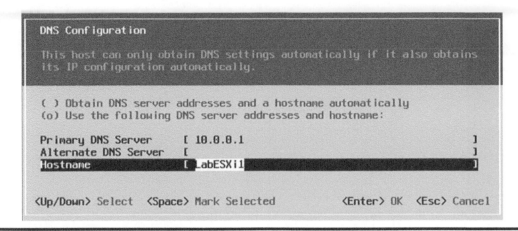

Figure 3.26   DNS settings.

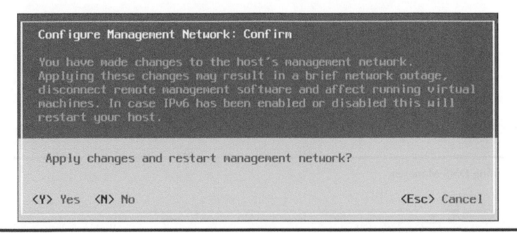

Figure 3.27   Applying changes.

14. Power on the **LabESXi2** server. Follow Steps 3 through 10 in Task 2 and Steps 1 through 13 in Task 3 to install and configure the LabESXi2 server. You need to add the NIC vmnic1 and configure the NIC with the IP address **10.0.0.20**, the subnet mask still 255.0.0.0, and the host name **LabESXi2**. The Default Gateway and DNS Server IP address are still **10.0.0.1,** and the DNS host name is still **dc.lab.local**.

15. After the installation is complete, log on to the **DC**. Click on the ESXiPXE window (Figure 3.16) and press the **Enter** key to turn off the PXE server.

In the following, you will need to configure the DNS server DC to add the machine names of the ESXi servers and the related IP addresses to Active Directory:

1. Log on to the **DC** virtual machine as the administrator.
2. To open the DNS Manager, click the **Tools** menu and select **DNS,** as shown in Figure 3.28.
3. In the DNS Manager dialog, under the node **Forward Lookup Zones**, right-click the node **lab.local** and

select **New Host (A or AAAA),** as shown in Figure 3.29, to open the New Host dialog.

4. In the New Host dialog, create a DNS record with the host name **LabESXi1** and the fully qualified domain name **labesxi1.lab.local,** which has a corresponding IP address **10.0.0.10,** as shown in Figure 3.30. You also need to create the corresponding pointer (PTR) record by checking the option **Create the associated pointer (PTR) record**. The PTR record is used for reverse lookup. Then, click the **Add Host** button.

5. Similarly, you can create a DNS record for the LabESXi2 virtual machine with the host name LabESXi2 and the corresponding IP address 10.0.0.20.

6. After the records are created, you should be able to see the newly created records in the lab.local domain, as shown in Figure 3.31.

7. To remotely access the ESXi server from your DC, you can download client software from the ESXi server. To do so, in the DC, open your browser and enter the following Uniform Resource Locator:
https://10.0.0.10

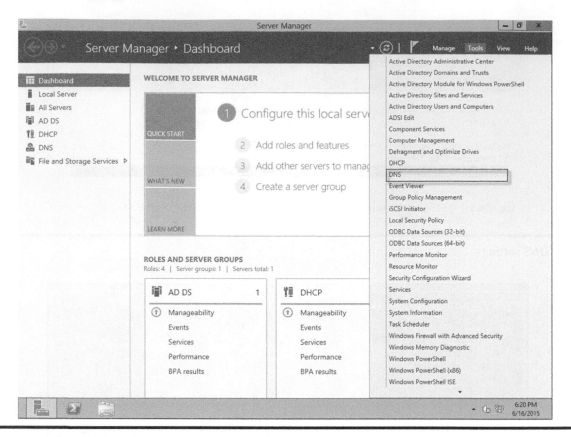

Figure 3.28 Opening DNS Manager.

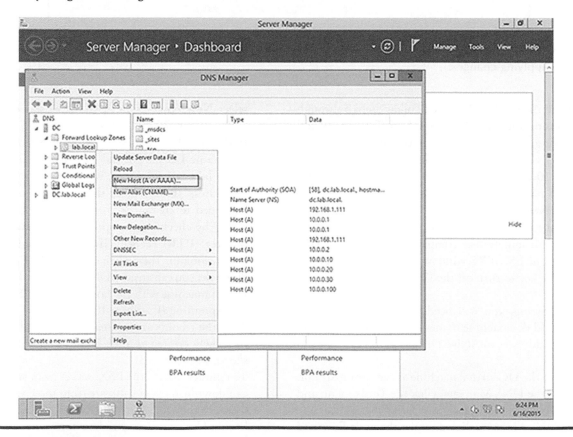

Figure 3.29 Opening New Host dialog.

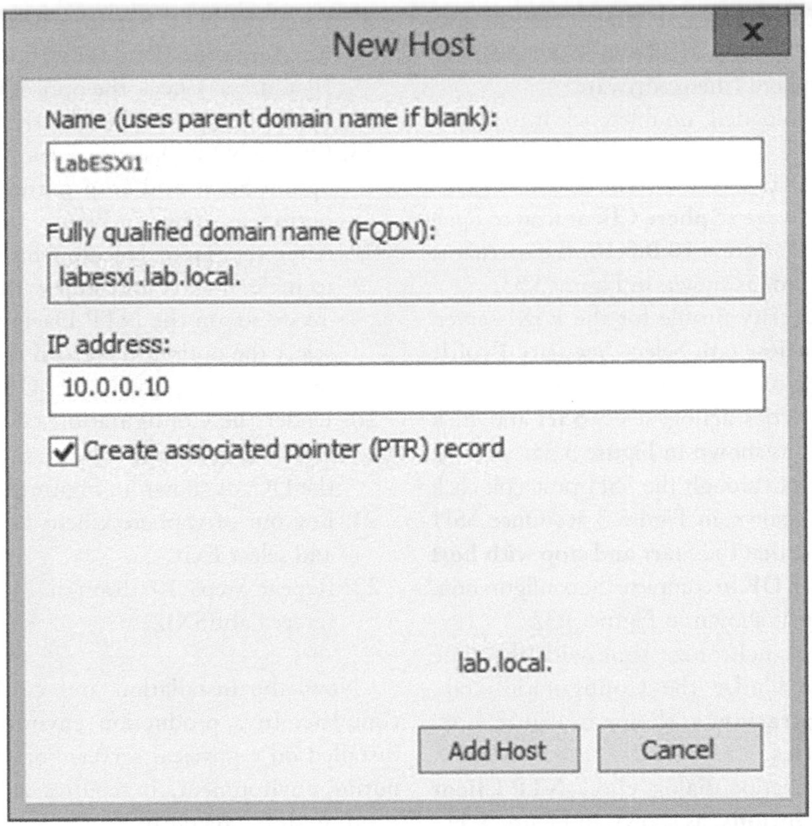

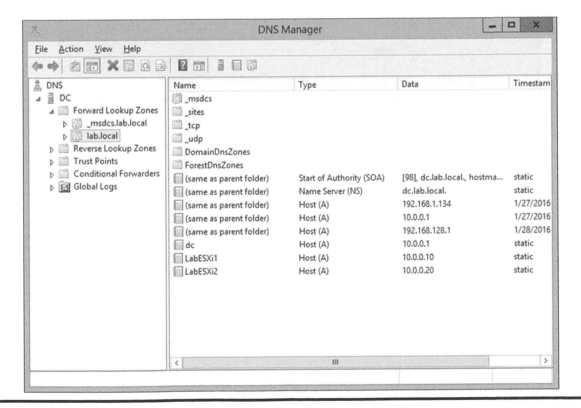

Figure 3.30 New Host DNS record.

Figure 3.31 Newly created DNS records.

8. On the VMware ESXi Welcome page, click the link **Download vSphere Client,** as shown in Figure 3.32. Then, install the vSphere Client software.
9. After the file is downloaded, double-click it to install vSphere Client.
10. Power on the **LabESXi1** server. On the desktop of DC, double-click the **VMware vSphere Clien**t icon to open it. Then, enter the IP address **10.0.0.10**, the username **root,** and the password, as shown in Figure 3.33.
11. To configure the security profile for the ESXi server, click the **Configuration** tab. Select **Security Profile** and click **Properties,** as shown in Figure 3.34.
12. In the Services Properties dialog, select **SSH** and click the **Options** button, as shown in Figure 3.35.
13. To allow remote access through the SSH protocol, click the **Start** button, as shown in Figure 3.36. Once SSH has started, make sure that the **Start and stop with host** option is selected. Click **OK** to complete the configuration.
14. SSH is now running as shown in Figure 3.37.
15. The next task is to synchronize time with the time server on the DC. Under the Configuration tab, select **Time Configuration,** as shown in Figure 3.38. Then, click **Properties**.
16. In the Time Configuration dialog, check **NTP Client Enabled** and click **Options,** as shown in Figure 3.39.

17. Click the **NTP Settings** link and click the **Add** button. Enter the IP address **10.0.0.1** as the NTP server's IP address. Check the option **Restart NTP service to apply changes** and click **OK**.
18. On the NTP Daemon (ntpd) Options page, select the option **Start and stop manually** and click the **Start** button, as shown in Figure 3.40.
19. After the Time Daemon has started, you also want to make it start and stop with the host automatically. To do so, on the NTP Daemon (ntpd) Options page, select the option **Start and stop with host,** as shown in Figure 3.41. Then, click **OK** twice.
20. Under the Configuration tab, you can see that NTP Client is running; it finds the NTP server created in the DC, as shown in Figure 3.42.
21. Log out of vSphere Client by clicking the **File** menu and select **Exit**.
22. Repeat Steps 10 through 21 to configure the ESXi server LabESXi2.

Now, the installation and configuration of ESXi are complete. In a production environment, ESXi should be installed on a physical server. For the enterprise-level computing environment, it requires at least two ESXi servers running simultaneously.

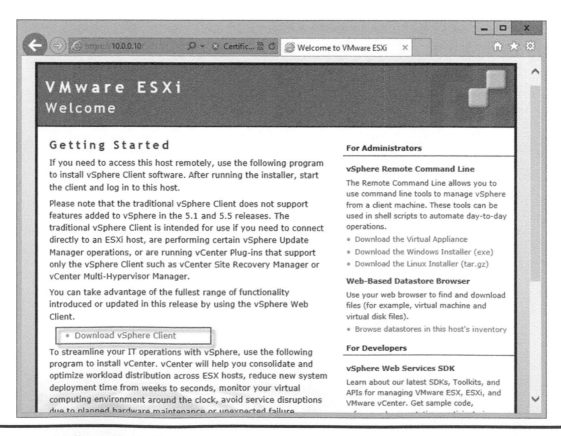

Figure 3.32 Downloading vSphere Client.

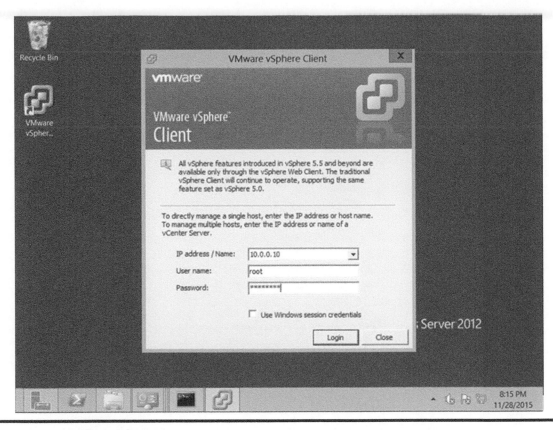

Figure 3.33   VMware vSphere Client.

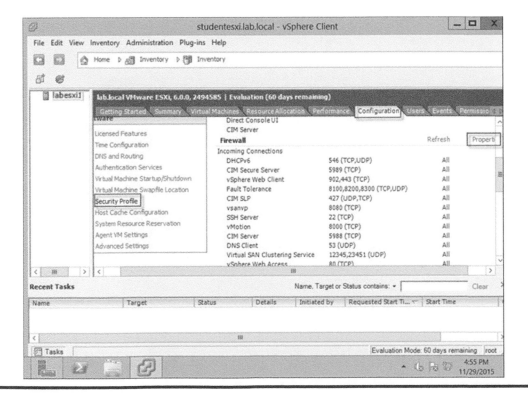

Figure 3.34   Security profile configuration.

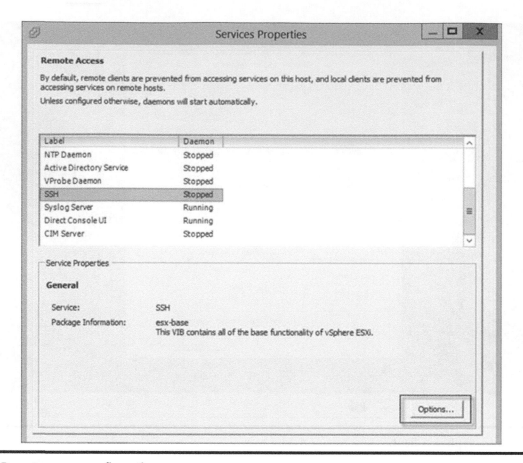

Figure 3.35   Remote access configuration.

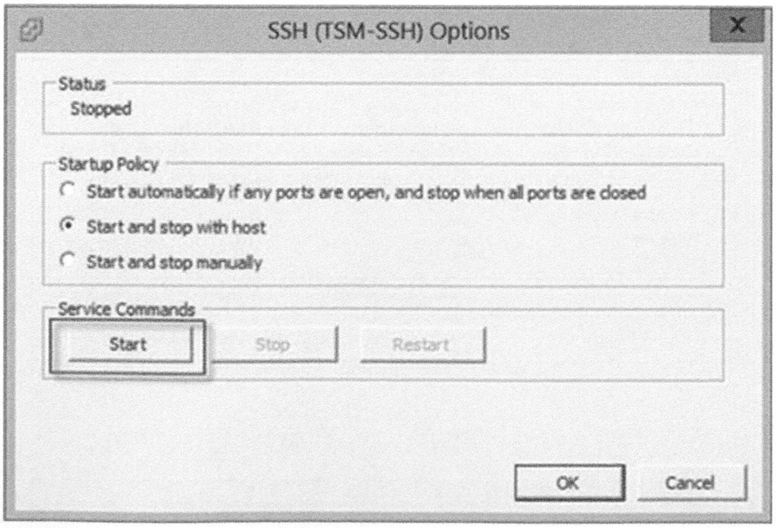

Figure 3.36   Configuring SSH options.

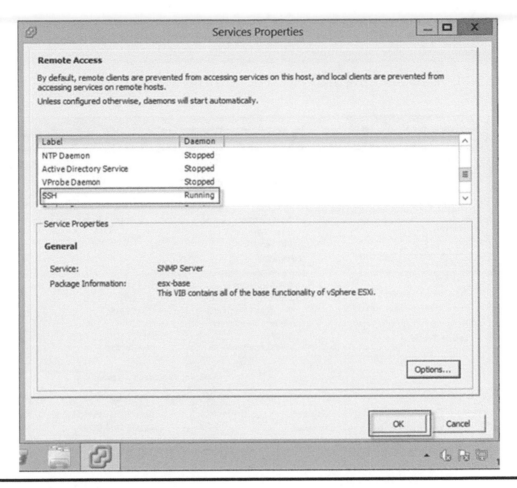

Figure 3.37   Running SSH.

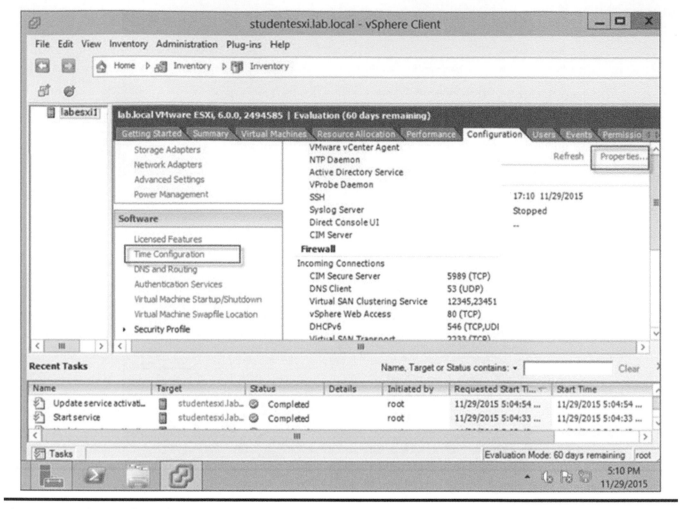

Figure 3.38 Time configuration properties.

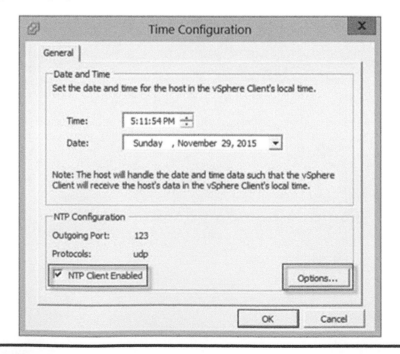

Figure 3.39 Time configuration properties.

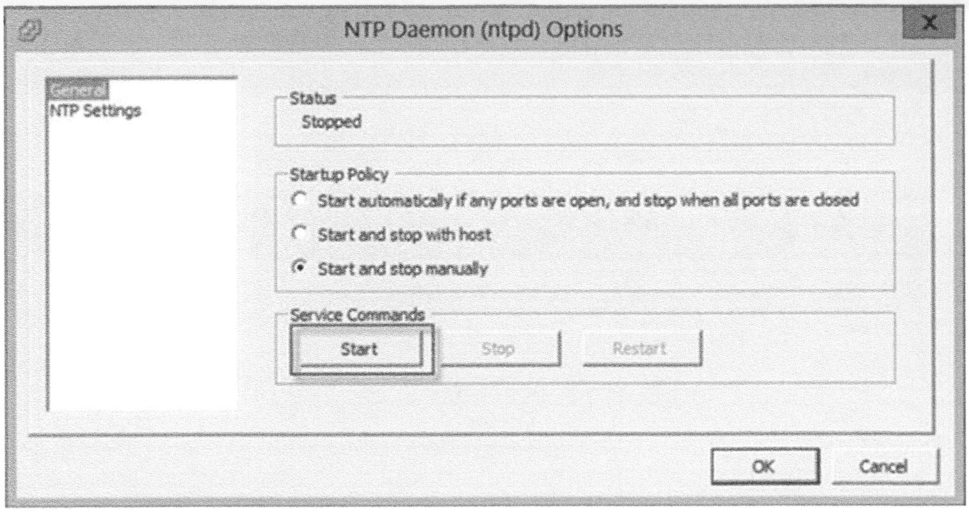

Figure 3.40   Start and stop manually option.

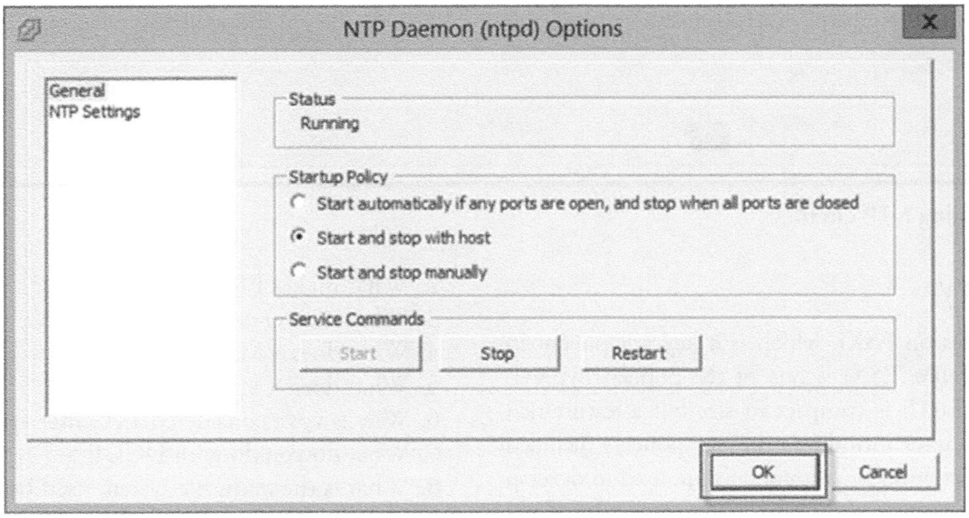

Figure 3.41   Start and stop with host option.

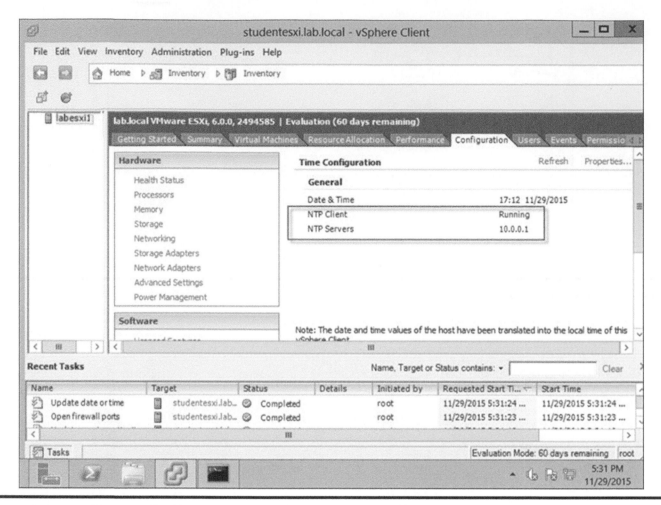

Figure 3.42   Running NTP client.

3.6 Summary

This chapter focuses on ESXi, which is a key component in VMware vCloud Suite. ESXi is one of the popular hypervisors for virtualization. It is compact in size but a feature-rich hypervisor. This chapter introduces the components included in ESXi. It describes how the components are used to develop a virtualized environment. In cloud computing, the cloud services are supported by the virtualized IT infrastructure. Virtualization is a technology that can significantly reduce the cost of IT infrastructure. It can also improve availability and security. This chapter explains how to prepare and conduct the installation and configuration of ESXi. The hands-on activity in this chapter provides the steps for the network-based installation of ESXi. It also demonstrates how to configure ESXi through the vSphere Client software. In the next chapter, you will learn a powerful centralized management tool called vCenter.

REVIEW QUESTIONS

1. What are the differences between a general-purpose operating system and ESXi?
2. What makes ESXi less vulnerable?
3. What do you do with VMkernel?
4. What does VMX do?
5. What does VMM do?
6. Why is vpxa considered a vCenter agent?
7. What do you do with DCUI?
8. What is the main file system used by VMkernel?
9. Describe "user world" in the ESXi architecture.
10. What is ballooning?
11. How does memory sharing work?
12. Explain the function of swapping.
13. What are the advantages of the Native Device Driver model?
14. How does CPU virtualization work?
15. How does memory virtualization work?
16. How does I/O virtualization work?
17. What tasks can be carried out by ESXi?
18. Describe how virtual machine cloning works.
19. What is desktop virtualization?
20. What tasks can virtualization management tools handle?

Chapter 4

vCenter Installation and Configuration

Objectives

- Understand the roles played by vCenter
- Install and configure vCenter
- Manage vCenter

4.1 Introduction

A cloud computing environment consists of a large number of servers, virtual machines, storage devices, and network devices. It is important to manage these cloud computing components at a centralized location. vCenter is such software through which the administrator can manage the virtual information technology (IT) infrastructure. When a host server is added to vCenter, all its virtual machines can be managed by vCenter. The related virtual networks and storage devices can also be managed by vCenter. In addition, vCenter is used for managing advanced features such as High Availability (HA), Fault Tolerance, and Load Balancing. Components such as vCloud Networking and Security (vCNS) and vCloud Director in VMware vCloud Suite also depend on vCenter. vCenter can be used for creating, managing, and importing or exporting virtual machines. It can also be used for monitoring performance, taking snapshots, recovering failed virtual machines, and displaying error messages. This chapter covers some basics about vCenter. It also provides hands-on practice for installing and using vCenter.

4.2 vCenter Components

The components included in vCenter form an integrated service for managing VMware vCloud Suite and many other third-party services. Tools and features are also provided by vCenter for optimizing virtualization and the cloud environment at the enterprise level. The following are some of the components that will be installed during the installation of vCenter:

- *vCenter Single Sign-On (SSO):* vCenter SSO offers the authentication service for the objects and services included in the VMware cloud infrastructure.
- *vCenter Inventory Service:* It is designed to reduce communication workload between vCenter Server and its clients.
- *vSphere Web Client:* It allows users to remotely access vCenter Server through a Web browser.
- *vCenter Server:* vCenter Server is the centralized management tool for managing the VMware computing environment.

vCenter SSO: To access an individual server, the user may need to be authenticated. In a multiple-server environment, to access multiple servers, the user has to be authenticated many times at multiple locations. vCenter SSO provides a centralized authentication environment. The following are some benefits of using SSO:

- Instead of letting each software or server authenticate the user individually, SSO centralizes the authentication task.
- The software and servers connected to vCenter are allowed to communicate with each other. SSO also makes the software and servers trust each other.
- SSO supports third-party authentication resources such as Microsoft Active Directory, OpenLDAP, and Network Information Service repositories. In addition, SSO even supports an authentication mechanism mixed with these authentication resources.
- SSO supports multiple instances of an authentication resource. The multiple authentication instances can be configured differently and be located in multiple geographical locations.

vCenter Inventory Service: To reduce communication workload between vCenter Server and a Web client, vCenter Inventory Service can be installed on a separate server that is located near a Web client. In such a way, the Web client does not have to retrieve information from vCenter Server directly. By reading or writing the content from the Inventory Service nearby, the response time can be reduced significantly. For a large enterprise-level computing environment, the Inventory Service can really be beneficial. Another benefit is that the Inventory Service allows users to make their own inventory object–level tags for better organizing and quicker searching inventory objects. Multiple coexisting Inventory Service servers can also be created for multiple administrators located in different locations. When an Elastic Sky X Integrated (ESXi) host is viewed under the Inventory View, you will see a list of tabs on the top part of the screen, as shown in Figure 4.1.

Brief descriptions of these tabs are given as follows:

■ *Summary:* The Summary tab presents information about the physical hardware such as the storage device and network device. It also provides the status of vMotion and vSphere Fault Tolerance.

■ *Virtual Machines:* This tab provides the usage information about the virtual machines that are running on an ESXi host.
■ *Performance:* This tab provides information about the performance of an ESXi host.
■ *Configuration:* This tab allows the administrator to configure storage devices, networks, and security measures.
■ *Tasks & Events:* This tab lists information about the tasks and events on vCenter Server.
■ *Alarms:* This tab provides information about the alarms and their definitions. When an error occurs, the health of an ESXi host is in a dreadful condition, or the ESXi host is about to run out of computing resources an alarm is issued.
■ *Permissions:* This tab lists permissions granted by an ESXi host.
■ *Maps:* This tab displays maps about the relations among the ESXi hosts, virtual machines, and other computing resources.
■ *Storage Views:* This tab displays information related to storage devices such as the used disk space, the amount of space used by snapshots, the status of network interface cards (NICs), and the paths to a storage device.

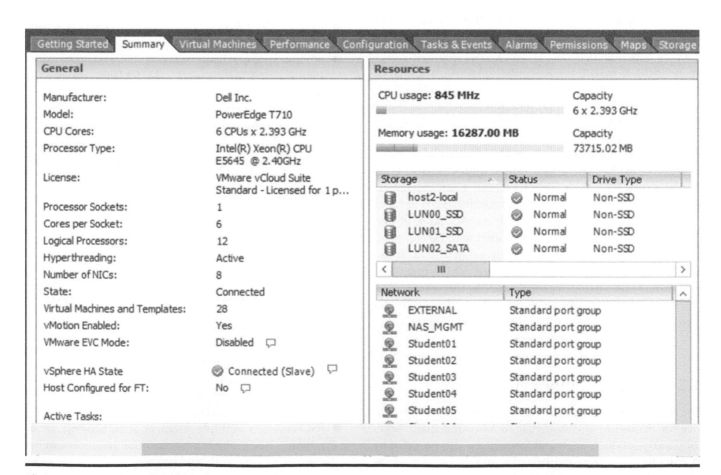

Figure 4.1   vCenter Inventory View.

- *Hardware Status:* This tab provides hardware information such as power supplies and central processing unit (CPU) temperature.

vSphere Web Client: vSphere Web Client is a Web browser–based client software (Figure 4.2). It can be used to connect a client to vCenter Server for managing databases, storage devices, ESXi hosts, virtual machines, virtual networks, licenses, users, roles, and many other VMware objects. As client software, vSphere Web Client offers the following features:

- It can be used to access vCenter Server installed on the server with either the Windows operating system or the Linux operating system.
- It is able to manage VMware objects through the Internet at any time and from anywhere.
- It can be customized to meet different requirements from different users.

When a log-on request is issued by a user, the user's credentials will be sent to vCenter SSO for authentication. Once the user is verified by the authentication mechanism, a security token will be issued to the user to log on to vCenter and to access the VMware objects managed by vCenter.

vCenter Server: vCenter Server is an application that provides a centralized management tool. vCenter can be used to manage virtual machines hosted by multiple VMware ESXi hosts. Once logged on to vCenter, the administrator can access all the hosts and all the virtual machines. The following are some of the major tasks that can be accomplished by vCenter Server:

- *User management:* Centralizing user management
- *Virtual machine management:* Creating, viewing, and managing virtual machines
- *Virtual machine migration:* Migrating virtual machines between hosts, between a host and storage, between datacenters, and between storage devices
- *Resource management:* Creating and managing host clusters for load balancing, power management, and virtual machine placement
- *HA management:* Supporting computing resource HA
- *Template management:* Creating and managing virtual machine templates
- *Alarm management:* Monitoring and reacting to alarms and error messages
- *Logging management:* Providing logging services

User management: vCenter provides SSO for the user and group authentication. Users can access vCenter through vSphere Client (Figure 4.3) or through vSphere Web Client.

When vCenter receives a logon request from a user, it verifies the username and password against Active Directory on the domain controller. Once the user is verified, the user

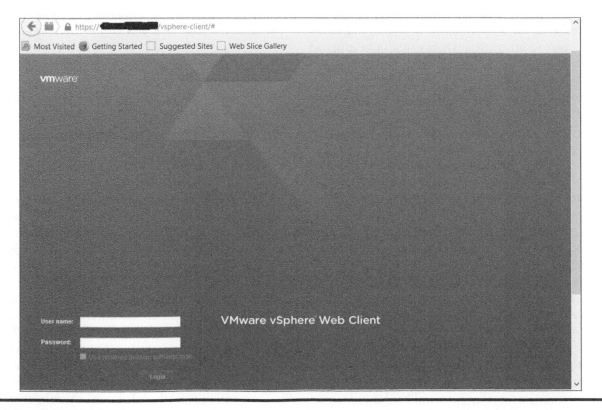

Figure 4.2   vSphere Web Client.

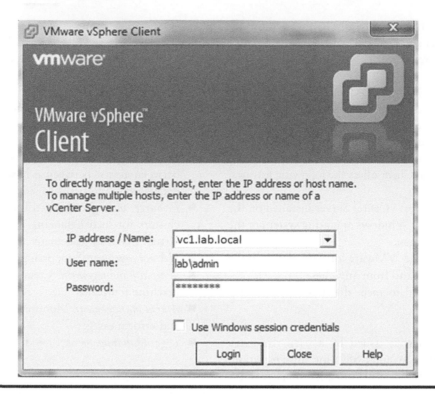

Figure 4.3   vSphere Client.

gets permission to access vCenter. Once logged on to vCenter, the user with the administrator permission can manage datacenters, ESXi hosts, and virtual machines. With the administrator permission, the user can create new users and assign proper privileges to other users. Users can also be assigned permissions at the at the ESXi host level, virtual machine level, and datacenter level.

To manage a large number of users, one can group these users based on their roles and privileges. vCenter provides 11 commonly used roles, each assigned at different levels of privilege. Table 4.1 lists the roles and privileges.

After a new user is created, the user can be added to one or more groups assigned with these roles. Once a role is assigned, the user will have the privilege to perform certain tasks. Figure 4.4 illustrates users created in vCenter.

Virtual machine management: In vCenter, a user with proper permission can view and manage an individual virtual machine or a group of virtual machines. With the administrator permission, a user can do the following:

- Create a new virtual machine and install guest operation system and application software on a newly created virtual machine
- Create a virtual machine by cloning an existing virtual machine or a template
- Add, remove, and configure virtual hardware devices
- Organize the virtual machine file system

- Monitor virtual machine performance
- Start, shut down, suspend, or resume a virtual machine, or take a snapshot of a running virtual machine
- Reset the properties of a virtual machine and rename the virtual machine
- Remove a virtual machine from the inventory or delete it from the hard disk
- Migrate virtual machines from one host to another host manually through the hot migration tool vMotion
- Allocate and enforce constraints of computing resources, such as CPU time and virtual hard disk space, on virtual machines

Through vSphere Client or through vSphere Web Client, a console can be launched to display a virtual machine's desktop, as shown in Figure 4.5. Through the console, the user can manage the guest operating system, application software, system service, and the file system of the virtual machine.

Virtual machine migration: In vCenter, virtual machines can be migrated from one host to another host or from a host to a network storage device and vice versa. Table 4.2 describes some methods to migrate virtual machines.

The migration of powered-off virtual machines is known as cold migration, which can be performed manually or according to a scheduled task. The migration of suspended or powered-on virtual machines is known as hot

Table 4.1   vCenter Roles and Privileges

Role	Privilege
Administrator	Users and groups assigned with this role are allowed to access, view, and modify all the objects in vCenter.
Read-only	Users or groups assigned with this role are allowed to view and examine the state of an object in vCenter. However, these users are not allowed to modify an object.
No access	Users or groups assigned with this role are not allowed to view and modify an object in vCenter.
VM administrator	Users or groups with this role are allowed to access, view, move, and modify a virtual machine in vCenter.
VM user	Users or groups with this role are allowed to access and run software on a virtual machine. The users with this role can also power on or off and reset a virtual machine.
VM power user	In addition to using a virtual machine, users or groups with this role are allowed to alter the hardware settings and create snapshots of a virtual machine.
Resource pool administrator	Users or groups with this role are allowed to create and assign resource pools to virtual machines.
Datacenter administrator	Users or groups with this role are allowed to manage datacenter objects.
Consolidated Backup user	Users or groups with this role are allowed to run VMware Consolidated Backup.
Datastore consumer	Users or groups with this role are allowed to use the storage of a datastore.
Network consumer	Users or groups with this role are allowed to connect a virtual machine or a host to a network.

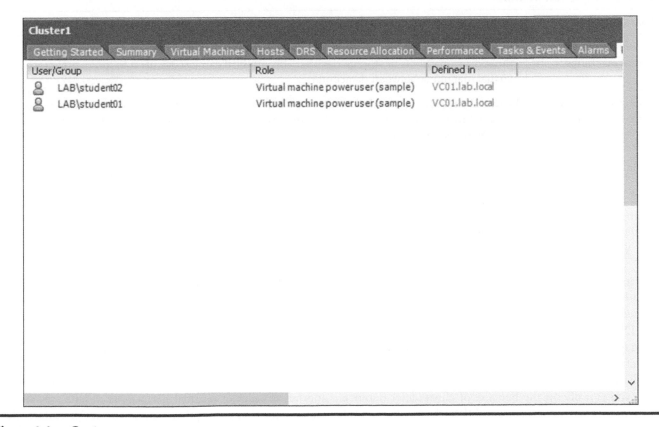

Figure 4.4   vCenter users.

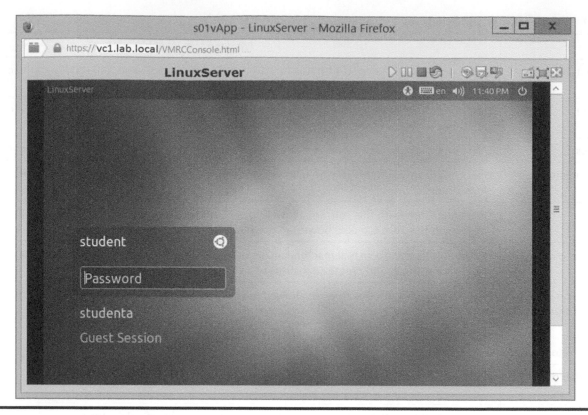

Figure 4.5 Virtual machine console.

Table 4.2 Migration Methods

Migration Method	Description
Moving powered-off virtual machines	With this method, powered-off virtual machines, configuration files, or virtual disks can be moved among hosts or storage devices. This method can also be used to move powered-off virtual machines between datacenters.
Moving suspended virtual machines	With this method, suspended virtual machines, configuration files, or virtual disks can be moved among hosts and storage devices. This method can also be used to move suspended virtual machines between datacenters.
Moving powered-on virtual machines with vMotion	With vMotion, powered-on virtual machines can be moved to another host without any interruption. However, vMotion cannot move virtual machines between datacenters.
Moving powered-on virtual machines with Storage vMotion	Virtual disks or configuration files of a powered-on virtual machine can be moved among datastores without any interruption.

migration. Figure 4.6 illustrates the network configuration for vMotion.

Resource management: VMware ESXi includes a feature called Distributed Resource Scheduler (DRS), which is used to manage computing resources. A VMware DRS cluster is a collection of ESX/ESXi hosts, associated virtual machines with shared resources, and a shared management interface. Before you can obtain the benefits of cluster-level resource management, you must create a DRS cluster. Figure 4.7 illustrates the DRS properties page.

The DRS service can be used to group ESXi hosts into clusters. Once a host becomes a member of a cluster, its resource is integrated into the cluster's resources. A cluster-wide resource allocation policy can be set for resource distribution. The cluster-wide load balancing monitors the usage of CPUs and memory by the hosts in the cluster. The load-balancing service moves the workload from one host to another to achieve optimal performance. This service also makes sure that appropriate computing resources are allocated to the virtual machines on each host.

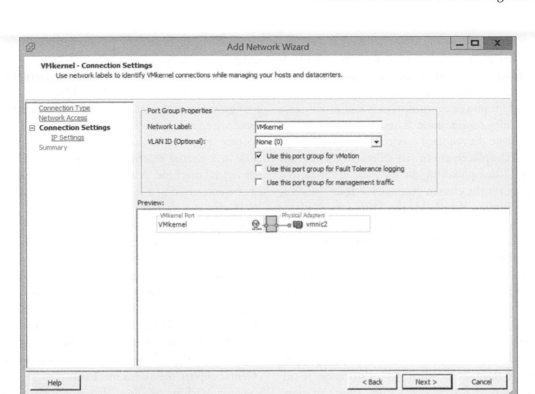

Figure 4.6   Network configuration for vMotion.

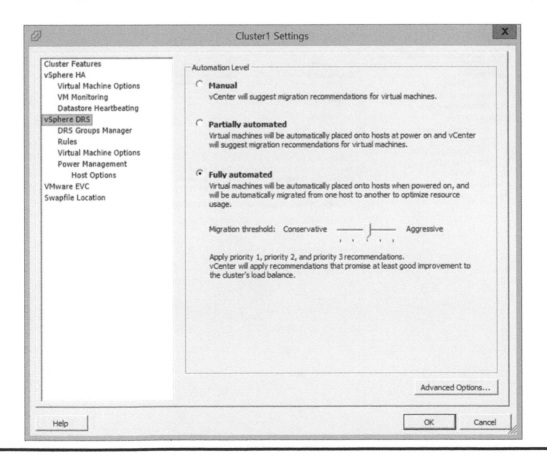

Figure 4.7   Properties of DRS.

The DRS service compares the power demand of each host in a cluster. It manages power consumption dynamically. It optimizes power consumption by keeping the power on for the host whose power consumption demand is high. Otherwise, when the demand for power consumption is low, it will place the host in the standby power mode. It makes sure to power on enough hosts to make the required services function properly.

DRS controls the placement of virtual machines on hosts within a cluster. When powering on a virtual machine in a cluster, depending on the chosen automation level, which is known as the migration threshold, the DRS service places the virtual machine on an appropriate host.

HA management: During the event of host failure, HA provides protection against the host operating system or hardware failure. In a cluster, HA monitors the hosts. In the case that a host fails, HA moves its virtual machines to other hosts that have room to accommodate more virtual machines. Figure 4.8 illustrates the properties of HA.

Template management: A VMware template can be used as a model for cloning more virtual machines. A template can be made from an existing virtual machine. It can be used as a backup of a virtual machine. One can clone a virtual machine from another virtual machine directly or from a template. The difference is that a template cannot be modified and powered on; therefore, the configuration of the template can be protected. Figure 4.9 illustrates the configuration of a template.

With vCenter, one can convert a virtual machine to a template and deploy a virtual machine from a template. The configuration of the template cannot be modified. However, there are some situations where it is necessary to update an existing template. In such a case, one can convert a template back to a virtual machine and make necessary changes on the virtual machine. After the virtual machine is updated, it can be converted to a template again.

Alarm management: vCenter provides mechanisms to monitor vSphere performance and to actively react to alarms. It monitors virtual machines, hosts, storage, servers, virtual networks, and other objects in the system. It issues alarms to the administrator in case of network problems, performance issues, storage capacity shortage, or hardware failure. The mechanisms provided by vCenter include performance charts, command-line tools, and alarm notifications. Figure 4.10 illustrates an alarm for a network connection problem.

To alert the administrator of VMware infrastructure, vCenter applies the alarm mechanism to each object such as a virtual machine or a host. It sets alarms on abnormal performance and the usage of computing resources. vCenter provides the resource usage information through the Summary page. Each host or virtual machine has its own Summary

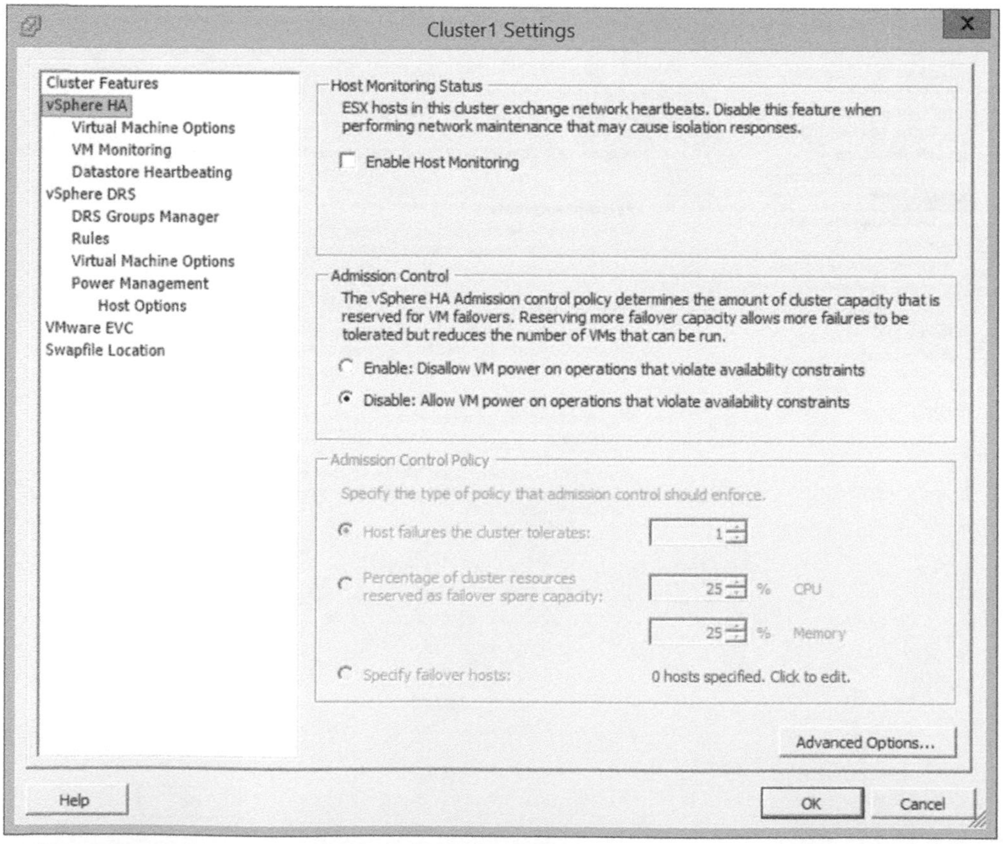

Figure 4.8 Properties of HA.

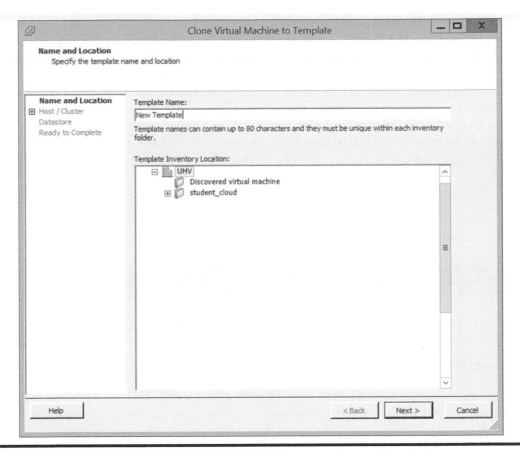

Figure 4.9 Template configuration.

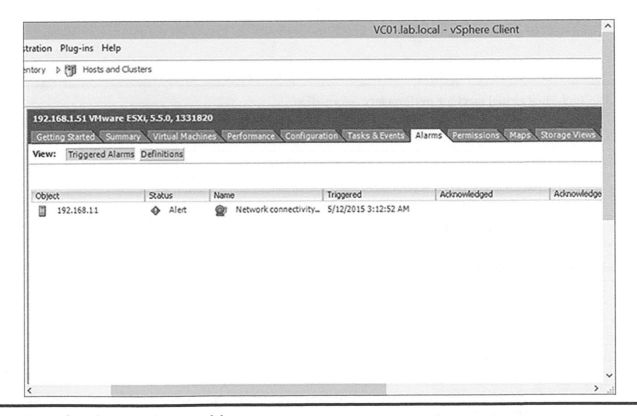

Figure 4.10 Alarm for network connectivity.

page. On the Summary page, the administrator can find the summarized information about the performance and resource usage. Each individual object managed by vCenter also provides performance information, as shown in Figure 4.11.

Based on the object, the performance data are collected and organized into logical groups. The data collection can be configured to have a specified duration and the type of data to be collected. Statistics for one or more logical groups can be displayed in a chart.

Logging management: In vCenter, a log file records actions carried out by machines and users. Log files are grouped according to their components and purposes. The log files can be used for troubleshooting and tracking user activities. Table 4.3 lists and describes some commonly used log files.

One can find many other log files in vCenter. Detailed coverage of the log files is beyond the scope of this book. Figure 4.12 shows the vCenter Server client log file.

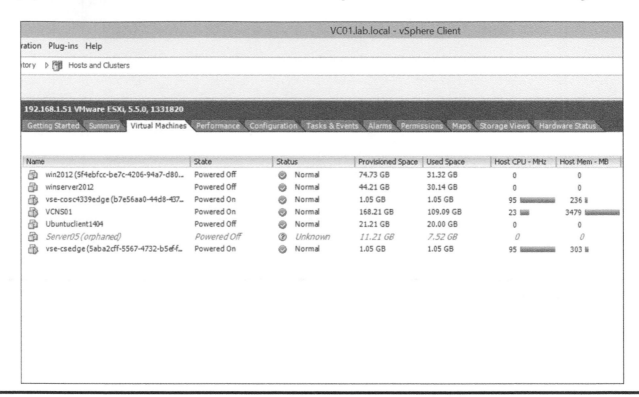

Figure 4.11 Individual virtual machine performance information.

Table 4.3 Log Files

Log File	Description
vmware-vpx\vpxd.log	vpxd.log is the main vCenter Server log that includes information about connection, communication, tasks, and events related to vCenter activities.
vmware-vpx\vpxd-alert.log	vCenter vpxd-alert.log includes nonfatal information about the vpxd process.
perfcharts\stats.log	It is the performance chart log including information about chart loading and displaying activities.
invsvc	The Inventory Service log includes information about changes of inventory formats and locations.
vmdird	The Directory Service daemon log includes information about Lightweight Directory Access Protocol operations and replication within SSO.
vsphere-client	The vSphere Web Client log includes information about Web Client activities such as start, status, or crash.
vws	The System and Hardware Health Manager log includes information about hardware activities such as start, status, or crash.

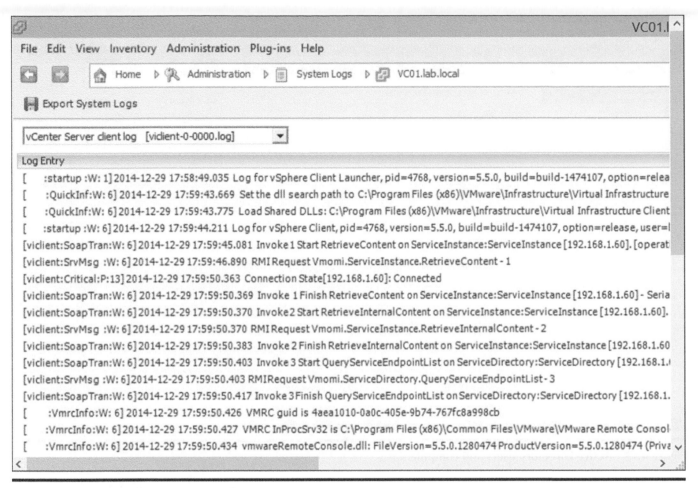

Figure 4.12 vCenter Server client log file.

4.3 Activity 1: Installing and Configuring vCenter Appliance 6

There are two ways to install vCenter Appliance. One way is to install it on a virtual machine with 8-GB random access memory, 140-GB storage space, and two NICs. The other way is to install it on an ESXi host, which is installed in Chapter 3. In this section, you will install and configure vCenter Appliance, which is a virtual machine with vCenter installed. Before installing vCenter Appliance, make sure that the domain controller has been installed and properly configured, as shown in Chapter 2. The installation and configuration of vCenter Appliance can be accomplished with the following tasks:

- *Task 1:* Installation preparation
- *Task 2:* vCenter Server installation
- *Task 3:* Accessing vCenter Appliance with vSphere Web Client

4.3.1 Task 1: Installation Preparation

Before the vCenter Server installation process gets started, prepare your virtual machines with the following steps:

- The domain controller DC is connected to an ESXi host in the same network.
- The vCenter Appliance ISO file is saved in the Document folder in the domain controller DC.
- In Active Directory, create a user vmadmin who has the administrator privilege. In DNS server, enter a new record vc.uhv.edu <—> 10.0.0.3.

The following steps are used to prepare for the installation:

1. Start the DC virtual machine. On the Server Manager page, click the **Tools** menu and click **Active Directory Users and Computers** to open the Active Directory Users and Computers dialog, as shown in Figure 4.13.

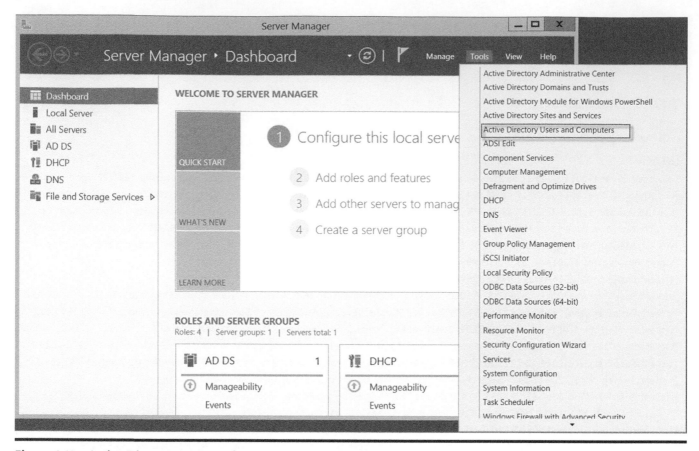

Figure 4.13 Active Directory users and computers.

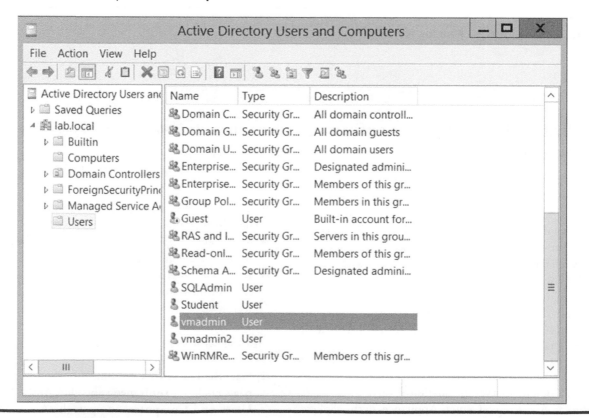

Figure 4.14 Creating new user vmadmin.

2. Create a new user **vmadmin** by right-clicking the **Users** link and selecting **New** and then **User**.
3. In the New Object—User dialog, specify the user logon name as **vmadmin** and click **Next**. Enter the password, click **Next** and then **Finish**. The newly added user is shown in Figure 4.14.
4. To make the user vmadmin a member of the administrators' group, right-click the user **vmadmin** and select **Properties**. Click the tab **Member Of** and click the **Add** button. In the Select Groups dialog, click the button **Advanced** and the button **Find Now**. Select **Administrators**. Similarly, add groups **Domain Admins** and **Enterprise Admins** for the user vmadmin. Then, click **OK** twice.
5. Assume that the vCenter Appliance ISO file has been copied to the Documents directory of your domain controller DC, as shown in Figure 4.15.
6. Double-click the ISO file. After the file is expanded, you will see the plug-in file, as shown in Figure 4.16, in the folder **vcsa**. Double-click the file **VMware-ClientIntegrationPlugin-6.0.0** to install the plug-in.

7. On the Welcome page, click **Next**.
8. On the End-User License Agreement page, accept the license agreement terms and then click **Next**.
9. On the Destination Folder page, take the default destination location, as shown in Figure 4.17. Then, click **Next**.
10. On the Ready to Install the Plug-in page, click **Install**.
11. You need to create a new DNS record for vCenter virtual machine in your domain controller. To do so, click the **Tools** menu. Then, click **DNS**.
12. After the DNS dialog is opened, right-click your domain lab.local and select **New Host (A or AAAA)**, as shown in Figure 4.18.
13. In the New Host dialog, enter **vc** as the vCenter server name, **vc.lab.local** as the fully qualified domain name, and 10.0.0.3 as the IP address (Figure 4.19). Then, click the **Add Host** button.
14. In the DNS Manager dialog, you should be able to see that the record for the new host is added, as shown in Figure 4.20. Then, close the dialog.

You are now ready to install vCenter Appliance.

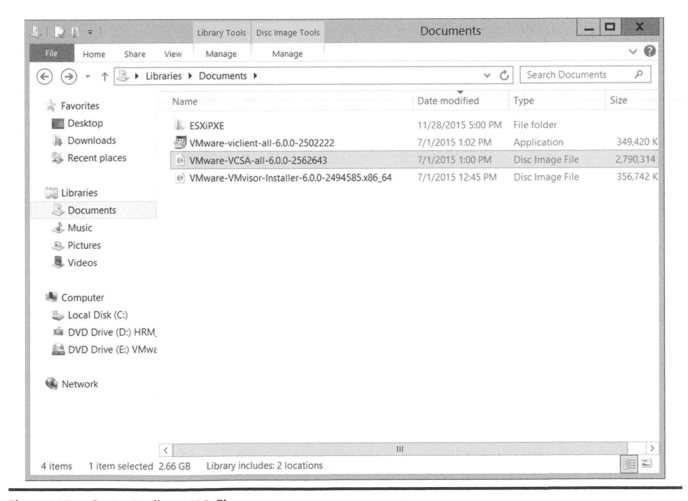

Figure 4.15   vCenter Appliance ISO file.

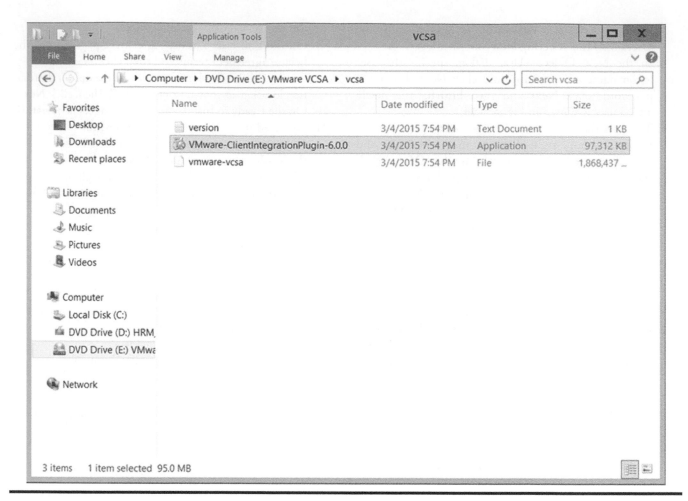

Figure 4.16 Installing plug-in file.

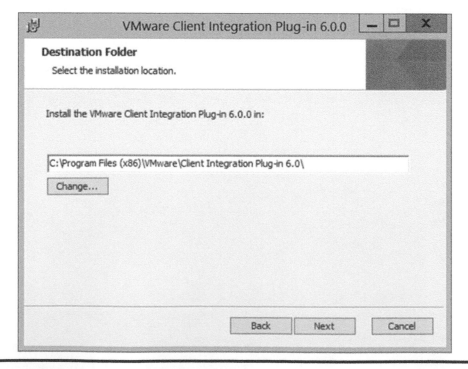

Figure 4.17 Destination folder for Client Integration Plug-in.

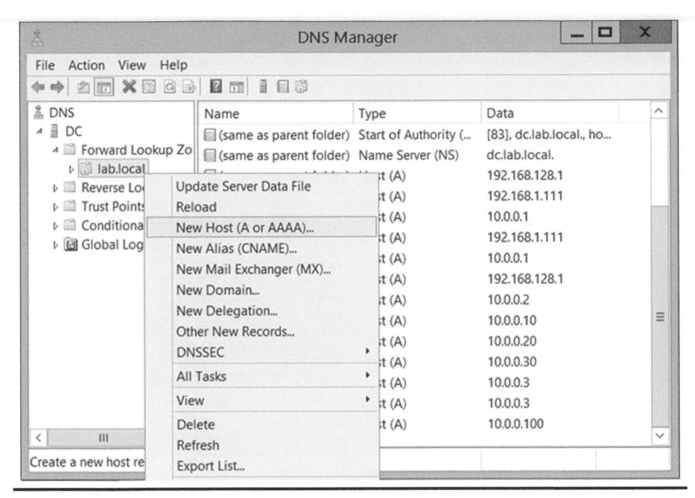

Figure 4.18 Creating new host.

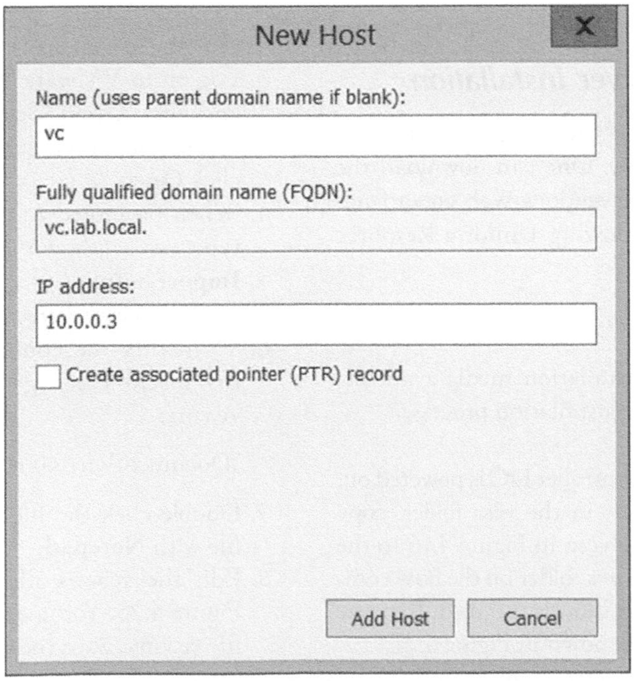

Figure 4.19 New host.

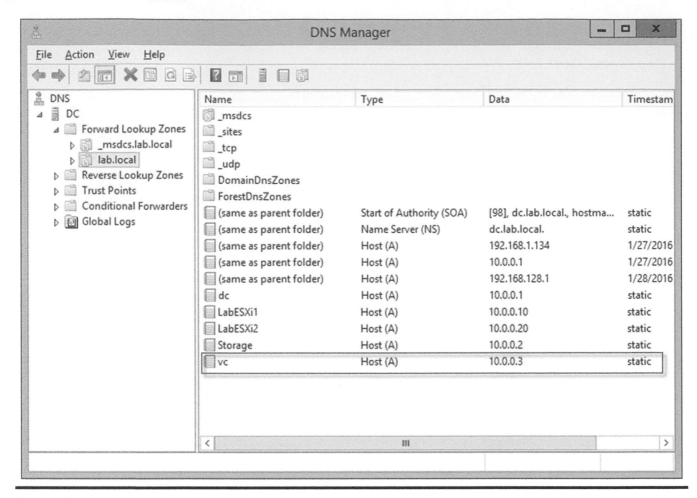

Figure 4.20   New host record.

4.3.2 Task 2: vCenter Server Installation

To install vCenter Appliance, you need to get the installation media downloaded and ready. One can download the installation media from a software vendor's Web site or from VMware directly through the following Uniform Resource Locator (URL):

http://www.vmware.com/download/

Assume that you have the installation media available; follow the steps below to start the installation process.

1. Make sure that the domain controller DC is powered on.
2. To install vCenter Appliance, in the vcsa folder, copy and paste the folder **vmware-vcsa** in Figure 4.16 to the **Documents/Virtual Machines** folder on the host computer where VMware Workstation is installed. Rename the file **vmware-vcsa.ova**, as shown in Figure 4.21.

3. Log on to VMware Workstation, click the **File** menu and click **Open**. Select the **vmware-vcsa** file in the Documents directory, as shown in Figure 4.22. Then, click **Open**.
4. When prompted to enter the virtual machine name, type **vc**, as shown in Figure 4.23. Then, click the **Import** button.
5. On the License Agreement page, click the **Accept** button.
6. To modify the configuration of the installed vc virtual machine, navigate to the folder containing the file vc.vmx:

   \Document\virtual machines\vc\vc.vmx

7. Double-click the file vc.vmx (Figure 4.24). Open the file with **Notepad**.
8. Edit the vc.vmx file by adding the lines shown in Figure 4.25. You may enter your own password in the file vc.vmx. Save the changes and exit.

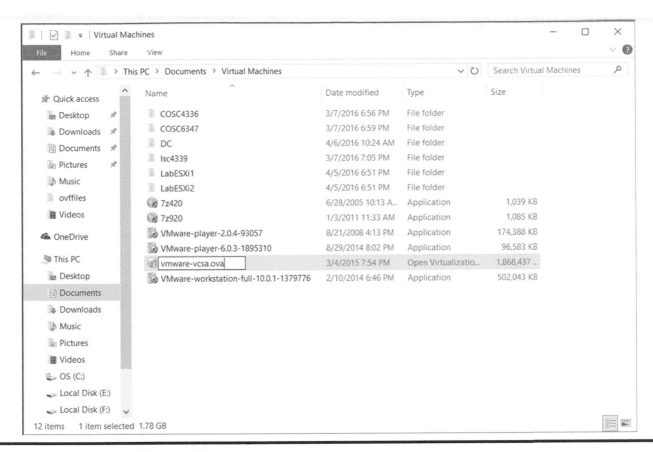

Figure 4.21 Executing installation file.

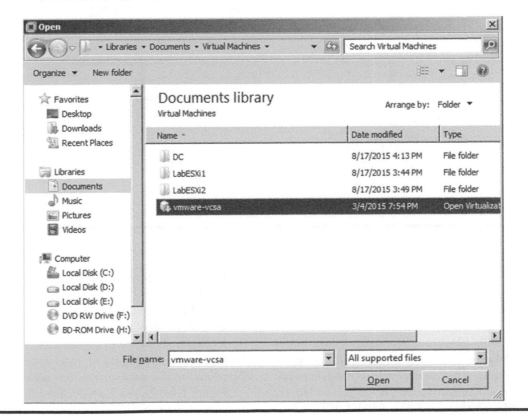

Figure 4.22 Opening vmware-vcsa file.

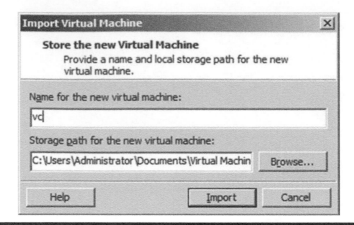

Figure 4.23 Name for new virtual machine.

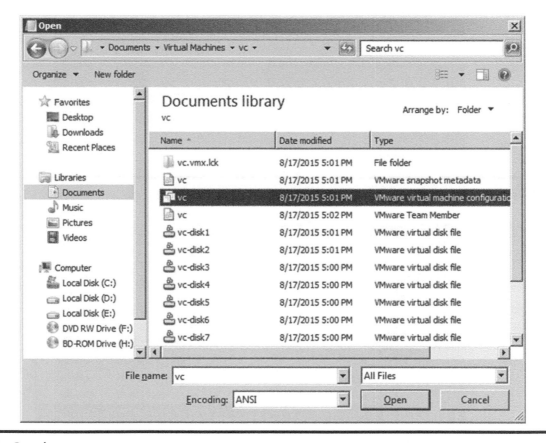

Figure 4.24 Opening vc.vmx.

9. To make sure that the virtual machine vc is connected to the domain controller DC, right-click the virtual machine vc in VMware Workstation and select **Settings**.

10. In the Virtual Machine Settings dialog, select **Network Adapter** in the left pane and check the option **Custom**. Then, select the virtual network where the domain controller DC is connected to, such as **VMnet2** (Figure 4.26). Click **OK** to accept the configuration.

11. You can now power on the virtual machine vc (Figure 4.27).

12. Press **F2** and enter the user name **root** and the password **Passw0rd!** (or your password) to log on to vCenter Server, as shown in Figure 4.28.

13. Once you have logged on to vCenter Server, you may configure the password or the network, as shown in Figure 4.29. As you have done the network configuration in the vc.vmx file, you may press **Esc** key to log out.

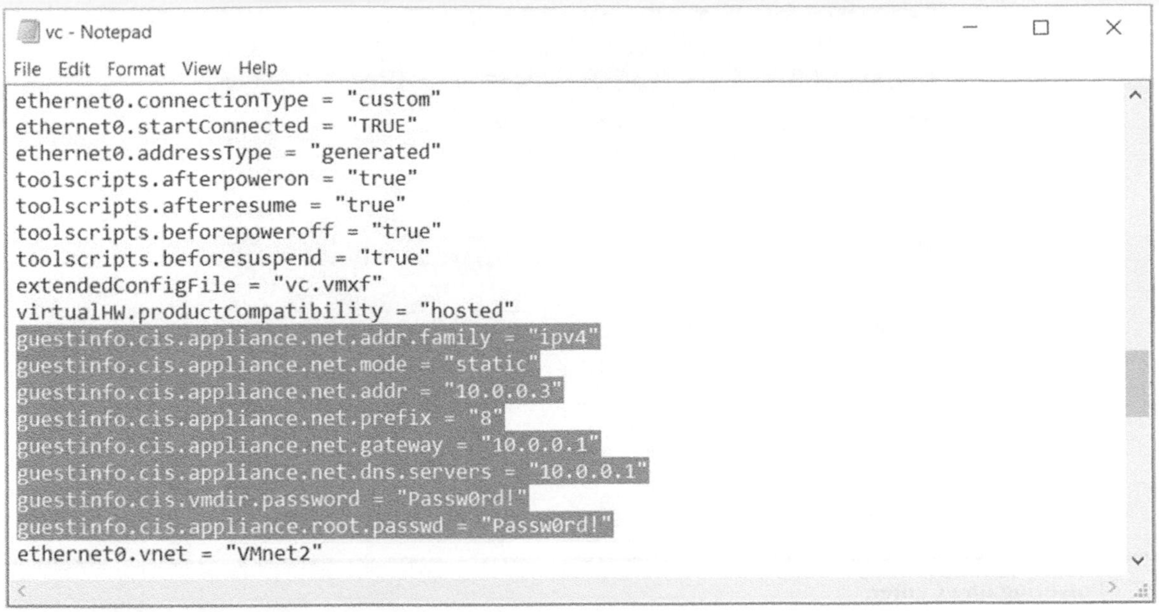

vc - Notepad
File Edit Format View Help
ethernet0.connectionType = "custom"
ethernet0.startConnected = "TRUE"
ethernet0.addressType = "generated"
toolscripts.afterpoweron = "true"
toolscripts.afterresume = "true"
toolscripts.beforepoweroff = "true"
toolscripts.beforesuspend = "true"
extendedConfigFile = "vc.vmxf"
virtualHW.productCompatibility = "hosted"
guestinfo.cis.appliance.net.addr.family = "ipv4"
guestinfo.cis.appliance.net.mode = "static"
guestinfo.cis.appliance.net.addr = "10.0.0.3"
guestinfo.cis.appliance.net.prefix = "8"
guestinfo.cis.appliance.net.gateway = "10.0.0.1"
guestinfo.cis.appliance.net.dns.servers = "10.0.0.1"
guestinfo.cis.vmdir.password = "Passw0rd!"
guestinfo.cis.appliance.root.passwd = "Passw0rd!"
ethernet0.vnet = "VMnet2"

Figure 4.25 Editing vc.vmx.

Virtual Machine Settings
Hardware
Options
Device
Summary
Memory 8 GB
Processors 2
Hard Disk (SCSI) 12 GB
Hard Disk 2 (SCSI) 1.3 GB
Hard Disk 9 (SCSI) 1 GB
Hard Disk 10 (SC... 10 GB
Hard Disk 11 (SC... 5 GB
Hard Disk 3 (SCSI) 25 GB
Hard Disk 4 (SCSI) 25 GB
Hard Disk 5 (SCSI) 10 GB
Hard Disk 6 (SCSI) 10 GB
Hard Disk 7 (SCSI) 5 GB
Hard Disk 8 (SCSI) 10 GB
CD/DVD (IDE) Auto detect
Network Adapter Bridged (Automatic)
Display Auto detect
Device status
Connected
Connect at power on
Network connection
Bridged: Connected directly to the physical network
Replicate physical network connection state
NAT: Used to share the host's IP address
Host-only: A private network shared with the host
Custom: Specific virtual network
VMnet2 (Custom)
LAN segment:
LAN Segments...
Advanced...
Add...
Remove
OK
Cancel
Help

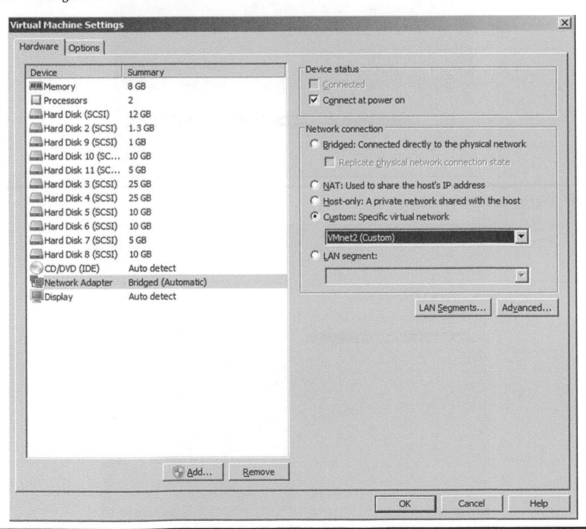

Figure 4.26 Virtual machine network adapter settings.

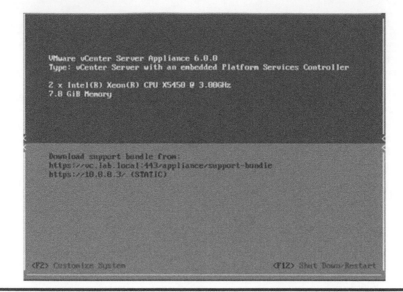

Figure 4.27 Powering on vCenter.

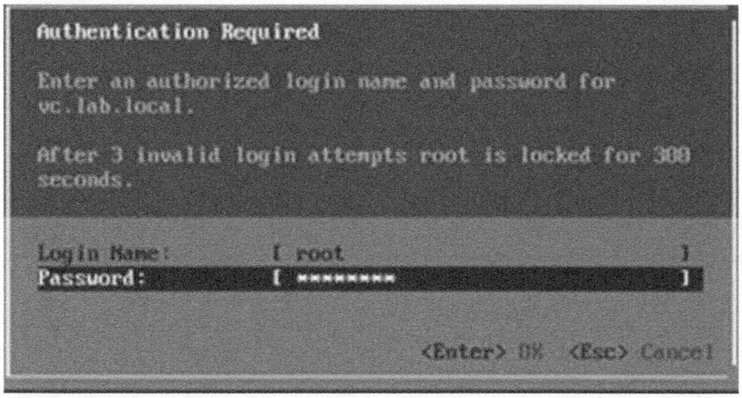

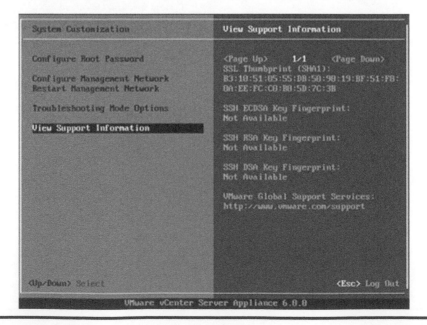

Figure 4.28 Logging on to vCenter Server.

Figure 4.29 vCenter Server configuration.

4.3.3 Task 3: Accessing vCenter Appliance with vSphere Web Client

In this task, you will use the vSphere Web Client software to access vCenter Appliance. The following are the steps to accomplish this task:

1. To log on to vCenter through vSphere Web Client from the domain controller DC, you need to install the Desktop Experience feature on DC. Log on to **DC**, on the Server Manager page, click **Add roles and features**.
2. Click **Next** several times until you get to the Select features page. Expand **User interfaces and infrastructure** and select **Desktop Experience**, as shown in Figure 4.30.
3. Click **Next** and click **Install** to complete.
4. In your browser, enter the following URL:

   https://vc.lab.local

5. A warning message may appear. Accept the warning to continue to the Web site.

6. You will be prompted to enter the logon credentials for SSO, as shown in Figure 4.31. Enter the user name **administrator@vsphere.local** and your password.
7. Once logged on, you should be able to see the home page shown in Figure 4.32. Click the **Hosts and Clusters** icon.
8. To add a datacenter, click the **vc.lab.local** node in the Navigator pane. Click the tab **Getting Started** and click the link **Create Datacenter**, as shown in Figure 4.33.
9. Keep the name as **Datacenter** and click **OK**, as shown in Figure 4.34.
10. To add a cluster, click **Datacenter** in the Navigator pane. Then, click the link **Create a cluster**, as shown in Figure 4.35.
11. Enter **Cluster** as the name and turn on the features **DRS** and **vSphere HA**, as shown in Figure 4.36. Then, click **OK**.
12. To add an ESXi host to vCenter for management, right-click the **Cluster** node and select **Add Host**, as shown in Figure 4.37.

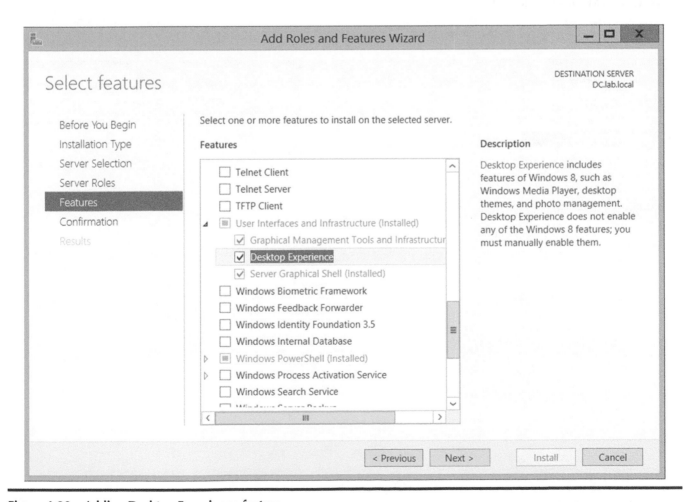

Figure 4.30   Adding Desktop Experience feature.

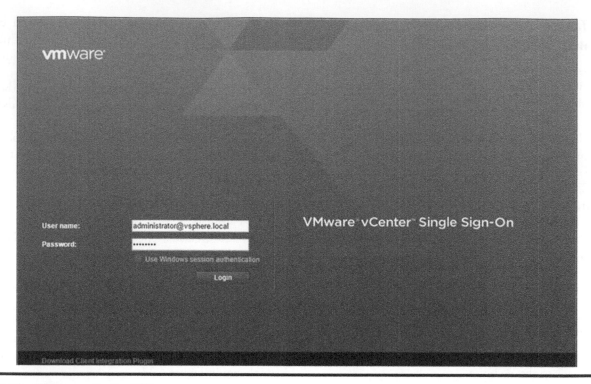

Figure 4.31 VMware vCenter SSO.

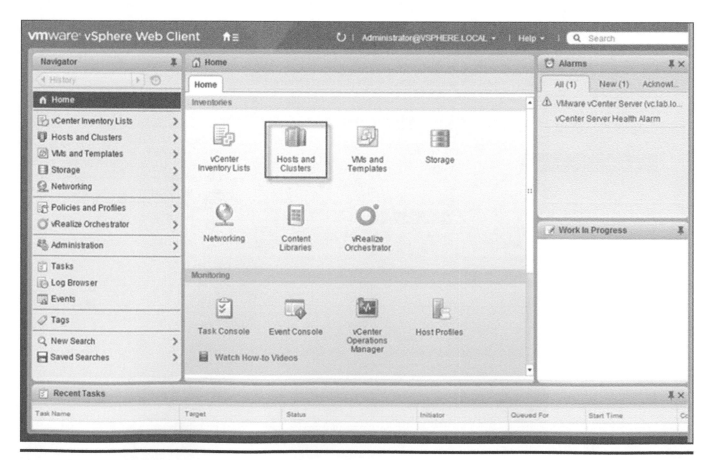

Figure 4.32 vCenter home page.

Figure 4.33 Creating Datacenter.

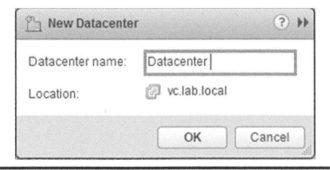

Figure 4.34 Datacenter name.

13. Enter the host name or IP address such as **LabESXi1**. Then, click **Next**.
14. Enter the host user name **root** and your password, as shown in Figure 4.38. Then, click **Next** a few times and click **Finish**.
15. Similarly, add the host LabESXi2 to vCenter. Figure 4.39 shows that two hosts are added.
16. To create a virtual machine on the host LabESXi1, click the node **labesxi1.lab.local** and click the link **Create a new virtual machine**, as shown in Figure 4.39.

17. On the Select a creation type page, select **Create a new virtual machine**, as shown in Figure 4.40, and click **Next**.
18. On the Select a name and folder page, name the virtual machine **myvm**, as shown in Figure 4.41, and click **Next**.
19. On the Select a compute resource page, select **labesxi1. lab.local**, as shown in Figure 4.42, and click **Next** twice.
20. On the Select compatibility page, select **ESXi 5.5 and later**, as shown in Figure 4.43, and click **Next**.

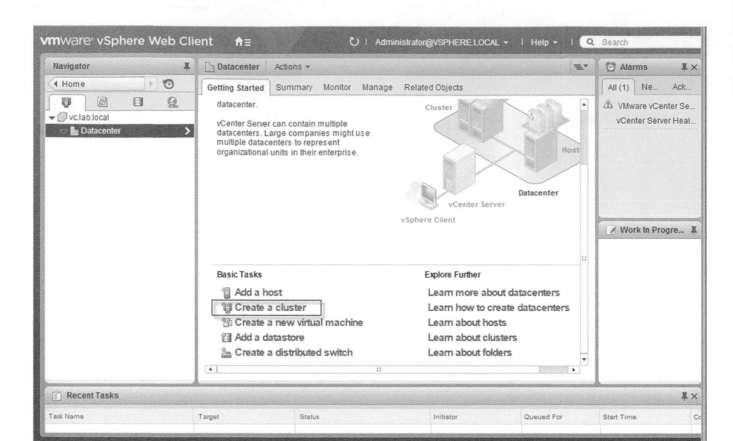

Figure 4.35 Creating cluster.

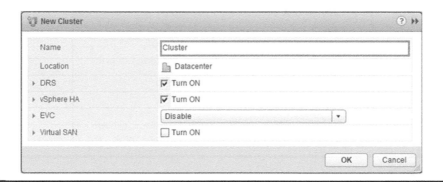

Figure 4.36 Cluster name.

21. On the Select a guest OS page, specify Guest OS Family as **Linux** and Guest OS Version as **Ubuntu Linux (32-bit)**, as shown in Figure 4.44. Then, click **Next**.
22. On the Customize hardware page, specify CPU, Memory, and New Hard Disk, as shown in Figure 4.45, and click **Next**.
23. On the Ready to complete page, click **Finish**, as shown in Figure 4.46.

24. After the virtual machine myvm is created, you can see it on the list under the Cluster node, as shown in Figure 4.47.

In the above, the necessary components of vCenter are installed. Now, you have the interface to access and manage the vSphere objects such as virtual machines hosted by the ESXi servers.

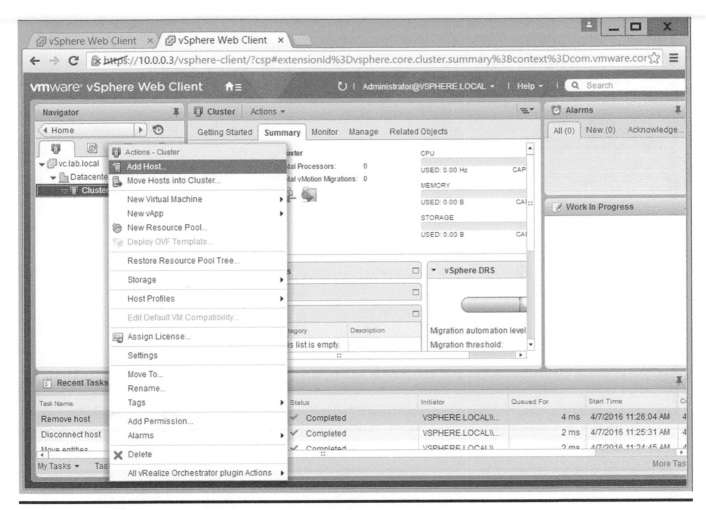

Figure 4.37 Adding host.

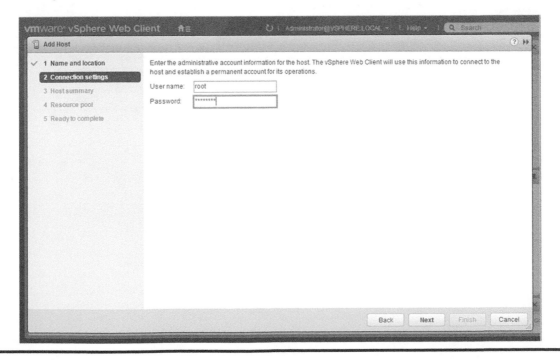

Figure 4.38 Entering host user name and password.

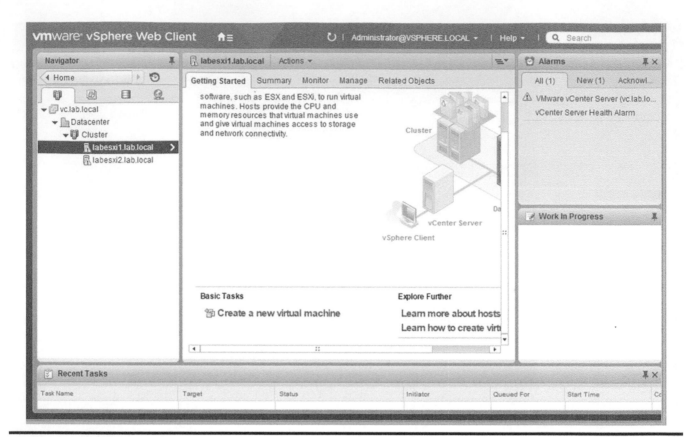

Figure 4.39   Added hosts.

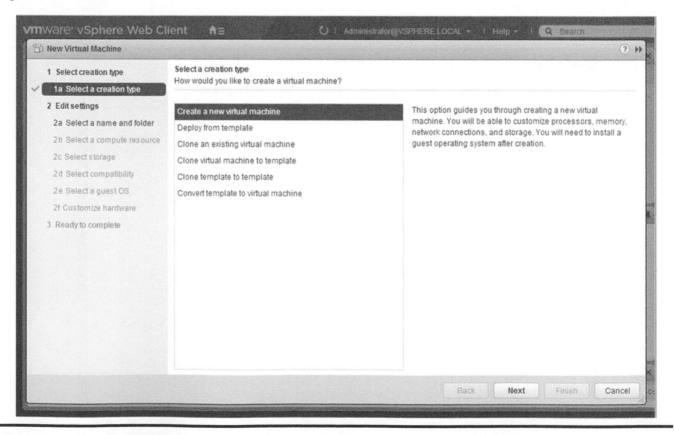

Figure 4.40   Creating new virtual machine.

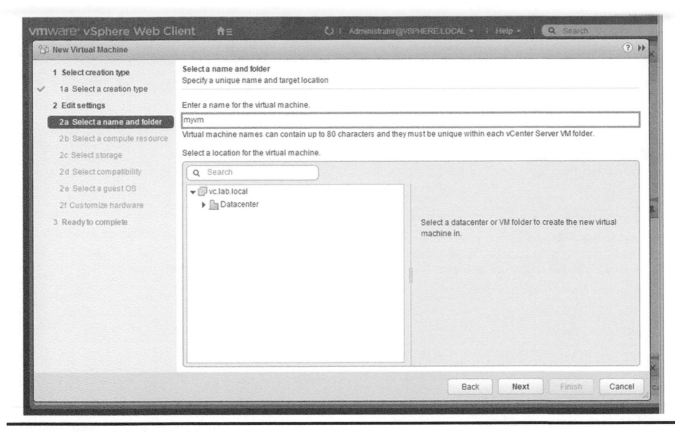

Figure 4.41   Naming virtual machine.

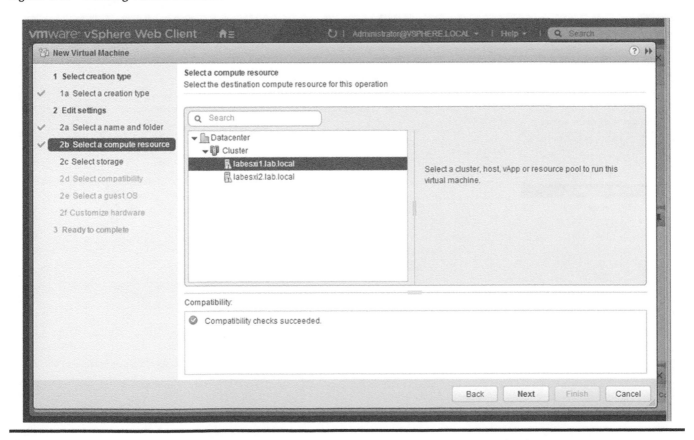

Figure 4.42   Selecting compute resource.

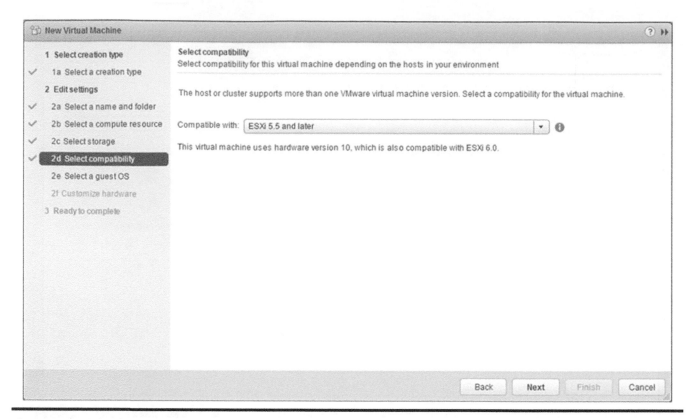

Figure 4.43 Selecting compatibility.

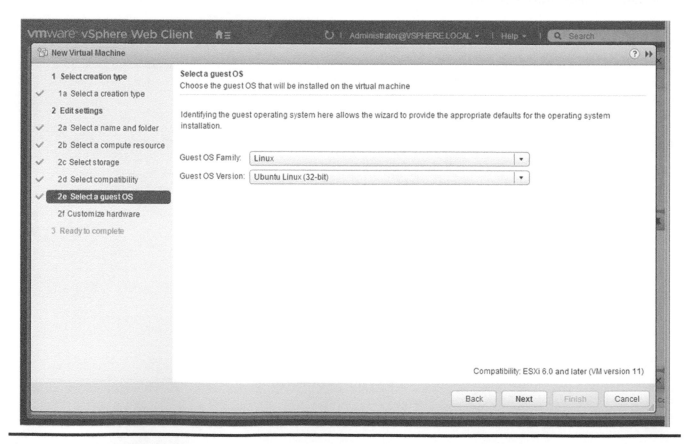

Figure 4.44 Selecting guest OS.

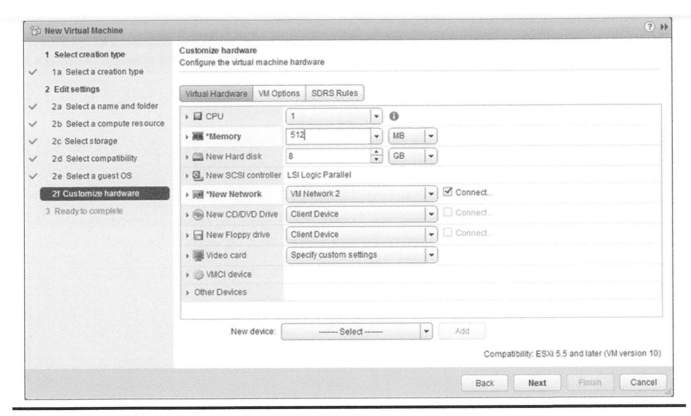

Figure 4.45 Customizing hardware.

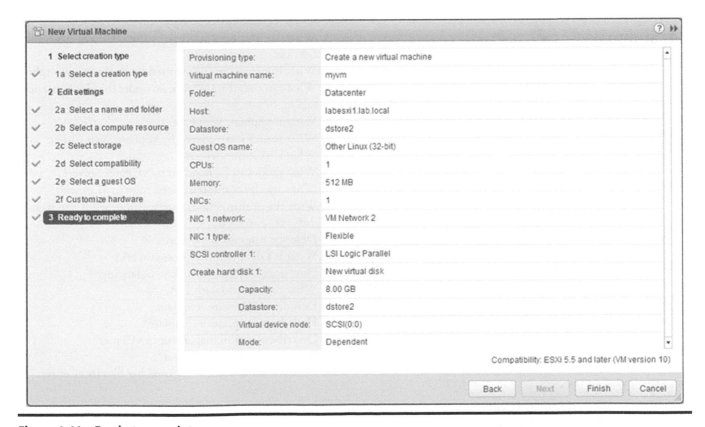

Figure 4.46 Ready to complete.

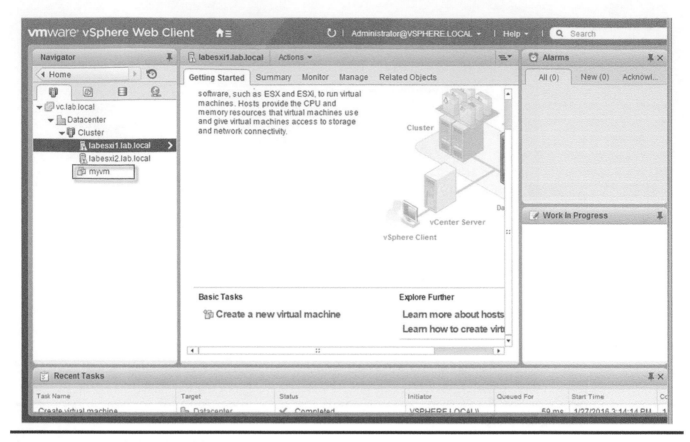

Figure 4.47   Created virtual machine.

4.4 Summary

This chapter introduces the centralized management software vCenter. By using vCenter, administrators can manage multiple ESXi hosts at a centralized location. vCenter can also be used to manage virtual machines and virtual networks. It is the key software to manage advanced features such as HA, Fault Tolerance, and Load Balancing, which are necessary for a private cloud. vCenter can also be used to monitor performance, take snapshots, recover failed virtual machines, and display error messages. This chapter describes the main components of vCenter including SSO, vCenter Inventory Service, vSphere Web Client, and vCenter Server. The installation and configuration of vCenter Appliance is also covered in this chapter. For the hands-on activity, this chapter provides the step-by-step instruction of vCenter Appliance installation. It also demonstrates how to link an ESXi host server to vCenter and how to create virtual machines with vCenter. In the next chapter, you will learn how to create and manage virtual networks with vCenter.

REVIEW QUESTIONS

1. What kind of software is vCenter?
2. What are the benefits of using SSO?
3. What are the benefits by of using vCenter Inventory Service?
4. What information is presented by the Summary tab?
5. What can the administrator do under the Configuration tab?
6. What is vSphere Web Client?
7. What features are offered by vSphere Web Client?
8. What is vCenter Server?
9. What tasks can be handled by vCenter Server?
10. What are the commonly used roles in vCenter?
11. With the administrator's permission, what can a user do?
12. Describe migration methods.
13. What is DRS, and how does it work?
14. How does DRS perform load balancing?
15. What can you do with HA?
16. Describe a VMware template.
17. How do you update a template?
18. Describe alarm management in vCenter.
19. What is a log file in vCenter?
20. Describe some commonly used log files in vCenter.

Chapter 5

Virtual Networks

Objectives

- Understand virtual networks
- Create and configure virtual networks
- Manage virtual networks

5.1 Introduction

In the VMware computing environment, virtual networks are used to link domain controllers (DCs), Elastic Sky X Integrated (ESXi) host servers, vCenter Servers, and virtual machines so that they can communicate with each other. Through the virtual networks, the virtual machines are able to use the data stored in the datacenter.

Virtual networks facilitate the centralized management of the virtualized computing system. They allow vCenter to manage ESXi hosts and other virtual machines. They are used to link the virtualized computing environment to physical networks so that the virtual machines can access the external networks. When linked to a physical network, the virtual machines can exchange data with physical machines. Through the physical network, the virtual machines can be connected to the Internet and allow users to work on the virtual machines through a Web page. Also, the virtual networks allow the virtual machines hosted by the ESXi servers to access external storage devices. Data can be retrieved and stored from and into an external data storage device.

5.2 Virtual Network Components

A virtual network is a software-based network. In this book, two types of virtual networks will be discussed. One is hosted by VMware Workstation, and the other is constructed on an ESXi host. The virtual network hosted by VMware Workstation has the following components.

Virtual switch: Like a physical switch, a virtual switch is used to construct a network. In VMware Workstation, the virtual switches are named (a) VMnet0 Bridged, which is used to connect a virtual machine directly to a physical network, (b) VMnet1 Host-only, which allows a virtual machine to communicate with the virtual machines created on the same host computer, (c) VMnet8 NAT (network address translation), which allows the virtual machines created on the same host computer to share the Internet Protocol (IP) address of the host, and (d) VMNetX (where X can be 2, 3, 4, and so on), which is a customized virtual switch. On a Windows host, 20 virtual switches can be created. A Linux host can have up to 255 virtual switches.

Virtual network adapter: Like a physical network adapter, a virtual network adapter enables a virtual machine to exchange data with a network. During the creation of a virtual machine, virtual adapters can be created. A virtual machine can have up to 10 virtual adapters. As shown in Figure 5.1, a network adapter is also labeled by the name of a virtual switch.

Virtual Dynamic Host Configuration Protocol (DHCP) server: VMware Workstation includes a virtual DHCP server to automatically assign an IP address to a newly created virtual machine.

Virtual NAT device: VMware Workstation has an NAT device that allows multiple virtual machines on the host to share a single IP address of a host.

A virtual network constructed on an ESXi host has the following components:

vSphere Standard Switch (vSwitch): This is a virtual switch constructed on an ESXi host. It is used to connect virtual machines to form a network. As this type of switch is constructed on a host, it can only be managed individually on each ESXi host.

vSphere Distributed Switch (vDS): This type of virtual switch is a distributed switch created on a group of different hosts that are centrally managed by a vCenter Server. Administrators can manage virtual networks and virtual

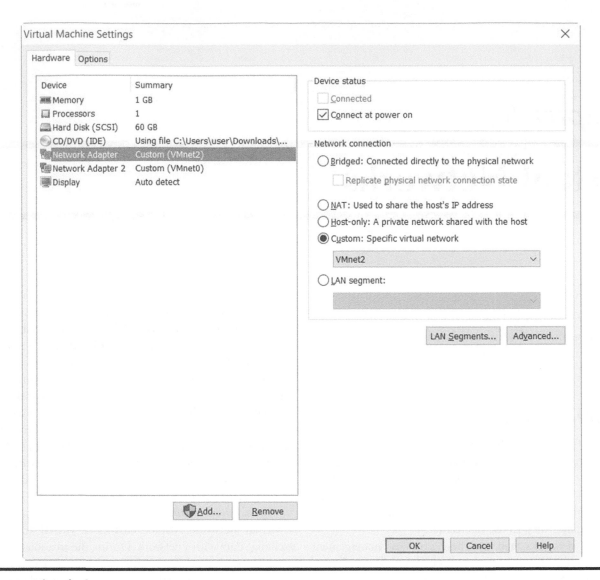

Figure 5.1 Virtual adapter.

machines across multiple hosts. Therefore, this type of switch can greatly simplify the configuration and management of virtual networks in a virtualized computing environment.

Port: Like a physical switch, a virtual switch also has ports through which virtual machines can be connected to the virtual switch. A port group is a collection of ports created on a virtual switch. A port group can be identified by a network label. That is, the virtual machines connected to the ports in the same port group belong to the same network. The broadcasting traffic cannot be passed from one port group to another port group with a different label. The following are some commonly used ports:

■ *VMkernel port:* This type of port is for the network traffic to travel in and out of an ESXi host server. It is used to connect a host to IP-based storage including Internet Small Computer System Interface (iSCSI) and Network File System. This type of port is also used for

moving a virtual machine from one host to another and for fault tolerance.
■ *VM port:* This type of port is for virtual machines. Through the port, a virtual machine can communicate with another virtual machine or with a physical machine. VM ports are used to construct a virtual local area network (VLAN), which forms a virtual subnet for better security, reliability, and performance.
■ *Trunk port:* Trunk ports are used to connect two switches. A trunk port can pass traffic for multiple VLANs. At a trunk port, different VLANs are distinguished with tags.
■ *Access port:* Unlike the trunk port, an access port passes traffic for only a single VLAN. When passing traffic, an access port also hides the information about the VLAN.

Virtual network adapter: Virtual network adapters are used to connect virtual machines to the virtual network. There are two types of virtual network adapters available. The first type is called an emulated virtual network adapter, which includes E1000 and E1000E. The emulated virtual network adapter is the virtual hardware that emulates a physical network adapter. As the drivers of physical network adapters are often preinstalled with an operating system, this type of virtual network adapter often works *out of the box*. The downside of this type of virtual network adapter is that emulation slows down performance. Figure 5.2 illustrates the properties of the E1000 virtual network adapter in a virtual machine.

The second type of virtual network adapter is called a paravirtualized virtual network adapter, which includes VMXNET 3. The paravirtualized network adapter is created during the installation of a guest operating system. It only operates inside the guest operating system, and no driver is actually working on this type of network adapter. By working inside the guest operating system, this type of network adapter has better performance. Figure 5.3 illustrates the use of VMXNET 3 network adapter in a virtual machine.

The following are some commonly used virtual network adapters:

- *Vlance network adapter:* This is an emulated version of a basic 10-Mbps physical network adapter. The driver for this 10-Mbps network adapter is preinstalled in most of the 32-bit guest operating systems. It is taken by VMware as the default network adapter unless VMware Tools is installed.

- *E1000 network adapter:* This virtual network adapter emulates the Intel E1000 network adapter, which has the 1-Gbps data transmission rate. This adapter is most commonly used for 64-bit virtual machines.

- *E1000E network adapter:* This virtual network adapter emulates the Intel Gigabit NIC, which is a newer version of the E1000 network adapter. It is used for Windows Server 2012 and later.

- *VMXNET 3 network adapter:* This type of network adapter is designed for performance. In addition, VMXNET 3 includes a number of new features such as multiqueue support, IPv6 offloads, and Message-Signaled Interrupts/Message-Signaled Interrupts Extension delivery. On the other hand, as it has no driver preinstalled in the guest operating system, VMXNET 3 network adapter requires VMware Tools to be installed.

- *Flexible network adapter:* As the name indicates, a flexible network adapter can identify itself either as a Vlance network adapter or a VMXNET adapter. This type of network adapter works like a Vlance network adapter when a virtual machine boots. Once the virtual machine has booted up, if VMware Tools is installed,

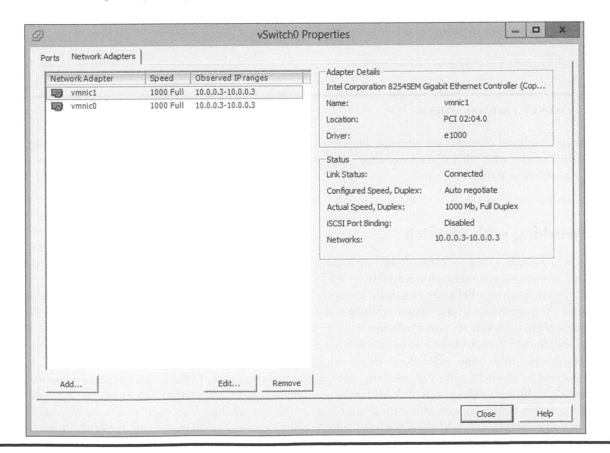

Figure 5.2 E1000 virtual network adapter.

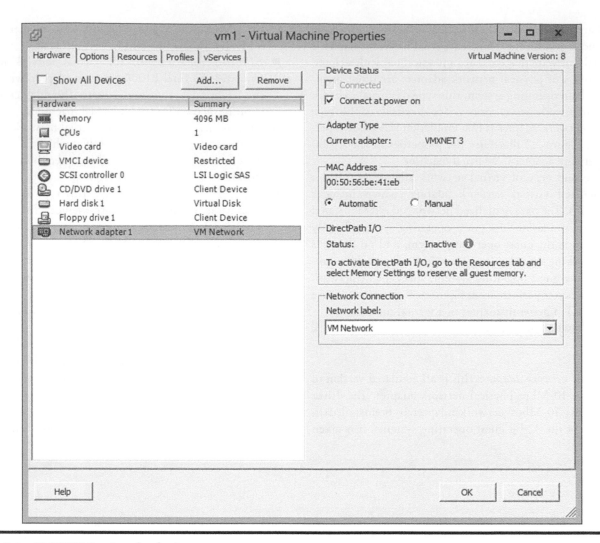

Figure 5.3   VMXNET 3 network adapter.

the virtual machine changes the network adapter to VMXNET. Otherwise, the Vlance network adapter will be used by the virtual machine.

5.3 Networking with vSwitch

With a vSwitch, various types of network infrastructures can be created to connect virtual machines within an ESXi host server, virtual machines between two host servers, a host server and a storage device, and a virtual machine and a physical machine. Figure 5.4 shows two vSwitches.

As shown in Figure 5.4, each of the virtual switches has a number of virtual machines connected to the switch through the virtual ports. On vSwitch1, you can see two types of ports: (1) virtual machine port group and (2) VMkernel port.

In Figure 5.4, vSwitch1 connects the virtual machines to the external physical network. On the right-hand side of vSwitch1, there are two uplinks that connect vSwitch1 to the physical network adapters on the host server. Through these

physical network adapters, the virtual machines can communicate with other virtual machines on a different host server. If a networked storage device is connected to the host server, the virtual machines can access the storage device through the uplinks. Also, through the uplinks, the virtual machines can be migrated from one host server to another host server. Figure 5.5 illustrates how the virtual machines on a host server communicate with the virtual machines on a different host server.

With vSwitches, different virtual networks can be constructed for various tasks such as the network for management, the network for connecting host servers and storage devices, and the network for connecting virtual machines. The following briefly describes these networks.

Management network: This type of network is for the management of traffic generated by external management software such as vSphere Client, vCenter Server, and Simple Network Management Protocol Client. By default, the management network is set up during the installation of ESXi. Once ESXi is installed, the user can configure the

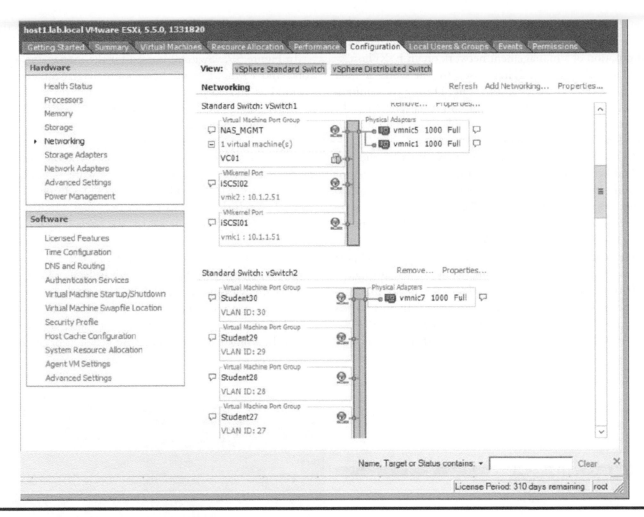

Figure 5.4 vSwitches.

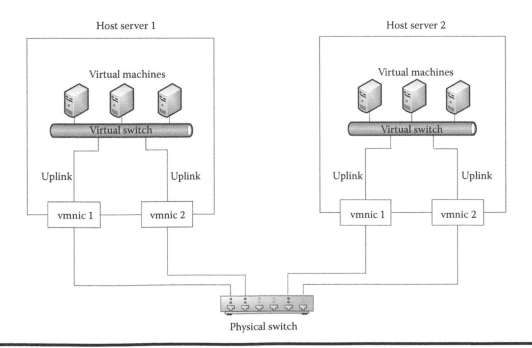

Figure 5.5 Virtual network components.

management network so that the host server can be reached by external management software. Figure 5.6 illustrates the configuration of a management network on an ESXi host.

By default, an ESXi host uses the network adapter vmnic0 for the management of traffic. During the configuration, other network adapters can also be specified for the management of traffic. It is also possible to use multiple network adapters for traffic management.

VMkernel network: This type of network is for the network traffic originated by an ESXi host. It can be used for vMotion, which moves virtual machines from one host to another host, for vSphere Fault Tolerance, and for storage device management. There are two types of VMkernel ports, one for the management network traffic and one for the nonmanagement network traffic. By default, the VMkernel port for network management is automatically created during the installation of ESXi. The VMkernel port for the nonmanagement needs to be created by the user. The VMkernel port is associated with the interface that is assigned an IP address. Figure 5.7 illustrates the two types of VMkernel ports, one

for management network and the other one for connecting to the storage device.

In Figure 5.7, vSwitch0 is used for the management network, and vSwitch1 is used for nonmanagement network. vSwitch1 is created by the user and is used to connect to an iSCSI storage device. The associated IP address for the management network is 10.0.0.10, and the IP address for the nonmanagement network is 10.0.1.10.

Virtual machine network: Unlike the VMkernel network, the port used in a virtual machine network is not associated with a specified IP address. It works like an unmanaged physical switch that has no IP address. Figure 5.8 shows a virtual machine network in which the ports have no associated IP address.

Virtual local area network: The VLAN is a virtual network technology. VLANs are used to isolate a group of virtual machines from another group of virtual machines. In such a way, network traffic within one VLAN cannot be passed on to another VLAN without a router. A VLAN is created by using a subset of ports on a switch or by using a

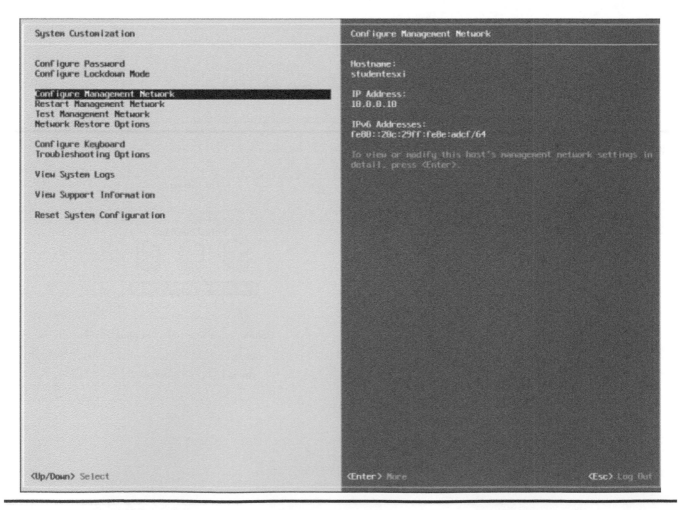

Figure 5.6 Configuration of management network.

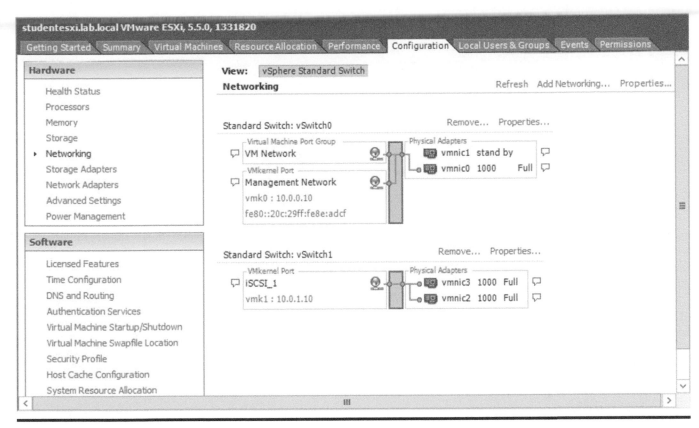

Figure 5.7   VMkernel ports.

set of ports from multiple switches. Figure 5.9 illustrates the VLAN technology.

The switch used to form a VLAN has two types of ports: (1) access port and (2) trunk port. The access port is used to connect a virtual machine, and the trunk port is used to connect another switch. When a VLAN is created over two switches, trunk ports are used to link the switches. A frame delivered through a switch has a tag to indicate which VLAN the frame originated from. The switch only delivers the frame to the virtual machines that belong to that VLAN. When a frame arrives at a switch, the switch examines the frame. The frame may or may not have a tag. If the frame comes directly from a virtual machine, it has no tag. If the frame is from another switch, it already has a tag assigned by the sending switch. If there is no tag in the frame, the switch will place a tag to that frame.

By using VLAN, multiple VLAN segments can be created on a switch. On the other hand, a group of virtual machines can be configured to be in the same VLAN even if the virtual machines are connected to different switches. On the same VLAN, the virtual machines on different physical networks can communicate with one another as if they were on the same network. In this way, the network traffic on a large switch can be limited to a specific VLAN segment. The VLAN technology provides the flexibility of forming different types of virtual networks. It can also be used to improve

network security and manageability. For better resource management of VMware networks, one may consider the VLAN technology.

NIC teaming: The NIC teaming technology is used for redundancy and load balancing. In NIC teaming, through the uplinks, multiple physical NICs are connected to the same virtual switch. These multiple physical NICs are teamed up to form a virtual NIC for better bandwidth and fault tolerance. Figure 5.10 illustrates NIC teaming.

In Figure 5.10, there are two virtual switches. These two switches communicate with the external physical switches. The virtual machines only know the virtual NICs configured on the ESXi host. They are not aware of the underlying physical NICs. When it arrives, the internal network traffic will be dispatched through one of the physical NICs. On the other hand, when the external network traffic arrives at the physical switch, it will be directed to the appropriate logical NIC based on the destination IP address. It is required that all uplinks be connected to physical switches that are in the same broadcasting domain. If multiple switches are involved in NIC teaming, these physical switches need to be configured as one logical switch.

One of the benefits of NIC teaming is load balancing. When NIC teaming is configured on a virtual switch in an ESXi host, load balancing is applied only to the outgoing network traffic. Based on the available network connections

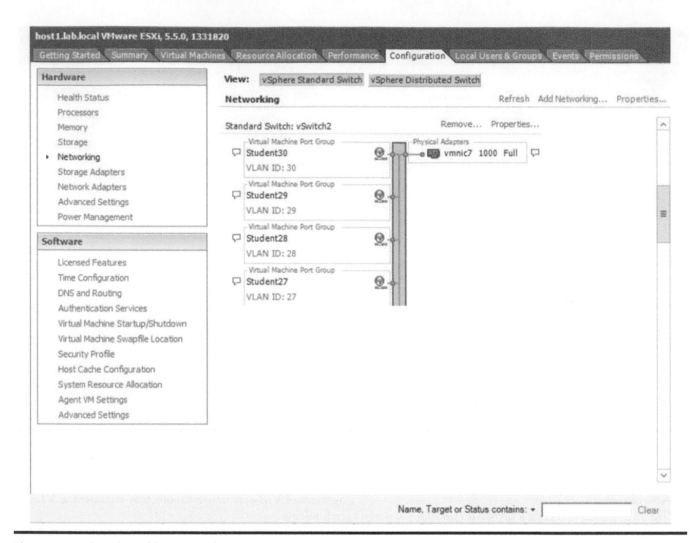

Figure 5.8 Virtual machine network.

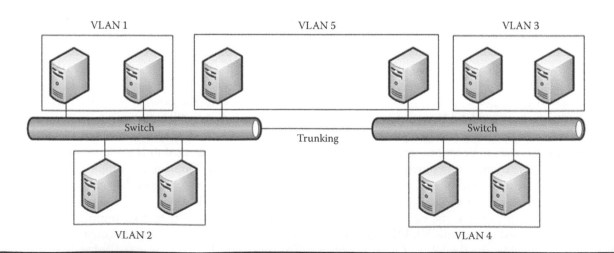

Figure 5.9 VLAN technology.

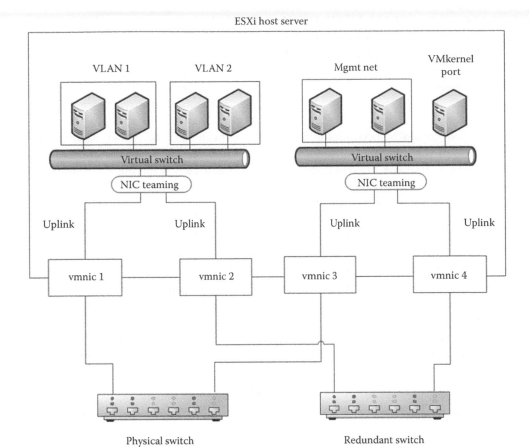

Figure 5.10 NIC teaming.

available from a virtual switch to a destination address, the outgoing network traffic is automatically load-balanced among these connections. On a virtual switch, the NIC teaming for load balancing can be configured according to the following four policies:

1. *vSwitch port-based load balancing:* This is the default policy that assigns each physical NIC in the team with an equal number of vSwitch ports. When an NIC fails, the ports related to that NIC will be reassigned to a different NIC.
2. *Source media access control (MAC)–based load balancing:* Each virtual network adapter on a virtual machine has a unique MAC address. This type of load balancing assigns an equal number of MAC addresses to the physical NICs in NIC teaming.
3. *IP hash-based load balancing:* This policy uses the source and destination IP addresses to calculate a hash that determines which uplink in the NIC team to use. This policy allows a virtual machine with multiple network adapters to communicate with multiple destination hosts.
4. *Explicit failover order:* With this policy, the virtual switch sends beacons out to detect upstream failures. Once a failure is detected, this policy determines how

a network adapter in the NIC team will be used. It always uses the highest-order uplink from the list of active adapters, standby adapters, and unused adapters.

Although an ESXi host does not handle load balancing on the incoming network traffic, the load balancing on the incoming network traffic can be implemented on a physical switch.

5.4 Networking with vDS

While the vSwitch is used to construct a network within an ESXi host, the vDS can be used to construct a network across multiple associated ESXi hosts. The vDS can accomplish the following tasks across multiple ESXi hosts in a datacenter:

- The vDS can be used to form various networks such as management networks or VMkernel networks.
- It can be used to connect virtual machines.
- It can be used to connect physical NICs that lead to external physical networks.
- On the vDS, VLANs can be formed for better flexibility, performance, and security.

As the vDS is constructed across multiple ESXi hosts in a datacenter, it is not necessary for each individual ESXi host to have its own vSwitch. This feature can greatly reduce the complexity in the network structure. In summary, the vDS provides the following benefits:

- *Simplifying virtual network configuration:* The vDS provides the centralized control on network configuration and operation. NIC teaming can be implemented across multiple ESXi hosts. The vDS provides the health check throughout the entire datacenter.
- *Enhancing virtual network management:* The vDS monitors network traffic distributed over the entire datacenter. It provides centralized network traffic–capturing service. It also provides protocols for network traffic analysis and protocols for network management. It provides mechanisms for the backup, rollback, and recovery of network configurations. It also provides centralized log service for troubleshooting.
- *Providing more advanced virtual network features:* The vDS provides a number of tools and services to enhance network capabilities. For example, it provides tools for network input/output (I/O) control. It also provides tools for enabling low-latency and high-I/O workloads. It enables centralized firewall service and is able to capture the network traffic directly in a particularly identified path. It is able to move virtual machines across multiple ESXi hosts. While doing so, it can keep the virtual machines' runtime state. It can also prevent virtual machines from sending messages used for calculating the spanning tree topology to a physical switch.

To be able to centralize the control of networks across multiple ESXi hosts, the vDS should be constructed in vCenter, so the network configurations can be distributed to all associated ESXi hosts connected to the vDS. Figure 5.11 illustrates the network infrastructure constructed with the vDS.

As shown in Figure 5.11, the configuration and management of the virtual switches have been moved from the ESXi host servers to vCenter. Through vSphere Client or vSphere Web Client, the network administrator can log on

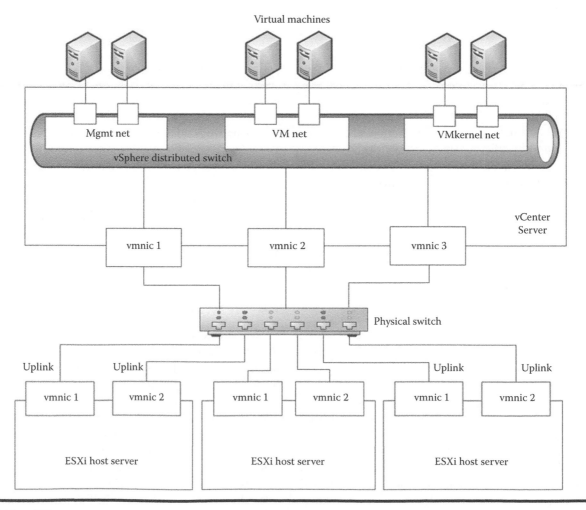

Figure 5.11 vDS.

to vCenter. In vCenter, the network administrator can create the connection to all the ESXi host servers and create the vDS across these ESXi host servers. The port group on the vDS can be distributed across multiple ESXi host servers. Within this structure, virtual machines can be easily moved from one ESXi host to another ESXi host. The vDS is suitable for network troubleshooting and monitoring across the entire virtualized computing environment. It also improves consistency and security.

5.5 Activity 1: Creating Network to Connect Host Servers to Storage Device

In this activity, you will create a network to connect the host servers LabESXi1 and LabESXi2 so that these two host servers can share the iSCSI storage device. The following are the tasks to be accomplished:

- *Task 1:* Preparation
- *Task 2:* Network configuration

5.5.1 Task 1: Preparation

This task starts with the preparation of an iSCSI server used as a shared storage device. Later, you will create a network to link the iSCSI server to the host servers.

1. Suppose that the Windows Server 2012 R2 ISO file has been downloaded to the Downloads folder on your DC virtual machine from the following Web site: https://www.dreamspark.com/Student/Default.aspx
2. To prepare the DC server so that it can be used to distribute the Windows Server 2102 R2 ISO file for installation, log on to **DC** and click the **Administrative Tools** tile. Then, double-click **Services**.
3. In the Services dialog, right-click **DNS Client** and select **Start** if the service is not already started. Similarly, start the services **Function Discovery Resource**

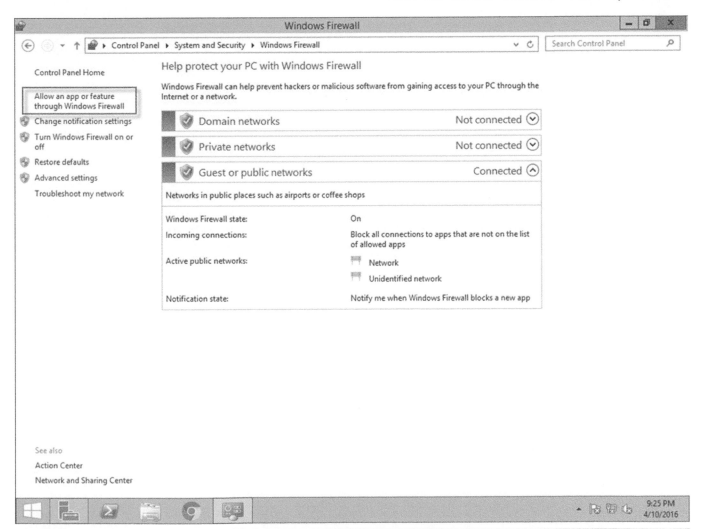

Figure 5.12 Allowing app or feature through Windows Firewall.

Publication, **SSDP Discovery**, and **UPnP Device Host**. Right-click the service and select **Properties**. You may need to change Startup Type to **Automatic (Delayed Start)** in the Properties dialog for the services Function Discovery Resource Publication, SSDP Discovery, and UPnP Device Host. Click the **Apply** button and the **Start** button so that they can be started. Then, close the Services dialog.

4. At the top part of the Administrative Tools dialog, click the link **System and Security**. Click **Windows Firewall**. Then, click the link **Allow an app or feature through Windows Firewall**, as shown in Figure 5.12.

5. In the Allow apps dialog, make sure that **Network Discovery** is checked, as shown in Figure 5.13. Then, click **OK**.

6. At the top part of the Administrative Tools dialog, click **Control Panel, Network and Internet, Network and Sharing Center**, and **Change advanced sharing settings**. Expand the Guest or Public node. Make sure

to click the options **Turn on network discovery** and **Turn on file and printer sharing**, as shown in Figure 5.14. Similarly, click Turn on network discovery and Turn on file and printer sharing for Private and Domain. For the All Networks node, make sure that the option Turn on sharing is checked so that anyone with network access can read and write files in the Public folder. Then, click the **Save changes** button. For security reasons, you can change back to the default setting after the guest operating system is installed. Your DC server is ready to deliver the ISO image file for installation.

7. If you have not done so, add two network adapters for each ESXi host. To do so, in VMware Workstation, right-click the **LabESXi1** virtual machine and select **Settings**. In the Virtual Machine Settings dialog, click the **Add** button. In the Hardware Type dialog, select **Network Adapter** and click **Next**. In the Network Adapter Type dialog, click the option **Custom** and

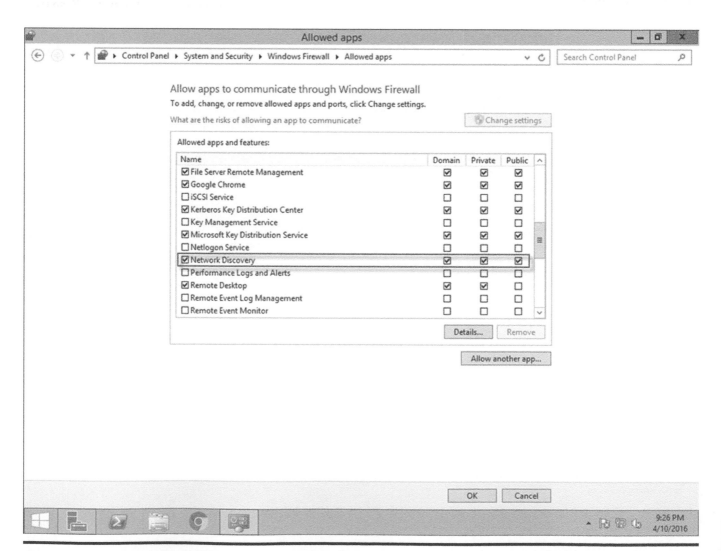

Figure 5.13 Allowing network discovery.

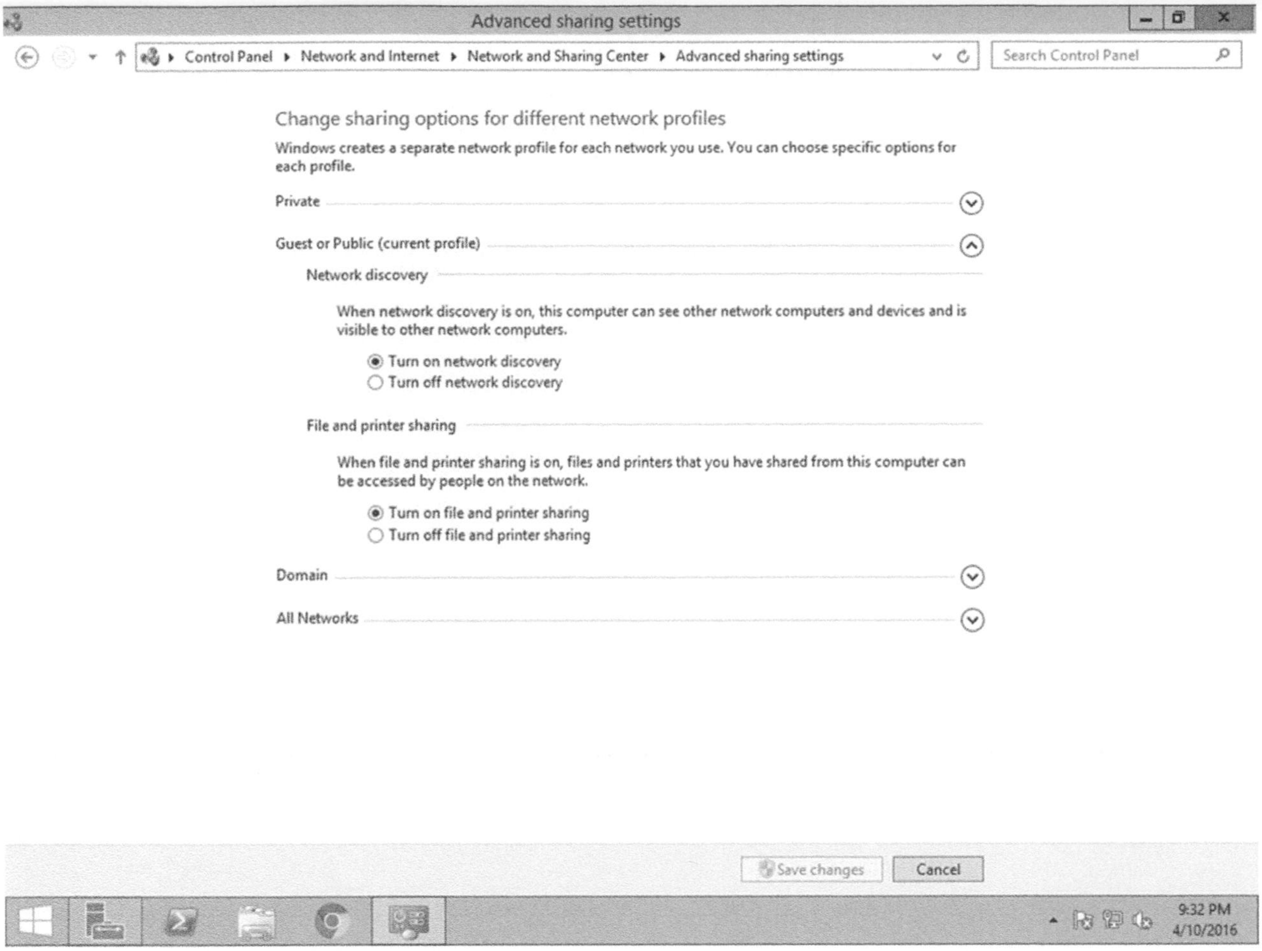

Figure 5.14   Turning on network discovery.

select **VMnet3** as the customized network. Then, click **Finish**. Use the same steps to add another network adapter in LabESXi1. Repeat the above steps to add two more network adapters to the LabESXi2 virtual machine.

8. In VMware Workstation, create a new virtual machine called **Storage** by clicking **Files** and **New Virtual Machines**. Check the option **Custom** and click **Next**.

9. On the Hardware Compatibility page, select **Workstation 11.x**. Then, click **Next**.

10. On the Guest Operating System Installation page, select the option **I will install the operating system later**. Then, click **Next** (Figure 5.15).

11. In the Select a Guest Operating System page, check the option **Microsoft Windows** and select **Windows Server 2012** on the Version dropdown list, as shown in Figure 5.16. Then, click **Next**.

12. On the Name the Virtual Machine page, enter the name **Storage**, as shown in Figure 5.17. Then, click **Next** three times to go to the Network Type page.

13. On the Network Type page, select the **Do not use a network connection** option, as shown in Figure 5.18. Then, click **Next**.

14. Click **Next** three times to go to the Specify Disk Capacity page. Select the option **Store virtual disk as a single file**, as shown in Figure 5.19. Then, click **Next** twice to go to the Ready to Create Virtual Machine page. Then, click **Finish**.

15. Right-click the newly created virtual machine **Storage** and select **Settings**. Click the **Add** button. On the Hardware Type page, click **Network Adapter** and click **Next**. On the Network Adapter Type page, click **Custom** and select **VMnet2**; then, click **Finish**. You should be able to see the added Network Adapter shown in Figure 5.20.

16. Click the link **CD\DVD** and check the option **Use ISO image file** shown in Figure 5.21. Then, click **Browse**.

17. In the Browse for ISO Image dialog, expand the **Network** node and click the **DC** node, as shown in Figure 5.22.

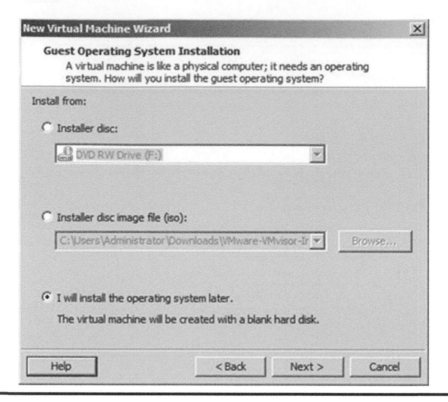

Figure 5.15 Installing guest operating system later.

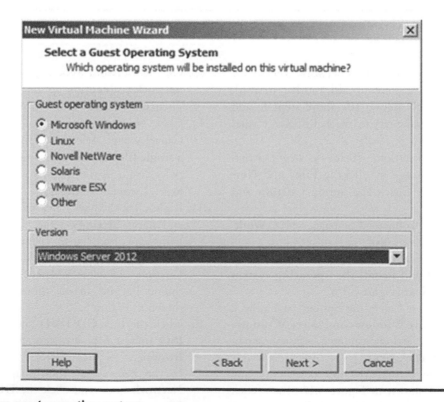

Figure 5.16 Selecting guest operating system.

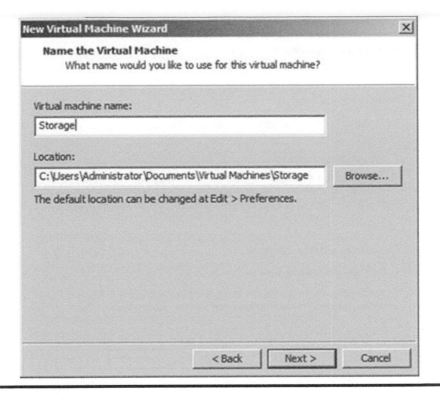

Figure 5.17   Naming virtual machine.

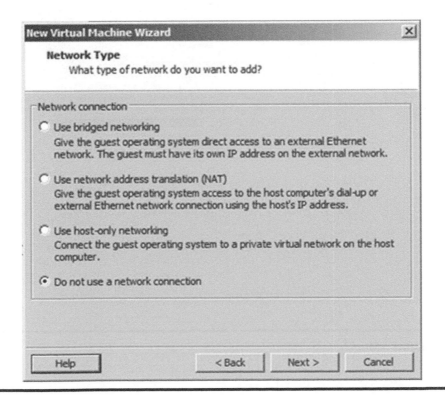

Figure 5.18   Selecting network type.

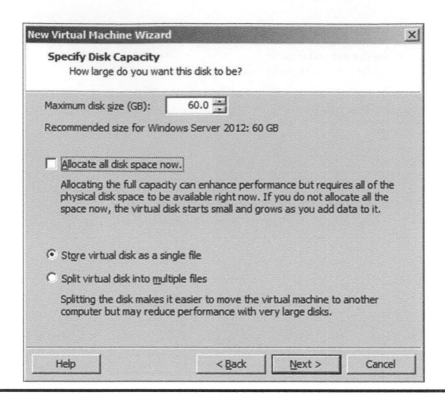

Figure 5.19 Specifying disk capacity.

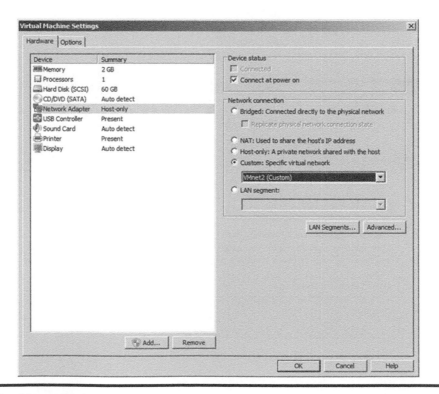

Figure 5.20 Network adapter VMnet2.

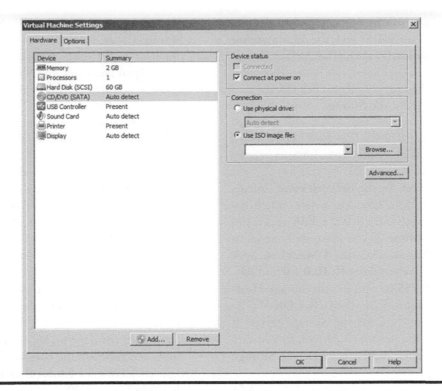

Figure 5.21 Using ISO image file.

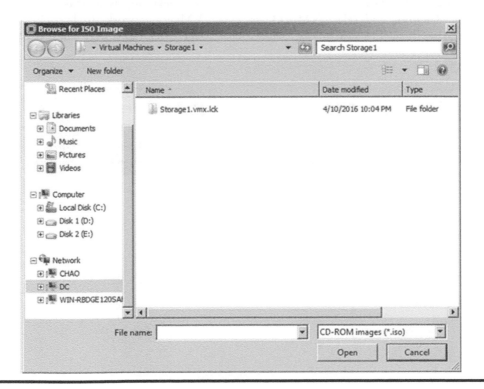

Figure 5.22 Browsing for ISO image file on DC.

18. Enter the user **Administrator** and your password. Once logged on, click the **User Share** folder, the **Administrator** folder, and the **Downloads** folder. Find the ISO file previously downloaded in the Downloads folder. Then, click **Open**, as shown in Figure 5.23. Then, click **OK** twice.

19. Now, you can power on the **Storage** virtual machine to start the installation process. Make sure to install the Windows Server 2012 R2 Standard (server with a graphical user interface) version. You also need to enter the password such as Passw0rd!.

20. To prepare the network for the network-based storage, in VMware Workstation, select the newly created virtual machine **Storage**, and click the **Edit** menu and **Virtual Network Editor**. If you have not done so, in Virtual Network Editor, select the **VMnet3** network and configure it with the subnet IP **10.0.1.0** and subnet mask **255.255.255.0**. Specify the option **Host-only**, as shown in Figure 5.24. Then, click **OK**.

21. You need to add an NIC to the Storage server in order to connect to the network VMnet3. In VMware Workstation, right-click the virtual machine **Storage** and select **Settings**.

22. In the Virtual Machine Settings dialog, click the **Add** button.

23. Once the Add Hardware Wizard is open, click **Network Adapter** and click **Next**.

24. Click the option **Custom** and select **VMnet3**, as shown in Figure 5.25. Then, click **Finish**.

25. To rename the newly added NIC, log on to the **Storage** virtual machine, right-click the network monitor icon at the lower-right corner of the screen and select **Open Network and Sharing Center**. Click the **Change adapter settings** link to open the Network Connection dialog.

26. In the Network Connection dialog, right-click the newly added NIC Ethernet 1 and rename it as **iSCSI** (Figure 5.26).

27. Right-click the **iSCSI** NIC and select **Properties**. Select **Internet Protocol Version 4** and click **Properties**.

28. Configure the NIC to have IP address **10.0.1.3** and the subnet mask **255.255.255.0**, as shown in Figure 5.27. Then, click **OK**.

29. Also, the NIC in the vmnet2 network is shown in Figure 5.28.

30. Repeat Steps 2 through 6 on the Storage server to make the Storage server able to be discovered on the network.

31. If you have not done so, log on to the DC server, click **Tools** and **DNS**. In the Forward Lookup Zones folder, right-click the zone **lab.local** and select **New Host**, as shown in Figure 5.29.

32. Add the host **Storage.lab.local** with the IP address **10.0.0.2**, as shown in Figure 5.30.

33. The next step is to make the ESXi hosts share the VMnet3 network. To do so, in VMware Workstation, right-click **LabESXi1** and select **Settings**.

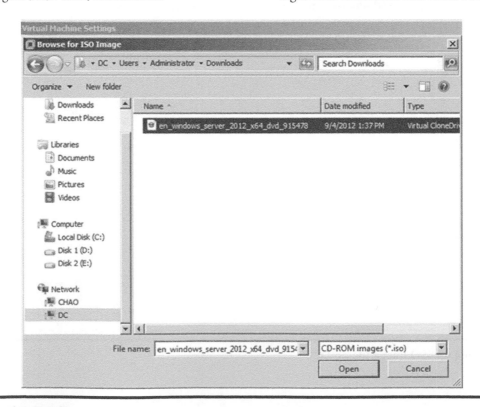

Figure 5.23 Opening ISO file.

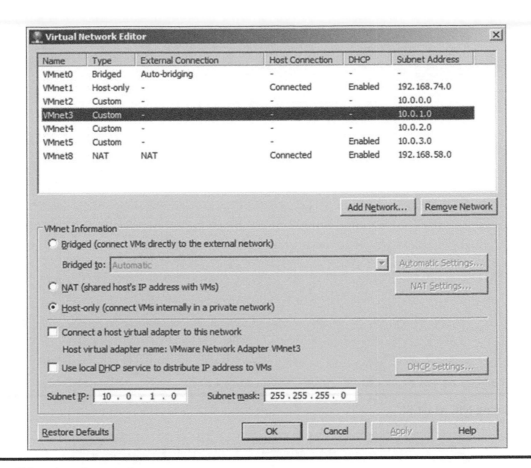

Figure 5.24   Editing virtual network.

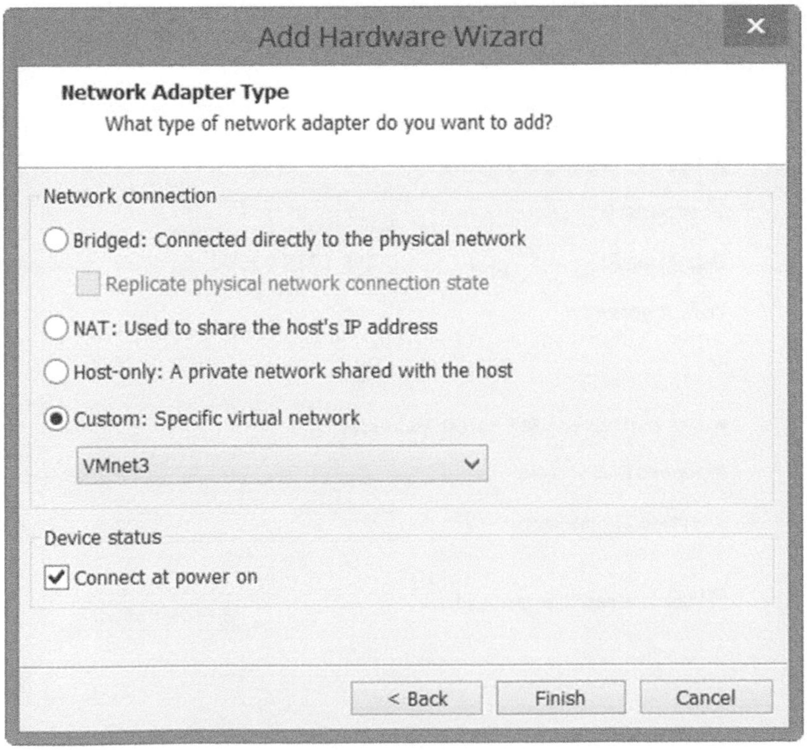

Figure 5.25   Network adapter type.

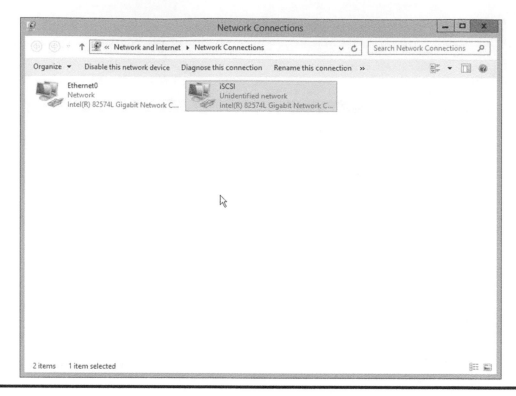

Figure 5.26 Renaming NIC as iSCSI.

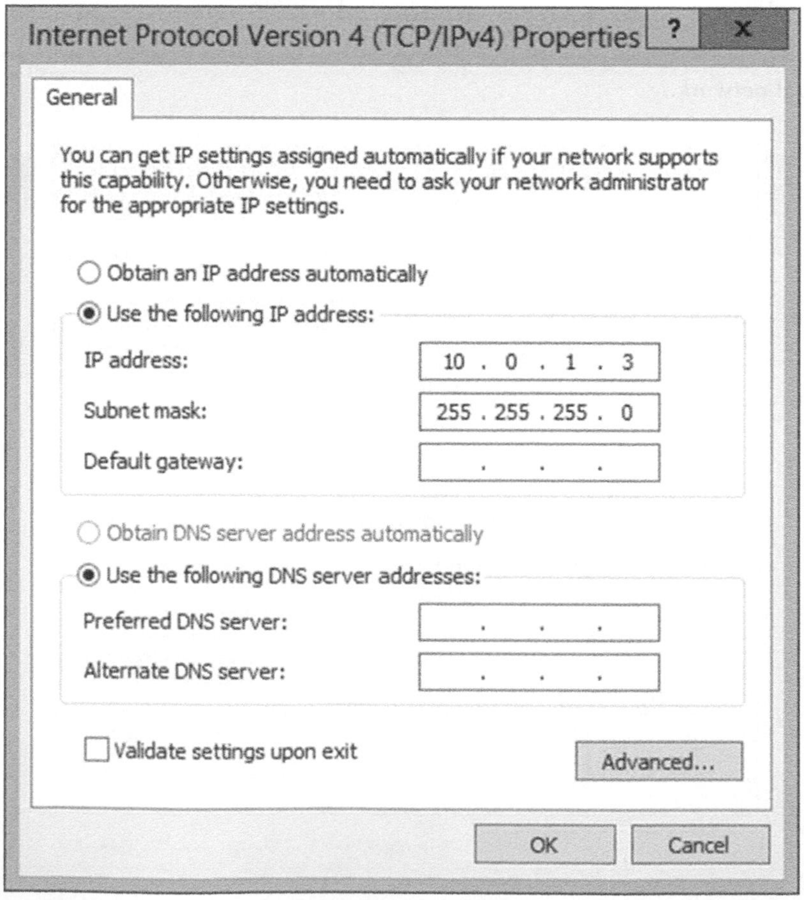

Figure 5.27 Configuring iSCSI NIC.

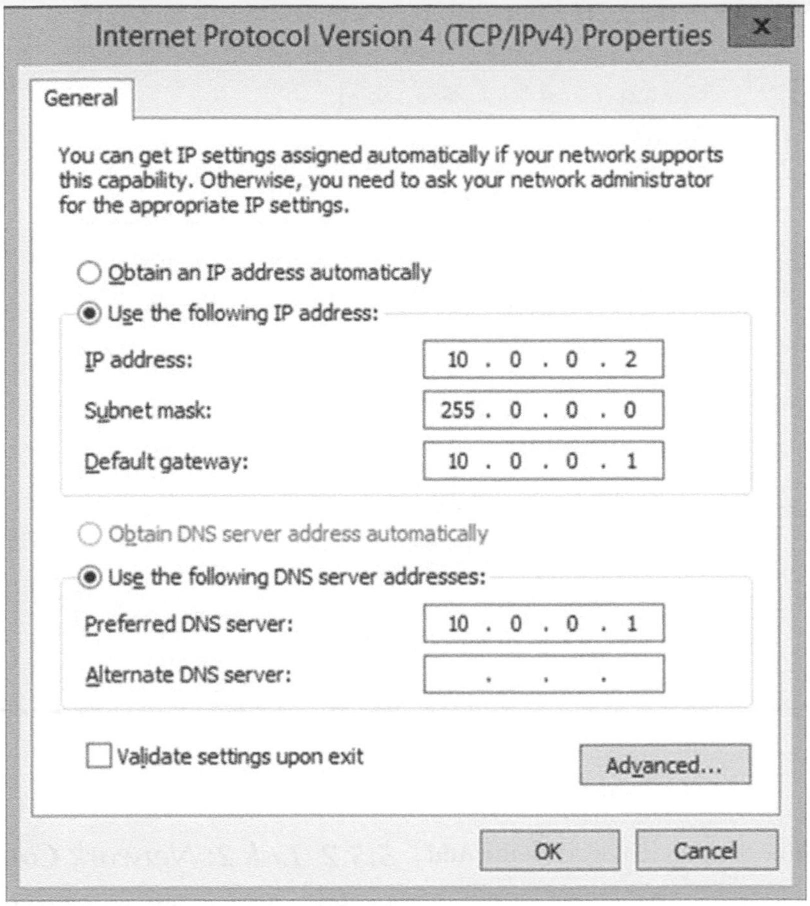

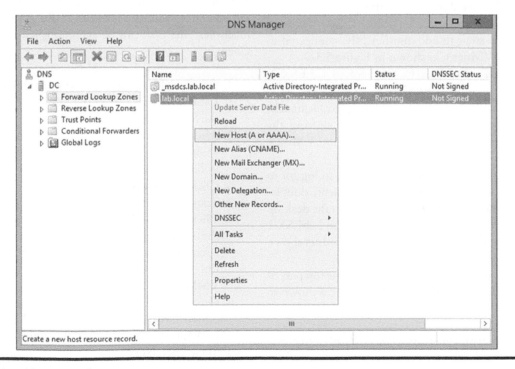

Figure 5.28   Configuring second NIC.

Figure 5.29   New Host record.

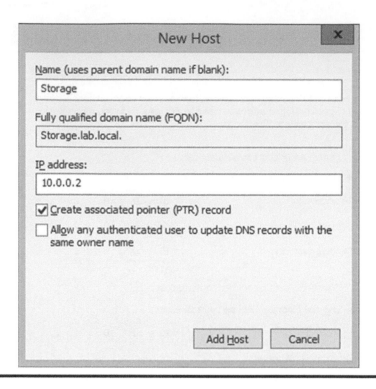

Figure 5.30 New Host.

34. In the Virtual Machine Settings dialog, click the **Add** button.
35. In the Add Hardware Wizard dialog, click **Network Adapter** and click **Next**.
36. Select the option **Custom** and select **VMnet3** on the dropdown list, as shown in Figure 5.31. Then, click **Finish**.
37. Use the same steps to add another NIC connected to the network VMnet3, as shown in Figure 5.32.
38. Similarly, add two NICs in VMnet3 to LabESXi2. Now, power on both **LabESXi1** and **LabESXi2**.
39. Log on to the **DC** server. When prompted for installing VMware Tools, you may do so by clicking the Update Tools button at the bottom of the VMware Workstation window.
40. After you have installed VMware Tools, to log on to the LabESXi1 host through vSphere Client, double-click the **VMware vSphere Client** icon on the desktop of DC; enter the host name or IP of the LabESXi1 server, the root user name, and the password, as shown in Figure 5.33. Then, click **Login**.
41. Once logged in, click the **Home** link on the top part of the screen. Then, click the **Inventory** icon, as shown in Figure 5.34.

After the Inventory page opens, your next task is to create and manage a network.

5.5.2 Task 2: Network Configuration

In this task, you will create VMkernel ports. VMkernel ports are used for iSCSI and other network traffic such as management, vMotion, and Fault Tolerance, which are generated by an ESXi host. These types of network traffic are separated from the network traffic generated by virtual machines. The task can be accomplished by using vSphere Client.

1. Continue from Task 1; make sure to power on **DC**, the **LabESXi1** host server, the **LabESXi2** host server, and the **Storage** server.
2. After logged on to the LabESXi1 server through vSphere Client, click the **Configuration** tab, as shown in Figure 5.35.
3. Click the **Networking** link, and you will see the default virtual network (Figure 5.36).
4. Click the **Add Networking** link, which is located on the upper-right part of your screen (Figure 5.36) to open the Add Network Wizard.
5. On the Connection Type page, select the option **VMkernel,** as shown in Figure 5.37, and click **Next**.
6. On the VMkernel—Network Access page, select the option **Create a vSphere standard switch**, as shown in Figure 5.38. Check both **vmnic2** and **vmnic3**. Then, click **Next**.

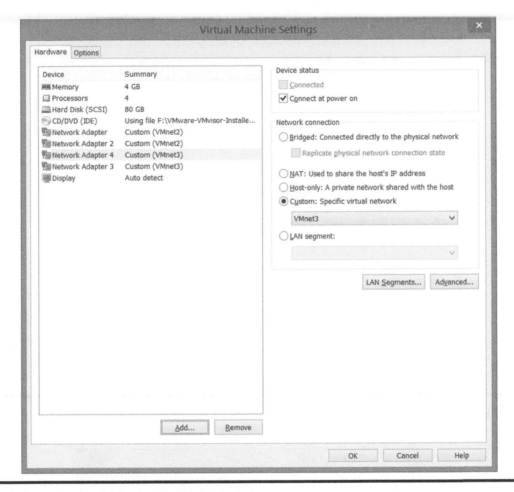

Figure 5.31   Adding network adapter to LabESXi1 server.

7. On the VMkernel—Connection Settings page, enter **iSCSI_1** for Network Label, as shown in Figure 5.39. Then, click **Next**.

8. On the VMkernel—IP Connection Settings page, enter **10.0.1.10** for IP Address, **255.255.255.0** for Subnet Mask, and **10.0.0.1** for VMkernel Default Gateway, as shown in Figure 5.40. Then, click **Next**.

9. On the Ready to Complete page, check the settings and click **Finish** (Figure 5.41).

10. You can see that the new network vSwitch1 with two uplinks, vmnic2 and vmnic3, is created, as shown in Figure 5.42.

11. Back to the LabESXi1 host server. Click the **Properties** link located on the right-hand side of vSwitch1 (Figure 5.42) to open the vSwitch1 Properties dialog.

12. In the vSwitch1 Properties dialog, click the **Add** button to add a VMkernel network.

13. On the Connection Type page, select the option **VMkernel,** as shown in Figure 5.43, and click **Next**.

14. On the VMkernel—Connection Settings page, specify Network Label as iSCSI_2 (Figure 5.44). Then, click **Next**.

15. On the VMkernel—IP Connection Settings page, set IP Address as **10.0.1.11** and Subnet Mask as **255.255.255.0**, as shown in Figure 5.45. Then, click **Next**.

16. On the Ready to Complete page, click **Finish**.

17. Click the **Properties** link located on the right-hand side of vSwitch1, as shown in Figure 5.42, to open the vSwitch1 Properties dialog.

18. In the vSwitch1 Properties dialog, click iSCSI_1 and click the **Edit** button (Figure 5.46).

19. In the iSCSI_1 Properties dialog, click the **NIC Teaming** tab. Check **Override switch failover order**. Then, use the Move Up and Move Down buttons to arrange **vmnic2** for Active Adapters and **vmnic3** for Unused Adapters, as shown in Figure 5.47. Then, click **OK**.

20. Similarly, for iSCSI_2, under the NIC Teaming tab, set **vmnic3** for Active Adapters and **vmnic2** for Unused Adapters, as shown in Figure 5.48. Then, click the **OK** button.

Figure 5.32   Adding another NIC to VMnet3.

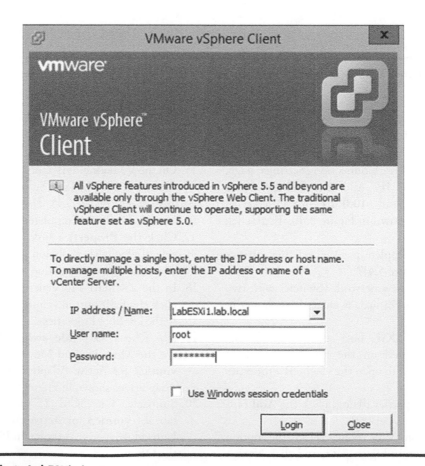

Figure 5.33   Logging in to LabESXi1 host.

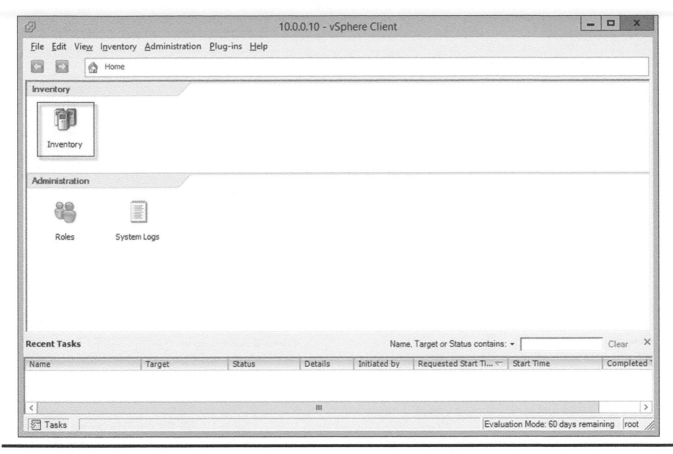

Figure 5.34 Home view of LabESXi1 host.

21. You now have the network layout, as shown in Figure 5.49.

22. Now, repeat the steps from Steps 2 through 21 to add the virtual network vSwitch1 for the host server **LabESXi2** with the port name iSCSC_1 and IP address **10.0.1.20**, and the port name iSCSI_2 and IP address **10.0.1.21**. The network layout on the LabESXi2 server is shown in Figure 5.50.

23. Log on to the LabESXi1 host server through vSphere Client. Click the **Configuration** tab and click the **Storage Adapters** link. Then, click the **Add** link, as shown in Figure 5.51.

24. In the Add Storage Adapter dialog, select the option **Add Software iSCSI Adapter**, as shown in Figure 5.52. Then, click **OK**.

25. Select the newly created storage adapter **vmhba33** and click **Properties**, as shown in Figure 5.53.

26. In the iSCSI Initiator (vmhba33) Properties dialog, highlight **iqn,** which is the name of the iSCSI Initiator, right-click it, and copy it, as shown in Figure 5.54. Save **iqn** in a text file. Then, click **Close**.

27. Repeat Steps 23 through 26 for the LabESXi2 server.

28. The tool VM-King can be used to verify that the network has been established between the Storage server and the ESXi host. Select the host server **LabESCi1** in VMware Workstation. Press **F2** to log on to LabESXi1. Move the cursor to **Troubleshooting Options** and press the **Enter** key (Figure 5.55).

29. Select the link **Enable ESXi Shell** and press **Enter**. Press the **ESC** key twice.

30. Press the **Alt+F1** keys; you will see the screen that prompts you to enter the user name and password, as shown in Figure 5.56.

31. Once logged on, to check the VMkernel network configuration, run the vmkping command, as shown in Figure 5.57.

    ```
    vmkping 10.0.1.3
    ```

32. To test the connection to the iSCSI server, run the following ping command. The results are given in Figure 5.57.

    ```
    ping 10.0.1.3
    ```

    If no error is displayed, your network is correctly configured.

33. After the network is checked, press the **Alt+F2** keys to exit the command window. You can now log out of vSphere Client.

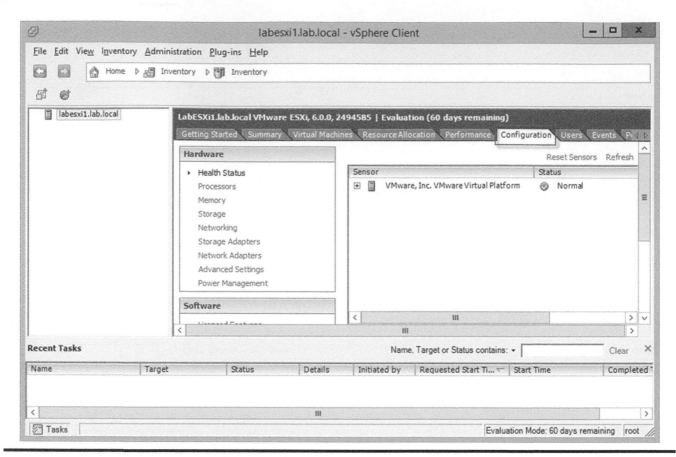

Figure 5.35   Logging on to LabESXi1 server.

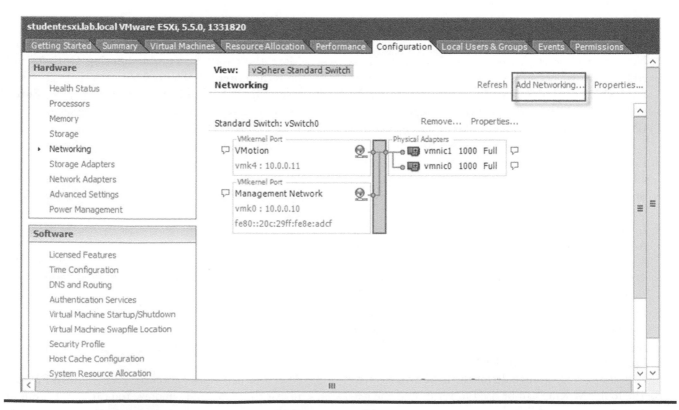

Figure 5.36   Default virtual network.

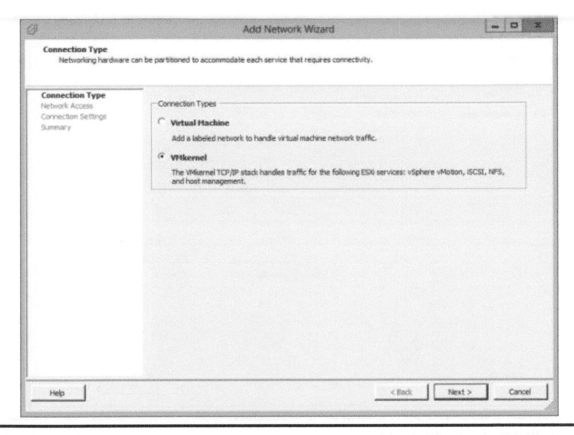

Figure 5.37 Connection Type.

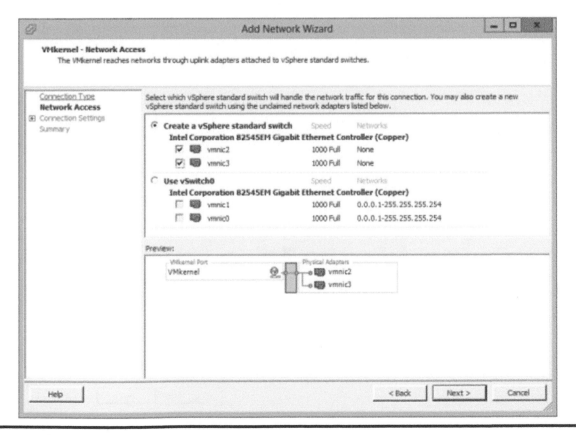

Figure 5.38 VMkernel Network Access.

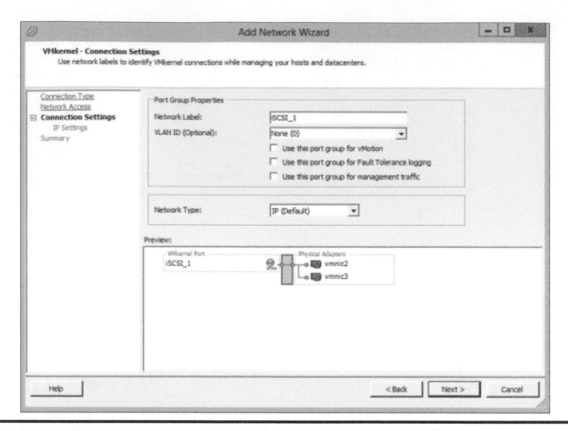

Figure 5.39   VMkernel—Connection Settings.

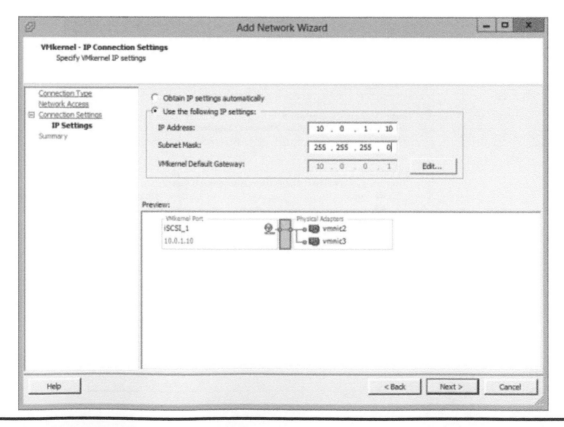

Figure 5.40   IP Connection Settings.

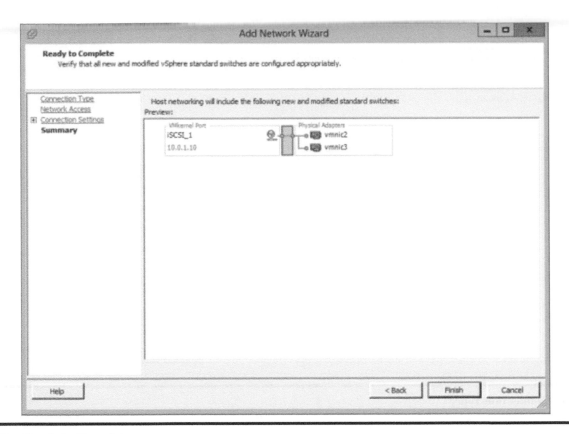

Figure 5.41 Ready to Complete.

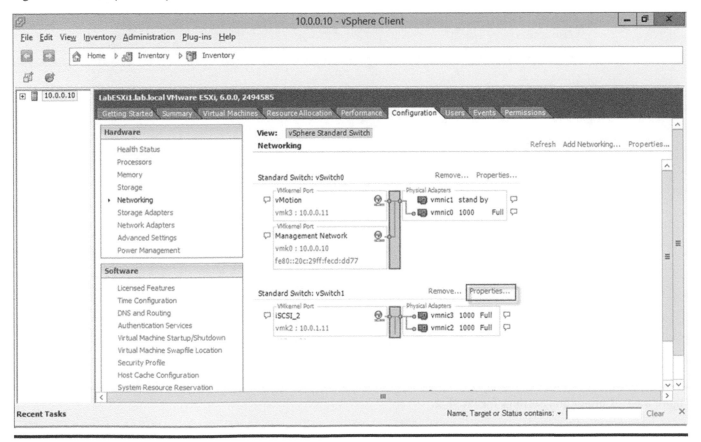

Figure 5.42 New network.

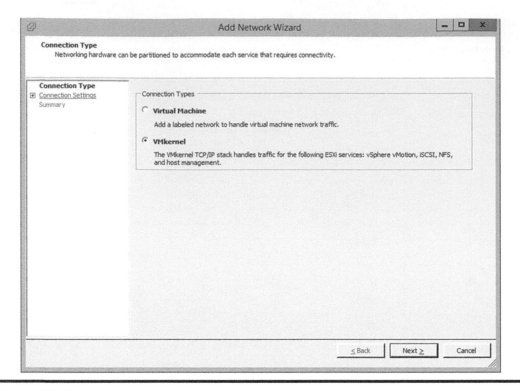

Figure 5.43   Connection Type.

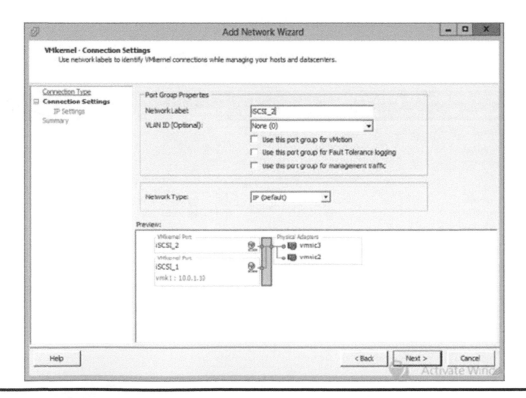

Figure 5.44   Connection Settings for iSCSI_2.

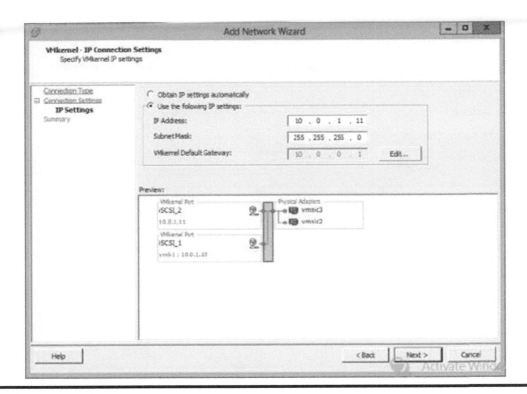

Figure 5.45   IP Settings for iSCSI_2.

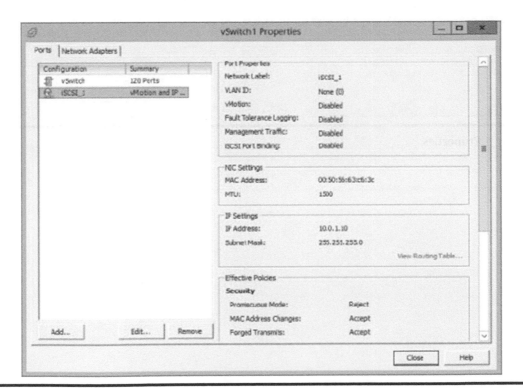

Figure 5.46   Editing iSCSI_1.

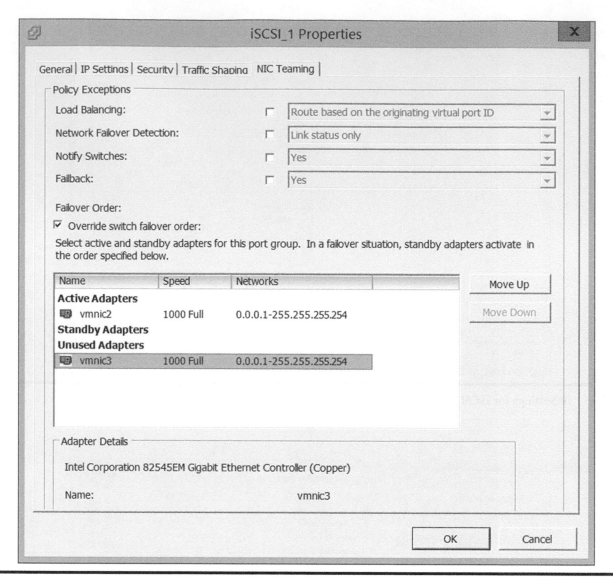

Figure 5.47 iSCSI_1 Properties.

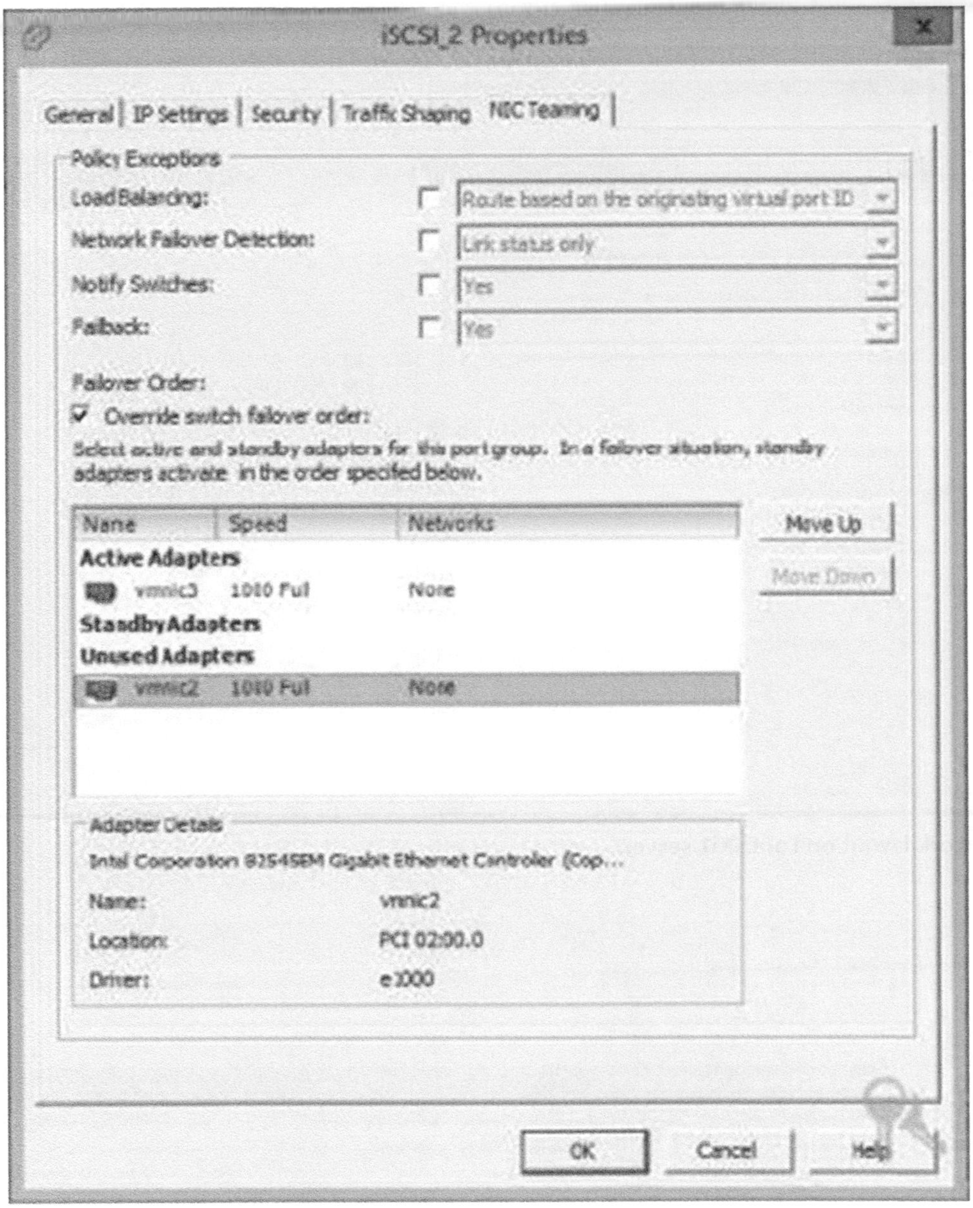

Figure 5.48   iSCSI_2 NIC Teaming Properties.

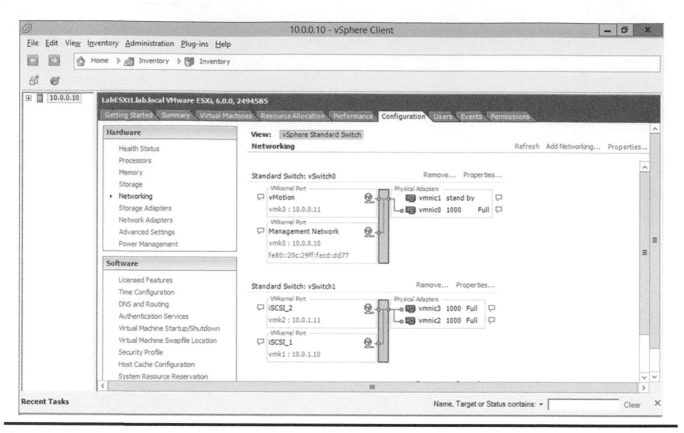

Figure 5.49   Network layout on LabESXi1 server.

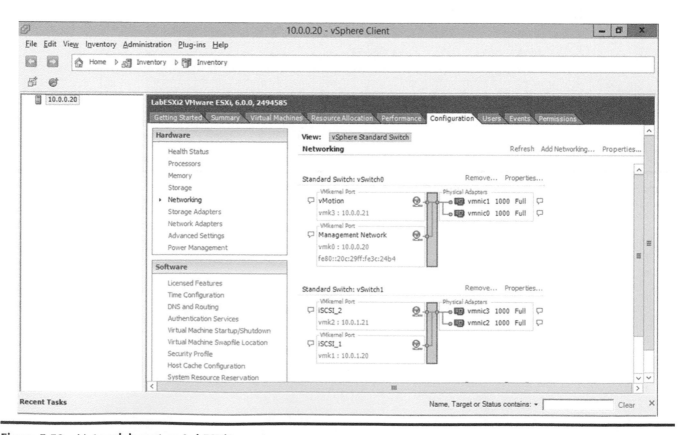

Figure 5.50   Network layout on LabESXi2 server.

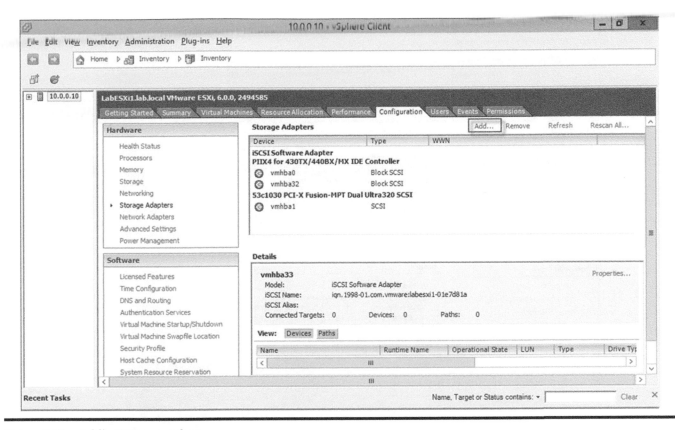

Figure 5.51 Adding Storage Adapter.

Figure 5.52 Adding Software iSCSI Adapter.

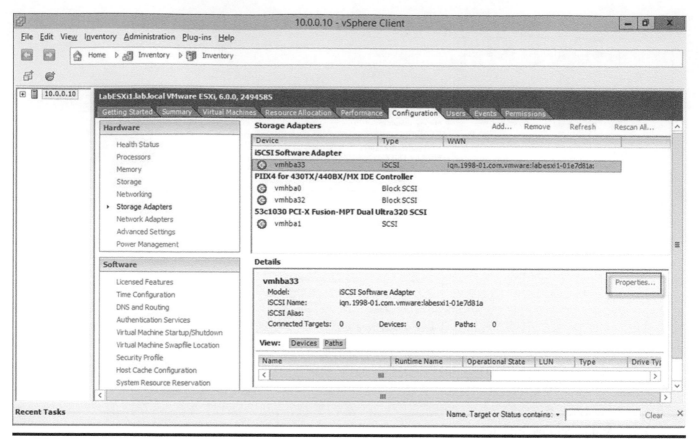

Figure 5.53 Storage Adapter Properties.

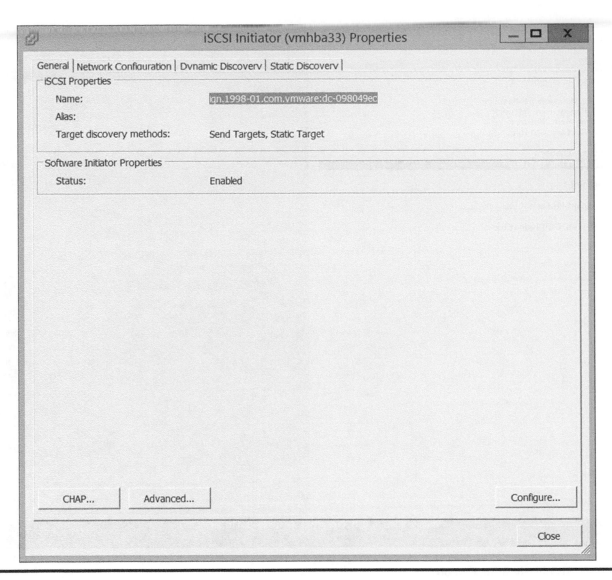

Figure 5.54   Copying iqn.

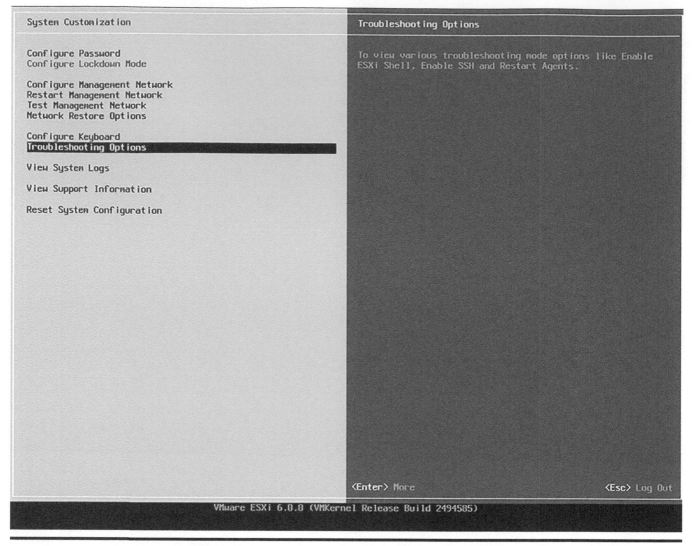

Figure 5.55 **Troubleshooting Options.**

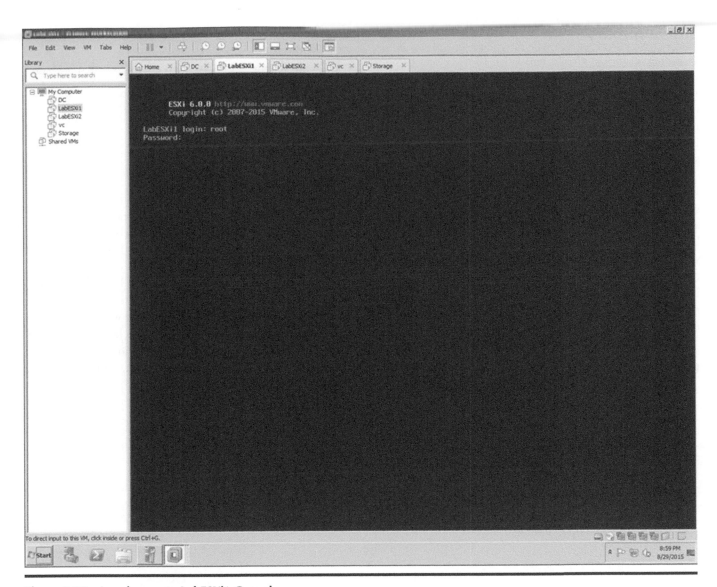

Figure 5.56 Logging on to LabESXi1 Console.

```
[root@LabESXi1:~] vmkping 10.0.1.3
PING 10.0.1.3 (10.0.1.3): 56 data bytes
64 bytes from 10.0.1.3: icmp_seq=0 ttl=128 time=0.917 ms
64 bytes from 10.0.1.3: icmp_seq=1 ttl=128 time=24.593 ms
64 bytes from 10.0.1.3: icmp_seq=2 ttl=128 time=1.167 ms

--- 10.0.1.3 ping statistics ---
3 packets transmitted, 3 packets received, 0% packet loss
round-trip min/avg/max = 0.917/8.892/24.593 ms
[root@LabESXi1:~] ping 10.0.1.3
PING 10.0.1.3 (10.0.1.3): 56 data bytes
64 bytes from 10.0.1.3: icmp_seq=0 ttl=128 time=0.808 ms
64 bytes from 10.0.1.3: icmp_seq=1 ttl=128 time=0.756 ms
64 bytes from 10.0.1.3: icmp_seq=2 ttl=128 time=0.760 ms

--- 10.0.1.3 ping statistics ---
3 packets transmitted, 3 packets received, 0% packet loss
round-trip min/avg/max = 0.756/0.775/0.808 ms
```

Figure 5.57 Testing network.

5.6 Summary

This chapter covers virtual networks. In the cloud computing environment, virtual networks are used to connect DCs, ESXi host servers, vCenter Servers, storage devices, and virtual machines. They are used to link the virtualized computing environment to the physical networks. This chapter introduces virtual network components. Two types of virtual switches, the vSwitch and vDS, are described in this chapter. These switches are used to construct virtual networks. The vSwitch is used to construct a virtual network hosted by a single ESXi host server. The vDS can be used to construct a virtual network across multiple ESXi host servers. The hands-on activity illustrates how to create a virtual network with the vSwitch. To prepare for the hands-on practice for the next chapter, a storage server is installed and configured in this chapter so that it can communicate with the virtual network. In the next chapter, you will learn how to implement and manage network-based storage devices.

REVIEW QUESTIONS

1. Describe how virtual networks can be used to facilitate the centralized management in the virtualized IT infrastructure.
2. Describe how a virtual switch works in a VMware Workstation.
3. What does a virtual network adapter do in a VMware Workstation?
4. What is a vSwitch?
5. What is a vDS?
6. Describe a port group.
7. What is a VMkernel port used for?
8. What is a VM port used for?
9. What is a trunk port used for?
10. What is an access port used for?
11. Describe an emulated virtual network adapter.
12. Describe a paravirtualized virtual network adapter.
13. What are differences between the E1000 network adapter and E1000E network adapter?
14. What are the new features built in a VMXNET 3 network adapter?
15. How does a flexible network adapter work?
16. What is a management network, and how does it work?
17. What is a VMkernel network, and how does it work?
18. What is a virtual machine network, and how does it work?
19. What is NIC teaming, and how does it work?
20. What are the benefits of a vDS?

Chapter 6

Network Shared Storage

Objectives

- Understand the role played by shared storage devices
- Install and configure a networked storage device
- Share the storage device among Elastic Sky X Integrated hosts

6.1 Introduction

Shared storage is a vital component of the VMware computing environment. In shared storage, the unused storage space is available to every Elastic Sky X Integrated (ESXi) host. On the other hand, by sharing data, the data do not have to be duplicated on each individual ESXi host's hard drive. It is also true that the virtual machines stored on a shared storage device can run on any ESXi host in a cluster of ESXi hosts. The shared storage allows application software to be shared by multiple ESXi hosts. Once an application is stored in the shared storage, it can be run by any virtual machines hosted by different ESXi hosts. Therefore, the shared storage is more efficient. More importantly, the shared storage allows advanced features such as vMotion to live-migrate virtual machines from one ESXi host to another ESXi host without disrupting the operation. When an ESXi host is offline for maintenance, the virtual machines hosted by the ESXi host can be moved to another ESXi host. In addition, in a vSphere system, many resource management tools depend on the shared storage. For example, the vSphere High Availability (HA) tool needs the shared storage for virtual machine recovery.

The goal of this chapter is to understand the infrastructure of a shared storage system. You will learn about shared storage concepts and architecture. You will also learn about shared storage software, shared storage hardware, and protocols used in shared storage. This chapter examines the role played by a storage array in supporting virtualization and

cloud computing. It shows how to design a storage array to meet the requirements of a VMware infrastructure. This chapter also covers the implementation and configuration of shared storage.

6.2 Network Shared Storage Architecture

Shared storage usually consists of the following components:

- *Storage processor (SP):* It is used to process storage input/output (I/O) and run storage software.
- *Storage software:* The software is included for storage management tasks such as making snapshots, data recovery, data archiving, data migration, data replication, storage quality of service (QoS), allocating storage space on demand, and so on.
- *Cache memory:* It is used by the SP to improve performance.
- *Storage disks:* They can be hard drives. These disks are used to store virtual machines and application software.
- *Network interfaces:* They are used to connect ESXi hosts and storage devices. Fibre Channel (FC) and Ethernet are commonly used for establishing connectivity.

In the VMware computing environment, a storage array is required to store virtual machines created by ESXi hosts. For an enterprise, the storage array used to support e-commerce consists of a number of network storage devices that form an array. Multiple ESXi hosts can share the same storage array. Each ESXi host can also use its own hard drive for storage. The storage system can be managed by vCenter. Figure 6.1 illustrates the storage system in a VMware computing environment.

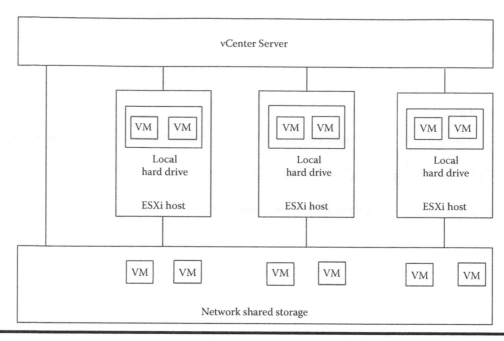

Figure 6.1 Storage system.

There are a large number of storage devices to choose on the market, and the storage devices can be configured in many ways. The ultimate goal of the design of a storage system is to make sure that the storage system meets the requirements. As a key component of the VMware computing environment, the storage array should meet the requirements of reliability, capacity, connectivity, compatibility, affordability, and performance. The following paragraphs briefly describe these requirements.

Reliability: It is required that the storage array be highly dependable. Reliability has a great impact on the VMware computing environment. The availability of virtual machines and virtual networks depends on the storage array. vCenter and ESXi hosts depend on the storage array to implement features such as vMotion, HA, and Distributed Resource Scheduler (DRS).

Capacity: The storage array must have adequate capacity to store all the virtual machines. It should be able to handle a large workload on data storage and data transmission. The storage array should be expandable for future growth.

Connectivity: It is also required that the storage array be able to communicate with every ESXi host on the network for the management of virtual machines. The storage array should support network devices with high network bandwidth. The operation of the VMware ESXi host relies on the storage array connection attributes such as bandwidth and the latency of the connection and the storage I/O transmission rate, also called throughput.

Compatibility: It is required that the storage array be compatible with the ESXi hosts. Not all the storage devices are supported by an ESXi host. The storage devices should be carefully selected based on the hardware compatibility guide provided by VMware.

Affordability: One of the requirements is to meet the budget limitation. The storage array should be evaluated by its cost and whether it can meet all the other requirements.

Performance: It is critical for the storage array to meet the performance requirement of the ESXi host. The performance of the ESXi host is directly impacted by the performance of the storage array. The performance of the virtual machines and virtual network devices also depends on the storage array. The performance is also based on the applications running on the storage array. Some of the applications may require intense update on the data content. This type of application may require the storage to have faster response time and be able to handle a large number of I/O activities. On the other hand, some of the applications may require a large storage space, but require less update on the data content. In this case, the storage device can have slower response time and a smaller number of I/O activities. However, the kind of application may require high throughput to handle a large block of data transmission in each I/O activity.

Often, there is a trade-off between the cost and the demand for high performance and reliability.

Not all storage arrays require high performance and reliability; therefore, some storage arrays can be built with low cost and still meet the requirements. The requirements can be classified at the following levels:

■ *High-level requirement:* A storage array is required to have high performance and HA. To meet the high-level requirement, the storage array should support multiserver replication, point-in-time restoration, snapshots for backup, host server clustering, multiple solid-state drive (SSD) disk drives for forming a redundant array of independent disks (RAID) system, FC storage area network (SAN), and the high-end server machines and network equipment.

- *Mid-level requirement:* A storage array is required to have mid-level performance and availability. To meet the mid-level requirement, the storage array should support server replication, snapshots for backup, multiple hybrid disk drives for forming a RAID system, FC or Internet Small Computer System Interface (iSCSI) SAN, and the mid-level server machines and network equipment.
- *Low-level requirement:* A storage array is required to have low-level performance and availability. To meet the low-level requirement, the storage array should support snapshots for backup, multiple Serial Advanced Technology Attachment (SATA) disk drives, iSCSI network-attached storage (NAS) or Network File System (NFS), and affordable server machines and network equipment.

The requirements may change from different time periods. Requirement changes may follow the changes in an organization's infrastructure, in the technology trend, and in the organization's IT policies. Without upgrading, a high-end storage array may become a storage array with low performance. As time passes by, a mission-critical requirement may no longer be required. On the other hand, the storage array may be started for lab experiments, and then it is upgraded to meet the mission-critical requirement later.

6.3 Storage Array System

For the storage system design, let us first investigate the technologies used in the storage system infrastructure. The pros and cons of the technologies of the storage system will be examined in this section. The following will be covered in the discussion:

- Description of storage system
- RAID technology
- Storage array technology
- Storage network
- Datastore

6.3.1 Description of Storage System

Virtual machines can be stored either in the local storage or shared network storage. The local storage is the hard drive installed on an ESXi host. As the local storage cannot be used

to implement VMware features such as vMotion, vSphere DRS, and vSphere HA, it is not recommended to store virtual machines for daily operations. On the other hand, the local storage can be used to store backups or snapshots. Therefore, the network shared storage is the choice for the VMware computing environment. The following describes some of the storage technologies.

Network shared storage: There are two types of standard network storage: (1) storage area network (SAN) and (2) network-attached storage (NAS). As the name indicates, SAN is a network that may connect multiple storage arrays. On the other hand, an NAS array is a storage device connected to a network. A qualified end user is allowed to save data directly to an NAS device. In contrast, end users are not allowed to save data directly to an SAN. Data need to be saved through an application installed on a host server. For a relatively small datacenter, the NAS device is the choice. NAS is less expensive and easy to manage and provides better security. It is especially suitable for small businesses.

On the other hand, SAN is designed for handling large data transfers. The installation of an SAN can be complicated. Installing the SAN involves storage devices, SAN controllers, network routers and switches, and the cables specially designed for the SAN technology. As the SAN connects multiple high-performance servers to multiple disk arrays, it allows servers installed with different types of operating systems to share the data stored on multiple disk arrays, as shown in Figure 6.2. SAN switches are used to connect various components of the SAN such as ESXi hosts and storage arrays. In the SAN system, multiple storage devices can be integrated so that the data appear to be stored in a single network storage device. When multiple network storage devices are connected to the ESXi hosts, a logical unit number (LUN) is used to identify a network storage unit, a storage device, or a hard disk.

The SAN fabric is a physical network connecting physical devices in an SAN. For handling the large data transfer, the SAN uses the FC fabric technology, which is specially designed for faster communication among storage devices. The FC protocol is primarily used for data communication among ESXi servers, SAN switches, and data storage. An SAN may include two or more fabrics for redundancy.

For a host to access a storage device on the SAN, the host sends out an access request. The request is encapsulated into FC packets and sent to a host bus adapter (HBA), which is a network adapter that provides I/O processing and physical connection between an ESXi host and a storage device. Through the HBA, the FC packets are transmitted to the fiber optic cable that leads to one of the SAN switches. The SAN switch forwards the request to the storage device, which will process the request.

Server Cluster: In Figure 6.2, multiple ESXi servers are connected to multiple switches, which are connected to

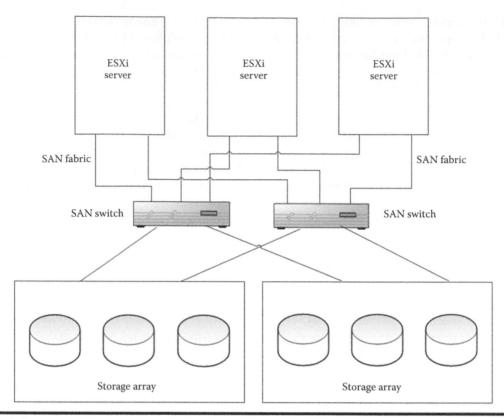

Figure 6.2   SAN architecture.

multiple storage arrays for HA. To achieve HA, it is required that the storage network be configured so that

- The ESXi hosts, network switches, and storage arrays are connected with redundant paths.
- All of the ESXi hosts in a cluster should be able to access the same storage array.

To prevent failure, multiple ESXi servers are used to form a server cluster, as shown in Figure 6.2. In a cluster, two or more ESXi servers are connected with a high-speed network and work together like a single logical server. In the case that one of the servers fails, the operation on the failed server can be continued on the other ESXi servers in the same cluster. VMware supports different ways of implementing a cluster, as shown in the following:

- *Cluster in a Box:* This type of cluster implementation is at the operating system and application level. That is, when two virtual machines on the same host are configured as the failover server for each other, if one of them fails, the other one will take over. At the operating system and application level, this type of cluster has no protection during the failure of an ESXi host server.
- *Cluster across Boxes:* This type of cluster implementation is at the host level. For this type of cluster, a

virtual machine on one host is clustered with another virtual machine on a different host. These two virtual machines are configured as the failover server for each other. This type of cluster can provide protection during the failure of an ESXi host server.

- *Physical to virtual clustering (N+1 clustering):* N+1 clustering means that an extra standby ESXi server is needed to host a group of virtual machines, each of which is clustered with a virtual machine on an ESXi host. In case that one of the host servers or a virtual machine hosted by the server fails, the virtual machine on the standby host will take over.

Clustering virtual machines can reduce the hardware cost and provide failure protection on software and hardware. Clustering even provides protection on the failure of an ESXi host service. The implementation of a cluster requires all the ESXi host servers to be able to access the same storage. Therefore, SANs are commonly used to build the network between ESXi host servers and storage arrays. All LUNs used to construct the cluster should be connected to all the ESXi hosts.

Hard disk: Four types of hard disks can be used in a storage device. The first type is known as Integrated Drive Electronics (IDE). This type of hard disk has a lower transmission rate and is a bit complicated to install. Nowadays, this type of hard disk is being substituted by the SATA hard disk. The SATA hard disk has a much faster data transmission rate and is easier to install. It also uses less electricity. The disadvantage of the SATA disk is that it gets loose easily and falls out of its socket. The third type of hard disk is the Small Computer System Interface (SCSI) hard disk. The SCSI hard disk has a higher spin speed at 10,000–15,000 rpm, while the IDE and SATA hard disks generally spin at 7,200 rpm. The higher the revolutions per minute (rpm) is, the faster the data access. On the other hand, the higher the rpm, the quicker it is worn out. The fourth type of hard disk is the solid-state drive, which is a newly developed hard disk technology. Unlike the other three types of hard disks, the SSD has no moving component. In a SSD hard disk, data are moved electronically. Since there are no moving parts, the SSD hard disk is much faster and less likely to wear out. The SSD disk can be more than 10 times faster than a 10,000-rpm hard drive. As the price of the SSD is moving down significantly, it is recommended to install SSD hard disks in a network storage device.

6.3.2 RAID Technology

Clustering can be used to provide protection for the software and hardware on an ESXi host server. The RAID system can be used for the protection of physical desks in case of failure and for performance improvement. In a network storage device, the RAID system is constructed with multiple hard disks for redundancy and performance improvement.

In a RAID system, data are distributed over multiple hard disks. The advantages of distributing data over multiple disks are briefly described in the following:

■ Multiple disk drives work together for better performance and reliability.
■ Data are spread across multiple disk drives for better I/O throughput.
■ Data redundancy provides better fault tolerance.
■ RAID can be formed at different levels.

The commonly used RAID levels are RAID 0 (striping) for improving performance, RAID 1 (mirroring) for better fault tolerance, RAID 5 (striping with parity) for better fault tolerance and performance, and RAID 10 (striping and mirroring) for better fault tolerance and performance. The description of each RAID level is given as follows.

RAID 0: This RAID structure divides a set of data into multiple blocks and stores these data blocks on multiple hard drives, as shown in Figure 6.3. Using multiple hard drives means that there will be multiple I/O channels. Therefore, the I/O performance can be improved. The RAID 0 technology is also called *disk striping*. A data block in disk striping is called a stripe. The multiple disk drives work together like a single logical disk drive.

As shown in Figure 6.3, two hard drives are used to improve performance. On the other hand, RAID 0 is not used as mission-critical storage since the RAID 0 structure has no data redundancy. This means that if any of the disks fails, the entire logical disk fails with it.

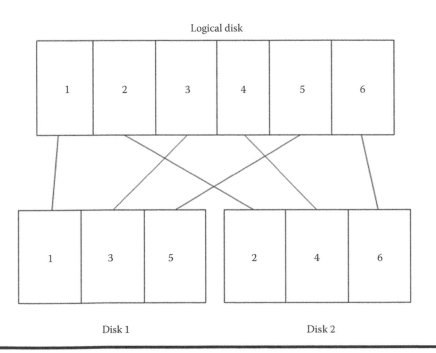

Figure 6.3 RAID 0 structure.

RAID 1: This RAID 1 structure provides fault tolerance by duplicating a set of data to multiple disks, as shown in Figure 6.4. If one disk drive fails, the other hard disk will continue to function so that no data are lost.

As shown in Figure 6.4, two hard drives are used to improve fault tolerance. On the other hand, RAID 1 degrades performance and raises the cost. This is due to the fact that every operation must be performed twice, and the cost on the disk drives is doubled.

RAID 5: By using the additional parity bits, the RAID 5 structure improves performance, as well as fault tolerance (Figure 6.5). In RAID 5, the data blocks are stored on multiple hard drives to improve performance. In the case that a disk drive fails, the parity bits can be used to recover the lost data.

As shown in Figure 6.5, RAID 5 provides fault tolerance with parity bits. Unlike RAID 1, which uses twice as much disk space for fault tolerance, RAID 5 achieves the same goal by using only a fraction of a disk drive to store parity bits. It also has better reading performance with disk striping. However, its written performance is degraded a bit due to the calculation and storing of the parity bits.

Table 6.1 illustrates how the lost data can be recovered by using odd parity. Suppose that RAID 5 is constructed with two disks. Each disk stores the binary bit values, either 1 or 0. Being the odd parity, for each pair of the Disk 1 bit and Disk 2 bit, the parity bit is added so that the sum is as follows:

Disk 1 bit + Disk 2 bit + parity bit = an odd number

Similarly, for the even parity, the sum should be an even number. Table 6.1 lists the possible combination of the bit values from both disks, the corresponding values for the parity bit, and the sum for the odd parity.

In the case that Disk 2 crashed, the bit values in Disk 2 can be recovered by using the Disk 1 bit and the parity bit with the following formula:

Disk 2 bit = sum − Disk 1 bit − parity bit

Table 6.2 illustrates the recovered Disk 2 bit values by using the above formula.

As RAID 5 is able to restore a crashed disk, it can be used as a mission-critical data storage infrastructure. RAID 5 is a particularly useful solution for small businesses due to its cost-efficient nature.

RAID 10: As the name indicates, RAID 10 is a combination of RAID 1 and RAID 0. It provides the features from both RAID 1 and RAID 0. That is, data striping provided by RAID 0 is used for better performance, and data duplication provided by RAID 1 is used for improving reliability. The structure of RAID 10 is illustrated in Figure 6.6.

With the improvement on both performance and reliability, RAID 10 can be considered a mission-critical data storage structure. On the other hand, RAID 10 has twice as many disks and takes more time to write to the disks. Even so, RAID 10 is still faster than RAID 5.

The RAID architecture can be used to improve performance and protect physical disks in case of failure. In the next section, the discussion will focus on the storage array technology for better performance and protection.

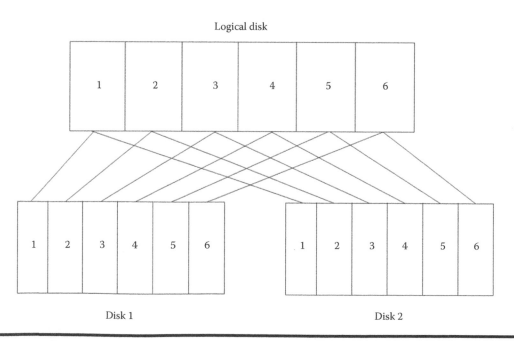

Figure 6.4 RAID 1 structure.

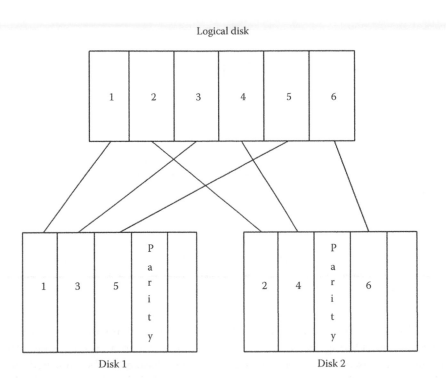

Figure 6.5 RAID 5 structure.

Table 6.1 Odd Parity in RAID 5 Structure

Disk 1 Bit Value	Disk 2 Bit Value	Parity Bit Value	Sum of Bits
0	0	1	1
0	1	0	1
1	0	0	1
1	1	1	3

Table 6.2 Recovered Disk Bits

Recovered Disk 2 Bit Value
Sum – disk bit – parity bit = 1 – 0 – 1 = 0
Sum – disk bit – parity bit = 1 – 0 – 0 = 1
Sum – disk bit – parity bit = 1 – 1 – 0 = 0
Sum – disk bit – parity bit = 3 – 1 – 1 = 1

6.3.3 Storage Array Technology

A storage array is a pool of storage devices shared by multiple servers. The storage array allows data to be moved from one storage device to another storage device. Although storage arrays vary from vendor to vendor, they all include components such as the SP, array software, cache memory, and network connection. The following provides some information about these components.

Storage processor: An SP may also be called a controller, a head, an engine, or a node. Often, pairs of SPs are working together to improve reliability. The SP is considered the brain of the storage array. It is used to run the storage array software and handle the storage array I/O. It works like a general-purpose CPU such as those produced by Intel and AMD. The SP may have as much memory as 4 GB, most of which is used for cache.

Storage array software: The software included in a storage array is mainly for management. The software can be used for data backup and recovery, testing, performance management, capacity management, thin provisioning, and storage quality service.

■ A major storage array vendor may provide tools such as data backup and recovery applications. The backup tool may include reporting, auditing, and predictive analysis services. The vendor may also provide error logs and dashboard views to reveal the backup/recovery job status.

■ A storage array may also include tools for snapshots and the cloning of virtual machines for testing and recovery. A snapshot preserves the state of a storage device at a particular time. The snapshot is available

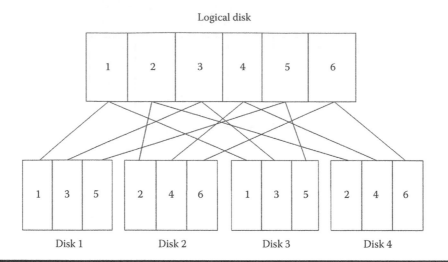

Logical disk

Figure 6.6   RAID 10 structure.

as a backup copy, and the preserved state can be used to restore failed data storage. During the creation of a snapshot, the cloning tool is used to create a complete copy of the data in a background operation.

■ Storage array vendors often provide storage resource management software. This kind of tool can illustrate how much disk space is left, the distribution of the storage usage, and the capacity transfer information. When there is a capacity shortage, the tool can reduce the capacity by archiving and deduplicating.

■ Thin provisioning is a technology that allocates storage on demand. This technology allows a virtual machine to shrink and expand virtual hard disk files to accommodate storage needs. Initially, thin provisioning may allocate a small portion of physical disk space to get started. Later, more physical disk space can be added when demand for physical storage space is increased by applications.

■ The performance monitoring and troubleshooting software may be included in a storage array. The software can be used to identify storage performance bottlenecks and fine-tune the applications running on the storage array. It tracks the I/O of resources and recommends possible improvement on the storage capacity. The administrator will be alerted about potential performance thresholds.

■ The storage QoS software is used to properly manage resources so that applications can maintain top performance. A cloud computing environment may host multiple tenants. These tenants may be ranked based on the policies. For each tenant, the software is used to prioritize the resources by specifying the maximum number of I/O per second and the latency acceptance. The software can set both a lower bound and an upper bound on storage performance.

The application software adds many useful features and functionalities to a storage array. The decision on storage array purchasing can be impacted on what application software is included and on if the third-party application software is allowed.

Cache memory: Most of the SP memory is run as cache memory. The cache memory is used for a SP to quickly access data required for calculation. The cache memory is typically integrated with the SP. The performance of the cache memory is critical to the storage array. In the SP, the cache memory is used to hold the data inputted from the ESXi server and the result of the calculation performed by the SP. When running an application, it is much faster for the SP to read from and write to the cache memory. Using the cache memory is even more efficient when an application requests the same data multiple times. For example, many virtual machines are generated with the same template.

Cache memory is commonly constructed with dynamic random access memory, which is a type of random access memory used in personal computers (PCs). It may also be constructed with NAND (NOT AND) flash memory. NAND flash memory is a type of storage technology that does not require power to retain data. This feature is also called nonvolatile, which makes NAND flash memory more reliable and easier to recover data during power failure. Another advantage of NAND flash memory is its low cost, which allows the SP to have a cost-efficient large cache memory.

There are different types of cache memory: (a) write-around cache, (b) write-through cache, and (c) write-back cache.

■ The write-around cache is loaded with the most used data for quick access.

■ The write-through cache writes data to the cache and through to the underlying permanent storage, which is good for frequently writing data.

■ The write-back cache writes data first to the cache and then acknowledges the write to the application immediately for low latency and high throughput for write-intensive applications.

6.3.4 Storage Network

A storage array includes devices for communicating with networks outside the array. Through external network connections, a storage network can accomplish the following tasks:

■ Allowing users from external networks to access the data stored in a storage array
■ Making it easier for data backup and disaster recovery
■ Connecting multiple storage arrays to an SAN

Properly configuring storage network devices can improve performance, reliability, and availability. As a critical device for the data I/O, the high-speed storage network is necessary for fast performance.

vSphere supports various storage network technologies such as FC, Fibre Channel over Ethernet (FCoE), iSCSI, NFS, and others. To have a better understanding of the storage network connection technologies, look at the following descriptions.

Fibre Channel: FC is a technology designed to connect computer servers to shared storage devices. It is the first technology used on an SAN, although other technologies can also be used on an SAN. The FC technology uses the optical interconnection, which has the data transfer rate up to 16 Gbps. In addition to the high data transfer rate, the use of optical fiber allows it to transfer data to as far as 6 mi. away, which is much longer than that of the Ethernet cable. FC may also work with twisted-pair Ethernet cables.

In the FC technology, the term *initiator* means the data consumer of storage. The network adapter on a server is the initiator, which initiates the connection to a storage array. The term *target* means the data provider, which is a volume of data or a storage array targeted by the initiator. The data volume or storage array accessible through FC or other storage network technologies can be identified by an LUN. The LUN is necessary for a host to identify a data volume so that it can be mounted individually as a storage device. In a storage array, a hard disk drive can be represented by an LUN, or an LUN can represent a portion of a hard drive, or an LUN can even represent a full storage array.

An initiator does not directly communicate with another initiator. The same is true for targets. Therefore, an initiator on a server is not directly connected to an initiator on another server. Figure 6.7 illustrates the connections of initiators and targets.

A World Wide Name (WWN) is used to uniquely identify a network interface card (NIC) port on a storage device

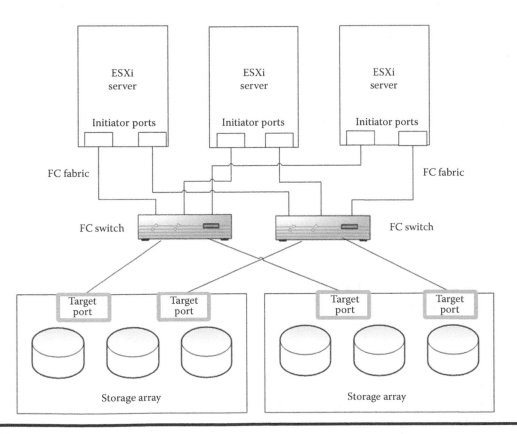

Figure 6.7 Initiator and target ports.

or a network node such as a switch. Similar to the media access control address of an NIC, the WWN is a number of 16 hex digits.

Zoning is used to define which initiator is connected to which target. A zone contains a list of initiator's port IDs and a list of target IDs to be connected by the initiator port IDs. The zone can contain many initiator ports, as well as many target ports (Figure 6.8). To allow each ESXi host to access every LUN stored on multiple storage arrays, the zone should be configured to include the initiator ports of all the ESXi hosts and the target ports of all the storage arrays. Zoning can accomplish the following tasks:

■ Zoning makes the targets visible to the initiators. That is, zoning makes the LUNs visible to the ESXi hosts.
■ Like virtual local area network (VLAN), zoning restricts network traffic to a specified route so that it prevents errors from being transmitted to other zones. If no zone is defined, there is no network traffic between the initiator and the target.

Zones can be configured either by a WWN or a port. In WWN-based zoning, the initiator's WWN and target's WWN are added to the same zone. As a WWN can be an identifier for a switch, the initiator is allowed to communicate with any port on the same switch.

Fibre Channel over Ethernet: FCoE is a technology that encapsulates FC frames into Ethernet frames so that the FC frames can be transmitted over an Ethernet network. The reason for doing so is to pass FC frames through an existing Ethernet network. Instead of building a new FC network, one can use FCoE on the existing Ethernet network. Also, as FC lacks the ability to resend lost data, it may want to take advantage of the Transmission Control Protocol (TCP). Transmission Control Protocol is an Ethernet technology that can resend lost packets. FCoE works with a single converged network adapter, which can deal with the Ethernet network traffic, as well as the FC network traffic.

Internet Small Computer System Interface: Developed by IBM, iSCSI is designed to be used by storage arrays to transmit data blocks over an Ethernet network. iSCSI allows the storage data to be encapsulated into Transmission Control Protocol/Internet Protocol (TCP/IP) packets, which are then passed through local area networks (LANs), wide area networks (WANs), or the Internet. Instead of using zoning like FC, VLANs are used to restrict the network traffic in iSCSI.

Similar to FC, data blocks are transmitted between an iSCSI initiator and an iSCSI target. The iSCSI initiator can be a software initiator or a hardware initiator. The software initiator encapsulates the iSCSI payload into a TCP/IP packet. Once the destination is reached, the TCP/IP packet is disassembled by iSCSI, and the content in the iSCSI payload will be processed by the storage operating system. ESXi hosts support the software initiator. Operating systems such as Windows XP or later, as well as Linux, all support the software initiator. The hardware iSCSI initiator is a third-party add-in adapter such as an HBA, which is treated by an operating system as a storage device. Generally, an iSCSI initiator can be identified by an iSCSI Qualified Name (IQN).

An iSCSI target is a storage device that hosts LUNs. It can also be implemented with software and hardware. Unlike FC where a target is related to a port, the iSCSI target can be related to a port or to an LUN, which is visible from multiple ports. It may be related to one or more LUNs. Like an iSCSI initiator, an iSCSI target or an LUN can be identified by an IQN.

Windows Server 2012 or later provides software-based iSCSI targets, which make virtual hard drives hosted by servers available to iSCSI initiators. Figure 6.9 illustrates the use of iSCSI targets.

Windows Server 2012 is able to support multiple iSCSI targets, each of which can be accessed by multiple iSCSI initiators. Although multiple initiators can make connections to the same target, this only works with the cluster configuration, which allows multiple initiators to access the target one at time to avoid the same data block to be updated simultaneously.

Network File System: Developed by Sun Microsystems, the NFS technology is designed to share files across a UNIX-like network system. NFS works like a client–server system where the initiator is considered as the client and the target is considered as the server. On the target side, a portion or an entire file system can be made available to the qualified initiators. On the initiator side, the exported file system can be mounted on the client machine. On the client machine, the mounted file system appears and behaves just like the one on the local computer.

When NFS is used with vSphere, it is not necessary for an ESXi server to have its own local file system. The ESXi server can mount the file system from a target storage array. By mounting the file system directly from the storage array, NFS is one of the easiest storage technologies since it does not require the configuration of zoning and VLAN. On the other hand, NFS does not support some of the high-performance and availability features.

Network technology comparison: The design of a storage array depends on the needs of an organization and budget constraints. It depends on the IT staff members' skills. It also depends on the available technology and the existing IT infrastructure. The software tools included in the storage array can also be a decision factor. Most of the time, an iSCSI storage architecture meets the requirements of a small- and medium-sized business. For a large enterprise, the FC architecture can be the solution.

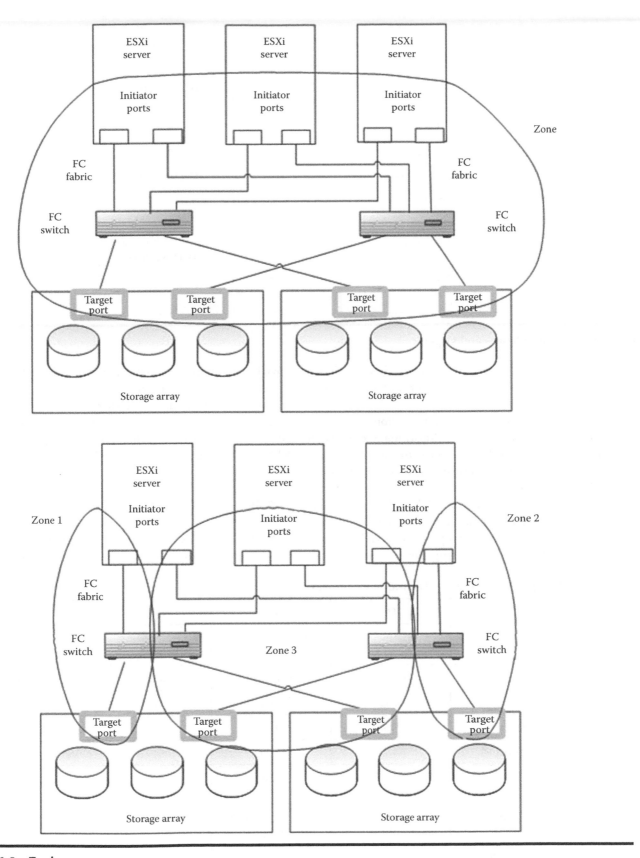

Figure 6.8 Zoning.

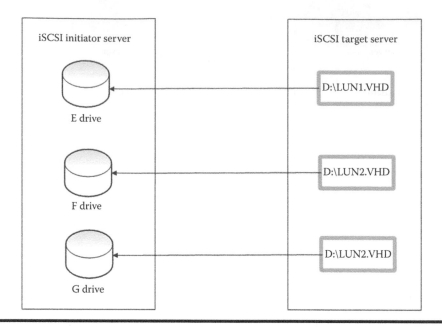

Figure 6.9 iSCSI initiators and targets.

To help with the selection of a storage technology, Table 6.3 provides a comparison of the features of storage array network technologies.

In Table 6.3, PSA stands for pluggable storage architecture. The goal of PSA is to make multipathing flexible. With PSA, any ESXi host can be connected to multiple storage arrays at any given time. Multipathing maintains multiple connections between ESXi hosts and storage arrays. It can be implemented by connecting multiple HBAs to multiple switches, and multiple switches are connected to multiple storage arrays. NIC teaming groups several NICs to form a single logical NIC. NIC teaming can increase network capacity and support passive failover in case that one of the NICs in the team goes down.

As shown in Table 6.3, rather than booting up ESXi from the local storage on the host server, the storage array allows ESXi to boot up from a boot image stored on an SAN. Booting up ESXi from the SAN may have the following benefits:

■ It is relatively simple to do cloning directly on a storage array.
■ It meets the diskless requirement on an ESXi host. Some of the blade systems have the diskless configuration.

Table 6.3 Storage Array Network Technology Features

Feature	FC	FCoE	iSCSI	NFS
ESXi boot from an SAN	Yes	Yes, only from hardware	Yes	No
Ease of configuration	Difficult	Difficult	Medium	Easy
Dynamic extension	Yes	Yes	Yes	Yes
Raw device mapping (RDM)	Yes	Yes	Yes	No
Max device size supported	64 TB	64 TB	64 TB	Vendor dependent
Max number of devices supported	256	256	256	Default 8, Max 256
Multipathing and scaling	PSA for failover and multipathing	PSA for failover and multipathing	PSA for failover and multipathing	NIC teaming and routing
Support DRS, HA, FT, and vMotion for vSphere and storage	Yes	Yes	Yes	Yes

- When booting up ESXi from the SAN, there is no need to do the maintenance of the local storage on the ESXi host.
- Booting from the SAN can use the disk space more efficiently.
- A diskless ESXi server costs less and consumes less power.
- When SSD disks are used in the storage array, booting from the SAN can achieve better performance.
- It is easier to build a replication system in the SAN architecture. This means that, during an event of failure, the ESXi host can be rapidly recovered.

In some cases, one should not consider booting up from the SAN; for example,

- Some of the SAN storage arrays do not support booting from the SAN.
- Putting everything in the SAN may cause a single-point-of-failure problem. If the SAN or its network fails, no ESXi host can be booted up.
- When a large number of ESXi hosts on the same storage array try to boot at the same time, it may cause congestion on the storage network.
- There is an I/O contention between ESXi VMkernel and ESXi services in the storage network.
- Booting from the SAN can add additional complexity.

6.3.5 Datastore

From a user's point of view, a datastore is where virtual machines are stored. The datastore allows users to access the virtual machines without knowing the technical details, such as the specifications about file systems, hard disks, data volume structures, and the storage network structure. Based on the file system used, the datastore can be Virtual Machine File System (VMFS) based or NFS based. The datastore can use storage space on one physical storage array or on several physical storage arrays, which may have different storage array technologies. The datastore simply allocates storage space for the virtual machines so that the users do not have to deal with the complexity of the physical storage technologies. Figure 6.10 illustrates datastores and their relations to the physical storage arrays. Figure 6.11 illustrates datastores viewed from a vCenter Server.

In Figure 6.10, VMX stands for VMware Configuration File, which keeps a log of key activities generated by VMware Workstation. VMDK stands for VMware Virtual Machine Disk, which is a virtual hard disk of a VMware virtual machine.

Figure 6.11 shows four datastores: one is located on the local hard drive; three are located on a storage array. Among the three, one is configured using the SATA hard drive, and the other two are using the SSD drive. Figure 6.11 also shows that the VMFS is used in the datastores. The Datastore

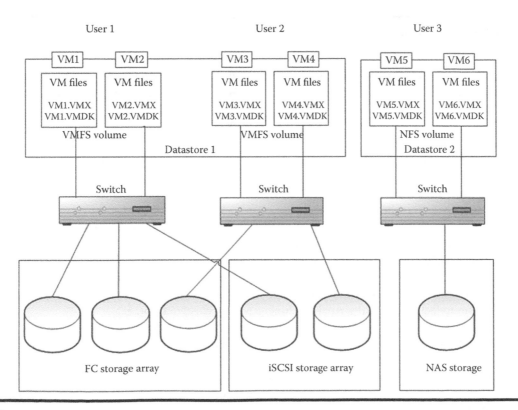

Figure 6.10   Datastores.

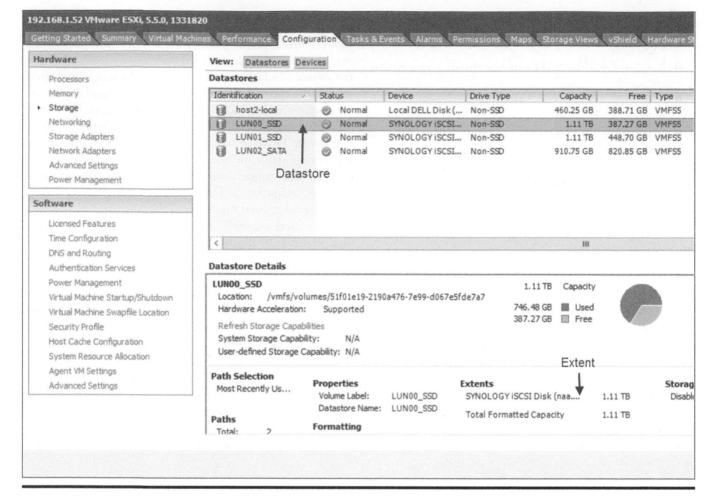

Figure 6.11 Datastores and extents.

Details pane shows that a 1.11-TB extent (partition) is configured on the datastore LUN00_SSD.

Physically, a datastore is just a set of VMFS volumes or a set of NFS directories mounted on NFS client machines. VMFS is a file system commonly used in a datastore. It is designed to work with ESXi hosts and block storage. The purpose of VMFS is to efficiently store VMDK images. Compared with file systems such as NTFS used by Windows and ext3 used by Linux, VMFS has the following features:

- VMFS is a clustered file system that allows multiple ESXi hosts to read/write in the same file system simultaneously.
- VMFS provides a simple and transparent distributed locking mechanism to lock individual virtual machine files for update.
- Multiple VMFS volumes can be integrated to form a larger VMFS volume.
- The size of a single partition in VMFS can be increased to 64 TB.
- VMFS can support more than 100,000 files.

- VMFS supports large VMDKs of up to 2 TB in size.
- VMFS can use a small subblock size of only 8 KB to reduce the amount of unused space.
- VMFS supports vSphere vStorage API for Array Integration primitives such as Atomic Test & Set for the improvement in performance and scalability, cloning blocks for mirroring LUNs, zeroing file blocks for thin provisioning, and so on.

VMFS is the key component in every storage array. It is optimized for the virtualization computing environment to handle tasks such as multiple ESXi hosts spanning, vMotion, and HA. It increases the efficacy on resource utilization by allowing multiple virtual machines to share a consolidated pool of clustered storage.

For ESXi host users, the datastore is a logical representation of storage space where virtual machines are stored. On the other hand, the LUN is a logical representation of physical storage disks, which can be constructed with various storage technologies such as FC, iSCSI, and NFS. The datastore can use LUNs, local disks, or exported NFS volumes to store virtual machines.

A VMFS datastore can consist of multiple extents (partitions) across multiple LUNs. With this design, even when an extent is missing due to the loss of a metadata section, the other parts of the datastore will still be available for operation. A datastore can be modified by adding, removing, or renaming the extents.

When virtual machines are created, they will be stored in a datastore. For better performance and reliability, one may not want to place too many virtual machines on a single LUN. The limit for the number of virtual machines placed to a single LUN can be determined by the following factors:

- The I/O activities of the virtual machines. The rate of I/O is defined by input/output operations per second (IOPS).
- The size of the virtual machines and the size of the metadata for virtual machines.
- The throughput of the LUN.
- The maximum tolerable time needed to recover the critical systems. The tolerable time for a system failure is measured by recovery time objective.

With these design considerations, VMware recommends creating LUNs with RAID 5 as the starting point. To make it easier, one may store all types of files to a single RAID 5 storage array. However, doing so is not efficient. Later, as workloads increase, based on different workloads, different RAID technologies can be used to build different LUNs. For files generated by intense update activities, consider RAID 0 for better performance. For some of the intensely updated files, which are also mission critical such as transaction log files, RAID 10 should be considered. For virtual machines that are large in size and require reasonable performance, RAID 5 is a good choice. A RAID array may contain one or more LUNs. When files in LUNs are accessed independently by multiple users, mapping these LUNs to a single RAID array may improve performance. When the update on one LUN requires the content from other LUNs in the same array, mapping these LUNs to a single RAID array may also improve performance.

In addition to VMFS, VMware supports the NFS. In a Network File System, NFS volumes can be exported by an NFS server to NFS clients. As storage clients, ESXi hosts can mount the NFS volumes exported by the storage array. In such a way, the virtual machine files stored in the NFS volumes will be available for the users. Instead of directly using the VMFS file system, a virtual machine can directly access and use a storage device through a mechanism called raw device mapping. RDM maps VMFS to a raw volume so that the raw volume appears as a VMFS volume. In such a way, the raw volume can be used to run virtual machines. The use of RDM can take advantage of VMFS when storing the virtual machines. Also, RDM can benefit from directly accessing a physical storage disk.

6.4 Activity 1: Developing Storage Array

In this activity, there will be two jobs. The first job is to determine a storage device through a case study. The second job is to implement an iSCSI storage array.

Storage array system case study: In this section, a case study is used to illustrate the implementation of a storage array system.

To design a storage array system for the hands-on practice, let us first conduct some investigations on the requirements for the availability, performance, and capacity. During the hands-on practice, students will use virtual machines to construct a VMware computing environment. By the end of the semester, these virtual machines will be deleted. During the learning process, it is likely that the students will make some mistakes that may cause the system to shut down. However, this may not necessarily be a bad thing for the learners who may gain some experience from troubleshooting. In the worst-case scenario, the students can delete and recreate the virtual machines. Therefore, the availability requirement for the storage array system is relatively low. The RAID architecture may not be necessary. A replication is also not necessary for this small project. FC is designed for working with an SAN to gain the enterprise-level performance and availability. For such a small project, the SAN and FC are not required. The storage technologies iSCSI and NFS will be able to meet the requirements.

For the performance, one can estimate the throughput of a virtual machine by using performance-monitoring tools provided by the vCenter Server. For the lab project, the virtual machines are active during the start-up process. Otherwise, they are idle most of the time. For a light ESXi server, it is estimated that, on average, each ESXi server may have about 50 IOPS. For the other virtual machines, the IOPS should be less than 50 IOPS. An Ethernet-based network should be able to handle such a workload. It has been tested that an NAS-based iSCSI storage array can handle 20 virtual machines that are booted up simultaneously at the beginning of a class. The NAS storage array has 7,200-rpm SATA hard drives installed. It will take extra time for the virtual machines to boot up if SATA hard drives are used. It is recommended that SSD drives should be considered if they are available.

For the capacity, each group of students needs at least three virtual machines for ESXi host servers: one for vCenter, one for vShield, and one for vCloud Director. Depending on the implementation plan, a few more virtual machines, such as a database server, may be needed. Overall, each group may not need more than 10 virtual machines. Assume that, on average, each virtual machine requires 60-GB storage space. Then, each group of students may require 500-GB storage space. Suppose that a class has 10 groups of students. A total of 5-TB storage space is required. If an NAS storage array is available for the lab project, a set of hard drives with 5-TB capacity should be installed. Another solution is to use the local storage space. Suppose that, in a computer lab, there are 10 PCs, each with a minimum of 500-GB storage space available. The created virtual machines can be stored locally on the PCs. In such a case, there is no need for an NAS device. The use of storage space can be significantly reduced if the virtual machines are created as thin-provisioned virtual machines. The size of the virtual disk file in a thin-provisioned virtual machine is only as much as is actually used. Most of the virtual machines in the lab project are not fully loaded. Therefore, the 500-GB storage space is enough for each physical PC in the lab.

For the low-level project described, the storage array can be a separate NAS device or simply a local hard disk. It is the best if the local hard disk is an SSD disk. Otherwise, if slow performance can be tolerated, a SATA local hard disk may also work. For the lab activity, a PC with 500-GB SATA hard drive can meet the storage requirement. Dell Precision T1700 with a 500-GB hard drive installed will work for this project, too.

For the storage network technology, we have three choices: (1) FC, (2) iSCSI, and (3) NFS. FC requires different network devices such as NICs, cables, and the FC switch. Replacing the existing Ethernet network with FC can significantly increase cost. In reality, FC is not considered for our small project. Both iSCSI and NFS can be built on the Ethernet network. As a storage technology on Ethernet with lower cost, iSCSI and NFS can achieve some degree of high performance and availability as FC does.

Between iSCSI and NFS, iSCSI is a block-based storage technology. The block-based storage technology delivers data as a block to the ESXi server. On the other hand, NFS is a file-based storage technology. The ESXi host server can share the files exported by the network storage array. iSCSI and NFS have their own pros and cons. The block-based storage technology has the following benefits for constructing a storage array:

- The block-based storage technology offers better performance than the file-based storage technology.
- It is usually more reliable and more efficient than file-based storage.
- Block storage can be formatted with VMFS, which is designed for VMware vSphere virtualization.
- Block storage allows ESXi to boot up from a boot image stored on an SAN.
- Each individual block can be formatted with different file systems to meet the requirements.
- Each individual block can be dealt with as an individual hard disk and can be controlled by an external operating system for flexibility.

For those who have PC experience, NFS is relatively easy to set up and maintain. The following are some of advantages of the NFS technology:

- NFS can lower the cost even further as it can use an existing server as an NAS server to export files to ESXi host servers.
- NFS works well with PC file systems such as NTFS for Windows and ext3 for Linux. Therefore, it is easy to integrate NFS with an existing IT infrastructure.
- NFS works well with an NAS-based storage array. It is relatively easy to set up the NAS device and configure the access control.
- Once mounted on an ESXi host, the NFS storage can be easily accessed by the ESXi host.

For learning purposes, iSCSI is selected for the hands-on activity in this chapter. By doing so, you will learn about block-based storage, which is a commonly used storage technology. For PC users who are unfamiliar with block-based storage, it is an opportunity to learn about this important technology. Also, the software target can be implemented with the widely available Windows Server 2012. In such a way, one does not have to purchase a separate physical storage array for the lab activity.

iSCSI storage implementation: In this section, you will install and configure the iSCSI storage. Before implementing the iSCSI storage, you need to add hard drives to the storage server and prepare the network for management. Then, you will create software targets with Windows Server 2012 and add hard drives to the targets. You will also need to configure the target so that it is available to the initiators. The installation and configuration of the iSCSI storage can be accomplished with the following tasks:

- *Task 1:* Installation preparation
- *Task 2:* Storage adapter and target creation
- *Task 3:* Initiator configuration

Let us start with Task 1.

6.4.1 Task 1: Installation Preparation

In this task, you will add hard disks to the Storage server created in Chapter 5. Once the hard drives have been added, you need to format the hard drives.

1. Start VMware WorkStation by right-clicking the **VMware WorkStation** icon on the desktop and select **Run as Administrator**.
2. Before you start the project, check your physical server to see how many physical hard disks are available to implement the network storage array. For example,

Figure 6.12 shows three hard drives on the physical machine. The C drive is used to host the operating system and applications for the physical machine. The D and E drives are available for the network storage array.

3. Right-click the newly created virtual machine **Storage** and select **Settings**. In the Settings dialog, click the **Add** button to open the Add Hardware Wizard. Select **Hard Disk**, as shown in Figure 6.13, and click **Next** twice to go to the Select a Disk page.

4. Click the option **Use a Physical Disk**, as shown in Figure 6.14. Then, click **Next**.

5. On the Select a Physical Disk page, select an available physical disk such as **PhysicalDrive1** in Figure 6.15 and click **Next**.

6. On the Specify Disk File page (Figure 6.16), click **Finish**.

7. Similarly, you can add another physical hard drive if it is available, as shown in Figure 6.17.

8. Power on the virtual machine **Storage**. After logging on, you may see that the physical hard disk is not shown on the Storage server. (If the hard drive is shown, skip the next two steps.)

9. To fix the problem, open the **Command Prompt** window; enter the command **diskpart** to check if the SAN is set as offline (Figure 6.18).

10. If the SAN is set as offline, on the Start menu, type **Create and format hard disk partitions**. Right-click the offline disk name and select **online**, as shown in Figure 6.19.

11. Similarly, add another physical hard drive.

12. Now, you should be able to see the physical hard disks shown in File Explorer (Figure 6.20).

6.4.2 Task 2: Storage Adapter and Target Creation

After the data storage is assigned to an iSCSI target, this data storage is available to the iSCSI initiator. The following steps illustrate how to create initiators and targets:

1. Start the virtual machines, DC, LabESXi1, LabESXi2, Storage, and vc. Log on to the Storage server. To install a target, in the Server Manager dialog of the Storage virtual machine, click **Add Roles and Features**.

2. In the Add Roles and Features Wizard, click **Next** three times to go the Select server roles page. Expand the nodes **File and Storage Services** and **File and iSCSI Services**. Then, check the option **iSCSI Target Server**, as shown in Figure 6.21. Then, click **Next** a few times to go to the Confirm installation selections page.

3. On the Confirm installation selections page, click **Install**.

4. In Server Manager, click the **File and Storage Services** link, as shown in Figure 6.22.

5. Click the **iSCSI** link, and then click the link **To create an iSCSI virtual disk, start the New iSCSI Virtual Disk Wizard** (Figure 6.23).

6. On the Select iSCSI virtual disk location page, select the option **Select by volume**. Click the volume **E**, as shown in Figure 6.24. Then, click **Next**.

7. On the Specify iSCSI virtual disk name page, enter the name **Datastore1** (Figure 6.25). Then, click **Next**.

8. On the Specify Virtual Disk Size page, specify the virtual disk size based on the available capacity, as shown in Figure 6.26. Check the option **Dynamically expanding**. Then, click **Next**.

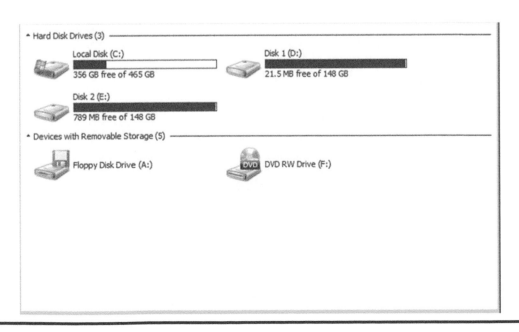

Figure 6.12   Hard drives available for storage device.

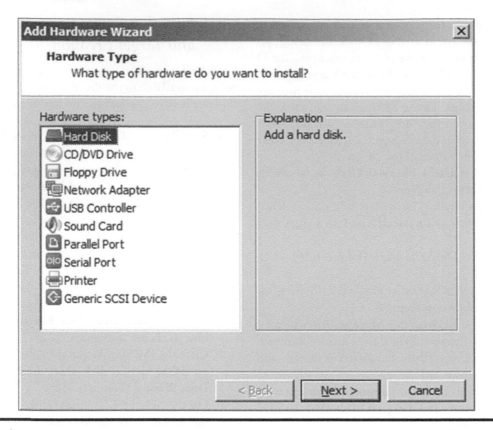

Figure 6.13 Hardware type.

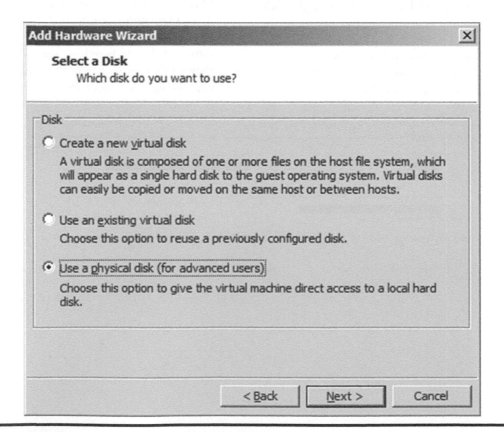

Figure 6.14 Disk selection.

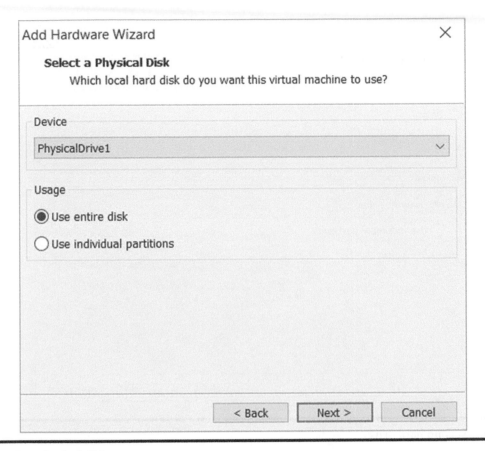

Figure 6.15   Selecting physical disk.

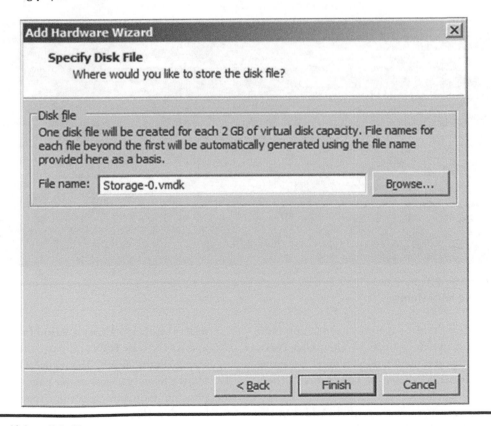

Figure 6.16   Specifying disk file.

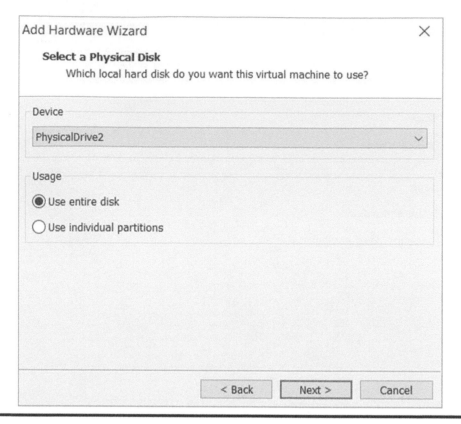

Figure 6.17   Adding second hard drive.

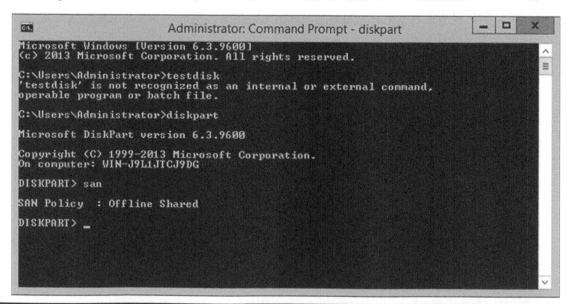

Figure 6.18   Checking SAN status.

9. On the Assign iSCSI target page, select the option **New iSCSI target**, as shown in Figure 6.27. Then, click **Next**.

10. On the Specify target name page, enter the name **LabESXi1.lab.local**, as shown in Figure 6.28. Then, click **Next**.

11. On the Specify access server page, click **Add**. On the Select a method to identify the initiator name page,

select the option **Enter a value for the selected type**. Specify the type **IQN** and paste the **iqn** value copied in Step 4 (Figure 6.29). Then, click **OK**.

12. On the Specify access server page, click **Next** twice.

13. On the Confirm selections page, check the configuration (Figure 6.30) and click **Create**. Then, click **Close**.

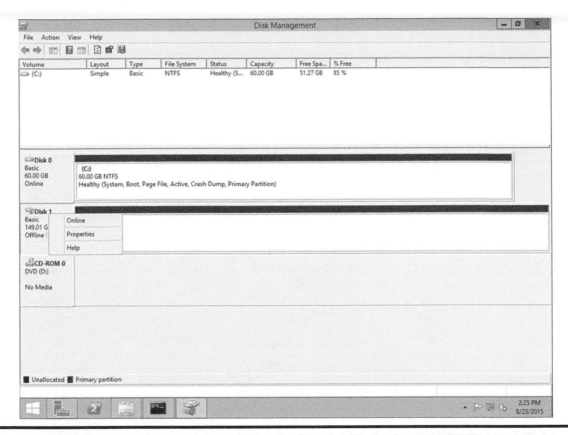

Figure 6.19   Bringing disk online.

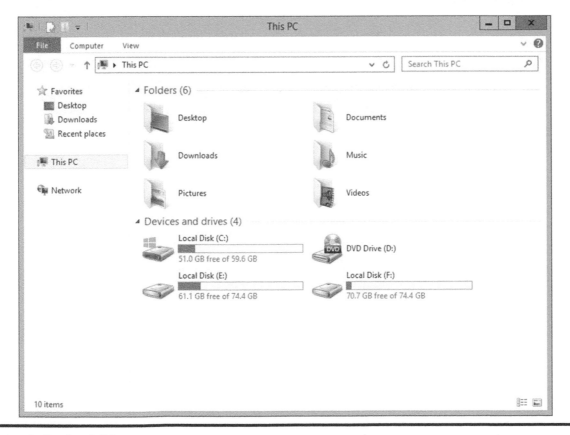

Figure 6.20   Online hard disks.

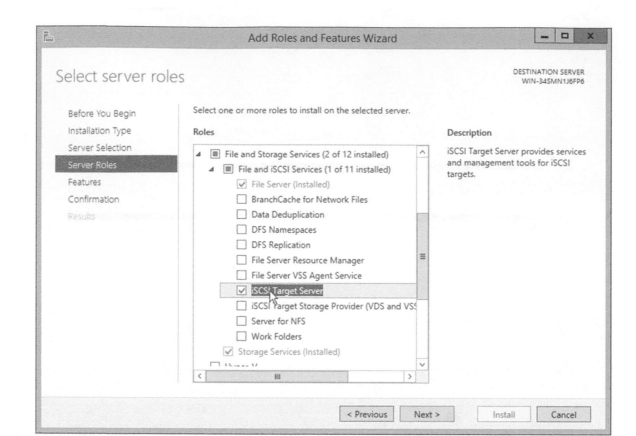

Figure 6.21 Adding iSCSI target.

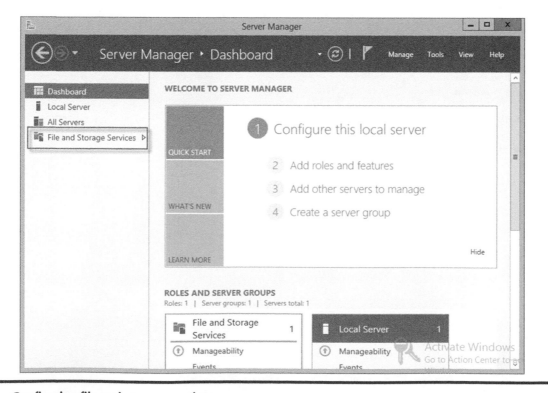

Figure 6.22 Configuring file and storage services.

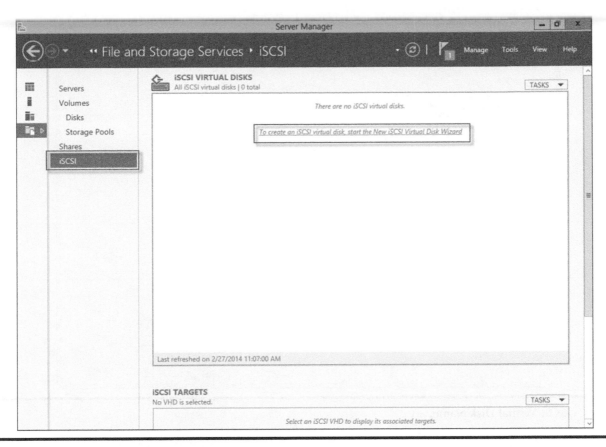

Figure 6.23 Starting New iSCSI Virtual Disk Wizard.

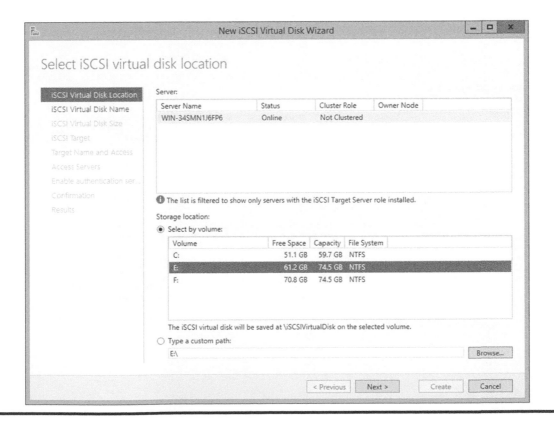

Figure 6.24 Selecting iSCSI Virtual Disk Location.

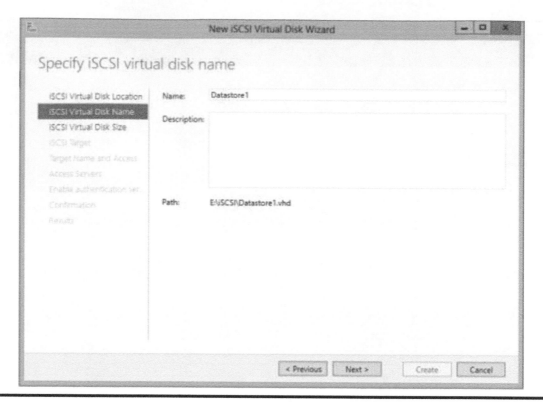

Figure 6.25   iSCSI Virtual Disk Name.

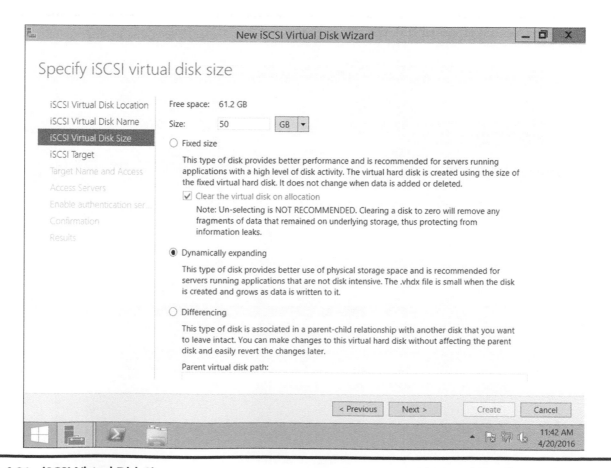

Figure 6.26   iSCSI Virtual Disk Size.

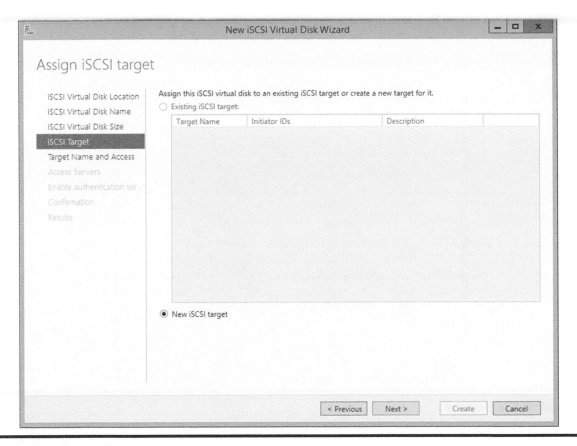

Figure 6.27   Assigning iSCSI Target.

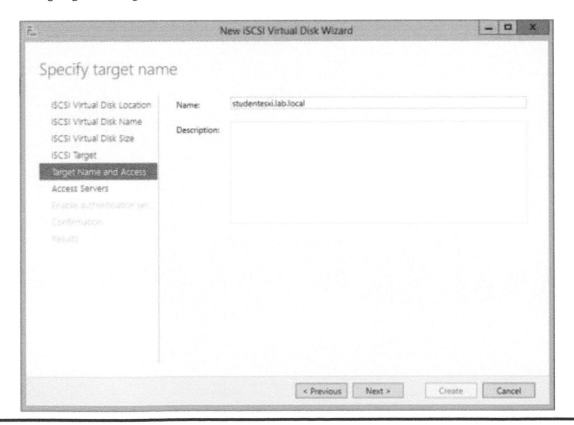

Figure 6.28   Specifying target name.

Figure 6.29 Identifying initiator.

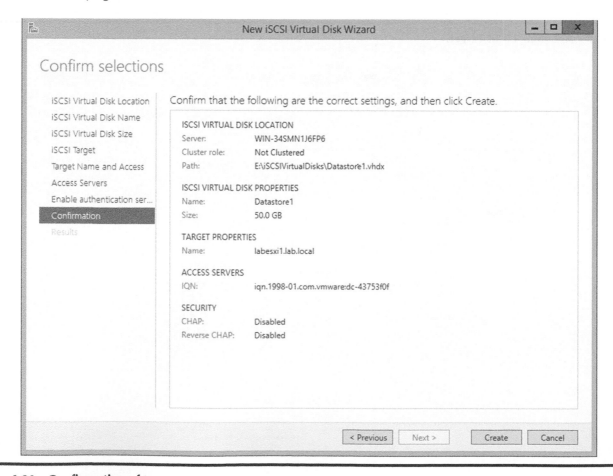

Figure 6.30 Configuration of target.

14. To install the target for the second hard disk, click **iSCSI**, you will see the target and the initiator. Click the **TASKS** dropdown list and select **NEW iSCSI Virtual Disk** (Figure 6.31).
15. On the Select iSCSI virtual disk location page, choose the option **Select by volume**, as shown in Figure 6.32. Then, click **Next**.
16. On the Specify iSCSI virtual disk name page, enter the second datastore name **Datastore2**, as shown in Figure 6.33. Then, click **Next**.
17. On the Specify iSCSI virtual disk size page, specify the disk size for the second datastore, as shown in Figure 6.34. Check the option **Dynamically expanding**. Then, click **Next**.
18. On the Assign iSCSI target page, select the option **New iSCSI target**, as shown in Figure 6.35. Then, click **Next**.
19. On the Specify target name page, name the second target **LabESXi2.lab.local**, as shown in Figure 6.36. Then, click **Next**.
20. Click the **Add** button to add the iqn ID for LabESXi2. On the Select a method to identify the initiator page, select the option **Enter a value for the selected type**.

Specify the type as **IQN** and paste the **iqn value** copied in Step 4, as shown in Figure 6.37. Then, click **OK**. Click **Next** twice to go to the Confirm selections page.
21. On the Confirm selections page, check the configuration shown in Figure 6.38 and click **Create**. Then, click **Close**.
22. You will see that two iSCSI virtual disks are created (Figure 6.39).

Once these two targets are created, the next task is to configure the initiators so that they can communicate with the targets.

6.4.3 Task 3: Initiator Configuration

For this task, you will configure the initiators (which are the ESXi hosts) to communicate with the targets. The following steps accomplish the task:

1. Now, on the DC server, from VMware vSphere Client, log on to vCenter Server, as shown in Figure 6.40.
2. Select **LabESXi1.lab.local** and click the **Configuration** tab and **Storage Adaptors**, as shown in Figure 6.41.

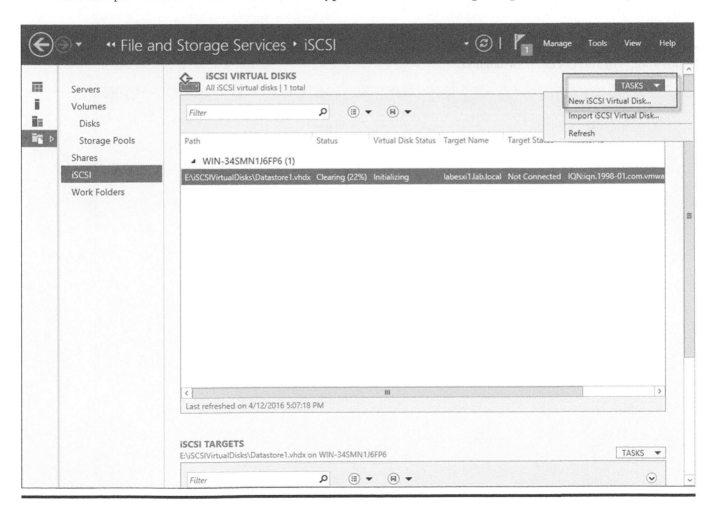

Figure 6.31 Target and initiator.

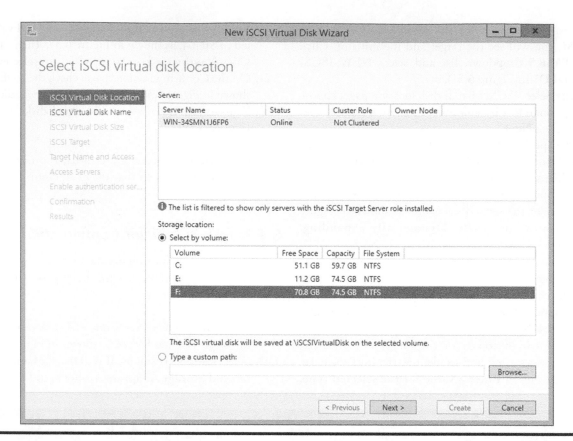

Figure 6.32   Location of iSCSI virtual disk.

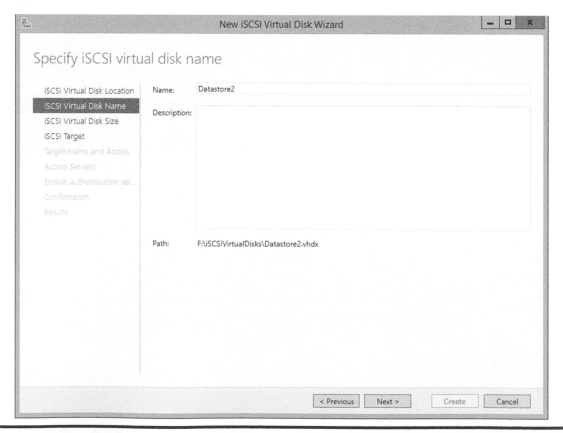

Figure 6.33   Name of Datastore.

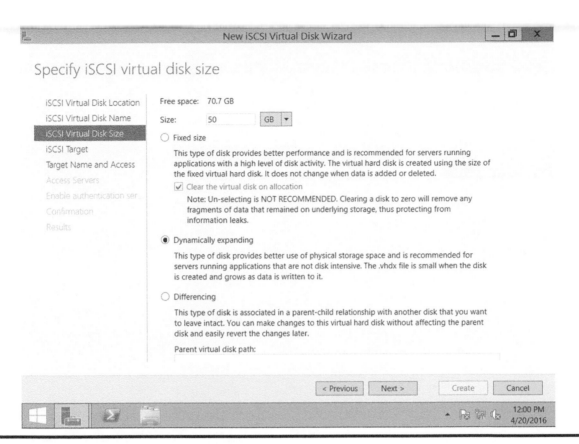

Figure 6.34 Size of Datastore2.

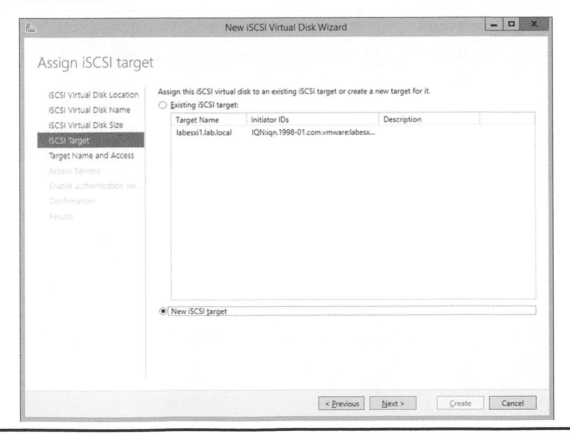

Figure 6.35 New Target for Datastore2.

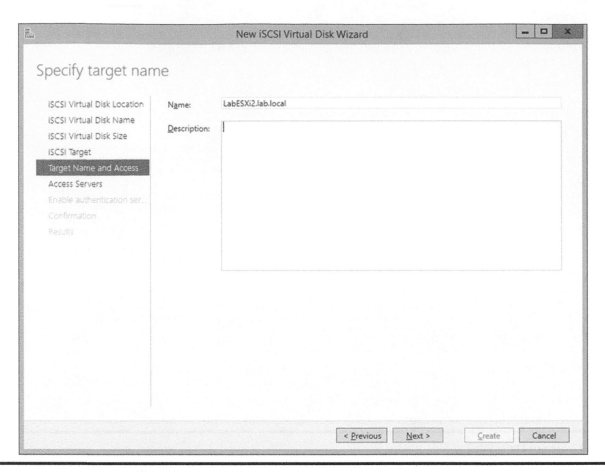

Figure 6.36 Name of second target.

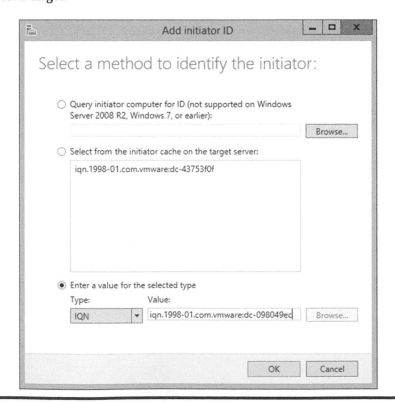

Figure 6.37 Identifying initiator.

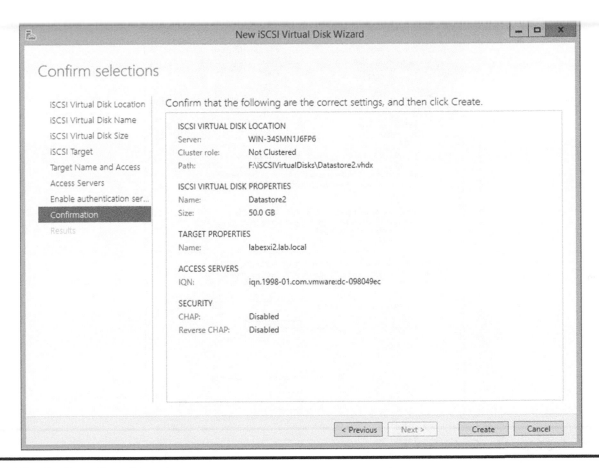

Figure 6.38   Configuration of target.

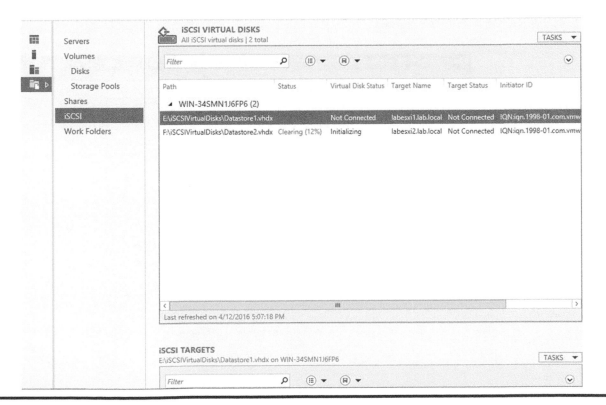

Figure 6.39   iSCSI virtual disks.

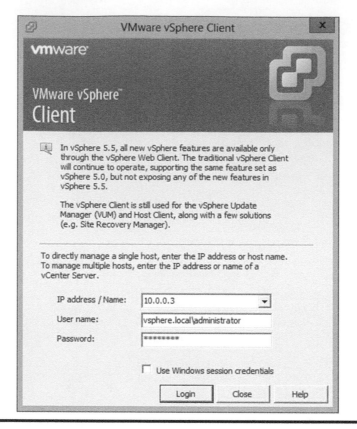

Figure 6.40   Logging on to vCenter Server.

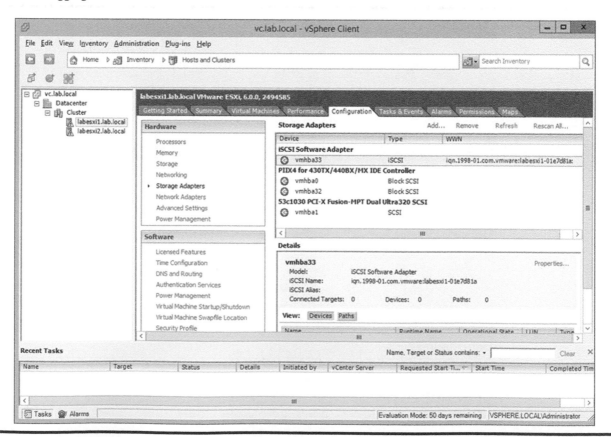

Figure 6.41   iSCSI Initiator.

3. Click the **Rescan All** link to rescan the ESXi host storage.

4. After rescanning has completed, click **Properties** in the Details pane.

5. Under the **General** tab, click the **Configure** button, as shown in Figure 6.42.

6. Make sure that the **Enabled** check box is checked, as shown in Figure 6.43. Then, click **OK**.

7. Under the **Dynamic Discovery** tab, click the **Add** button (Figure 6.44).

8. On the Add Send Target Server page, enter the iSCSI server's IP address **10.0.1.3** created in Chapter 5. Then, click **OK** (Figure 6.45).

9. Now, you can see the added IP address and port number, as shown in Figure 6.46. Click **Close**.

10. In the iSCSI Initiator (vmhba33) Properties dialog, under the **Network Configuration** tab, click the **Add** button to add both the **iSCSI_1** and **iSCSI_2** port groups, as shown in Figure 6.47. Then, click **Close**. When prompted to rescan, click **Yes**.

11. Under the Configuration tab, click the **Storage** link on the left-hand side of your screen. If you do not see the iSCSi storage that is added to your ESXi host server, click the **Add Storage** link on the upper part of your screen to open the Add Storage wizard. On the Select Storage Type page, select the option **Disk/LUN**, as shown in Figure 6.48. Then, click **Next**.

12. You should be able to see the iSCSI storage device created earlier. Select the storage device and click **Next**, as shown in Figure 6.49.

13. On the Current Disk Layout page, take the default and click **Next**.

14. On the Properties page (Figure 6.50), enter the name **dstore1** for LabESXi1 (for LabESXi2, enter the name **dstore2**), and click **Next**.

15. On the Disk/LUN - Formatting page, you can decide how much space can be used by the ESXi host. In our case, select the option **Maximum available space**, as shown in Figure 6.51, and click **Next**.

16. On the Ready to Complete page, verify the configuration and click **Finish** (Figure 6.52).

17. Repeat Steps 2 through 17 for the host LabESXi2.lab. local.

18. Back to the **Storage** server, on the Server Manager page, click **File and Storage Services**. Then, click **iSCSI**. You will see that both LabESXi1 and LabESXi2 storage targets are connected, as shown in Figure 6.53.

19. At this point, each initiator has only one target connected to it. To connect an initiator to two targets, click on the virtual disk **Datastore1.vhdx**, as shown in Figure 6.54. In the iSCSI TARGETS pane, right-click the target and select **Properties**.

20. To add the labesxi2.lab.local initiator to Datastore1, click the **Initiators** link on the left pane (Figure 6.55). Then, click the **Add** button.

21. On the Select a method to identify the initiator page, select the option **Select from the initiator cache on the target server**. Click the initiator related to labesxi2, as shown in Figure 6.56. Then, click **OK**.

22. As shown in Figure 6.57, Datastore1 is linked to the initiators related to both labesxi1 and labesxi2. Then, click **OK**.

23. Go back to the iSCSI dialog; click on the virtual disk **Datastore2.vhdx**, as shown in Figure 6.58. In the iSCSI TARGETS pane, right-click the target and select **Properties**.

24. To add the labesxi1.lab.local initiator to Datastore2, click the **Initiators** link on the left pane. Then, click the **Add** button.

25. On the Select a method to identify the initiator page, select the option **Select from the initiator cache on the target server**. Click the initiator related to labesxi1. Then, click **OK** twice (Figure 6.59).

26. You will see that Datastore2 is linked to the initiators related to both labesxi1 and labesxi2. Then, click **OK**.

27. Assume that you are still logged in vCenter through vSphere Client. Select one of the hosts on the left pane (Figure 6.60). Under the Configuration tab, click **Storage Adapters**. Right-click the **vmhba33** link and select **Rescan**. In the Details pane, you can see there are two devices and four connections from the initiators.

28. Click the **Storage** link in the Hardware pane; you will see that the host has three datastores (Figure 6.61); one is the local hard disk, and the other two are the network based-storage devices, which are in the Storage server.

29. Click on the other host, and you will have a similar result; one datastore is the local hard disk, and the other two are network based (Figure 6.62).

In this hands-on activity, you convert a Windows Server 2012 server to a network-based shared storage device. The ESXi hosts are configured as initiators connected to the targets that are provided by the Windows Server 2012 server. Two ESXi servers, LabESXi1 and LabESXi2, are configured to share the dstore1 and dstore2. The virtual machines stored in the shared storage can be hosted by either LabESXi1 or LabESXi2.

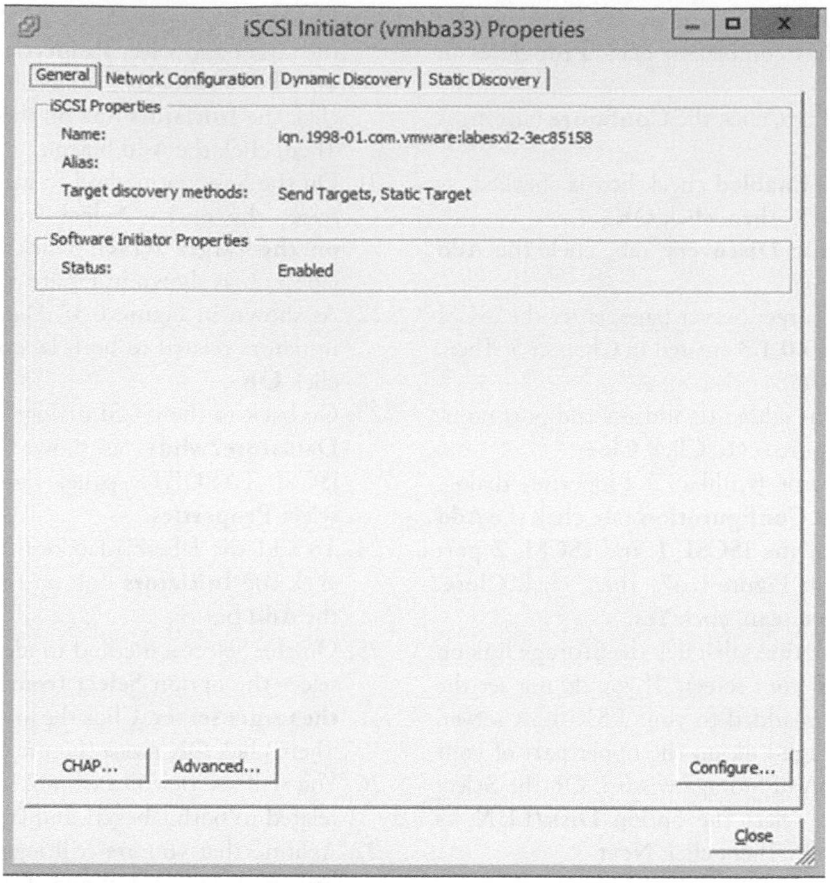

Figure 6.42   Configuring iSCSI Properties.

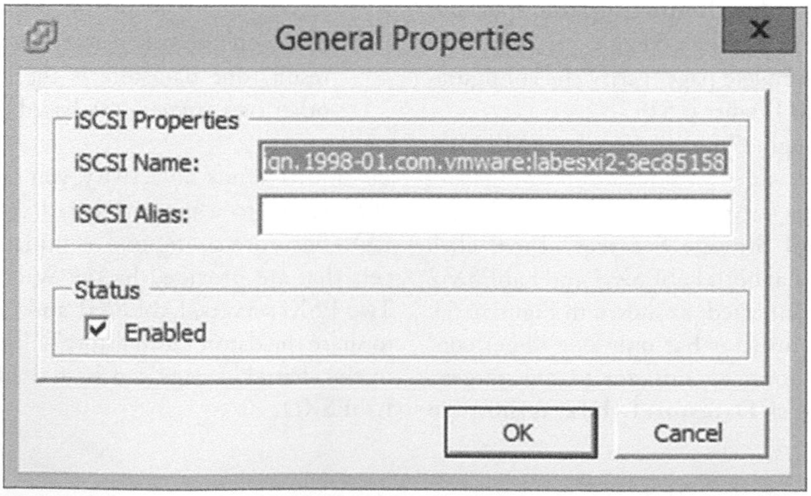

Figure 6.43   Enabling iSCSI.

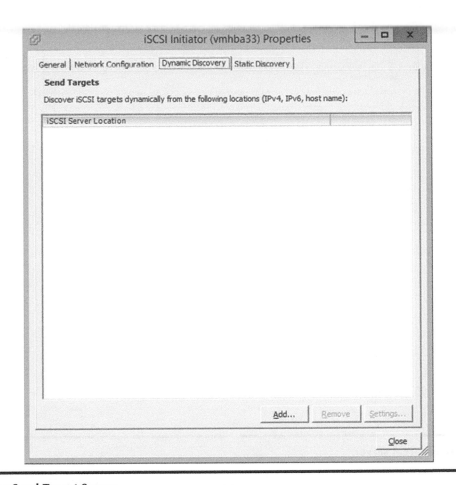

Figure 6.44 Adding Send Target Server.

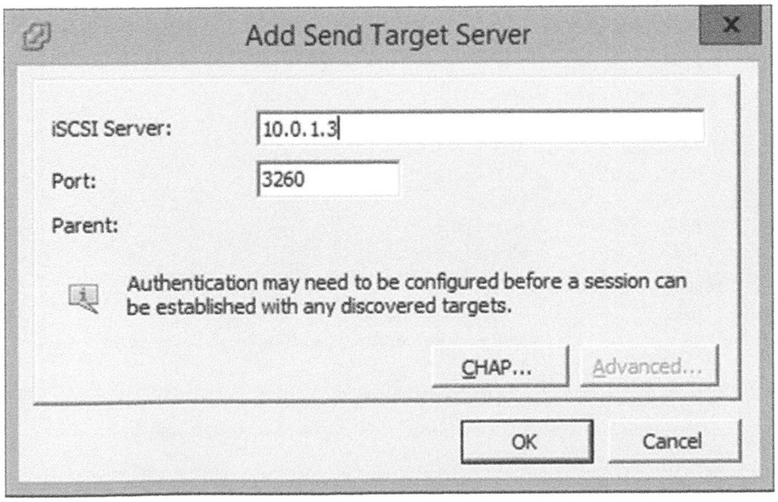

Figure 6.45 Specifying iSCSI server IP.

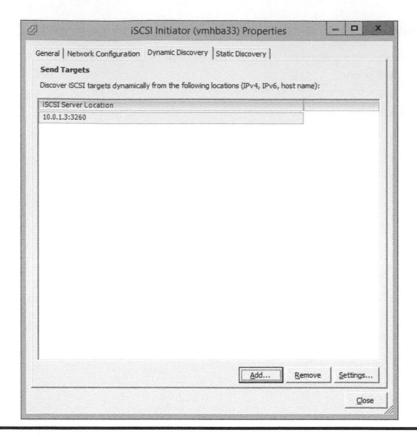

Figure 6.46   Added send target server.

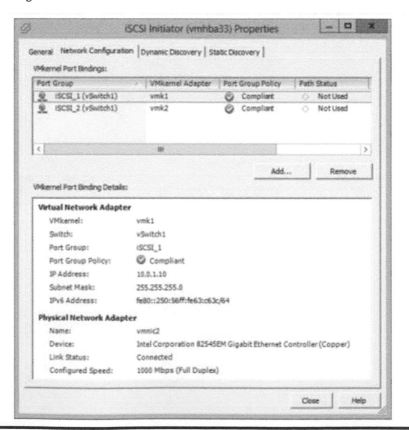

Figure 6.47   Adding VMkernel port groups.

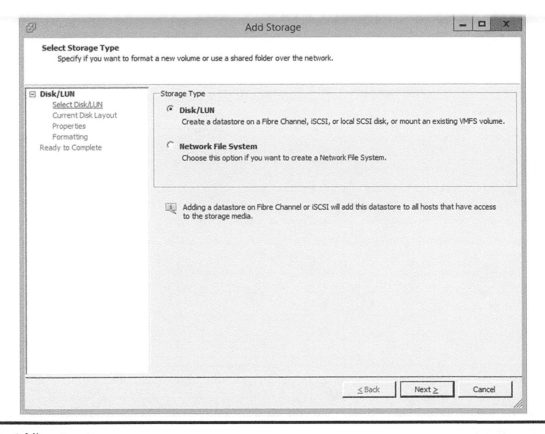

Figure 6.48 Adding storage.

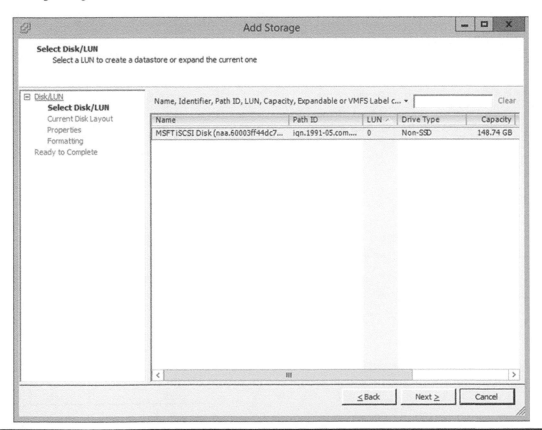

Figure 6.49 Selecting disk/LUN.

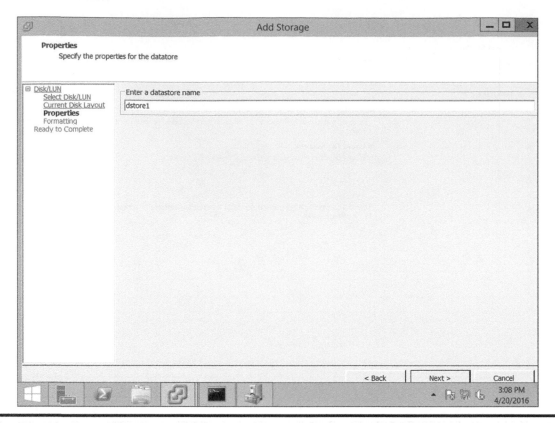

Figure 6.50 Naming datastores.

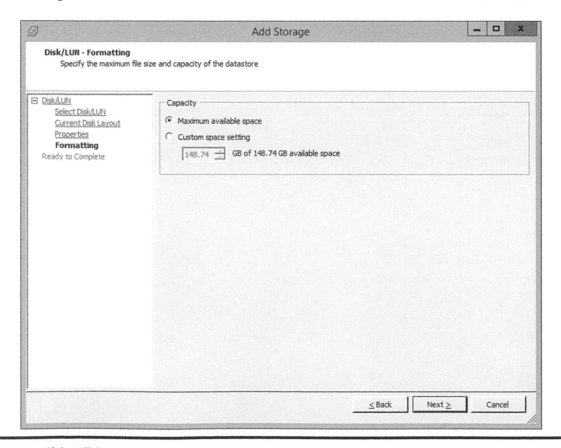

Figure 6.51 Specifying disk/LUN capacity.

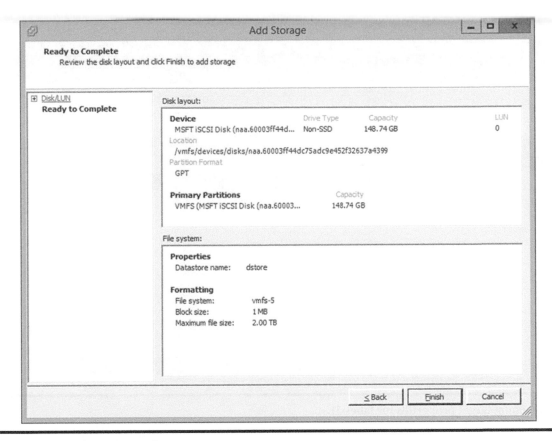

Figure 6.52   Reviewing datastore options.

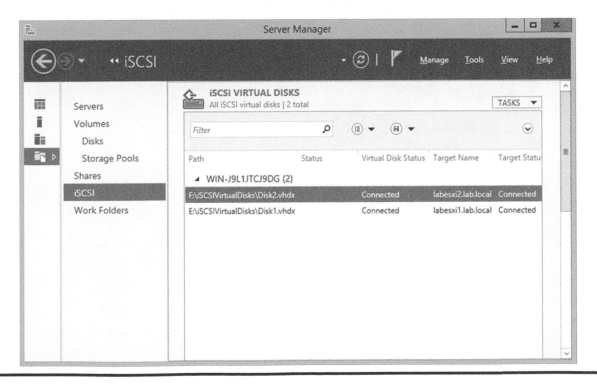

Figure 6.53   Connected targets.

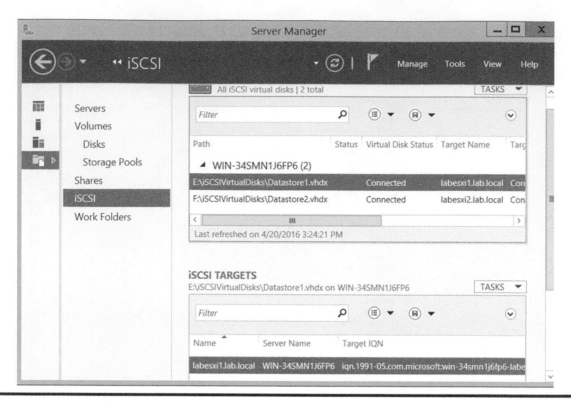

Figure 6.54 Opening target properties for labesxi1.

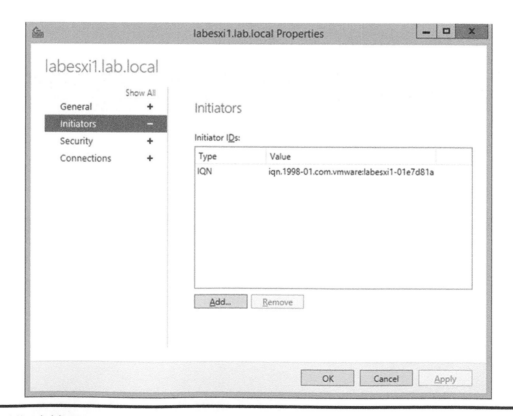

Figure 6.55 Adding initiator.

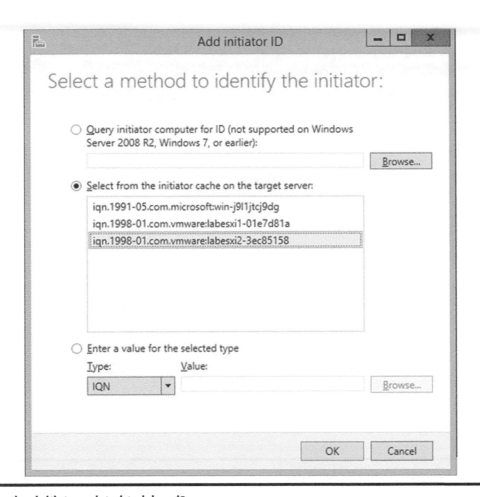

Figure 6.56 Selecting initiator related to labesxi2.

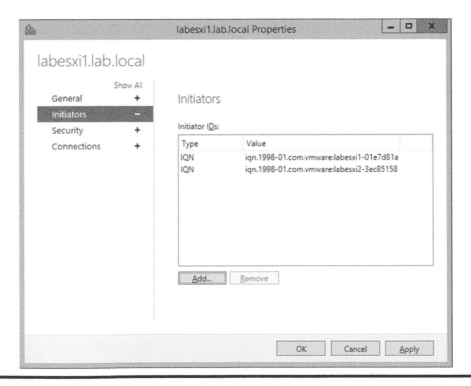

Figure 6.57 Initiators linked to Datastore1.

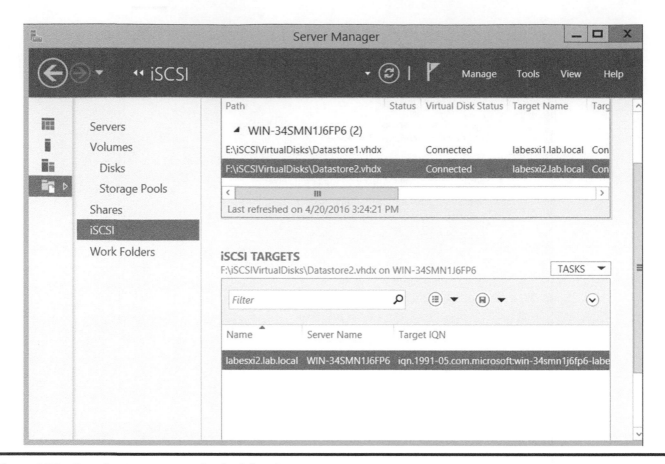

Figure 6.58 Opening target properties for labesxi2.

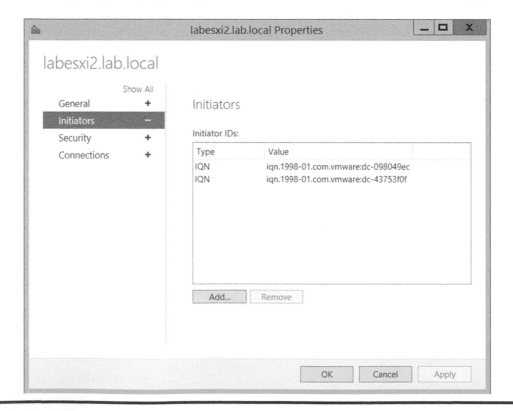

Figure 6.59 Selecting initiator.

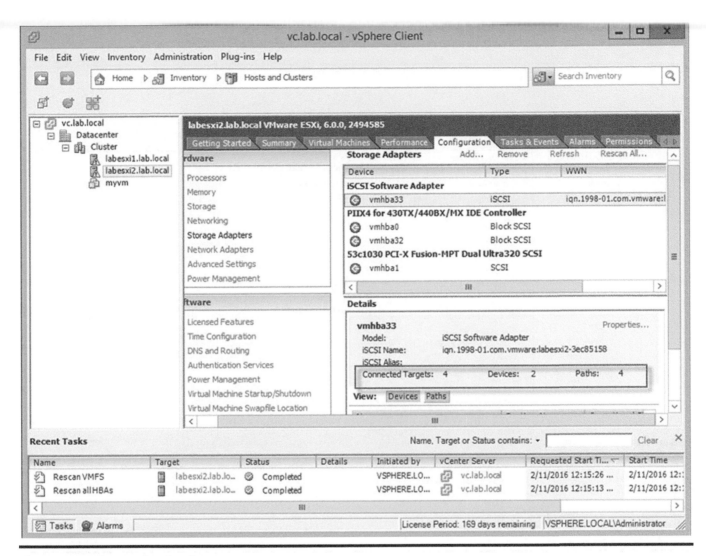

Figure 6.60 Connection details.

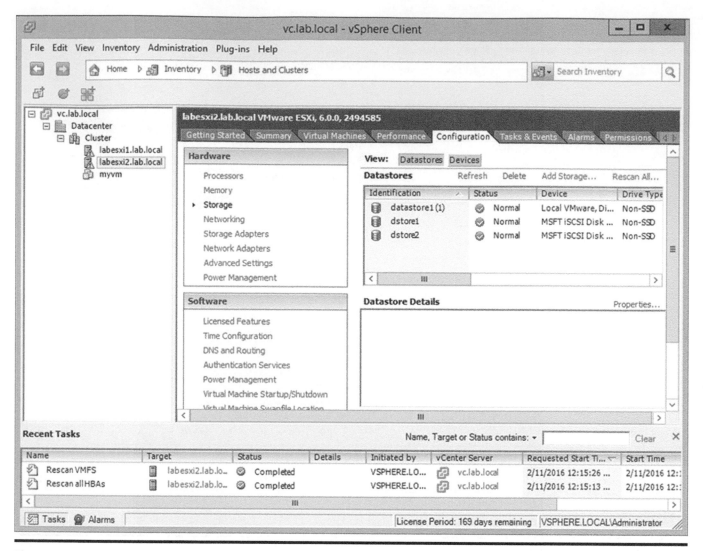

Figure 6.61   Datastores on LabESXi2 host.

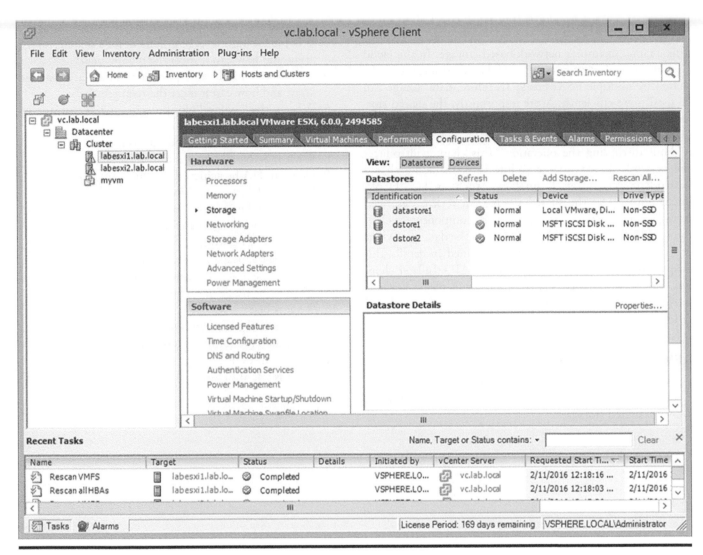

Figure 6.62   Datastores on LabESXi1 host.

6.5 Summary

This chapter examines network-based storage. In the cloud computing environment, network-based storage can be shared by multiple ESXi hosts. Therefore, data storage can be used more efficiently. More importantly, the shared storage allows advanced features such as vMotion to live-migrate virtual machines from one ESXi host to another ESXi host without disrupting the operation. This chapter introduces the network shared storage architecture, including shared network storage array technologies such as FC, FCoE, iSCSI, and NFS. The shared storage network is described in this chapter. Shared storage network components such as the initiator and target are also covered. The datastore where the virtual machines are stored is explained in detail. This chapter also introduces the concept of RAID. In later chapters, the network-based shared storage will play a key role in the implementation of VMware features such as HA and vMotion.

REVIEW QUESTIONS

1. Why is shared storage more efficient?
2. What are the advanced features that can be performed on shared storage?
3. Describe the components included in shared storage.
4. What is the high-level requirement for a shared storage array, and how can it meet the requirement?
5. What is the mid-level requirement for a shared storage array, and how can it meet the requirement?
6. What is the low-level requirement for a shared storage array, and how can it meet the requirement?
7. What is an NAS array, and how is it used?
8. What is SAN, and how is it used?
9. How can HA be achieved in a shared storage system?
10. What is a Cluster in a Box, and how does it work?
11. What is a Cluster across Boxes, and how does it work?
12. What is physical to virtual clustering (N+1 clustering), and how does it work?
13. Describe the usage of a storage processor.
14. What is the usage of storage array software?
15. What is the usage of cache memory?
16. What is FC?
17. What does the term *initiator* mean?
18. What does the term *target* mean?
19. What is an LUN?
20. What is iSCSI designed for, and what is its advantage?

Chapter 7

Virtual Machines, Templates, and vApps

Objectives

- Create and configure virtual machines, templates, and vApps
- Import and export virtual machines, templates, and vApps
- Use virtual machines, templates, and vApps

7.1 Introduction

After the network shared storage is created, it is time to create virtual objects such as virtual machines, templates, and vApps. A virtual machine is a software emulation of a physical computer. In a virtual machine, the virtualized computer hardware devices are a set of files. These files are used to run an operating system (OS) or applications like a physical computer. A template is a master copy of a virtual machine. With a template, one can make multiple copies of a virtual machine. These copies have the same hardware configuration, the same OS, and the same application software. When cloning a template, you are given the option to customize the OS such as the computer name and network settings. A vApp is a set of virtual machines preconfigured to form a computing environment. For example, a vApp can be used to construct a three-tier client–server infrastructure to support a database system. Through a vApp, you can control the computing resources distributed to each virtual machine in the vApp. Within the vApp, a virtual network can be created to connect the virtual machines. A vApp can be made as a template that can clone multiple similar vApps.

7.2 Virtual Machines

In this section, more details about virtual machines are provided. This section describes the following components of a virtual machine:

- Guest OS
- Virtual memory
- Virtual processor
- Virtual storage
- Virtual network adapters
- Virtual video cards
- VMware Tools
- Virtual machine snapshots
- Virtual machine files

Guest operating system: A virtual machine is a collection of virtual hardware devices used to run a guest OS. The VMware-supported guest OSs may include the following:

- Windows Vista or later (32 bit or 64 bit),
- Windows Server 2003 or later (32 bit or 64 bit),
- Ubuntu Linux (32 bit or 64 bit),
- Red Hat Enterprise Linux 3/4/5/6 (32 bit or 64 bit),
- SUSE Linux Enterprise Server 8/9/10/11 (32 bit or 64 bit),
- CentOS 4/5 (32 bit or 64 bit),
- FreeBSD (32 bit or 64 bit), and so on.

When Elastic Sky X Integrated (ESXi) is installed on certain Macintosh servers such as the Macintosh server with OS X 10.11.x, ESXi can support the Mac OS X virtual machines.

In addition to Macintosh, vSphere 6 supports many versions of Linux and UNIX guest OSs.

To support the installation of guest OSs, there are several ways for virtual machines to access the guest OS installation materials. A virtual machine is able to access the compact disc/digital videodisc (CD/DVD) drive of the computer where vSphere Client is installed. When an installation CD/DVD is inserted into the local CD/DVD drive, the virtual machine can be configured to use the local CD/DVD drive as its own CD/DVD drive. When the installation CD/DVD is inserted in the CD/DVD drive in the ESXi host server, the virtual machine can use the CD/DVD drive of the ESXi host server as its own CD/DVD drive. The virtual machine can also use the installation ISO file stored in the local computer. Moreover, the virtual machine can install a guest OS through the network-based Preboot Execution Environment server.

Versions of virtual hardware: Different versions of the VMware hypervisor vSphere support different versions of virtual hardware. For example, vSphere 6 supports the hardware version 11. vSphere also supports earlier hardware versions. Table 7.1 lists different versions of hardware.

In Table 7.1, the VMware product with a higher hardware version can power on a virtual machine with lower hardware virtual support. By doing so, some of the features provided by the higher hardware version will be lost. On the other hand, the VMware product with a lower hardware version cannot power on a virtual machine with a higher hardware version.

Virtual memory: A virtual machine includes a set of virtualized hardware devices, as shown in Figure 7.1.

As shown in Figure 7.1, 3-GB memory is presented to the OS of the virtual machine. However, it is not the actual physical memory allocated to the virtual machine. In some cases, the actual amount of physical host memory allocated to a virtual machine may be less than 3 GB. It depends on the memory resource settings. A virtual machine may share some of the actual physical memory with other virtual machines. It may also take some of the unused physical memory from other idle virtual machines. The memory presented in Figure 7.1 is the maximum amount available to the virtual machine. If the configured amount is more than the available physical memory, the swap file on a hard disk will be used as memory. Using the swap file as memory can significantly reduce the performance of a virtual machine.

Virtual processor: In Figure 7.1, there is one virtual processor, which is a physical central processing unit (CPU) assigned to the virtual machine. The virtual processor in the virtual machine appears to the OS as a single-core CPU. A physical processor can have more than one operation unit, called a core. As an operation unit, the core can also be considered a processor. A physical processor with two cores can be considered two processors, each with one core. If the Hyper-Threading Technology is supported, a core can handle two threads at the same time. This means that a core can handle two logical processors at the same time. With the hardware version 11, a virtual machine can have as many as 128 cores depending on the vSphere license.

Virtual storage: A virtual machine can have four Small Computer System Interface (SCSI) controllers. An SCSI controller can be used to connect up to 15 SCSI devices to a computer bus. A SCSI device can be a printer, a disk drive, a scanner, or other peripherals to a virtual machine. Figure 7.1 shows that two hard drives are connected to the SCSI controller. In addition to the SCSI controllers, a virtual machine can have four Serial Advanced Technology Attachment (SATA) controllers. An SATA controller can connect up to 30 storage devices. A virtual machine can also support up to four Integrated Drive Electronics (IDE) storage devices. Figure 7.1 shows that the virtual machine has an IDE CD/DVD device. When creating a new virtual disk, there are three disk provision options: (1) thick provision lazy zeroed, (2) thick provision eager zeroed, and (3) thin provision. Disk provisioning is a process to allocate storage to virtual machines to achieve better performance. In the process, logical unit numbers are assigned within a network to a datastore, the datastore and recovery routes are made available to users, and the allocated storage space is kept in virtual disk files. The description of these three provision options is given in Table 7.2.

Table 7.1 Virtual Machine Hardware Versions

Hardware Version	Description
12	The VMware products Fusion 8.x, Workstation Pro 12.x, and Workstation Player 12.x require this version.
11	The VMware products Fusion 7.x, Workstation 11.x, Player 7.x, and ESXi 6 require this version.
10	The VMware products Fusion 6.x, Workstation 10.x, Player 6.x, and ESXi 5.5 require this version.
9	The VMware products Fusion 5.x, Workstation 9.x, Player 5.x, and ESXi 5.1 require this version.
8	The VMware products Fusion 4.x, Workstation 8.x, Player 4.x, and ESXi 5.0 require this version.

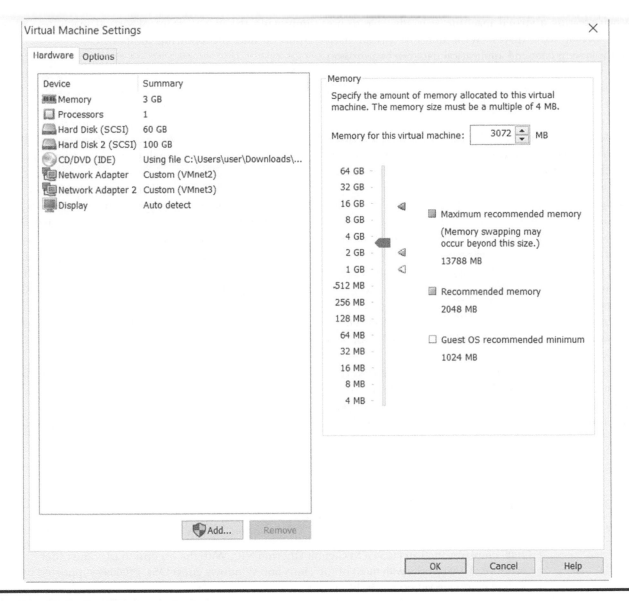

Figure 7.1 Virtualized hardware devices.

Table 7.2 Supported Virtual Disk Provisions

Virtual Disk Provision	Description
Thick provision lazy zeroed	Thick provision means that all the space specified for the virtual disk files is reserved at the creation of a virtual machine. Lazy zero means that the unused storage space is not cleared. The old data in the unused storage space will be overwritten when the new data are added to the storage space for the first time.
Thick provision eager zeroed	This provision option also reserves all the storage space specified to a virtual disk. Eager zero means that the full storage space is cleared out during the provisioning process. vSphere Fault Tolerance requires the thick eager-zeroed option.
Thin provision	Thin provision creates a virtual disk on an as-needed basis. The virtual disk only uses as much datastore space as needed. The thin-provisioned virtual disk starts small at first. Later, the virtual disk grows depending on the amount of data actually stored in it, up to the size configured for the virtual disk.

When creating a virtual machine, it is advisable to use multiple virtual hard drives. With multiple virtual hard drives, the system data and application data can be stored on different virtual hard disks for better performance.

Virtual network adapters: As shown in Figure 7.1, there are two virtual network adapters. The virtual network adapters are used to connect virtual machines to virtual networks. In Figure 7.1, there are two virtual networks: (1) VMnet2 and (2) VMnet3. The VMware virtual machines support the virtual network interface cards (NICs) listed in Table 7.3.

Virtual graphic card: Some of the virtual machines require high-end graphic capability. To meet this requirement, vSphere 6 provides the Virtual Shared Graphics Acceleration (vSGA) technology. This technology allows multiple virtual machines to leverage physical graphics processing units (GPUs) installed in an ESXi host to accelerate three-dimensional (3D) graphics. This technology offloads the processing of 3D rendering to the physical GPU. In such a way, it can reduce the workload of the CPU on the ESXi host.

VMware Tools: As mentioned in Table 7.3, VMXNET 2 (Enhanced) and VMXNET 3 depend on VMware Tools. VMware Tools is a collection of tools used for enhancing virtual machines' performance. It also includes some tools for improving the management of virtual machines. VMware Tools includes the following components:

- *VMware Tools Service:* The service manages the interaction between the guest and the host OS. It handles jobs such as time synchronization, power state change, processing message exchange, and so on.
- *VMware Device Drivers:* The drivers can be used to replace the original guest OS drivers for better performance.
- *VMware User Process:* This component can be used to enhance the management of the user process such as copying and pasting text between a virtual machine and its host computer.
- *VMware Tools Control Panel:* This component can be used to alter the settings of VMware Tools such as connecting virtual devices or shrinking virtual disks.

Once VMware Tools is installed, a guest OS can get the following benefits:

- Improving sound, graphics, and networking performance
- Improving the mouse operation
- Allowing file and folder sharing
- Allowing copy-and-paste and drag-and-drop files

Table 7.3 Supported Virtual NICs in vSphere 6

Virtual NIC Types	Description
E1000	E1000 emulates the Intel 82545EM Gigabit Ethernet NIC. With the exception of some older versions, E1000 works with most of the Linux and Windows guest OSs. E1000 is supported by the virtual hardware versions 8, 9, 10, and 11.
E1000e	E1000e emulates a newer model of Intel Gigabit NIC (Number 82574) in the virtual hardware. It is known as the "e1000e" vNIC. e1000e works with Windows 8 and later guest OSs. It does work with Linux guest OS. E1000e is supported by the virtual hardware versions 8, 9, 10, and 11.
Flexible	Flexible emulates the AMD 79C970 PCnet32 NIC. If VMware Tools is not installed, Flexible identifies itself as a Vlance adapter. When VMware Tools is installed, it identifies itself as a VMXNET adapter, which has better performance. Flexible is supported by the virtual hardware versions 8, 9, 10, and 11.
VMXNET 2 (Enhanced)	VMXNET 2 is optimized for virtual machines to achieve better performance. It has no physical counterpart and has no driver from OS vendors. To use this NIC adapter, VMware Tools needs to be installed. VMXNET 2 (Enhanced) is a 10-Gb virtual NIC. It is supported by the virtual hardware versions 8, 9, 10, and 11.
VMXNET 3	VMXNET 3 offers all the features available in VMXNET 2 and adds several new features like multiqueue support, IPv6 offloads, and MSI/MSI-X interrupt delivery. For IPv6, VMXNET 3 has much better performance than VMXNET 2 (Enhanced). As a 10-Gb NIC, VMXNET 3 is more stable than VMXNET 2 (Enhanced). VMware Tools is also required for VMXNET 3. VMXNET 3 is supported by the virtual hardware versions 8, 9, 10, and 11.

- Taking quiesced snapshots of the guest OS to prevent inconsistencies
- Synchronizing time between a virtual machine and its host computer
- Moving into and out of the virtual machine console seamlessly without pressing the Ctrl+Alt combination key

In VMware Workstation or VMware Player, the VMware Tools installation ISO file is built in. VMware Tools installation can be done by selecting the item **Install VMware Tools** on the VM menu. By doing so, the installation ISO file will be mounted on a virtual CD/DVD drive, and the installation process will begin. For virtual machines hosted by an ESXi host, the ISO file is automatically placed in the folder vmimages/tools-isoimages on the ESXi host during the installation. The installation of VMware Tools can be done through the vSphere Web Client software. Once vSphere Web Client is opened, select **Install/Upgrade VMware Tools** under the Configuration menu to begin the installation process.

Virtual machine snapshots: Taking a snapshot records the current state of a virtual machine at a specific time. A snapshot can be used in many ways. For example, it can be used to recover a failed virtual machine due to the misconfiguration in a hands-on activity. It can also be used as the before-image in a virtual machine upgrading process. If the upgrade fails, the virtual machine can be reset to its before-image. Often, a power failure of a host server may damage some virtual machines. In such a case, snapshots can be used as the backup to recover the damaged virtual machines. A snapshot only consumes minimal storage space. However, as more and more snapshots are created, they will eat up a considerable amount of storage space. In such a case, some of the snapshots need to be removed. ESXi provides the tool Snapshot Manager for removing snapshots.

Virtual machine files: From the ESXi host's point of view, virtualized computer hardware devices are a set of files, as shown in Figure 7.2.

Among these files, one is the configuration file with the file extension .vmx, and the other one is the hard disk file with the file extension .vmdk. The content of the .vmx file defines the virtual hardware used by a virtual machine. It specifies the number of virtual processors, the number of network adapters, the network configuration, the amount of random access memory, and the configuration of the virtual hard disk used by the virtual machine. The data of the virtual machine are stored in the .vmdk file, which is used as the virtual hard disk. Figure 7.2 shows some other files, too. The .nvram file stores the state of a virtual machine's basic input/output system (BIOS). The .vmsd file stores the information and metadata of the snapshots. The .vmxf file is a supplemental configuration file used by VMware Workstation for virtual machine teaming. A team of virtual machines can start or stop together.

7.3 Virtual Machine Templates

In this section, templates will be introduced. This section will start with the description of the templates. Then, it will introduce the Open Virtual Machine Format (OVF) and Open Virtual Appliance (OVA). At the end of this section, the concept of content libraries will be introduced.

7.3.1 Templates

In a cloud computing environment, sometimes, a specially configured virtual machine needs to be cloned and distributed to many other users. For example, in a networking class, three virtual machines are created and configured

Name	Date modified	Type	Size
caches	2/24/2014 4:23 PM	File folder	
VC.nvram	9/1/2015 6:45 PM	VMware Virtual M...	9 KB
VC.vmdk	12/22/2014 3:29 PM	VMware virtual dis...	7,744 KB
VC.vmsd	2/26/2014 3:31 PM	VMware snapshot ...	1 KB
VC.vmx	9/1/2015 6:45 PM	VMware virtual ma...	4 KB
VC.vmxf	12/1/2014 9:07 PM	VMware Team Me...	4 KB
vmware.log	9/1/2015 6:45 PM	Text Document	285 KB
vmware-0.log	8/26/2015 10:48 PM	Text Document	284 KB
vmware-1.log	7/10/2015 12:17 PM	Text Document	284 KB
vmware-2.log	6/16/2015 9:59 PM	Text Document	282 KB
WindowsServer2012_Base-cl1.vmdk	9/1/2015 6:45 PM	VMware virtual dis...	14,374,016 ...

Figure 7.2 Virtual machine files.

for carrying out the networking tasks. The set of virtual machines needs to be distributed to many students. To make the virtual machine distribution task easier, a master copy of a virtual machine called a virtual machine template can be created for cloning and distributing identically configured virtual machines to students. Figure 7.3 illustrates a set of templates created in a cloud computing environment. Per class requirements, students can select one or more templates to create virtual machines for their hands-on practice. As shown in Figure 7.3, some of the templates have a gold plate. The gold plate indicates that a created virtual machine is business critical. Its computing resources are protected. A virtual machine can also choose a different level of protection such as silver, bronze, or no protection.

A template can be created by converting an existing virtual machine designed for accomplishing certain tasks. The virtual machine is preinstalled with necessary application software and is configured with adequate computing resources. The virtual machine should also be installed with the latest VMware Tools. vCenter or VMware Workstation allows a user to export a virtual machine as a template. Once exported as a template (master copy), the virtual machine configuration in the template cannot be changed. To update a template, you need to convert the template back to a virtual machine. After the virtual machine is updated, convert it back to the template. In addition to converting a virtual machine to a template, a physical machine can be converted to a template with the free-download software VMware vCenter Converter.

7.3.2 OVF and OVA

Templates can help a great deal with the deployment of virtual machines. However, when deploying a template to another host with a different version of ESXi or a host managed by a different vCenter, the template may not be transported correctly. The same is true when deploying a template made in VMware Workstation to an ESXi host. To help with the deployment of a template across multiple platforms, the industry-standard OVF can be used. Figure 7.4 displays files in an OVF package. An OVF standard package contains several files, which are described in the following:

- *Descriptor file:* This file has an .ovf extension. This file contains the information about an OVF template. It includes the metadata for an OVF package. It also comprises the information about the licensing, product details, the links to other files in the OVF template, and the requirements for the virtual hard disks.
- *Manifest file:* This file has an .mf extension. It includes the Secure Hash Algorithm 1 (SHA1) digest, which is a cryptographic hash function. After an OVF template is transported, the SHA1 digest will be recalculated for the transported OVF template. The newly calculated SHA1 digest is then compared with the original SHA1 digest included in the manifest file for integrity checking.
- *Disk image file:* This file has a .vmdk extension. It is a virtual machine disk image file or other types of supported disk image files. Multiple disk image files can be included in one OVF template package.

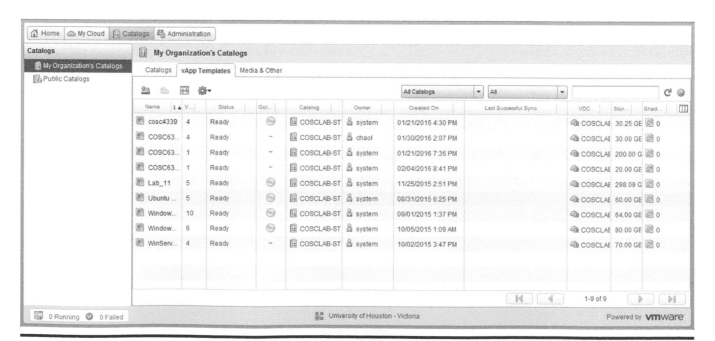

Figure 7.3 Templates.

Name	Date modified	Type	Size
cosc4339.mf	12/29/2015 5:29 PM	MF File	1 KB
cosc4339.ovf	12/29/2015 5:29 PM	Open Virtualizatio...	36 KB
cosc4339-disk1.vmdk	12/29/2015 5:19 PM	VMware virtual dis...	3,602,590 ...
cosc4339-disk2.vmdk	12/29/2015 5:19 PM	VMware virtual dis...	1,896 KB
cosc4339-disk3.vmdk	12/29/2015 5:29 PM	VMware virtual dis...	6,521,811 ...

Figure 7.4   Files in OVF package.

■ *Certificate file (optional):* This file has a .cert extension. This file is used for authenticity checking. It contains a signed digest for the manifest file and an X.509 certificate.

■ *Resource file (optional):* The ISO file can be a type of resource file.

Compared with an OVF package, OVA is a single file that includes all the files in the OVF package. It is easier to download the OVA package for installation. Figure 7.5 illustrates a set of OVA files distributed by VMware.

In VMware Cloud Suite, an OVF/OVA package can be used in three ways:

1. When transporting virtual machines to a different vCenter instance or to a different hypervisor, it is advisable to export these virtual machines as OVF templates.

2. After an OVF template is exported, it can be imported to another vCenter, ESXi host, or VMware Workstation for cloning virtual machines.

3. An OVF template can be made available for the public to download it.

In a large enterprise, there may be a large number of OVF templates or other resources. Often, it is required that these files be accessed from multiple sites. To help with the management of these templates and files, VMware provides Content Libraries, which will be described next.

7.3.3 Content Libraries

The Content Library is a shared storage to which users can publish OVF templates, ISO files, text files, and installation

VMware-vShield-Manager-5.5.3-2081508 (2).ova	Date modified: 1/1/2016 11:19 AM	
C:\Users\user\Downloads	Type: Open Virtualiza...	Size: 1.37 GB
vCloud-Director-VA-OP-5.5.1.0-2170358_OVF10 (2).ova	Date modified: 1/1/2016 11:15 AM	
C:\Users\user\Downloads	Type: Open Virtualiza...	Size: 1.47 GB
vRealize-Operations-Manager-Appliance-6.1.0.3038036_OVF10.o...	Date modified: 10/27/2015 5:29 PM	
C:\Users\user\Downloads	Type: Open Virtualiza...	Size: 1.77 GB
VMware-vShield-Manager-5.5.3-2081508 (1).ova	Date modified: 4/1/2015 9:57 PM	
C:\Users\user\Downloads	Type: Open Virtualiza...	Size: 1.37 GB
vCloud-Director-VA-OP-5.5.1.0-2170358_OVF10 (1).ova	Date modified: 4/1/2015 9:53 PM	
C:\Users\user\Downloads	Type: Open Virtualiza...	Size: 1.47 GB
vCloud-Director-VA-OP-5.5.1.0-2170358_OVF10.ova	Date modified: 12/25/2014 3:55 PM	
C:\Users\user\Downloads	Type: Open Virtualiza...	Size: 1.47 GB
VMware-vShield-Manager-5.5.3-2081508.ova	Date modified: 12/15/2014 9:14 PM	
C:\Users\user\Downloads	Type: Open Virtualiza...	Size: 1.37 GB
vCloud-Director-VA-OP-5.5.1.0-2170358_OVF10.ova	Date modified: 11/30/2014 3:10 PM	
C:\Users\user\Downloads\VMware2015	Type: Open Virtualiza...	Size: 1.47 GB
VMware-vShield-Manager-5.5.2-1740418.ova	Date modified: 11/30/2014 2:58 PM	
C:\Users\user\Downloads\VMware2015	Type: Open Virtualiza...	Size: 1.35 GB
VMware-vShield-Manager-5.5.0a-1473628.ova	Date modified: 11/27/2014 4:53 PM	
C:\Users\user\Downloads\VMware2015	Type: Open Virtualiza...	Size: 1.35 GB

Figure 7.5   OVA files.

media files. Once published, these files can be consumed across multiple vCenter Servers. A storage device used by the Content Library can be a local hard disk attached to a vCenter Server or a datastore located in a network-based storage. Using a datastore for the Content Library makes it easier to deploy a large OVF template. For the Content Library that requires frequent updates, using a local hard disk can improve performance. The Content Library can be configured into two types of libraries: (1) local library or (2) subscribed library. The local and subscribed libraries are described as follows.

Local library: When the Content Library is configured for the use by a single vCenter instance, it is a local library. The local library allows users of a vCenter instance to upload OVF templates or other files to the Content Library. The local library can be published so that users from other vCenter instances can subscribe to it. When published, an authentication mechanism is used to verify the subscribers.

Subscribed library: A subscribed library downloads the content from a published library. It can be created in the same vCenter instance where the published library is. It can also be created in a different vCenter instance. The subscribed library can be configured to download changes as soon as they are available in the published library. Or, it can be configured to download metadata without actual data. Later, based on the needs, the full content of a selected item can be downloaded to the subscribed library. The subscribed library is automatically synchronized with the published library on a regular basis to keep the library content up to date.

7.4 vApps

In a cloud computing environment, cloud subscribers may require a specially designed IT infrastructure to accomplish some tasks. For example, a networking course may require the IT infrastructure to consist of servers and routers for hands-on practice. In this case, a set of virtual machines and virtual network equipment can be combined to form a vApp. These virtual machines and network equipment are preconfigured per the requirement of the IT infrastructure. A vApp offers the following features:

■ It provides the resource control for the virtual machines included in a vApp.
■ Various private networks can be constructed in a vApp.
■ vApps are portable. They can be exported as OVF templates and be transported to other virtual infrastructures such as XenServer or Hyper-V.
■ The components in a vApp can be powered on, powered off, suspended, or shut down in predefined order.
■ A vApp can be edited, updated, and cloned.

Figure 7.6 illustrates a vApp, which consists of two virtual machines, one router, and four subnets designed for networking hands-on practice.

In VMware, a vApp can be created in two steps. First, create a vApp container. Then, add virtual machines and network equipment into the vApp. The vApp owner can edit

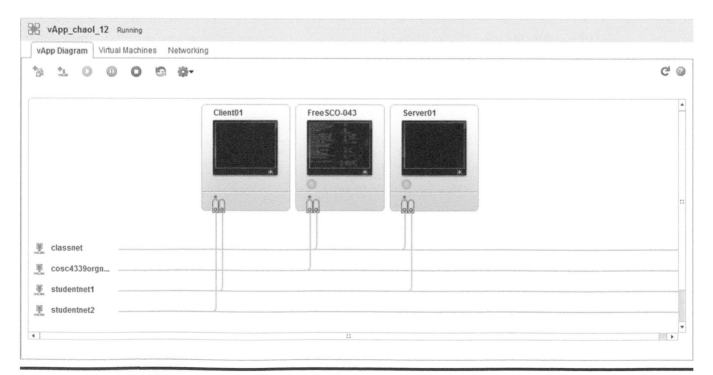

Figure 7.6 vApp for networking.

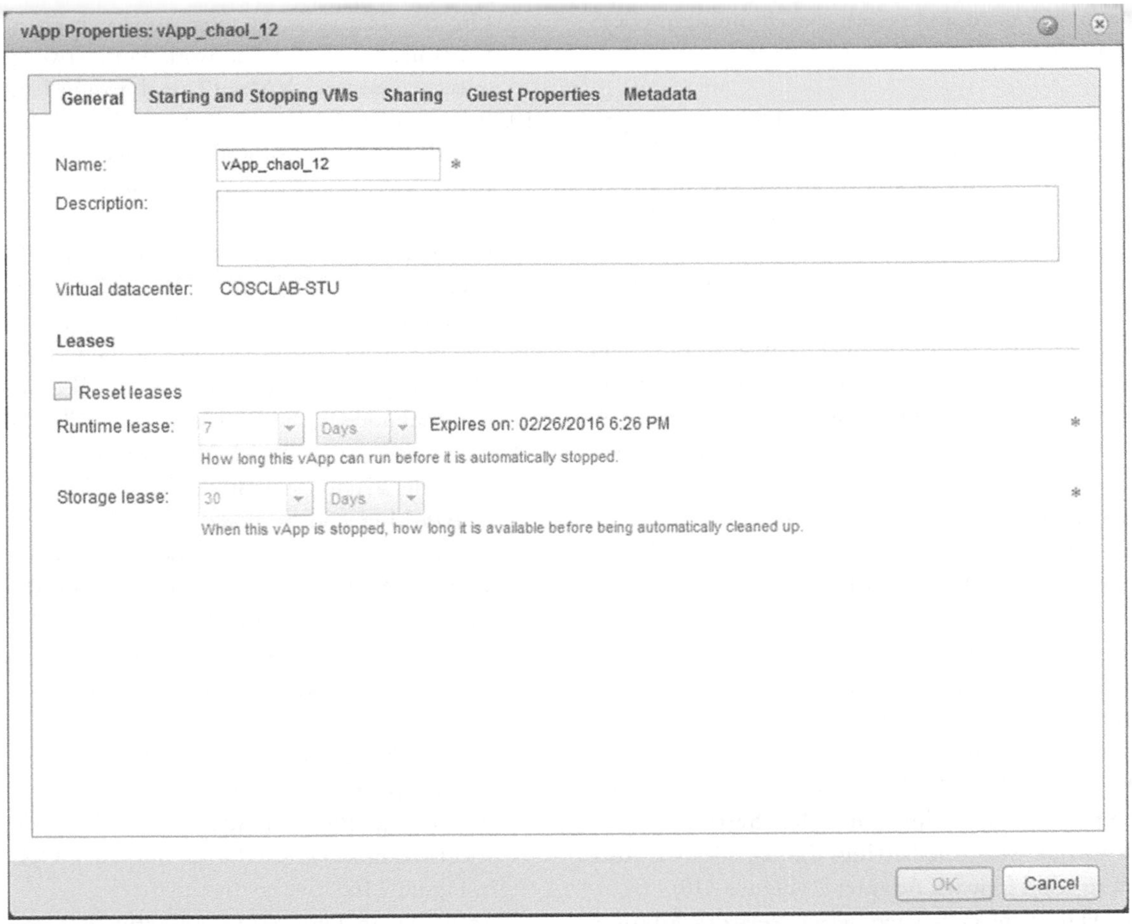

Figure 7.7 vApp Properties.

the vApp properties or edit the settings of the components included in the vApp. Figure 7.7 shows the editable properties of a vApp.

In a vApp, the starting and stopping of virtual machines can be configured to follow a predefined order. One can specify the elapsed time between the starting of two virtual machines. Similarly, the elapsed time between the shutting down of two virtual machines can also be specified.

In a vApp, there are three ways to assign an Internet Protocol (IP) address to an NIC of a virtual machine. The NIC can be configured to have a fixed IP address, which is manually assigned by the vApp developer. An IP address can also be assigned by selecting one of the IP addresses from a vCenter-managed range of IP addresses. Also, an IP address can be assigned by a Dynamic Host Configuration Protocol server.

A vApp can be exported as an OVF template or imported from an OVF template. While importing an OVF template, the user can specify the network settings, product information, upgrade instruction, vApp name, and vApp virtual hardware.

7.5 Activity 1: Developing Virtual Machine, Template, and vApp

In this activity, you will learn how to develop a virtual machine, template, and vApp. The following are the tasks to be accomplished in this section:

- *Task 1:* Installing guest OS on virtual machine
- *Task 2:* Exporting and importing OVF template
- *Task 3:* Creating and transporting vApp

7.5.1 Task 1: Installing Guest OS on Virtual Machine

In this task, you will first download the Ubuntu ISO and OVF files for installation. You will create a virtual network to connect to the virtual machine. You will also upload the installation ISO file to the shared storage so that it can be linked to the CD/DVD drive for installation. The following are the steps to download and install the Ubuntu Linux OS on a virtual machine:

1. In VMware Workstation, start the DC server. If you have not done so, download the installation file (the Ubuntu 14.04.4 LTS Desktop [32 bit] ISO file) from the following Web site: http://www.ubuntu.com/download/desktop
2. As shown in Figure 7.8, download Ubuntu 14.04.4 LTS Desktop (32 bit).
3. To illustrate the installation of the OVF package, you may also download the Ubuntu Server 12.04 LTS (32 bit) OVF file from the following Web site: http://iweb.dl.sourceforge.net/project/firstdigest/ubuntu/ubuntu-server-12.04-i386-0VF.7z
4. Download the freeware 7z from the Web site http://www.7-zip.org/download.html and extract the 7z file, ubuntu-server-12.04-i386-0VF.7z, to a folder (Figure 7.9).
5. If you have not done so, you also need to download the file VMware ClientIntegrationPlugin.
6. To install the downloaded ISO file, you need to create a virtual machine network on one of the ESXi hosts. To do so, in VMware Workstation, right-click the **LabESXi1** virtual machine and select **Settings**.
7. In the Virtual Machine Settings dialog, click the **Add** button to add Network Adapter 7 (Figure 7.10).
8. On the Hardware Type page, select **Network Adapter** and click **Next**.
9. On the Network Adapter page, check the option **Custom** and select the network. For Network Adapter 7, select the network **VMnet2**, as shown in Figure 7.11.
10. Repeat Steps 6 through 9 to add Network Adapter 5, Network Adapter 6, and Network Adapter 7 to the LabESXi2 host. Then, start the servers in the order of DC, Storage, LabESXi1, LabESXi2, and vc.
11. Log on to the server DC. In the Chrome Web browser, enter the following Uniform Resource Locator, and log on to the vCenter server: https://10.0.0.3
12. You will first create a network for the virtual machines. Once logged on to the vCenter server, select the **labesxi1.lab.local** node in the navigation pane. Click **Manage** on the main menu and click **Networking** in the submenu. Select the **Virtual switches** link and select the **Add Host Networking** icon, as shown in Figure 7.12.
13. On the Select connection type page, check the option **Virtual Machine Port Group for a Standard Switch** and click **Next**, as shown in Figure 7.13.
14. On the Select target device page, check the option **New standard switch** and click **Next**, as shown in Figure 7.14.
15. On the Create a Standard Switch page, click the **+** sign to add a physical NIC (Figure 7.15).
16. In the Add Physical Adapters to the Switch dialog, select the newly created NIC and click **OK**, as shown in Figure 7.16.
17. As shown in Figure 7.17, an active adapter is added. Then, click **Next**.

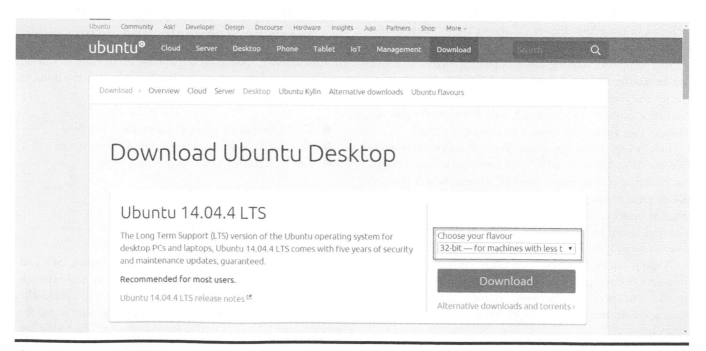

Figure 7.8 Downloading Ubuntu OS.

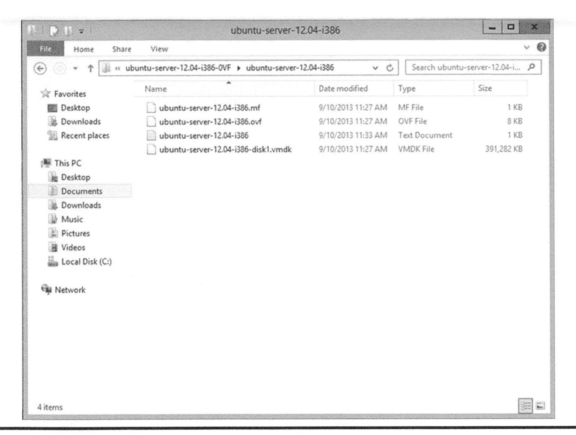

Figure 7.9 OVF files for installation.

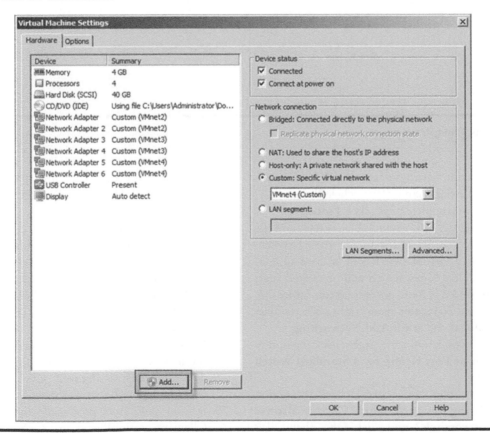

Figure 7.10 Adding network adapter.

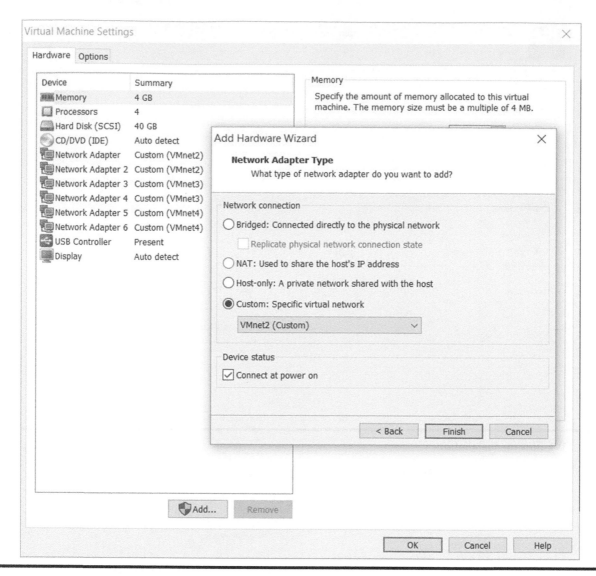

Figure 7.11   Network adapter type.

18. On the Connection Settings page, enter **VM Network 2** as the virtual switch name. Then, click **Next**.
19. On the Ready to complete page, click **Finish**.
20. As shown in Figure 7.18, vSwitch2 is created, and the uplink physical NIC is added to the virtual switch. The newly added virtual switch will be used to connect the virtual machines, which will be created later.
21. You can also add a few more port groups for future use. To do so, in the Navigator pane, right-click the host **labesxi1.lab.local** and select **Add Networking**.
22. On the Select connection type page, check the option **Virtual Machine Port Group for a Standard Switch** and click **Next**.
23. On the Select target device page, check the option **Select an existing standard switch**. Click the **Browse** button; select **vSwitch2** and click **OK**. Then, click **Next**.

24. On the Connection Settings page, enter **Student Network** for the Network label box. Then, click **Next.**
25. On the Ready to complete page, click **Finish**.
26. Repeat Steps 12 through 25 to add a standard virtual network on the LabESXi2 host server.
27. To install a guest OS, your next task is to make the ISO file available for the installation. To do so, click the **Storage** submenu and click the **Rescan** icon, as shown in Figure 7.19.
28. Click the **Storage** icon in the Navigator pane to show the files in the storage. Then, select one of the shared datastores such as **dstore2**. Click the **Files** tab and click the **Upload** icon, as shown in Figure 7.20.
29. If you are not prompted to install VMware-ClientIntegrationPlugin, go to Step 30. Otherwise, Click **Yes** to get started. Browse the folder to find the

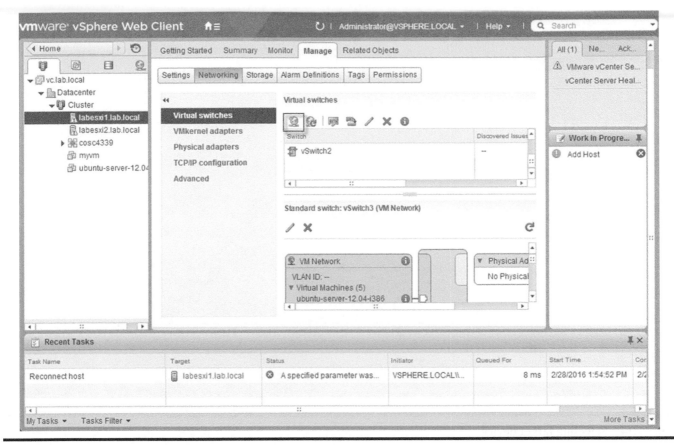

Figure 7.12   Adding virtual switch.

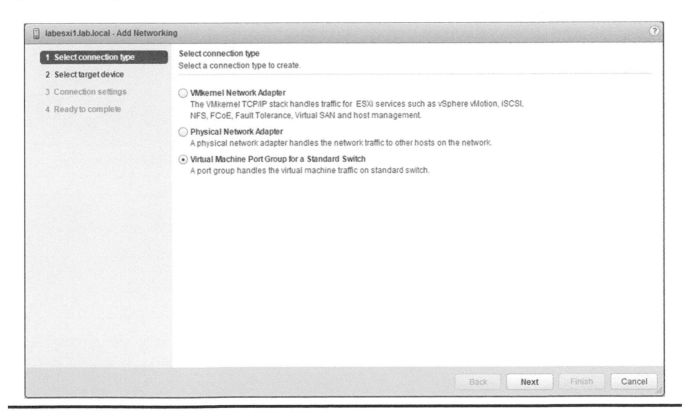

Figure 7.13   Selecting connection type.

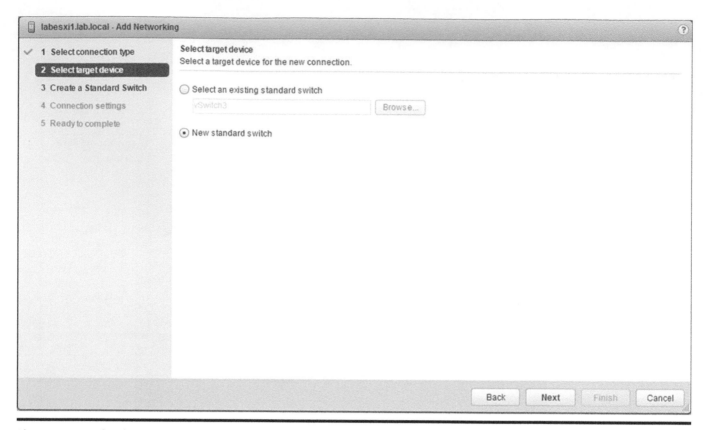

Figure 7.14   Selecting target device.

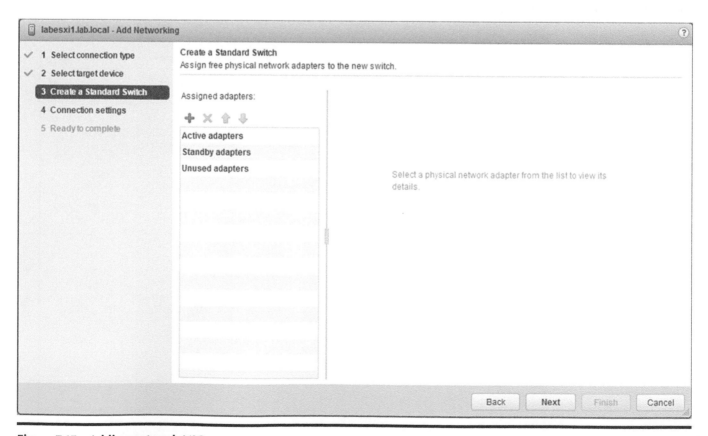

Figure 7.15   Adding network NIC.

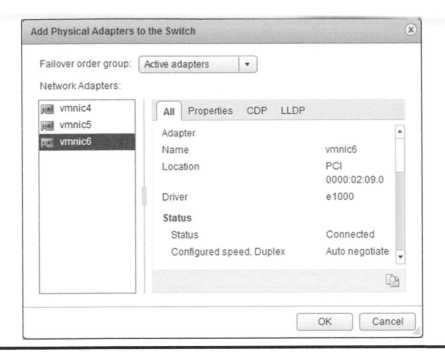

Figure 7.16   Selecting available NIC.

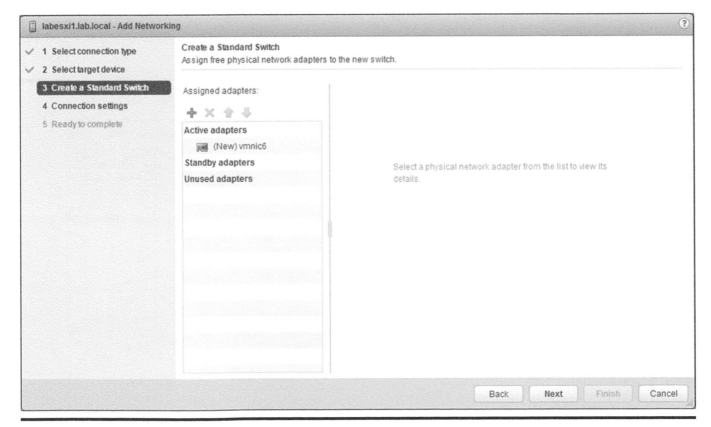

Figure 7.17   Added active adapter.

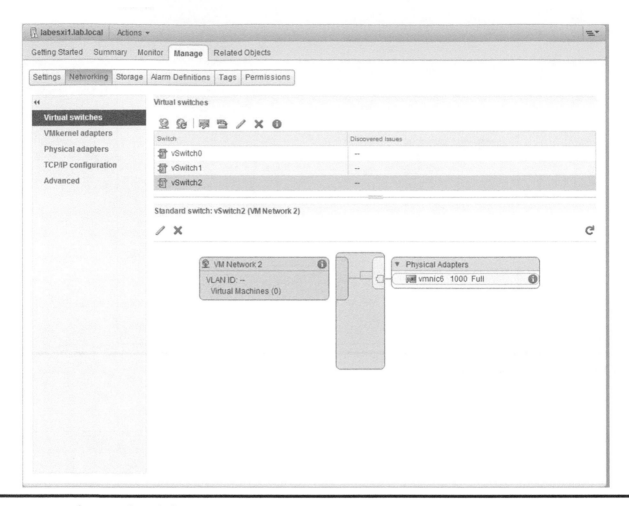

Figure 7.18   Newly created vSwitch.

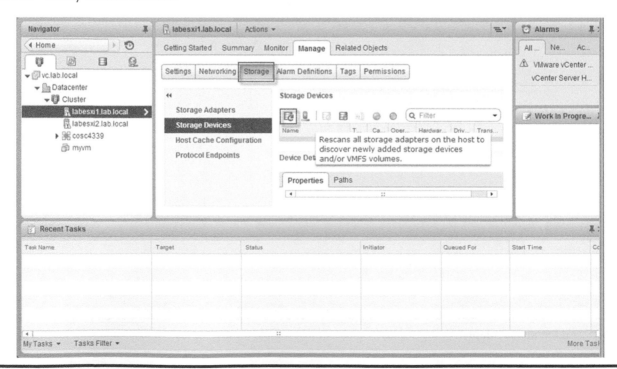

Figure 7.19   Storage connection.

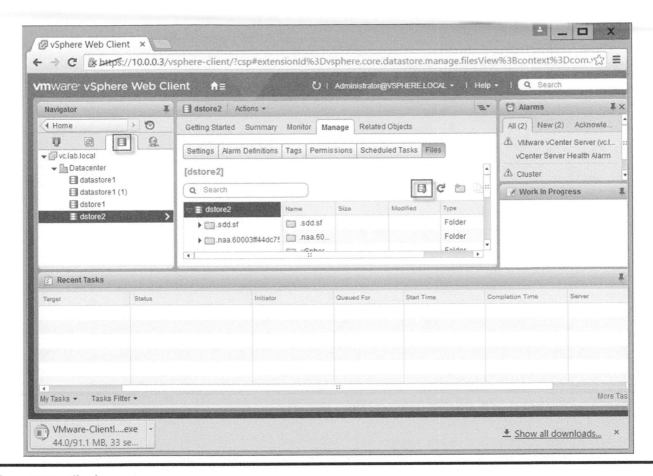

Figure 7.20 Files in storage.

file, as shown in Figure 7.21. The installation may require you to close the Web browser.

30. Double-click the file to open the installation wizard. On the Welcome page, click **Next**.

31. On the End-user License Agreement page, check the option **I accept the terms in the license agreement**. Then, click **Next**.

32. On the Destination folder, take the default. Then, click **Next**.

33. On the Ready to Install the Plug-in page, click **Install**.

34. After the installation is complete, click **Finish**. Then, restart the Web browser.

35. Select **dstore2** in the Navigation pane. Click the **Add Folder** icon to create an **ISO** folder (Figure 7.22).

36. Click the **Upload** icon, as shown in Figure 7.23, to upload the ISO file to the shared datastore.

37. In the Open dialog, select the ISO file, as shown in Figure 7.24. Then, click **Open**.

38. After the file is uploaded, you will see the file in the ISO folder, as shown in Figure 7.25.

39. To install the guest OS on the virtual machine myvm created earlier, click the **Host and Cluster** icon in Navigation pane. Right-click the virtual machine **myvm** and select **Edit Settings**, as shown in Figure 7.26.

40. On the CD/DVD dropdown list, select the item **Datastore ISO File**, as shown in Figure 7.27.

41. As shown in Figure 7.28, attach the ISO file to the CD/DVD drive. Then, click **OK**.

42. After the ISO file is attached to the CD/DVD drive, check the checkbox **Connect at Power On**, as shown in Figure 7.29. Then, click **OK**.

43. To install the guest OS, right-click the virtual machine **myvm** and select **Power**. Then, click **Power On**, as shown in Figure 7.30.

44. To interact with the installation process, right-click the virtual machine myvm and select **Open Console**, as shown in Figure 7.31.

45. In the console, you can observe the installation process (Figure 7.32).

46. On the Welcome page, click **Install Ubuntu**, as shown in Figure 7.33.

47. On the Preparing to Install Ubuntu page, verify that you have enough storage space. Then, click **Continue**. (You may need the Tab key to move the cursor.)

48. On the Installation Type page, click **Install Now**.

49. In the Write the changes to disks dialog, click **Continue**.

50. On the Where are you page, select your time zone and click **Continue**.

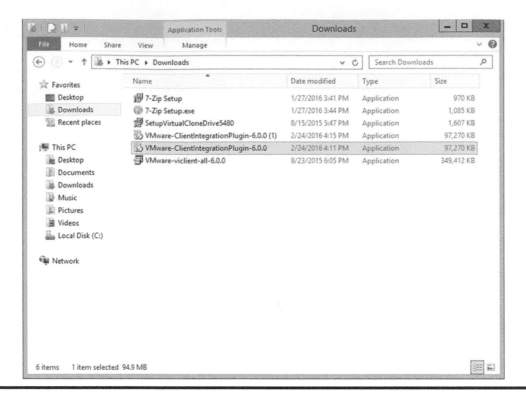

Figure 7.21   Finding VMware-ClientIntegrationPlugin File.

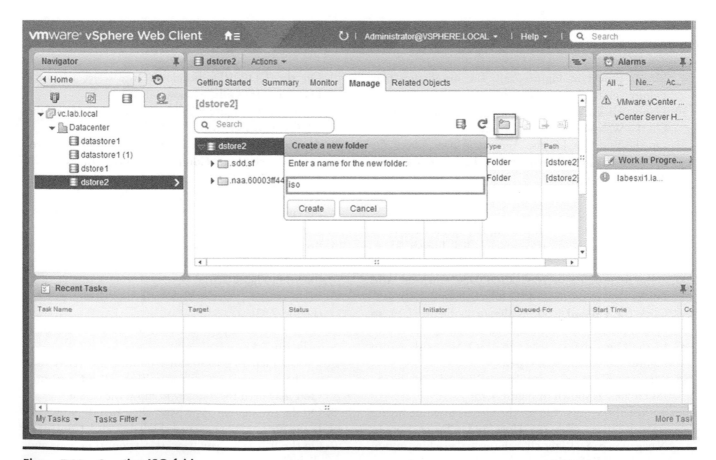

Figure 7.22   Creating ISO folder.

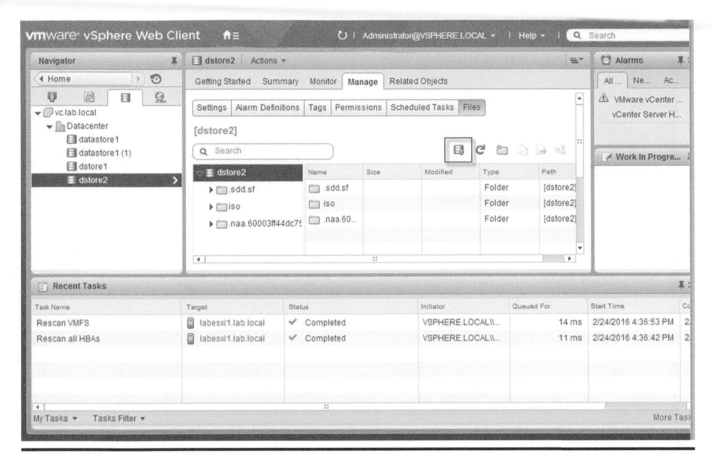

Figure 7.23   **Uploading ISO file.**

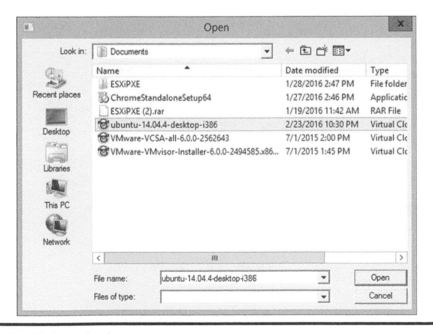

Figure 7.24   **Opening ISO file for upload.**

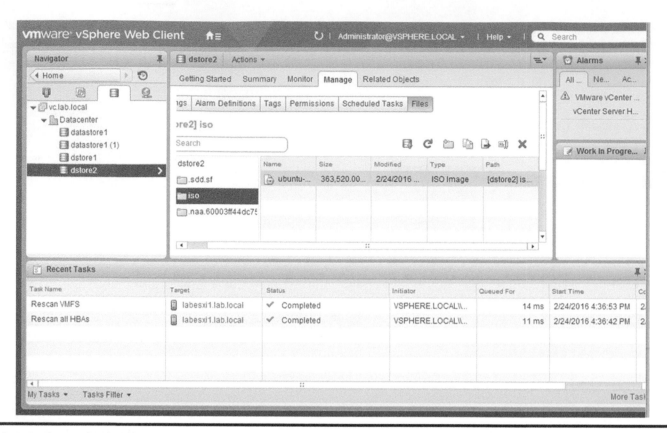

Figure 7.25 Uploaded ISO file.

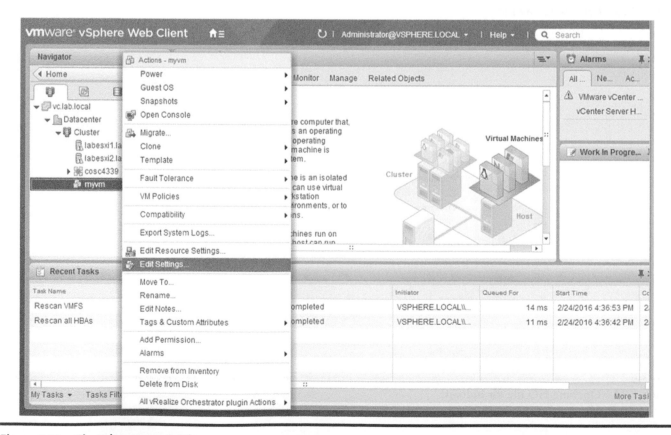

Figure 7.26 Changing myvm Settings.

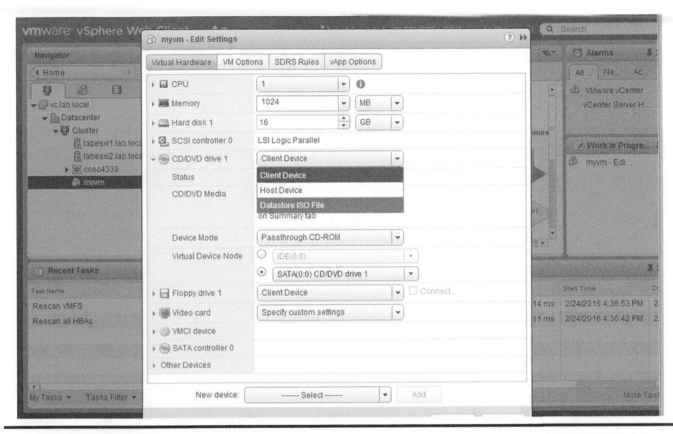

Figure 7.27   Configuring CD/DVD.

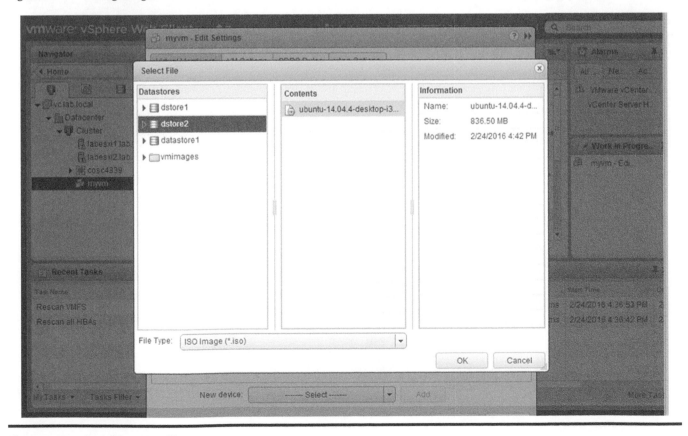

Figure 7.28   Attaching ISO file.

Figure 7.29 Connecting at power on.

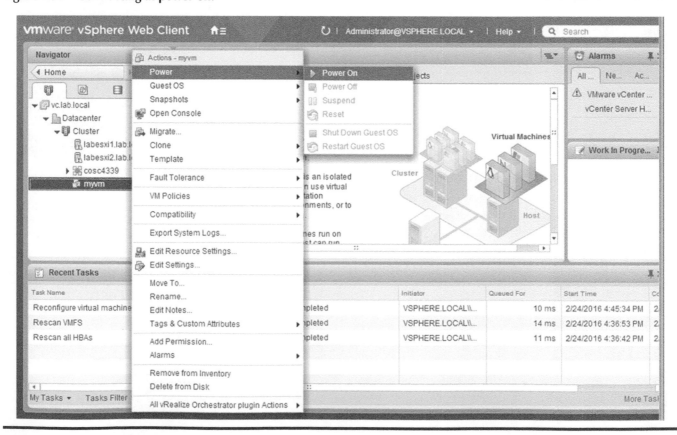

Figure 7.30 Powering on virtual machine myvm.

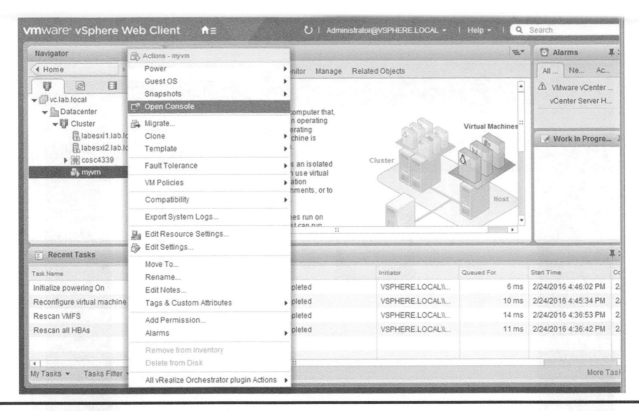

Figure 7.31　Opening console.

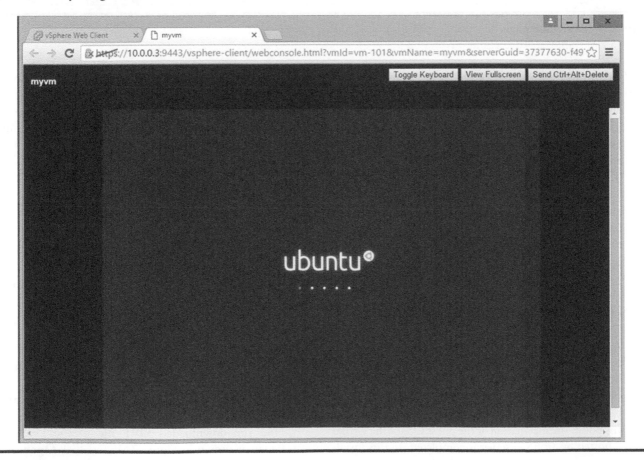

Figure 7.32　Installation process.

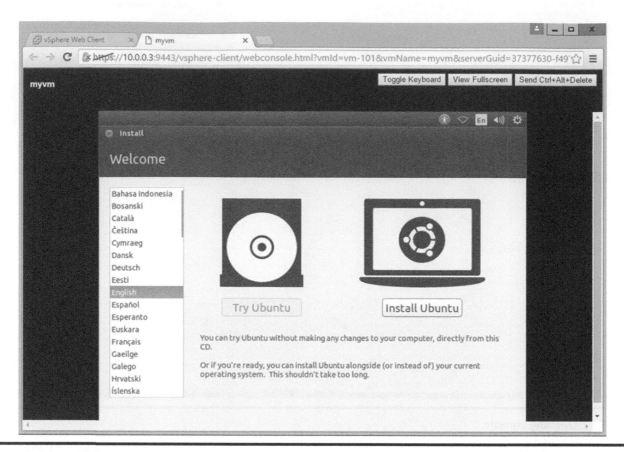

Figure 7.33   Welcome page.

51. On the Keyboard layout page, select your keyboard layout style and click **Continue**.
52. On the Who are you page, enter the user name and password. Then, click **Continue**. The installation process begins (Figure 7.34).
53. Once the operation is complete, click **Restart Now**. After the system restart is complete, you should be able to see the installed guest OS shown in Figure 7.35.
54. Enter your password to log on to the guest OS. Once you have logged on, you will see that the network is not connected, as shown in Figure 7.36. Click the **Network** icon and click **Edit Connections**.
55. Select **Wired connection 1** and click **Edit**. In the Editing wired connection 1 dialog, click the **IPv4 Settings** tab. Click the **Add** button, and then enter the configuration of the network adapter, as shown in Figure 7.37. Then, click **Save**.
56. As shown in Figure 7.38, the network is connected. Close the **Network Connections** dialog and shut down the virtual machine.

At this point, the installation of the guest OS for the virtual machine hosted by an ESXi server is completed. In this installation process, the installation ISO file is placed on the shared storage so that it can be accessed by the virtual machines. A separate virtual network is also created for the virtual machines. In addition to manually creating virtual machines, you can import and export virtual machines. The next task will illustrate how to export and import an OVF template.

7.5.2 Task 2: Exporting and Importing OVF Template

In the previous task, you have downloaded the OVF template, which is a master copy of the Ubuntu server. In this task, you will learn how to create a virtual machine by importing the OVF template. You will also learn how to export a virtual machine as an OVA file. Follow the steps below to accomplish this task.

1. Assume that you are still logged on to vSphere Web Client. Right-click the **Cluster** node and select **Deploy OVF Template**, as shown in Figure 7.39.
2. On the Select source page, check the option **Local file** and click **Browse**, as shown in Figure 7.40.
3. Find the downloaded OVF file in the Document folder, as shown in Figure 7.41, and click **Open**. After the OVF file is opened, click **Next**.

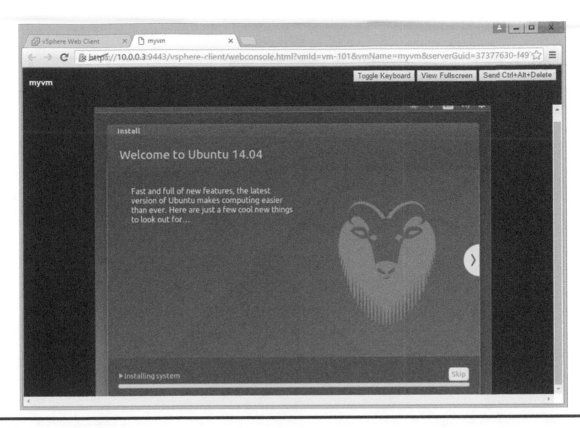

Figure 7.34 Starting installation.

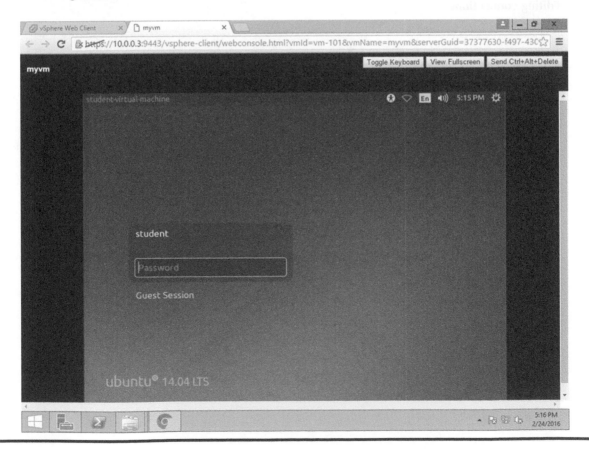

Figure 7.35 Installed guest OS.

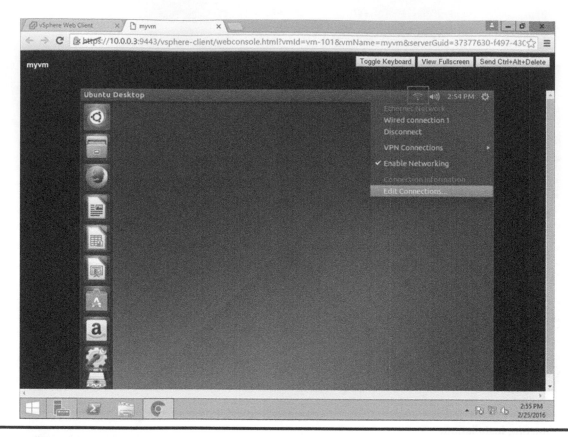

Figure 7.36 Editing connections.

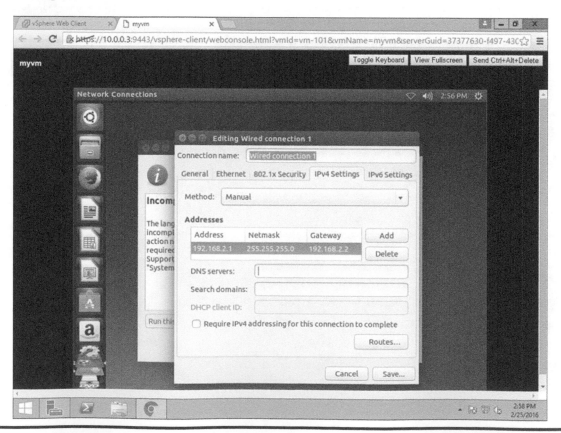

Figure 7.37 Network adapter configuration.

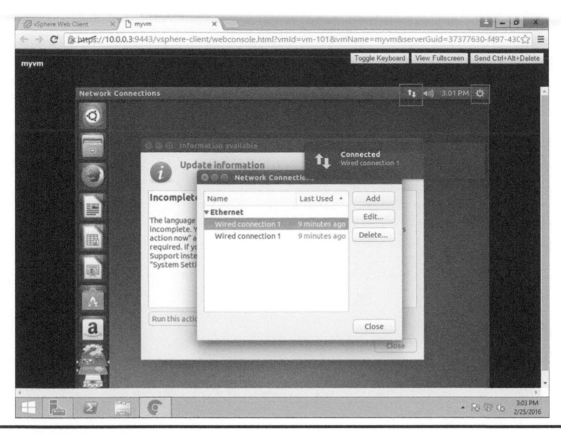

Figure 7.38   Networked virtual machine.

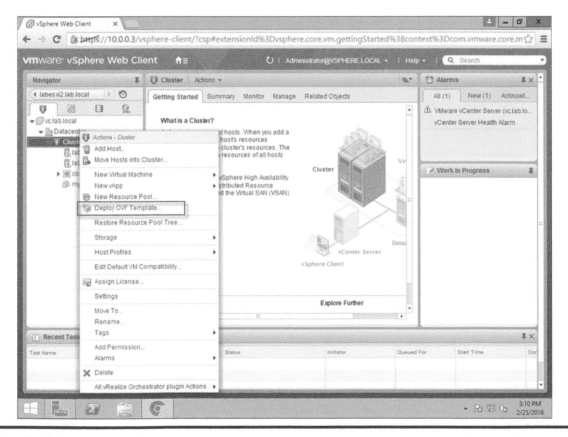

Figure 7.39   Deploying OVF template.

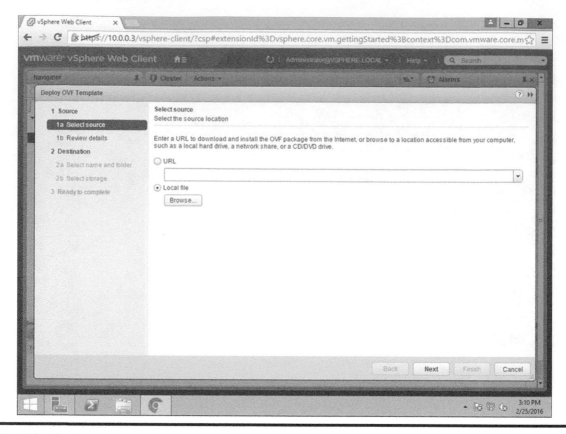

Figure 7.40 Selecting source.

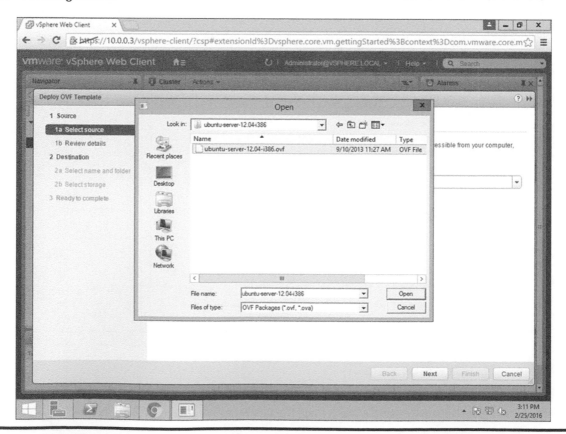

Figure 7.41 Opening OVF file.

4. On the Review details page, review the OVF file information and click **Next**.
5. On the Select name and folder page, select **Datacenter**, as shown in Figure 7.42, and click **Next**.
6. On the Select storage page, select the available shared storage such as **dstore2** (Figure 7.43). Then, click **Next**.
7. On the Setup networks page, make sure that **VM Network** is selected (Figure 7.44). Then, click **Next**.
8. On the Ready to complete page, click **Finish**. After the OVF template is deployed, a new virtual machine is created, as shown in Figure 7.45.
9. To export a virtual machine as an OVA file, right-click the virtual machine **myvm** and select **Template,** and then select **Export OVF Template**, as shown in Figure 7.46.
10. In the Export OVF Template dialog, select **Single file (OVA)** on the Format dropdown list, as shown in Figure 7.47. Click the **Choose** button and specify the destination in the Document folder. Then, click **OK**.
11. Once exported, you should be able to see the OVA file, as shown in Figure 7.48.

7.5.3 Task 3: Creating and Transporting vApp

In this task, you will create a vApp that includes two virtual machines to form a client–server infrastructure. After the vApp is created, you will learn how to import and export it.

1. Assume that you are still logged on to vSphere Web Client. To create a vApp, right-click the **Cluster** node and select **New vApp** and then **New vApp**, as shown in Figure 7.49.
2. On the Select a creation type page, select the option **Create a new vApp**, as shown in Figure 7.50. Then, click **Next**.
3. On the Select a name and location page, enter **cosc4339** as the vApp name and select **Datacenter**, as shown in Figure 7.51. Then, click **Next**.
4. On the Resource allocation page, take the default. Then, click **Next**.
5. On the Ready to complete page, verify the configuration and click **Finish**.
6. As shown in Figure 7.52, the newly created vApp cosc4339 has appeared in the Navigation pane.

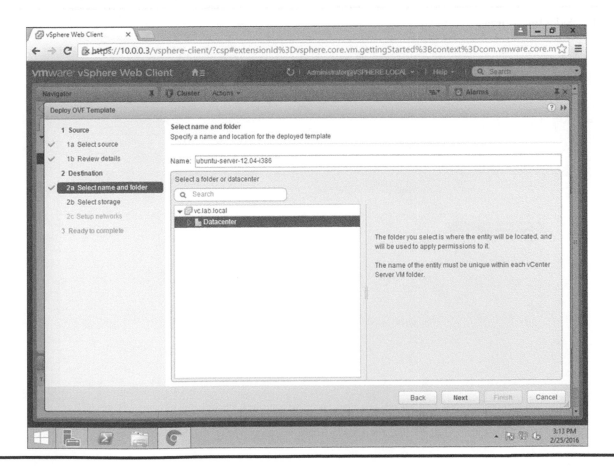

Figure 7.42 Selecting Datacenter.

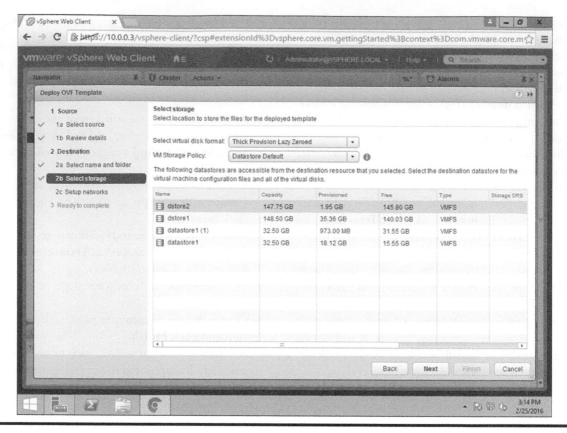

Figure 7.43 Selecting storage.

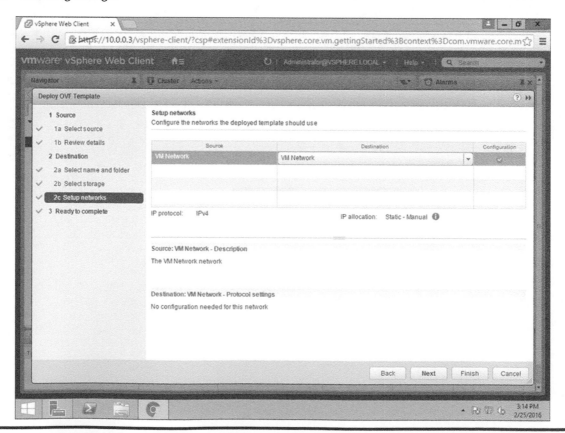

Figure 7.44 Setting up network.

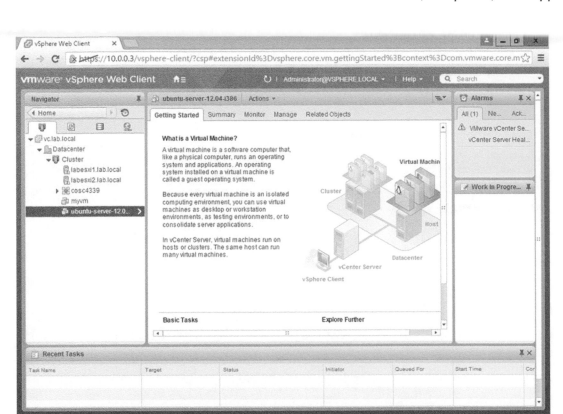

Figure 7.45 Deployed OVF template.

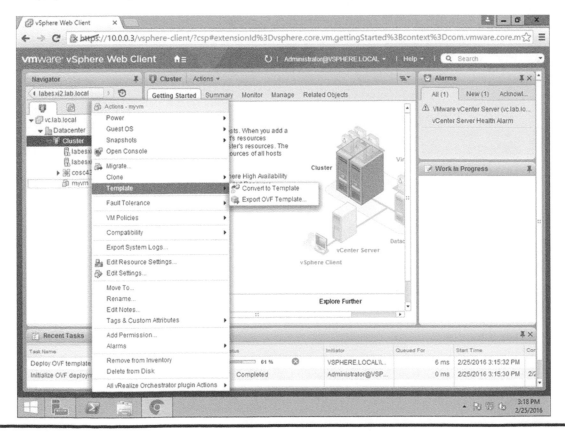

Figure 7.46 Exporting OVF template.

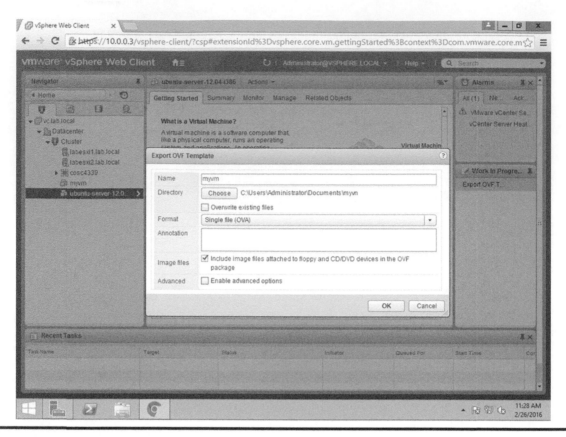

Figure 7.47 Specifying export format.

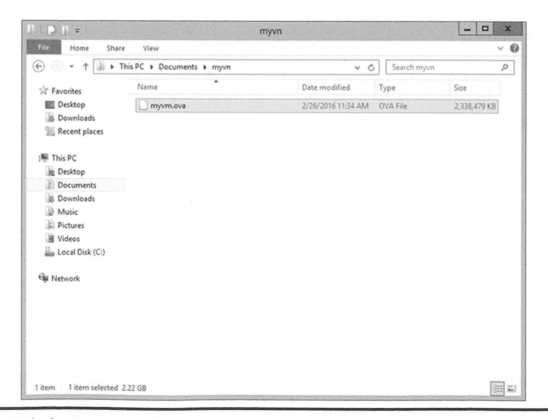

Figure 7.48 Reviewing exported OVA file.

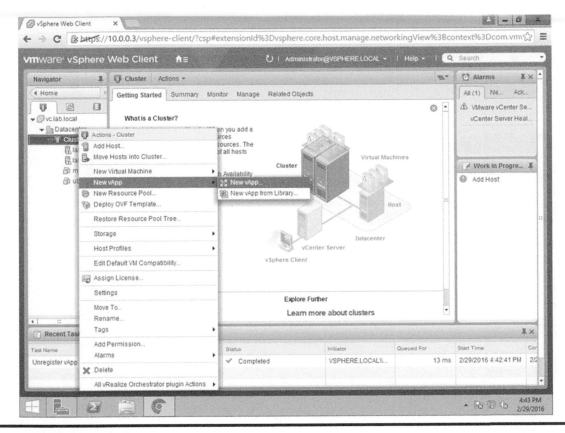

Figure 7.49   Creating New vApp.

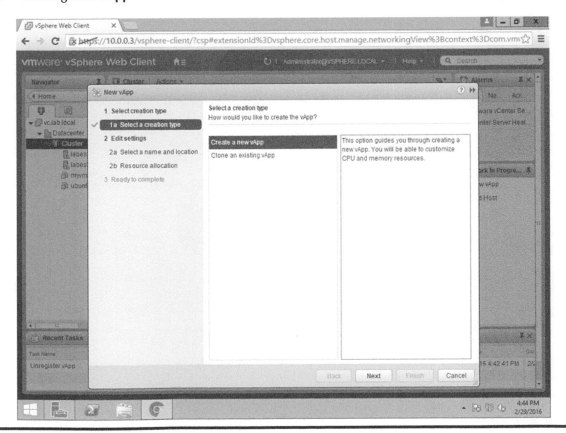

Figure 7.50   Selecting creation type.

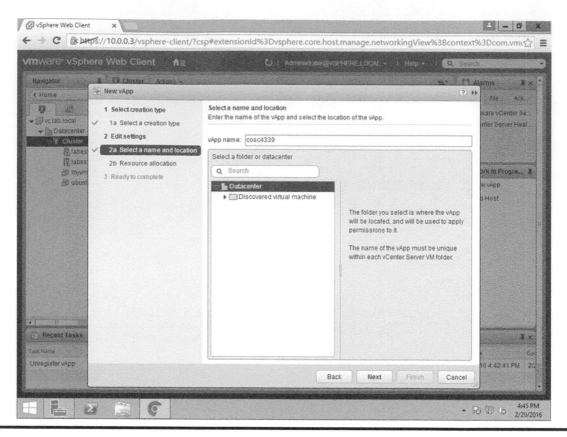

Figure 7.51 Selecting name and location.

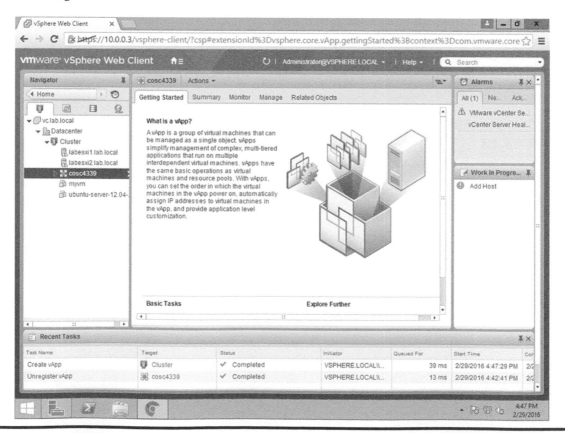

Figure 7.52 Newly created vApp.

7. To add the virtual machines to the vApp, drag both **myvm** and **ubuntu-server** to the vApp cose4339, as shown in Figure 7.53.

8. You can now power on the vApp by right-clicking **cosc4339** and select **Power** and **Power On**, as shown in Figure 7.54.

9. As you can see, both virtual machines are powered on. To power off the vApp cosc4339, select **Power** and **Shut Down**, as shown in Figure 7.55.

10. To export the newly created vApp, right-click the vApp **cosc4339** and select **OVF Template** and **Export OVF Template**, as shown in Figure 7.56.

11. In the Export OVF Template dialog, click the **Choose** button. In the Select Folder dialog, create and select

the folder **cosc4339**, as shown in Figure 7.57. Then, click the **Select Folder** button.

12. In the Export OVF Template dialog, name the exported vApp as **cosc4339**, as shown in Figure 7.58. Then, click **OK**.

13. As shown in Figure 7.59, you can find the exported OVF files in the folder cosc4339.

14. Repeat Steps 1 through 8; in Task 2, you can import vApp OVF files.

In this task, you have created a vApp with two virtual machines. The vApp is exported as the OVF template. In later chapters, you will learn how to make the vApp available to subscribers in a cloud computing environment.

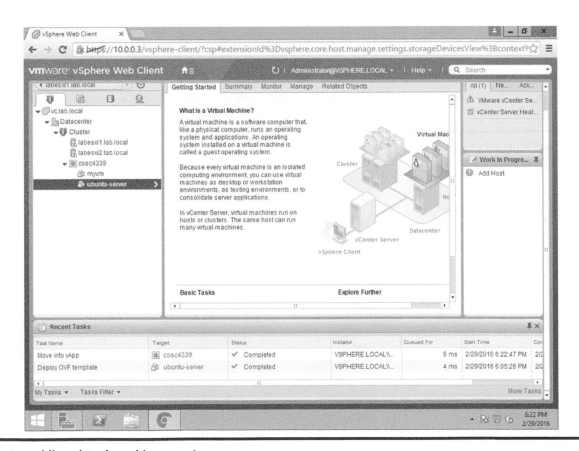

Figure 7.53 Adding virtual machines to vApp.

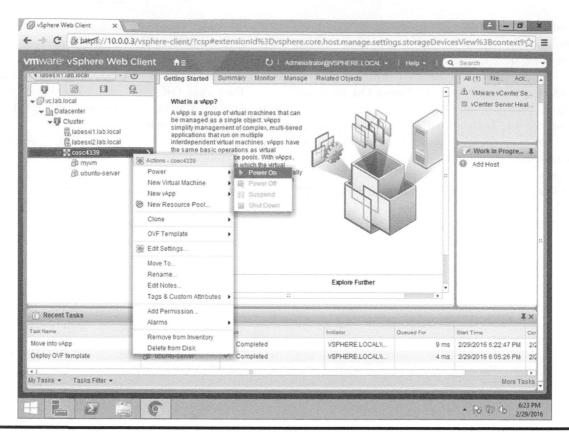

Figure 7.54 Powering on vApp.

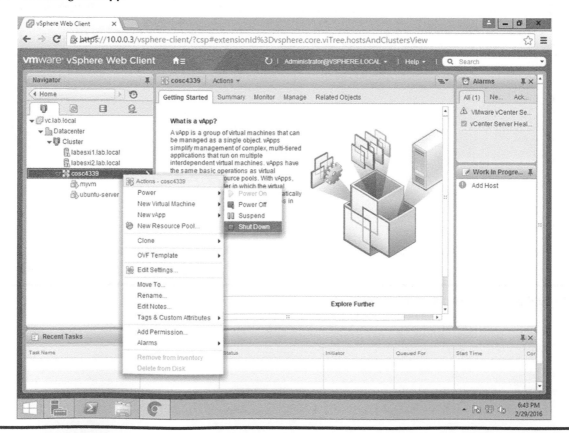

Figure 7.55 Powering off vApp.

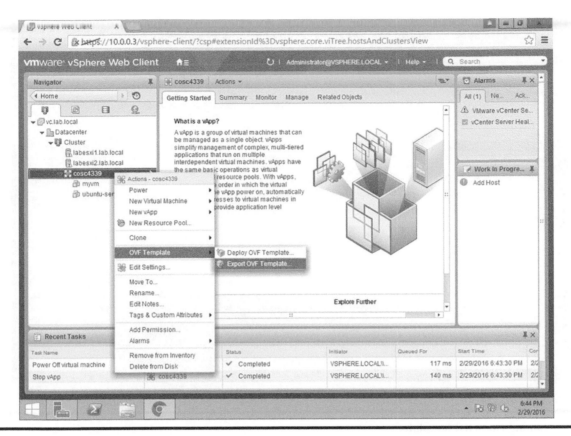

Figure 7.56 Exporting OVF template.

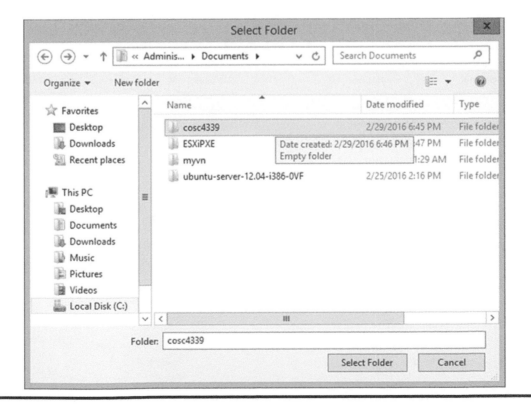

Figure 7.57 Selecting folder.

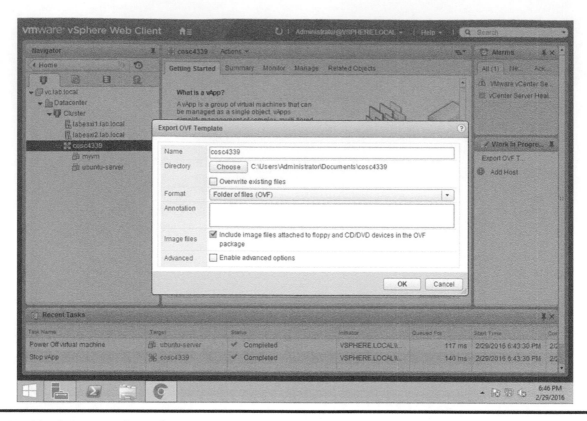

Figure 7.58 Naming exported template.

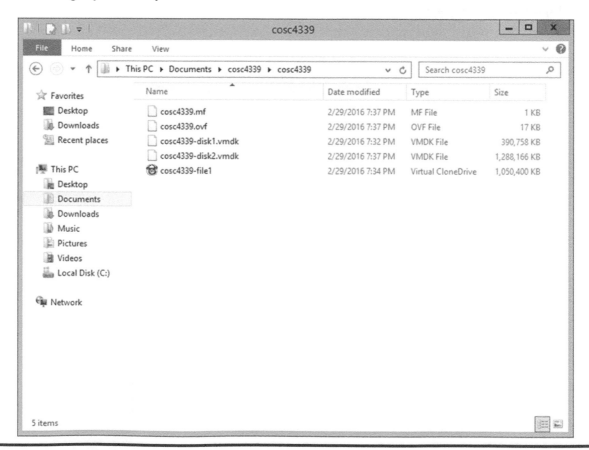

Figure 7.59 Exported OVF files.

7.6 Summary

This chapter covers the ESXi-hosted virtual objects such as virtual machines, templates, and vApps. In a virtual machine, the hardware is virtualized with the software. These virtualized hardware devices are used to support the guest OS. This chapter covers the template that is used as the master copy for virtual machine cloning. It introduces vApp, which is a set of virtual machines preconfigured to form an IT infrastructure. Virtual networks can also be built in a vApp. Like a virtual machine, a vApp can be exported as an OVF or OVA file to be transported to another virtualized computing environment. The hands-on practice of this chapter covers the tasks such as installing the guest OS, importing and exporting the OVF and OVA files, and creating and transporting vApps. In later chapters, virtual machines, templates, and vApps will be used to provide infrastructure as a service in a cloud computing environment.

REVIEW QUESTIONS

1. What is a vApp, and how does it work?
2. How can a virtual machine access the guest OS installation materials?
3. Describe virtual machine hardware versions.
4. Explain why, sometimes, the actual amount of physical memory allocated to a virtual machine may be less than the configured amount.
5. If the Hyper-Threading Technology is supported, a physical processor with six cores can be considered as how many single-core processors?
6. Describe the three disk provision options.
7. What is the usage of vSGA?
8. What are the benefits a guest OS can get from VMware Tools?
9. How is VMware Tools installed?
10. What is the usage of a snapshot?
11. Describe the content of a .vmx file.
12. Where are the data of the virtual machine stored?
13. Where is the information about a virtual machine's BIOS stored?
14. For templates, what does the symbol of the gold plate indicate?
15. How do you update a template?
16. Describe the files contained in an OVF standard package.
17. What are the uses of an OVF/OVA package in VMware Cloud Suite?
18. What is Content Library, and how does it work?
19. What are the features offered by a vApp?
20. How is an IP address to an NIC of a virtual machine assigned in a vApp?

Chapter 8

High Availability and Resource Balancing

Objectives

- Understand Clustering
- Comprehend VMware High Availability
- Apply VMware Fault Tolerance
- Configure vMotion
- Get familiar with Distributed Resource Scheduler

8.1 Introduction

During business operations, the information technology (IT) infrastructure may experience server crash, storage failure, network disconnection, power outage, or inaccessible application software. Due to these problems, the business supported by the IT infrastructure will go down, which cannot be tolerated by a company of any size. Therefore, the high availability (HA) of the IT infrastructure is critical for a business to be successful. The term *high availability* refers to the services on the IT infrastructure to keep running for a long period of time. One of the benefits of VMware is that it provides tools to keep the HA of a virtualized IT infrastructure. This chapter introduces the following three commonly used HA tools:

1. *Clustering:* VMware supports *network load balancing (NLB) clustering* and *Windows failover clustering*. Clustering makes a group of servers act like a single system in order to achieve HA.
2. *VMware High Availability:* It is an HA tool to prevent virtual machine failure. It can get a failed virtual machine up and running with very little disturbance.
3. *VMware Fault Tolerance (FT):* It is an HA tool for virtual machines that require zero downtime.

For the VMware projects covered in this book, we focus on HA for services delivered by the following layers in the IT infrastructure:

- *Application layer availability:* In this layer, HA is to make the application software installed on the virtual machines available to the end users. The application layer availability highly depends on the availability of other HA layers.
- *Operating system layer availability:* In this layer, HA is applied to the virtual machine guest operating system and the Elastic Sky X Integrated (ESXi) host operating system.
- *Virtualization layer availability:* In this layer, HA is applied to the ESXi hypervisor and the virtualized IT infrastructure.
- *Physical structure layer availability:* In this layer, HA is applied to the hardware such as storage and network devices. To achieve HA in the physical structure, redundancy is the most used technique, for example, the use of redundant power supplies to prevent power failure and the use of redundant switches to prevent network failure.

For many businesses, HA is necessary. The failure of an IT infrastructure can have a significant negative impact on a company. The company will lose its customers and have a bad reputation. The IT infrastructure failure may stop the business operation, which will reduce the revenue and profit.

It is critical for a company to make the core components of its IT infrastructure highly available. The tools provided by VMware can make the company more resilient to the failure occurred in each of the layers in the IT infrastructure.

8.2 Clustering

Redundancy is one of the measures to keep HA in the application layer. In the VMware computing environment, the application redundancy can be implemented by creating a cluster including multiple servers. To make the core applications highly available, clustering can be accomplished by using NLB clustering and the Microsoft Cluster Service (MSCS).

Network load balancing: By nature, an NLB cluster is used to enhance performance and availability. In an NLB cluster, all the servers can be configured as active nodes. These servers work together to handle requests from the clients. Each server in the NLB cluster can be configured to take a certain percentage of the total workload. The administrator can also configure the servers to take specific types of workload. The cluster presents a single Internet Protocol (IP) address and a single name to the clients. Based on the workload, the client requests can be redirected to a particular server. If the performance of one of the nodes goes down, NLB can do a dynamic analysis about the health and capacity levels of the application servers. Based on the analysis, the client requests will be redirected to other active nodes. Figure 8.1 illustrates an NLB cluster.

Being able to redirect the client requests to other servers, the NLB cluster is suitable for services such as the virtual private network and Web server. Using a virtual machine to host the application software makes it easier to restore the application and operating system. The NLB cluster supported by VMware can run in a multicast mode or unicast mode. The multicast mode allows the ESXi hosts within the cluster to communicate with each other. When running in the unicast mode, the virtual machines are required to run on a single ESXi host server.

Microsoft Cluster Service: The cluster technology is often used to achieve HA in the operating system layer. The HA of the application layer depends on the HA of the operating system layer. Further, the HA of the operating system layer depends on the HA of the virtualization layer and the physical layer. MSCS is the tool that can be used for operating system redundancy. VMware supports the MSCS clustering. In the MSCS clustering, a node is configured either as an active node or a passive node. Only the active node can be accessed by the clients. The passive node assumes ownership if the active node fails. Both the active node and passive node share the same IP address and name. Figure 8.2 illustrates an MSCS cluster. The private network in Figure 8.2 is used for checking the heartbeat of the cluster nodes. An MSCS cluster is often used to protect application servers such as the Dynamic Host Configuration Protocol (DHCP) server, email server, and database server.

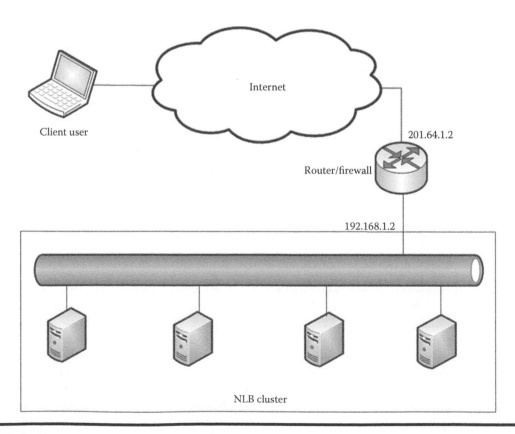

Figure 8.1 NLB cluster.

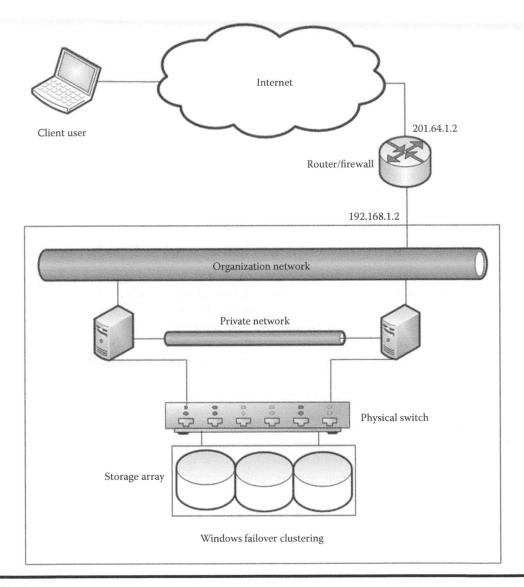

Figure 8.2 MSCS cluster.

Virtual machine clustering with MSCS: To form multiple servers into a cluster with MSCS, the servers should be configured to meet the following requirements:

- A virtual machine should have the Windows Server Enterprise Edition or Datacenter Edition operating system installed.
- Only two nodes are allowed in each cluster.
- All virtual machines in the cluster should be able to access the network shared storage.
- Every virtual machine in the cluster should have two network interface cards (NICs): one connected to the organization network and one connected to the private network. The NICs of the virtual machine should be configured with LSI Logic SAS and VMXNET adapters.
- All ESXi hosts should be installed with the same version of ESXi.

In addition to these requirements, one needs to understand that virtual machine clustering may not support the following elements in VMware:

- NIC teaming
- Datastores configured with Fibre Channel over Ethernet, iSCSI, or Network File System (NFS)
- Other HA mechanisms such as vMotion, VMware HA, VMware FT, and vSphere Distributed Resource Scheduler (DRS)

Like the clustering at the ESXi level, MSCS clustering can also be implemented in three different configurations: (1) Cluster in a Box, (2) Cluster across Boxes, and (3) physical to virtual clustering. The following gives a quick review of the three configurations.

Cluster in a Box: Cluster in a Box is the easiest way to implement clustering since there is no extra configuration required. The private network carries the network traffic used for checking the heartbeat of the cluster nodes. The organization network is used for the communication between the cluster and other systems in the IT infrastructure. On the other hand, this configuration has no protection in the event of ESXi server failure. Therefore, this configuration is often used in the experiment or testing scenarios. The two virtual machines are connected to a storage disk formatted with Virtual Machine File System (VMFS). The storage disk can be the local disk on the ESXi host server or on the network shared storage array. Figure 8.3 illustrates the Cluster-in-a-Box configuration.

Cluster across Boxes: In this configuration, two virtual machines in a cluster are hosted by two different ESXi host servers. However, for vSphere 4 or a newer version of vSphere, the virtual machine disk (VMDK) files and the virtual machine's boot drive or C drive are allowed to be stored in a storage area network storage device. For the older version of vSphere, the boot drive or C drive must be stored in the host's local hard drive. Also, the shared storage must be constructed on Fibre Channel external disks. The storage is required to use raw device mapping (RDM), which presents the storage device directly to a virtual machine. This configuration provides good protection if one of the ESXi host servers fails. In case one of the ESXi host servers fails, the cluster node on the other host server will continue responding to client requests. The Cluster-across-Boxes configuration requires Fibre Channel shared storage external to the ESXi host servers. Figure 8.4 demonstrates how the Cluster-across-Boxes configuration works.

The configuration of Cluster across Boxes is more complicated than that of Cluster in a Box. An external physical switch is required for connecting the ESXi host servers and the network shared storage array. It is also required that the two cluster nodes can communicate through the private network and the organization network.

Physical to virtual clustering: In this configuration, one physical machine and one virtual machine are used to form a cluster. The virtual machine node and physical machine node share the same network storage. They should be able to communicate through the organization network and the private network. This configuration provides protection in case the ESXi host server or the physical machine fails. One of the advantages of physical to virtual clustering is that it allows an ESXi host server to handle multiple clusters, each paired with a virtual machine on the ESXi server and an external physical machine. Figure 8.5 shows a physical-to-virtual-clustering configuration.

In addition to NBL and MSCS, there are many other third-party redundancy tools available. For example, F5 is a company producing a range of integrated products for load balancing and application delivery networking. Oracle has a product called Oracle Real Application Clusters, which is a clustered version of Oracle Database. It can be used to enhance the availability, scalability, and agility of an application server.

One of the key measures for enforcing HA is redundancy on the network and storage devices. The network is one of the weakest links in an IT infrastructure. Network redundancy ensures that the end users can remotely access the applications. If one of the routes has an access problem, the network traffic can take another route. Some of the routers

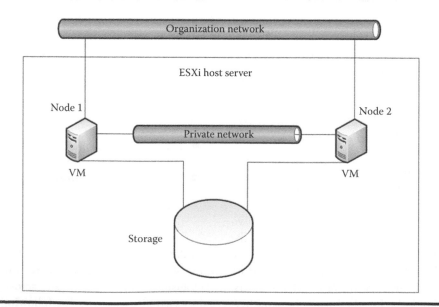

Figure 8.3 Cluster in a Box.

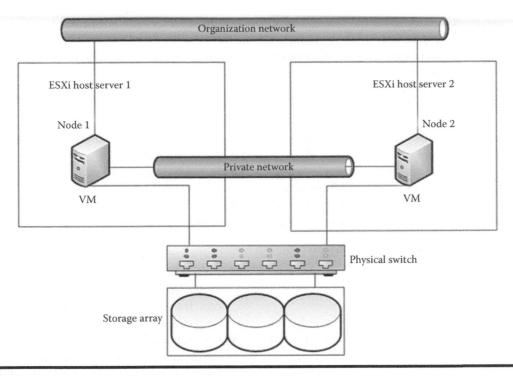

Figure 8.4 Cluster across Boxes.

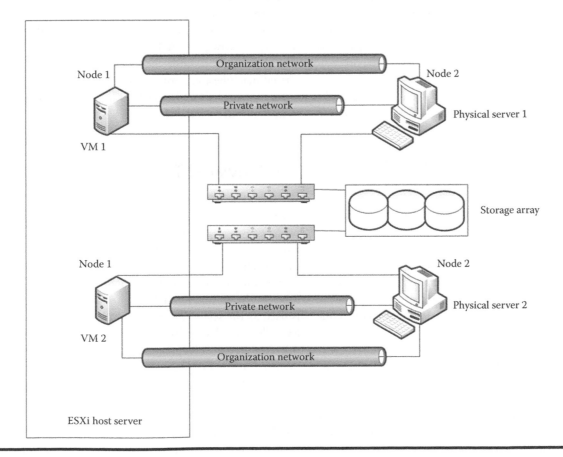

Figure 8.5 Physical to virtual clustering.

include the Hot Standby Router Protocol or Virtual Routing Redundancy Protocol. These protocols allow a secondary router to take over if the primary router fails. NIC teaming is another network redundancy mechanism. In NIC teaming, a virtual machine communicates with an external device through multiple physical NICs. If one of the physical NICs fails, the network traffic can still pass through other physical NICs. Redundant storage can be implemented through the redundant array of independent disks technology.

On the downside, redundancy consumes more resources, processing power, and network capacity. Redundancy increases the workload and cost. Therefore, we should consider using redundancy only for applications that are critical for the business operation.

8.3 VMware HA

VMware HA is a component of VMware that provides the automatic failover of virtual machines. VMware HA can protect virtual machines hosted by an ESXi host server running in a VMware HA–enabled cluster. VMware HA is an affordable and easy-to-use HA in addition to clustering. Another benefit of VMware HA is that it can be deployed uniformly across multiple physical ESXi host servers.

Suppose that multiple ESXi host servers are configured so that they belong to the same cluster. To enable the VMware HA service across the host servers in the cluster, the host servers are required to meet the following requirements:

- All the ESXi host servers in the cluster need to be configured with static IP addresses or reserved DHCP addresses.
- All the ESXi host servers in the cluster should have an identical vSphere Standard Switch configuration, or all the ESXi host servers should connect to the same vSphere Distributed Switch.
- All the ESXi host servers in the cluster must have access to the same management network.
- All the ESXi host servers in the cluster must have access to the same network shared storage device.
- All the ESXi host servers in the cluster must be configured so that their short host names can be resolved to the corresponding IP address by the domain name system server.

A virtual machine may fail due to the failure of the ESXi host server or due to the failure of the guest operating system or the application software on the virtual machine. In the event of the ESXi host server failure, the VMware HA mechanism can restart the affected virtual machines from another host server. In the event of the guest operating system or application software failure, the VMware HA mechanism can restart the virtual machine on the same ESXi host server. VMware HA can also be used to check the capability of an ESXi host server to make sure that the server has enough resources for its virtual machines. During the operation, VMware HA performs the following tasks:

- It identifies abnormal configuration settings and potential error conditions.
- It reports the health status and provides suggested remediation steps.
- It elects a master host among all the host servers in a cluster and makes other host servers as slave hosts.
- It automatically detects ESXi host server failures and initiates the reboot of virtual machines.
- It automatically detects operating system failures in a virtual machine by monitoring the heartbeat information. If a failure is detected, it initiates the reboot of the virtual machine.
- It continuously monitors the capacity utilization and the resources available for restarting virtual machines.
- It automatically deploys a virtual machine to an ESXi host server that has the most available resources.

Although VMware HA is a powerful HA tool, it relays the reboot of the affected virtual machines. From the time a virtual machine fails to the time the virtual machine is rebooted, VMware HA has a short downtime. Therefore, VMware HA is suitable for protecting non-mission-critical virtual machines. For mission-critical virtual machines, one needs to consider another HA tool, VMware FT, which provides continued availability.

8.4 VMware FT

VMware FT is another component of VMware that provides continuous availability. Unlike VMware HA, which protects every virtual machine in the cluster, VMware FT works on an individual virtual machine. To protect the virtual machine, the VMware FT mechanism automatically creates an identical virtual machine; the original one is used as the primary machine, and the newly created one is used as the secondary machine. VMware FT uses a utility called vLockstep. To get the identical result, vLockstep matches the secondary machine with the primary machine, instruction for instruction and memory for memory. The heartbeat ping is used to check on the primary and secondary machines for the instantaneous detection of a failure. If zero downtime is required for a virtual machine, VMware FT should be considered. However, VMware FT has more requirements on computing resources. Since the secondary virtual machine is created to match the primary virtual machine when VMware FT is enabled, running both the primary and secondary virtual machines consumes twice the random access memory and some additional central processing unit (CPU) overhead. Therefore, there is no need to use VMware FT on every virtual machine.

In order to enable VMware FT in a cluster, the following requirements must be met at the cluster level:

- VMware HA must be enabled in the cluster before one can power on a VMware FT–enabled virtual machine.
- Make sure that the host certificate checking is enabled for all the hosts that used VMware FT. By default, the host certificate checking is enabled in a vCenter Server.
- It is required that at least two ESXi host servers in a cluster are running the same version of VMware FT.
- It is required that at least two ESXi host servers have processors from the same compatible processor group.

At the ESXi host server level, enabling VMware FT has the following requirements:

- All the ESXi host servers in the cluster should be installed with the same ESXi version and patch level.
- All the ESXi host servers in the cluster should have access to the same datastores and networks.
- All the ESXi host servers in the cluster should be VMware Hardware Compatibility List certified.
- All the ESXi host servers in the cluster should have Hardware Virtualization enabled in the basic input/output system. All the ESXi host servers in the cluster should have FT logging network connection configured.

At the virtual machine level, enabling VMware FT has the following requirements:

- The affected virtual machine should be configured with a single virtual CPU and configured with thick provisioning. The NIC used by the virtual machine should be configured with VMXNET 2, VMXNET 3, or E1000 network driver.
- The affected virtual machine should not have any snapshots and should not be a linked clone. Also, the virtual machine should not be configured with a Universal Serial Bus drive, a sound device, a CD-ROM drive, a floppy drive, serial ports, and parallel ports.
- The affected virtual machine is connected to all the ESXi host servers participating in the VMware FT.
- The virtual machine should be stored in virtual RDM or VMDK files. The virtual machine files should be stored in the network shared storage device.
- The virtual machines should be running on one of the supported guest operating systems such as various

editions of the Windows Server operating system and the Linux operating systems from the major Linux distributions.

During the operation, VMware FT does not work with the following vSphere components:

- During the operation, it is not possible to take snapshots of virtual machines on which FT is enabled.
- During the vMotion operation, Storage vMotion cannot be invoked for virtual machines with FT turned on.
- The DRS features are automatically disabled on a VMware FT–enabled virtual machine.
- During the operation, hot-plugging is not supported. Therefore, one cannot add or remove a piece of hardware such as an NIC on a VMware FT–enabled virtual machine.

In order to enable VMware FT on a virtual machine, the VMware HA service must be enabled. The operation of VMware FT depends on the VMware HA service. For example, when both the primary and secondary machines in VMware FT fail, VMware FT depends on VMware HA to restart the primary machine.

8.5 vMotion

vMotion is a mechanism that enables the live migration of running virtual machines from one ESXi host server to another with zero downtime. During the migration, the end user will not experience any interruption. When an ESXi host server is about to go down, with vMotion, all of the virtual machines on the server can be moved to another server for continued operation. vMotion can be used to balance the workload among ESXi host servers. The virtual machines on a heavily used ESXi host server can be moved live to a lightly used ESXi host server.

There is another type of vMotion called Storage vMotion. vMotion migrates running virtual machines. During a vMotion process, the CPU and memory usage are moved from one ESXi host server to another ESXi host server. However, the running virtual machine's hard drive is left unmoved. On the other hand, Storage vMotion migrates the running virtual machine's hard drive from one datastore to another datastore.

During the migration process, each type of vMotion works differently. The following briefly describes each type of vMotion. Let us start with the migration process for vMotion.

- After the migration order is issued, vMotion begins the process by making a copy of the running virtual machine's active memory page on the source ESXi host server.

■ Then, it places the copied active memory page to the memory of the destination ESXi host server.

■ During the migration process, the active memory page may be changed. If so, the changes will be recorded in a transaction log file.

■ Once the active memory page is copied to the destination ESXi host server, the virtual machine on the source host server stops responding to clients' requests.

■ The next step is to transfer the log file to the destination ESXi host server. The memory on the destination ESXi host server will be updated according to the log file.

■ Once the memory is updated, the virtual machine will be running on the destination ESXi host server. Then, the memory used by the virtual machine on the source ESXi host server can be deleted.

Storage vMotion has the following migration process:

■ After the migration order is issued, Storage vMotion begins to copy the metadata of a running virtual machine to an alternative datastore.

■ Then, the virtual machine's disk file will also be copied from the source datastore to the destination datastore with the tool Changed Block Tracking (CBT). With CBT, the data integrity can be preserved during the migration.

■ If changes are made to the source during the copying process, the data blocks that have changed will again be copied to the destination until the source and destination are synchronized.

■ Once the disk copy is completed, the virtual machine is suspended. Then, the virtual machine will be quickly pointed to the disk files on the destination. After that, the virtual machine can be resumed.

■ Once the virtual machine is successfully resumed, the source home directory and disks can be deleted.

To migrate disk files from a source datastore to a destination datastore, Storage vMotion can be used to move virtual disks when replacing an existing storage device with a newly purchased storage device. Or, it can be used to move disk files off a storage device that is under maintenance to another storage device. The user can also use Storage vMotion to move disk files from an ESXi host server's local hard drive to a network shared storage device.

In order to successfully implement vMotion, ESXi host servers, virtual networks, and virtual machines are required to meet certain requirements. The following lists some of the configurations required for the ESXi host servers:

■ The source and destination ESXi host servers should be connected to a shared storage device.

■ All the ESXi host servers in a cluster should be configured with identical virtual switches and identical port groups.

■ All the ESXi host servers in a cluster should be able to communicate through the vMotion-enabled VMkernel ports.

■ All the ESXi host servers in a cluster should belong to the same physical network or virtual local area network.

■ The processors used by the ESXi host servers in a cluster should be compatible. That is, the processors should be from the same processor family and same vendor and have the same features. It is also required that the processors must have the virtualization technology (Intel VT or AMD-v) enabled.

In addition to the requirements on ESXi host servers, there are some requirements on virtual machines. The following are some of them:

■ A virtual machine to be migrated should not be connected to any physical devices such as CD/DVD drives, floppy drives, and serial/parallel ports.

■ The virtual machine should not bind its CPU to a specific process and not be connected to an internal-only virtual switch.

■ The virtual machine's disk files, log files, configuration files, and nonvolatile memory should be stored on a datastore formatted as VMFS or NFS.

Like vMotion, Storage vMotion has its requirements for successful virtual hard disk file migration. For an ESXi host server, the following are some of the requirements:

■ The ESXi host server should be licensed to perform Storage vMotion.

■ The ESXi host server should have access to both the source and destination datastores.

The affected virtual machines should also meet the resource and configuration requirements shown as follows:

■ The running virtual machines should have no snapshots.
■ The running VMDKs should be configured in the persistent mode or with RDMs.
■ Storage vMotion cannot be performed on a virtual machine that is in the process of installing VMware Tools.

With vSphere 5.1 or a newer version, vMotion and Storage vMotion can be combined to conduct a unified migration. The combined vMotion allows a running virtual machine to change its datastore and host server at the same time as long as two ESXi host servers are connected to the same local network. The newer version vSphere also allows the migration of a virtual machine between clusters.

8.6 DRS

DRS is a component of vCenter Server. DRS allows users to set up rules for allocating resources for a computing task. It can be used to establish resource pools for different computing tasks. The main function of DRS is to automatically balance computing workload among a group of ESXi host servers. DRS supports the intelligent placement, which determines which nodes of a cluster should be used to run a virtual machine. It uses vMotion to automatically move virtual machines to a host server with more computing resources. In addition, DRS centralizes the control of hardware parameters and provides continued monitoring of hardware utilization. It is able to prioritize the utilization of resources according to the importance of an application. DRS can also be used to optimize the use of energy efficiency and the use of hardware resources when the computing circumstance has changed.

If the user wants more control of resource distribution, DRS can be set to the manual mode. In the manual mode, after a virtual machine is powered on, the user will be prompted to select the ESXi host server to host the virtual machine. When imbalance is detected among ESXi host servers, DRS will send recommendations to the user for rebalancing the workload.

8.7 Activity 1: Implementation of vMotion and FT

In this activity, the following tasks will be performed:

- *Task 1:* Creating vMotion Network on LabESXi1 Host Server
- *Task 2:* Creating vMotion Network on LabESXi2 Host Server
- *Task 3:* Testing vMotion and HA
- *Task 4:* Implementing FT

8.7.1 Task 1: Creating vMotion Network on LabESXi1 Host Server

To accomplish the first task, follow the steps below to get started.

1. Start the servers in the order of DC, Storage, LabESXi1, LabESXi2, and vc. Log on to the **vCenter** Server through vSphere Client, Select the first ESXi Server **labesxi1.lab.local** and click the **Configuration** tab, and then click **Storage**. If dstore1 and dstore2 are missing, click **Rescan All**. Click **Networking** in the Hardware pane (Figure 8.6).

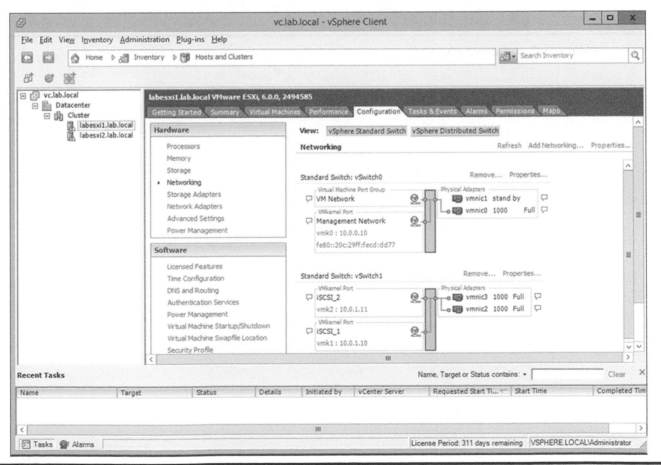

Figure 8.6   Selecting LabESXi1 host server.

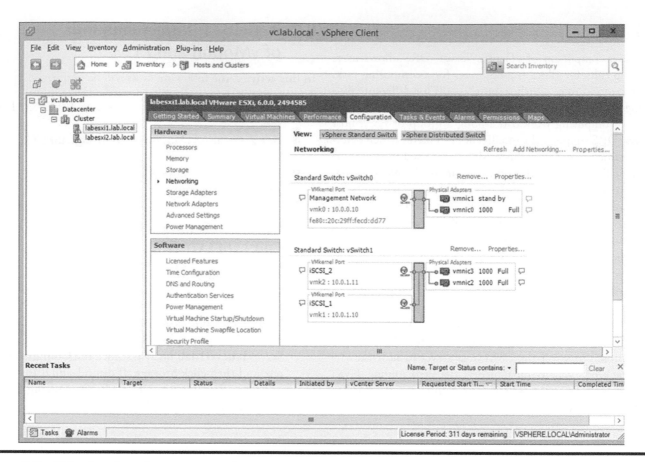

Figure 8.7 VM network port group removed.

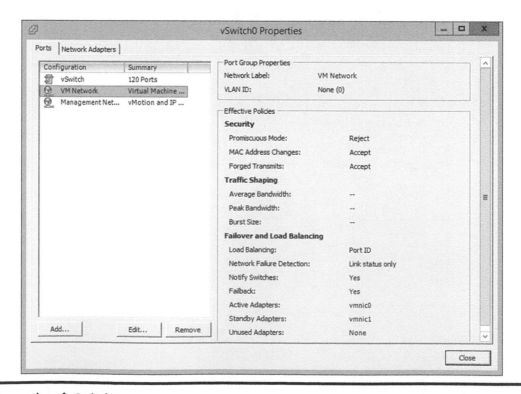

Figure 8.8 Properties of vSwitch0.

In Figure 8.6, you can see two virtual standard switches.

2. To remove the port group VM Network from vSwitch0, click the **Properties** link next to vSwitch0.
3. Under the Ports tab, select **VM Network** and then click the **Remove** button. Close the vSwitch0 Properties dialog; you will see that the VM Network port group has been removed, as shown in Figure 8.7.
4. Your next step is to create a **vMotion** interface. To do so, click the **Properties** link next to vSwitch0.
5. In the vSwitch0 Properties dialog, click the **Ports** tab and then double-click the **vSwitch** link in the left pane, as shown in Figure 8.8.
6. Click the **NIC Teaming** tab, as shown in Figure 8.9.
7. Select the NIC **vmnic1** and use the **Move Up** button to move **vmnic1** to **Active Adapters**, as shown in Figure 8.10. Then, click **OK**.

8. Now, double-click the **Management Network** link in the vSwitch0 Properties dialog, as shown in Figure 8.11.
9. Set **vmnic0** as active and **vmnic1** as standby (Figure 8.12). Then, click **OK**.
10. To add a new **VMkernel** interface on vSwitch0, click the **Add** button shown in Figure 8.11. On the Add Network Wizard page, select VMkernel option, as shown in Figure 8.13. Then, click **Next**.
11. On the VMkernel—Connection Settings page, name the network **vMotion** and check the box **Use this port group for vMotion** (Figure 8.14). Then, click **Next**.
12. On the VMkernel—IP Connection Settings page, set the IP address as **10.0.0.11** with the subnet mask as **255.255.255.0**, as shown in Figure 8.15. Then, click **Next**.
13. On the Ready to Complete page, click **Finish** (Figure 8.16).

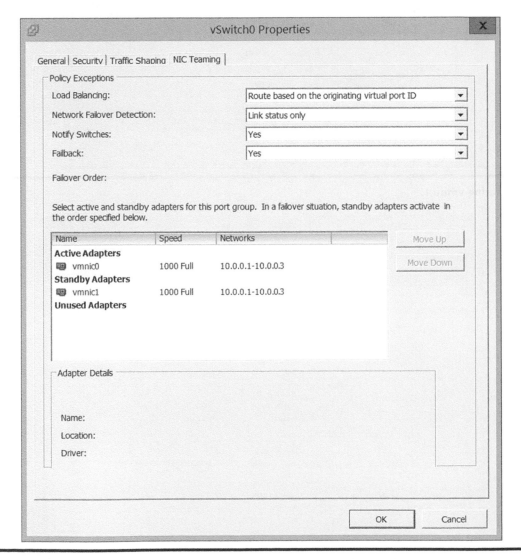

Figure 8.9   NIC teaming.

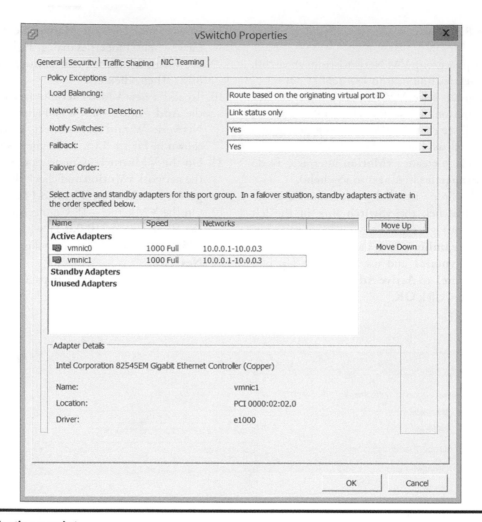

Figure 8.10 Activating vmnic1.

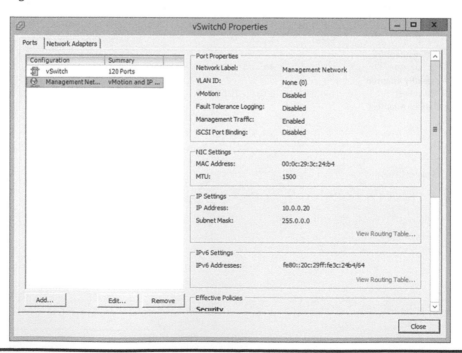

Figure 8.11 Opening Management Network Properties Dialog.

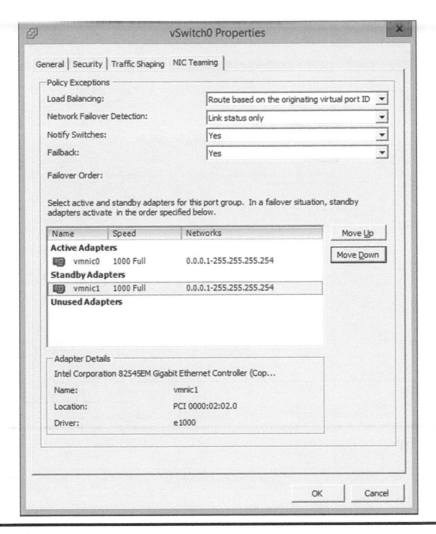

Figure 8.12   Adapter Setting.

14. On the vSwitch0 Properties page, double-click the **vMotion** link to open the Properties page (Figure 8.17).

15. Click the **NIC Teaming** tab and click **Override switch failover order**. Set the NIC order so that **vmnic1** is active and **vmnic0** is standby, as shown in Figure 8.18. Click **OK** and then click **Close**.

8.7.2 Task 2: Creating vMotion Network on LabESXi2 Host Server

The second task is to create a vMotion network on the LabESXi2 host server. The vMotion network carries the migration traffic between the two ESXi host servers. Follow the steps below to get started.

1. Assume that you are still on vCenter. Select the second ESXi server **labesxi2.lab.local** and click the **Configuration** tab. Click the **Networking** link in the Hardware pane, as shown in Figure 8.19.

2. To remove the port group VM Network from vSwitch0, click the **Properties** link next to vSwitch0.

3. Under the Ports tab, select **VM Network** and then click **Remove** button. Close the vSwitch0 Properties dialog, and you will see that the VM Network port group has been removed.

4. Your next step is to create a **vMotion** interface. To do so, click the **Properties** link next to vSwitch0.

5. In the vSwitch0 Properties dialog, click the **Ports** tab and then double-click the **vSwitch** link in the left pane.

6. Click **NIC Teaming** tab.

7. Select the NIC **vmnic1** and use the **Move Up** button to move **vmnic1** to **Active Adapters**, as shown in Figure 8.20. Then, click **OK**.

8. Now, double-click the **Management Network** link in the vSwitch0 dialog.

9. Set **vmnic0** as active and **vmnic1** as standby. Then, click **OK**.

10. To add a new **VMkernel** interface on vSwitch0, click the **Add** button in the vSwitch0 Properties dialog. On

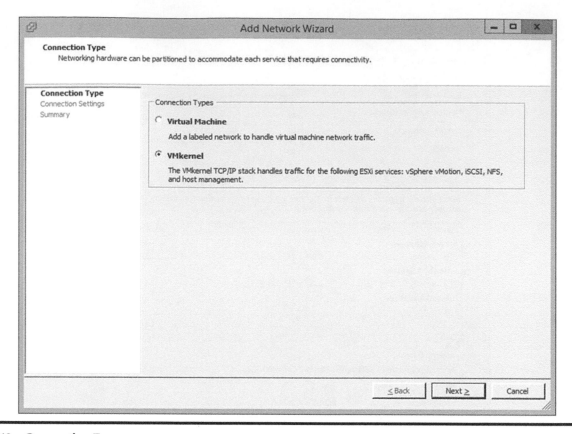

Figure 8.13 Connection Type.

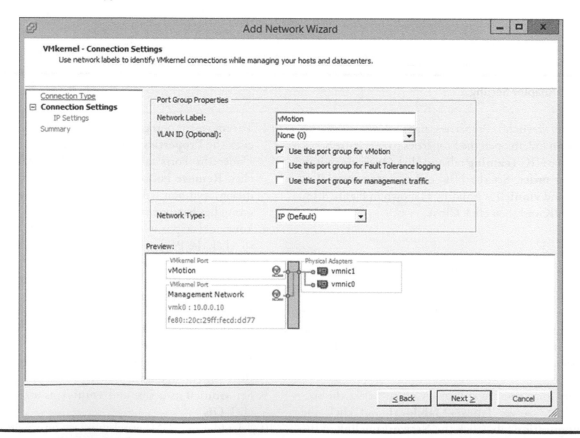

Figure 8.14 Configuring vMotion.

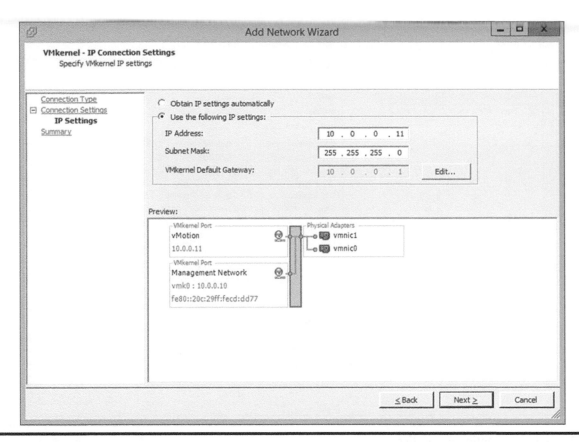

Figure 8.15 IP Connection Settings.

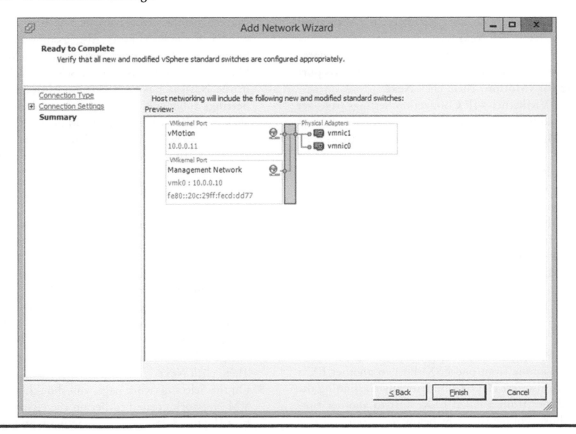

Figure 8.16 vMotion Settings.

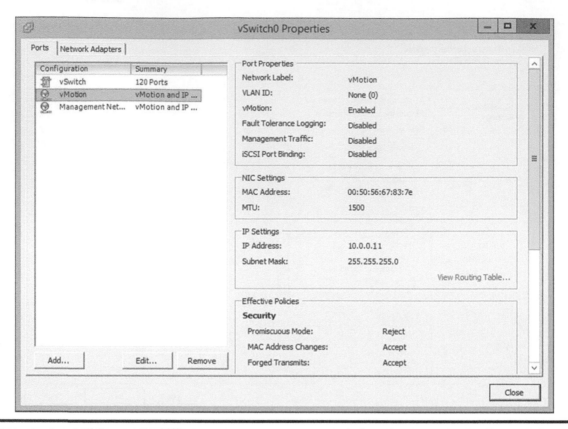

Figure 8.17   Opening vMotion Properties.

the Add Network Wizard page, select the **VMkernel** option. Then, click **Next**.

11. On the VMkernel—Connection Settings page, name the network **vMotion** and check the box **Use this port group for vMotion**. Then, click **Next**.

12. On the VMkernel—IP Connection Settings page, set the IP address as **10.0.0.21** with the subnet mask as **255.255.255.0**, as shown in Figure 8.21. Then, click **Next**.

13. On the Ready to Complete page, click **Finish**.

14. In the vSwitch0 Properties page, double-click the **vMotion** link to open the Properties page.

15. Click the **NIC Teaming** tab and click **Override switch failover order**. Then, set the NIC order so that **vmnic1** is active and **vmnic0** is standby, as shown in Figure 8.22. Click **OK** and then click **Close**.

8.7.3 Task 3: Testing vMotion and HA

In this task, you will test vMotion by manually moving a live virtual machine from one ESXi host to another ESXi host. You will also test HA by automatically reassigning the virtual machines from a failed ESXi host to another running ESXi host. Follow the steps below to accomplish this task.

1. Assume that the virtual network VM Network is created on each of the ESXi hosts. Also, assume that you have logged on to the vCenter Server through Web Client. On the Hosts and Clusters page, select the **Cluster** node in the Navigator pane. Click the **Manage** menu and **Settings** submenu. Click the link **vSphere DRS** and click the **Edit** button, as shown in Figure 8.23.

2. In the vSphere DRS editing dialog, select **Manual** on the DRS Automation dropdown list (Figure 8.24). Then, click **OK**.

3. To migrate a virtual machine, expand the **Cluster** node and power on the vApp **cosc4339**.

4. Click the virtual machine **ubuntu-server**. In Figure 8.25, you can see that **ubuntu-server** is hosted by labesxi1.lab.local.

5. Right-click the virtual machine **ubuntu-server** and select **Migrate**, as shown in Figure 8.26.

6. On the Select migration type page, select the option **Change compute resource only** and click **Next**.

7. On the Select a compute resource page, check the option **labesxi2.lob.local**, as shown in Figure 8.27. Then, click **Next**.

8. On the Select network page, you should be able to see **VM Network** created earlier on the labesxi2.lab.local host (Figure 8.28). Select the network and click **Next** twice.

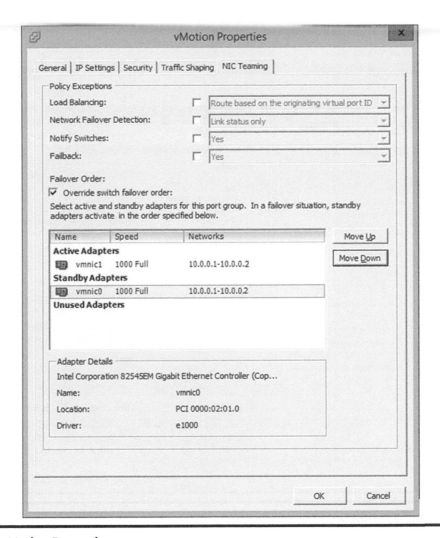

Figure 8.18   Setting vMotion Properties.

9. On the Ready to complete page, click **Finish**.
10. As shown in Figure 8.29, **ubuntu-server** is now hosted by the ESXi server **labesxi2.lab.local**.
11. To test HA, you can set the LabESxi2 host to the maintenance mode. By doing so, HA will move all the virtual machines on the LabESXi2 host to the LabESXi1 host so that these virtual machines will be continuously available to users. Right-click the host **labesxi2.lab. local** and select **Maintenance Mode**, and then select **Enter Maintenance Mode**, as shown in Figure 8.30.
12. As shown in Figure 8.31, the virtual machine ubuntu-server is sent back to the host labesxi1.lab.local when the labesxi2.lab.local host was in the maintenance mode.
13. Now, right-click the host **labesxi2.lab.local** and select **Maintenance Mode,** and then select **Exit Maintenance Mode**.
14. Also, click the **Cluster** node. Then, click the **Manage** menu and click the **Settings** submenu. Select the link **vSphere DRS** and then click **Edit**, as shown in Figure 8.32.

15. In the Edit cluster settings dialog, change DRS Automation to **Fully Automated**. Then, click **OK**.

In this task, you have tested vMotion and HA. The next task is to implement FT.

8.7.4 Task 4: Implementing FT

In this task, you will activate the FT mechanism. Follow the steps below to accomplish this task.

1. First, you need to shut down vc and both of the ESXi host servers.
2. If you have not done so, edit the NIC settings in Steps 2 through 7. Otherwise, go to Step 8 to continue. In VMware Workstation, click **Edit,** and then click **Virtual Network Editor**. In the Virtual Network Editor dialog, create a network **VMnet4** with the subnet IP address **10.0.2.0 and the subnet mask 255.255.255.0**, as shown in Figure 8.33. Then, click **OK**.

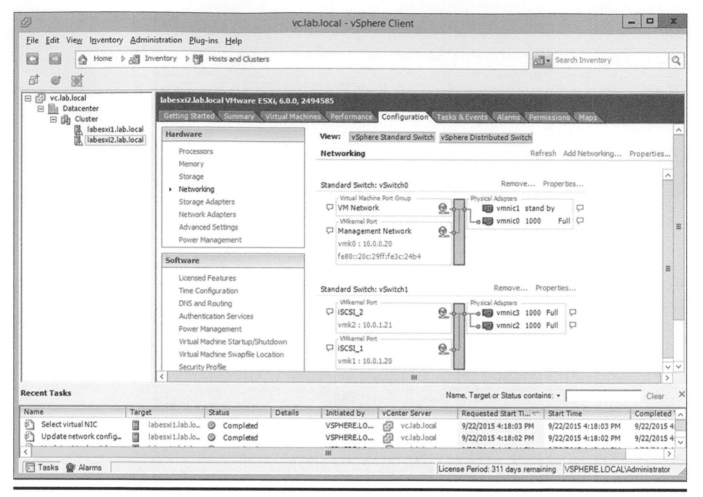

Figure 8.19   Selecting LabESXi2 Host Server.

3. Right-click the LabESXi1 host server in VMware Workstation and select **Settings**. Click the **Add** button (Figure 8.34).

4. On the Hardware Type page, select **Network Adapter** and click **Next** (Figure 8.35).

5. On the Network Adapter Type page, select **Custom** and select **VMnet4** on the dropdown list, as shown in Figure 8.36. Then, click **Finish**.

6. Similarly, add another network adapter. Figure 8.37 shows that Network Adapter 5 and Network Adapter 6 are added.

7. Similarly, add the network VMnet4 and the two new network adapters to the LabESXi2 host server.

8. Now, you can power on the LabESXi1, LabESXi2, and vc servers. Then, log on to the vCenter Server through vSphere Client. Select **labesxi1.lab.local**; click the **Configuration** tab and click the **Networking** link, as shown in Figure 8.38.

9. To add a new vSwitch, click the **Add Networking** link.

10. On the Connection Type page, select **VMkernel**, as shown in Figure 8.39. Then, click Next.

11. On the VMkernel—Network Access page, select **vmnic4** and **vmnic5**, as shown in Figure 8.40. Then, click **Next**.

12. On the VMkernel—Connection Settings page, name the new vSwitch **Fault Tolerance** and check the option **Use this port group for Fault Tolerance logging**, as shown in Figure 8.41. Then, click **Next**.

13. On the VMkernel—IP Connection Settings page, choose the option **Use the following IP settings** and specify the IP address as **10.0.2.10 with the subnet mask 255.255.255.0** (Figure 8.42). Then, click **Next**.

14. On the Ready to Complete page, check the configuration and click **Finish**, as shown in Figure 8.43.

15. Under the Configuration tab, you should be able to see the newly created FT vSwitch shown in Figure 8.44.

16. Repeat Steps 8 through 15 to create an FT Standard vSwitch for LabESXi2. This time, on the VMkernel—IP Connection Settings page, specify the IP address as **10.0.2.20** with the subnet mask 255.255.255.0 (Figure 8.45).

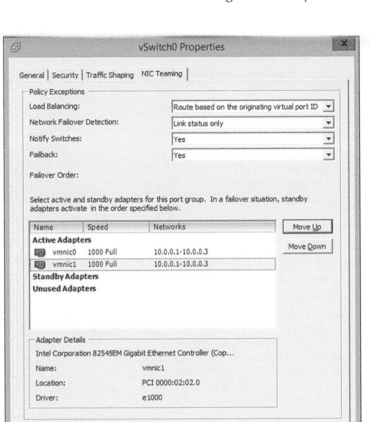

Figure 8.20   Activating vmnic1 on LabESXi1 Host Server.

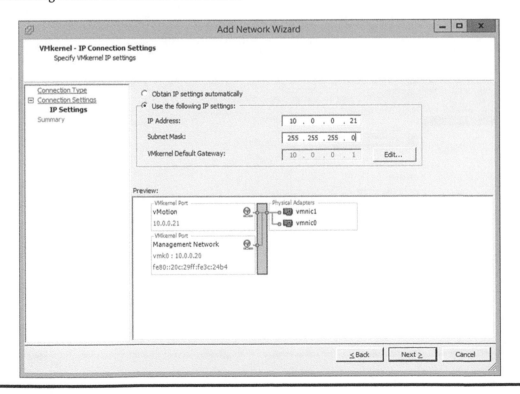

Figure 8.21   IP Connection Settings.

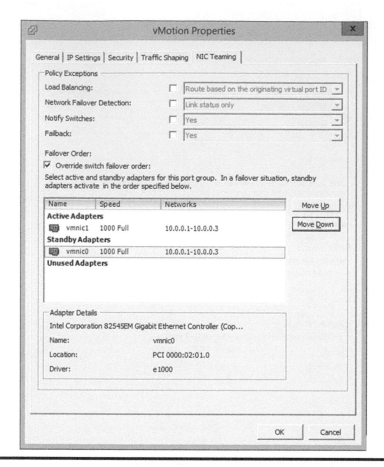

Figure 8.22   Setting vMotion Properties on LabESXi2 Host Server.

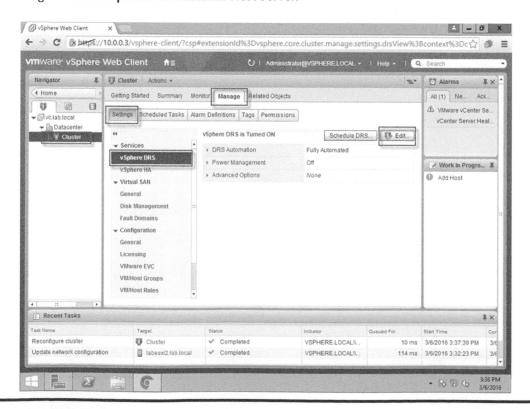

Figure 8.23   Editing vSphere DRS.

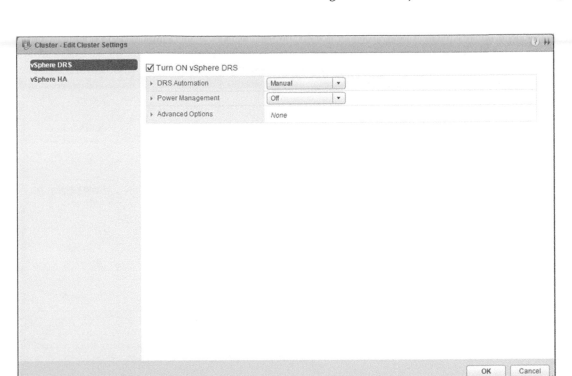

Figure 8.24 Configuring DRS Automation as Manual.

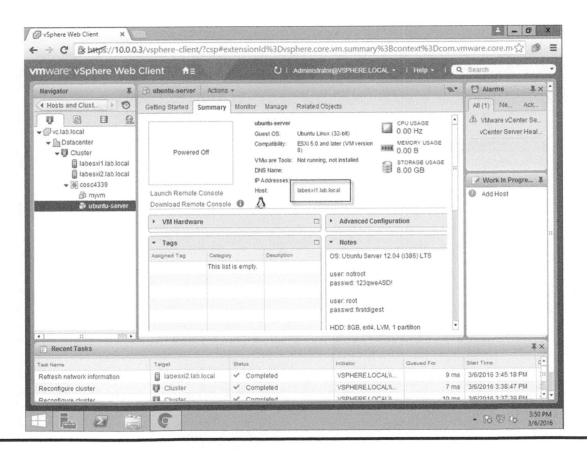

Figure 8.25 ubuntu-server Hosted by labesxi1.lab.local.

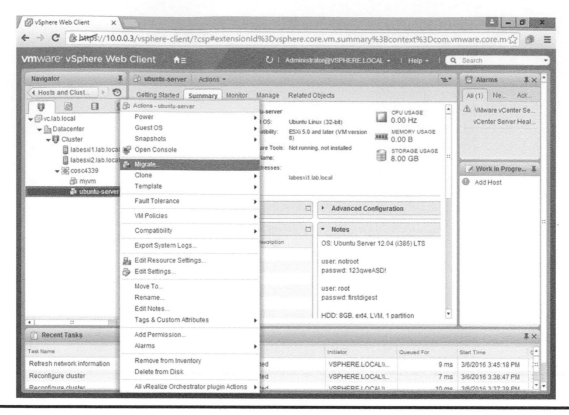

Figure 8.26 Migrating virtual machine.

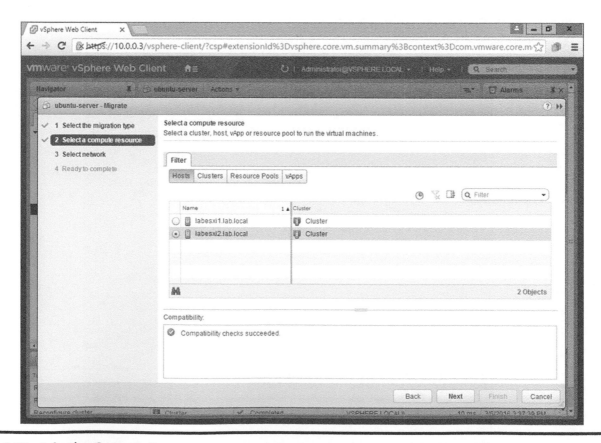

Figure 8.27 Selecting Compute Resource.

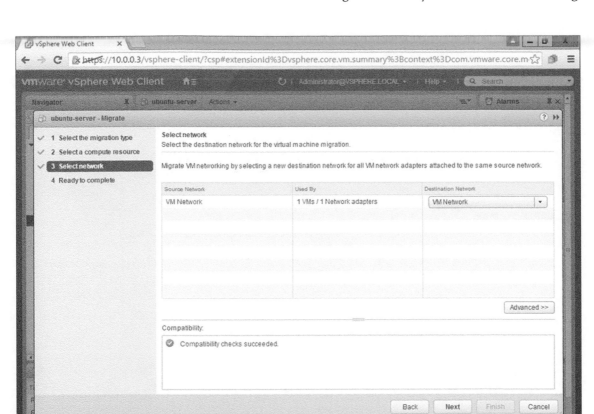

Figure 8.28 Selecting Network.

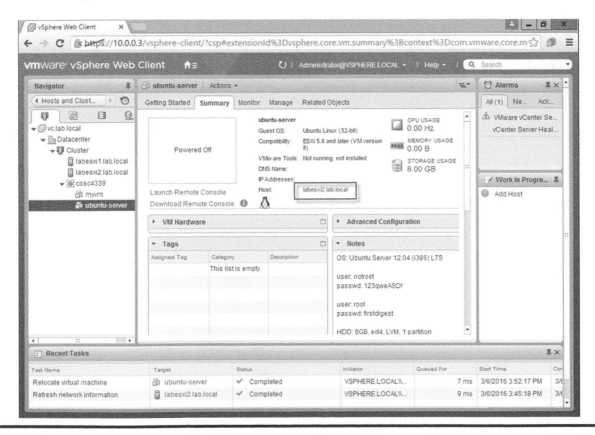

Figure 8.29 ubuntu-server Hosted by labesxi2.lab.local.

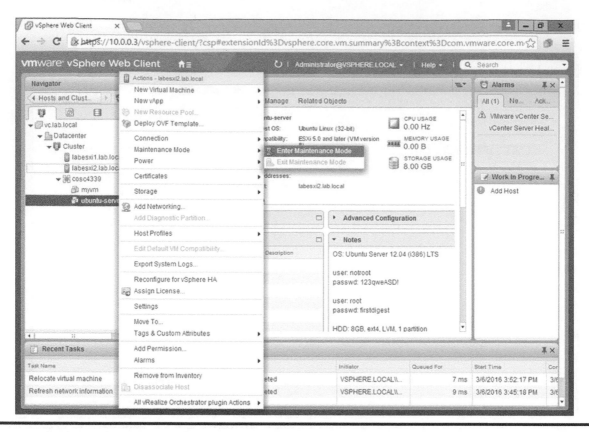

Figure 8.30 Selecting Maintenance Mode.

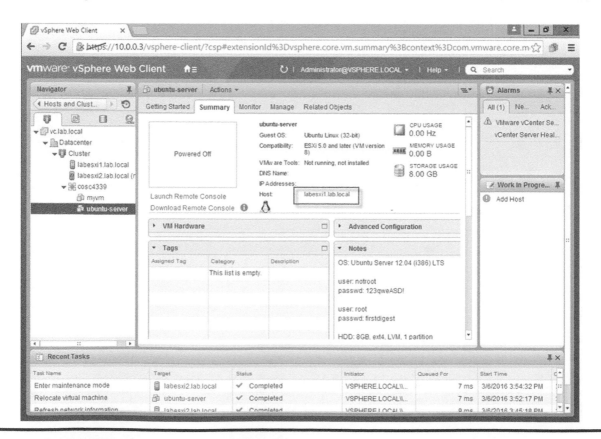

Figure 8.31 ubuntu-server migrated to labesxi1.lab.local.

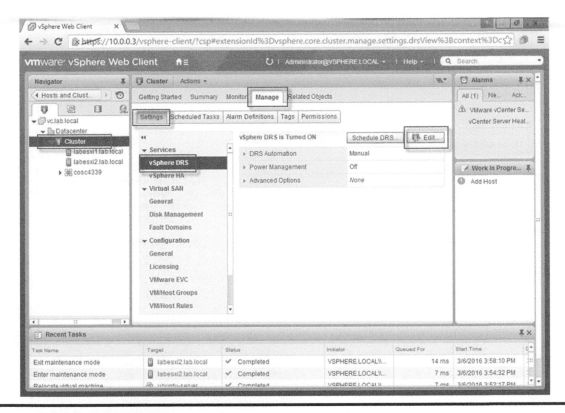

Figure 8.32   Editing Cluster Settings.

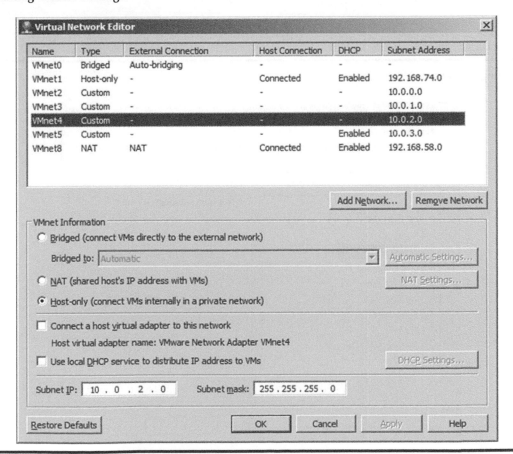

Figure 8.33   Creating VMnet4 Network.

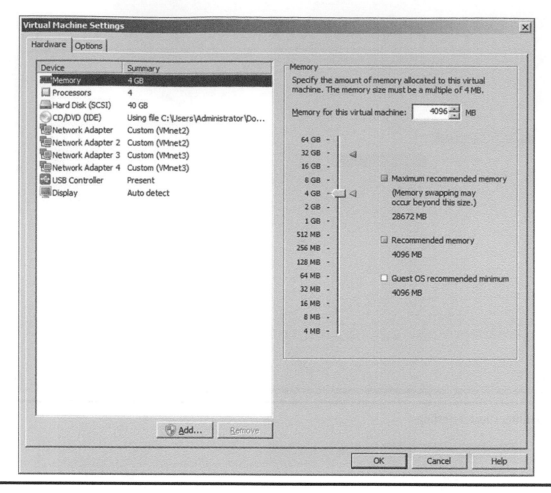

Figure 8.34   Adding Hardware.

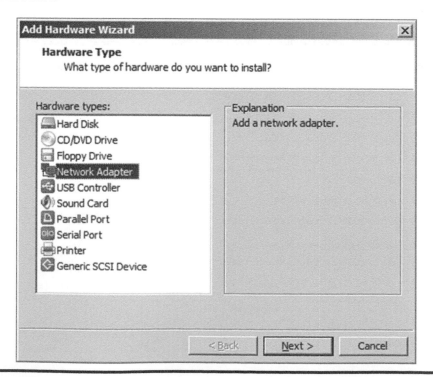

Figure 8.35   Adding Network Adapter.

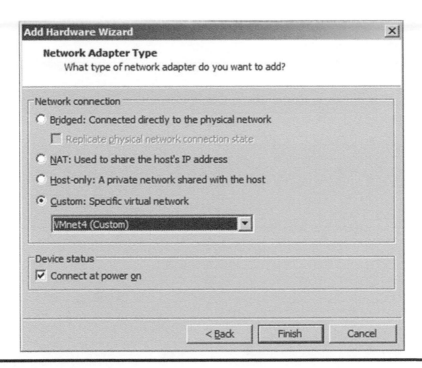

Figure 8.36   Network Connection.

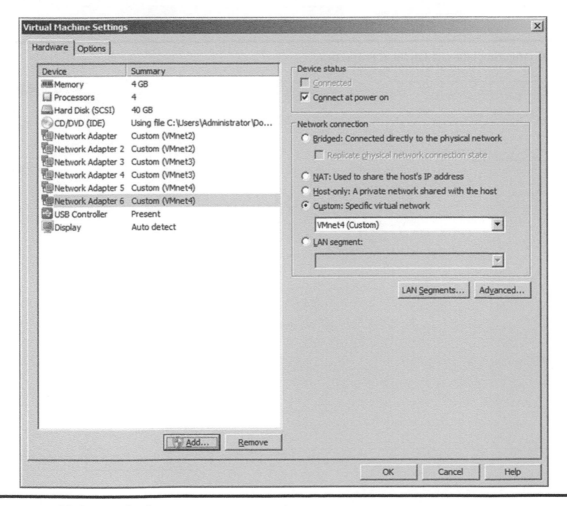

Figure 8.37   Two added network adapters.

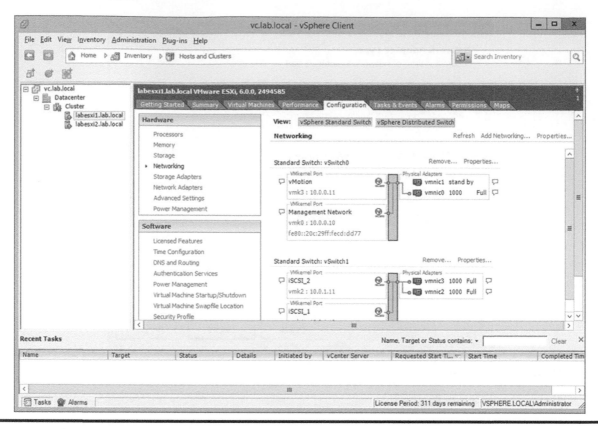

Figure 8.38   Configuring labesxi1.lab.local Properties.

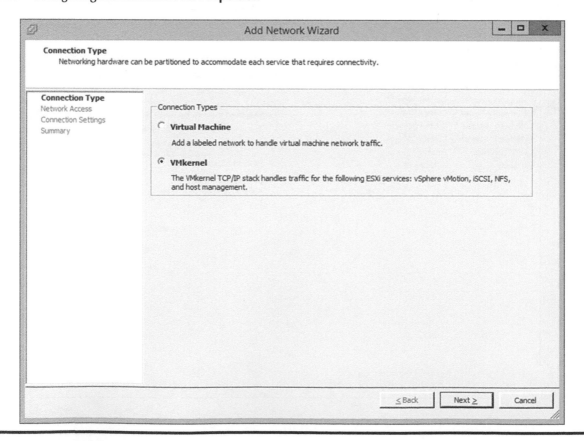

Figure 8.39   Connection Type.

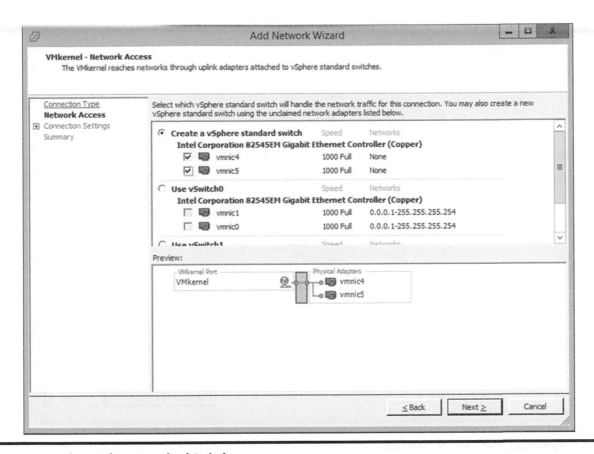

Figure 8.40   Creating vSphere Standard Switch.

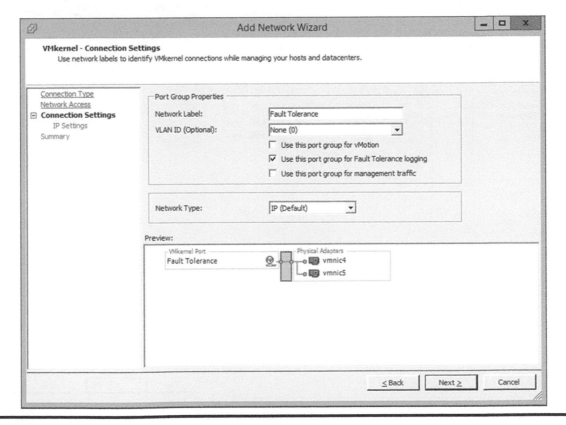

Figure 8.41   Port Group Properties.

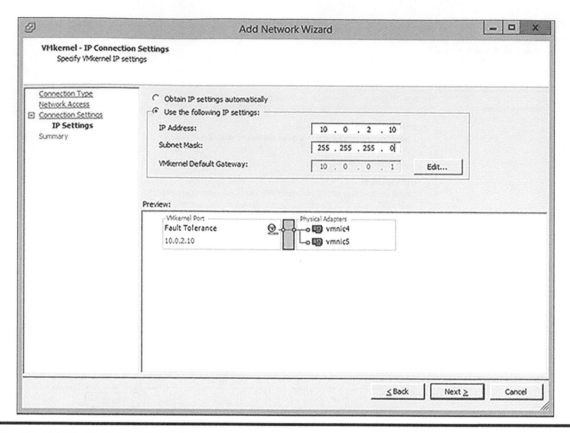

Figure 8.42 Specifying VMkernel IP Settings.

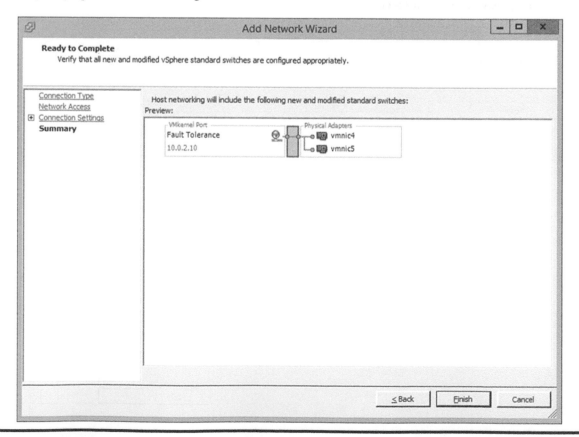

Figure 8.43 FT vSwitch summary.

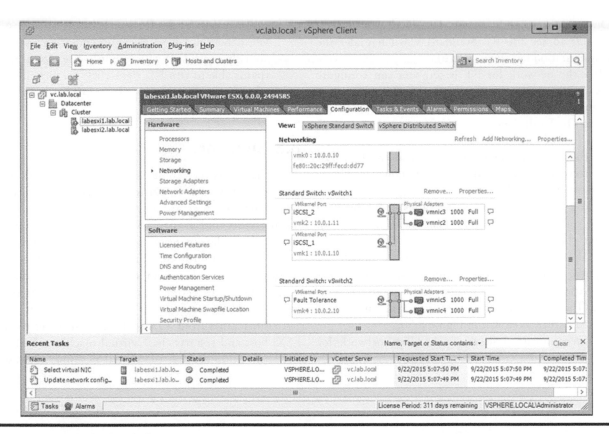

Figure 8.44   FT Standard Switch.

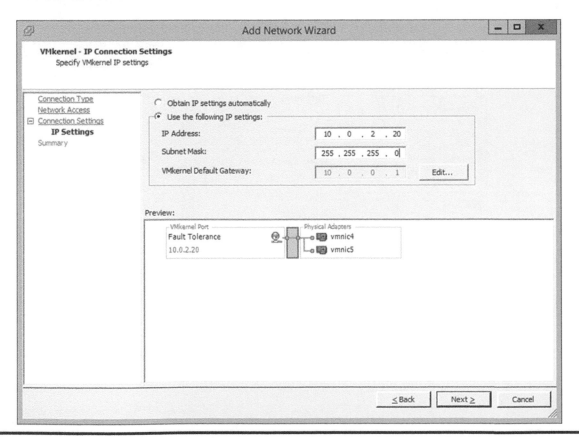

Figure 8.45   Specifying VMkernel IP settings for LabESXi2 host server.

17. Once the configuration is completed, you should be able to see the FT Standard vSwitch under the Configuration tab (Figure 8.46).

18. After the network for FT is set, you can configure the virtual machine ubuntu-server for FT protection. Right click **ubuntu-server**, select **Fault tolerance** and **Turn On Fault Tolerance**, as shown in Figure 8.47. Then, click **Next**.

19. On the Select datastores page, select **dstore1** to host the secondary virtual machine, as shown in Figure 8.48. Then, click **Next**.

20. On the Select host page, select **labesxi1.lab.local** to host the secondary virtual machine (Figure 8.49). Then, click **Next**.

21. On the Ready to complete page, click **Finish**. In vSphere Web Client, you should be able to see that the virtual machine ubuntu-server is protected with FT. (The icon of the ubuntu-server virtual machine is turned darker, as shown in Figure 8.50.)

22. It is recommended to use a 10-Gbps network for FT. Also, the ESXi host server needs to have enough memory to carry out the operation. As a demonstration lab, it may not have enough computing resources to actually run FT. If you do not have a virtual machine that is able to run FT, right-click the virtual machine **ubuntu-server** and select **Turn Off Fault Tolerance**.

8.8 Summary

This chapter covers some of the topics related to business continuity such as clustering, HA, vMotion, FT, and DRS. These features are provided by VMware for improving reliability and availability. In an enterprise computing environment, the downtime of an IT infrastructure must be reduced to the minimum. Clustering makes a group of servers to act like a single system in order to achieve redundancy. Clustering creates a computing environment for implementing other HA measures. HA is a measure that migrates virtual machines from a failed ESXi host server to another ESXi host and restarts these virtual machines. It may take a short downtime. After the virtual machines are restarted,

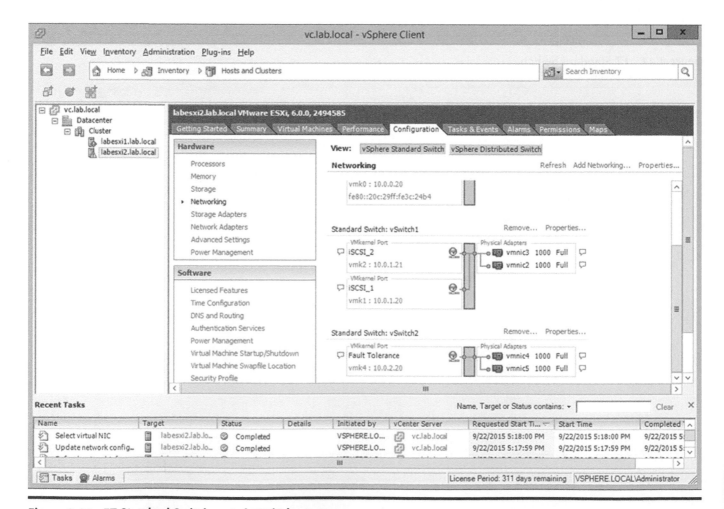

Figure 8.46 FT Standard Switch on LabESXi2 host server.

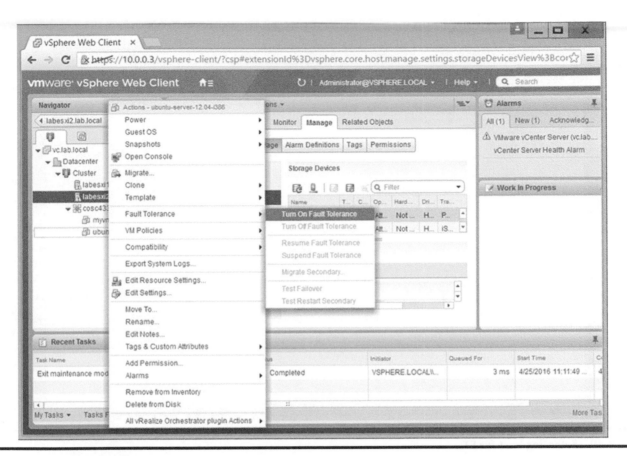

Figure 8.47   Turning on FT.

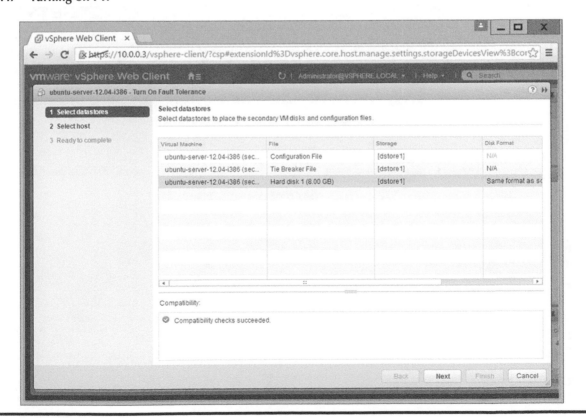

Figure 8.48   Selecting datastore for FT.

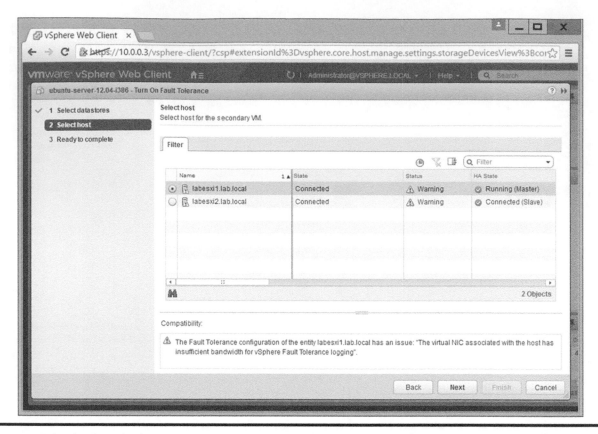

Figure 8.49 Selecting host for FT.

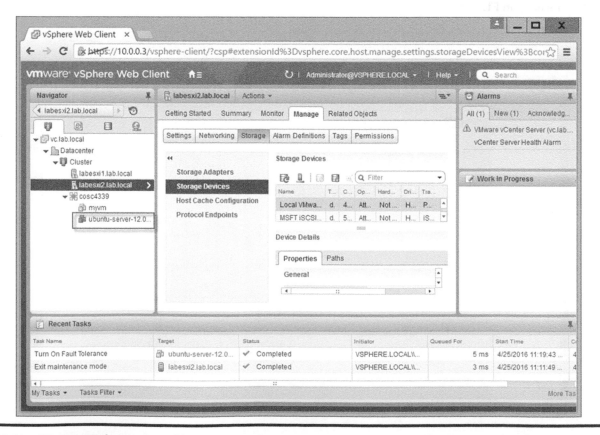

Figure 8.50 FT-protected virtual machine.

they can continue to handle the computing tasks. FT can be used for virtual machines that require zero downtime. This technique runs two identical virtual machines at the same time. If one of them fails, the other one will continue to run. vMotion live-migrates virtual machines from one host to another host with no downtime. The hands-on practice of this chapter carries out tasks such as implementing clustering, HA, FT, and vMotion. In the hands-on practice, a separate network is created for the implementation of vMotion and FT. The hands-on practice also tests the implementation of HA and vMotion.

REVIEW QUESTIONS

1. Why is the HA of the IT infrastructure critical for a business to be successful?
2. What are the HA tools provided by VMware?
3. How can core applications be made highly available?
4. What is NLB, and how does it work?
5. What is MSCS, and how does it work?
6. For MSCS clustering, in what scenarios is Cluster in a Box often used?
7. For MSCS clustering, in what scenarios is Cluster across Boxes often used?
8. For MSCS clustering, in what scenarios is physical to virtual clustering often used?
9. What is VMware HA, and how can IT benefit from this technology?
10. To enable the VMware HA service in a cluster, what are the requirements to ESXi hosts?
11. What are the activities performed by VMware HA?
12. How does VMware FT provide continued availability?
13. To enable VMware FT in a cluster, what requirements must be met?
14. To enable VMware FT at the host level, what requirements must be met?
15. To enable VMware FT at the virtual machine level, what requirements must be met?
16. What is vMotion and how is it used?
17. Describe the migration process for vMotion.
18. Describe the migration process for Storage vMotion.
19. In order to successfully implement vMotion, what are the requirements to ESXi hosts?
20. How is DRS used?

Chapter 9

Managing vSphere Security

Objectives

- Understand security issues in a virtualized information technology infrastructure
- Overview security measures provided by VMware vCloud Suite
- Secure vSphere components

9.1 Introduction

Security is always a top consideration for an information technology (IT) infrastructure. The security weakness in a virtualized IT infrastructure can pass the vulnerability to virtual machines (VMs) or even the physical computers. A virtualized computing environment may have the following vulnerabilities:

- *Remote login console:* It includes the host management console such as the Elastic Sky X Integrated (ESXi) command shell and secure shell (SSH), VM remote login console, remote service management console, and application program interfaces (APIs). As these remote consoles can be accessed through the Internet, hackers may find a way to illegally access the vSphere components.
- *Virtual machine datastore:* It contains VM files and data files. Once it is hacked, hackers can transfer or delete these files.
- *Virtual networks:* They are various virtual networks created on an ESXi host. They also include virtual networks created in a vApp. When a virtual network is not properly configured, it is possible for hackers to make unauthorized access to the virtual network. The hackers can modify, destroy, and misuse the virtual network.
- It is also possible that the virtualized IT infrastructure is infected by computer virus.

Therefore, the virtualized IT infrastructure has to be protected to avoid various security breaches. In general, the security rules applied to physical machines are also applied to the VMs. The administrator is required to update security patches timely. The log files should be stored in a safe location. Users should also be authenticated and authorized according to a specific rule. The firewall also needs to be properly set up.

In addition to these general security measures, the vSphere virtualized computing environment has its own specific security measures. To make the VMware computing environment secure, VMware vCloud Suite provides many security features such as firewalls, user authentication, and server certification. While considering how to secure the vSphere virtual environment, this chapter focuses on the subjects related to the user authentication and authorization, and certification. Other virtual network–related security topics will be discussed in Chapter 10.

An authentication process provides a way of identifying a user by checking the user's name and password. The authentication is mainly done through vCenter. ESXi also handles the authentication process. In an enterprise computing environment, the authentication is often integrated with the directory service.

Once users are authenticated, they need to be authorized for different types of access or activities. The authorization process determines what a user can do after logging on to a virtualized IT infrastructure. Users need to be assigned roles to carry out certain tasks. Based on the users' roles, they may get permissions to run certain commands or access certain servers.

One of the often-performed security tasks is the management of certificates. A certificate contains information about the owner of the service provided by vSphere virtualization. It ensures the service users that they are dealing with a legitimate service owner. Therefore, each vSphere virtualization service needs a certificate. During the installation, a certificate is automatically generated for ESXi. The same is true for vCenter. By default, ESXi or vCenter uses a self-generated certificate for providing services. A certificate should be verified by a trusted certificate authority. Self-generated certificates are vulnerable to possible man-in-the-middle attacks. vSphere 6 provides two certificate packages: (1) VMware Endpoint Certificate Store (VECS) and (2) VMware Certificate Authority (VMCA). Details about these two packages will be given in later sections.

Securing the vSphere virtual environment means that you need to secure the components included in VMware vCloud Suite. The commonly used components are ESXi hosts, vCenter, VMs, storage devices, virtual networks, vShield, vCloud Director, and so on. Each of the components included in VMware vCloud Suite has additional security measures. More details about the security management of ESXi hosts, vCenter, and VMs will be given in the next few sections.

9.2 ESXi Host Security Management

Out of the box, an ESXi host provides many security measures. By default, the ESXi host turns off remote access mechanisms such as ESXi Shell and SSH. It only allows the root user to access the ESXi host through Direct Console

User Interface (DCUI). ESXi opens the firewall port only when the related service is started. A lockdown mode is used by ESXi hosts to enforce the host security. ESXi provides vSphere Installation Bundle for checking integrity. For the certificate management, vSphere 6.0 (or later) provides the tools VMCA and VECS. VMCA provisions each ESXi host with a signed certificate. By default, this certificate has VMCA as the root certificate authority (CA). If it is required, the self-signed CA can be replaced by a trusted third-party CA. vSphere 6.0 (or later) provides the account lockdown to prevent repeated failed attempts trying to log on to an ESXi server. The allowed maximum number of failed attempts is 10.

Figure 9.1 illustrates an implementation blueprint of security measures to protect ESXi hosts. The security implementation blueprint is also called the security model. In the security model, there are five objects: (1) user, (2) user group, (3) permission, (4) role, and (5) privilege. Each user has a user account in the local host or in Active Directory. The user account contains information such as the user name and password for authentication. Users can be grouped together to form user groups based on the operations to be allowed. A user needs to get permissions such as read only, read/write, no access, or full control of data and operations. The operations to be allowed are called privileges. A role is

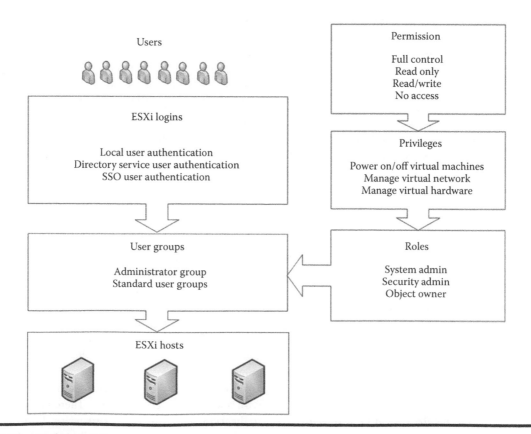

Figure 9.1 ESXi security model.

a list of privileges allowed to accomplish a task. A role can be assigned to a user or to a user group so that the user can perform certain operations. An ESXi host provides some built-in roles. Administrators can also create their own roles. For example, a system admin role gets all the permissions for every operation. Based on the role assigned to a user, the user may be able to create VMs, open a remote login console, or configure a virtual network.

To access an ESXi host server requires user authentication. Although user authentication can be done through vCenter, ESXi host authentication is necessary in case that an ESXi host is not connected to vCenter. The ESXi host authentication is also required when you try to link an ESXi host to vCenter. The user authentication on an ESXi host can be done in two ways: (1) authenticating users locally on each individual ESXi host or (2) authenticating users centrally through a directory service such as Active Directory.

When user accounts are created locally on each individual ESXi host, to access an ESXi host, a user can be authenticated through vSphere Client or through a command-line interface (CLI). Figure 9.2 illustrates user accounts created locally on an ESXi host with vSphere Client. It also shows the dialog used to create a new user on the ESXi host. For

better security, it is recommended not to create too many user accounts on an ESXi host.

The ESXi host allows the administrator to remotely access it with SSH. SSH is a secure protocol for remote access. One of the popular SSH clients is PuTTY, which can be downloaded free from the Internet. Figure 9.3 illustrates the user authentication for an SSH connection to an ESXi host through PuTTY.

ESXi CLI and SSH are command-line utilities. Once a user logs on to an ESXi server through ESXi CLI or SSH, the user can perform system management tasks with two sets of commands: (1) esxcfg and (2) esxcli. esxcfg is a set of commands used for system management of the older versions of ESXi hosts. esxcfg is often used for backward compatibility. After vSphere 4 was released, much of the functionalities of esxcfg can be done through esxcli. Both esxcfg and esxcli focus on the management of the hypervisor ESXi. They can be used to manage infrastructure-related objects such as hardware, storage, networks, ESXi software, and so on. They can be used to control the operation of VMs, configure the properties of kernels, manage ESXi software images and packages, maintain virtual networks on ESXi hosts, handle VMware storage, and so on.

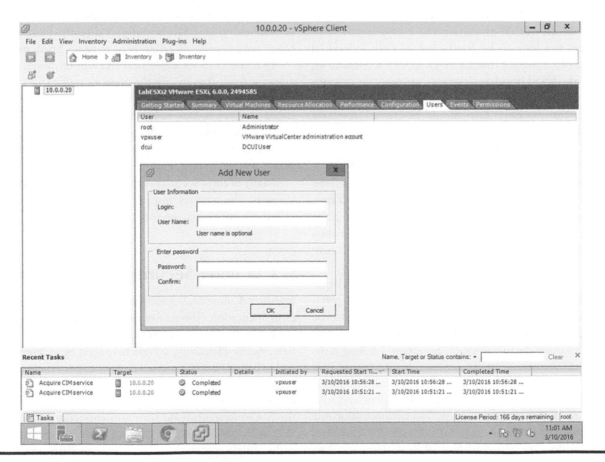

Figure 9.2   User management with vSphere Client.

Figure 9.3   User authentication for SSH connection.

In an enterprise computing environment, user authentication is done through a directory service such as Active Directory. Active Directory provides a centralized user authentication service. With Active Directory, user authentication does not have to be conducted on each individual ESXi server. To integrate the Active Directory services to an ESXi host, the ESXi host has to be able to access the domain controller, which provides the Active Directory services. The user accounts of the ESXi host should be created in Active Directory as well.

The fully qualified domain name (FQDN) of ESXi hosts should be registered in the domain name system (DNS) service, and the system time should be synchronized among the domain controller and ESXi hosts. Once an ESXi host meets these requirements, through vSphere Client, the ESXi host can be integrated into Active Directory. Figure 9.4 illustrates the ESXi configuration tools for integrating the Active Directory services.

The authorization process determines what privileges are assigned to an ESXi object. An object can get its privileges through the role assigned to it. An object can also be assigned permissions directly by the administrator. An ESXi host provides three default roles: (1) no access, (2) read-only, and (3) administrator. The no-access role prevents a user from accessing an ESXi object. The read-only role allows the user to view the ESXi objects but does not allow the user to perform operations on the objects. The administrator role allows the user to perform every task. Figure 9.5 illustrates the built-in roles, and the Add New Role dialog is used to create a custom role.

When a role is assigned to a user, a set of privileges is assigned to that user. That is, the user gets a set of permissions to perform some operations. The permissions can also be assigned to an ESXi host object directly. Figure 9.6 illustrates the permissions assigned to the user **Student**.

In addition to authentication and authorization, ESXi provides the firewall to control the network traffic in and out of an ESXi host. By default, ESXi only allows the network traffic generated by services such as DNS, vSphere Client, API management, service discovery, vMotion, and SSH. The administrator can also configure the firewall to allow other network traffic in or out of an ESXi host. Figure 9.7 shows the firewall properties.

Many of these security measures can also be done through vCenter. The next section provides more information about vCenter security management.

9.3 vCenter Security Management

Figure 9.8 illustrates a security model for vCenter security implementation. The security model includes objects such as vSphere Client, vCenter Server, single sign-on (SSO), database, Active Directory, servers managed by vCenter, storage, and other related vCenters.

User authentication can be done through Active Directory or through SSO for local users. vCenter provides the SSO mechanism for user authentication. Once authenticated by SSO, a user is allowed to access multiple servers and multiple applications. For user authentication, SSO provides the domain vsphere.local. Through vCenter, the user's

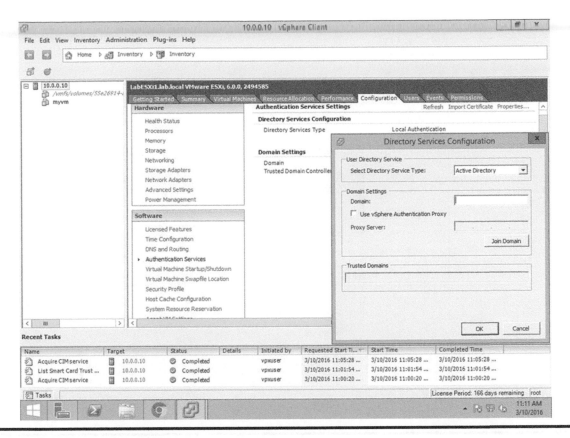

Figure 9.4   **Active Directory integration.**

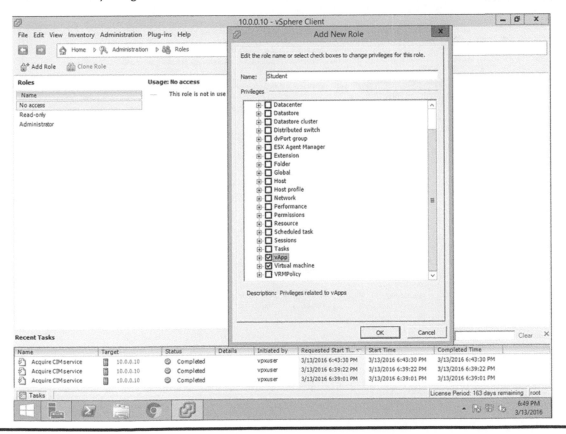

Figure 9.5   **Adding new role.**

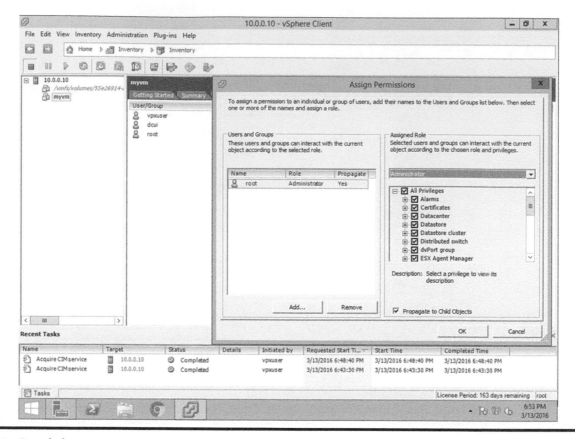

Figure 9.6   Permissions.

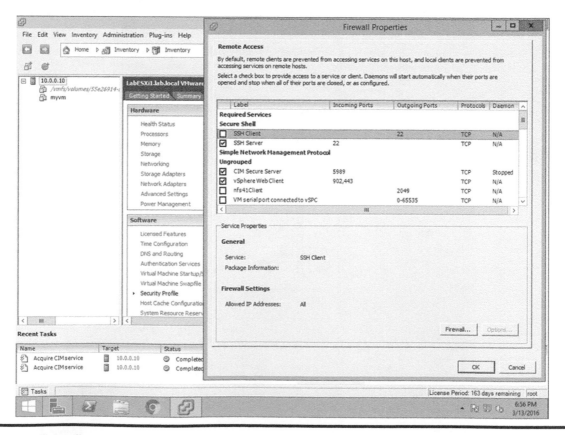

Figure 9.7   ESXi firewall.

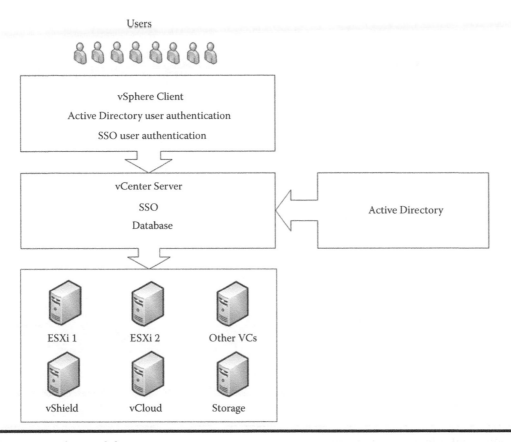

Figure 9.8 vCenter security model.

privileges can be configured for performing different tasks. vCenter provides predefined roles for grouping users with similar permissions. The administrator can create a specially designed role for a group of users with the same privileges. SSO can also use directory services such as Active Directory and Lightweight Directory Access Protocol. When a host server of vCenter is configured to join the Active Directory domain, vCenter can take advantage of Active Directory for user authentication. Some users in Active Directory can be assigned roles or permissions to perform operations in vCenter. Through SSO, the users on a local computer that hosts vCenter can also be given permissions to perform operations in vCenter. Figure 9.9 illustrates the configurations of joining vCenter to Active Directory.

To allow users to perform various tasks, vCenter provides different roles, which are summarized in Table 9.1.

vCenter provides the Certificate Manager for managing the certificate service. The Certificate Manager is a command-line utility used to perform all common certificate tasks. Certificate management can also be done with CLIs. The complexity of certificate management can be greatly reduced by using VECS and VMCA. A certificate assigned by VMCA is created for each ESXi host and other servers in the environment. VECS stores all the certificates and private keys for vCenter Server and its associated services.

vCenter 6 (or later) supports a new service: VMware Platform Services Controller (PSC). PSC handles tasks such as vCenter SSO, licensing, certificate management, and server reservation. Therefore, PSC can be considered as SSO, plus certificate management, and plus more. vCenter allows certificates to be assigned by trusted third-party CAs. The third-party CAs can also be stored in VECS. As certificates depend on time stamps, vCenter provides tools for setting up the NTP service to synchronize time among servers in the virtual environment. By using vSphere Web Client, the administrator can conduct a good amount of certificate management tasks. Figure 9.10 illustrates the active certificates viewed from vCenter.

Now that you have learned about the measures used to secure vCenter, next, you will learn how VMs are secured.

9.4 VM Security Management

Securing VMs is about securing guest operating systems and securing the environment where VMs are running. To enhance the guest operating system security, administrators should consider the following measures:

- Keeping VMs patched timely.
- Virtual machines should be protected with antivirus software.

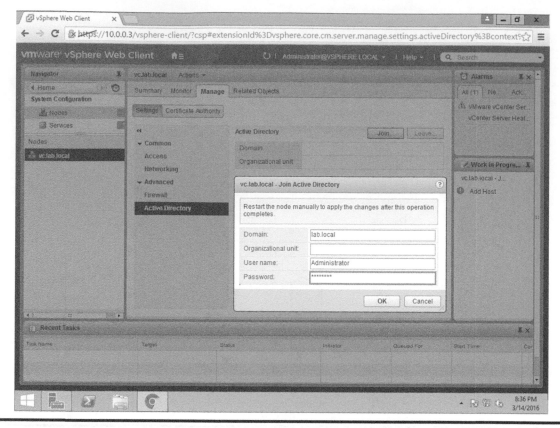

Figure 9.9   Joining vCenter to Active Directory.

Table 9.1   vCenter Roles

Roles	Description
Administrator	A user with the administrator role has full control of the vCenter objects assigned to that user.
Read-only	A user with the read-only role is able to view the objects in a vCenter inventory. However, the user is not allowed to interact with these objects.
No-access	A user with the no-access role is prevented from viewing and interacting with a vCenter object.
Content Library administrator	A user with this role has the permission to manage Content Library.
Datastore consumer	A user with this role can allocate space from a datastore.
Network administrator	A user with this role has the permission to manage a network.
Resource pool administrator	A user with this role has the permission to manage a resource pool including VMs, alarms, and tasks.
Tagging administrator	A user with this role has the permission to interact with tags.
VMware consolidated Backup user	A user with this role has the permission to back up a VM.
VMware machine power user	A user with this role can interact with a VM and change some of its configurations, except a few system administration operations.
VMware machine user	A user with this role has the permission to interact with a VM but is not able to change its configurations.

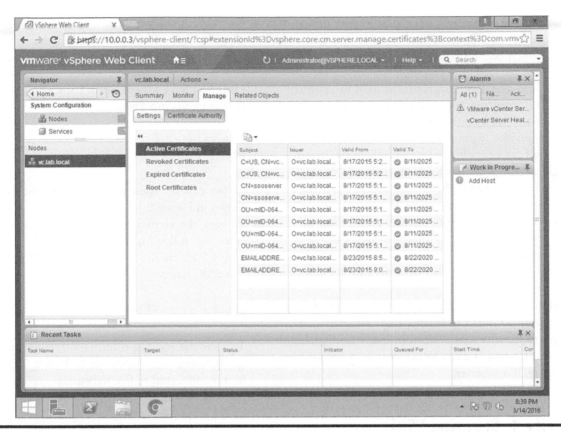

Figure 9.10   Active certificates.

- Properly configuring the firewall to restrict the access to the VMs.
- Applying the principle of least privilege so that the users are given the least amount of privilege necessary to do their jobs.
- Auditing and monitoring VM operations.

To protect the VMs, the following security measures should be considered:

- To prevent VMs from overconsuming the computing resources, which may cause an outage, a resource pool can be created to allow the VMs to share the computing resources.
- To avoid multiple users from logging on the same VM simultaneously, the VM can be configured so that only one user can log on to it at a time.
- Once the VM is protected with the properly configured guest operating system and antivirus software, it can be exported as a template. The template can be used as the master copy for cloning other VMs protected with the same security measures.
- It is also recommended to limit the use of the remote login console to access the VM. Through the remote login console, a hacker may damage the power

management system of the VM. The hacker may also harm the connection of a removable device.

When trying to secure VMs, make sure to keep the network security in mind. More details about securing the network are given in the next section.

9.5 Virtual Network Security Management

A virtual network may include elements such as virtual local area network (VLAN), virtual network adapters, virtual switches, distributed virtual switches, ports, and port groups. vSphere provides tools for securing the elements in the virtualized infrastructure. A set of network management utilities is provided for virtual network configuration.

VLAN is used to implement network isolation. A virtual network can be isolated from other virtual networks. The access of a virtual network can be configured at different isolation levels. Network traffic generated by vSphere Client, the ESXi management shell, API, or third-party software can be isolated. The network connecting networked storage devices can also be isolated from other network traffic.

A virtual private network (VPN) helps secure private network traffic over the unsecured Internet. The encryption and authentication mechanisms are provided by the VPN to protect the traffic on virtual networks. Data are encrypted for confidentiality. The digital signature is used to validate the authority and integrity. The authentication mechanisms are used to validate VPN users and computers.

A firewall is provided to protect virtual networks at different levels. The firewall can be configured to make the network traffic go through certain ports, block certain protocols, or block the traffic coming from certain hardware addresses. VMware recommends rejecting all the network traffic at first, and then only allowing the necessary network traffic to pass the firewall.

VMware vShield is a product that provides a group of networking and security services for protecting the cloud computing environment. More discussion about vShield will be given in Chapter 10.

In addition to the security measures mentioned in Section 9.4, administrators can further improve security by using third-party security tools. When properly configured, the virtualized infrastructure can be as secure as any physical IT infrastructure, if not better.

9.6 Activity 1: Securing ESXi Hosts and vCenter

In this activity, you will perform the following tasks to enhance the security of ESXi hosts and vCenter:

- *Task 1:* Introducing ESXi shell and SSH
- *Task 2:* Securing ESXi hosts
- *Task 3:* Securing vCenter
- *Task 4:* Managing certificates

To begin, you need to enable ESXi Shell and SSH on the ESXi hosts.

9.6.1 Task 1: Introducing ESXi Shell and SSH

In this task, if you have not done so, you will first enable ESXi Shell including SSH and CLI. Then, you will try some system management commands.

1. Start the VMs DC, Storage, LabESXi1, LabESXi2, and vc. Log on to the ESXi host **LabESXi2** through DCUI (Figure 9.11).
2. Click **Troubleshooting Options**, as shown in Figure 9.12, and press the **Enter** key.
3. Make sure that both ESXi Shell and SSH are enabled, as shown in Figure 9.13. If ESXi Shell is enabled, Press the **Esc** key to exit. Do the same for the SSH. Then, press the **Esc** key again to log out.

4. To start ESXi Shell, press the key combination ALT+F1. You will be prompted to enter the username and password. Enter **root** as the username and enter your password to log in.
5. Once you have logged on to LabESXi2, enter the following two commands:

```
cd/usr/bin
ls
```

You can see the commands with the esxcfg prefix shown in Figure 9.14.
6. To view the virtual NICs created on this ESXi host, enter the following esxcfg command. As shown in Figure 9.15, there are seven virtual NICs installed on this ESXi host.

```
esxcfg-nics —list
```

7. To view the routing information, enter the following esxcfg command. As shown in Figure 9.15, the ESXi host is connected to five networks.

```
esxcfg-route —list
```

8. To view functions of virtual switches, enter the following command. Figure 9.16 shows that you have four virtual switches. vSwitch0 is used for vMotion and management. vSwitch1 is used for storage devices. vSwitch2 is used for fault tolerance, and vSwitch3 is used for VMs.

```
esxcfg-vswitch —list
```

9. Instead of esxcfg, esxcli can also be used for system management. For example, to view the permissions of users, enter the following command. As shown in Figure 9.17, there are three users created on the ESXi host. All three users are assigned the role Admin and have full access rights.

```
esxcli system permission list
```

10. To view the current ESXi host version, enter the following command:

```
esxcli system version get
```

11. To exit ESXi Shell, enter the following command. Then, press the key combination **ALT+F2** to exit the ESXi host.

```
exit
```

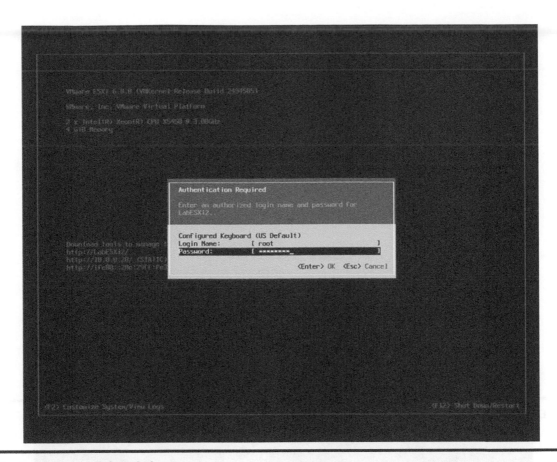

Figure 9.11 Logging on to labESXi2 host server.

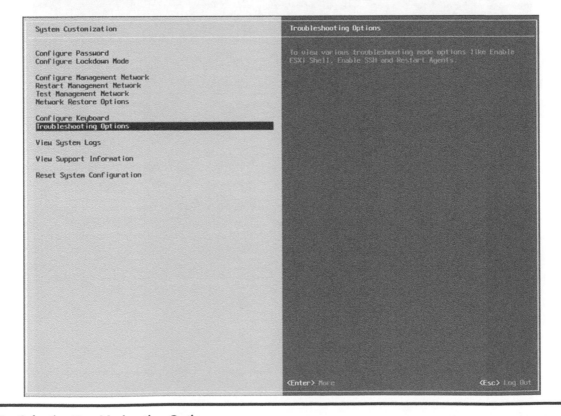

Figure 9.12 Selecting Troubleshooting Options.

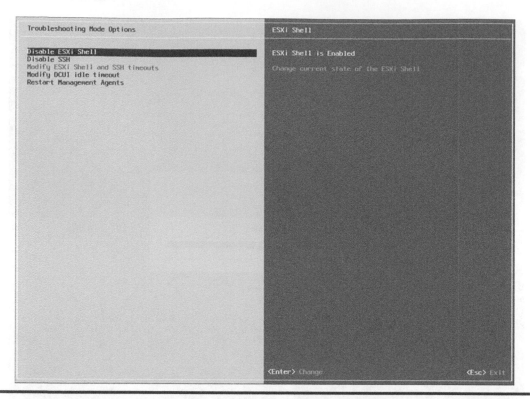

Figure 9.13　ESXi Shell and SSH are enabled.

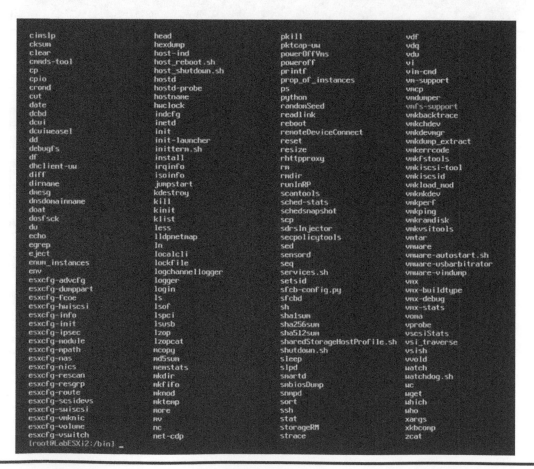

Figure 9.14　esxcfg commands.

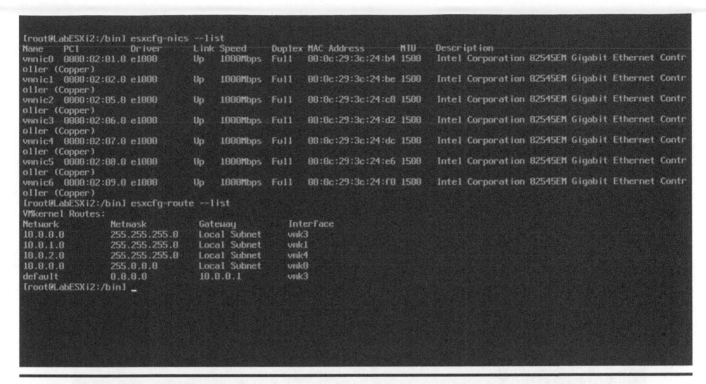

Figure 9.15 Virtual NICs and routes.

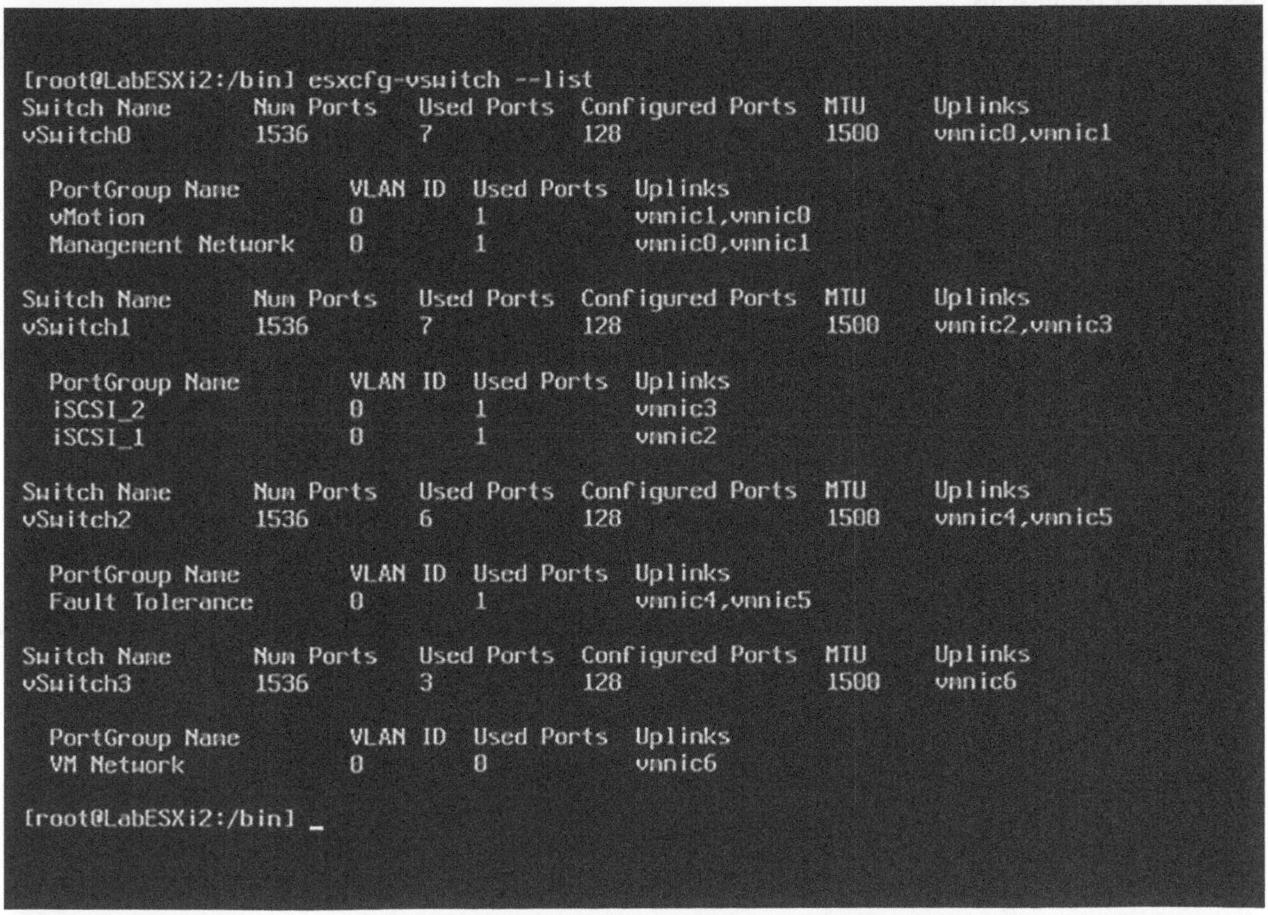

```
[root@LabESXi2:/bin] esxcfg-vswitch --list
Switch Name        Num Ports    Used Ports    Configured Ports    MTU        Uplinks
vSwitch0           1536         7             128                 1500       vnnic0,vnnic1

   PortGroup Name            VLAN ID    Used Ports    Uplinks
   vMotion                   0          1             vnnic1,vnnic0
   Management Network        0          1             vnnic0,vnnic1

Switch Name        Num Ports    Used Ports    Configured Ports    MTU        Uplinks
vSwitch1           1536         7             128                 1500       vnnic2,vnnic3

   PortGroup Name            VLAN ID    Used Ports    Uplinks
   iSCSI_2                   0          1             vnnic3
   iSCSI_1                   0          1             vnnic2

Switch Name        Num Ports    Used Ports    Configured Ports    MTU        Uplinks
vSwitch2           1536         6             128                 1500       vnnic4,vnnic5

   PortGroup Name            VLAN ID    Used Ports    Uplinks
   Fault Tolerance           0          1             vnnic4,vnnic5

Switch Name        Num Ports    Used Ports    Configured Ports    MTU        Uplinks
vSwitch3           1536         3             128                 1500       vnnic6

   PortGroup Name            VLAN ID    Used Ports    Uplinks
   VM Network                0          0             vnnic6

[root@LabESXi2:/bin] _
```

Figure 9.16 Virtual switches.

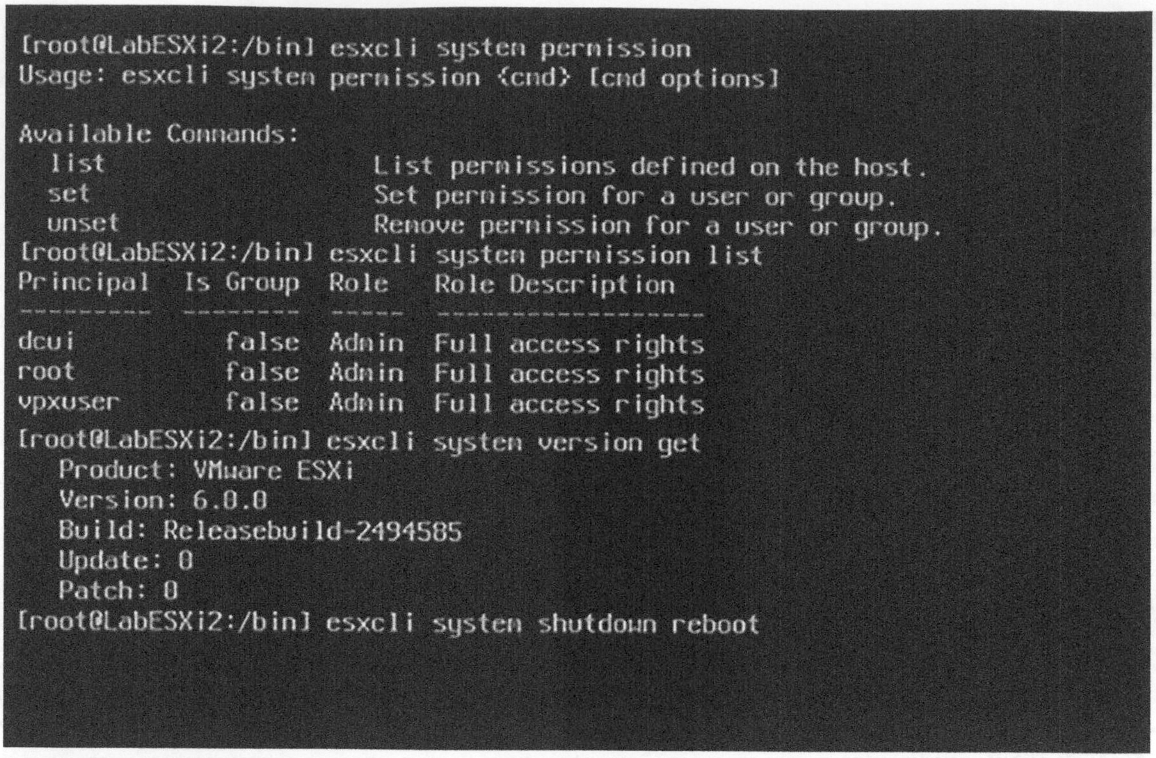

```
[root@LabESXi2:/bin] esxcli system permission
Usage: esxcli system permission <cmd> [cmd options]

Available Commands:
  list                 List permissions defined on the host.
  set                  Set permission for a user or group.
  unset                Remove permission for a user or group.
[root@LabESXi2:/bin] esxcli system permission list
Principal    Is Group    Role    Role Description
-----------  ----------  ------  -------------------
dcui          false      Admin   Full access rights
root          false      Admin   Full access rights
vpxuser       false      Admin   Full access rights
[root@LabESXi2:/bin] esxcli system version get
    Product: VMware ESXi
    Version: 6.0.0
    Build: Releasebuild-2494585
    Update: 0
    Patch: 0
[root@LabESXi2:/bin] esxcli system shutdown reboot
```

Figure 9.17   User permissions.

12. To use SSH for system management, if you have not done so, log on to DC and download putty.exe from the following Web site: http://www.chiark.greenend.org.uk/~sgtatham/putty/download.html

13. To open PuTTY, double-click the **PuTTY** icon on the Desktop of DC.

14. Once the PuTTY Configuration dialog is opened, enter the IP address **10.0.0.20** for the ESXi host LabESXi2, as shown in Figure 9.18, and click the **Open** button.

15. You will be prompted to enter the user name and password. Enter **root** as the user name and enter the password for the LabESXi2 host. Then, press **Enter**.

16. Once you have logged on to the host LabESXi2, enter the following command to change the directory to/usr/bin where you can locate the esxcfg and esxcli commands:

```
cd /usr/bin
```

17. The esxcli commands are arranged in a tree system. For example, to get the information about a host name, you can first enter the command

```
esxcli system hostname
```

A set of options will be displayed, as shown in Figure 9.19. After the get option is added as follows, you will get the host name (Figure 9.19).

```
esxcli system hostname get
```

18. With the esxcli command, you are able to set the firewall. To illustrate this, first, enter the command

```
esxcli network firewall
```

19. Among five options, add the get option to the command as

```
esxcli network firewall get
```

20. In Figure 9.20, you can see that the firewall is enabled and is loaded. The firewall's default action is DROP.

21. You can also run the commands in PuTTY to manage network services. To see the DNS server list, execute the following command, as shown in Figure 9.21:

```
esxcli network ip dns server list
```

22. To get the IP addresses assigned to the ESXi host servers, run the following command, as shown in Figure 9.22:

```
esxcli network ip interface ipv4 get
```

23. To check if the DNS server functions properly, execute the following command, as shown in Figure 9.23:

```
nslookup labesxi2.lab.local
```

24. To exit PuTTY, enter the following command:

```
exit
```

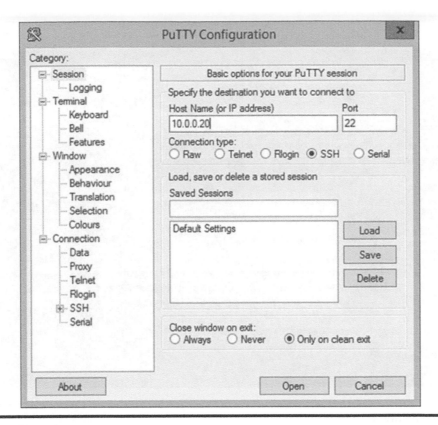

Figure 9.18 PuTTY configuration.

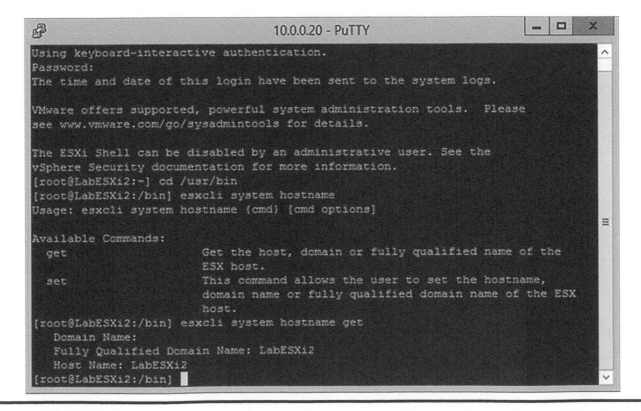

Figure 9.19 Getting hostname.

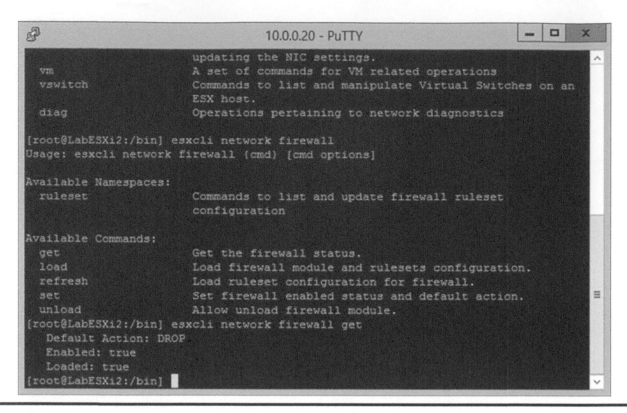

Figure 9.20 Firewall configuration.

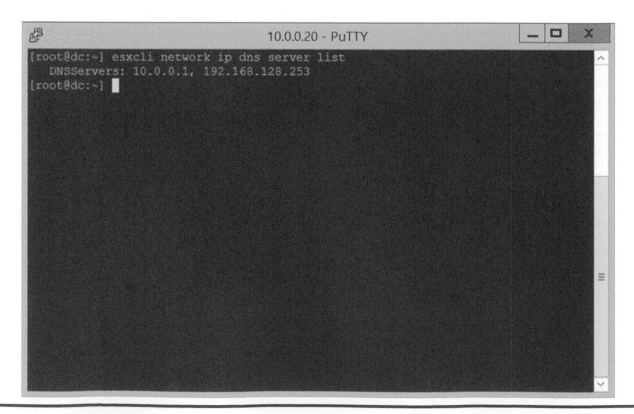

Figure 9.21 DNS server list.

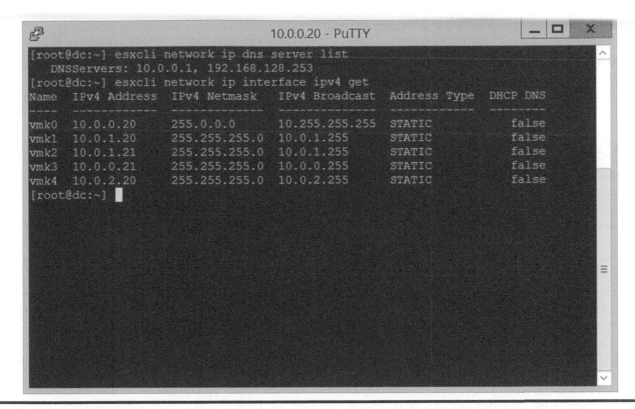

Figure 9.22 IP addresses.

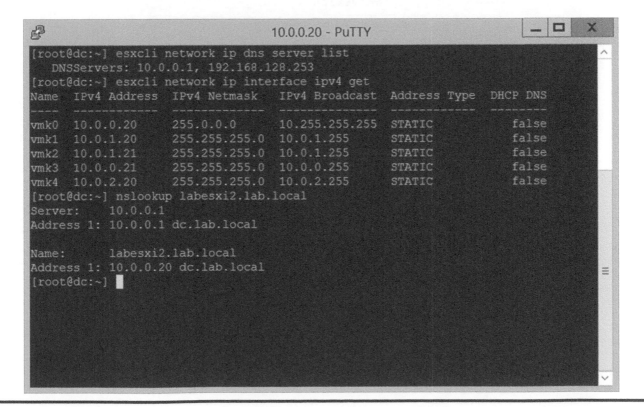

Figure 9.23 nslookup command.

In this task, you have learned to access an ESXi host through ESXi Shell and the SSH client PuTTY. You have also executed a few esxcfg and esxcli commands for system management. There are many books that cover the use of esxcfg and esxcli commands. Interested readers can refer to those books for more details.

9.6.2 Task 2: Securing ESXi Hosts

In this task, you will first create and edit a user object on an ESXi host. Then, you will learn how to configure a firewall. Lastly, you will create a role and assign permissions to the role. To accomplish these tasks, follow the steps below.

1. From vSphere Client, log on to the ESXi host **LabESXi1** as **root** (Figure 9.24).
2. To create a new user, select the host **10.0.0.10**. Click the **Users** tab. Right-click the empty space below the Users tab and select **Add**, as shown in Figure 9.25.
3. In the Add New User dialog, you can create a user **student1** with the password of your choice. The password should meet the complexity requirement. Then, click **OK**.
4. To edit the newly created user's settings, right-click the user **student1** (Figure 9.26) and select **Edit**.
5. In the Edit User—Student dialog, enter the user name and then click **OK**.

6. To configure the firewall on the ESXi host, under the **Configuration** tab, select **Security Profile** in the Software pane. In the Firewall pane, click **Properties**, as shown in Figure 9.27.
7. In the Firewall Properties dialog, you can configure the remote access. For example, you can check **SSH Client** to allow SSH outgoing traffic (Figure 9.28). Then, click **OK**.
8. To add a role, click the **View** menu, select **Administration** and **Roles**, as shown in Figure 9.29.
9. On the submenu, click **Add Role**.
10. In the Add New Role dialog, enter **student** as the role name. Check the privileges **Datastore**, **Folder**, **Host**, **Network**, **vApp**, and **Virtual Machine**, as shown in Figure 9.30. Then, click **OK**.
11. In vSphere Client, you can see that the new role **student** is added.
12. To grant a permission to a VM object, in vSphere Client, in the Inventory pane, right-click the VM **myvm** and select **Add Permission**, as shown in Figure 9.31.
13. In the Assign Permissions dialog, click the **Add** button. In the Select Users and Groups dialog, select the user **student1** and click the **Add** button, as shown in Figure 9.32. Then, click **OK**.
14. In the Assign Permissions dialog, select the role **student** to assign privileges such as **Datastore** and **Folder**, as shown in Figure 9.33. Then, click **OK**.

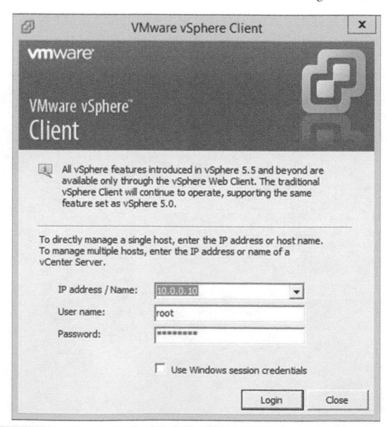

Figure 9.24 Logging on to LabESXi1.

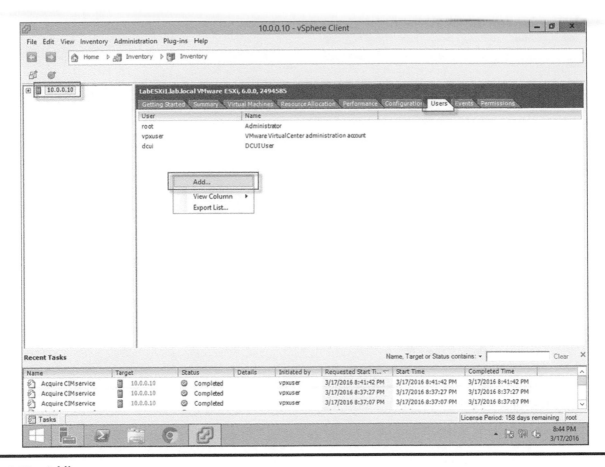

Figure 9.25 Adding user.

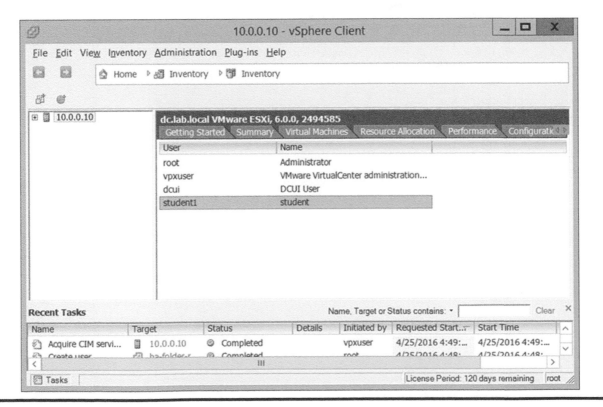

Figure 9.26 Editing user.

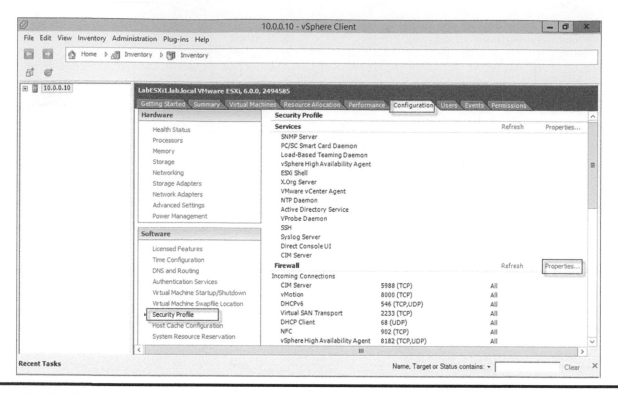

Figure 9.27 Configuring firewall properties.

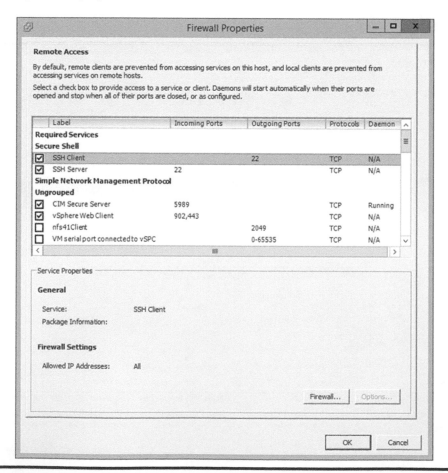

Figure 9.28 Configuring remote access.

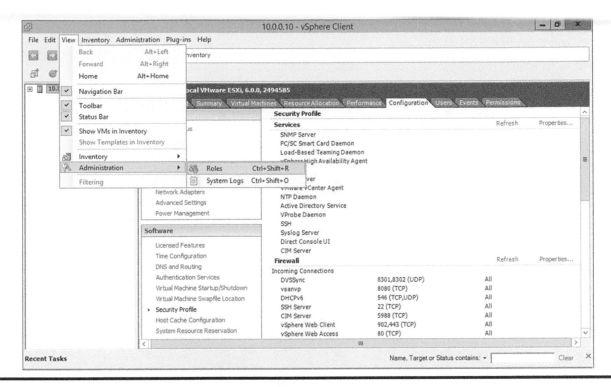

Figure 9.29   Adding role.

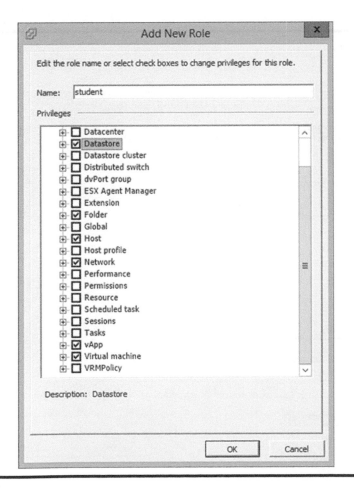

Figure 9.30   Configuring role.

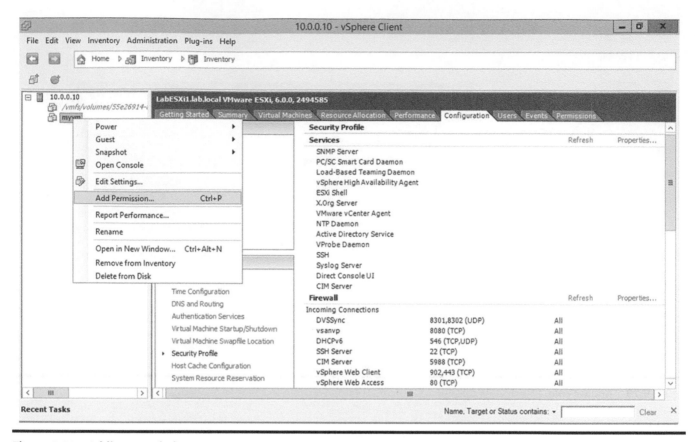

Figure 9.31   Adding permission.

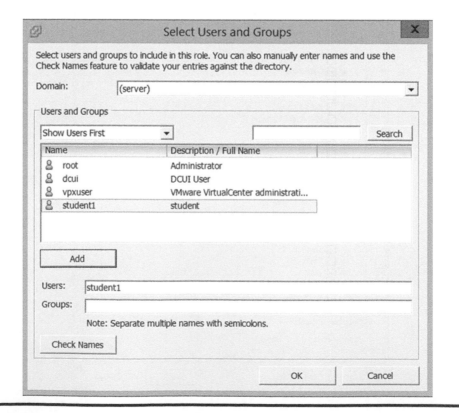

Figure 9.32   Adding user.

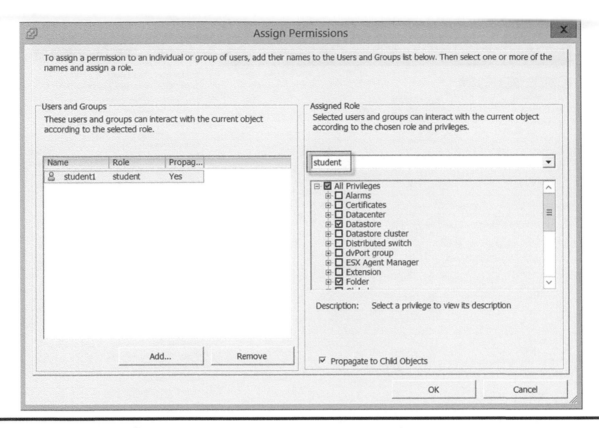

Figure 9.33 Assigning permissions.

In this task, you have made a few security measures such as creating a new user for the ESXi host, creating a new role on the ESXi host, and assigning permissions. In the next task, you will perform some activities to secure vCenter.

9.6.3 Task 3: Securing vCenter

To integrate Active Directory and vCenter, follow the steps below.

1. If you have not done so, create a user Student2 on your DC server. Log on to the DC server, click the Tools menu, and select Active Directory Users and Computers, as shown in Figure 9.34.
2. In the Active Directory Users and Computers dialog, right-click the **Users** node and select **New** and then **User** (Figure 9.35).
3. In the New-Object User dialog, enter **Student2** as the user name. Also, enter the domain name **@lab.local** (Figure 9.36). Then, click **Next**.
4. Enter your password and check the option **Password never expires** (Figure 9.37). Then, click **Next**.
5. Review the user configuration and click **Finish**.
6. You should be able to see the new user Student2. Right-click **Student2** and select **Properties**, as shown in Figure 9.38.

7. In the Student Properties dialog, click the tab **Member Of**. Then, click the **Add** button, as shown in Figure 9.39.
8. In the Select Groups dialog, click the **Advanced** button. Then, click the **Find Now** button and click the **Domain Admins** group, as shown in Figure 9.40.
9. Similarly, find **Enterprise Admins** (Figure 9.41). Then, click **OK** twice.
10. Next, you will work on the vCenter Server. In the Chrome Web browser, enter the Uniform Resource Locator **https://10.0.0.3** and press **Enter**. Log on to vCenter through vSphere Web Client with the user **administrator@vsphere.local** and your password.
11. To integrate Active Directory to vCenter, on the Home page, click the **System Configuration** icon, as shown in Figure 9.42. Then, click the **Home** icon on the top part of your screen and click **Administration**.
12. In the Navigator pane, select **Nodes** and then click **vc.lab.local**. Under the **Manage** tab, click **Active Directory**, as shown in Figure 9.43.
13. Click the **Join** button. As shown in Figure 9.44, in the Join Active Directory dialog, enter the domain name **lab.local**, the user name **Administrator**, and the password. Then, click **OK**.
14. To apply the change, right-click the node **vc.lab.local** and select **Reboot** to restart the node manually (Figure 9.45).
15. Once the node is rebooted, click the **Home** icon on the top part of your screen and select **Administration**.

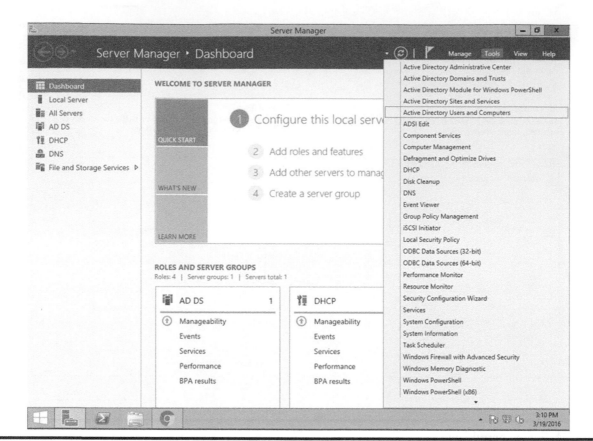

Figure 9.34   Opening Active Directory users and computers.

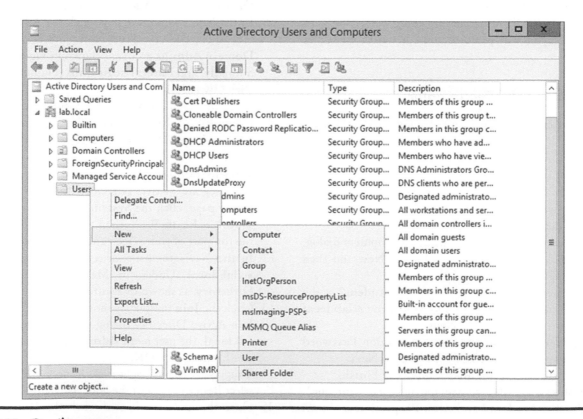

Figure 9.35   Creating new user.

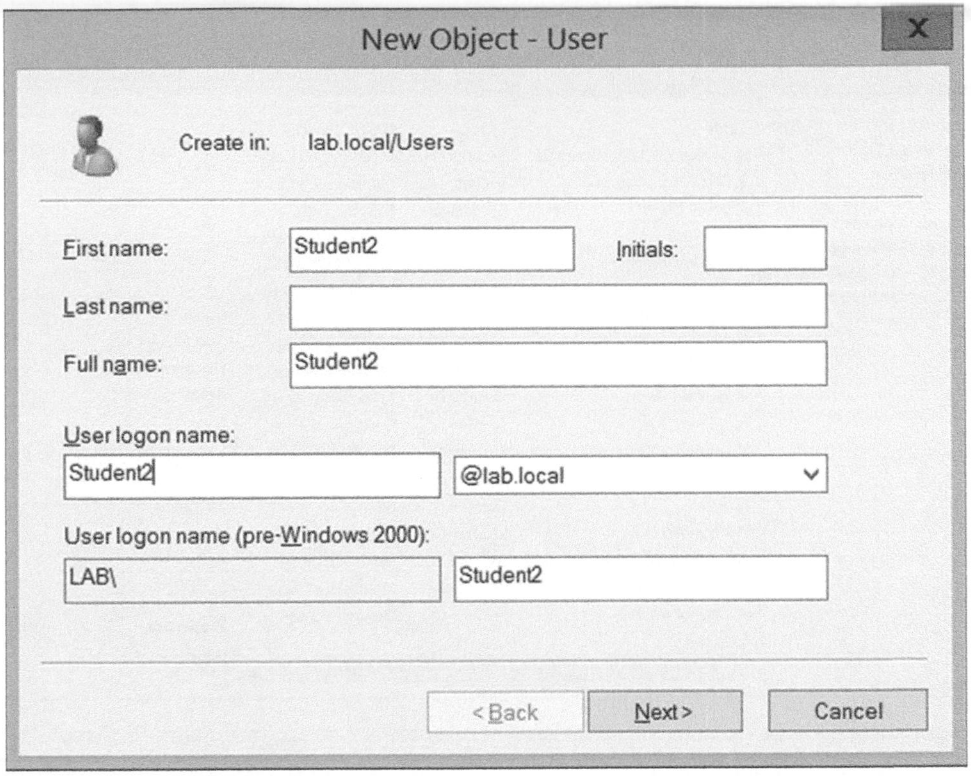

Figure 9.36   Entering new user information.

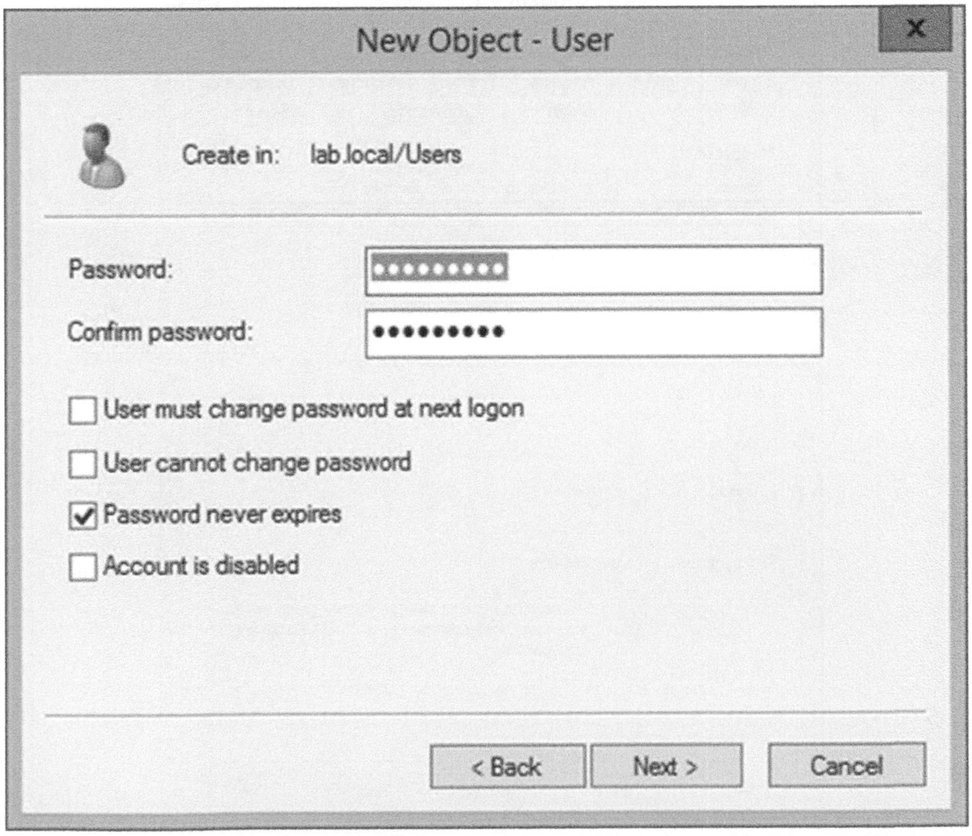

Figure 9.37   Configuring password.

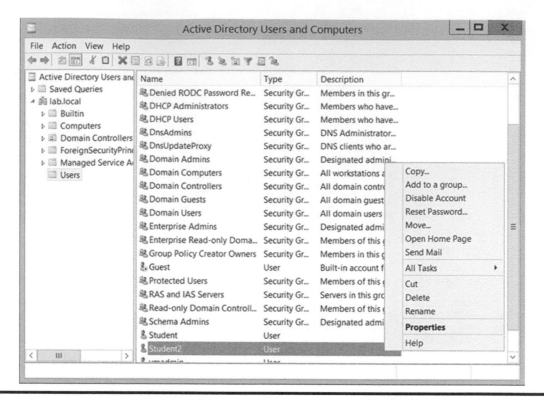

Figure 9.38 New user property configuration.

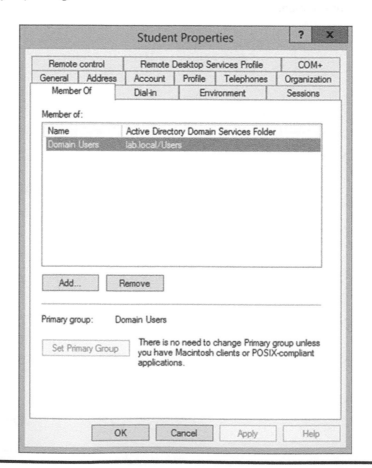

Figure 9.39 Adding member.

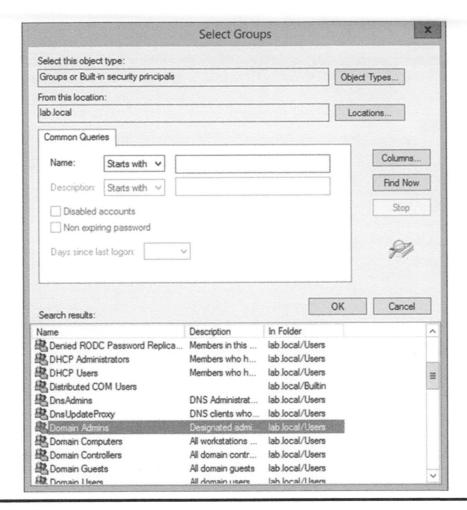

Figure 9.40   Selecting Domain Admins Group.

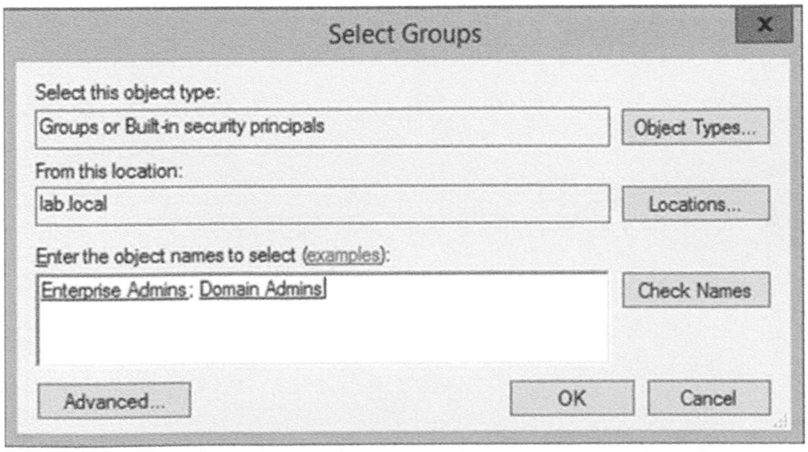

Figure 9.41   Finding Enterprise Admins Group.

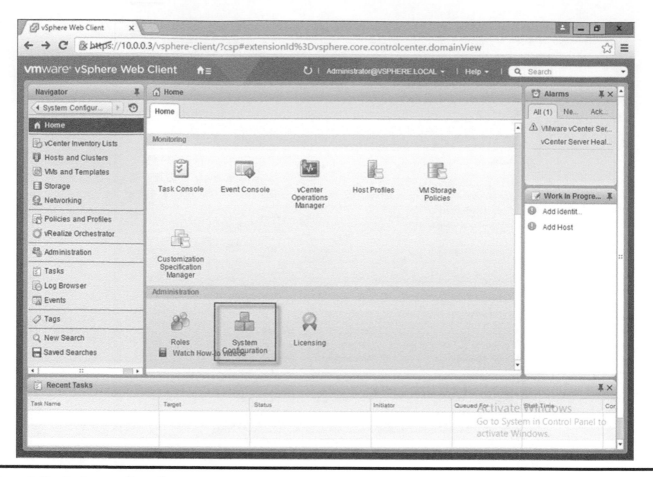

Figure 9.42   System configuration.

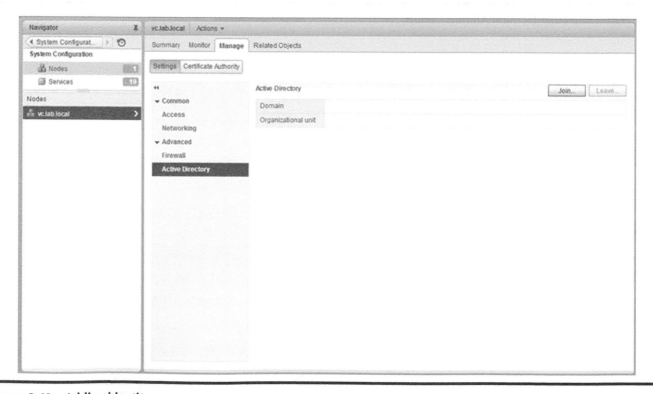

Figure 9.43   Adding identity source.

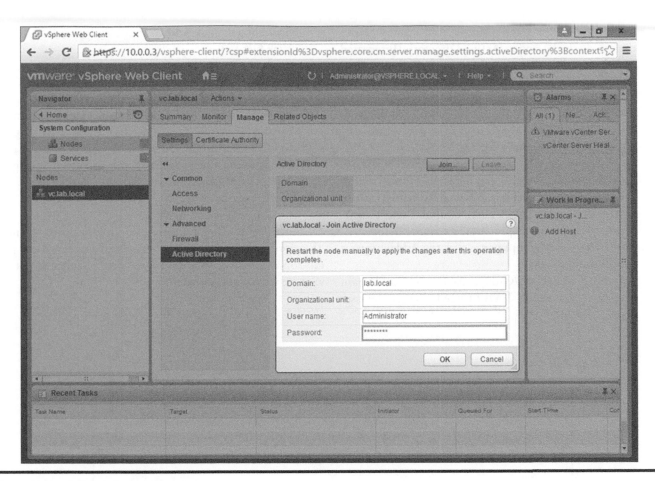

Figure 9.44 Joining Active Directory.

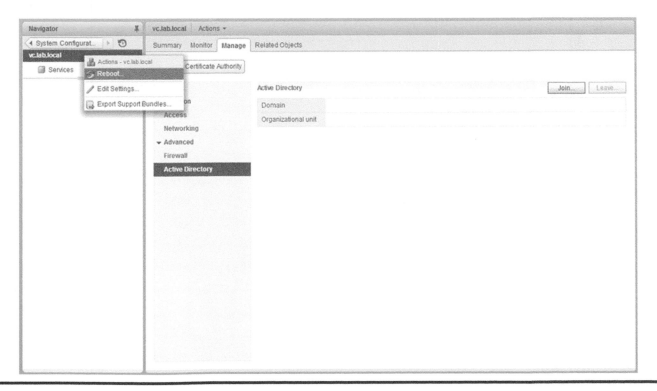

Figure 9.45 Rebooting vc.lab.local.

Click the green plus sign **+**. In the Add Identity Source dialog, check the option **Active Directory (Integrated Windows Authentication)** and you will see that the domain name LAB.LOCAL is added (Figure 9.46). Then, click **OK**.

16. Click the newly added domain **lab.local** and click the **Set as Default Domain** icon, as shown in Figure 9.47. Click **Yes** to confirm the setting.

17. To assign permissions to the Student user in Active Directory to access vCenter, click the **Home** icon on the top part of your screen and click **Administration**. In the Navigator pane, click **Global Permissions**. Then, click the green plus sign **+** (Figure 9.48).

18. In the Users and Groups pane, click the **Add** button, as shown in Figure 9.49.

19. On the Select Users/Groups page, on the Domain dropdown list, select **LAB.LOCAL**. Select the user **Student** and click **Add**, as shown in Figure 9.50. Then, click **OK** twice.

20. As shown in Figure 9.51, the user **Student** is added as a vCenter administrator. It shows that **Student** is from the domain LAB.LOCAL.

21. To verify if the user Student from Active Directory can log on to vCenter, log off vCenter. Then, log on to vCenter through vSphere Web Client with the user **lab\Student** and your password, as shown in Figure 9.52. Once logged in, you should be able to see the Home page.

In this task, Active Directory is integrated with vCenter. Therefore, an Active Directory user can be assigned the permission to access vCenter for centralized management of the vSphere virtual environment.

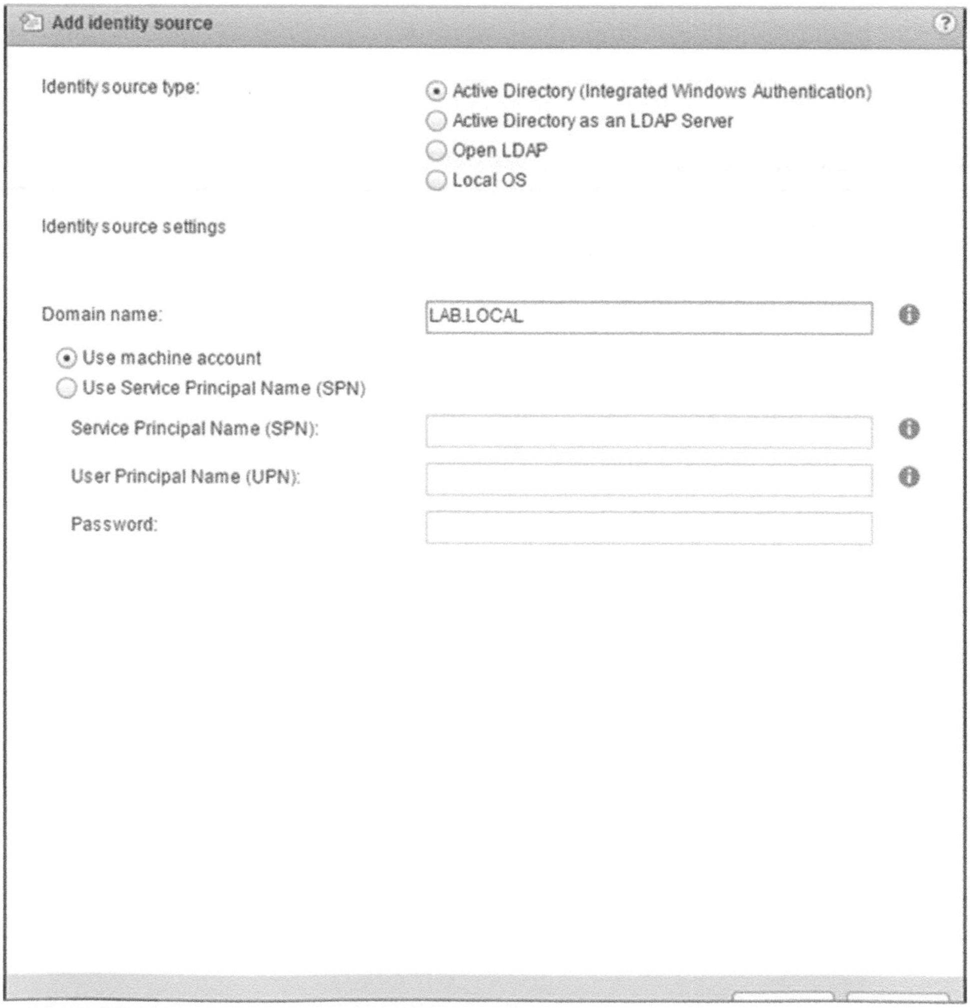

Figure 9.46 Integrating Active Directory.

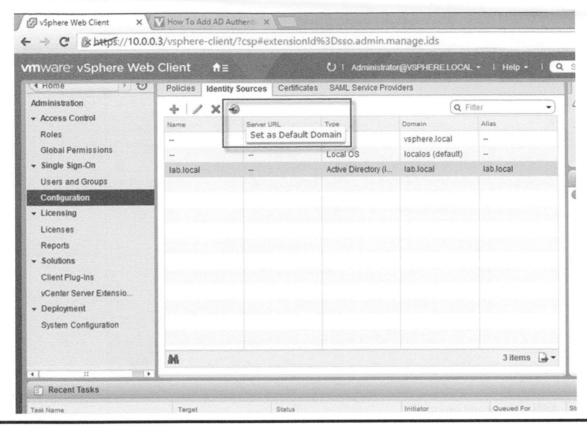

Figure 9.47 Setting default domain.

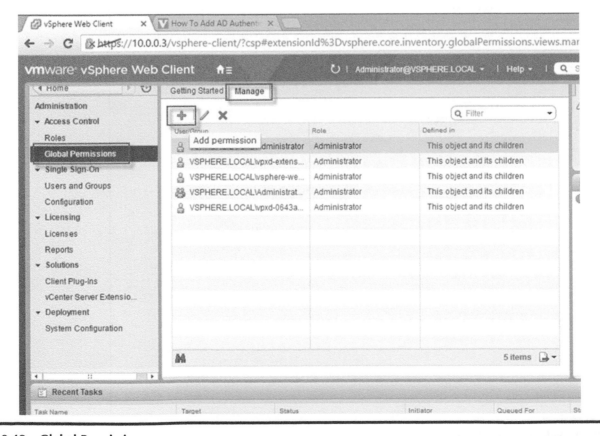

Figure 9.48 Global Permissions.

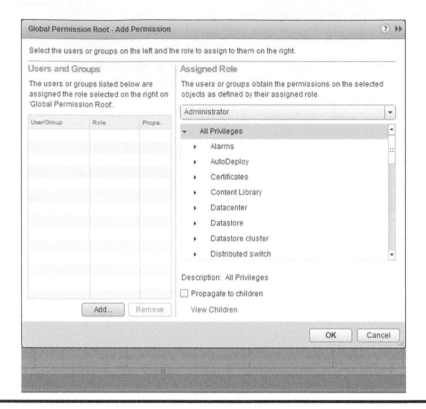

Figure 9.49 Adding users and groups.

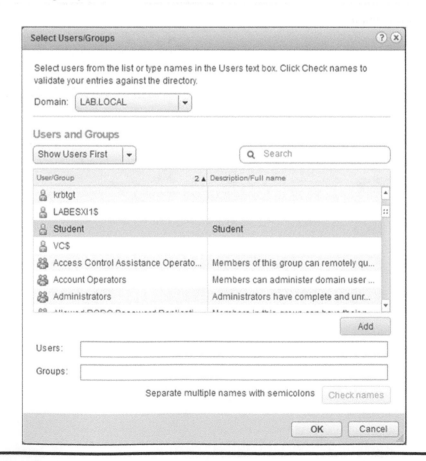

Figure 9.50 Selecting user Student.

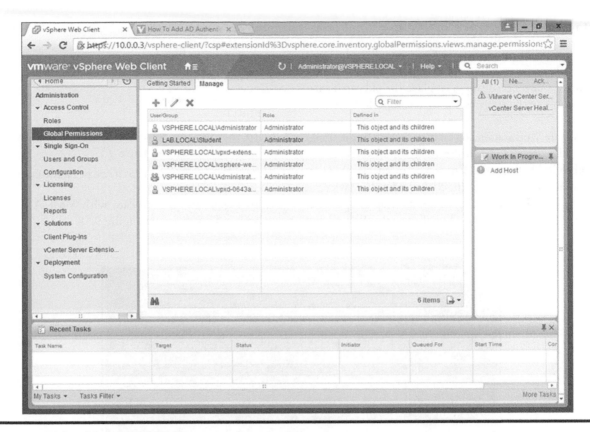

Figure 9.51   Newly added user Student.

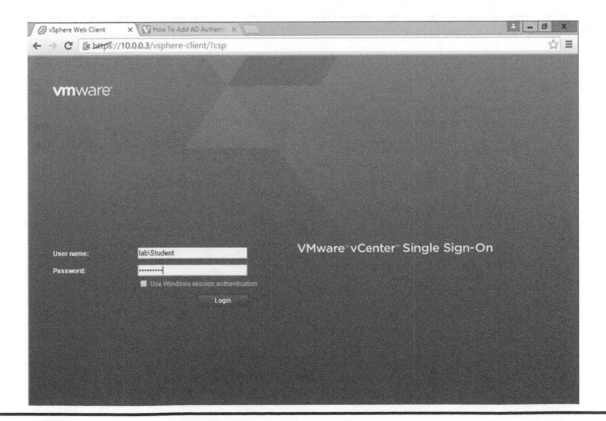

Figure 9.52   Logging on to vCenter as lab domain user.

9.6.4 Task 4: Managing Certificates

In this task, you will first configure vCenter to allow the SSH connection. Then, you will create a certificate store. Next, you will create a new certificate to replace the old certificate for vCenter. Follow the steps below to accomplish this task.

1. In VMware Workstation, log on to vc as root (Figure 9.53).
2. Click the link **Troubleshooting**, and then select **Disable SSH**. Press the **Enter** key to enable SSH, as shown in Figure 9.54. Then, click the **Esc** key twice.
3. Double-click **PuTTY** icon on the desktop to open the PuTTY Configuration dialog. Enter the IP address of the machine vc.lab.local, as shown in Figure 9.55. Then, click **Open**.
4. Through PuTTY, log on to vc as **root** (Figure 9.56).
5. To enable the shell, run the following two commands:

```
shell.set —enabled True
shell
```

6. To manage the certificates, run the following command, as shown in Figure 9.57:

```
/usr/lib/vmware-vmca/bin/certificate-manager
```

7. To regenerate a certificate with VMCA, choose the option **4**, as shown in Figure 9.58.

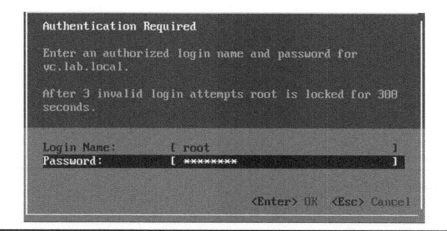

Figure 9.53 Logging on to vCenter Server.

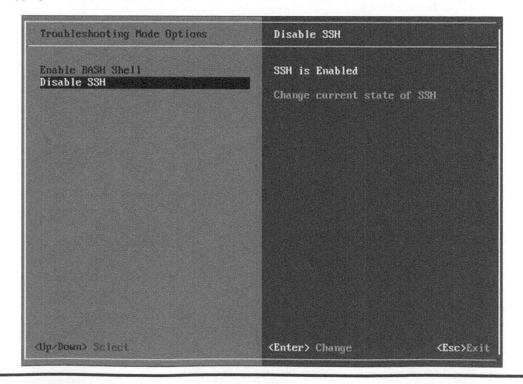

Figure 9.54 Enabling SSH.

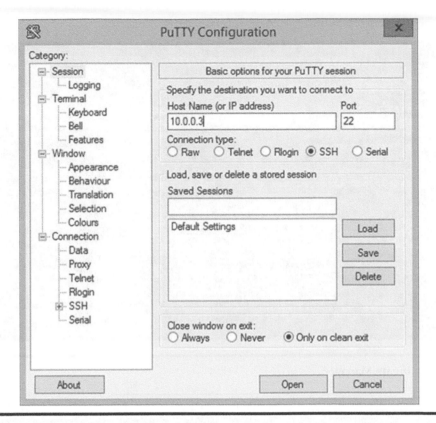

Figure 9.55 **Configuring PuTTY for remote login.**

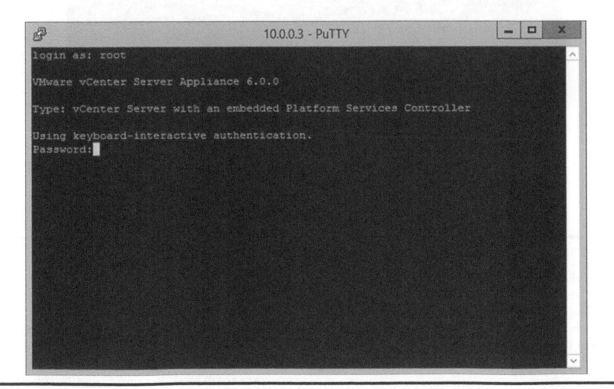

Figure 9.56 **SSH Logging on to vc.**

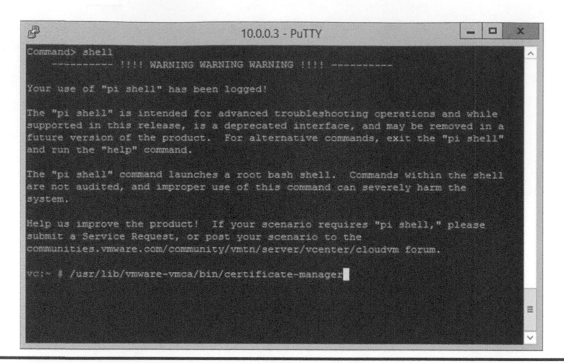

Figure 9.57 **Starting Certificate Manager.**

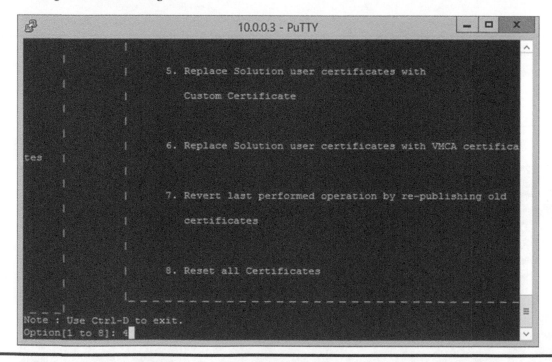

Figure 9.58 **Regenerating new certificate.**

8. Enter the specifications about your new certificate similar to those displayed in Figure 9.59. When asked if to regenerate the certificate, enter **y** and press the **Enter** key.

9. Exit the certificate manager by pressing the key combination **Ctrl+D**. Then, run the following command to exit the shell:

```
exit
```

10. To view the newly generated certificate, log on to vc through vSphere Client. On the Home page, click the **System Configuration** icon (Figure 9.60).

11. When prompted to verify the password, enter your password and press **Enter**.

12. In the System Configuration pane, select **Nodes** and then select **vc.lab.local**, as shown in Figure 9.61. The newly regenerated certificate has the latest validation date.

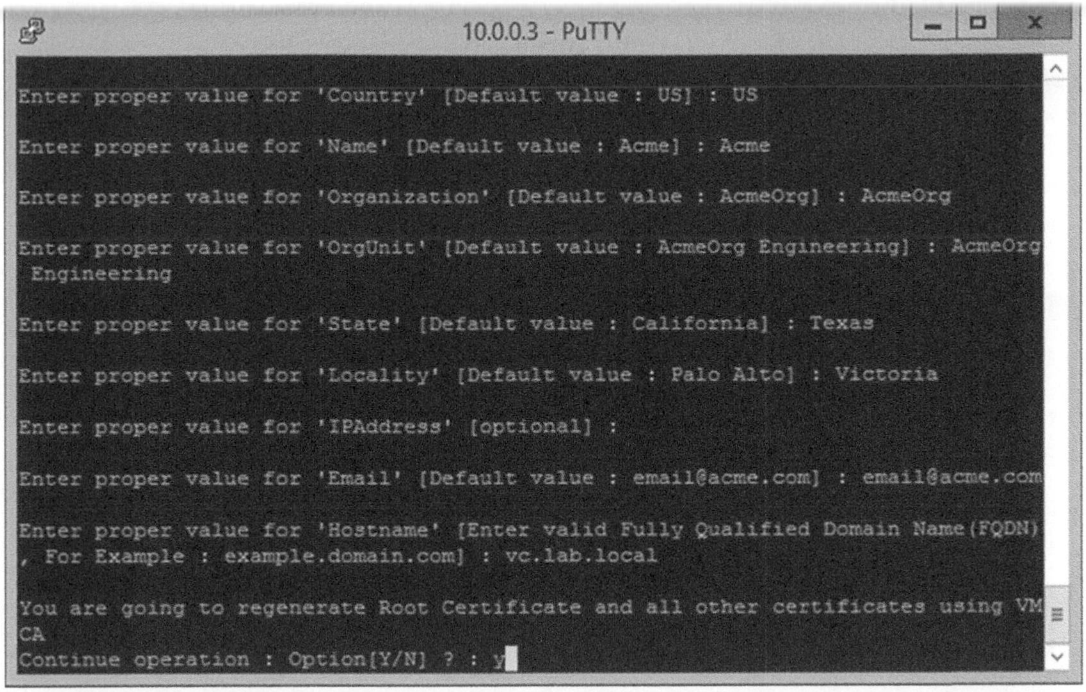

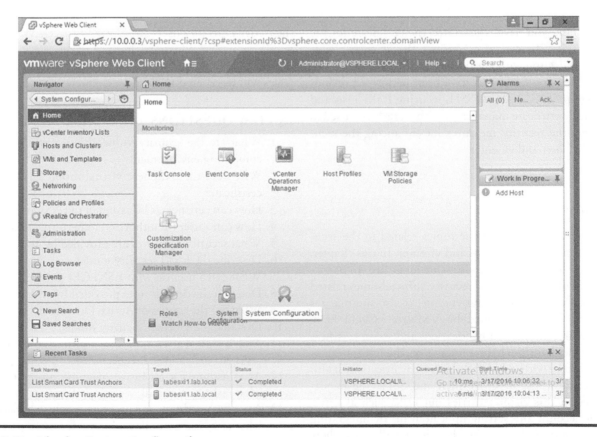

Figure 9.59   Certificate specifications.

Figure 9.60   Viewing System Configuration.

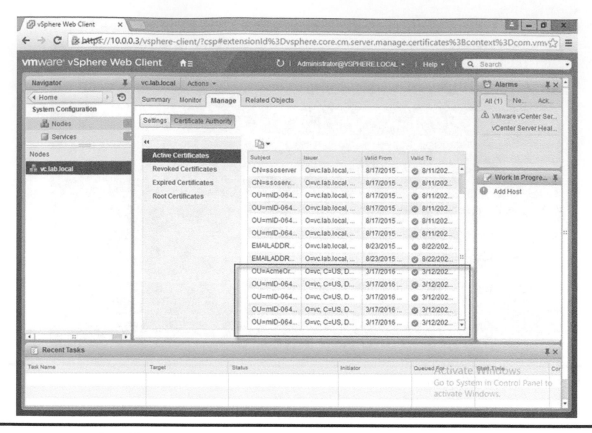

Figure 9.61 Regenerated certificate.

In this task, you have regenerated the certificate for the vCenter Server. The certificate ensures the vCenter clients that they are dealing with a legitimate vCenter owner.

In this activity, four tasks have been performed including setting up ESXi Shell and SSH, securing ESXi hosts and vCenter, and certificate management. These tasks are used to demonstrate the security measures for enhancing the security of ESXi hosts and vCenter.

9.7 Summary

This chapter covers some of the topics related to the security management of ESXi hosts and vCenter. In this chapter, some general security vulnerabilities are identified. In particular, this chapter identifies the security vulnerabilities related to the vSphere virtual IT infrastructure. It also summarizes the security features provided by VMware vCloud Suite such as the firewall, user authentication, and server certification. In particular, this chapter focuses on the integration of Active Directory with vCenter for user authentication. It also demonstrates the use of ESXi Shell and SSH. The hands-on practice in this chapter carries out tasks such as creating a user account and setting up a firewall. By integrating Active Directory with vCenter, this chapter illustrates how

the Active Directory users are allowed to access vCenter. The hands-on activity illustrates how to regenerate a certificate for vCenter by using SSH. More network-related security issues will be covered in the next chapter.

REVIEW QUESTIONS

1. What are the security vulnerabilities in a virtualized computing environment?
2. Why does each vSphere virtualization service need a certificate?
3. How can certificates be assigned to ESXi and vCenter?
4. How can a user be authorized to perform certain tasks?
5. What security measures are provided by an ESXi host?
6. Describe the ESXi security model.
7. What can a user do with ESXi CLI or SSH?
8. Describe the default roles provided by an ESXi host.
9. What are the usages of Active Directory?
10. Describe the vCenter security model.
11. After assigned a resource pool administrator role, what tasks is a user allowed to perform?
12. After assigned a VMware machine power user role, what tasks is a user allowed to perform?
13. After assigned a Content Library administrator role, what tasks is a user allowed to perform?

14. After assigned a VMware-consolidated backup user role, what tasks is a user allowed to perform?
15. What is VMware PSC, and how does it work?
16. What is VECS, and what can be done with it?
17. To enhance the guest operating system security, what security measures should be considered?
18. To protect VMs, what security measures should be considered?
19. What is a VPN, and how does it work?
20. What is the recommendation by VMware on setting up a firewall?

Chapter 10

vCloud Networking and Security

Objectives

- Understand vCloud Networking and Security
- Apply vCloud Networking and Security to enhance network security
- Implement security measures for a private cloud

10.1 Introduction

A physical information technology (IT) infrastructure has its limitations. It is not flexible for dynamically allocating network resources to meet computing requirements. It is not easy to reconstruct a physical network structure. It is also expensive to construct a physical network. A virtualized IT infrastructure created with VMware is able to meet these challenges. The virtualized IT infrastructure is flexible. It is much easier to reconstruct a virtualized network structure. The cost of constructing a virtualized IT infrastructure is low. It takes much less time to deploy a virtualized IT infrastructure. Using a virtualized IT infrastructure allows an organization to respond faster to changing business requirements.

Once a virtualized IT infrastructure is implemented, the next task is to configure the remote access mechanism so that customers can safely access the IT infrastructure. If multiple customers are allowed to access the virtualized IT infrastructure, each customer accessing the IT infrastructure should have its own isolated computing environment. The customer should have its own segment of the virtual network and its own set of virtual machines. The virtualized IT infrastructure may face the following security issues:

- The first challenge is the remote access management. As the virtualized IT infrastructure is accessible worldwide, hackers may find a way to penetrate the virtualized IT infrastructure.

- The second challenge is protecting the underlying physical IT infrastructure from being hacked through the virtualized IT infrastructure. A security layer is needed to separate the physical IT infrastructure and the virtualized IT infrastructure.

Included in VMware vCloud Suite, VMware vCloud Networking and Security (vCNS) is a product that provides the solution to the above-mentioned issues. With vCNS, an enterprise can effectively manage remote access. vCNS can be used to isolate users' networks from each other. It provides protection for the private cloud. It also provides security shields to protect virtual machines and virtual networks. The use of vCNS will lower the cost by simplifying the provisioning of gateway services.

To simplify the implementation of the software-defined network and reduce the requirements on the underlying physical network, VMware NSX is recommended by VMware for the future. Similar to vCNS, NSX virtualizes the network and security features. It is designed to expand the vCNS service to any general-purpose Internet Protocol (IP) network hardware, including mobile virtual networks. However, at the time of writing, VMware NSX is not included in VMware vCloud Suite for academic users. Therefore, vCNS will be used for the hands-on practice in this chapter. vCNS can be considered the stepping-stone to VMware NSX.

10.2 Applying vCNS

Without vCNS, isolation is accomplished with hardware that is expensive, not flexible, and has a complicated installation process. Without changing the existing physical infrastructure, vCNS can logically partition and isolate a part of the IT infrastructure. The partition can be isolated with logical firewalls and routers. vCNS provides the integrated security service including the firewall, gateway, virtual private network (VPN), network address translation (NAT), and Dynamic Host Configuration Protocol (DHCP). The shield formed by using logical firewalls and routers is flexible and easy to implement. With vCNS, the critical applications and hardware can be protected by isolating them from the less secure components in the IT infrastructure.

To meet business requirements, vCNS can quickly add the security service to exactly where it is needed without hardware upgrades. It provides the virtual extensible local area network (VXLAN) technology, which can form an overlay network on the existing network. With VXLAN, vCNS can cross physical network boundaries. In this way, it is more elastic to allocate computing resources across clusters. VXLAN can be used to automatically scale up or scale down the network service to react to business changes.

Protecting the business-critical IT infrastructure requires finer traffic flow control and monitoring. By providing the gateway for the network, vCNS has the advantage for better network traffic control and monitoring. It is easier for vCNS to enforce the rules to control the network traffic. When the virtual machines are migrated from one host server to another host server, vCNS allows the security measures enforced on the virtual machine to be carried with the virtual machine.

vCNS is built on top of the vSphere Distributed Switch, which can connect virtual machines hosted by multiple Elastic Sky X Integrated (ESXi) hosts. Therefore, vCNS is fully integrated with vCenter Server and vCloud Director. vCNS links vCloud Director to vCenter Server so that it can take advantage of this integration. It can control and monitor security services across vCenter Server and vCloud Director. The integration can simplify the service deployment and management. It works seamlessly with the existing private cloud hosted on vCloud Director. vCNS can be used to support load balancing across multiple clusters. It can also be used to improve network security and performance by including some third-party services.

In a virtualized IT infrastructure, vCNS can be used to control remote access. It can be used to verify if a user can log on to a virtual machine. A virtual machine can be isolated so that no user can access it without being authenticated by vCNS. Once a user logs on to a virtual machine, vCNS only allows the user to use certain applications authorized to the user. Unauthorized users are prevented from accessing the data stored in an organization's datacenter.

10.3 vCNS Architecture

vCNS is used for centralized network and security management in a cloud environment. It consists of two types of virtual devices: (1) firewall and (2) edge gateway.

These devices can also be used for connecting to third-party devices.

The edge gateway device routes the network traffic between two networks. It controls network traffic to enter and leave a virtual datacenter (VDC). It provides several security mechanisms such as the IPsec site-to-site VPN and stateful inspection firewall. It can be configured to provide services such as NAT, static routing, DHCP, and the domain name system (DNS). The edge gateway can also be used for load balancing.

While the edge gateway is used to protect a network, the app firewall can be quickly deployed to protect a critical app within the network. The firewall device provides protection for apps such as virtual machines and other objects in a private cloud. The firewall device examines the network traffic in and out of an app and determines if the network traffic is allowed to pass the firewall based on the firewall rules.

Figure 10.1 illustrates the architecture of vCNS.

vCNS includes the following major components: (a) vShield Manager, (b) vShield Edge, (c) vShield App, and (d) vShield Endpoint. The following briefly describes these components.

vShield Manager: It is the management and control software for vShield. Through the Web interface, a user can deploy, configure, and monitor all other vShield components. It can also be used to manage the plug-ins for vCenter Server. The administrator can install, configure, and run vShield Manager on different ESXi hosts.

vShield Edge: By using vShield Edge, one can isolate virtual networks from each other in a multitenant environment to improve security and performance and efficiently use IP addresses. vShield Edge can also isolate port groups to protect them. It provides the security measures to protect a VDC. vShield Edge has external and internal network interfaces. It can be connected to external networks through the uplink port group. Through vShield Edge, services such as load balancing, NAT, and VPN can communicate with the external networks. If there is only a single external IP address, the network traffic will be overlaid to that eternal IP address. For better performance, multiple external IP addresses should be used to implement the services.

vShield Edge can be deployed with a port group or a virtual local area network (VLAN). When deployed with the port group, vShield Edge isolates a network from other networks. In an isolated network, the virtual machines can communicate with each other in the same network. However, the network traffic in and out of the network will be controlled by vShield Edge. When vShield Edge is deployed with a VLAN, the virtual machines in the VLAN are isolated by the vShield Edge. Figure 10.2 shows an example of vShield Edge.

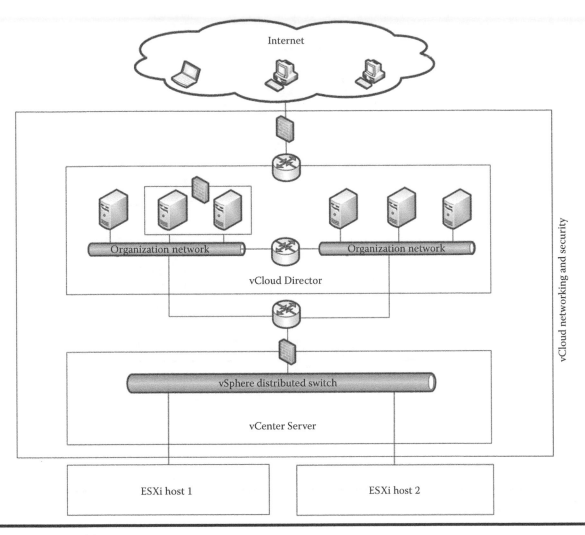

Figure 10.1   vCNS architecture.

vShield Edge provides network gateway services such as the firewall, DHCP, VPN, NAT, and load balancing. The following briefly describes these services:

- *Stateful firewall:* A stateful firewall is a second-generation firewall. Aside from using the criteria such as the IP address, port, and protocol, the stateful firewall uses the data and connection state as its acceptance criteria. The vShield Edge stateful firewall can be configured to allow or block the network traffic in and out of an isolated network. It can be used to block the network traffic based on a set of source or destination IP addresses. It can also block certain network protocols such as Hypertext Transfer Protocol (HTTP), File Transfer Protocol (FTP), Internet Control Message Protocol (ICMP), and so on.
- *Dynamic Host Configuration Protocol:* This service can automatically assign an IP address to a virtual machine. It can specify a range of IP addresses to be assigned and a range of IP addresses to be reserved. In addition to IP addresses, it provides other parameters to a virtual machine, including the IP of a gateway, IPs of DNS servers, and search domains. It can assign an IP address that matches the hardware address of a virtual machine so that the virtual machine has a permanent IP address.
- *Network address translation:* This service is used to translate a private IP address to a public IP address so that the virtual machine on the private network can have access to the Internet. A source NAT is used to translate a private internal IP address to a public IP address, and a destination NAT is used to translate a public IP address to a private internal IP address.
- *Virtual private network:* It is a network technology that creates a VPN over a public network such as the Internet. vShield Edge supports a site-to-site IPSec VPN, which connects a vShield Edge instance at a remote site. The VPN is protected by security measures

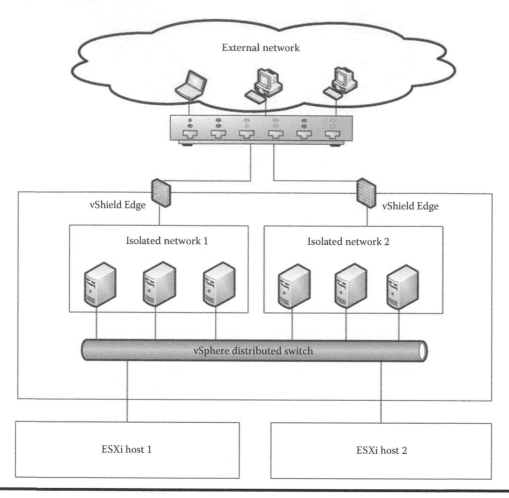

Figure 10.2   vShield Edge.

such as encryption and authentication provided by the protocol IPSec.

■ *Web load balancer:* The load balancer is designed for load balancing for the HTTP. With the load balancer, the computing resources can be redistributed among Web applications.

vShield App: vShield App is a firewall used for protecting virtual machines and virtual apps. vShield App provides a cost-effective solution without reconfiguring the existing network. This component can be used to implement an IP-based stateful firewall and a gateway in the application layer of a network infrastructure. This vShield App–based firewall has the advantage that it does not require network modifications of IP addresses. Another vShield App advantage is that it can be used to create a custom container known as a security group. The security container can be formed by placing the firewall on individual virtual network interface cards (NICs) of virtual machines. By doing so, it can provide a broad range of protection for the applications running on those virtual machines. It can be used to control the access to the virtual

machines or datastores. Hence, it prevents attacks from the Internet or from other internal or external networks.

vShield App is widely applied in the virtualized IT infrastructure. For example, in an isolated network, as shown in Figure 10.3, remote access from the Internet is not allowed. In such a case, vShield App can be used to create a demilitarized zone (DMZ), which is a network section between the Internet and the secured internal network. The vShield App firewall rules have a higher priority than the firewall rules provided by vShield Edge. vShield App checks each traffic session against the priority order in the firewall rule table. The vShield App firewall rules will be enforced first. The network traffic from the Internet can only reach the DMZ. The DMZ prevents the Internet traffic from directly getting to the isolated internal network.

As another example, the firewall rules provided by vShield App can be applied to a security group container. The members of a security group will all be protected by the firewall rules. There is no need to create rules for an individual member or individual protocol. This can significantly simplify the firewall configuration. The membership of a security group can be altered dynamically. This feature can further simplify

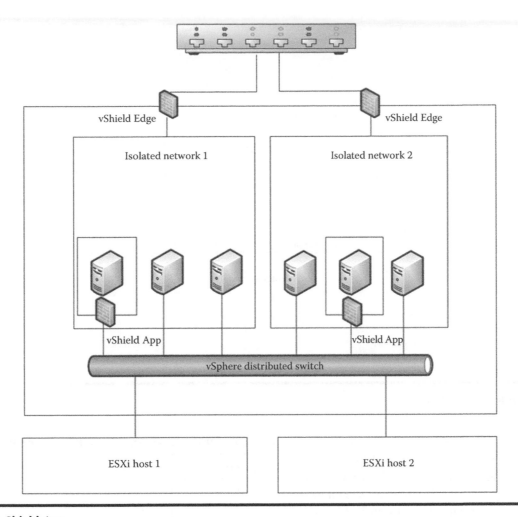

Figure 10.3   vShield App.

the firewall configuration since it is not required to rewrite the firewall rules as the members move in and out of a security group container. Figure 10.3 illustrates vShield App.

In Figure 10.3, although the servers protected by vShield App are connected to the same isolated network, vShield App limits the access from other servers in the same network.

vShield Endpoint: To protect virtual machines from viruses and malware, vShield Endpoint provides a virus-scanning engine. vShield Endpoint also stores the antivirus signature, which can be continuously updated. vShield Endpoint provides interfaces that allow a third-party tool to be used to protect virtual machines with antimalware, intrusion prevention, and deep packet inspection. Third-party tools can also be used for file scanning and memory and process scanning. The antivirus and antimalware activities are logged for troubleshooting or for further analysis. Figure 10.4 illustrates the vShield Endpoint architecture.

vShield Endpoint supports multiple third-party partners. Each partner has its own virus-scanning mechanism. The searching and filtering algorithms are used to catch viruses.

To reduce the burden of searching, some of the partners may only check the files that have been modified recently. Once a virus is detected, the partners have their own ways to remove the virus. For example, some of them will delete the infected file, and others will quarantine the virus, and still others may attempt to clean up the infected file.

10.4 vCNS Implementation

vShield Manager is the software that manages the components of vShield. vShield Manager can be downloaded from VMware's Web site. VMware provides a wizard to assist the installation. VMware also provides the ready-made vShield Manager server, which is built on a virtual machine called appliance. All the components of vShield Manager can be packaged into an Open Virtualization Appliance (OVA) file, which contains all the vShield components. The use of the appliance can simplify the implementation of vCNS for small projects. The deployment of the appliance is straightforward.

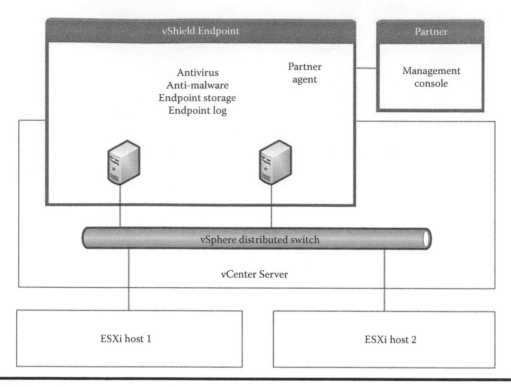

Figure 10.4 vShield Endpoint.

During the implementation of vCNS, it is required that at least one vShield Manager is installed for each vCenter. vShield Edge should be implemented for a port group or a VLAN. vShield App or vShield Endpoint should be implemented for a security group hosted by an ESXi host server. Approximately, a vCNS appliance is required to meet the requirements shown in Table 10.1.

During the installation process, the user needs to provide the information about the name of vShield Manager and the ESXi host server to be connected. Once the vShield Manager OVA file is deployed, it needs to be enabled. The virtual NIC and network need to be configured to connect to vShield Manager. For better security, vShield Manager should be connected to an isolated management network that links to the vCenter Server. Once connected to the vCenter Server, vCNS can be configured through vCenter. In vCenter, the vShield Manager can view the inventory that contains the ESXi host server, virtual NIC, and virtual machines. vShield Manager can also be accessed through a Web interface. Through the Web page, a user can specify the network settings such as the DNS service and Network Time Protocol (NTP) service. The user can also configure the network segments and specify the multicasting process.

As vShield Edge is used to control the network traffic between two networks; two network interfaces, one for the internal network and one for the external network, should be configured for it. The internal network interface is connected to a port group on a virtual switch. For

Table 10.1 vCNS Appliance Requirements

Item	Component	Requirement
Memory	vShield Manager	8 GB
	vShield Edge	Small: 256 MB, large: 1 GB
	vShield App	1 GB
	vShield Data Security	512 MB
Disk space	vShield Manager	60 GB
	vShield Edge	Small: 320 MB, large: 4.4 GB
	vShield App	5 GB/host server
	vShield Data Security	6 GB/host server
Virtual central processing unit (CPU)	vShield Manager	2
	vShield Edge	Small: 1, large: 2
	vShield App	2
	vShield Data Security	1

virtual machines on a network formed with the port group, vShield Edge is the gateway for accessing the external network. The internal network interface should be configured with the IP address and subnet mask that match the internal network. The external network interface is connected to the external network. The external network can be a company's physical network, or the Internet, or an uplink network formed by another port group. Like the configuration of the internal network interface, the configuration of the external network interface is also required to match the external network specifications. When vShield Edge provides multiple network services such as the VPN, NAT, and load balancing, multiple external network interfaces can be configured for better performance. vShield Edge can have as many as 10 virtual network interfaces. A firewall can also be configured on vShield Edge. The default setting of a firewall blocks all the incoming network traffic. vShield Edge can also be configured to run simultaneously on two servers for high availability so that it can always provide service.

vShield App is basically used to protect a virtual machine container by setting up firewalls. A virtual machine container can be a datacenter, a cluster, or a security group. The firewalls prevent attacks from the outside of a virtual machine container or between two containers. They can be configured to control network traffic flow and monitor the traffic in and out of a virtual machine container.

The firewall rules are enforced based on the container level at the datacenter, cluster, and security group. At the datacenter level, the rules configured at the datacenter are also applied to the cluster level and the security group level. Similarly, the rules configured at the cluster level can also be applied to the security group containers within the cluster. Therefore, one needs to make sure that the rules configured at the lower level do not conflict with the rules configured at the higher level. At each container level, one can configure the default rule that allows or denies all network traffic. When the default rule is set to allow all network traffic, special rules can be configured to deny some network traffic when certain conditions are met. On the other hand, when the default rule is set to deny all network traffic, special rules can be configured to allow some network traffic when certain conditions are met. For example, when the datacenter-level default rule is set to deny all network traffic, the administrator should create some special rules to allow HTTP traffic in and out of the datacenter. Rules should also be created to allow the DNS and DHCP traffic in and out of the security group container if the DNS and DHCP servers are created outside the security group container.

Through vShield Endpoint, IT administrators can manage antivirus and antimalware policies for virtualized environments. After vShield Manager is installed and connected to vCenter, it enables the functionality needed to manage vShield Endpoint. To manage the antivirus and antimalware policies supplied by third-party vendors, vShield Endpoint provides the following components:

- A third party–secure virtual device
- A thin agent used to offload tasks such as file, memory, and process scanning from virtual machines to the third party–secure virtual device
- A vShield Endpoint Elastic Sky X module to enable communication between the first two components so that the virus-scanning activities can be offloaded to the secure virtual device

For the configuration and management of a third party–secure virtual device, a management console is provided by the VMware partner. By doing so, there is no need for the IT infrastructure administrator to frequently update the antivirus software on each virtual machine. vShield Endpoint can significantly reduce the IT administrator's workload by offloading the antivirus agent to the third party–secure virtual device.

Now that you have learned about vCNS, the following hands-on activity is provided to illustrate the installation of vCNS. The hands-on activity also shows how to configure vCNS to get ready for the private cloud computing environment.

10.5 Activity 1: Implementing vCNS

In this activity, the following tasks will be performed:

- *Task 1:* Installing VMware vShield Manager appliance
- *Task 2:* Configuring vShield Manager

10.5.1 Task 1: Installing VMware vShield Manager Appliance

As a centralized network management component of vCNS, vShield Manager provides security protection of VDCs and cloud environments. vShield Manager can be distributed as a prebuilt appliance. In the first task, you will install the vShield Manager appliance in vCenter.

1. On the desktop, right-click the icon of VMware Workstation and select **Run as Administrator**.
2. Start the virtual machines in the order of DC, Storage, LabESXi1, LabESXi2, and vc.
3. Log on to **DC**. From vSphere Client, and log on to **vCenter**. Once logged on to vCenter, click the **labesxi1.lab.local** node, click the **Configuration** tab, click **Storage** in the Hardware pane, and then click

the **Rescan All** link, as shown in Figure 10.5. (Note: If there is an error, you may need to restart the vc server. Then, log on to vc through vSphere Client again.)

4. Do the same for labesxi2.lab.local.
5. Your next job is to deploy vShield Manager. To do so, click the **File** menu and select **Deploy OVF Template**, as shown in Figure 10.6.
6. On the Source page, click the **Browse** button (Figure 10.7).
7. Assume that the vShield Manager appliance file is saved in the Documents folder; select the **OVA** file in the Open dialog and click **Open**, as shown in Figure 10.8. After the file is open, click **Next**.
8. On the OVF Template Details page, click **Next**.
9. On the Accept License Agreement page, click **Accept**, and then click **Next**.
10. On the Name and Location page, take the name **vShield** and select **Datacenter**, as shown in Figure 10.9. Then, click **Next**.
11. On the Resource Pool page, select **Cluster**, as shown in Figure 10.10, and click **Next**.

12. On the Storage page, select **dstore1**, as shown in Figure 10.11, and click **Next**.
13. On the Disk Format page, check the option **Thin Provision** (Figure 10.12). Then, click **Next**.
14. On the Properties page, enter your password such as **Passw0rd!** (Figure 10.13). Then, click **Next**.
15. On the Ready to Complete page, click **Finish**.
16. Once the installation is complete, you should be able to see the newly installed vShield Manager named **vShield** (Figure 10.14).

10.5.2 Task 2: Configuring vShield Manager

Once vShield Manager is installed, your next task is to configure vShield Manager so that it can be connected to the network VMnet2.

1. As vShield Manager takes a lot of resources, our first step is to adjust some resource usage. Assume that you are still logged on to vCenter through vSphere Client. Right-click the **Cluster** node and select **Edit Settings** (Figure 10.15).

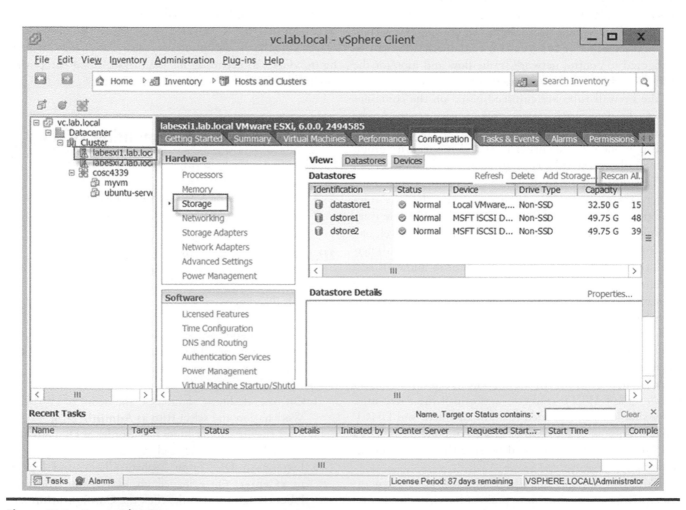

Figure 10.5 Rescanning Storage.

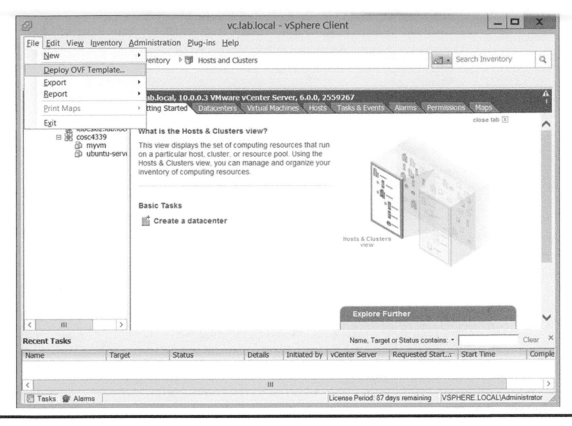

Figure 10.6   Deploying OVF Template.

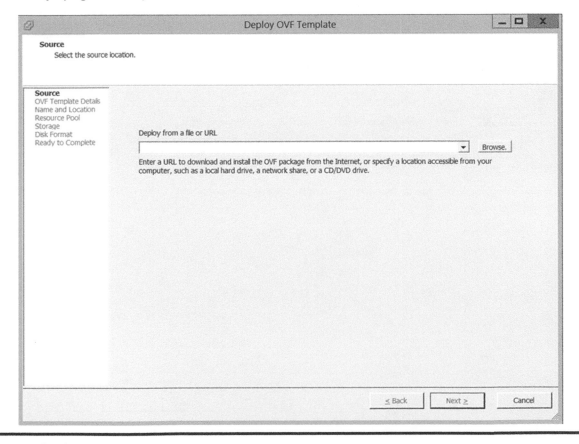

Figure 10.7   Selecting Source.

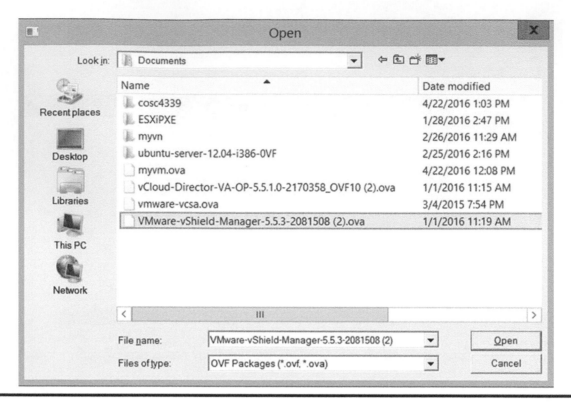

Figure 10.8   Opening OVA file.

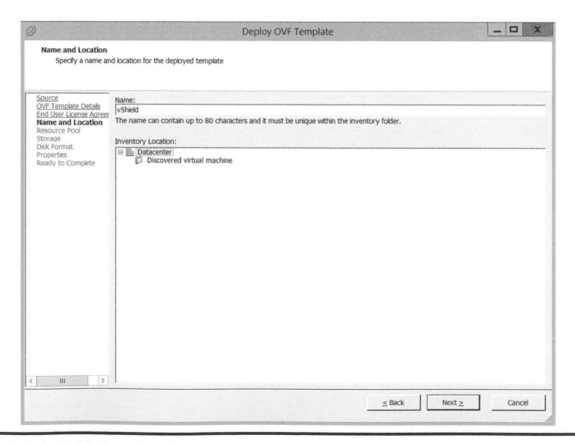

Figure 10.9   Selecting Name and Location.

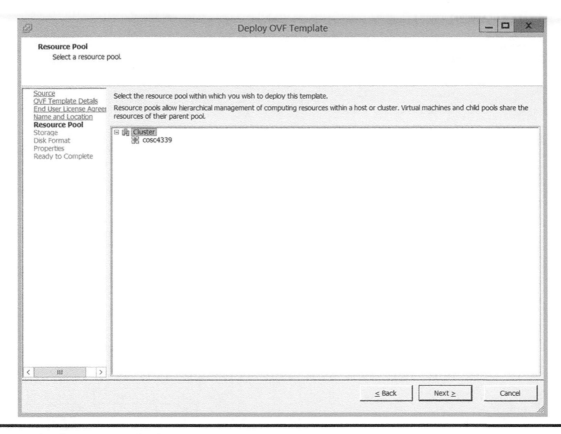

Figure 10.10 Selecting Resource Pool.

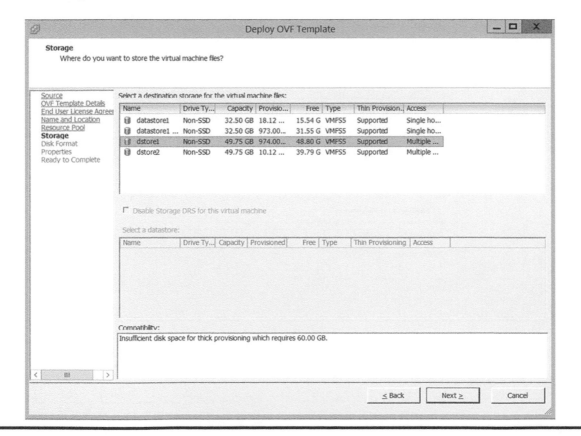

Figure 10.11 Selecting datastore.

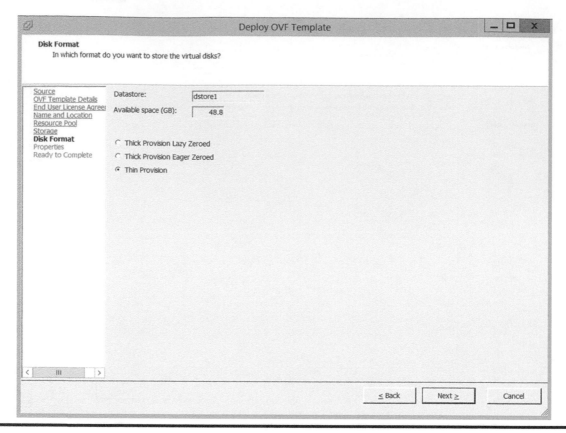

Figure 10.12 Specifying Disk Format.

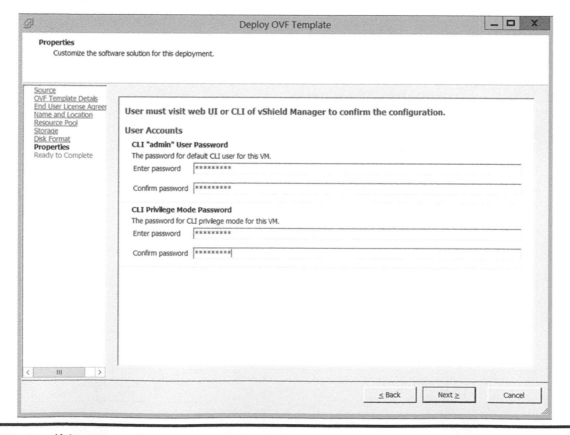

Figure 10.13 Specifying Password.

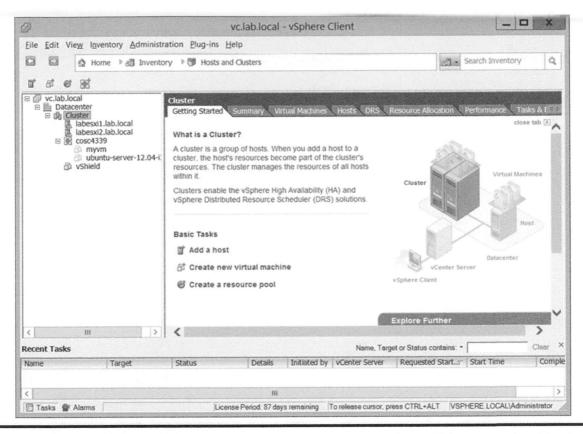

Figure 10.14 Newly installed vShield Manager.

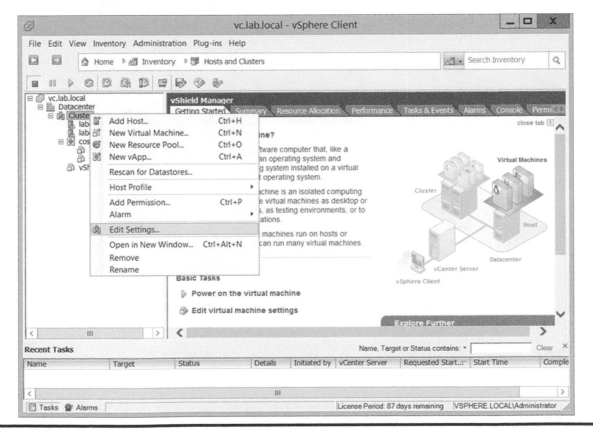

Figure 10.15 Editing cluster settings.

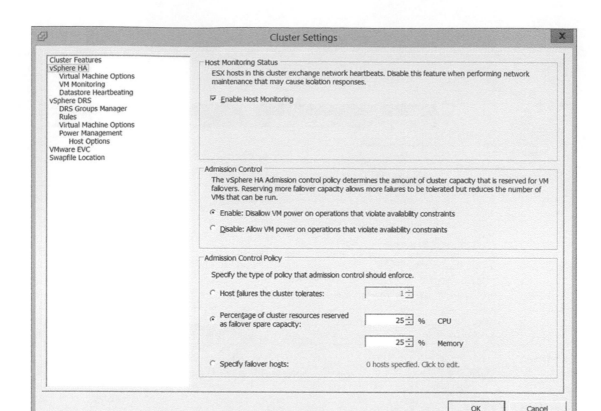

Figure 10.16 Adjusting reserved CPU and memory resources.

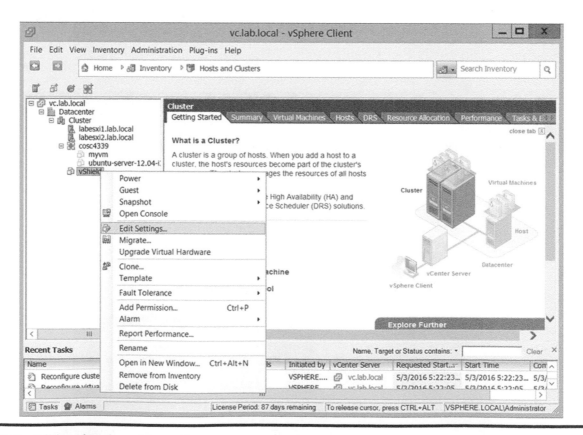

Figure 10.17 Editing virtual machine settings.

2. In the Cluster Settings dialog, click the node **vSphere HA** and click the option **Percentage of cluster resources reserved as failover spare capacity**. Specify the reserved CPU and Memory, each as **25%** (Figure 10.16). Then, click **OK**.

3. To reduce the memory usage of vShield Manager, right-click the virtual machine **vShield** and select **Edit Settings**, as shown in Figure 10.17.

4. In the vShield—Virtual Machine Properties dialog, adjust the memory size to **4GB**, as shown in Figure 10.18. Then, click **OK**.

5. Click the **Resources** tab. Click **Memory** and change the memory reservation to **0**, as shown in Figure 10.19. Then, click **OK**.

6. To power on vShield Manager, right-click **vShield** and select **Power** and then **Power on**, as shown in Figure 10.20.

7. Once vShield Manager is powered on, right-click **vShield Manager** and select **Open Console**, as shown in Figure 10.21.

8. In the console, log on vShield Manager with the default user name **admin** and your password (Figure 10.22).

9. Enter the command

   ```
   enable
   ```

   and press the **Enter** key. When prompted, enter your password and press the **Enter** key.

10. Run the command

    ```
    setup
    ```

    to configure vShield Manager, as shown in Figure 10.23. When prompted to save the configuration, enter **y** and

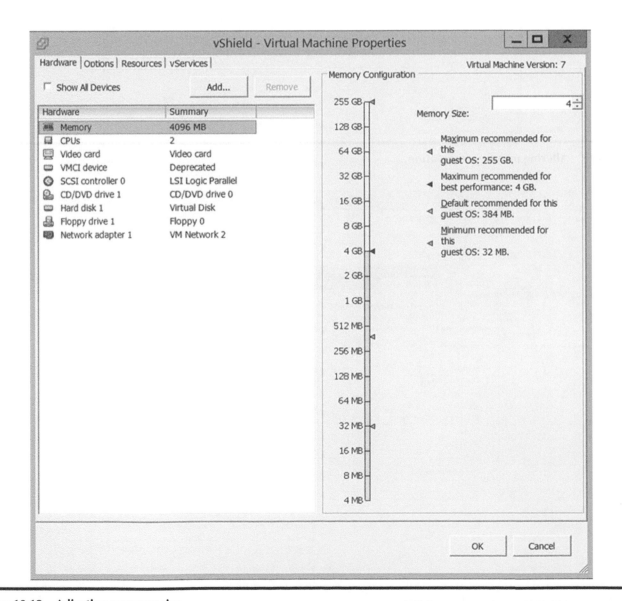

Figure 10.18   Adjusting memory size.

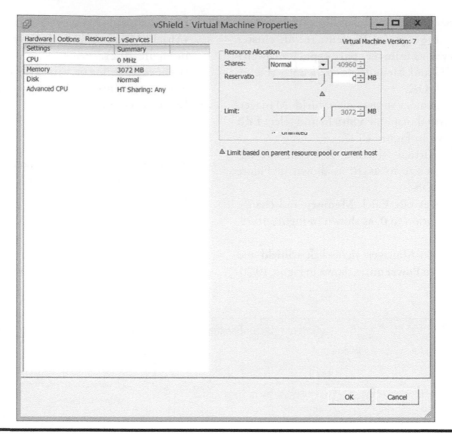

Figure 10.19   Altering memory reservation.

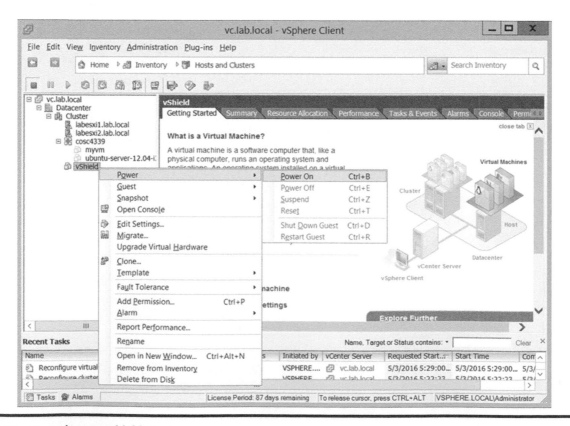

Figure 10.20   Powering on vShield Manager.

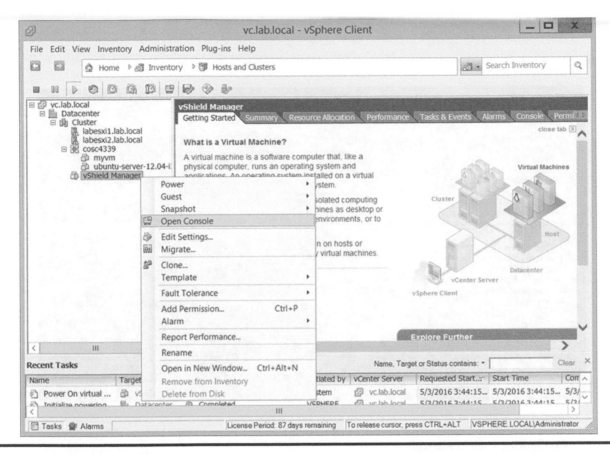

Figure 10.21 Opening console.

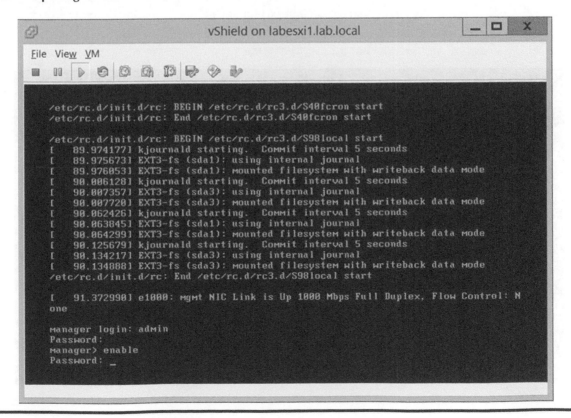

Figure 10.22 Logging on to vShield Manager.

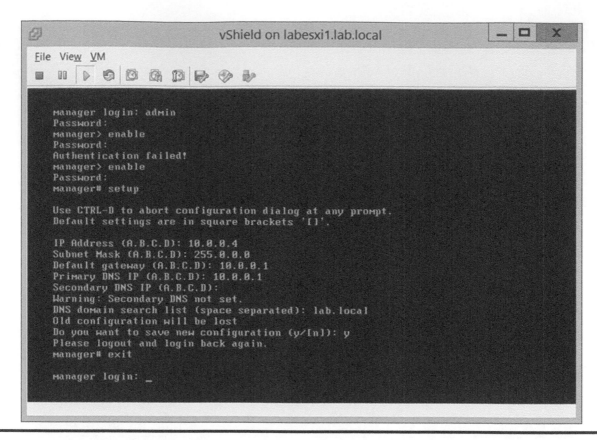

Figure 10.23 Configuring vShield Manager.

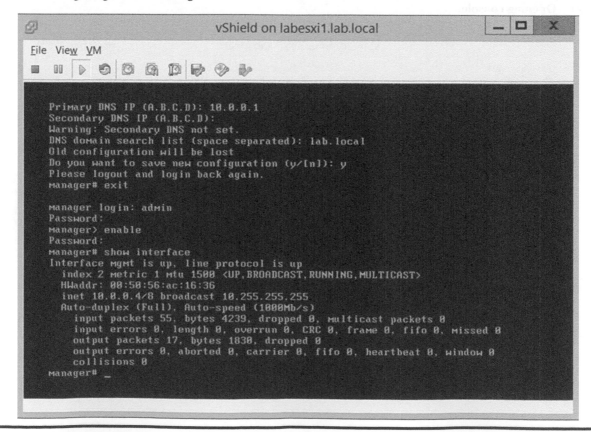

Figure 10.24 Showing interface.

press the **Enter** key. When prompted to log out, enter **exit** and press the **Enter** key.

11. Log on to vShield Manager again as **admin** and run the command **enable**. Once vShield Manager is enabled, run the following command, as shown in Figure 10.24:

```
show interface
```

12. Run the command **exit** to log out. Then, close the console.

13. You may need to add a DNS record for vShield Manager. To do so, on the Server Manager page of the DC server, click **Tools** and select **DNS**. In the DNS Manager dialog, right-click the lab.local node and select **New Host**, as shown in Figure 10.25.

14. In the New Host dialog, enter **vShield** as the name and **10.0.0.4** as the IP address (Figure 10.26). Make sure the option **Create associated pointer (PTR) record** is checked. Click **Add Host**. Once the DNS record is added, exit DNS Manager.

15. To check if the vShield Manager can be accessed from a Web browser, start **Chrome** and enter the Uniform Resource Locator **https://10.0.0.4**, as shown in Figure 10.27. Click the **Advanced** link and click the **Proceed to 10.0.0.4** link.

16. Log on to vShield Manager with the user name **admin** and the default password **default** (Figure 10.28).

17. Next, you need to configure Lookup Service, which is hosted by your vCenter Server. To do so, click the **Edit** button for Lookup Service, as shown in Figure 10.29.

18. In the Lookup Service Information dialog, click the check box **Configure Lookup Service**. Enter the information about the vCenter Server, as shown in Figure 10.30. Then, click **OK**. (Note: If there is an error, you may need to restart the vCenter Server.)

19. You should be able to see that the vCenter Server is connected, as shown in Figure 10.31.

20. To configure the vCenter Server, click the **Edit** button. Enter the information, as shown in Figure 10.32. Here, the Active Directory user **lab\student** is entered, and the password is **Passw0rd!**. Then, click **OK**.

21. As shown in Figure 10.33, vCenter is configured.

22. To synchronize the machine between vCenter and vShield Manager, you need to configure vShield Manager to use the same NTP server as the one used by vCenter. To do so, click the **Edit** button for the NTP server.

23. In the NTP Server Information dialog, enter the IP address of the NTP server, as shown in Figure 10.34. Then, click **OK**.

24. Before you leave the configuration of vShield Manager, you need to change the default password. Click the **Change Password** link on the top part of the screen.

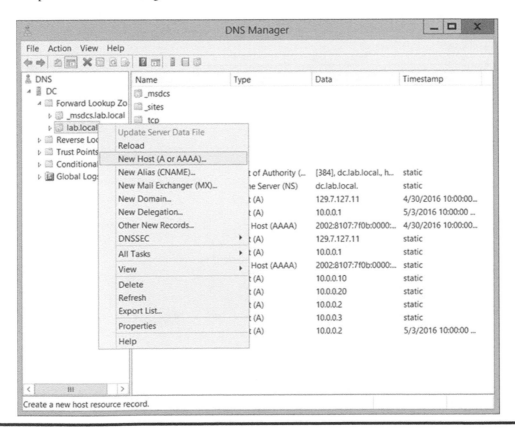

Figure 10.25   New Host.

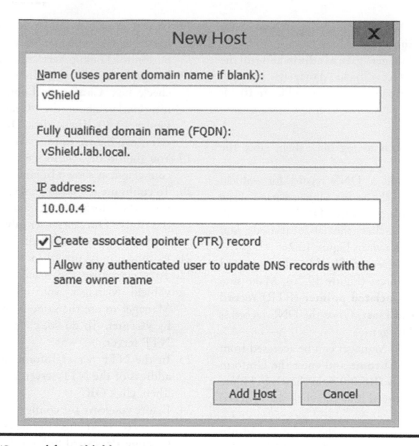

Figure 10.26   New DNS record for vShield.

Figure 10.27   Connecting to vShield Manager.

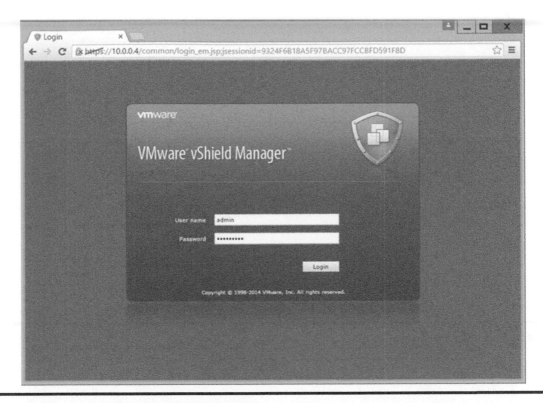

Figure 10.28 Logging on to vShield Manager through browser.

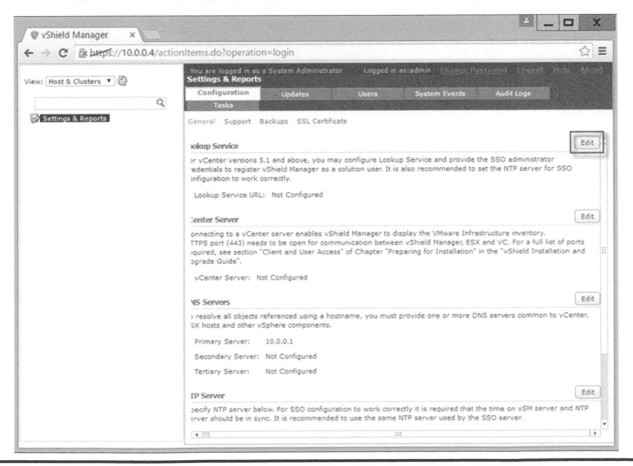

Figure 10.29 Editing Lookup Service.

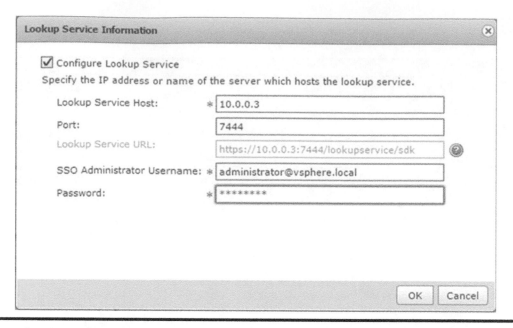

Figure 10.30   Configuring Lookup Service.

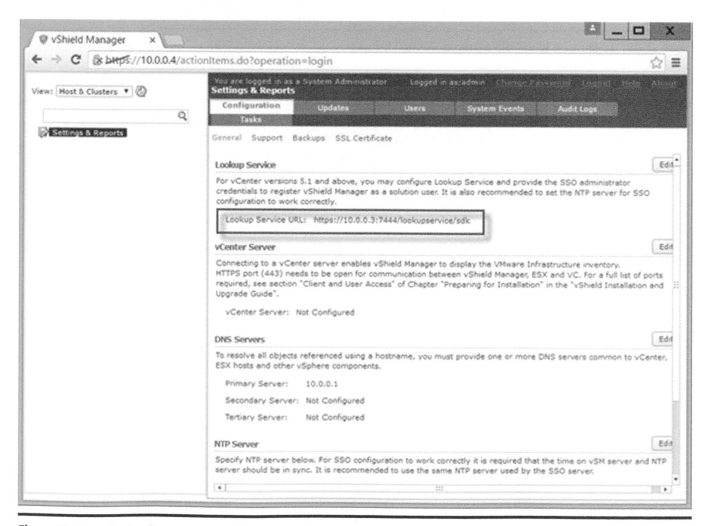

Figure 10.31   vCenter Server connected.

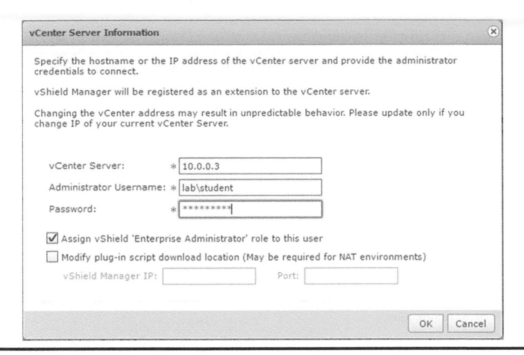

Figure 10.32   vCenter Server information.

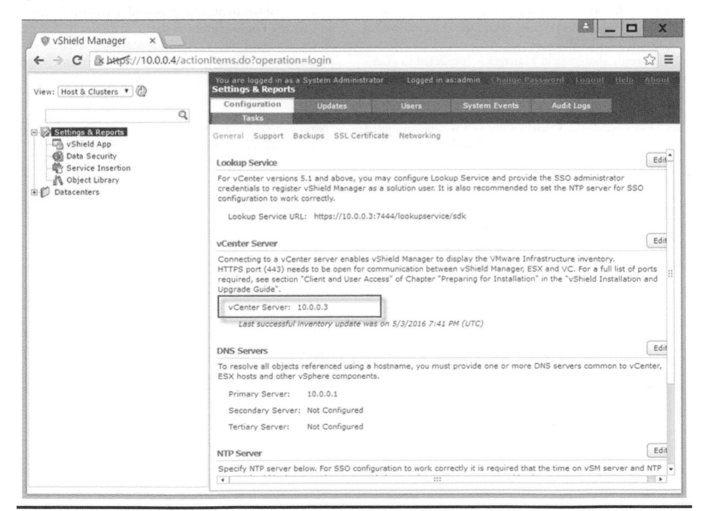

Figure 10.33   Configured vCenter.

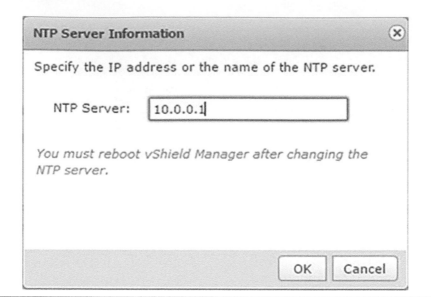

Figure 10.34 NTP Server Information.

Enter **default** as the old password and your new password (Figure 10.35). Then, click **OK**. You can now log out of vShield Manager.

25. To verify that vShield Manager is connected to vCenter, log on to vCenter through vSphere Client. On the Home page, you should be able to see the vShield icon shown in Figure 10.36.
26. Double-click the **vShield** icon; you will be prompted to enter the user name and password. Enter the user name **lab\student** and password **Passw0rd!**. Then, click the **Login** button, as shown in Figure 10.37.
27. Once logged on to vShield Manager, expand the Datacenter node; you will see the hosts and vApp cosc4339 connected to vCenter (Figure 10.38).

Now, vShield Manager is installed and configured. It is ready to provide the network security for vCloud Director.

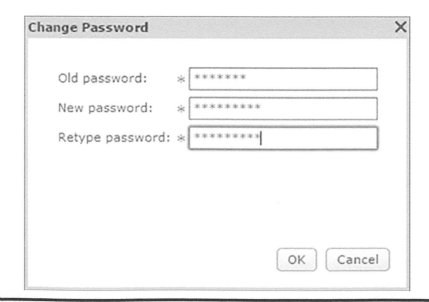

Figure 10.35 Changing default password.

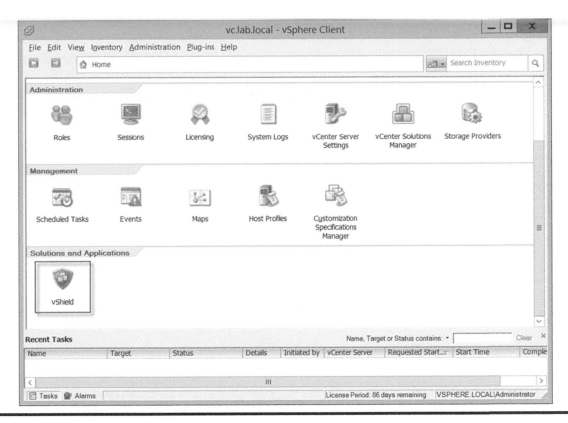

Figure 10.36 vShield Manager connected to vCenter.

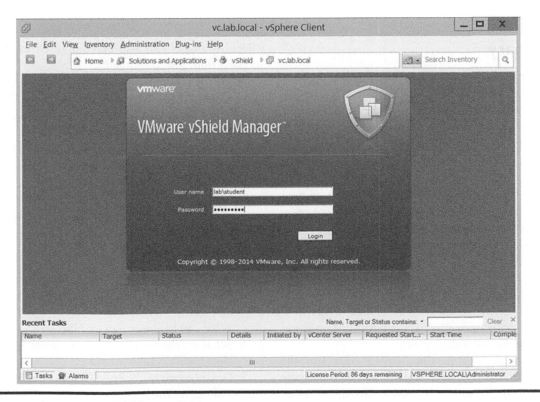

Figure 10.37 Logging on to vShield from vCenter.

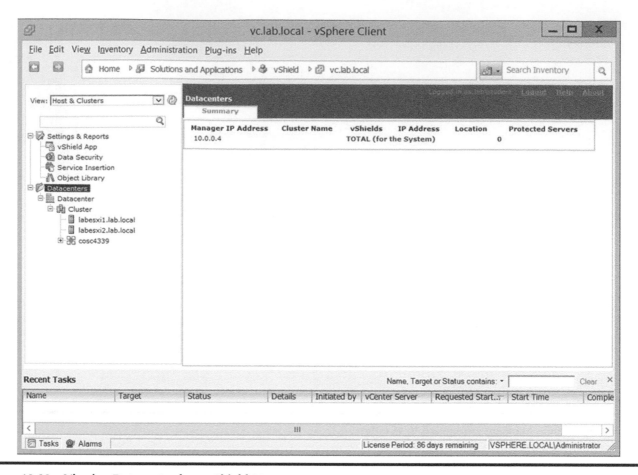

Figure 10.38 Viewing Datacenter from vShield Manager.

10.6 Summary

This chapter provides an overview about vCNS. It illustrates how vCNS can be used to efficiently manage remote access, isolate users' networks from each other, and protect the private cloud. vCNS provides security shields to protect virtual machines and virtual networks. vCNS centralizes the network and security management in a cloud environment. It accomplishes the task with two types of virtual devices: (1) firewall and (2) edge gateway. The firewall can be used to control the network traffic between vApps, between organizations' networks, or between a virtual network and a physical network. The edge gateway is used to control the network traffic that enters and leaves a VDC. This chapter also introduces other vCNS components such as vShield App and vShield Endpoint. An overview about vCNS implementation is also given in this chapter. vShield Manager is introduced. The chapter provides detailed information about vShield Manager appliance deployment.

The hands-on activity in this chapter illustrates the installation of vShield Manager appliance. Once properly configured, vShield Manager is accessible through vCenter.

vShield Manager can also be configured so that it can be accessed from a Web browser.

After the configuration is completed, vShield Manager will be ready for vCloud Director. During the implementation of vCloud Director, the edge gateway will be used to isolate an organization's network from other organizations' networks. The edge gateway can also be used to isolate the virtual network from the physical network. With vShield Manager, IT administrators can create firewall, VPN, and NAT services for remote access. The topics related to vCloud Director will be covered in the next chapter.

REVIEW QUESTIONS

1. What security issues may a virtualized IT infrastructure face?
2. What can be done with vCNS?
3. What are the security services provided by vCNS?
4. How does VXLAN work?
5. Describe how vCNS performs finer traffic flow control and monitoring.

6. What are the advantages of linking vCloud Director to vCenter Server with vCNS?

7. How does vCNS control remote access?

8. What types of virtual devices are included in vCNS?

9. What are the usages of an edge gateway?

10. What are the usages of a firewall device in vCNS?

11. What are the major components of vCNS?

12. What do you do with vShield Manager?

13. What can be done with vShield Edge?

14. How can vShield Edge be deployed?

15. What is a stateful firewall, and how does it work in vCNS?

16. What are the usages of NAT in vCNS?

17. What are the usages of a VPN in vCNS?

18. What do you do with vShield App?

19. What can be done with vShield Endpoint?

20. What components are provided by vShield Endpoint to manage the antivirus and antimalware policies?

Chapter 11

vCloud Director

Objectives

- Understand vCloud Director (vCD)
- Install and configure vCD
- Implement cloud services with vCD

11.1 Introduction

Previously, the components of VMware vCloud Suite such as Elastic Sky X Integrated (ESXi) and vCenter have been used to create a virtualized information technology (IT) infrastructure. The virtualized IT infrastructure consists of datacenters, clusters, ESXi hosts, virtual machines (VMs), and vApps. It provides a platform for implementing a cloud computing environment. Cloud computing provides on-demand services such as software as a service (SaaS), platform as a service (PaaS), and infrastructure as a service (IaaS). The following are requirements for a cloud computing environment:

- It should be accessible to cloud subscribers anywhere and anytime.
- It should provide resources based on cloud service subscribers' demands.
- It should provide flexible and scalable services for fast provisioning.
- It should provide a billing system for the use of the services.
- It should allow each cloud service subscriber to work in its own secure and exclusive computing environment.

In the VMware vCloud Suite package, vCloud Director (vCD) is such software used to fulfill these requirements. vCD provides a provider virtual datacenter (vDC), which can be used to define a resource pool for a cloud provider. The resource pool may include datastores, virtual networks, central processing units (CPUs), memory, and so on. On top of the provider vDC, multiple organization vDCs can be created. For example, for each cloud subscriber, vCD can be used to create an organization vDC (which is a portion of one or more provider vDCs) specially designed for a cloud subscriber. With the resources allocated in the organization vDC, the subscriber can create vApps that are virtualized IT infrastructures, each of which consists of a group of VMs connected with virtual networks.

In an organization, a catalog can be created to store the templates of vApps that can be shared by the users within the organization or, if allowed, shared cross multiple organizations. In the organization, an isolated computing environment can be created for each cloud subscriber. By connecting to vCenter, vCD can obtain computing resources such as hosts, datastores, and port groups, needed for a resource pool for the provider vDC. However, the administrator of vCD cannot view or administrate the vCenter.

A cloud subscriber can access its own organization through a Web browser such as Chrome. One area of vCD that needs to be improved is the Web portal used to interact with vCD. The Web portal is not flexible enough, so the cloud subscriber cannot customize it for its business activities. vCD also lacks some features for automating the provisioning of the subscriber's IT infrastructure. At the time of writing this book, the software VMware vRealize Automation has been included in VMware vCloud Suite. However, the VMware vCloud Suite for academic users still includes only vCD. Therefore, you will work on vCD in the hands-on practice. VMware vRealize Automation also provides Resource Reservation similar to Organization in vCD, Service Blueprint similar to Catalog in vCD, and so on. Once available, VMware vRealize Automation can be used to integrate vCD. vCD vApps and templates can be imported into vRealize Automation and made available to cloud subscribers. vRealize Automation considers vCD as its endpoint. In fact, vRealize Automation is designed to deploy and provision cloud services across physical servers, or used to deploy other private and public cloud platforms such as Hyper-V and OpenStack.

11.2 vCD Architecture

As described in Section 11.1, vCD is cloud management software. vCD depends on vCenter to provide computing resources. Figure 11.1 illustrates the relationship between vCenter and vCD.

In Figure 11.1, vCD is used to manage the computing resources for the cloud subscribers. vCenter provides the computing resources for vCD and other internal IT infrastructures. Multiple instances of vCD can be installed on multiple servers. Each vCD server is called a vCD cell and is configured to provide certain cloud services. vCD cells are configured to share the same database. The computing resources for vCD are isolated from the computing resources for the internal IT infrastructure through vShield Manager for better security. The isolation of vCD from vCenter also makes troubleshooting easier. vCD can manage the resources provided by multiple vCenter Servers. By making the computing resources available to subscribers, vCD provides a cloud-based IT infrastructure where the subscribers can carry out their computing tasks.

Based on the needs of cloud subscribers, vCD regroups the computing resources provided by vCenter and delivers the cloud services to the subscribers. By regrouping the computing resources provided by vCenter, vCD can create a vDC. The vDC allows the cloud subscribers to establish

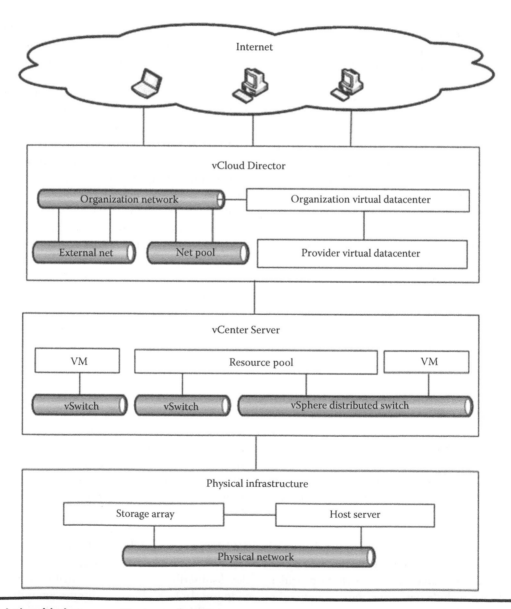

Figure 11.1   Relationship between vCenter and vCD.

their own IT infrastructure including VMs, storage, and network resources. This kind of vDC is scalable based on the needs of the subscribers. A vDC contains the following virtual components.

Provider virtual datacenter: A provider vDC groups computing resources such as ESXi hosts, networks, and memory provided by vCenter with the storage resources provided by datastores to form a resource pool for cloud computing. A provider vDC can collect computing resources from multiple vCenters and collect storage resources from multiple datastores. Through the provider vDC, multiple ESXi hosts can be integrated with multiple storage arrays. A provider vDC can be shared by multiple cloud subscribers. It can be configured to provide three different levels of services: (1) Gold, (2) Silver, and (3) Bronze. Each level of services is configured to guarantee a certain amount of resources.

Organization: For each cloud subscriber, an organization is created for sharing resources and for user management. An organization vDC can collect computing resources from multiple provider vDCs. An organization is the unit for managing a group of users belonging to the same cloud subscriber. The organization serves as a security boundary so that only the users from the same organization can access the computing resources assigned to the organization. By using organizations, vCD can support a secure multitenant computing environment. Figure 11.2 illustrates the relationship between the provider vDC and the organization vDC.

vApp: In an organization, various vApps can be created. A vApp is a container that includes VMs and virtual networks. It can even include other vApps. It can be as simple as a single VM, or it can be built as a multitier client–server infrastructure to support network-based applications such as databases and Web services. If needed, a vApp can be easily cloned to produce multiple copies of the same vApp. A template is a master copy for cloning. Each cloud subscriber can use a template to produce vApps for its cloud users. The vApp is portable so that it can be carried to and run on other virtual infrastructures. To improve portability, the vApp can be exported as an Open Virtualization Format (OVF) or Open Virtual Appliance (OVA) file so that it can be imported to other cloud environments, including clouds created with vSphere, XenServer, or Hyper-V.

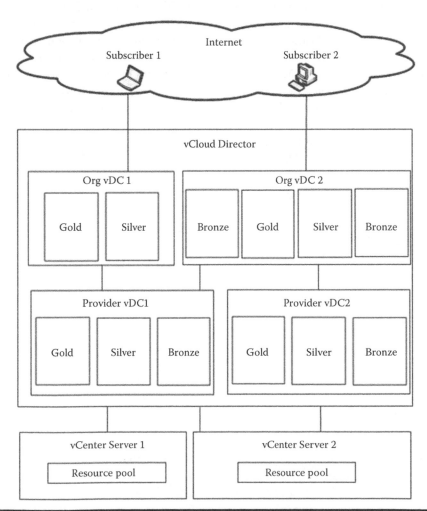

Figure 11.2 Relationship between provider vDC and organization vDC.

Catalog: In an organization, a catalog is used to store templates and vApps. These templates and vApps can be used by cloud subscribers to form their own vApps. The cloud subscribers can also publish their own templates and vApps for the users to share.

11.3 vCD Configuration

vCD is often built in a ready-made appliance that has vCD installed on a Linux VM with the 64-bit SUSE Enterprise operating system and an embedded version of Oracle 11g Express. The appliance is packaged into an OVA file. The OVA file can be downloaded from http://www.vmware.com. The deployment of the vCD appliance is straightforward. Once vCD is installed, there will be a few configuration tasks to be done. The following are some of the configuration tasks.

Connecting to vCenter and vShield Manager: vCD needs to be configured to connect to vCenter and vShield Manager. For vCD to use the computing resources managed by vCenter, vCD has to be attached to vCenter. After vCD is attached to vCenter, the cloud administrator can assign vCenter's resource pools, datastores, and networks to a provider vDC created on vCD. Figure 11.3 illustrates the configuration of the connection to vCenter.

vCD is also required to connect to vShield Manager for network security–related services. Therefore, each instance of vCD requires an instance of vShield Manager. Before the installation of vCD, an instance of vShield Manager should be installed and configured. It is also required that vShield Manager be registered to vCenter. Only after vShield Manager is registered in vCenter, can vCD be connected to vCenter. Through vShield Manager, the cloud administrator can create virtual networks among organizations and vApps. The cloud administrator can also create remote access mechanisms such as firewall, virtual private network (VPN), and network address translation (NAT) services. Figure 11.4 illustrates the configuration of the connection to vShield Manager.

Database configuration: vCD also needs to be configured to be able to access a database. The later version of vCD such as version 5.6.3 supports both Oracle 11g or later and Microsoft (MS) SQL Server 2008 Enterprise or later versions of databases. The database is used by vCD to store and share vCloud information. For database configuration, it is required that a dedicated database schema be created for vCD to use only. It is also required that a database instance and a vCD database user account be created for the installation of vCD. The installation of a vCD appliance does not require the installation and configuration of an Oracle or MS SQL database server. The appliance includes an embedded version of Oracle 11g Express database. The configuration of the database will be done during the installation of vCD. Figure 11.5 illustrates the database configuration during the installation of vCD.

Certificate configuration: To provide cloud services over the Internet, the Secure Sockets Layer (SSL) protocol is used to protect protocols such as Hypertext Transfer Protocol (HTTP).

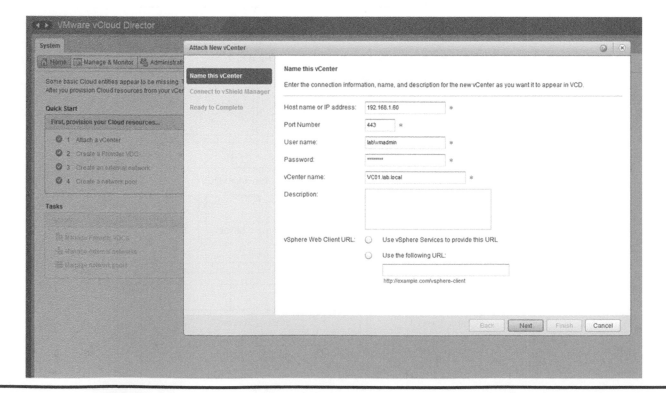

Figure 11.3 Connection to vCenter.

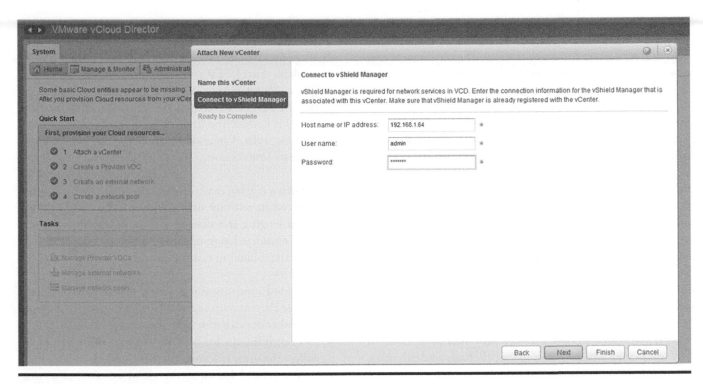

Figure 11.4   Connection to vShield Manager.

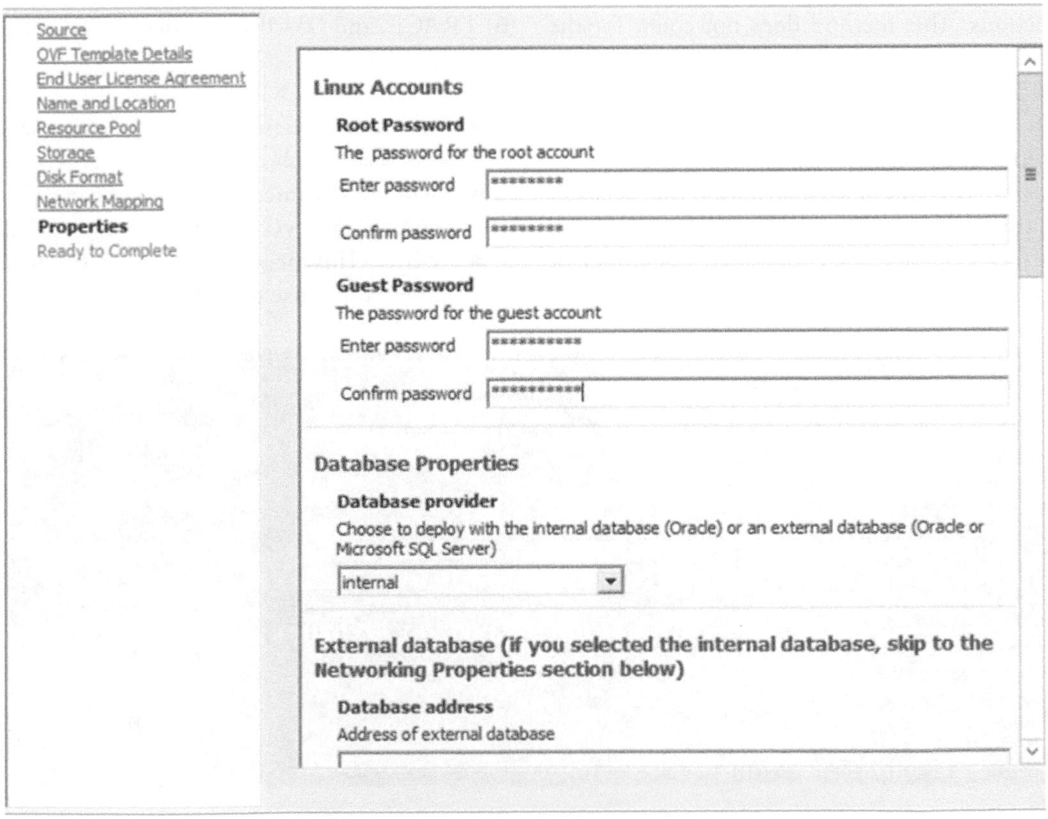

Figure 11.5   Database configuration.

Each vCD needs two SSL connections: one for the HTTP service and one for the console proxy service. vCD requires one certificate for each of these two services. The certificate can be signed by a trusted certification authority such as VeriSign or self-signed. In a production environment, a third-party certificate is required for the implementation of vCD. For self-signed certificates, some Web browsers will post a warning. A certificate creation tool, Java Keytool, is included in vCD. Figure 11.6 illustrates the content in a certificate file.

Multicell configuration: To improve scalability, multiple copies of vCD can be installed to form a server group. Each group member is called a cell. A network-based storage array is often required for a group to share its data. When multiple cells are installed, a load-balancing mechanism is commonly used to balance the workload of the cells. vShield Manager can be used for load balancing when an edge has multiple links connected to it. In a multicell environment, load balancing can be done through four different methods:

1. *IP_hash:* For an edge gateway with multiple uplinks, to determine which uplink to use, IP_hash load balancing performs a mathematical calculation on each network packet, the source IP address, and the destination IP address. In such a way, packets can be distributed to multiple uplinks for better use of the available bandwidth.
2. *Least_conn:* In a multicell environment, this method creates a new connection to the cell that has the fewest connections. This method does not count for the actual amount of network traffic in and out of a cell. Therefore, it may not be great for balancing the load for a cell with less connections, but each connection has a large amount of traffic.
3. *Round_robin:* This method distributes the network traffic in turn based on the weight assigned to each cell. This method does not count for the number of connections to a cell. As it distributes the network traffic in turn, some of the low-capacity cell may get more network traffic than it can handle.
4. *Uniform Resource Identifier (URI):* This method is only available for HTTP service load balancing. A URI is frequently referred to as a Web address. In this method, the left part of a URI (on the left side of the question mark) is hashed and divided by the total weight of the running cells. Once designated, the cell will handle requests from clients.

Centralized logging configuration: As an option, vCD can be configured to relocate its log files to a central location. Centralized logging is a desired feature in a multicell environment. Centralized logging allows the cloud administrator to perform the following tasks:

■ The cloud administrator can view the system log including the current running and failed processes. The cloud administrator can also view the completed tasks.
■ By examining the log files, the cloud administrator can collect the error information for troubleshooting.
■ At the central location, the cloud administrator can analyze the performance of each cell or even each organization.

In vCD, a log file contains seven levels of messages: (1) FATAL, (2) ERROR, (3) WARN, (4) INFO, (5) DEBUG, (6) TRACE, and (7) OFF. The descriptions of these levels are given as follows:

■ *FATAL:* This message level indicates that an event may lead to the crash of vCD.
■ *ERROR:* This message level indicates that an error has occurred, and vCD is still allowed to run.
■ *WARN:* This message level indicates that an event may potentially cause problems to vCD.

Figure 11.6 Content of certificate file.

- *INFO:* This message level provides information about an event.
- *DEBUG:* This message level provides detailed information about the events involved in debugging.
- *TRACE:* This message level traces the events and provides more detailed information about the processes in debugging.
- *OFF:* This message level indicates that logging is turned off.

In a multicell environment, each cell is attached to a vShield Manager. The log file in each vShield Manager can also be sent to the central location.

11.4 vCD Implementation

Once vCD is connected to vCenter, the vCenter resources are available for implementing vCD components such as the provider vDC, organization vDC, vApps, network pools, external networks, organization networks, and vApp networks. Figure 11.7 shows an available vCenter resource pool from vCD.

With the vCenter resource pool available, vCD should be able to access resources such as the ESXi hosts, datastores, and the network. From vCD, one can prepare a host so that it is ready for the provider vDC. Figure 11.8 illustrates two

available ESXi hosts used to support cloud computing. The host configuration options include Enable Host, Disable Host, Prepare Host, Properties, and so on.

Figure 11.9 illustrates the available datastores for vCD. Some of them are local datastores on the ESXi hosts. Others are network-based datastores.

Once connected to vCenter, the port groups on the virtual switches hosted by the ESXi hosts or vCenter will be available to vCD. To vCD, the networks connected to those port groups are called external networks. Each port group can provide a connection point for an external network. Figure 11.10 illustrates the external networks available in vCD. One of the external networks is connected to a computer lab on campus, and the other one is connected to a public network. The external networks can also be used to connect to the storage array and be utilized for network management.

After a provider vDC is created, the vCloud administrator can create organizations for cloud subscribers. The resources in the provider vDC can be shared by multiple organizations. In some cases, an organization vDC may take resources from multiple provider vDCs. Each organization has its own organization vDC. Figure 11.11 illustrates a provider vDC and organization vDCs.

In Figure 11.11, there is one provider vDC, labvdc, that includes two organization vDCs: (1) csorgvdc and (2) cosc4339org.

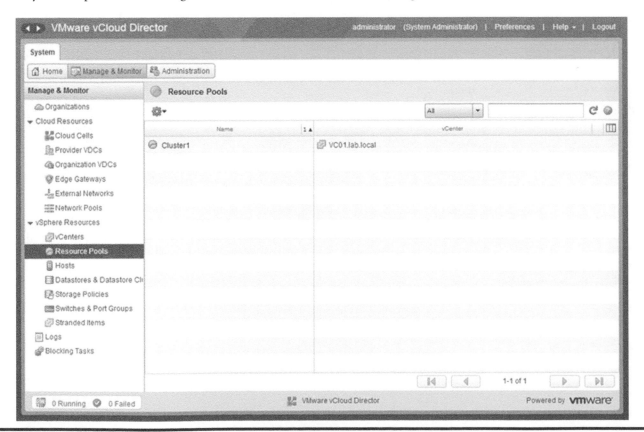

Figure 11.7 vCenter resource pool.

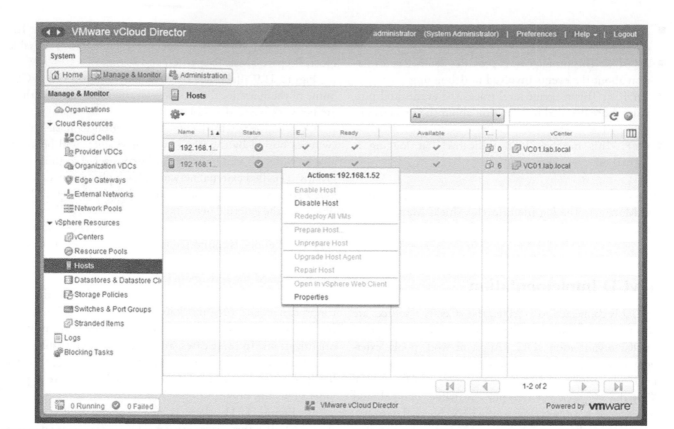

Figure 11.8   Available hosts and configuration options.

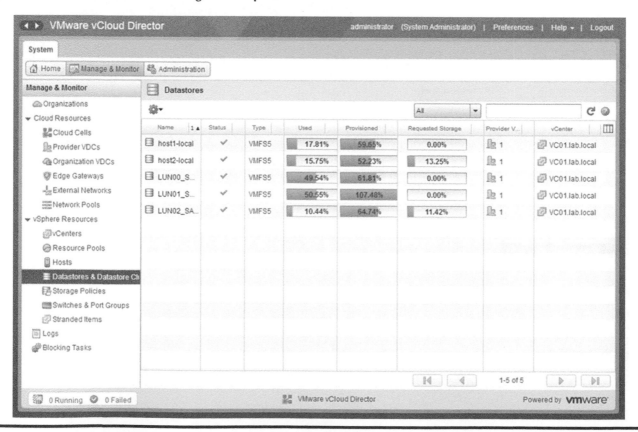

Figure 11.9   Available datastores.

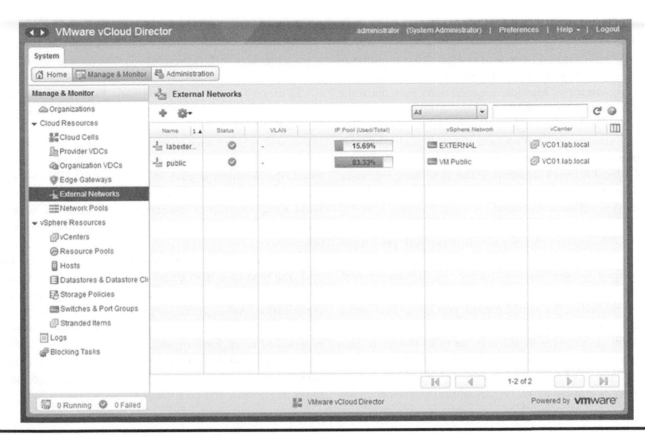

Figure 11.10 Available external networks.

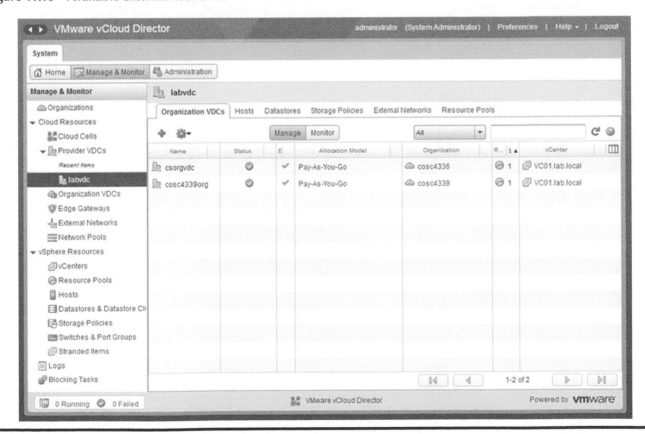

Figure 11.11 Provider vDC and organization vDCs.

To support different levels of vDCs, different levels of virtual networks, external networks, organization networks, and vApp networks can be created in vCD. To communicate through the VPN or Internet, an external network is required for an organization. Multiple organizations may share the same external network. Within an organization, data communication is done through the organization network. The vCloud administrator can create a network pool to support organization networks or vApp networks. A network pool includes local network segments, external network segments, virtual local area networks (VLANs), and port groups. There are four types of network pools:

1. *VLAN-backed network pool:* This network pool registers a set of unused VLANs for vCD to use.
2. *vCloud network isolation–backed (VCNI) network pool:* The network pool registers a set of cloud-isolated networks. It does not require prebuilt port groups in vCenter.
3. *Portgroup-backed pool:* The network pool registers prebuilt port groups in vCenter for vCD to use. It does not require a vSphere Distributed Switch (vDS).
4. *vSphere VXLAN network pool:* This kind of network pool is similar to VCNI. In addition, it allows VMs

from different clusters to communicate without a router. A VXLAN pool is automatically created when a provider vDC is created.

To create an organization network, the organization can use one of the network segments from the network pool. Figure 11.12 illustrates the port group–backed network pool labnetpool, which contains port groups (or L2 network segments). As shown in Figure 11.12, while working in a cloud-based lab environment, each student can have his or her own network segment, such as Student20, so that the student can build a vApp on top of the network segment. The network segments in a network pool are usually isolated from each other.

Once the provider vDC and the network pool are created, the next task is to create organizations. To support a multitenant computing environment, each tenant has its own organization. An organization provides a security boundary so that its computing resources are only available to a group of qualified users. Each organization has a unique Uniform Resource Locator (URL) used by its login portal. Each organization can have its own policies that define resource usage limits, set quotas, and create leases.

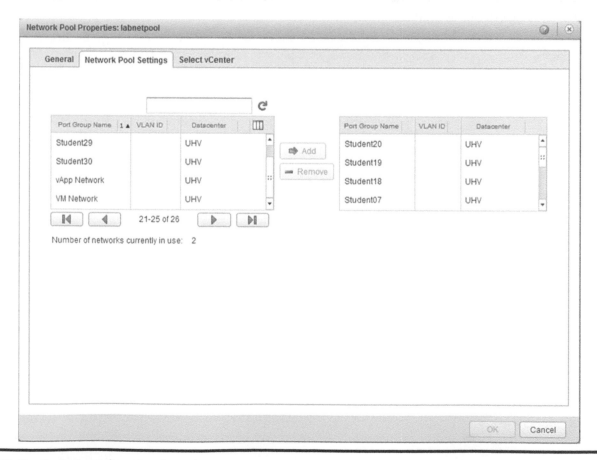

Figure 11.12 Port groups in network pool.

While creating an organization, an organization vDC can be created. An organization vDC has three allocation models:

1. *Allocation pool model:* This model allocates a subset of resources. However, only a certain percentage of the allocated resources is committed to the organization vDC. This model allows the provider to overcommit resources.
2. *Reservation pool model:* In this model, all of the allocated resources are committed to the organization vDC.
3. *Pay-as-you-go model:* This model allocates resources only when a vApp is powered on. If the vApp is powered off, the cloud subscriber will not be billed for resources. This model allows the administrator to specify the maximum amount of CPU and memory resources to commit to the organization vDC.

Figure 11.13 illustrates the pay-as-you-go model.

As shown in Figure 11.13, the CPU quota and Memory quota are set to unlimited. The CPU resources guaranteed and Memory resources guaranteed are set to 20%. 1-GHz virtual CPU speed is applied to VMs in the vApp. The maximum number of VMs allowed in this organization vDC is set to 100.

In an organization, a number of network services can be created to support its operations. The commonly used organization network services are as follows:

- *Dynamic Host Configuration Protocol (DHCP) service:* This service assigns an IP address to the VMs connected to an organization network.
- *VPN service:* This service provides a secure connection for remote access to the organization.
- *Firewall service:* This service is used to control the network traffic within vCD.
- *NAT service:* It maps an external IP address to an internal IP address within a vApp. Such mapping is called *destination network address translation*. Or, it can map an internal IP address to an external IP address. Such mapping is called *source network address translation*.
- *Routing service:* It creates static routes between two vApps or between two organizations.
- *Domain name system (DNS) relay service:* It forwards the DNS request from a VM within an organization to an external provider DNS server, and returns the response to the internal VM.

Networks are built in the organization vDC for the VMs and vApps to communicate with external networks or connect with each other. There are three types of organization vDC networks, which are described in the following:

Direct organization vDC network: This type of network connects to an external network directly. From the

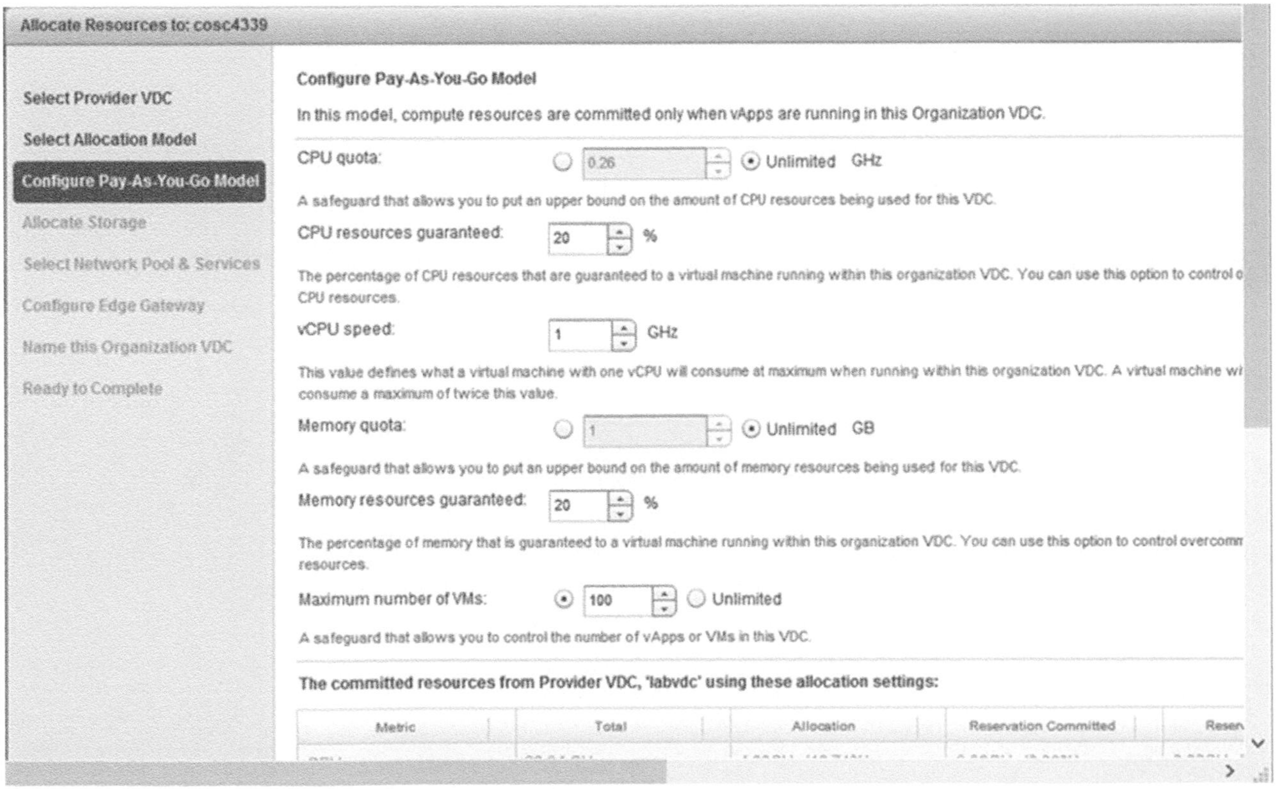

Figure 11.13   Pay-as-you-go allocation model.

Internet and the system outside of a cloud, one can connect to this network through a secure shell or a remote desktop. This network is created by the vCD system administrator and cannot be altered by the organization administrator.

Routed organization vDC network: This type of network connects to an external network through an edge gateway, which is created in vShield Manager. Once an edge gateway is created for an organization vDC, it can provide services such as connecting multiple routed organization vDC networks to the edge gateway, setting up firewalls, associating an organization vDC network with a network pool, specifying a DHCP range, routing the network traffic to external networks, performing load balancing, providing VPN services, configuring NAT features, and so on.

Isolated organization vDC network: This type of network is defined as a single subnet. It does not connect to an edge gateway, an external network, or other organization networks. There are no firewall and routing services provided by the edge gateway for this type

of network. The VMs in this type of network do not communicate with the machines outside this organization vDC. This type of network can be associated to a network pool. vApps created on this type of network can communicate through an internal vApp network edge device. For the VMs created in different vApps to communicate with each other, an NAT service needs to be configured on the vApp network edge device.

Figure 11.14 illustrates a routed organization vDC network. The network provides a set of static IP addresses ranging from 192.168.10.1 to 192.168.10.200. The network uses the DNS service provided by the edge gateway. Through the edge gateway, the organization vDC network can access the external networks.

After an organization is created, the next task is to create vApps, which can be used to implement a virtualized IT infrastructure. In vCD, a vApp is a package that consists of prebuilt VMs and vApp networks. A vApp can be made as a template for cloning by the cloud subscribers. Templates are

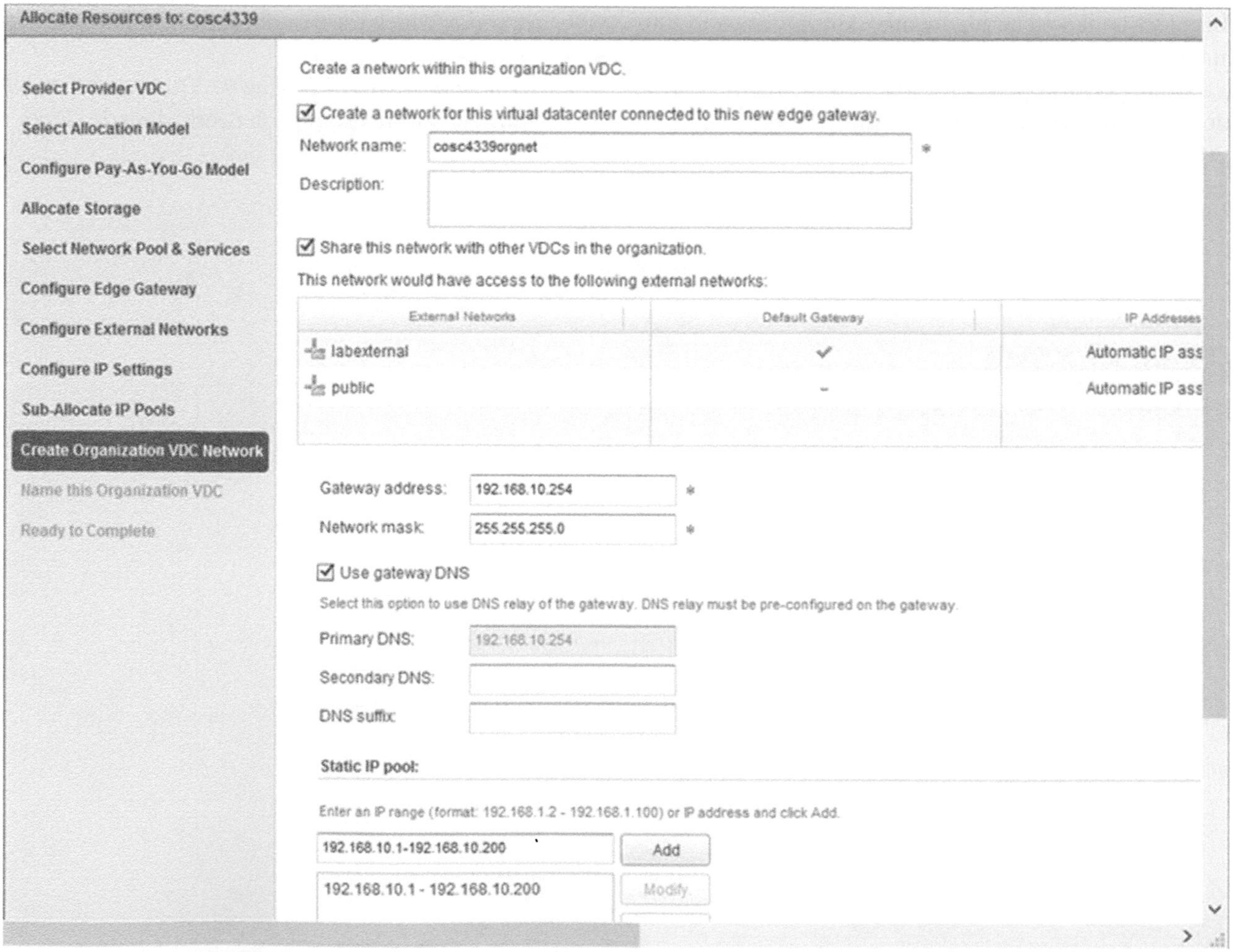

Figure 11.14 Organization vDC network.

stored in a container called a catalog, which is accessible by the cloud subscribers.

Creating a new vApp requires the organization vCD and the storage allocation policy. A vApp can be created by cloning an existing vApp template or building a new one. When a vApp is cloned from a template, vApp network may need to be reconfigured to fit the new computing environment. The IP addresses for VMs, gateways, and DNS servers need to be modified to meet the new requirements. The vApp network may need to connect to the new organization vDC network, which may connect to different external networks or connect to a different edge gateway. Figure 11.15 illustrates the relationships among different levels of networks.

The guest operating system may also need to be customized for the new computing environment. After the vApp is created, the administrator can add, edit, or delete VMs in it. The administrator can also configure the vApp to control the start or stop behavior of the VMs in the vApp.

A VM in a vApp can get its IP address in three different ways: (1) DHCP, (2) manual, and (3) static. For a VM to get a DHCP address, it is required that an edge gateway be built in vShield Manager, or from a DHCP server in an external network. If the DHCP address is used, the VM on the vApp network cannot communicate with the organization vDC network through the NAT service. It is because an external NAT IP cannot be set on an organization vCD network.

For a VM to use a static IP address, a range of static IP addresses should be specified while creating an organization vDC network. When a VM is created in a vApp, it is assigned a static IP address available in the static IP address range. When a static IP address is used in the vApp network, the organization network automatically assigns an NAT external IP address to simplify the NAT configuration.

The vCloud administrator can also manually assign IP addresses to VMs. When a VM in a vApp has a manually assigned IP address, the organization vDC network does not automatically create an external NAT IP address. Unlike DHCP, when an IP address is manually assigned to the VM, the vCloud administrator can manually set an external NAT IP address on the organization vDC network for the VM.

A vApp can be saved as a template for easy deployment. vApp templates are stored in a catalog, which can

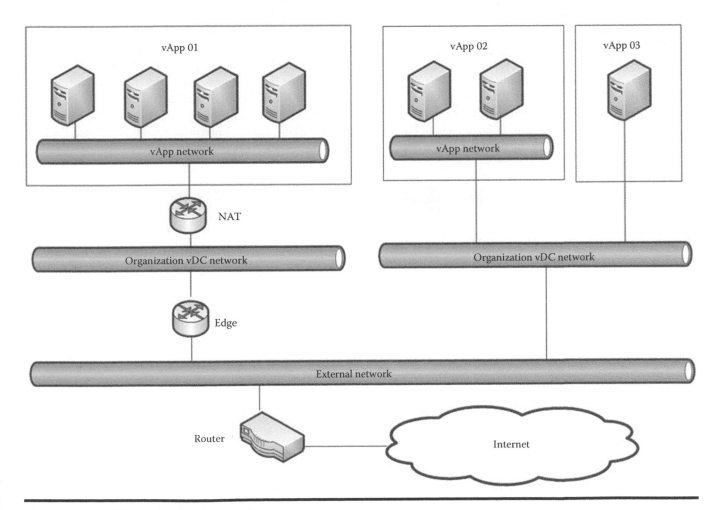

Figure 11.15 **Different levels of networks.**

be configured in four different ways: (1) private, (2) public, (3) shared, or (4) published.

1. *Private:* This type of catalog is only available to the vCloud administrator or catalog owner.
2. *Public:* This type of catalog is available to other organizations in the same vCD cell.
3. *Shared:* This type of catalog allows dedicated users in different organizations to share the vApp templates.
4. *Published:* This type of catalog can be made available to other vCD cells.

The vCloud administrator can upload an OVF package directly to a catalog or download a vApp template from a catalog as an OVF file. Figure 11.16 shows some catalogs and templates.

In Figure 11.16, there is a private catalog cosc4339cat and a public catalog. Two templates, Linuxclienttmp and Linuxservertmp, are stored in the private catalog cosc-4339cat. The organization users can create vApps and VMs with these templates. Figure 11.17 shows a vApp created with these two templates.

In Figure 11.17, the vApp s01vApp has two VMs: (1) LinuxClient and (2) LinuxServer. There are two vApp networks. The VM LinuxClient is directly linked to the organization vDC network cosc4339orgnet.

Now that vCD is briefly introduced, a hands-on activity is provided to practice the installation and configuration of vCD. The hands-on activity also shows how to create vCloud components for developing a private cloud computing environment.

11.5 Activity 1: Private Cloud Development with vCD

In this activity, the following tasks will be performed:

- *Task 1:* Installing and configuring vCD
- *Task 2:* Creating vCloud components
- *Task 3:* Implementing and managing cloud services

11.5.1 Task 1: Installing and Configuring vCD

To accomplish the first task, follow the steps below.

1. On the desktop, right-click the VMware Workstation icon and select **Run as Administrator**.
2. To reserve more memory for the cloud, right-click the **LabESXi1** host server and select **Settings**. Change the memory for this host to **6GB**. Do the same for the LabESXi2 host server.
3. Start the VMs in the order of DC, Storage, LabESXi1, LabESXi2, and vc.
4. Log on to vc through vSphere Client. In vSphere Client, power on **vShield Manager**.
5. Your next job is to deploy the vCD appliance. To do so, click the **File** menu and select **Deploy OVF Template**.
6. On the Source page, click the **Browse** button and select the vCD appliance file (Figure 11.18). In Figure 11.18, the OVA file has the vCD version 5.5.5 installed on SUSE Linux Enterprise Server 11 Service Pack 2. Then, click **Next**.

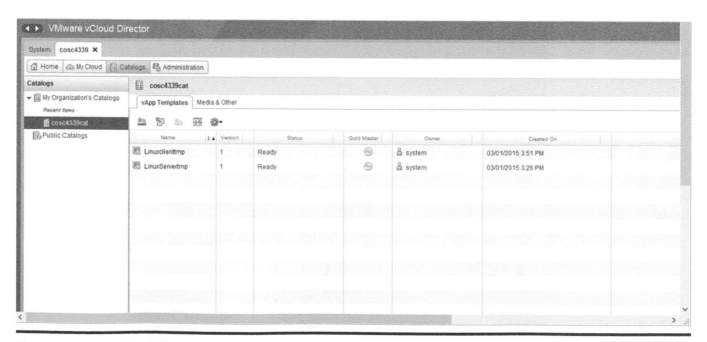

Figure 11.16 Catalogs and templates.

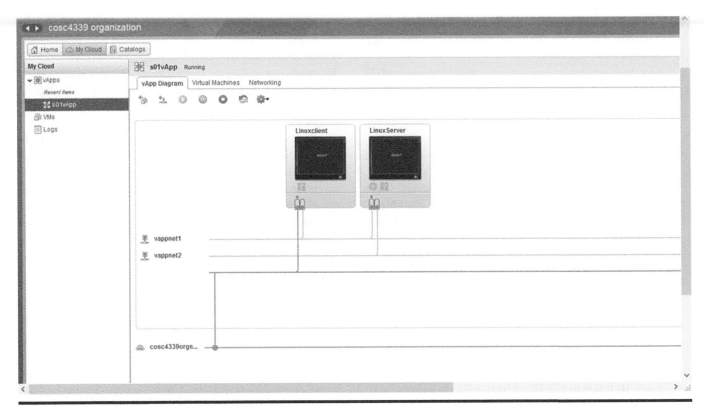

Figure 11.17   vApp and vApp networks.

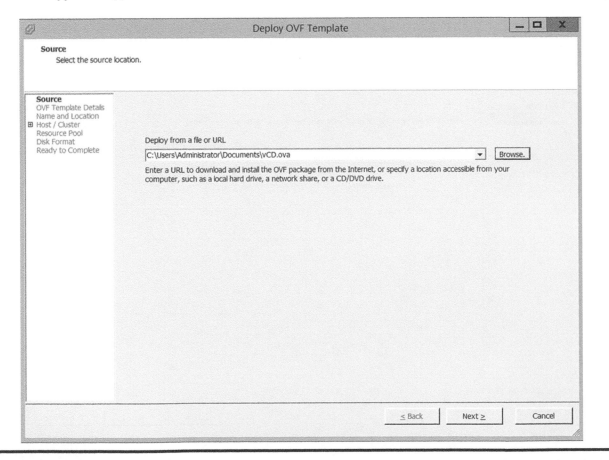

Figure 11.18   Selecting source location.

7. On the OVF Template Details page, click **Next**.
8. On the End User License Agreement page, click **Accept** and click **Next**.
9. On the Name and Location page, enter the name **vCD** and keep **Datacenter** as the inventory location (Figure 11.19).
10. On the Resource Pool page, click the **Cluster** resource and click **Next**.
11. On the Storage page, select **dstore1**, as shown in Figure 11.20, and click **Next**.
12. On the Disk Format page, select the option **Thin Provision**, as shown in Figure 11.21. Then, click **Next**.
13. On the Network Mapping page, take the default and click **Next**.
14. On the Database Properties page, select **Internal** in the dropdown list. Move the cursor down to the Linux Account section, and enter your password for Linux such as **Passw0rd!**. Also, enter the password for the guest account. The networking properties depend on your computing environment. Here, as shown in Figure 11.22, you may enter **10.0.0.1** as the gateway IP and **10.0.0.1** as the DNS server IP. For Network 1, enter **10.0.0.6** as the IP address with the subnet mask **255.0.0.0** (Figure 11.22). For Network 2, you may have

the IP address **10.0.0.101** and subnet mask **255.0.0.0**. Then, click **Next**.
15. On the Ready to Complete page, click **Finish**.
16. As shown in Figure 11.23, the vCD is installed.
17. Power on the VM vCD. Under the **Console** tab, it shows that, to manage vCD, you can log on to the vCD console, as shown in Figure 11.24.
18. In the Chrome browser, enter the URL **https://10.0 .0.101/cloud/** to log on to vCD with the username **administrator** and the password entered earlier. (If an error occurs, use the arrow key to move the cursor to **Configure Network**, as shown in Figure 11.24.) Press the **Enter** key. Then, follow the instruction to change the IP address of eth1 to **10.0.0.101**. Reboot the vCD VM. After you have logged on, you should be able to see the Welcome page, as shown in Figure 11.25.
19. On the Welcome page, click **Next**.
20. On the License Agreement page, click **Yes, I accept the terms in the license agreement**. Then, click **Next**.
21. On the Licensing page, enter the license key and click **Next**.
22. On the Create an Administrator Account page, enter your password and email information (Figure 11.26). Then, click **Next**.

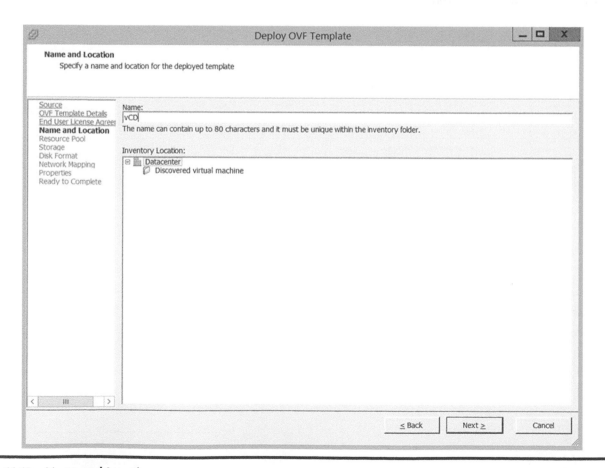

Figure 11.19 Name and Location.

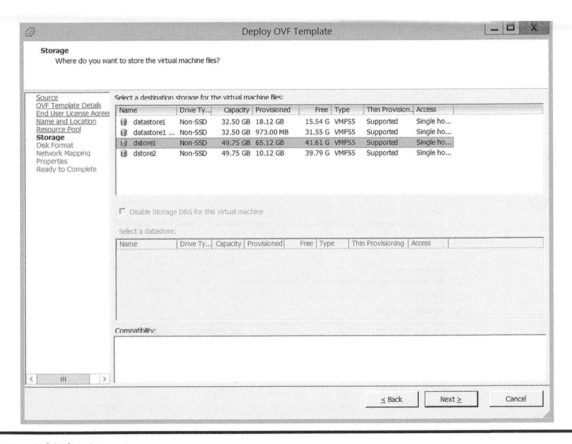

Figure 11.20 Selecting Storage.

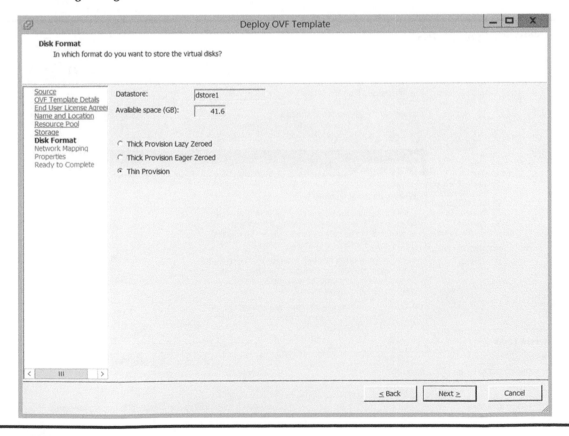

Figure 11.21 Disk Format.

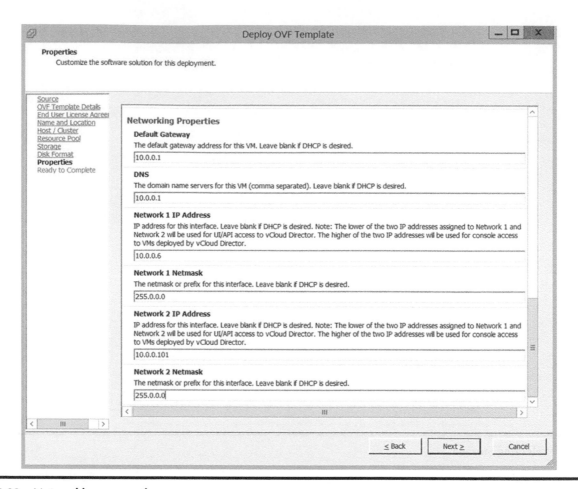

Figure 11.22   Networking properties.

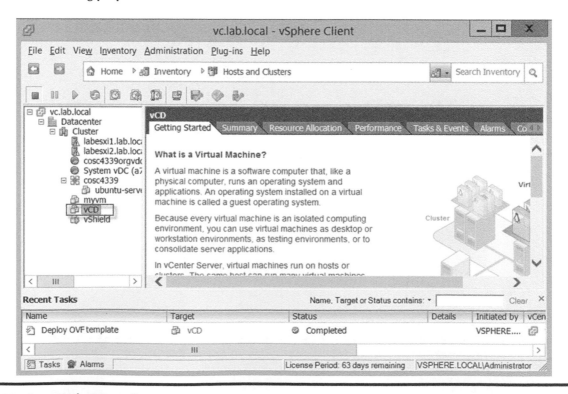

Figure 11.23   Imported vCD appliance.

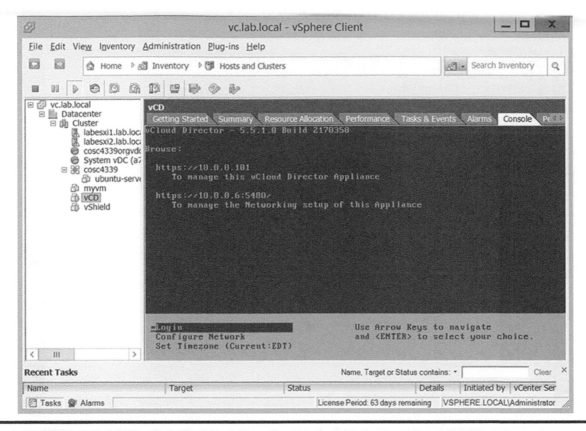

Figure 11.24   vCD console.

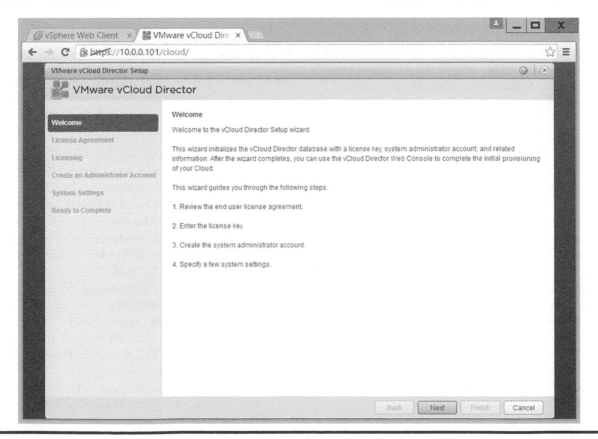

Figure 11.25   vCD.

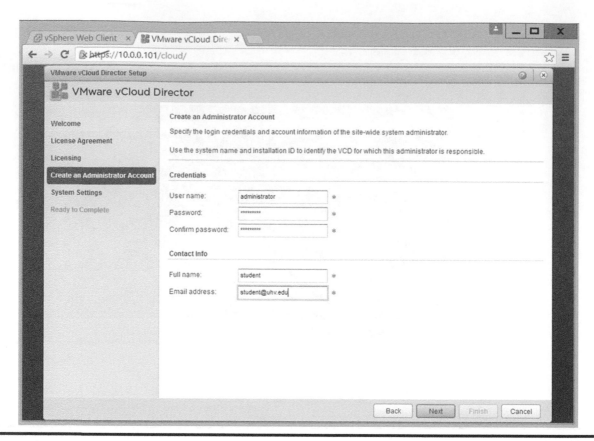

Figure 11.26 Creating administrator account.

23. On the System Settings page, enter **student_cloud** as the system name. Also, specify the number of identification ID as **3**. Then, click **Next** (Figure 11.27).
24. On the Ready to Complete page, click **Finish**. After the configuration is completed, start your Web browser and enter the URL https://10.0.0.101, as shown in Figure 11.28. You can now log on to vCD as **administrator**, as shown in Figure 11.28.
25. Once logged on, click the link **Attach a vCenter** to open the **Attach New vCenter** wizard. Specify the vCenter information, as shown in Figure 11.29, and click **Next**.
26. On the Connect to vShield Manager page, enter the information about vShield Manager, as shown in Figure 11.30. Then, click **Next**.
27. On the Ready to Complete page, click **Finish**. Click the **Manager & Monitor** tab, and click the link **vCenters**; you will see that the vCenter and vShield Manager are linked.

You have now installed and configured vCD. In the next task, you will create some vCloud components.

11.5.2 Task 2: Creating vCloud Components

The second task is to create vCloud components such as a provider vDC, organization, organization vDC, vApp, template, and catalog. Follow the steps below to get started.

1. To prepare the ESXi host for the provider vDC, the ESXi host needs to be set in the maintenance mode. To do so, you need to migrate all live VMs to another ESXi host. Click the host **LabESXi1** in vSphere Client. Under the **Virtual Machines** tab, right-click the VM **vShield** and select **Migrate**, as shown in Figure 11.31. In the Migrate Virtual Machine wizard, migrate the VMs to the LabESXi2 host.
2. Once vShield is live-migrated to the LabESXi2 host, right-click the **LabESXi1** host and select **Enter Maintenance Mode** (Figure 11.32).
3. Switch back to the vCD Web portal. Click the **Home** tab and click the link **Create a Provider VDC**, as shown in Figure 11.33.
4. On the Name this Provider VDC page, enter the name **labvdc** and specify **Hardware Version 10** as the

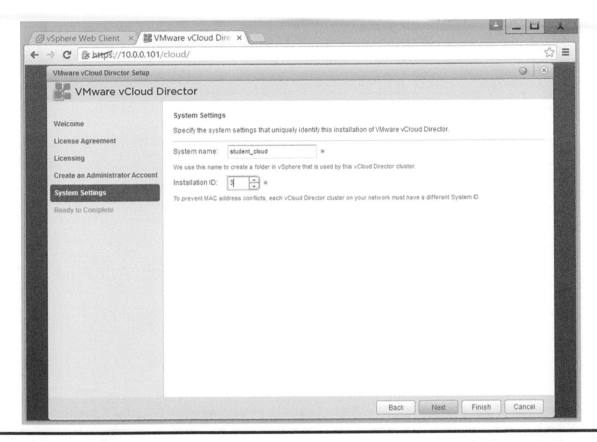

Figure 11.27 System settings.

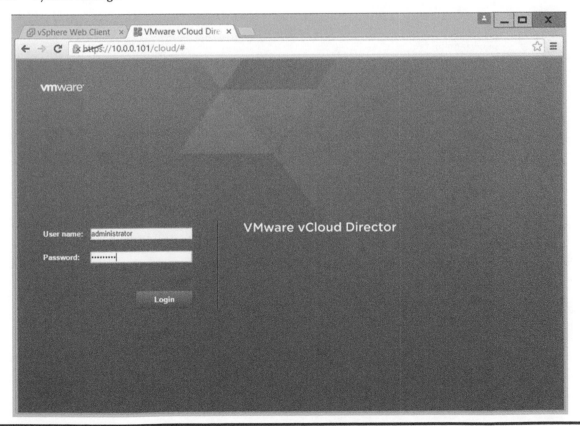

Figure 11.28 Logging on to vCD.

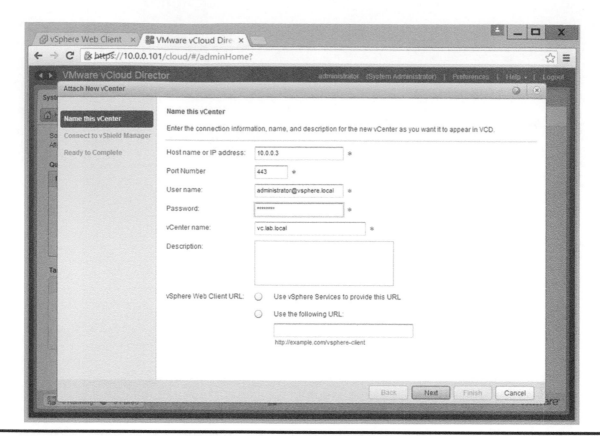

Figure 11.29 Attaching vCenter.

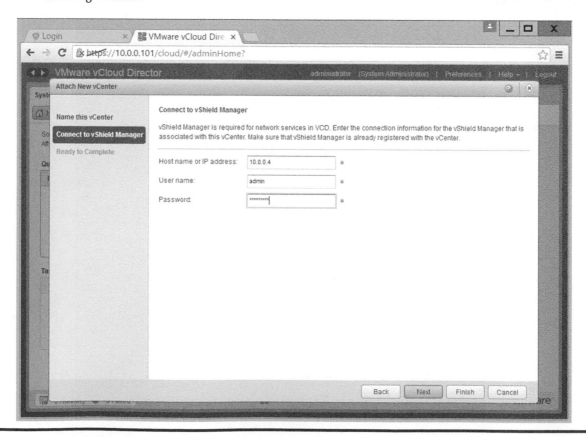

Figure 11.30 Connecting to vShield Manager.

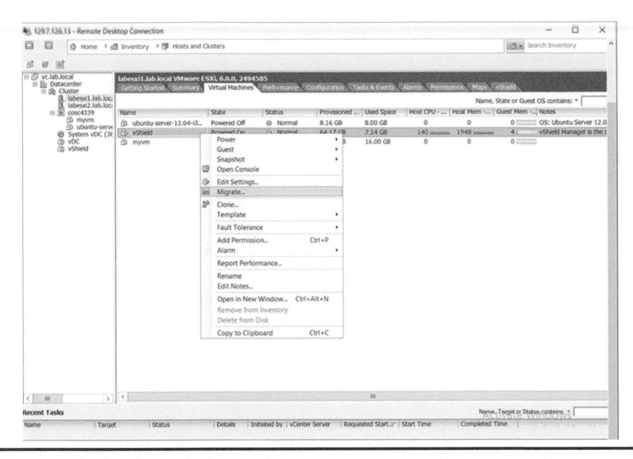

Figure 11.31 Migrating virtual machines.

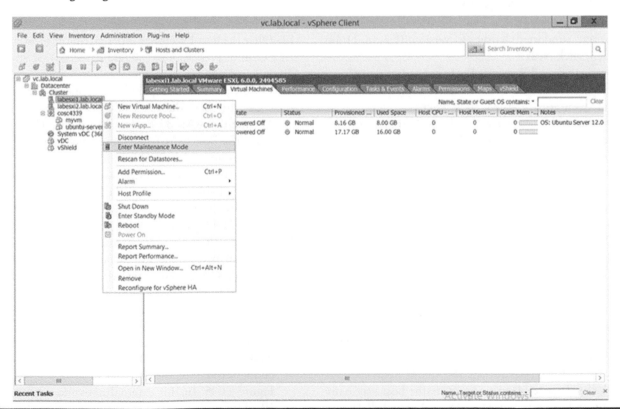

Figure 11.32 Entering maintenance mode.

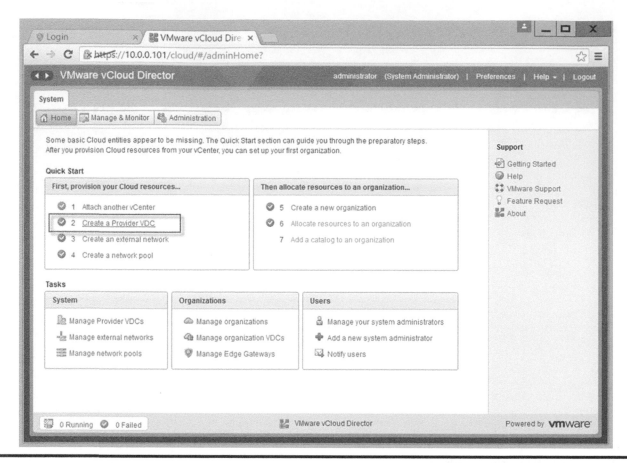

Figure 11.33   Creating provider vDC.

highest supported hardware version (Figure 11.34). Then, click **Next**.

5. On the Selected Resource Pool page, select the vCenter **vc.lab.local**. Also, select **Cluster** for Resource Pool and vCenter Path. Then, click **Next**.

6. On the Add Storage page, click the **Add** button to add **Any** storage, as shown in Figure 11.35. Then, click **Next**.

7. On the Prepare Hosts page, enter the root password for your ESXi host, as shown in Figure 11.36. Then, click **Next**.

8. On the Ready to Complete page, click **Finish**.

9. Click the **Manager & Monitor** tab and click the link **Hosts**. You may see the error message "Cannot prepare host" as shown in Figure 11.37. This is because the process cannot set the hosts into the maintenance mode to install the vDirector agent.

10. As LabESXi1 has been set to the maintenance mode, right-click **labesxi1.lab.local** and select **Prepare Host** (Figure 11.38). (You may need to do it twice if the VM is slow.)

11. On the Prepare Hosts page, enter the host user name **root** and your password, such as **Passw0rd!** (Figure 11.39). Click **OK** and then click **Finish**.

12. Once the host LabESXi1 is prepared, the error message "Cannot prepare host" should disappear, as shown in Figure 11.40.

13. Once the host is prepared, in vSphere Client, right-click the host **labesxi1.lab.local** and select **Exit Maintenance Mode**, as shown in Figure 11.41.

14. After the host exits the maintenance mode, you will have the host ready, as shown in Figure 11.42.

15. To prepare the host LabESXi2, migrate the live VMs from the LabESXi2 host to the LabESXi1 host. Repeat Steps 10 through 14 to prepare the host LabESXi2. Figure 11.43 shows that both hosts are prepared.

16. After the Provider vDC is created, the next job is to create an external network. Under the **Home** tab, click the link **Create an external network** to open the New External Network wizard. On the Select vSphere Network page, click **vc.lab.local** and **VM Network 2**, as shown in Figure 11.44. Then, click **Next**.

17. On the Configure External Network page, click the **Add** button. In the Add Subnet dialog, enter the configurations of the external network, as shown in Figure 11.45. In this external network, a set of static IP addresses is reserved for future VMs on the private cloud. Click **OK** and then click **Next**.

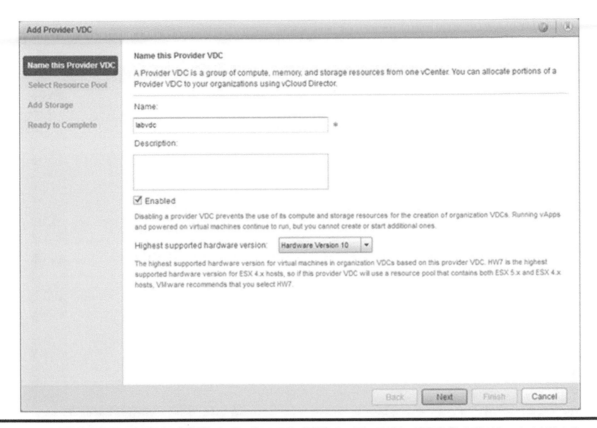

Figure 11.34 Name and highest supported hardware version.

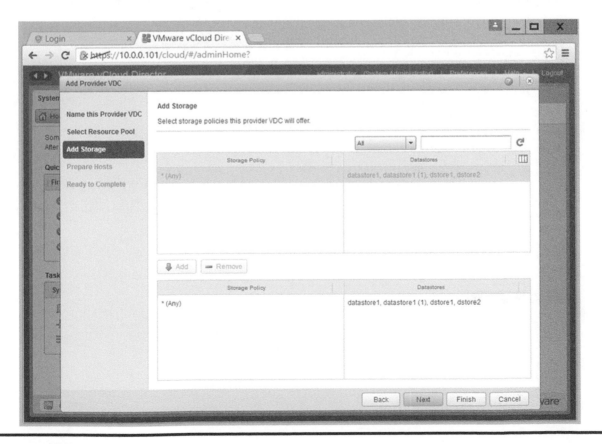

Figure 11.35 Adding storage.

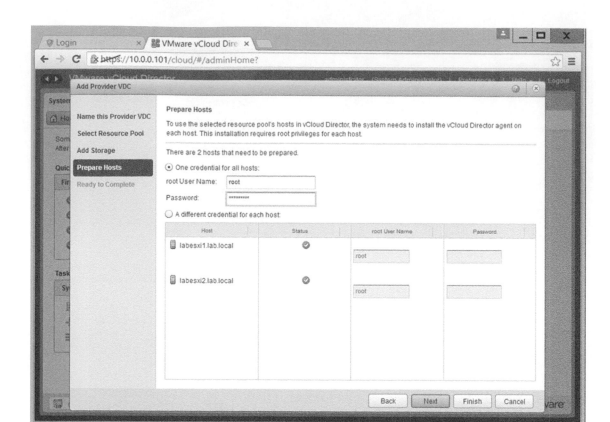

Figure 11.36 Preparing hosts.

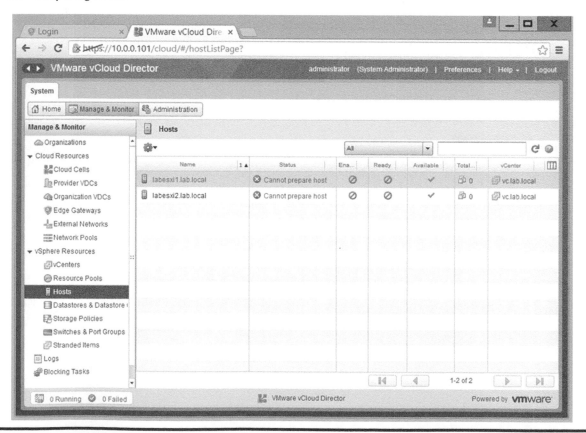

Figure 11.37 Error message.

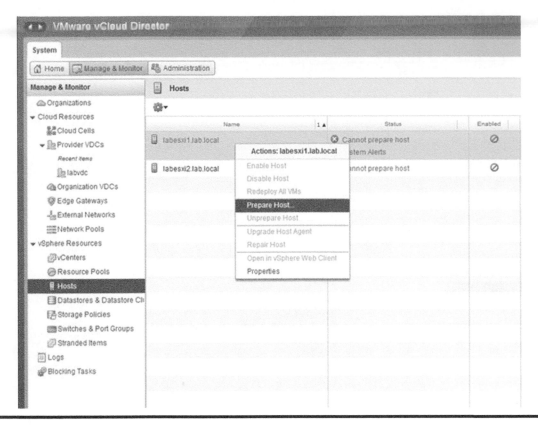

Figure 11.38 Preparing host.

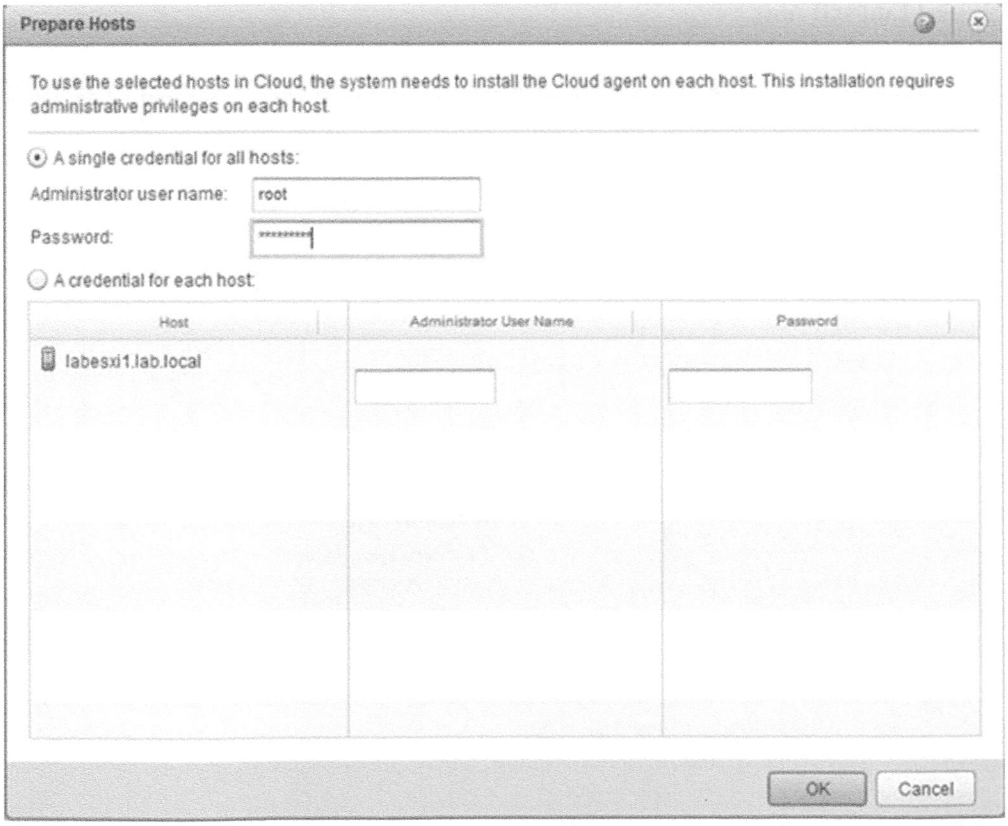

Figure 11.39 Host user name and password.

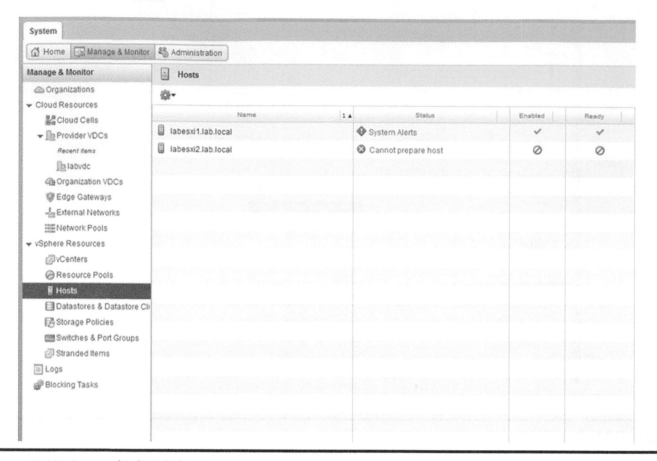

Figure 11.40   Prepared LabESXi1 host.

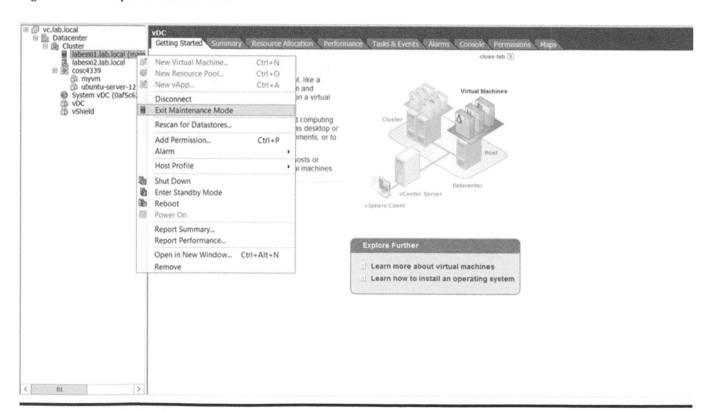

Figure 11.41   Exiting maintenance mode.

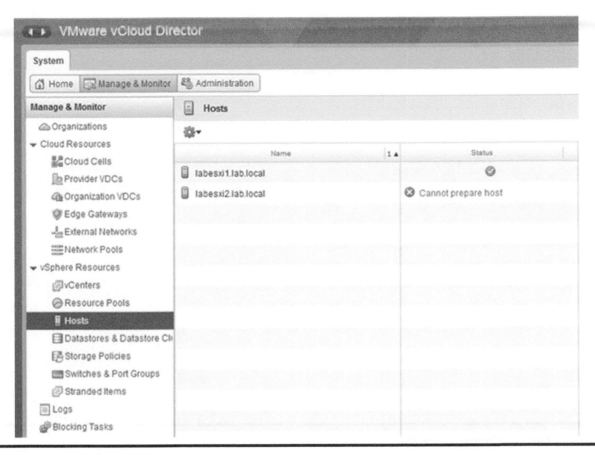

Figure 11.42 Prepared host.

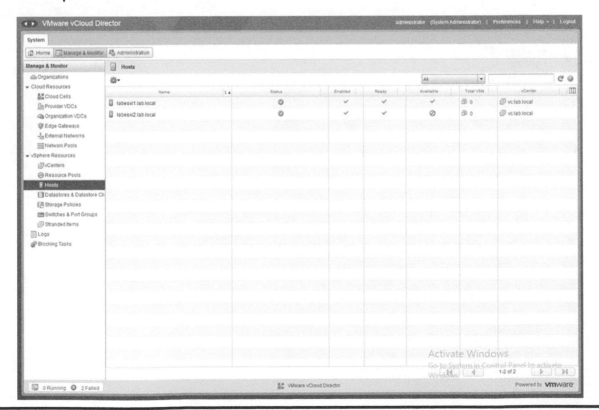

Figure 11.43 Two prepared hosts.

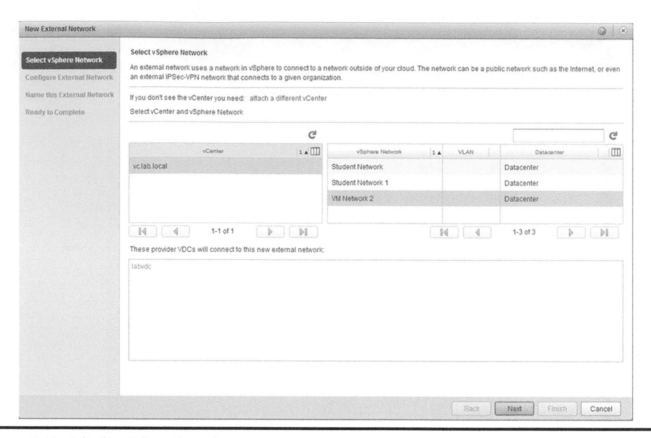

Figure 11.44　Selecting vSphere Network.

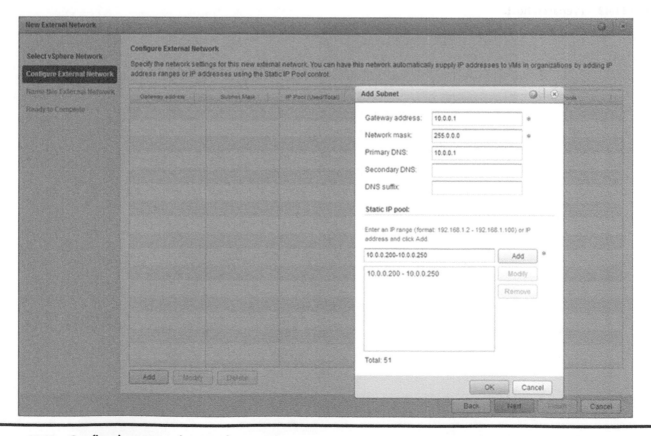

Figure 11.45　Configuring external network.

18. Name the external network **labexternal**. Then, click **Next**.

19. On the Ready to Complete page, click **Finish**.

20. The next job is to create a network pool. By default, vCD will automatically create a VXLAN network pool that works with a vDS. As a vDS has not been created, the default VXLAN network pool will fail. Under the **Home** tab, click the link **Create another network pool**. On the Network Pool Type page, select the option **vSphere port group-backed**, as shown in Figure 11.46. Then, click **Next**.

21. On the Select vCenter page, select **vc.lab.local** and click **Next**.

22. On the Configure Port Group-backed Pool page, add the available **Student Network,** as shown in Figure 11.47. Then, click **Next**.

23. On the Name the Network Pool page, enter the name **labnetpool** and then click **Next**.

24. On the Ready to Complete page, click **Finish**.

25. The next job is to create a new organization. Under the **Home** tab, click the link **Create a new organization** to open the New Organization wizard.

26. On the Name this Organization page, enter **cosc4339** as the organization name and **Private cloud for COSC4339** as the organization full name (Figure 11.48). Then, click **Next**.

27. On the LDAP Options page, take the default and click **Next**.

28. On the Add Local Users page, click the **Add** button, enter a user name such as **student**, and enter a password such as **Passw0rd!**. Click **OK** (Figure 11.49). Then, click **Next**.

29. On the Catalog page, check the option **Allow sharing catalog to other organizations**, the option **Allow publishing external catalogs**, and the option **Allow subscribing external catalogs**. Then, click **Next**.

30. On the Email Preferences page, take the default and click **Next**.

31. On the Policies page, choose Never Expires for several configuration items, as shown in Figure 11.50. Then, click **Next**.

32. On the Ready to Complete page, click **Finish**.

33. Your next job is to allocate organization resources. To do so, on the **Home** page, click the link **Allocate resources to an organization**. On the Select Organization page, click the organization **cosc4339**, as shown in Figure 11.51. Then, click **Next**.

34. In the Select Provider VDC page, click the provider vDC **labvdc**, as shown in Figure 11.52. Then, click **Next**.

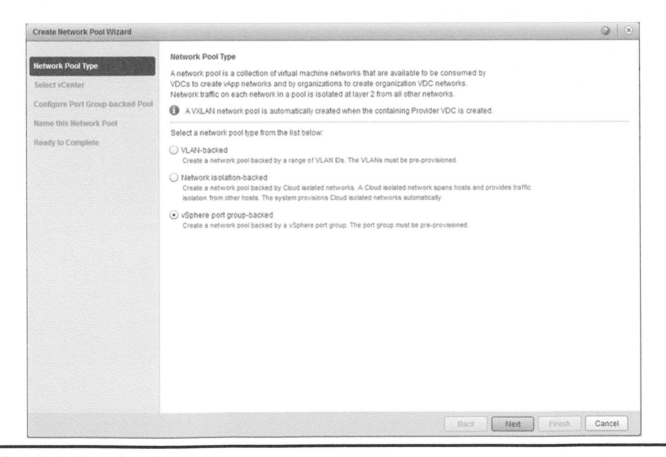

Figure 11.46 Network pool type.

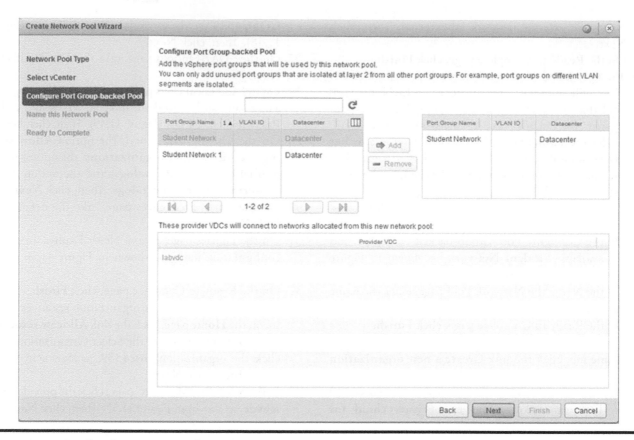

Figure 11.47 Configuring port group-backed pool.

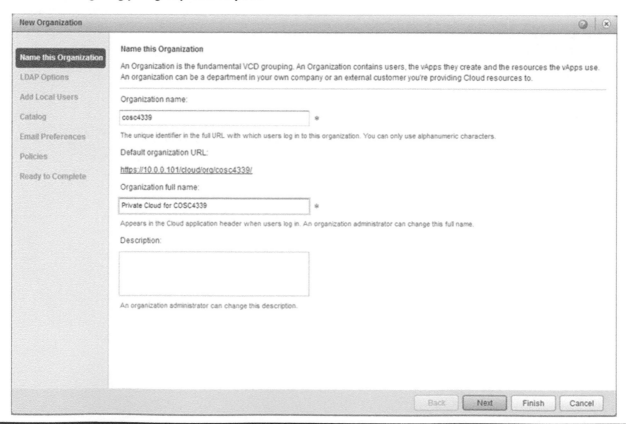

Figure 11.48 Naming organization.

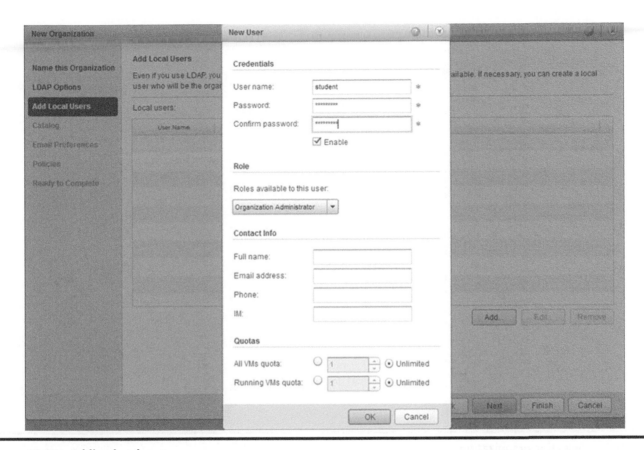

Figure 11.49 Adding local user.

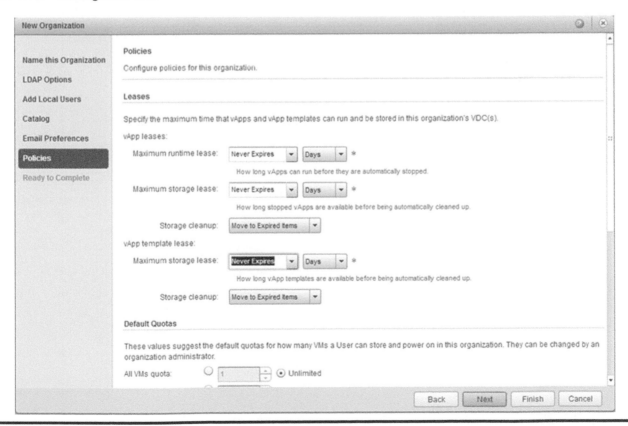

Figure 11.50 Policies.

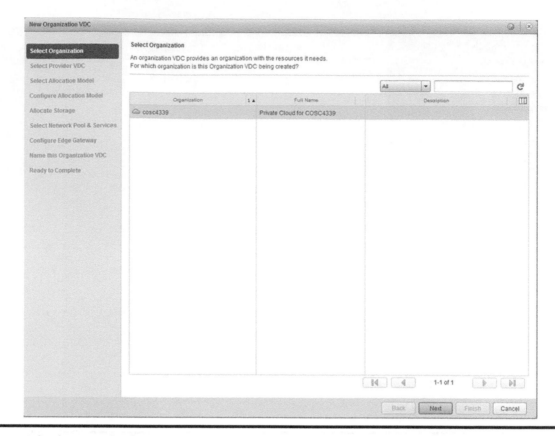

Figure 11.51   Selecting organization.

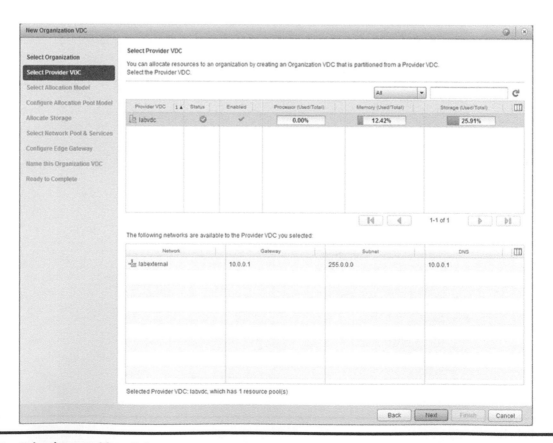

Figure 11.52   Selecting provider vDC.

35. On the Select Allocation Model page, check the option **Pay-As-You-Go** and then click **Next**.
36. On the Configure Pay-As-You-Go page, take the default and click **Next**.
37. On the Allocate Storage page, select **(Any)** and click the **Add** button. Check the option **Enable thin provisioning**, as shown in Figure 11.53. Then, click **Next**.
38. On the Select Network Pool and Services page, in the Network pool dropdown list, select **labnetpool**. In the Quota for this organization box, enter the value **1**, as shown in Figure 11.54. Then, click **Next**.
39. On the Configure Edge Gateway page, take the default and click **Next**.
40. On the Name this Organization VDC page, enter the organization vDC name **cosc4339orgvdc**. Then, click **Next**.
41. On the Ready to Complete page, click **Finish**.
42. Your next job is to configure the organization network. To do so, click the **Manage & Monitor** tab. In the Organizations pane, click the link **Organization VDCs**. Double-click the newly created **cosc4339orgvdc**. Click the **Administration** tab and click the **Org VDC Networks** submenu. Now, click the green + sign. On the Select Network Type page, check the option **Connect directly to an external network**, as shown in Figure 11.55. Select the **lab-external** network and click **Next**.
43. On the Name this Organization VDC Network page, enter network name **coscorgnet**. Then, click **Next**.
44. On the Ready to Complete page, click **Finish**.
45. Your next job is to create a catalog. To do so, click the **Catalogs** tab and click the green + sign. On the Name this Catalog page, name the catalog **cosc4339catalog**, as shown in Figure 11.56. Then, click **Next**.
46. On the Select Storage Type page, take the default and click **Next**.
47. On the Share this Catalog page, click the **Add Members** button. On the Share With Users and Groups page, check the option **Everyone in the organization** and click **OK**, as shown in Figure 11.57. Then, click **Next**.
48. On the Publish Settings page, check the option **Enable Publishing**. Enter your password such as **Passw0rd!** and confirm it. Also, check the option **Enable early catalog export to optimize synchronization**, as shown in Figure 11.58. Then, click **Next**.
49. On the Ready to Complete page, click **Finish**.

Now, you have created some vCD components that will be used to support the development of cloud services. In the

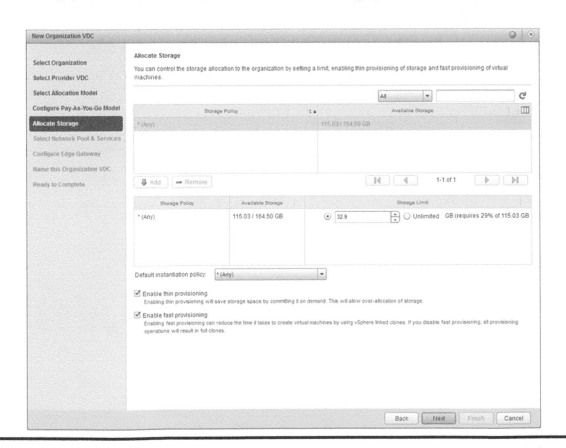

Figure 11.53 Allocating storage.

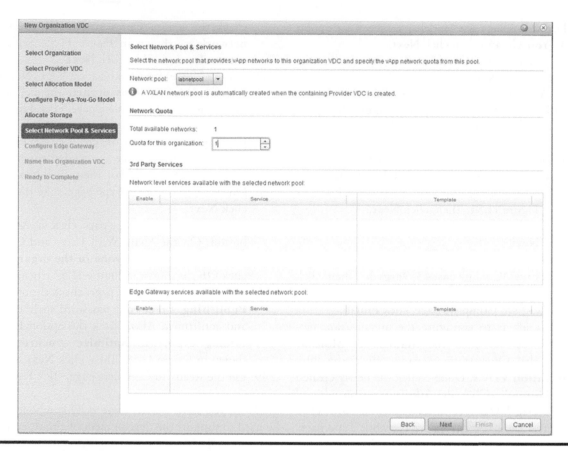

Figure 11.54 Selecting network pool and services.

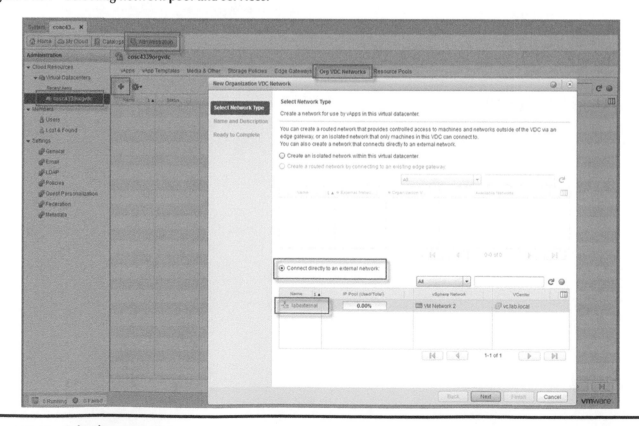

Figure 11.55 Selecting network type.

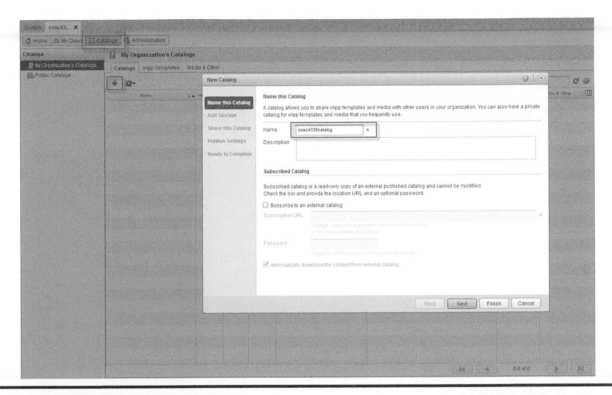

Figure 11.56 Naming catalog.

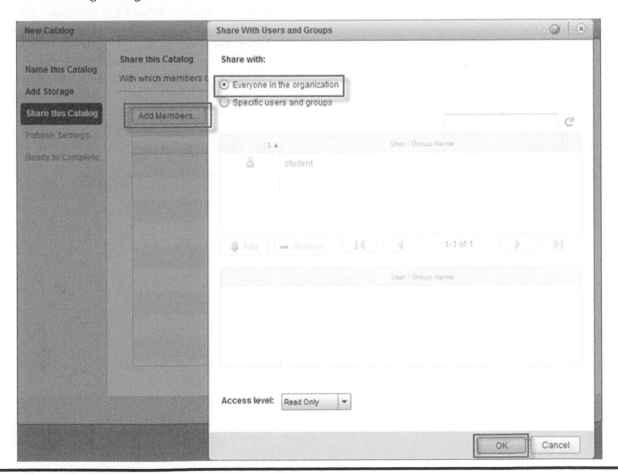

Figure 11.57 Sharing catalog.

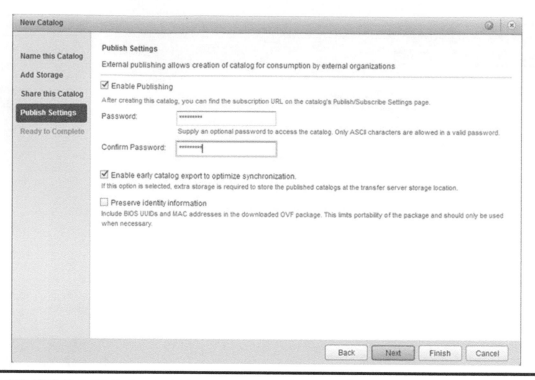

Figure 11.58 Publishing settings.

next task, you will create an IaaS service to support a networking computer lab.

11.5.3 Task 3: Implementing and Managing Cloud Services

In this task, you will create a vApp that includes a VM that is connected to an external network. Follow the steps below to accomplish this task.

1. First, you need to upload a VM created earlier as a template. Click the **Catalogs** tab and click the **vApp Templates** submenu. To upload the OVF file, click the **Upload** icon, as shown in Figure 11.59.
2. Click the option **Local file** and click the **Browse** button. Open the **myvm.ovf** file (Figure 11.60). Then, click **Upload**.
3. Once uploaded, the template myvm can be used to create new vApps. Click the **My Cloud** tab. Then,

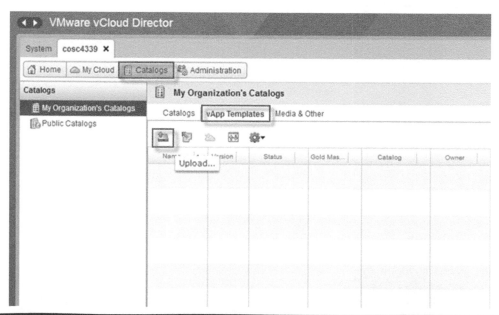

Figure 11.59 Uploading template.

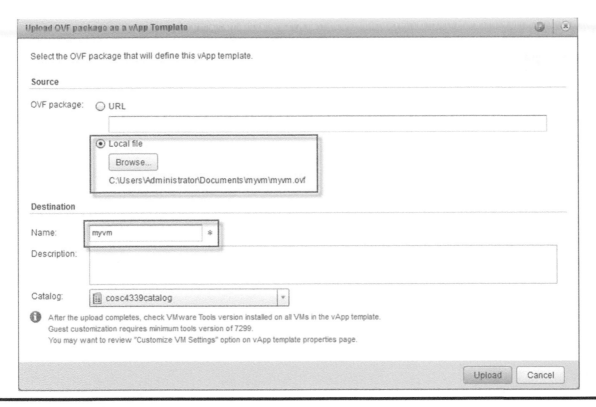

Figure 11.60 Uploading OVF file.

click the **Add vApp from Catalog** icon, as shown in Figure 11.61.

4. On the Select vApp Template page, click the **All Templates** tab and click **myvm,** as shown in Figure 11.62. Then, click **Next**.

5. On the Select Name and Location page, enter the vApp name **student2**. Then, click **Next**.

6. On the Configure Resources page, take the default and click **Next**.

7. On the Configure Network page, take the default and click **Next**.

8. On the Customize Hardware page, take the default and click **Next**.

9. On the Ready to Complete page, click **Finish**.

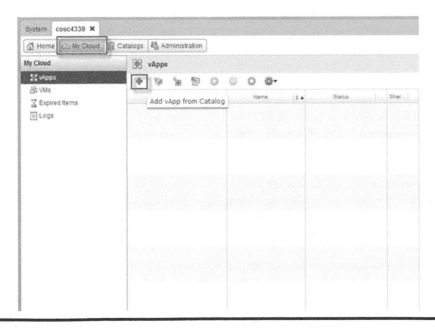

Figure 11.61 Adding vApp from catalog.

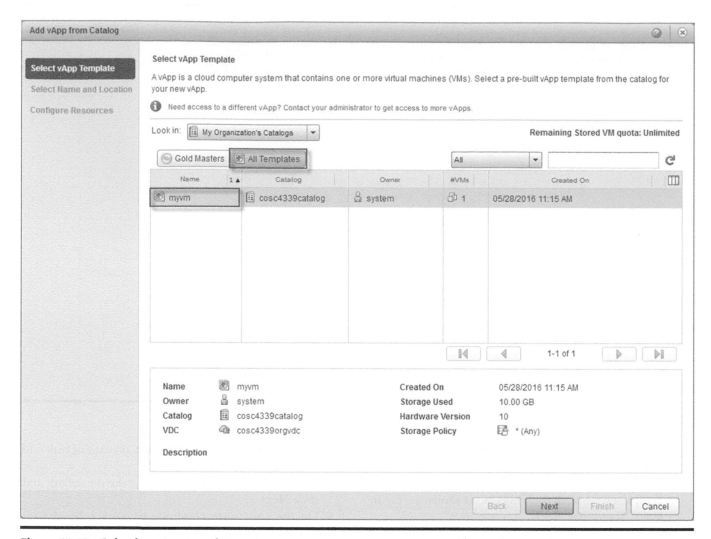

Figure 11.62 Selecting vApp template.

10. Once the vApp is deployed, you can power on the vApp by clicking the green arrow icon, as shown in Figure 11.63.
11. Once the vApp is on, click the VM icon to open the console. You may see the error message "Disconnected." This problem is due to the self-signed certificate used for the console proxy. To fix the problem, press the **F12** key. On the Developer Tools page, click the **Console** menu. Then, click the link similar to wss://10.0.0.6/902;*ticket* as shown in Figure 11.64.
12. In the opened Web page, in the URL, change wss to **https** and press **Enter**. You will get a warning about the use of a self-signed certificate. Click the **Advanced** button and the link **Proceed to 10.0.0.6 (unsafe)**, as shown in Figure 11.65.
13. Now, click the VM icon to open the console. When you see that the console is opened, you can access the VM's desktop, as shown in Figure 11.66. If the external network is configured to connect to the Internet, the cloud subscribers will be able to access

the vApp from the Internet with a proper permission. For better security, instead of directly connecting to the external network, you can create an edge gateway between the external network and vApp network. Then, users can access the vApp through the static route, NAS, or VPN from the external network. You can also set up the firewall between two networks.

14. In an organization, user authentication is centrally managed by a directory service. The next job is to configure vCD so that it can use Active Directory for user authentication. First, you need to create a record in the DNS about the vCD server. In the DC server, click the **Tools** menu in Server Manager and select **DNS**, as shown in Figure 11.67.
15. In the DNS Manager dialog, right-click the **lab.local** node and select **New Host** (Figure 11.68).
16. In the New Host dialog, enter the name **vcd** and the IP address **10.0.0.101**, as shown in Figure 11.69. Click **Add Host** and then click **Done**.

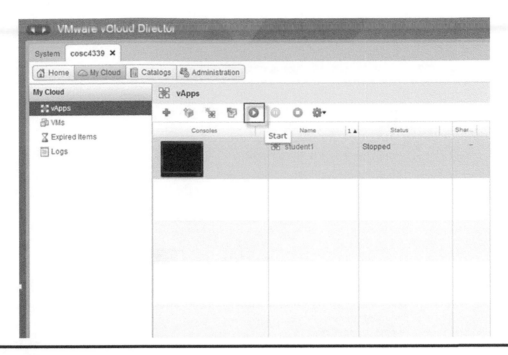

Figure 11.63 Powering on vApp.

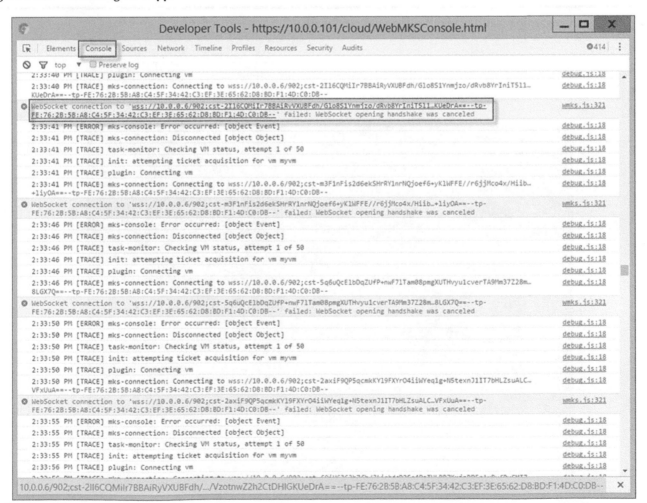

Figure 11.64 Console error.

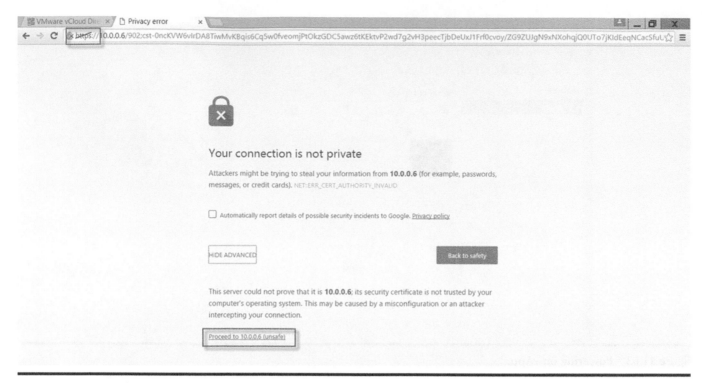

Figure 11.65 Disregarding warning about self-signed certificate.

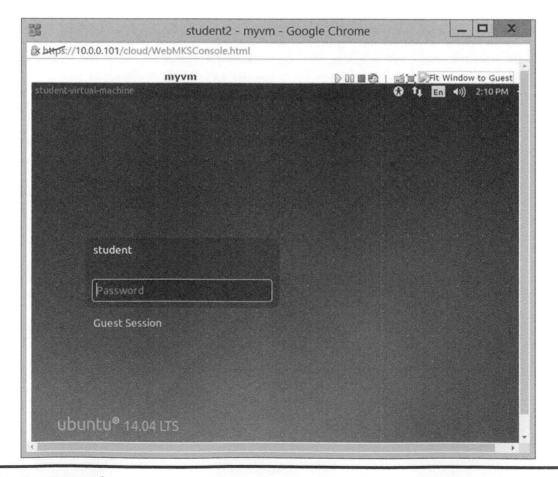

Figure 11.66 Remote console.

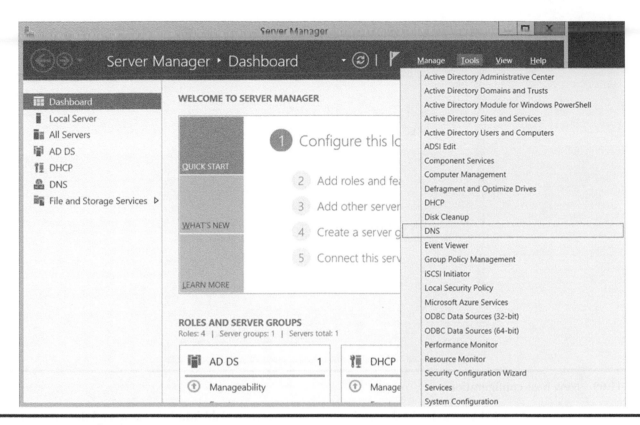

Figure 11.67   Opening DNS.

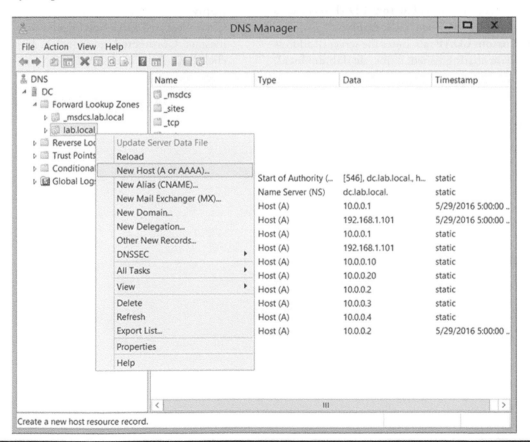

Figure 11.68   Adding new host.

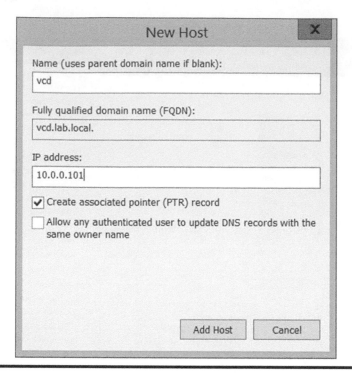

Figure 11.69   New host configuration.

17. Switch back to the vCD Web portal. Under the cosc4339 tab, click the **Administration** submenu. Click the link **LDAP** and select the option **Custom LDAP service**, as shown in Figure 11.70. Then, click **Apply**.
18. Click the **Custom LDAP** tab. Enter the server IP address **10.0.0.1**, base distinguished name **dc=lab,dc=local**, user name **lab\Administrator**, and the password such as **Passw0rd!**, as shown in Figure 11.71. Then, click **Apply**.
19. Click the **Test LDAP Settings** button. You will see the message **Connected**, as shown in Figure 11.72. If so, click **OK**. Then, click **Apply**.

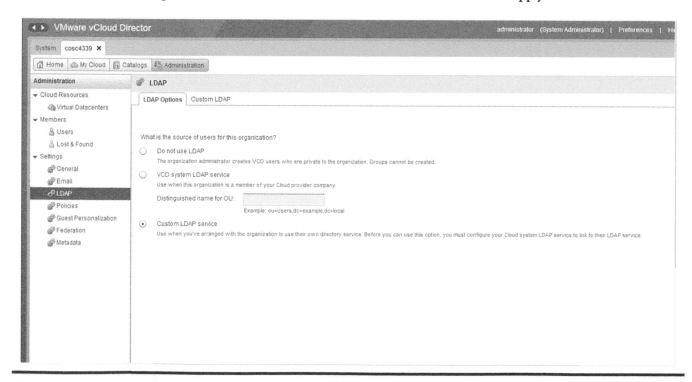

Figure 11.70   Custom LDAP service.

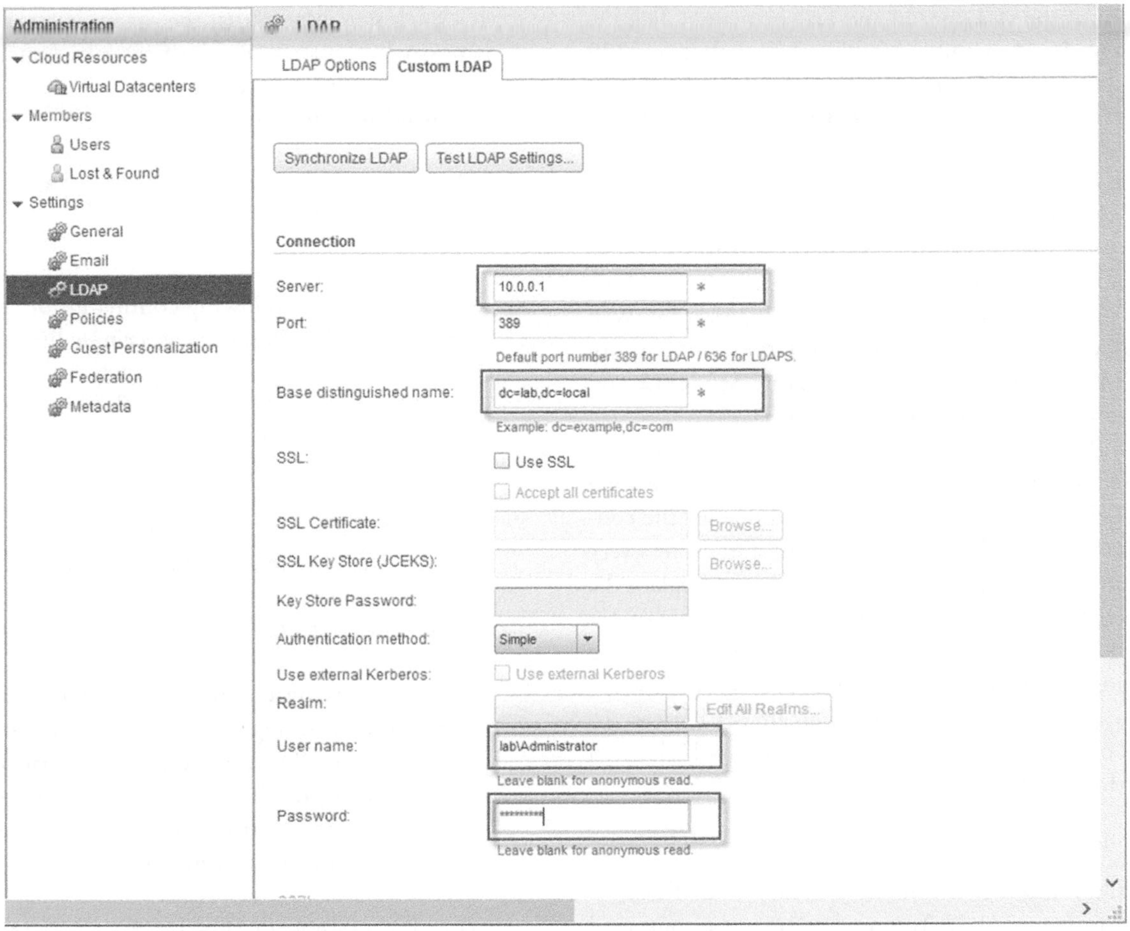

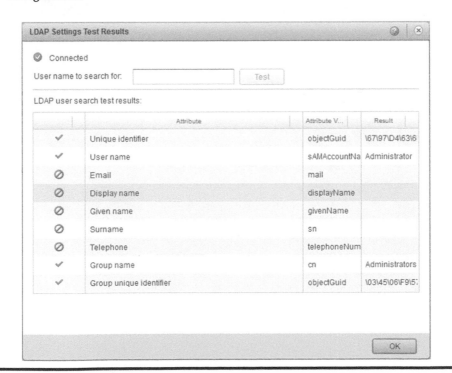

Figure 11.71   LDAP configuration.

Figure 11.72   Connected to domain controller.

20. Log out of the vCD portal and Log in again. Click the **Manage & Monitor** menu. Double-click **cosc4339** and click the **Administration** submenu. Click the **Users** link and click the **Import Users** icon, as shown in Figure 11.73.
21. In the Import Users dialog, click the **Search** button, select the user **Student2**, and click the **Add** button. In the Assign role dropdown list, select **vApp** Author, as shown in Figure 11.74. Then, click OK.
22. Now, Student2 can log on to the organization Web portal with the URL https://vcd.lab.local/cloud/org /cosc4339. Log in with the user name **Student2** and password such as **Passw0rd!** (Figure 11.75).
23. SSL will be used to secure the remote access to vCD. To use SSL, you need to create two certificates for each vCD cell: one for the Web portal and one for the console proxy. Since the self-signed certificates expire every three months, it requires the administrator to replace the old certificates with newly created certificates. To get started, log on to the vCD console with the user name **root** and password such as **Passw0rd!** (Figure 11.76).
24. You will use the Java keytool to create certificates. To do so, change the directory where the keytool is located with the following command:

```
cd /opt/vmware/vcloud-director/jre/bin
```

25. Run the following command to create a certificate, as shown in Figure 11.77. You need to enter the command as a single line. Notice that the password for the keystore is **passwd**. The keystore **certificates.ks** is stored in the directory/opt/vmware/vcloud-director/jre/bin. (Enter the command as a single line.)

```
./keytool -keystore certificates.ks
-storetype JCEKS -storepass passwd
-genkey -keyalg RSA -alias http
```

26. Similarly, run the following command for the console proxy: (Enter the command as a single line.)

```
./keytool -keystore certificates.ks
-storetype JCEKS -storepass passwd
-genkey -keyalg RSA -alias consoleproxy
```

27. Later, to replace the expired certificates, change to the directory with the following command:

```
cd /opt/vmware/vcloud-director/bin
```

28. Run the following command for certificate management, as shown in Figure 11.78. You need to enter the path to the certificate store as **/opt/vmware/vcloud -director/jre/bin**. The password for the keystore is **passwd**. After the certificates are replaced, you need to reboot vCD with the command `reboot`.

```
./cell-management-tool certificates
```

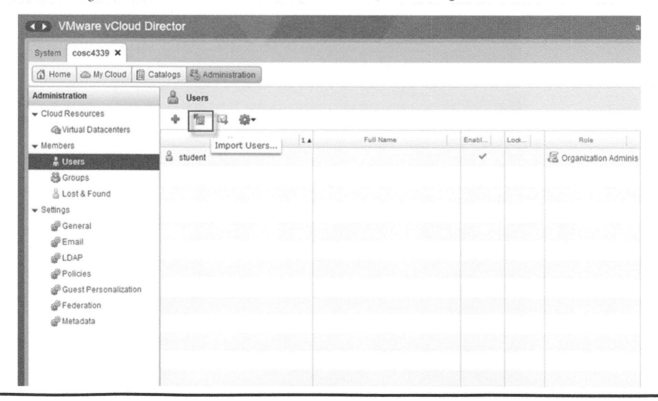

Figure 11.73 Importing user.

Figure 11.74   Importing Student2.

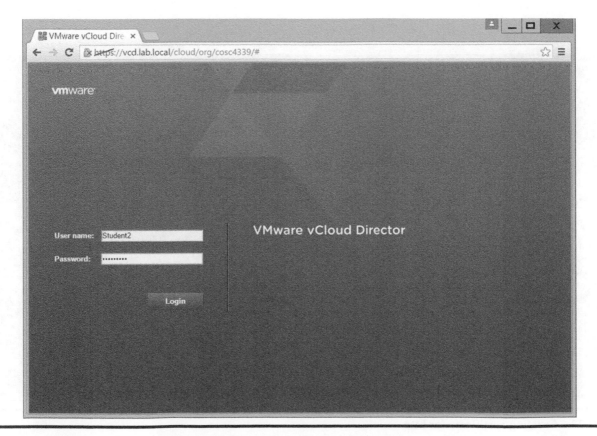

Figure 11.75   Logging on to cosc4339 organization.

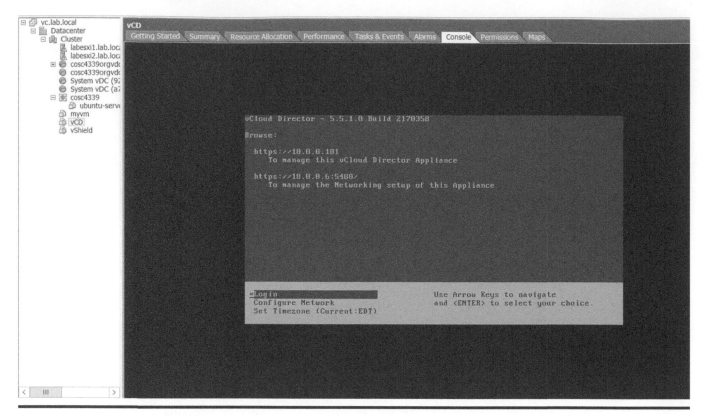

Figure 11.76   Logging on to vCD.

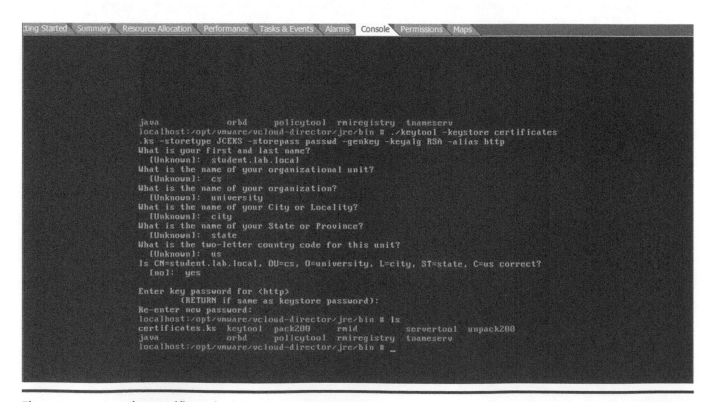

Figure 11.77   Creating certificate for http.

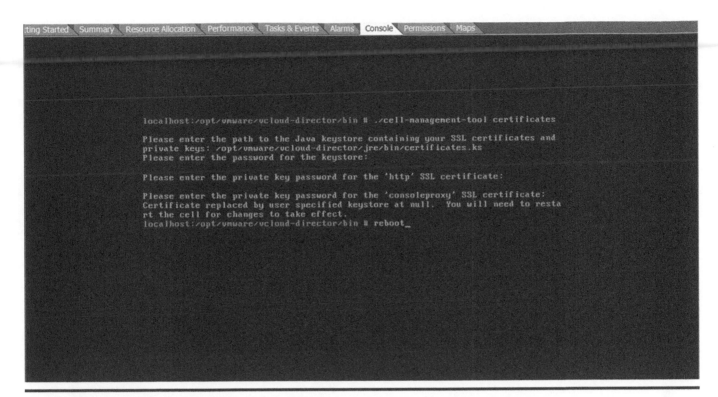

Figure 11.78 Replacing certificates.

In this task, you have completed three jobs to support the IaaS service. You created a vApp and made it accessible from an external network through a Web portal. You connected vCD to Active Directory for user authentication. You also learned how to create new SSL certificates and how to replace the old certificates.

11.6 Summary

This chapter provides an overview about vCD. It illustrates how vCD can be used to develop cloud computing services in the private cloud environment. vCD is designed to meet the requirements for a cloud computing environment. With vCD, administrators can allocate the computing resources for the cloud provider. This chapter covers the components of a provider resource pool such as datastores, virtual networks, CPUs, memory, and so on. With the provider resource pool available, administrators can distribute resources to organizations created for cloud subscribers. Once an organization has its computing resources, its administrator can create vApps to support cloud services such as IaaS, SaaS, and PaaS.

The hands-on activity in this chapter illustrates the installation and configuration of vCD. It also shows how to create components in vCD. The last task in the hands-on activity is about developing and managing cloud services. With limited resources in the lab environment, the vApp created for the IaaS service only includes a single VM. The vApp remote access takes the easiest way: direct connection to an external network. In a production environment, various vApps, including multiple VMs and their own networks, should be created to support various cloud computing services. Remote access security should be enhanced with the firewall, NAS, SSL, and VPN.

REVIEW QUESTIONS

1. What are the requirements for a cloud computing environment?
2. What is vCD?
3. What is the usage of vCD?
4. What is the relationship between vCenter and vCD?
5. What can we benefit from the isolation of vCD from vCenter?
6. What is a provider vDC, and how does it work in vCD?
7. What is an organization, and how does it work in vCD?
8. What is a vApp, and how does it work in vCD?
9. What is a catalog, and how does it work in vCD?
10. Describe the vCD appliance.

11. Why should vCD be connected to vCenter?
12. Why should vCD be connected to vShield Manager?
13. What databases are supported by vCD?
14. What is the usage of a database in vCD?
15. Why does vCD require certificates?
16. Describe the multicell configuration.
17. Describe the network pools used in vCD.
18. What are the resource allocation models in an organization vDC?
19. What are the commonly used organization network services?
20. What are the catalog types?

Appendix A: IT Infrastructure Preparation for Supporting Business

In this activity, an information technology (IT) infrastructure is prepared for installing VMware vCloud Suite. The infrastructure consists of physical server computers and network devices specified in Chapter 1. As an example, let us consider a basic implementation that costs about $10,000. The configuration of the IT infrastructure is shown in Figure A.1.

This implementation can be expanded in many ways. For example, one can use two lab switches and two storage switches to improve redundancy. Also, for a large project, one can add more Elastic Sky X Integrated (ESXi) servers and vCenter Servers. The state-of-the art server machines with powerful central processing units and random access memory can be used for the installation of ESXi. The network storage can be implemented with the fast solid-state drive disks and storage area network technology.

In Figure A.1, each volume in the network storage is formed as RAID 1 with two hard drives for better reliability. There is a direct connection between ESXi host 1 and ESXi host 2 without a switch. This type of design is for improving performance and security. Assume that the virtual machines in a vApp are hosted by different ESXi hosts. The direct link between two ESXi hosts provides a private connection for better performance and security. The direct connection is independent from other network traffic. It is also isolated from other network equipment such as network switches. To create a direct connection, a new virtual switch should be created on each ESXi host server. Then, associate the virtual switch with an uplink network interface card (NIC). Figure A.2 illustrates the virtual switch and the associated NIC for the direct connection between the two ESXi host servers. Now, for a virtual machine to communicate to other

virtual machines in a vApp over the direct connection, add a new virtual NIC to the virtual machine. Then, connect the new NIC to the newly created virtual switch.

Figure A.2 shows a standard virtual switch created for the network storage. The storage-related network traffic is delivered to the network storage device through two uplink NICs: (1) vmnic3 and (2) vmnic4.

Also, as shown in Figure A.2, vSwitch2 is created for direct connection. Student0x are vApps that support hands-on activities in an IT class. Each vApp includes a router, a server, and a client virtual machine. The communication between the server and client is done over the direct connection.

Figure A.3 illustrates the virtual network switch created for the virtual network and virtual machine management. Through this network, the ESXi host servers can communicate with other servers such as vCenter, vCloud Director, the domain controller, database server, and vCloud Networking and Security (vCNS) Server. This network is also used to communicate with the computers installed in a computer lab on campus.

Instead of being installed on physical machines, servers such as the vCenter Server, database server, and so on can also be implemented on virtual machines hosted by ESXi hosts. VMware vCloud Suite provides an appliance for vCenter, vCNS, and vCloud Director, respectively. An appliance is a ready-made virtual machine installed with vCenter, vCNS, or vCloud Director. The vCenter appliance and vCloud Director appliance even include a ready-built database. The appliance greatly simplifies the installation process. On the other hand, the appliance may not be suitable for a very large project.

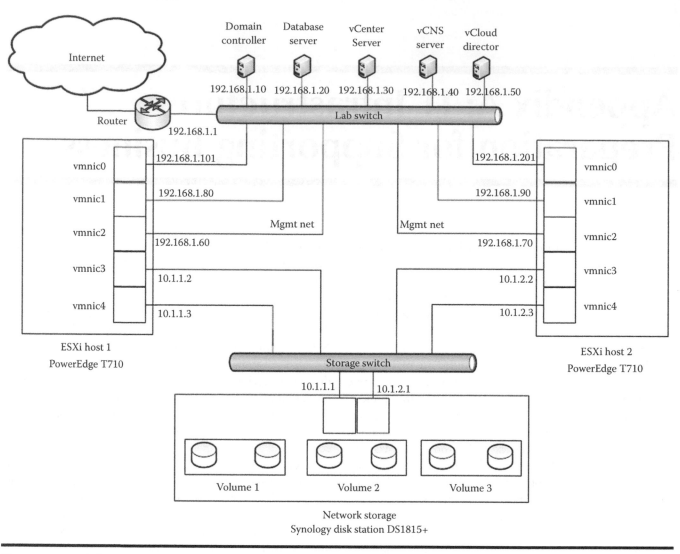

Figure A.1   IT infrastructure configuration.

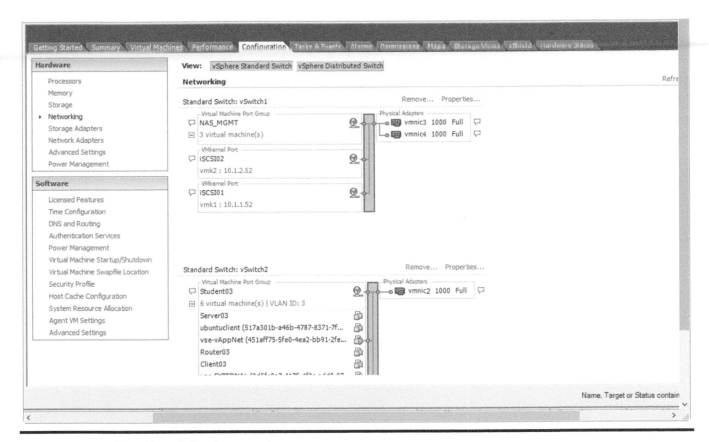

Figure A.2   Configuration of direct connection.

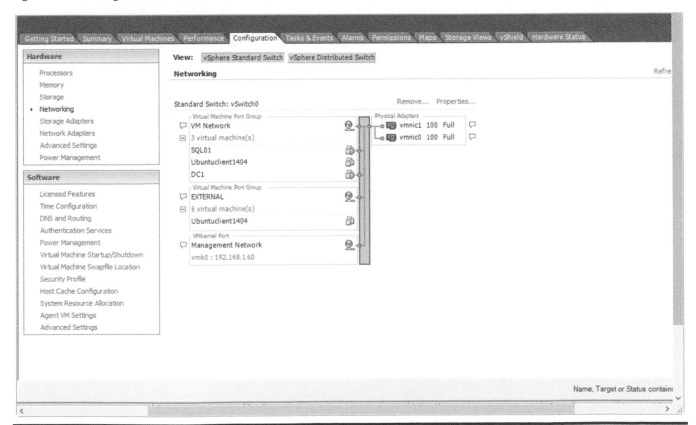

Figure A.3   Management network virtual switch.

Appendix B: SQL Server Database Installation and Configuration

vCenter stores its configuration data, task data, event data, performance data, monitoring data, and other statistic data in a database. The database is a key component of a vCenter Server. The vCenter Server communicates with the database during its operation. For reliability and security, the vCenter database can be installed on a separate machine. With the separate database, it is relatively easier to rebuild vCenter if it crashes.

As a key component of the vCenter Server, the database needs to be well maintained. The operation data, such as the task data, event data, and performance data, and statistic data grow over time. The administrator needs to closely monitor the storage space to make sure that the database has adequate space for growth. There should be a policy for aging and purging historical data. The administrator should frequently back up the database for database recovery in case of database failure.

vCenter supports database management systems from major database vendors. For example, vCenter supports IBM DB2, Microsoft SQL Server, and Oracle. When vCenter is installed on a personal computer (PC) with the Windows operating system, DB2, SQL Server, and Oracle are all supported by vCenter. On the other hand, the vCenter Server Virtual Appliance only supports DB2 and Oracle. For a small project, one can also use the embedded database provided by the vCenter Server Virtual Appliance.

We plan to install vCenter on a server with Windows Server 2012 installed. Microsoft SQL Server 2012 is chosen due to its large user base. The minimum requirement for a PC to run SQL Server is one central processing unit, 1-GB random access memory, and 4-GB storage.

As a front-end application, vCenter is connected to the back-end database with the Open Database Connectivity (ODBC) technology. Once connected to SQL Server through ODBC, with the database owner permission, vCenter users can access SQL Server to manage the data stored on the database.

Configuring SQL Server 2012: In this section, we will configure the server named SQL.lab.local to host databases that provide storage for vCenter. The following are the steps for the deployment of SQL Server:

1. Assume that the server to be used to install SQL Server has a solid-state drive (SSD) for better performance. Also, the server has a network interface card (NIC) with a fixed Internet Protocol (IP) address.
2. In Server Manager, click the **Local Server** link on the left-hand side of your screen. Then, click **IPv4 address assigned by DHCP, IPv6 enabled**, as shown in Figure B.1.
3. Assume that you have set up a domain controller with the server name dc.lab.local and the IP address 10.0.0.1. The domain name system (DNS) server is implemented on the domain controller. Before you can join SQL Server to a domain, for example, lab.local, you need to make sure that the NIC is configured to use dc.lab.local as its DNS server. To do so, right-click **Ethernet** and select **Properties**, as shown in Figure B.2.
4. Check **Internet Protocol Version 4 (TCP/IPv4)** and click **Properties**, as shown in Figure B.3.
5. In the Internet Protocol Version 4 Properties (TCP/IPv4) dialog, enter the IP address of dc.lab.local, which is **10.0.0.1** for the preferred DNS server, as shown in Figure B.4. Then, click **OK**.
6. After you are done with the configuration of the NIC, go back to the Local Server page. Click the **WORKGROUP** link, as shown in Figure B.5.
7. Once the configuration of the NIC is complete, click the **Change** button in the System Properties dialog.
8. In the Computer Name/Domain Changes dialog, check the **Domain** option and type the domain name **lab.local**, as shown in Figure B.6. Then, click **OK**. You will be prompted to enter the user name and password of the administrator of your domain controller DC. After connected to DC, click **OK** and restart the server hosting SQL Server.
9. Log on to the domain controller DC. In Server Manager, click the **Tools** menu and select **Active Directory Users and Computers**. Then, click **Users**, **New**, and **User**, as shown in Figure B.7.

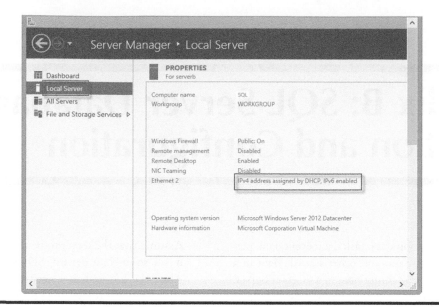

Figure B.1 SQL.lab.local server properties.

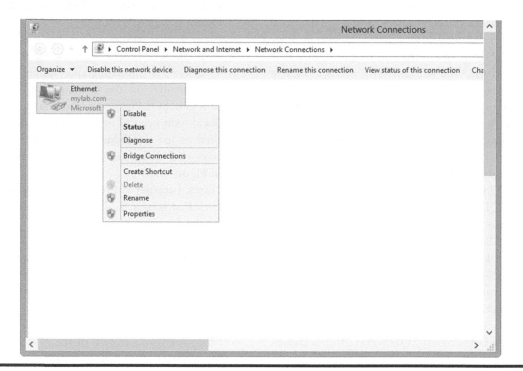

Figure B.2 Ethernet configuration.

10. In the New Object—User dialog, create a new user **SQLAdmin**, as shown in Figure B.8. Then, click **Next**.
11. You will be prompted to enter the password. Type in the password and check the option **Password never expires**, as shown in Figure B.9.
12. Right-click the newly created user **SQLAdmin** and select **Properties**. Add the user to the Administrators' group (Figure B.10).

13. Log on to the server hosting SQL Server with the user SQLAdmin. On the Server Manager page, click the **Tools** menu and select **Computer Management** and **Local Users and Groups**.
14. Click the **Groups** node and right-click **Administrators**. Select **Add to Group** and click the **Add** button.
15. Add the user **SQLAdmin** to the Administrators group, as shown in Figure B.11.

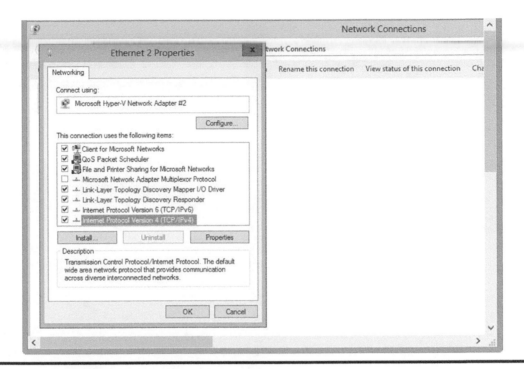

Figure B.3 Ethernet properties.

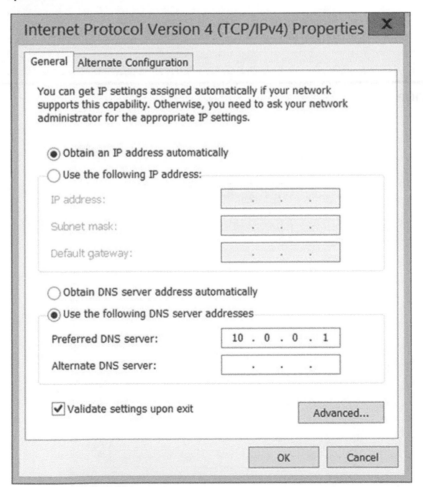

Figure B.4 IP address of preferred DNS server.

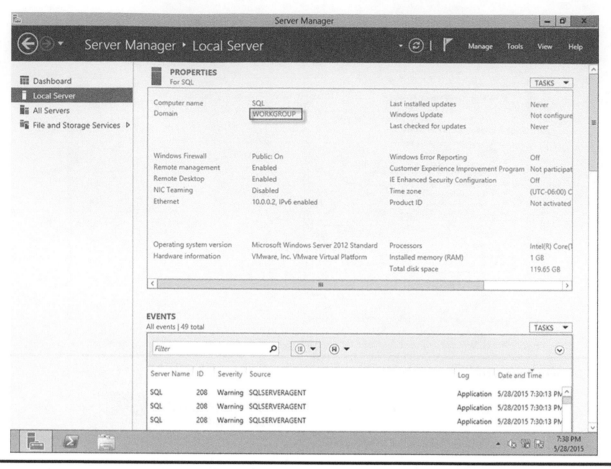

Figure B.5 WORKGROUP.

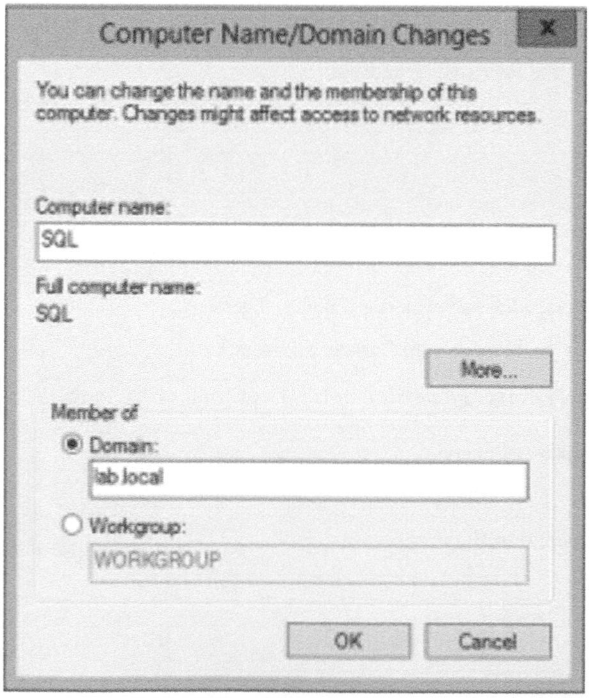

Figure B.6 Computer and domain names.

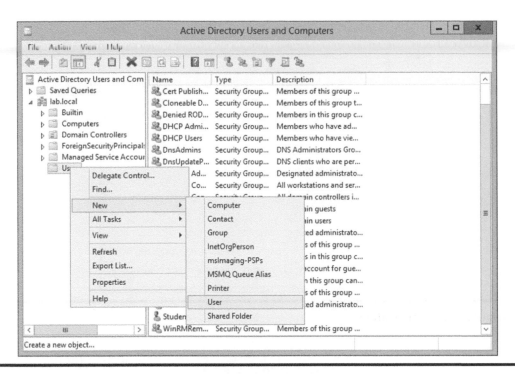

Figure B.7 Creating new user.

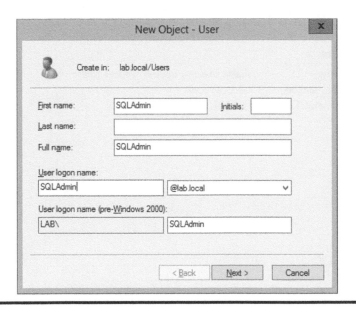

Figure B.8 New user configuration.

16. To install SQL Server 2012, download the Enterprise 64-bit version of SQL Server 2012 installation image file from the DreamSpark Web site: en_sql_server_2012 _enterprise_edition_x86_x64_dvd_813294.iso. The file needs to be burned to a digital videodisc (DVD).

17. Insert the DVD to the DVD drive on the server hosting SQL Server. When prompted, run the **SETUP .EXE** file (Figure B.12).

18. On the SQL Server Installation Center page, click the link **Installation** in the left pane. In the right pane, click the link **New SQL Server stand-alone installation or add features to an existing installation**, as shown in Figure B.13.

19. On the Setup Support Rules page, if successful, click **OK**.

20. On the Product Key page, make sure that the product key has been added and click **Next**.

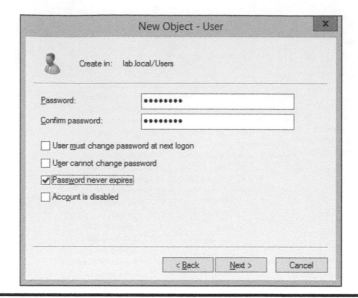

Figure B.9 Password and its specification.

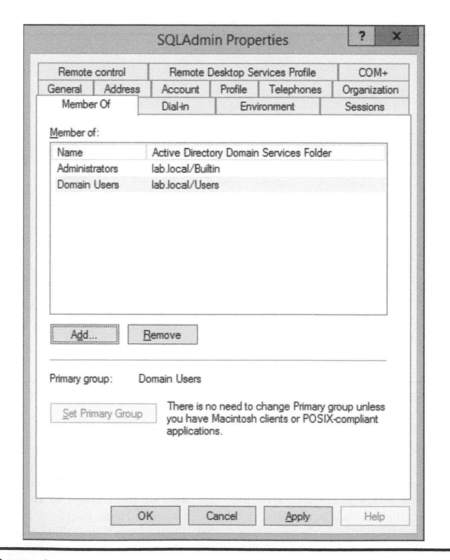

Figure B.10 Administrators' group.

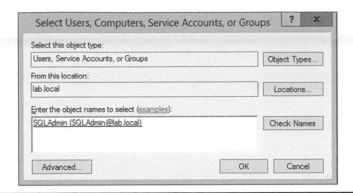

Figure B.11 Add user to administrators group.

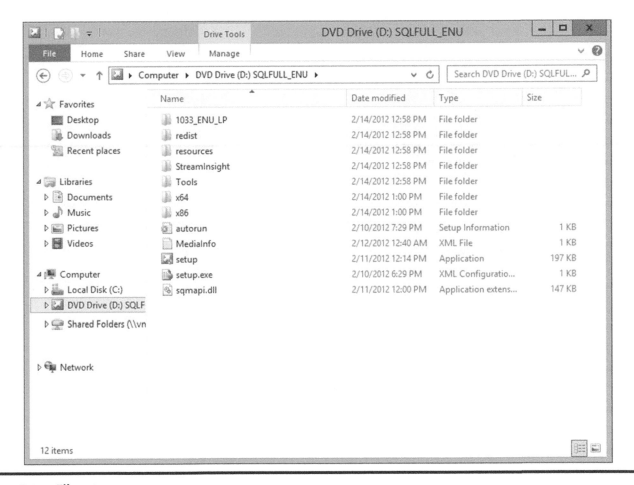

Figure B.12 File setup.

21. On the License Terms page, accept the license terms and click **Next**.
22. On the Product Updates page, click **Next**.
23. On the Setup Support Rules page, if there are no failures even with a few warnings, as shown in Figure B.14, click **Next**.
24. On the Setup Role page, check the option **SQL Server Feature Installation** and click **Next**.

25. On the Feature Selection page, select features, as shown in Figure B.15, and click **Next**. If you have an SSD disk, install SQL Server to the SSD disk (Figure B.15).
26. On the Installation Rules page, if there is no failure, click **Next**.
27. On the Instance Configuration page, take the default and click **Next**.

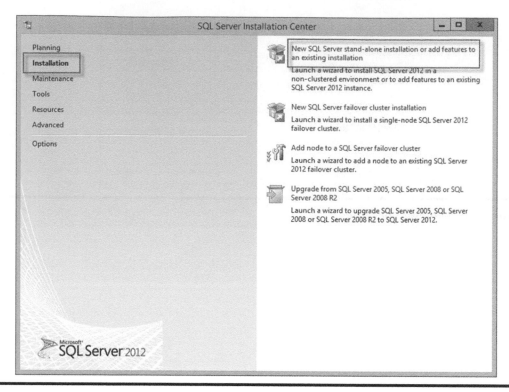

Figure B.13 SQL Server installation center.

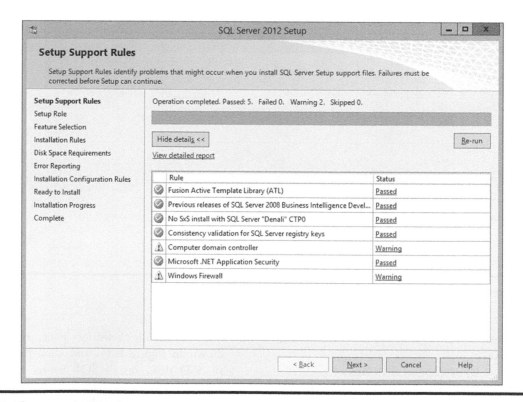

Figure B.14 Setting up support rules.

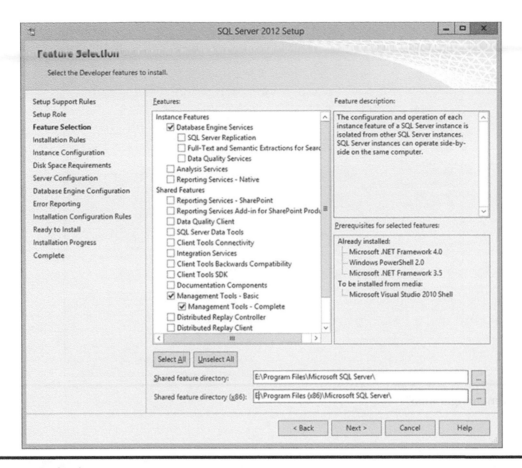

Figure B.15 Feature selection.

28. On the Disk Space Requirements page, if you have enough disk space, click **Next**.
29. On the Server Configuration page, make sure that the account name for SQL Server Agent and SQL Server Database Engine is set as **lab\SQLAdmin** and Startup Type is set as **Automatic** (Figure B.16). Click **Next**.
30. On the Database Engine Configuration page, make sure that **Windows authentication mode** is selected. If the current user is SQLAdmin, click the **Add Current User** button (Figure B.17). If not, click the **Add** button to add the user SQLAdmin (Figure B.18). Then, click **Next**.

31. On the Error Reporting page, click **Next**.
32. On the Installation Configuration Rules page, if there is no failure, click **Next**.
33. On the Ready to Install page, click the **Install** button.
34. On the Complete page, if the installation is successful, click **Close**.
35. To view the installed SQL Server, on the **Start** menu, type **SQL**. You will see the installed SQL Server components, as shown in Figure B.19. Right-click **SQL Server Management Studio** and select **Pin to Start**. You should be able to log on to SQL Server with the SQLAdmin account.

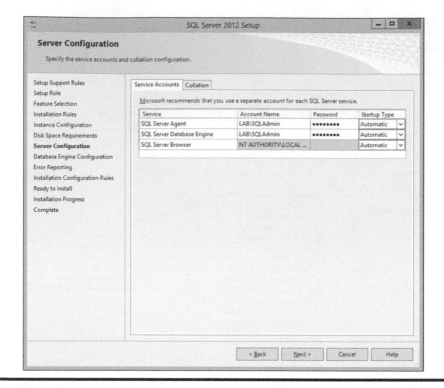

Figure B.16 Server configuration.

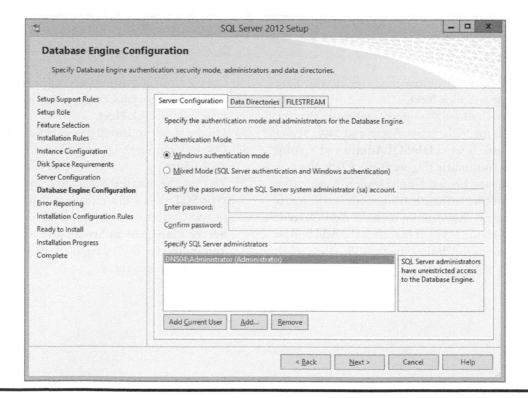

Figure B.17 Adding SQL Server administrator.

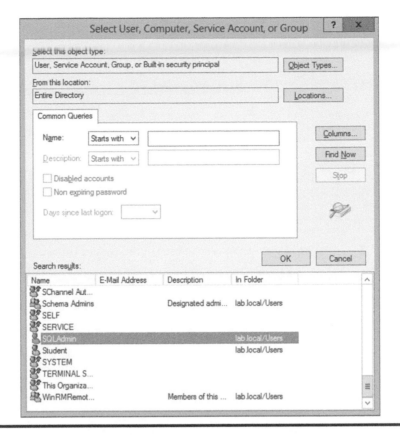

Figure B.18   User SQLAdmin.

Figure B.19   Installed SQL Server components.

Appendix C: Installing and Configuring vCenter Server with SQL Server Database

There are two ways to install vCenter. One way is to install vCenter on a physical machine named as VC, with at least 4-GB random access memory, 140-GB storage space, and two network interface cards (NICs). The other way is to install the vCenter appliance on an Elastic Sky X Integrated (ESXi) host, which is discussed in Chapter 4. Before the installation of vCenter Server, make sure that the domain controller has been installed and properly configured, as shown in Chapter 2. Also, suppose that the server used to host vCenter has Windows Server 2012 installed. The installation and configuration of vCenter Server can be accomplished with the following tasks:

- *Task 1:* Installation preparation
- *Task 2:* vCenter Single Sign-On (SSO) installation
- *Task 3:* Inventory service installation
- *Task 4:* vCenter Server configuration
- *Task 5:* vSphere Web Client installation

Let us start with Task 1.

Task 1: Installation Preparation

Before the vCenter Server installation process gets started, you need to make sure that the virtual machine prepared for vCenter Server is properly configured.

- Connect the VC virtual machine to the private network that connects to the domain controller DC and the server hosting SQL Server.
- In Active Directory, create a user who has the administrator privilege on the VC server.
- The VC virtual machine must be configured to join the domain lab.local.
- Create a database on SQL Server to store vCenter data.

- The software SQL Native Client needs to be installed on the VC server so that it can communicate with the SQL Server installed previously.
- Establish an Open Database Connectivity (ODBC) connection to the SQL virtual machine.

The following steps connect the VC server to the private network that connects the domain controller DC and the SQL Server:

1. Start the server and log in as the administrator. Click the link **Local Server** on the left-hand side of your screen.
2. A server needs a fixed Internet Protocol (IP) address. To assign the NIC connecting to the private network a fixed IP address, at the lower-right corner of the screen, right-click the network icon and select **Open Network and Sharing Center**, as shown in Figure C.1.
3. On the Network and Sharing Center page, click the link **Change adapter settings**.
4. Right-click the **Ethernet** icon for the NIC connecting to the private network and select **Properties**, as shown in Figure C.2.
5. After the Ethernet Properties dialog is opened, click **Internet Protocol Version 4**, as shown in Figure C.3. Then, click the **Properties** button.
6. In the Internet Protocol Version 4 Properties dialog, select the option **Use the following IP address** and specify the IP address as **10.0.0.3**, network mask as **255.0.0.0**, the default gateway as **10.0.0.1**, and the preferred DNS server as **10.0.0.1** (Figure C.4). Then, click **OK**.
7. You need to create a user with the administrator privilege for VC.lab.local, which is used to host vCenter. To do so, in Server Manager, click **Tools** and **Active Directory Users and Computers**.

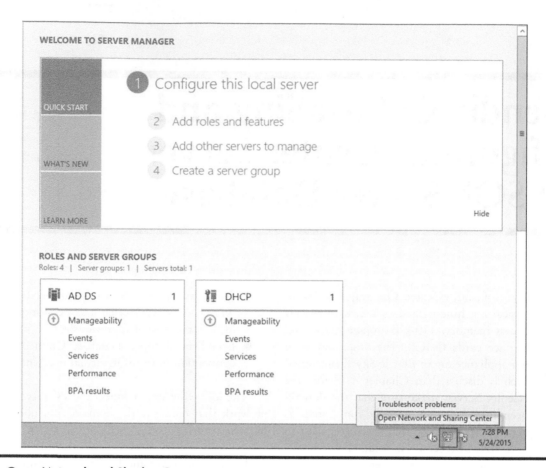

Figure C.1   Open Network and Sharing Center.

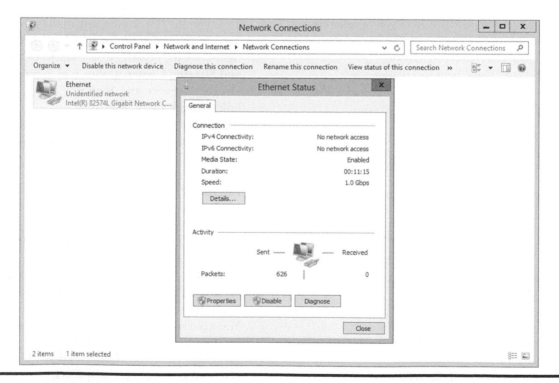

Figure C.2   Ethernet properties.

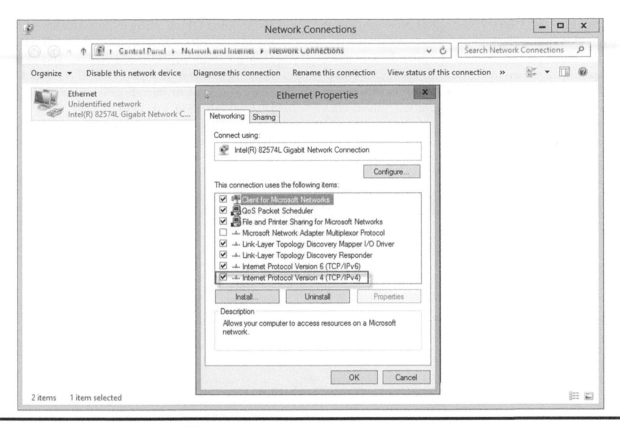

Figure C.3   Internet Protocol Version 4.

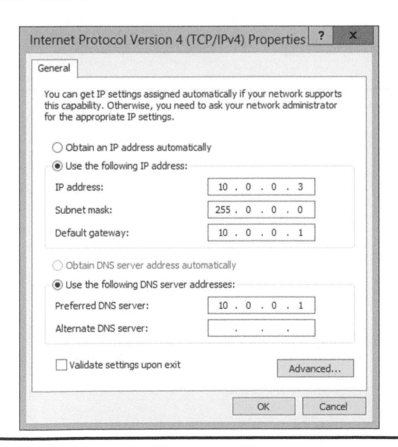

Figure C.4   Internet Protocol Version 4 Properties.

8. Right-click the **Users** node, select **New** and select **User**, as shown in Figure C.5.
9. In the New Object—User dialog, enter the user name **vmadmin**, as shown in Figure C.6. Then, click **Next**.
10. Enter your password and check the option **Password never expires**, as shown in Figure C.7. Then, click **Next** and click **Finish**.
11. Right-click the newly created user **vmadmin** and select **Properties**. In the vmadmin Properties dialog, click the **Member Of** tab. Then, use the **Add** button to make the user vmadmin be the member of Administrators, Domain Admins, Domain Users, and Enterprise Admins, as shown in Figure C.8. Then, click **OK**.
12. Next, you need to join the VC server to the domain lab.local. To do so, log on to VC.
13. On the Dashboard of Server Manager, click **Local Server** on the left-hand side of the screen. Then, click the computer name.

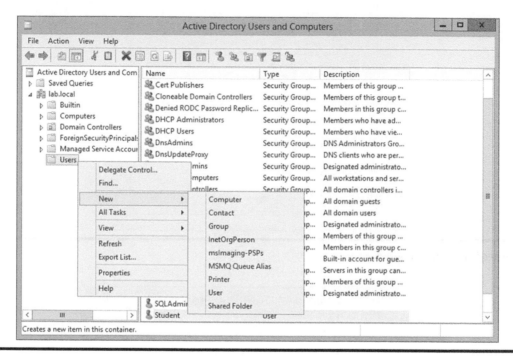

Figure C.5   Creating new user.

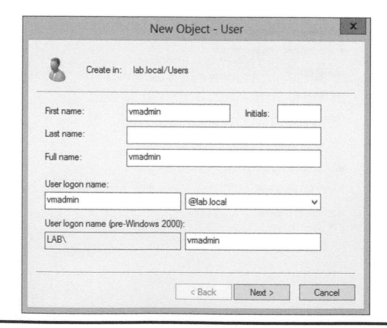

Figure C.6   User vmadmin.

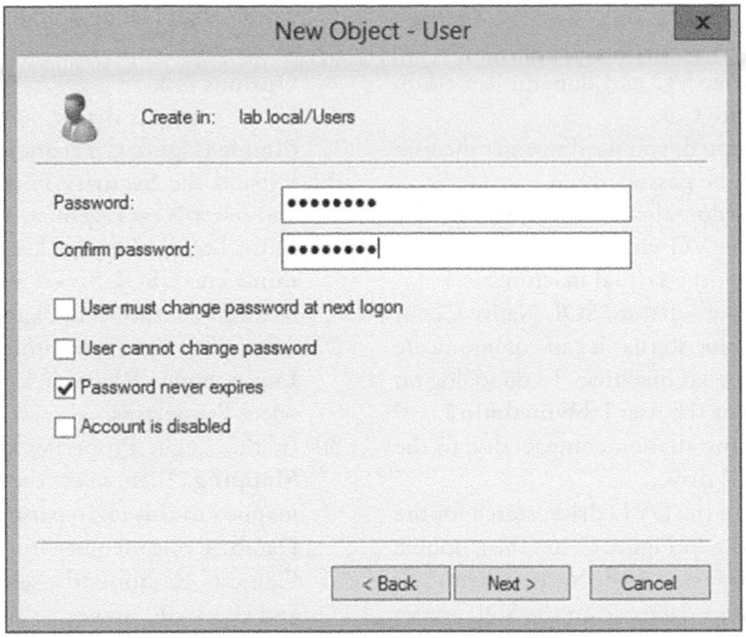

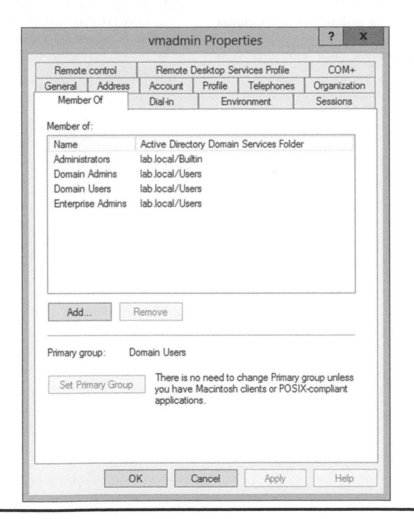

Figure C.7   Password.

Figure C.8   Memberships for user vmadmin.

14. In the System Properties dialog, click the **Change** button.
15. Enter the computer name **VC** and domain name **lab. local**, as shown in Figure C.9.
16. Click **OK**. When prompted, you need to enter the user name **vmadmin2** and the password.
17. Once connected to the domain controller, you will be prompted to restart the VC virtual machine. Follow the instruction to restart the virtual machine.
18. Next, you will install the software SQL Native Client on the VC virtual machine so that it can communicate with the SQL Server virtual machine. To do so, log on to the VC server again as the user **lab\vmadmin2**.
19. Insert the SQL Server installation compact disc to the digital videodisc (DVD) drive.
20. Back to the VC server, in the DVD drive, search for the **sqlncli.msi** file, as shown in Figure C.10. Then, double click the **x64** version to install SQL Native Client.
21. Now, you need to create a database on the SQL Server for vCenter. To do so, log on to the SQL Server.
22. On the Start menu, click **SQL Server Management Studio**, as shown in Figure C.11.
23. In the SQL Server login dialog, click the **Connect** button.
24. Right-click the **Databases** node and select **New Database**.
25. In the New Database dialog, enter the database name **vCenter02**, as shown in Figure C.12. Then, click the **Options** link.
26. In the Options dialog, specify the recovery model as **Simple** (Figure C.13) and then click **OK**.
27. Expand the **Security** node. Then, right-click **Logins** and select **New Login**, as shown in Figure C.14.
28. In the Login—New dialog, enter the login name **vmadmin2**, check **SQL Server authentication** and enter your password, as shown in Figure C.15. Then, click **OK**.
29. After the login vmadmin2 is created, expand the **Login** node. Right-click the login **vmadmin2** and select **Properties**.
30. In the Login Properties dialog, click the link **User Mapping**. Then, select the database **msdb** in the Users mapped to this login pane and check **db-owner** in the Database role membership for msdb pane, as shown in Figure C.16. Similarly, select the database **vCenter02** and check **db_owner**, as shown in Figure C.17.
31. On the Start menu, click **SQL Server Configuration** (Figure C.18).
32. In the SQL Server Configuration Manager dialog, make sure that **TCP/IP** and **Named Pipes** are enabled for Client Protocols and Protocols for MSSQLSERVER, as shown in Figure C.19. Then, exit SQL Server Management Studio.

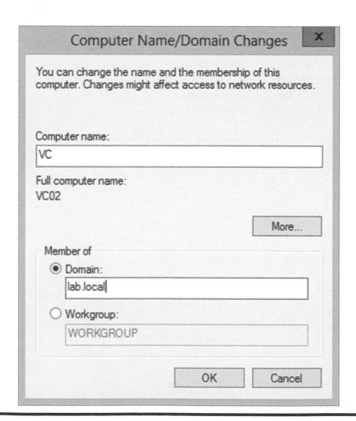

Figure C.9 Computer name and domain name.

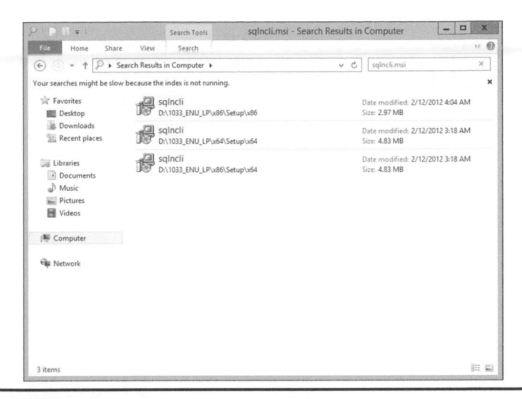

Figure C.10   sqlncli file.

Figure C.11   SQL Server Management Studio.

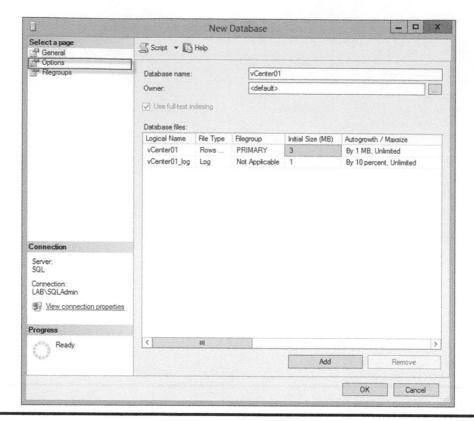

Figure C.12 New Database.

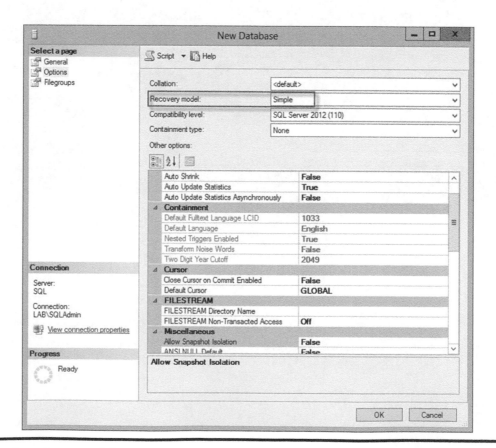

Figure C.13 Simple recovery model.

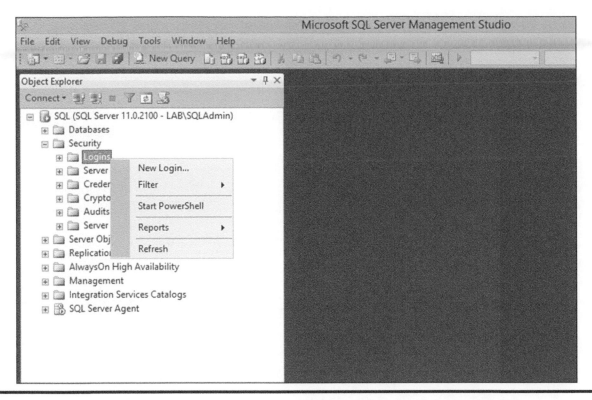

Figure C.14   New Login.

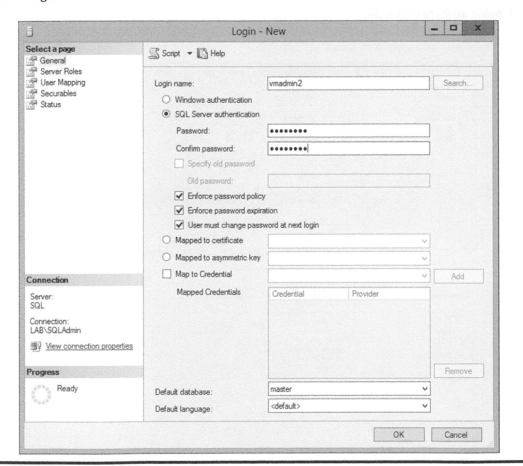

Figure C.15   New login vmadmin2.

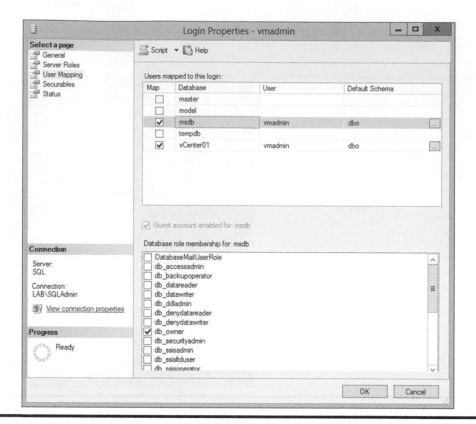

Figure C.16 Mapping msdb to vmadmin.

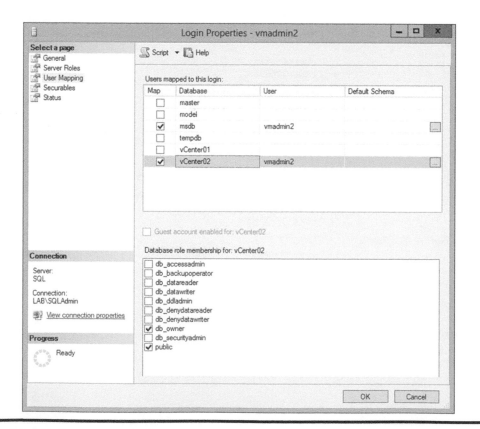

Figure C.17 Mapping vCenter02 to vmadmin.

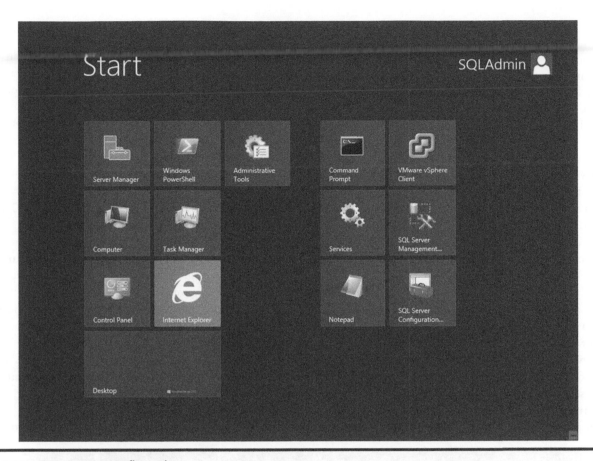

Figure C.18   SQL Server Configuration.

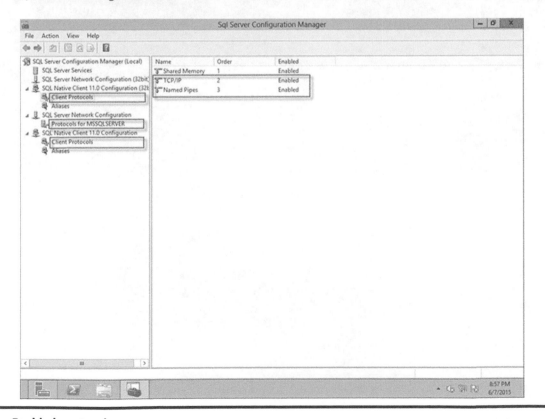

Figure C.19   Enabled protocols.

33. Now, from the VC virtual machine, you need to create an ODBC connection to the newly created database vCenter02. In the VC server, on the **Start** menu, click **Administrative Tools**, as shown in Figure C.20.

34. Once the Administrative Tools dialog is open, double-click **ODBC Data Sources (64bit)**, as shown in Figure C.21.

35. Click the **System DSN** tab and click the **Add** button.

36. In the Create New Data Source dialog, click **SQL Server Native Client 11.0**, as shown in Figure C.22 and then click **Finish**.

37. You will be prompted to create a new data source to SQL Server. In the DSN Configuration dialog, enter the data source name **vCenter** and make sure the server **SQL.lab.local** is selected, as shown in Figure C.23. Then, click **Next**.

38. In the Create a New Data Source to SQL Server dialog, select the option **With SQL Server authentication using a login ID and password entered by the user**. Then, enter the login ID **vmadmin2** and the password, as shown in Figure C.24. Then, click **Next**.

39. Then, click **Next** a few times and click **Finish** to get to the summary page (Figure C.25). Click the **Test Data Source** button. If successful, click **OK** to complete the configuration.

Task 2: vCenter SSO Installation

To install vCenter components, you need to get the installation media downloaded and make the media available in the DVD drive. You can download the installation media from a software vendor's Web site or from VMware directly through the following Uniform Resource Locator (URL): http://www.vmware.com/download

Assume that you have the installation media available; follow the steps below to go through the installation process.

1. Assume that the servers DC, SQL, and VC are still powered on. The installation DVD has been inserted into VC's DVD drive.

2. Log on to the VC virtual machine **lab\vmadmin2**. In the File explorer, double-click the DVD drive icon, as shown in Figure C.26.

3. On the vCenter for Windows page, click the **Install** button.

4. On the Welcome page, click **Next**.

5. On the End User License Agreement page, check **I accept the terms of the license agreement**. Then, click **Next**.

6. On the Select deployment type page, two types of deployment architectures, Embedded Deployment and

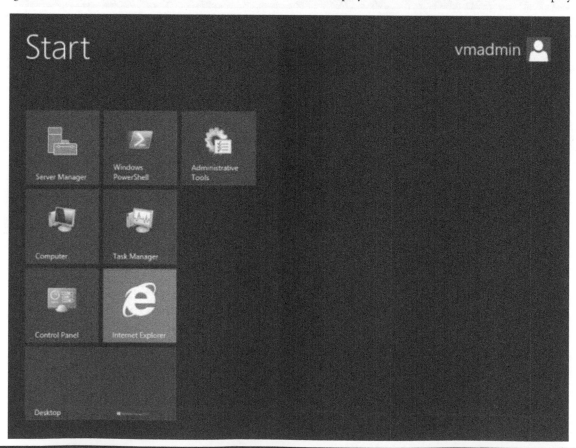

Figure C.20 Administrative Tools.

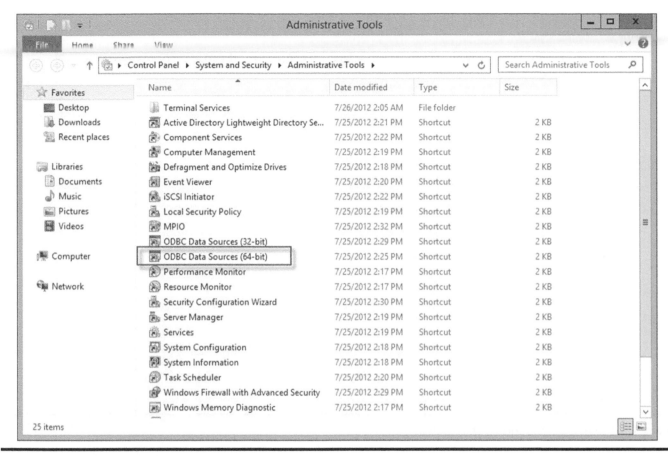

Figure C.21   ODBC Data Sources (64-bit).

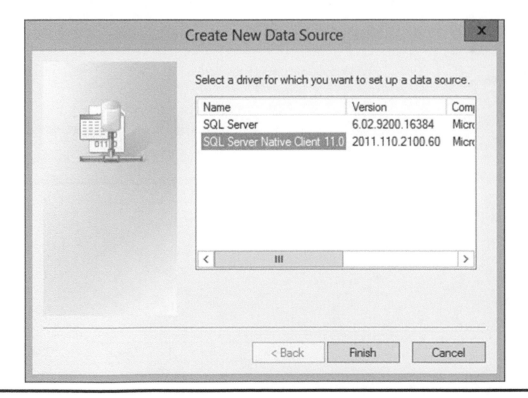

Figure C.22   SQL Server Native Client 11.0.

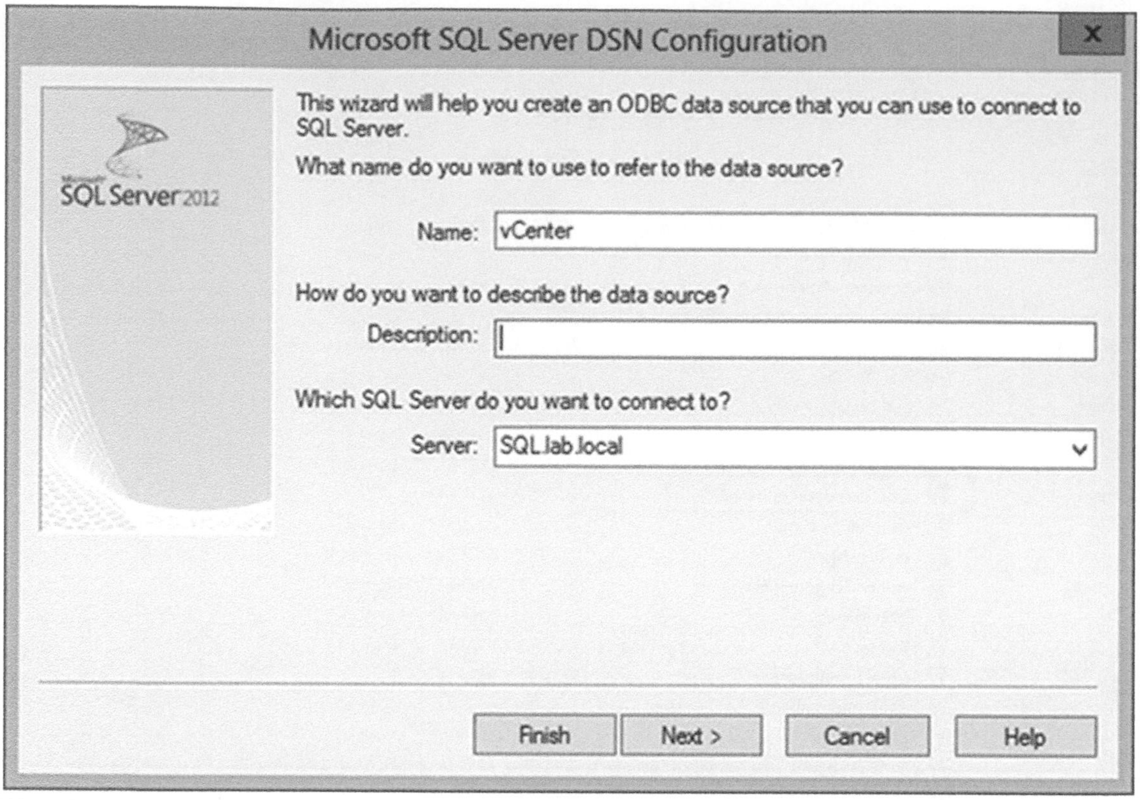

Figure C.23 ODBC data source configuration.

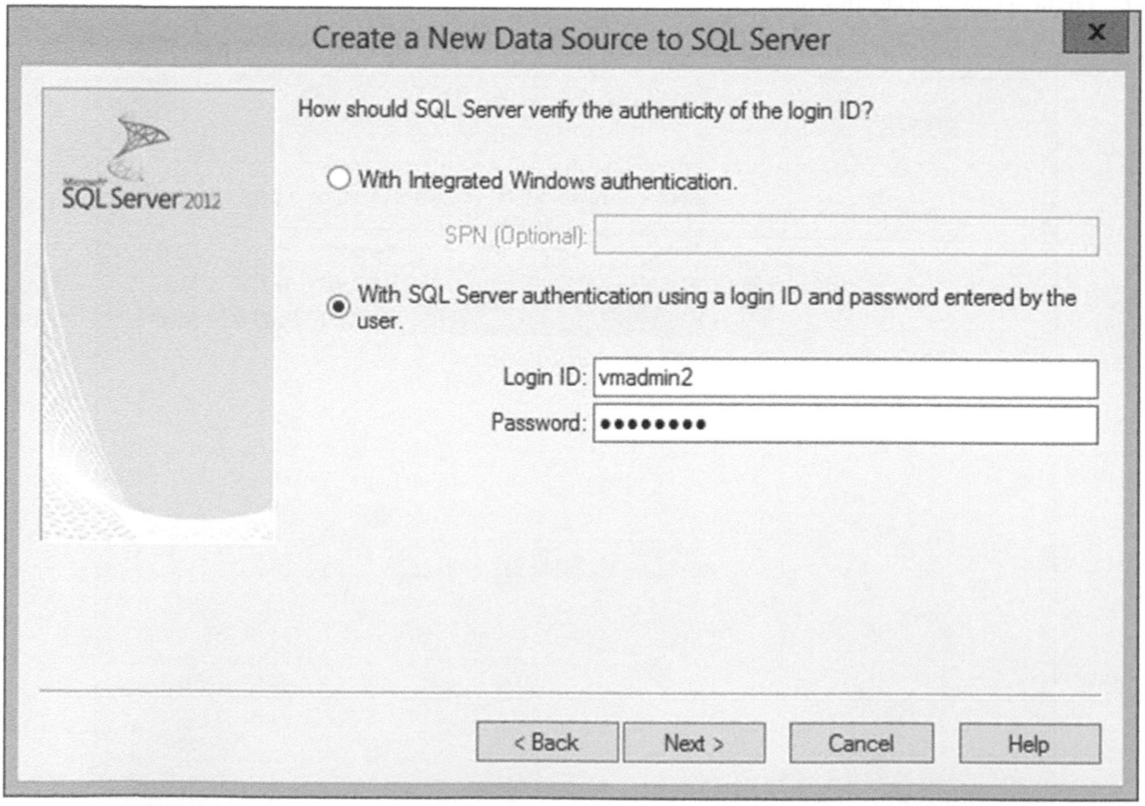

Figure C.24 SQL Server authentication.

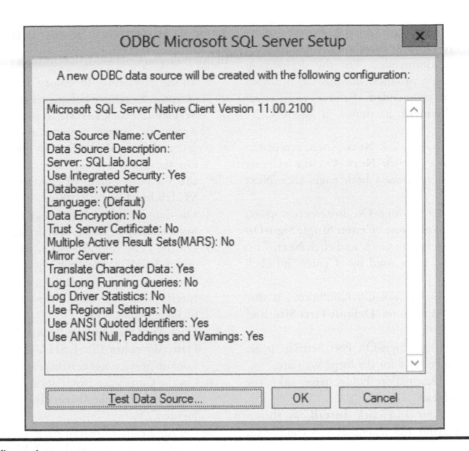

Figure C.25   Configuration summary.

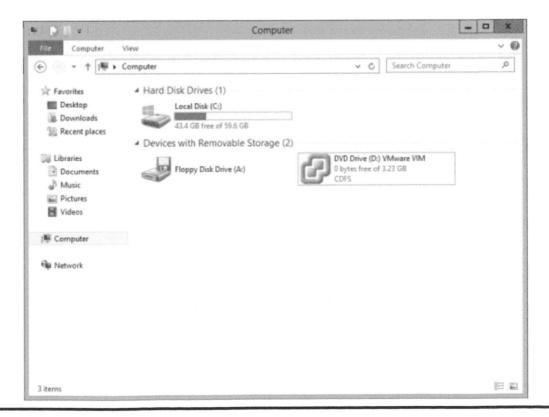

Figure C.26   Installation media in DVD Drive.

Centralized Deployment, are available. For the deployment with eight products or fewer installed, Embedded Deployment is recommended. For the deployment with more than eight products installed, Centralized Deployment is recommended. In our case, select **Embedded Deployment**, as shown in Figure C.27. Then, click **Next**.

7. On the Welcome page, click **Next**. Then, accept the license agreement and click **Next**. On the vCenter Single Sign-On Prerequisite Check page, click **Next** again.

8. On the vCenter Single Sign-On Information page, select the option **Standalone vCenter Single Sign-On Server**, as shown in Figure C.28, and click **Next**.

9. Enter the password to be used by vCenter and click **Next**.

10. On the vCenter Single Sign-On Configuration site, take the default site name **Default-First-Site** and click **Next**.

11. On the vCenter Single Sign-On Port Settings page, take the default port **7444** for the https Web site.

12. On the Change Destination Folder page, take the default and click **Next**.

13. Review the selections and click **Install**, as shown in Figure C.29. After the installation is completed, click **Finish**.

Task 3: Inventory Service Installation

In this task, you will install the Inventory Service component.

1. To install vCenter Inventory Service, in the VMware vCenter Installer dialog, click **vCenter Inventory Service** and click **Install**, as shown in Figure C.30.

2. Accept the license agreement and click **Next**. Also, accept the default destination folder and click **Next**.

3. On the Local System Information page, make sure that the Fully Qualified Domain Name is specified as **VC.lab.local** and click **Next**.

4. On the Configure Ports page, take the default port numbers (Figure C.31). Then, click **Next**.

5. On the JVM Memory page, select the inventory size option **Small**, as shown in Figure C.32 and click **Next**.

6. On the vCenter Single Sign On Information page, specify the SSO administrator's password (Figure C.33) and click **Next**.

7. Click **Yes** to accept the Secure Sockets Layer–Secure Hash Algorithm 1 (SSL SHA-1) fingerprint of the SSO Lookup Service leaf certificate.

8. On the Certificate Installation for Secure Connection page, click the **Install certificates** button, as shown in Figure C.34.

9. On the Ready to Install page, click **Install**. After the installation is completed, click **Finish**.

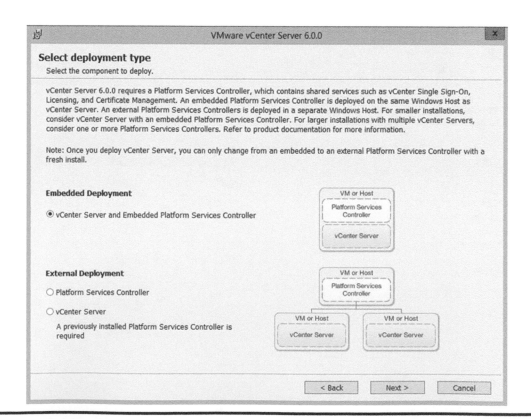

Figure C.27 **Selecting Embedded Deployment.**

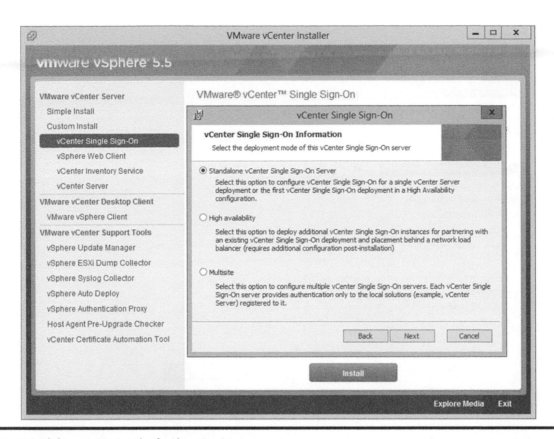

Figure C.28 Standalone vCenter Single Sign-On Server.

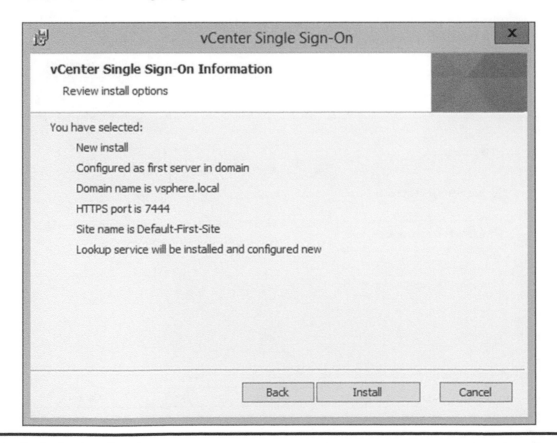

Figure C.29 Reviewing install options.

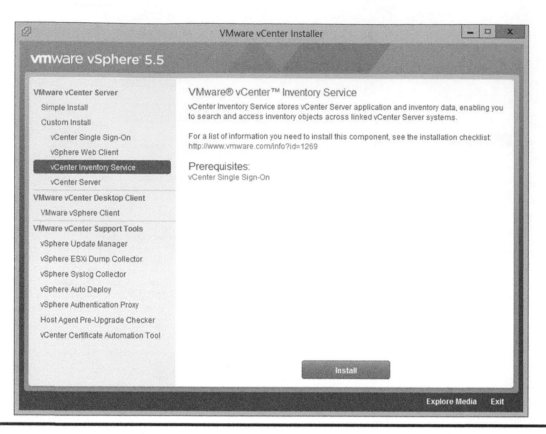

Figure C.30 **vCenter Inventory Service.**

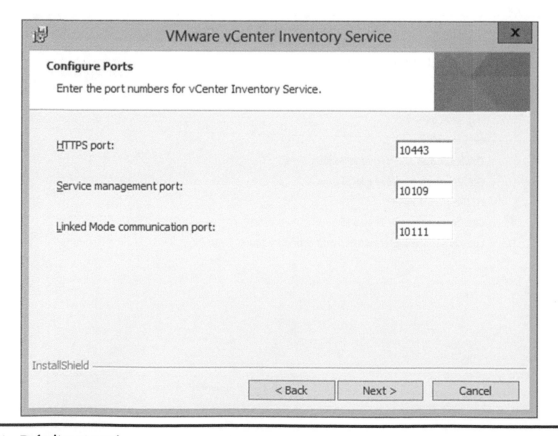

Figure C.31 **Default port numbers.**

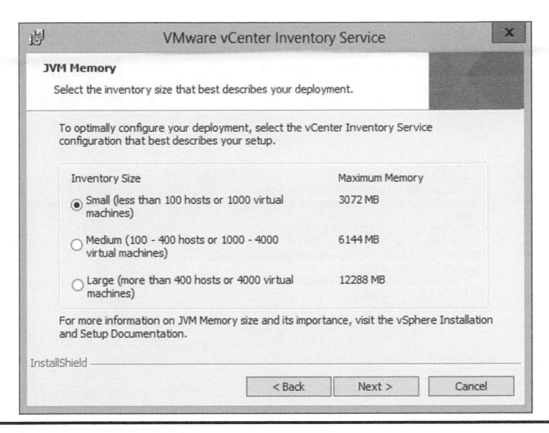

Figure C.32   Inventory size.

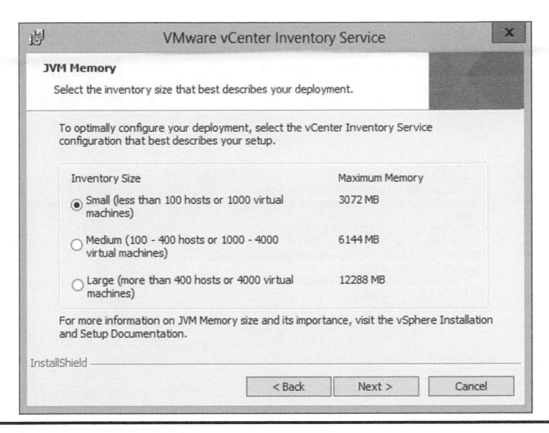

Figure C.33   Password for SSO administrator.

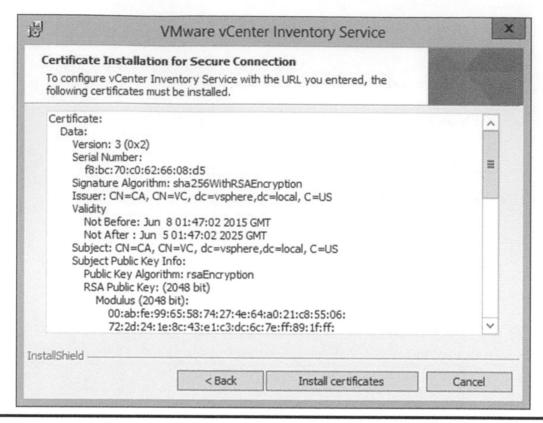

Figure C.34 Installing certificates.

Task 4: vCenter Server Configuration

With the SSO and Inventory Service installed, in this task, you will install vCenter Server. Follow the steps below to accomplish this task.

1. To install vCenter Server, in the VMware vCenter Installer dialog, click **vCenter Server** and click **Install**, as shown in Figure C.35.
2. On the Welcome page, click **Next**. Accept the license agreement and click **Next**.
3. If you have the license key, enter the key and click **Next**. Otherwise, simply click **Next**.
4. On the Database Options page, select the option **Use an existing supported database** and enter the data source name **vCenter (MS SQL)**, as shown in Figure C.36. Then, click **Next**.
5. Enter the database login name **vmadmin** and the password (Figure C.37). Then, click **Next**.
6. On the vCenter Server Service page, enter Account name, Account password, and Fully Qualified Domain Name, as shown in Figure C.38. Then, click **Next**.
7. On the vCenter Server Linked Mode Options page, select the option **Create a Standalone VMware**

vCenter Server Instance, as shown in Figure C.39, and click **Next**.
8. On the Configure Ports page, specify the default port numbers, as shown in Figure C.40, and click **Next**.
9. On the JVM Memory page, select the inventory size option **Small** and click **Next**.
10. On the Single Sign On Information page, enter the password for the SSO administrator and click **Next**.
11. Click **Yes** for the SSL SHA-1 fingerprint of the SSO Lookup Service leaf certificate.
12. On the Certificate Installation for Secure Connection page, click the **Install Certificates** button.
13. On the vCenter Single Sign On Information page, register the user **administrator@vsphere.local**, as shown in Figure C.41. Then, click **Next**.
14. On the vCenter Inventory Service Information page, take the default Lookup Service URL and vCenter Inventory Service URL, as shown in Figure C.42. Then, click **Next**.
15. On the Destination Folder page, take the default destination and click **Next**.
16. On the Ready to Install the Program page, click the **Install** button.

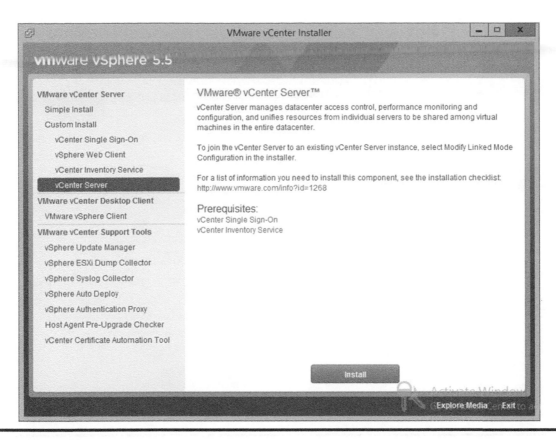

Figure C.35   vCenter Server.

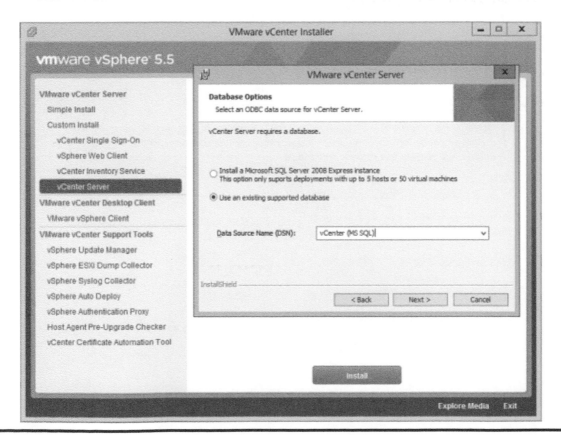

Figure C.36   Database option and data source name.

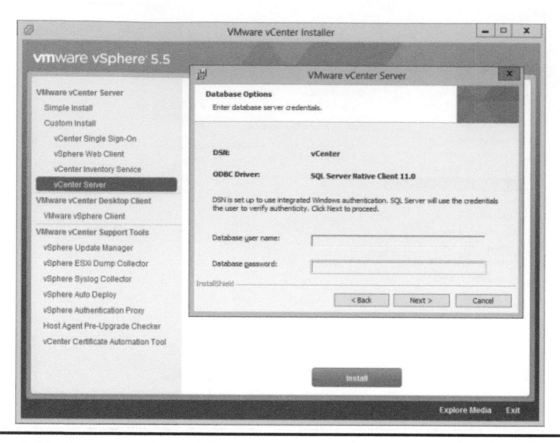

Figure C.37 Database user name and password.

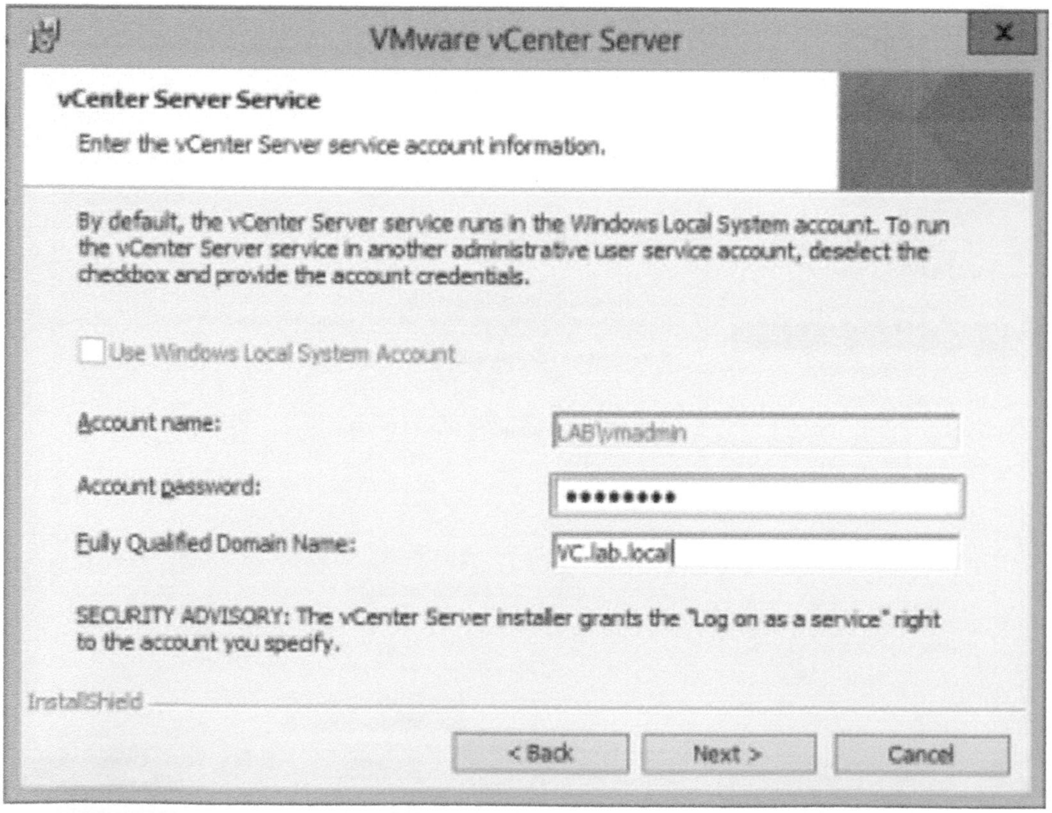

Figure C.38 vCenter Server Service account.

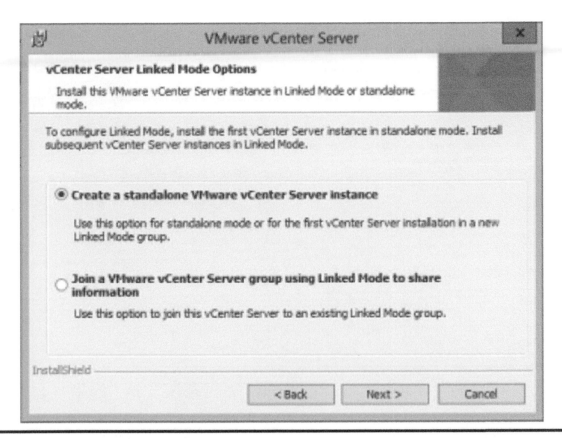

Figure C.39   vCenter Server Linked Mode Option.

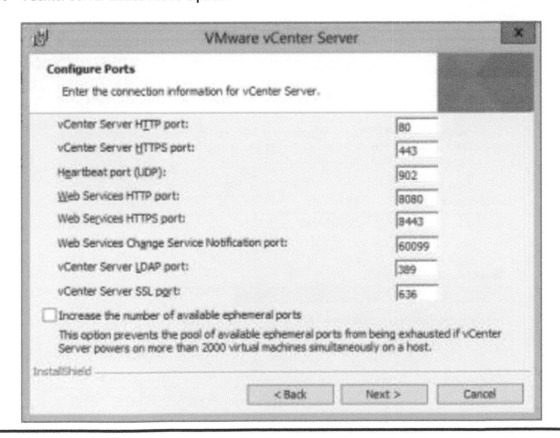

Figure C.40   Port configuration.

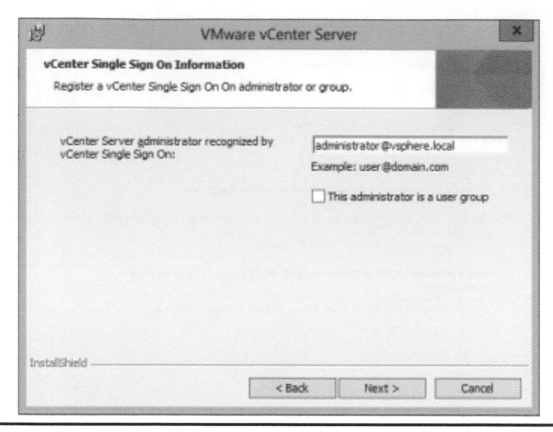

Figure C.41   Registering vCenter Single Sign On administrator.

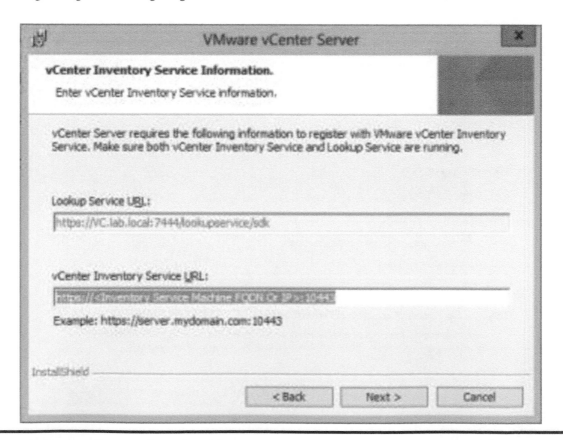

Figure C.42   vCenter Inventory Service Information.

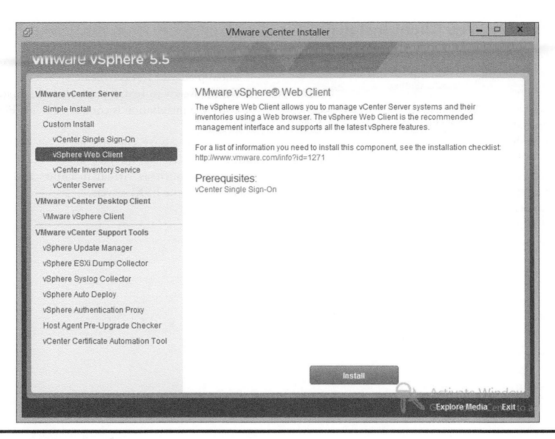

Figure C.43   vSphere Web Client.

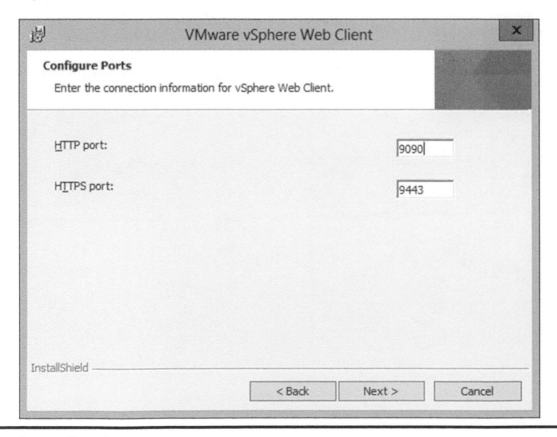

Figure C.44   Port configuration.

Task 5: vSphere Web Client Installation

In this task, you will install the vSphere Web Client software. The following are the steps to accomplish this task:

1. To install vSphere Web Client, in the VMware vCenter Installer dialog, click **vSphere Web Client** and click **Install**, as shown in Figure C.43.
2. On the Welcome page, click **Next**. Accept the license agreement and click **Next**.
3. On the Destination Folder page, take the default destination folder and click **Next**.
4. On the Configure Ports page, take the default port setup, as shown in Figure C.44, and click **Next**.
5. On the vCenter Single Sign On page, enter the password for the SSO administrator and click **Next**.
6. Click **Yes** for the SSL SHA-1 fingerprint of the SSO Lookup Service leaf certificate.
7. On the Ready to Install page, click the **Install** button.
8. Once the installation is completed, click **Finish**.

Now, the necessary components of vCenter for us are installed. You have the interface to access and manage the vSphere objects such as virtual machines and virtual networks hosted by the ESXi servers.

Bibliography

Web Sites

The following Web sites are about the recent development of cloud computing–related technologies:

- Web sites that provide comprehensive coverage of some major cloud providers:
  - http://www.ibm.com/solutions/education/cloud academy/us/en/cloud_academy_3.html
  - http://aws.amazon.com/
  - http://www.apple.com/icloud/
  - http://windows.azure.com
  - https://cloud.google.com/
  - http://windows.microsoft.com/en-US/skydrive /download

  Web sites that provide tutorials of Windows Azure:
  - http://pubs.vmware.com/vfabric5/index.jsp ?topic=/com.vmware.vfabric.sqlfire.1.0/getting _started/tutorial_chapter_intro.html
  - http://searchvmware.techtarget.com/feature/The -top-10-VMware-tutorials-and-tips-of-2014
  - http://searchvmware.techtarget.com/tip/Virtual -switch-tweak-optimizes-ESXi-networking
  - http://searchvmware.techtarget.com/opinion/Why -VMwares-vExpert-program-is-worth-applying-for
  - http://searchvmware.techtarget.com/tip/Mind -the-NUMA-node-when-adding-large-VMs
  - http://searchvmware.techtarget.com/tip/The-top -five-free-tools-for-managing-VMware-vSphere
  - http://searchvmware.techtarget.com/opinion/Is -the-Microsoft-VMware-marriage-on-the-rocks
  - http://searchvmware.techtarget.com/answer/How -secure-is-VMware-NSX
  - http://searchvmware.techtarget.com/opinion /What-VMware-needs-to-do-to-convert-the -vSphere-Web-Client-haters
  - http://searchvmware.techtarget.com/tip/How-to -stop-worrying-and-learn-to-love-the-new-vSphere -Web-Client
  - http://searchvmware.techtarget.com/tip/VMware -changing-vCenter-architecture-in-vSphere-6

- http://www.virtuallyghetto.com/2015/03/home -labs-made-easier-with-vsan-6-0-usb-disks.html
  - http://www.vmware.com/pdf/vi3_san_design _deploy.pdf
  - http://www.jpaul.me/2011/10/getting-started -with-a-vcloud-service-provider-a-customer-how -to/
  - https://blogs.vmware.com/management/2015 /03/comparing-vrealize-automation-vrealize -orchestrator.html
  - http://www.vmware.com/pdf/vi3_san_design _deploy.pdf
  - https://m1xed0s.wordpress.com/2014/01/16/remote -access-vcloud-director-vm-console/
- Cloud resource Web sites:
  - https://www.dreamspark.com/Product/Product .aspx?productid=8
  - http://content.dell.com/us/en/enterprise/dell -cloud-computing.aspx
  - http://blogs.msdn.com/b/sqlazure/
  - http://azure.microsoft.com/en-us/services/virtual -machines/
  - http://www.vmware.com/solutions/cloud -computing
  - http://channel9.msdn.com/Series/Windows -Azure-Virtual-Machines-and-Networking -Tutorials
  - http://technet.microsoft.com/en-us/library/dn 502517.aspx

Books

The following books provide in-depth coverage of cloud computing theories and related technologies:

- Pankaj Arora, Raj Biyani, and Salil Dave. 2012. *To the Cloud: Cloud Powering an Enterprise.* New York: McGraw-Hill Osborne Media.
- Nick Marshall. 2015. *Mastering VMware vSphere 6.* Indianapolis, Indiana: Sybex.

■ Lars Nielsen. 2011. *The Little Book of Cloud Computing*, 2011 Edition. Wickford, RI: New Street Communications, LLC.

■ Barrie Sosinsky. 2011. *Cloud Computing Bible*. Hoboken, NJ: Wiley.

■ John Rhoton and Risto Haukioja. 2011. *Cloud Computing Architected: Solution Design Handbook*. USA: Recursive, Limited.

■ Jothy Rosenberg and Arthur Mateos. 2010. *The Cloud at Your Service*. Greenwich, CT: Manning Publications.

■ Venkata Josyula, Malcolm Orr, and Greg Page. 2011. *Cloud Computing: Automating the Virtualized Data Center (Networking Technology)*. Indianapolis, IN: Cisco Press.

■ Vic (J.R.) Winkler. 2011. *Securing the Cloud: Cloud Computer Security Techniques and Tactics*. Waltham, MA: Syngress.

■ Lipika Pal. 2014. *VMware vCloud Director Essentials*. Birmingham, UK: Packt Publishing.

■ Kevin Jackson. 2012. *OpenStack Cloud Computing Cookbook*. Birmingham, UK: Packt Publishing.

■ Dave Crookes. 2012. *Cloud Computing in Easy Steps*. Warwickshire, UK: In Easy Steps Limited.

■ Christopher Wahl and Steven Pantol. 2014. *Networking for VMware Administrators*. Upper Saddle River, NJ: VMware Press.

Index

Page numbers with f and t refer to figures and tables, respectively.

Printed and bound by CPI Group (UK) Ltd, Croydon, CR0 4YY

21/10/2024

01777098-0011